The Official Dictionary of Unofficial English

A Crunk Omnibus for Thrillionaires and Bampots for the Ecozoic Age

Grant Barrett

McGraw-Hill

New York   Chicago   San Francisco   Lisbon   London   Madrid   Mexico City
Milan   New Delhi   San Juan   Seoul   Singapore   Sydney   Toronto

The *McGraw·Hill* Companies

Library of Congress Cataloging-in-Publication Data

Barrett, Grant.
        The official dictionary of unofficial English / by Grant Barrett.
                p.   cm.
        Includes bibliographical references.
        ISBN 0-07-145804-2 (alk. paper)
        1. English language—New words—Dictionaries.   2. English language—Terms
and phrases.   3. English language—Usage—Dictionaries.   I. Title.

PE1630.B34   2006
423'.1—dc22   2005055470

1 2 3 4 5 6 7 8 9 10 11 12 13 14 15 16   LBM/LBM   0 9 8 7 6

ISBN 0-07-145804-2

Illustrations by Brian Dow

McGraw-Hill books are available at special quantity discounts to use as premiums and sales promotions, or for use in corporate training programs. For more information, please write to the Director of Special Sales, Professional Publishing, McGraw-Hill, Two Penn Plaza, New York, NY 10121-2298. Or contact your local bookstore.

This book is printed on acid-free paper.

OCT 3 1 2006

Contents

Acknowledgments

Thanks to Erin McKean for her guidance, wisdom, and humor, and to Jonathan Lighter for demonstrating worthy models of both lexicography and a lexicographer. Special thanks to Laurence Urdang and the Dictionary Society of North America for their grant in support of my web site. For their suggestions, corrections, additions, notes, comments, and other help, thanks also are deserved by Gustavo Arellano, Nathan Bierma, Bill Brogdon, David Barnhart, Carlos Caga-anan II, Hunter Cutting, Jamie Davis, Paul Deppler, Steve Dodson, Connie Eble, Cathy Giffi, Yesenia Gutierrez, Sonya Kolowrat, Margaret Marks, Yisrael Medad, Bill Mullins, Johnny North, Mark Peters, Barry Popik, James Proctor, Michael Quinion, William Safire, Strawberry Saroyan, Jesse Sheidlower, Ava Swartz, Michael Volf, Steven I. Weiss, Douglas Wilson, David Wilton, Ben Zimmer, the online communities at Languagehat.com and Word Origins.org, and everyone on ADS-L, the American Dialect Society e-mail list. You all make it easier.

Introduction

This book is the result of hunting on the Internet for unrecorded words. In these pages, you'll find words you've never seen before—even though they've been around for decades. You'll find old words with new definitions. You'll find foreign words tiptoeing into foreign Englishes, sports jargon butting into politics, street slang bouncing out of California, and Spanish moving comfortably into mainstream American English. From dozens of countries, from politics and sports, slang and jargon, humdrum to extraordinary, new and old, what you'll read is language that deserves a little more attention.

Although it may look like it at first glance, not all of these words are new. Many are, but more than a few have histories spanning decades or even a century. They all share, however, two characteristics. One, they are undocumented or underdocumented. This means that there is more to be said about them than has so far appeared in other dictionaries. Two, they are interesting in and of themselves, either as cultural artifacts, for their history, or even just for the way they roll off the tongue.

The Why of the Word Hunt

Early in 1999 I began a Web blog called World New York. The web site's primary focus was New York City and things of interest to its inhabitants. I developed a series of complex Web searches that dug deep into the Internet and pulled out the new, the unusual, the pithy, and the funny and then posted them as extracts and links. In a casual fashion I also began recording interesting words as I came across them, presenting them mostly as curiosities. Because my readers sent messages saying they liked the interesting words, I spent extra time hunting them down. I soon realized that there were many zillions of useful and interesting words to be found if I looked hard enough and in the right way. But I also saw there was more to be done than I had the time for because there were many lexical items that seemed to be uncollected by *anyone*—at least, they didn't appear in any of the dozens of dictionaries I owned.

So in June 2004 I turned my blog into a dictionary-oriented web site, which I named Double-Tongued Word Wrester (double-tongued.org). It is what I call "a growing dictionary of old and new words from the fringes of English." With the goal of reaching into those uncharted waters and hooking the so-far uncaptured words, I began to think about the best way to collect the uncollected, to record the unrecorded, to document the undocumented and the underdocumented.

The How of the Word Hunt

When compiling dictionaries, there are two primary tasks. The first is identifying lexical items, be they new words or new meanings for old words. The second is substantiating lexical items: proving where they come from, what they mean, and how they are used.

Defining Terms

Throughout this book, I use *lexical item* to mean anything that is to be defined, be it a single word, phrase, term, or affix, including prefixes, suffixes, and infixes (syllables that are inserted into the middle of other words). I'll also use the term *reader*. In lexicography, a reader is someone who reads in an organized, consistent fashion with the intent of discovering new lexical items that warrant recording. When a lexical item is first found but not yet substantiated as a definable term, it is a *catchword*.

How the Corporations Do It

Most modern dictionary publishers of any size have archives, both paper and digital, of citations that have been collected by readers on the prowl for new language. Large dictionary operations, like that of the *Oxford English Dictionary (OED)*, have many paid and volunteer readers who can return thousands of new citations every year. Readers are usually assigned specific publications (including runs of periodicals) to read their way through. Each time they find something that strikes them as new, noteworthy, or worth investigation, they cite it. The results of this work can be substantial—editors at Merriam-Webster have more than sixteen million citations on paper. These citations include the catchword, the source (book, newspaper, transcript, etc.), the date, the author, who said or wrote it, and an exact quote of the words used. A few notes might be added to a citation to indicate a context or connotation that might not be immediately clear.

Once it's time to edit a particular part of a dictionary, the citation slips (or database records) are gathered. If there are, for example, a dozen slips for *crunk*, then a draft entry can immediately be written. New research is then done to further substantiate the word or to trace its origins. Words for which there is only a single citation slip get a more thorough investigation. Readers are sent to look at specific books, or to peruse the works of specific authors, or to make inquiries into journals on specific subjects, all in the hope of proving that a single citation represents a valid, recordable lexical item that deserves an entry in a dictionary.

In the past twenty or so years, this work of substantiating terms has grown easier. First with the appearance of digital databases such as Lexis Nexis, Dialog, and Westlaw, and now with the addition of others such as Proquest Historical Newspapers (and Proquest's American Periodical Series), NewspaperArchive.com, Dow Jones Factiva, Google's twenty-five-year archive of Usenet posts, the two Making of America databases at the University of Michigan and Cornell University, and many others. It's easy to spend a few minutes searching for a lexical item to find out if it has been used, by whom, and what the user intended it to mean. Particularly for recent lexical items, etymological work has never been easier.

Individuals unaffiliated with dictionary publishers, like a number of pro-am volunteers associated with the American Dialect Society, do this sort of history-hunting purely for the thrill of the hunt and can, in a matter of minutes, destroy longstanding theories on word origins, develop new possible etymologies, expand the understanding of new meanings for old words, and antedate lexical items by days or decades. As new databases come online and as thousands of new digitized pages are added to the existing databases, there is always new digital digging to be done. A much-anticipated newspaper digitization effort was announced by the National Endowment for the Humanities and the Library of Congress in 2004. It will preserve millions of periodical pages from 1836 to 1923 in searchable online archives.

But this sort of research only revolutionizes the second primary task of dictionary-making, the substantiation—the proving, vetting, and testing—of found words. The first task, identifying previously unrecorded lexical items, is still relatively complex.

Besides reading programs like the *OED*'s, dictionary publishers and third-party consortiums now develop corpora made up of hundreds of millions of words pulled from books, periodicals, conversation and media transcripts, and elsewhere. Specialized tools analyze them, looking for unique, new, or unusual patterns, associations, or usages. This brute force method, while effective, is also time-consuming, costly, and labor-intensive. It also requires specialized technical knowledge in a field where time, money, and manpower are often in short supply. Certainly this method, like a reading program, is probably inappropriate for a small dictionary-making operation, and definitely out of reach for a simple web site created for the joy of revealing interesting language.

What can a small operation—or a solitary lexicographer or word freak—do to participate in the hunt? As it turns out, quite a lot.

Wayne Glowka, with the help of others, is the latest neologian to collect new words for the "Among the New Words" column in the professional journal *American Speech*, a column that has been published for more than fifty years. William Safire, with the help of a series of able assistants and his readers, has been discussing new and novel language in a syndicated weekly column for more than twenty years, on top of writing political commentary and books (including at least one political thriller). He is probably the most-recognized writer on language in the United States. David Barnhart (of the famous Barnhart dictionary-making family) has been a part of publishing the quarterly *Barnhart Dictionary Companion* since 1982, in which he brings his word finds to the attention of subscribers. Paul McFedries's Word Spy (wordspy.com), Evan Morris's Word Detective (word-detective.com), and Michael Quinion's World Wide Words (worldwidewords.org) are three web sites that exploit their creators' penchants for constantly monitoring language change; all three solo word hunters have also turned out books.

Given those models of mostly solitary word-hunting, it's clear that keeping an eye on the malleability of English discourse doesn't require large budgets or manpower.

Tracking and Capturing the Wild Journalist

One of the characteristics shared by the best word hunters, both professional and amateur, is erudition. That is, they tend to be well-educated (even if that education is autodidactic), literate, and, therefore, thoroughly at home with the printed word.

In looking through the citations I had casually gathered for my old Web blog, I noticed a curious pattern: writers are predictable. Journalists—the source of most of my interesting words—have a tendency to flag words that are new to their vocabulary with such phrases as "known in military parlance as" or "referred to as" or "as they call it" or "known to fans as" or even the straightforward "coined the word" or even just "new word."

This means that journalists as a body are giving tips on new words to anyone who cares to pay attention. They're like accidental participants in a worldwide dictionary reading program, creating texts right and left that they sprinkle with found words from their daily interviews, research, and conversations. Therefore, when they introduce a new word with a phrase like "called in copspeak," it behooves the word-hunter to pay attention.

Thus, with the aforementioned digital databases (and many others) it's easy to search for these collocations—that is, to look for the juxtaposition of the identifying phrases such as "called by many" or "referred to as"—and then read nearby text to see if there is a word worth turning into a citation slip—not all that far off from the searching I did when looking for newsworthy bits about New York City for the old Web log.

Reading all these news stories is still time-consuming, but there are still other shortcuts. In order to speed the word-hunting, services such as Google News permit collocation searches to be automated. As of this writing Google News indexes more than 4,500 English-language periodicals and news-oriented web sites that publish on the World Wide Web. At no cost to the user, it permits the creation of automated alerts that conduct searches in real time and then delivers the results via an e-mail alert when there's a match.

It turned out to be just the ticket for finding interesting new lexical items for the Double-Tongued Word Wrester web site. Currently, with more than 800 collocations being searched, hundreds of e-mail messages arrive in my inbox daily, each of them containing at least one potentially citable lexical item. Google News also permits searches in foreign languages, so unique phrases in French, English, and other languages likely to lend or borrow from English can be searched for, too—phrases such as "jargon anglais" or "espanglish."

Although I have collected thousands of citations in this way since 2004, this method is far from perfect. For one thing, there are plenty of journalists who are culturally left behind, the kind of folks who are just now commenting on the novelty of "bling bling" even though it's a word that has spread far since B.G. and the Cash Money Millionaires made it a household word in 1999. It's so common, in fact, that it's also now appearing in overseas Spanish as "blin blin." These are the same journalists for whom the word "blog" is a novelty. Coined in 1999, I still regularly come across opinion pieces commenting on this newfangled "blog" thingy. Some journalists are on the cutting edge; some are still struggling to get out of the silverware drawer. This means that more than a few of the search results will be dead ends.

That's not a criticism of the journalism profession so much as it's an ordinary truth about all language speakers. Most words are new to most people most of the time. But most "newish" words that float about in the zeitgeist for any reasonable length of time will eventually come up using these collocation searches—even if it is five years later. Whenever they are encountered, whether they are brand-new or old hat, the most important thing is to get them on the record so they can begin the substantiation process.

In this way words that seem perfectly ordinary—like *huck* 'to make a short toss' or *heartsink* 'dismay or disappointment'—can come to light. These terms were undocumented, as of this writing, in any of the hundreds of dictionaries, major and minor, that I now own or have access to.

It's not just newspapers that can be searched this way. Online services such as Feedster, Technorati, Daypop, and PubSub also permit automated searching of material produced by nonjournalists who write on everyday subjects in Web logs, journals, and other personal sites. While blogs return far fewer good hits for each thousand search results than do newspapers—mainly because nonjournalist writers tend to be less formulaic than journalists and use less-common collocations or no collocations at all, but also because the education and age range skews much lower for run-of-the-mill personal web sites—blogs have the advantage of returning far more slang and nonstandard language. In English alone there are more blogs, covering more topics, from more places, written by more people, than there are newspapers published in the entire world in any language. This means the possibilities for new lexical items bubbling to the surface are immense.

A bonus of word-hunting by looking for journalistic flags is immediacy. Not only can new or newly popular terms be identified by lexicographers very soon after they bubble to the surface, but they can be captured before periodicals archive their online content in fee-based archives. Automated alerts mean getting while the getting is good. It's a financial and logistical nightmare to imagine even a large dictionary-making operation paying per article every time an editor wants to investigate a lexical item. Many of the larger periodicals do archive their content in Lexis Nexis or Factiva, where, although there are fees, at least the content is available. In an embarrassing number of cases, online stories are removed from periodicals' web sites after a week or month and aren't digitally archived *anywhere* that is easily accessible, for free or for fee. As far as the word-hunter is concerned, any unrecorded lexical items that could have been identified in those pages have vanished.

Personal web sites are also ephemeral. They are not only being created at a phenomenal rate, they are also going offline at a phenomenal rate, often with the entirety of their text disappearing forever. Sites like the Internet Archive (archive.org) have experimented with full-text searches of historical Internet archives, but there are logistical and legal complications with this, and even at their best, none of these Internet archive services can archive but a tiny fraction of the available content on the Internet. Again, instant alerts checked daily mean that any new word that is pointed out by a writer is more likely to be caught before the source disappears.

This method of word-hunting is by no means extraordinary. It's simply a matter-of-fact use of the tools available so that one word-hunter can have a far better chance of recording interesting words as they zip by. Many tens of thousands—millions? possibly!—still go unrecorded, but I've captured a few of them here in this book.

About This Dictionary

Criteria for Inclusion

A lexical item is first considered for inclusion in this book because it is interesting or new to me. Next, I check established works to see, first, if the item is there; second, if it is there, how it is defined; and third, if it is there, whether there is good reason to include it here, such as if the citation demonstrates a previously unrecorded sense, adds significantly to the history or understanding of the item, or clarifies a point previously in dispute. Most often consulted are the *Oxford English Dictionary (OED)* (online), *WordNet*, the *New Oxford American Dictionary*, *Merriam-Webster's Collegiate Dictionary* (11th ed.), the *Dictionary of American Regional English*, the *Historical Dictionary of American Slang*, and *Cassell's Dictionary of Slang*. (See the Bibliography for more consulted works.)

After that, lexical items continue to be considered if they can be shown to exist in word-based media over a nontrivial period. "Nontrivial" is variable, depending upon the lexical item, the niche in which it was found, and the types of sources it is found in.

Definitions

With a few exceptions, definitions are given only for those senses, including everyday and slang meanings, that are not well-covered by other dictionaries. *Whip*, for example, includes only the definition of "an automobile" and *not* definitions related to long cords used for beating, creating foam out of liquids, or a political figure in a deliberating body who persuades party members not to stray.

In a number of cases (such as with *squick*, *huck*, and *hot box*), more than one definition or part of speech is given together in a single entry. This usually indicates that the definitions or parts of speech are related and can be supported by the same batch of citations, although on occasion homonyms that have separate meanings for the same part of speech, as in the case of *merk*, are given together in a single entry.

Homonyms that have unrelated meanings for different parts of speech, such as the verb *gank* 'to rob, rip off, or con (someone)' and the noun *gank* 'fake illegal drugs sold as real,' are given in separate entries.

Parentheses are used in definitions to indicate a variable meaning. For example, at *bed head*, the definition is "a hairstyle in (intentional) disarray." This means that sometimes *bed head* is disarray that is accidental and sometimes it means disarray by design.

Words that are cross-references to other entries in this dictionary are in SMALL CAPS.

Each entry is marked with labels. These come in four types: references to place, such as Iraq or United States; references to language, such as Spanish or Japanese; references to subject, such as Crime & Prisons or Business; and references to register—the type of language in which the word tends to appear—such as Slang, Jargon, or Derogatory.

Citations

For this book, I've chosen a historical dictionary model, like that used by the *Oxford English Dictionary*, the *Dictionary of American Regional English*, and the *Historical Dictionary of American Slang*. In a historical dictionary (yes, I am American, and I believe *a historical* to be good American English; my *aitch* is very solidly pronounced), an entry is supported by citations of the headword in context over time, which can add nuance to the meaning, show the changing senses of the word, and give clues to the environments and situations in which it appears or has appeared.

Citation Coverage

It should not be assumed that a gap in citations represents a gap in usage, but that the lexical item was continuously used from at least as early as the first citation, through at least as late as the last one. However, it is not uncommon for a word to remain little-used for years or decades and then to spring to the fore. *Chad*, from the American presidential election of 2000, is a good example of this.

It also should not be assumed that the first cite is the first use ever of a lexical item. That kind of conclusive and certain statement can be made about very few words; at least, such statements about absolute firsts are not often made by reputable lexicographers. A work of this limited scope contributes to the understanding of the modern English lexicon, but it cannot presume to comprehensively and decisively determine the etymology or origin of all its headwords. Therefore, I have not made a life's work out of finding the absolute first citation for every entry. However, many entries include speculation as to origin or history, with many hedges and caveats, and, in nearly all cases, the existing digital resources mentioned earlier have been checked in as thorough a fashion as possible. I have also made a consistent effort with citations to cover a broad range of usages, spellings, nuances, and sources.

In rare cases, a definition or sense is given that is not fully supported by the citations shown. This could be because I used resources that cannot be quoted due to ownership or copyright restrictions. It also could be because I have found but not entered other citations that were difficult to document properly because they lacked important identifying information such as date or author.

Sometimes I included citations that are not exactly appropriate for the word as I have defined it. In these cases, the entire cite is contained within brackets [ ]. Such citations are included either because I *know* they are related to the definition given, though the citation insufficiently shows this (usually because it is a variation or another part of speech for the same concept), or because my lexicographical instincts suggest the citation and the headword are related. In the latter case, it is important to include such evidence so that the dictionary reader is aware that it exists and can judge it accordingly.

Citations are pulled from a variety of word-based media: periodicals, news wires, blogs, academic papers and journals, online bulletin boards, Usenet, my personal e-mail, books, television, movies, the wide-open Internet, radio and chat transcripts, and anything else I find. In the hunt for word histories, I have relied heavily on periodical databases and have cited periodicals more often than any other media. It should not be assumed that newspapers or other periodicals are the primary means by which new words are spread, just that they are where lexical items are the easiest to find.

Except for citations pulled from transcriptions of oral speech, there are no oral cites here. Such collection methods are beyond the scope of a book of this small size and given the free-form and free-flowing nature of much that is written on Internet discussion forums, the gap between oral language and the written record is not as large as it once was. In addition, requiring that a lexical item appear in print ensures at least some minimal level of widespread acceptance, which is useful for eliminating fly-by-night words and terms of passing fancy more likely to crop up in records of oral speech.

Bibliographic Information Included in Citations

As is the case with other historical dictionaries, sufficient information is included in the citations so that the scholar can re-find the original source, if desired. This means that titles are sometimes abbreviated in what I hope is a logical fashion.

In some cases, particularly on the Internet, bibliographic information is not available when citable text is found. I have done my best to determine this information, but in some cases it has proven impossible for sites of relatively high value. Therefore, authors of which I am not certain are included in brackets. Dates about which I am uncertain are marked with an asterisk. If anything else about a citation is questionable, a citation simply has not been used to support an entry.

Where author names are bracketed, it is often the case that it is known to be a pseudonym, especially in Internet citations. Online monikers or handles are common and in some cases, especially for prolific or well-known users, they are just as good at identifying a person as a real name. Mark Twain is a good historical example of this; Mimi Smartypants is a good Internet-era example.

The @ symbol is used in two ways in citations. First, when followed by a place, it indicates the dateline or place where the story was reported from. In the case of Web logs, this may mean that a soldier serving in Iraq has a dateline of Baghdad, although his web site is hosted in Santa Cruz, California. Second, when the work being cited was found within another work, such as a short story appearing in an anthology or a newspaper quoting from a novel, the @ symbol connects the two citations.

In cases where two dates are given for a citation—one at the head of the citation and another near the end, a citation has been pulled from a work that has been published more than once. The newest date is given to indicate the date of the edition we are citing from (and whose pagination we are using), while the oldest date is given to indicate the year the work was first published.

Digital Citations

All citations pulled from resources found on the Internet are marked with *Int.* Citations from print publications that republish their content on the Internet are treated stylistically as if they were print publications (meaning, for example, that the publication title is italicized), but they will include *Int.* in place of page numbers. A few publications do indicate in their online versions of articles on what page in the print edition they appeared. These page numbers are recorded with the citations when available.

I am necessarily required to trust that the information provided by digital databases is correct. This is often fine, as the actual page images can be viewed and the information verified there, but in the case of archives such as Factiva and Lexis Nexis, the bibliographic information is not always exact. However, given that access to both of those archiving services is widespread and that citations recorded in this book include strings of word-for-word text, the modern scholar will have little difficulty in searching for those citations on either database and thus turning up the original source with ease. I am assured by my fellow modern word-hunters that full-text searches are by far the preferred method for finding a specific, known quotation, much less going to microfilm or hard copy when a digital version is available.

In other cases, especially in the case of NewspaperArchive (newspaperarchive.com), while full page images are provided, they often do not include page numbers, especially in older periodicals, and the page numbers assigned by NewspaperArchive bear no real relation to the original pagination. I have done my best to correct for this, but there are bound to be citations for which my efforts have failed. However, as the quotation and everything else about the citation is correct, the citation has lost little of its value in supporting an entry.

Editing Citations

Punctuation is usually Americanized, but spelling is not. Double hyphens are converted to em-dashes. Spaces around em-dashes are removed. For readability, ellipses, em-dashes, quotes, and apostrophes are converted to the proper form: ellipses of more or less than three periods are made three, hyphens used where em-dashes are expected are turned into em-dashes, straight quotes are made curved. For space and appearance reasons, e-mail- or Usenet-style quoting of previous messages is usually silently removed and converted to standard double-curved quotes, as it would appear in a dialogue, leaving the words themselves intact. Multiple spaces after punctuation are made single. Line and paragraph breaks are not retained. Text is often elided or redacted in order to properly document a word without a lot of verbiage, and such cut text is replaced with an ellipsis. Headlines that appear in all capital letters are converted to initial caps; words in all caps that appear in quotes are made lowercase or initial capped, as necessary.

Obvious typographical or spelling errors are corrected when found in the bibliographic information of professional texts, but usually not if found in the quote itself, not when part of an eye-dialect or other form of intentional misspelling, not in a casual or personal communication (such as a blog entry, letter, or e-mail message), and not when there is uncertainty about what the correct text should be. Errors that are due to bad optical character recognition or other transcription methods are corrected in bibliographic information, but not in quotes. Some spelling errors in quotes are corrected with bracketed text in a small number of cases, as in the 1880 cite for *bull tailing*. These corrections contribute to a better overall readability, while not diminishing the ability to refind the original cite source, if it is so desired.

Changing English

Language change is consistent: soldiers—and any group of like-minded young men and women—have always developed a short-hand that both makes their tasks easier to do and establishes cama-raderie. In the time it took to compile a dictionary of this small size, thousands of new words have been coined and used. Some start on their way to word-lives of fame and fortune. Others die horri-ble deaths in places like the LiveJournals of young goth girls or the cheap column inches of a trend-watcher's marketing e-mail. Mil-lions of second-language English speakers will mix their mother tongue with their adopted one. A sportscaster will invent a witty new use for an old word he half-remembers from psychology. Three children in Ohio will call the new kid a new obscenity based upon a part of the body.

The following essays do a bit of digging and noodling on the subject of language change, covering such things as melanges of English and different appellations for the white man and Westerner around the world. They are dedicated to Arturo Alfandari of Bel-gium, who invented the rather nice, but mostly forgotten, little lan-guage of Neo. He demonstrated quite well that it doesn't matter how good a language invention is: it doesn't count unless people use it.

Words of the Latest War
One of the most productive areas of new American language has always been the military. This is partly due to the need for short-cuts for long ideas, and partly due to the natural jargon that arises from any group of persons with a common purpose, as well as the need to de-jargonize: they make acronyms out of phrases and nouns and verbs out of acronyms. Still other terms come from the dark humor, youthful rambunctiousness, and gung-ho spirit soldiers tend to have.

The 2003 American invasion of Iraq, still ongoing as of this writing, has been no less productive linguistically. It's too early to say with certainty whether any of these words will have staying power, but as long as such words continue to fill a need, they will continue to be used.

Motivated soldiers learn the local languages in order to foster more genial relations and demonstrate a willingness to understand the natives, but like *dinky-dau* "crazy," brought back from the Vietnam War, most foreign words are unlikely to survive except as historical footnotes. Refer to the dictionary for the citations of the words used in this article.

ali baba *n.* thief. After the government of Saddam Hussein was toppled, uncontrolled looting ravaged the country—anything of value, and many things that weren't, were stolen or destroyed. Looters, and, generally, any thieves, are called *ali baba*, by Iraqis, after the tale of "Ali Baba and the Forty Thieves," told by Scheherazade in the stories known in the West as *Thousand and One Nights*. American soldiers who have served in Iraq say they tend not to use the term as a noun, but as a verb meaning "to steal": "We're gonna ali baba some scrap metal from their junkyard."

angel *n.* among American military medical personnel in Iraq, a soldier killed in combat. It is probably a coincidence that Jose Angel Garibay was one of the first coalition soldiers, if not the first, killed in Iraq after the American invasion.

Eye-wreck *n.* a jocular name for Iraq; a cynical reflection on some observers' opinions of the state of the war.

fobbit *n.* a soldier or other person stationed at a secure forward operating base; (*hence*) someone who seeks the security and comfort of a well-protected military base. From *forward operating base* + hob*bit*. A variation is *FOB monkey*. A more common synonym is *rear-echelon motherfucker*, or *REMF*, which dates back to at least as early as the Vietnam War. Others synonyms are *pogue*, from the World War II or earlier, and the more recent *base camp commando*.

goat grab *n.* at gatherings or celebrations in the Middle East, a communal self-served meal of meat and vegetables eaten with the hands. This term is used informally by Anglophones not native to the culture. Such meals are usually convivial, and in the case of the current war in Iraq, they are seen by the coalition forces as an opportunity for improving community relations. The food eaten in a goat grab is often a form of *mansef*, which includes rice with almonds and pine nuts, *shrak* (a thin, round wheat bread), goat (sometimes with lamb and beef and usually cooked with yogurt), and *jammid* (a dry, hard cheese made of sheep's or goat's milk).

haji *n.* an Iraqi; any Muslim, Arab, or native of the Middle East. Originally an honorific given to Muslims who have made a pilgrimage to Mecca, during the British control of India and Persia (now Iraq), it was often used less as a title of honor than as a useful shorthand to refer to any pilgrim bound for or returned from Mecca. Because *haji* is often used as a title or form of address in Arabic, it occurs quite often in daily discourse and is likely to stand out to listeners who are not accustomed to it. Soldiers who have served in Iraq, however, are not necessarily familiar with the religious connotations of the word. Instead, they tend to associate it with Haji, a character on the cartoon television series "The Adventures of Johnny Quest," which has been in television syndication since 1964. Now, when used by coalition personnel in Iraq, *haji*, sometimes spelled *hajji* or *hadji*, is usually pejorative or scornful. It is often applied to any non-Western national, not just Iraqis. The plural is also sometimes *haji*, without a terminating *s*. Haji is also used in an attributive fashion, sometimes being clipped to *haj*, to create items like *haji mobile*, a beat-up or dilapidated automobile driven by an Iraqi, or *haji mart*, a flea market, bazaar, or roadside vendor.

hawasim *n.* a looter or thief. Arabic from the expression *Harb Al-Hawasim*, meaning the "final war" or "decisive battle," an expression used by Saddam Hussein to refer to the 2003 invasion of Iraq.

hillbilly armor *n.* scavenged materials used by soldiers for improvised bulletproofing and vehicle hardening, esp. in Iraq. American soldiers found that many military vehicles were capable of protecting them against small-arms fire only, leading to make-do and jerry-rigged attempts to harden the vehicles against larger weapons or explosives.

Mortaritaville or **Mortarville** *n.* a military base subject to regular attack. A *mortar* is 'a muzzle-loading high-angle gun with a short barrel that fires shells at high elevations for a short range.' *Mortaritaville* has usually referred specifically to Logistical Support Area (Camp) Anaconda Is near Balad, Iraq, fifty miles north of Baghdad, although an informant says that a giant, multicolored "Welcome to Mortaritaville" sign was displayed at Log Base Seitz (also known as Seitzkatraz or Impact Zone Seitz) in late 2003. Mortaritaville is a play on the Jimmy Buffett song "Margaritaville."

muj *n.* among (Anglophone) foreigners in Middle Eastern or Islamic nations, a guerrilla fighter or fighters. Clipped form of Persian and Arabic *mujahideen*, plural for *mujahid*, 'one who fights in a jihad or holy war.' *Muj* is used both in the singular and plural. The term was used before the 2002 American invasion of Afghanistan.

POI *n.* *p*issed-*o*ff *I*raqi; uncooperative Iraqi. While this term is not widespread and mostly seems to be used by pundits and policy-makers, it sometimes plays a role in demonstrating that, contrary to American hopes, invading troops were not necessarily seen as liberators.

sandbox *n.* the Middle East; a country in that region. There are many literal uses of *sandbox* to refer to any arid, desert, or sandy land or country, and in the military, to an area in which an exercise is held. The U.S. Army's National Training Center at Fort Irwin, in the Mojave Desert in California, is known as *the sandbox*. This term is usually constructed with the definite article: *the sandbox*. It's also enhanced by other senses of sandbox, such as 'a figurative or literal play area; an area for testing or planning; a sand-filled scale model of a war zone.'

shako mako *n.* Arabic, loosely translated as "what's up?" or more specifically, "what do and don't you have?" or "what's there and not there?" It's similar to *shoo fee ma fee* used in Lebanese Arabic. Commonly one of the first Iraqi Arabic expressions learned by coalition forces. A common response is *kulshi mako* "nothing's new."

ulug *n.* thug or lout. Arabic. Repopularized by the former Iraqi Minister of Information Muhammad Saeed Al Sahhaf as a term for Americans. The word had previously been rare.

Other military terms elsewhere in the dictionary include *armchair pilot, backdoor draft, bag drag, battle rattle, big voice, birth control glasses, counter-recruiter, boots on the ground, bullets and beans, C41SR, chalk, cross-decking, Dover test, flash-bang, fourth point of contact, fragged, FRAGO, gedunk, ghost soldier, hollow army, horse blanket, hot wash, interview without coffee, jointery, lily pad, mayor's cell, perfumed prince, purple, rat line, rat-racing, rehat, rice bowl,*

Rummy's Dummies, shack, teeth arm, thunder run, tiny heart syndrome, toe-popper, twidget, unass, wizzo.

Glishes: Englishes Around the World

No matter where English spreads, the grumbles of dissent are the same: with the widespread adoption of outside terms come foreign ideas that are a threat to identity. What's uncertain, in most cases, is whether the adoption of English words is the canary in the coal mine, the poisonous gas that kills the bird, or the coal itself. Are Anglicisms adopted because they are needed for new ideas, for new material goods, for new technologies, or for new fashions? Or, are they adopted because the tsunami of Anglophone-dominated worldwide media, entertainment, science, and politics is over-printing perfectly useful and usable existing terms? Are the new words bringing the new concepts, or are the new concepts bringing the new words?

Outside of Europe, English has imprinted itself in few places longer than it has in India. In an attempt to explain Indian English language poetry to outsiders, poet Keki Daruwala has described how before World War II and before Partition, the English language in India was already so Hindified, so Indian, that when he had his first conversation with an Englishman, "he had to repeat himself three times to make himself understood. What an exotic accent, I thought. Why couldn't the fellow speak English as she ought to be spoken?"[1]

It wasn't just accent, but vocabulary. Daruwala describes the schoolboy slang imported from the British Isles: "It was old slang of course, shipped some three decades ago, which had got lost on the seas, then lay rotting on the docks like dry fish, till it was dispatched by steam rail and later on mule back to those public schools in the mountains." But it was Indian, too, and to not know it, or to mangle it, made one an outcast.

That the word "Hinglish"—meaning a combination of English and Hindi, one of the most widely spoken Indian languages—was added to the *Oxford Dictionary of English (ODE)* in 2005 should not be a surprise to anyone who has experienced what Daruwala did, or even anyone who follows Indian cinema. *ODE* was simply

---

1. Daruwala, Keki. "On Writing in English: An Indian Poet's Perspective." *Daily Star* (Dhaka, Bangladesh). Accessed 13 July 2005. www.thedailystar.net/2004/08/21/d408212102104.htm.

acknowledging that, after four hundred–plus years of Anglophone influence on the Subcontinent, English and Hindi had become inextricably linked.

Despite the valid claim Indians have that Hinglish is not a back-alley dive joint ripping off the good name of a more successful franchise, but a fully functional regional office for the highly successful enterprise known as English, the integration of the language and the changes it has made to the Indian languages it has come into contact with have not come without complaint. Like the French, some Indians resist the crests and swells of Anglified language. Russians, Malays, and Israelis, too, sometimes find its continuous influence unsettling. The role of English is tied up in the question of Puerto Rican statehood, and its big-booted imprint is a matter that Ireland, Scotland, and Wales have been dealing with for centuries, as Welsh and varieties of Gaelic fade and decline. The various Englishes even battle among themselves: American English today so influences Australian English (or "Strine," as it's sometimes affectionately called) that complaint has been made about its effect on national character: *blokes* and *mates* aren't blokes anymore, they're *guys*. Within the United States, there's a renewed battle concerning whether Ebonics is a true dialect of Black Americans or just ungrammatical slang.

As the question of the legitimacy of Anglicisms in other language continues to be discussed, the influence of English spreads and these two-language mixtures take names: *Hinglish* in India, *Konglish* in South Korea, *Spanglish* or *Espanglish* in the Hispanophone world, *Swenglish* in Sweden, and a dozen or more others elsewhere. These names are often used in joking speech or to describe the mishaps of language students or grammatical errors made by immigrants.

These are more than clever names, however, although they are not necessarily sufficiently significant so as to represent new language or dialects. For one thing, these various language mixtures tend not to show the distinct and unique characteristics that would warrant calling them a language—for example, grammar and vocabulary that are so consistently and thoroughly different from the parent languages that they prevent mutual intelligibility.

For another thing, they might be called dialects, yet they are not strictly regional as a diaslect usually is (unless you count a country as a region), and their lexicons appear and disappear like slang rather than demonstrating sufficient accretion and transmission to successive generations. Of course, definitions of a dialect vary, even among linguists, though in general, a dialect is related historically, politically, and linguistically to a more widely spoken, higher-prestige language with which it shares enough grammar and vocabulary as to make speakers of the two languages sufficiently mutually comprehensible. This is true especially in formal or pedagogical situations where the dialect speakers are likely to use the prestige language, while still retaining in the dialect distinct features that permit its speakers to determine an insider from an outsider.

We could call these two-language mixtures *sociolects*, which is a broad, general term for languages spoken by cohesive, nonmainstream classes or subcultures, but each non-English language that forms the mixtures tends to span several classes and cultures, although that depends upon the language in question. Also, these language mixtures are identified closely with ideas and cultural shifts more than they are to cohesive ethnic groups. They also do not show the simplicity of a pidgin, in which grammar and lexicon are reduced to very simple forms.

So, for want of a better term, we'll call these English-influenced linguistic creations *glishes*. This term borrows the last syllable of English, like so many of the coinages for the mixtures do. A glish is created when words, ideas, and structures are borrowed from English by another language with increasing frequency, over a substantial period of time, up until such time as the mixture is clearly, by most definitions, a dialect.

A glish tends to have the following characteristics:

• It is a mixture of a language with English, including direct borrowings (a word is taken from English with the same spelling and meaning, though the pronunciation usually changes), modified borrowings (the spelling and/or meaning are altered, but the new form is still related to the original English), and calques (idiomatic terms that have been translated literally from English to the second language).

• It appears where two cultures come in constant contact with nearly equal force and endurance.

- It has transparency. When a word or term is borrowed or adapted from English, what is meant tends to be clear through context in the borrowing language.
- In conversations, its speakers demonstrate hybrid vigor, in which the most appropriate words, phrases, or constructions are used from the language in which they are the easiest to say or spell, or most likely to be understood by others.
- It may include grammatical errors when judged by the rules of the parent languages, but those errors are consistent, regular, and shared among multiple speakers.
- In general, its English-influenced words and structures can be discarded from the idiolect without impoverishing the speaker's ability to communicate in the non-English language.
- It has a tendency to create words, forms, and grammar that exist independent of the two parent languages, while still not qualifying as a fully formed dialect.
- In its simplest form, it is clearly not a fully formed dialect or language, meaning it does not have a distinct body of literature, is not used by an elite class, does not have prestige, is not taught in schools, is not the exclusive form of communication of its users, is not thoroughly exclusive of outsiders, and is not the exclusive language of a commonly recognized nation.
- Over the short term, it often contains instant borrowings that fill a momentary need for an idea or word that seems unavailable to the speaker of the non-English language. These borrowings might exist only for the length of a conversation (or only in a screenplay).
- Over the long term, it is distinguished from permanently but individually absorbed Anglicisms in that it has a large body of transient, unassimilated words that are culturally related, such as those dealing with trades or popular culture. While the influence of English may remain consistent, individual incidences of its influence tend to be temporarily popular, remaining well-used only as long as the cultural, technological, or political waves that brought them persist. These borrowings might exist in daily discourse for years or decades, depending upon such things as the endurance of a music fad, style of clothing, the availability of certain types of work, etc.

• At the very latest stages and in its most complex form, it includes a permanent lexicon of habitually borrowed words and forms. The lexicon is used by those who do not speak any English at all, it is transmitted to successive generations, and there is often no notion on the part of speakers that the language is adapted from English. At this stage, a glish meets some definitions of a dialect.

Spanglish

Spanglish is a well-known example of a glish. It was recognized as a distinct form of language as early as 1954 by Salvador Tío, a Puerto Rican journalist and writer. In *A Fuego Lento* he wrote, "Esta lengua nueva se llamará el 'Espanglish'. La etimología es clara. Viene de español y de english." Translated: "This new language will be called 'Espanglish.' The etymology is clear. It comes from Spanish and English."

In 1970 Rose Nash summarized Spanglish in a way that applies to the other varieties that have since appeared. It is, she wrote, "a gradual relexification of...Spanish through borrowings, adaptations, and innovations of the kind observable in every living language."[2]

Spanglish, as she defines it, generally could be said to be a variety of Spanish that contains English words in a Spanish sentence structure. The differences between the two parent languages and Spanglish have most to do with borrowed words and rather little to do with borrowed grammar. So word order, pronunciation, emphasis, and sentence rhythm are typically Spanish, and English verbs may be conjugated according to Spanish rules. "To like" becomes *likear* (*gustarse* in Spanish) and "to delete" becomes *deletear* (*suprimir* or *eliminar* in Spanish).

A glish like Spanglish is not "bad" Spanish resulting from a momentary confusion of rules nor is it the intentional mixing of the two languages for comic effect. It's ordinarily unconscious and done out of need, although it is not the same as code-switching, in which a speaker moves back and forth between two languages while retain-

2. Nash, Rose. "Spanglish: Language Contact in Puerto Rico." *American Speech*. 45.3 (1970) 223–333; "Englanol: More Language Contact in Puerto Rico." *American Speech*. 46.1 (1971) 106–122.

ing the integrity of each language without inventions, changes, or coinages.

Like Singlish, the English hybrid spoken in Singapore, Spanglish has sometimes been called a dialect of English. Both of these, while still showing many of the characteristics of glishes, are well-developed enough that they might match certain definitions of a dialect. For one thing, both are regional, although Spanglish is multiregional, with variants in New York, Puerto Rico, Texas, California, and elsewhere. Spanish spoken on beaches in Spain by British holidaymakers meets a few characteristics of a glish—mainly, it features the best use of words from either language for the purposes at hand—but it is English borrowing Spanish, not the other way around. For another, Spanglish and English are often used institutionally in media and by government.

Certainly the Spanish used in public service advertisements on behalf of New York City's Metropolitan Transit Authority or on the city's talk radio stations is not strict Castilian Spanish, nor is it completely Puerto Rican, Dominican, or Mexican—but it is comprehensible to the city's large body of Hispanophones, or *nuyoricans* (also sometimes called *nuyorricans* or *nuyoriqueños*). New York's Spanish-speakers, even those that are third-generation speakers who have never been outside of the five boroughs, can still make themselves understood when speaking to Spaniards, Chileans, or other speakers of other Spanish variants. This is especially true when they speak slower, since the number one complaint is that they speak too fast, pretty much the same complaint outsiders have of New York's English-speakers, too. The Spanish language as spoken in New York City certainly has undergone changes, but only those words that are derived from encounters with English qualify as a glish. The others merely demonstrate natural language change and its possible status as a dialect.

Singlish, too, is not just a mix of English and one other language. It also includes Hokkien Chinese, Malay, and a big dose of words from other languages. So, technically, while some facets of Singlish are glish-like, it is not a perfect example of a glish.

Various Glishes

Many of the following glishes are rarely used. Others, like Spanglish, Japlish, Hinglish, and Franglais, can be found in standard dictionaries. Many of them are joke terms, especially when they are used informally to describe someone who either speaks heavily accented or ungrammatical English, or to describe an Anglophone who is mangling and bastardizing a foreign tongue.

Amlish: American English
Anglicaan: Afrikaans
Anglikaans: Afrikaans
Anglonorsk: Norwegian
Arablish: Arabic
Benglish: Bengali
Bonglish: Bengali
Camfranglais: English and French mixed in Cameroon
Changlish: Chinese
Chinglish: Chinese
Denglish: German
Deutschlish: German
Dutchlish: Dutch
Englañol: Spanish and British English
Englog: Tagalog
Espanglish: Typically, English borrowings into Spanish
Eurolish: European English
Finglish: Finnish
Fingliska: Finnish and American English
Franglais: French
Frenglish: French
Gerlish: German
Germerican: German and American English
Germish: German
Gernglish: German
Greeklish: Greek
Gringoñol: Spanish
Hindlish: Hindi
Honglais: Hong Kong English
Hunglish: Hungarian
Indlish: Subcontinental Indian English
Indoglish: Bahasa Indonesia
Indonglish: Bahasa Indonesia
Italglish: Italian

Jamlish: Jamaican English
Janglish: Japanese
Japanglish: Japanese
Japenglish: Japanese
Japglais: Japanese
Japlish: Japanese
Konglish: Korean
Krautlish: German
Malish: Malay
Manglish: Malay
Minglish: Manx Gaelic, Maltese, mangled English (mixed with any
    other language)
Punglish: Punjabi
Punjlish: Punjabi
Runglish: Russian
Russlish: Russian
Simlish: Language of characters in the multiplayer video game "The
    Sims"
Singlish: Singaporean English (Most linguists would agree that this
    is a dialect of English.)
Spanglish: Spanish
Swedlish: Swedish
Swenglish: Swedish
Taglish: Tagalog
Tamlish: Tamil
Tanglish: Tamil, especially in the written form where the Roman
    alphabet is used instead of the Tamil
Thanglish: Tamil
Tinglish: Tamil
Wenglish: Welsh
Yinglish: Yiddish

Words to Watch

Zillions—no, gazillions—of new words are coined every year, but
only a few catch on. Here are a few that have yet to catch fire.

agnotology *n.* the science or study of ignorance caused by the characteristics, beliefs, or actions of a society or culture. *Agnotology*
includes the breaking of the chains of passed-along knowledge due

to modern advances (such as how to perform breech births or use plants in folk remedies), corporate whitewash campaigns that instill doubt about valid scientific evidence, and information that is not disseminated due to blacklists, bans, or gag rules. Probably coined by Robert Proctor, though there is a similar word, *agnoiology*, the science or study of ignorance. The antonym of both *agnoiology* and *agnotology* would probably be *epistemology*, 'the science of the nature and foundations of knowledge.'

folksonomy *n.* an accreted classification system whose levels, branches, and nodes are created informally and collaboratively by all users who submit data to a system. The most common application of this word is to describe *tagging*, used by some web sites to permit users to classify posts, pictures, questions, or other user-submitted items. From *folk* + *taxonomy*. Coined by Thomas Vander Wal.

gayhawk *n.* similar to a *fauxhawk*, in that one's hair stands on end across the top of the head, front to back, while the sides are combed upward toward the peak. The head is not shaved as it is in a Mohawk, from which both *gayhawk* and *fauxhawk* are derived using the portmanteau *-hawk*.

grandclerk *n.* the child of someone who clerked for a judge. Used by former U.S. Supreme Court Justice Sandra Day O'Connor to describe the children of her former clerks. A *law clerk* is an American term for an up-and-coming lawyer or law student who assists a judge or lawyer.

groantone *n.* an erotic or sexually suggestive ring tone for a portable telephone. Also known as a *moantone*.

honeymonkey *n.* an insecure computer designed to attract crackers, viruses, and other Internet threats so that they may be studied. Popularized, if not coined by, employees at Microsoft Corporation.

infartillery *n.* a military unit that serves the traditional functions of both artillery and infantry units. Probably coined by soldiers in the U.S. Army's Third Infantry Division's 4th Brigade Combat Team (Unit of Action) while training at the Joint Readiness Training Center at Fort Polk, LA. From *infantry* + *artillery*.

skoyc *n.* an acronym for "soft kiss on your cheek." Used mainly in online discussions but if said aloud, it is usually pronounced as "skoyk."

snazzual *adj.* fashionable and trendy, but suitable for most nonformal occasions. Usually said of clothing. From *snazzy* + *casual*.

solastalgia *n.* nostalgia or a sense of loss about rapid (negative) changes to one's community or surroundings. From Latin *solacium* 'solace' and *algos* 'pain.' Probably coined by Australian Glenn Albrecht in 2004.

splitter *n.* a public spittoon made of a potted plant attached to a lamppost, intended to keep public expectorations off the pavement. Coined by Kirtisagar Bollar in India. From *spit* + *litter.*

spluckle *n.* a split-fingered fastball pitch in baseball, also known as a *splitter*, that suddenly drops before it reaches the batter. Coined by Adam Melhuse of the Oakland A's. From *spl*it + kn*uckle*ball.

spreadmart *n.* a computer spreadsheet that exists in multiple unreconciled versions throughout an organization. Coined by Wayne Eckerson in 2002. From *spread*sheet + data *mart* 'a static collection of data of a specific time, place, and criteria.'

stay rape *n.* when a guest overstays a visit. Something akin to a gate-crasher with aphilophrenia, the kind of person that stays until the last dog is hung. It's a classic slang word: it demonstrates irreverence for the host-guest relationship and treads in taboo territory by trivializing the idea of rape.

vegepreferian *n.* someone who prefers vegetarianism but is not adamant about it. Coined by Elizabeth Bromstein in Toronto, Can. A slightly more common term is *flexitarian*.

Y V Ulluq Q *n.* a prism effect of cold ground air and higher warm air that creates a lingering band of bright light at the horizon even when the sun has set. Coined by Canadian Wayne Davidson, from the initials of his fellow scientists, Andrew Young and Siebren Van der Werf, and the Inuktitut words *ulluq*, meaning "day" or "daytime," and *qausuittuq*, meaning "the place with no dawn or no tomorrow."

On the Inside, On the Outside

One interesting subniche of slang is derogatory terms used within an ethnic group or race to insult its own members, but inside that, there's a sub-subniche of food-related derogatory terms that all follow the pattern "X on the outside; Y on the inside."

These terms share common characteristics. They are shapers of self. They reflect the way a cultural community believes one must act in order to be identified with that group, and they compare it to the way outsiders—usually a dominant Caucasian or Western culture—act. They demonstrate the conflict between a need to assimilate with mainstream culture and a need to assert one's membership in an ethnic or racial group. They describe a person's appearance and a person's behavior. They charge a person with betraying his or her true identity and community—charges that are almost impossible to defend against, making this particular kind of insult especially effective. Such name-calling leaves the subject only two choices: One, conform to the expected racial or ethnic behavior. Two, abandon a racial or an ethnic identity.

Below is a list of such terms and three similar political terms. Be warned: these are the sorts of expressions that might be used jokingly among friends but never between strangers.

apple *n.* a person who is ethnically American Indian but culturally American. In the Navajo language, the word *bilasáana* 'apple' is used.

banana *n.* a white-acting East Asian person. A typical comment: "He's a banana and posts to soc.couples.intercultural trying to brag that he's a ladies man who dated Latinas. I think he wants a white girl." (From the Usenet group soc.culture.korean, Mar. 21, 1997.)

Bounty bar *n.* in the United Kingdom, a white-acting black person. Bounty bars are a chocolate bar made with a coconut filling by Mars, Inc. They are not sold in the United States, but are similar to the Almond Joy chocolate bars made and sold by Hershey's, Inc.

cedar *n.* a white-acting American Indian, most likely in the Southeast. Rare.

coconut *n.* a white-acting black, Hispanic, or South Asian person.

egg *n.* a white-acting East Asian person.

Oreo *n.* a white-acting black person. From the Oreo-brand dessert cookie, which has two dark chocolate wafers filled with white icing.

potato *n.* a white-acting Hispanic or South Asian person.

radish *n.* a capitalist person or institution masquerading as a communist; a Chinese person who behaves like a Westerner.

rotten banana *n.* a black-acting East Asian person; a white-acting black person.

turnip *n.* a Russian communist who is secretly a royalist. From the post World War I period.

Twinkie *n.* a white-acting East Asian person. From the brand name of a yellow cake-like treat filled with white icing.

watermelon *n.* a communist or socialist masquerading as an environmentalist.

Colorful Names for Whitey

In any language, there's no shortage of epithets or nicknames for anyone who's a little different. Minorities are called with hate, the powerful get terms of resentment, foreigners get names of disgust, and outsiders get nicknames of exclusion. That means, too, that there's no shortage of terms for white Westerners.

As always, the most important factor as to whether someone is offended is context, so keep in mind that these are not words to be used lightly.

ang moh *n.* Singapore. From Hokkien Chinese for "red-haired" but describes anyone Caucasian or anything Western. Common especially in Singlish, where it is used derogatively to describe someone who is trying to act non-Asian. A more severe form is *ang moh sai*, meaning "red-haired shit."

béké *n.* French West Indies, including Dominica and Martinique. A French Creole word for a resident descending from white Europeans, especially someone in authority; the boss or owner. There are numerous supposed origins for this word, none of which can be completely proven or disproven. One claims there is a similar word in the African language Igbo and that it came to the islands with slaves. Another claims that it formerly was a term for sailor's quarters in the front of a ship. Still another claims that small rations of food known as *becquée*, 'a beakful,' were given to laborers by the plantation owners, and by transference the term was applied to the givers themselves. And last and least likely, the phrase *eh bé qué?* was said to be a corruption of *eh bien quoi?* (roughly, "so, what's this?") a French phrase used so often by white colonizers that it was corrupted into béké. The writings of Patrick Chamoiseu are excellent explorations of the cultural implications behind the white and black encounters in the Antilles.

buckra *n.* United States, a boss or master; any white person, especially one of low standing. Both the *Dictionary of American Regional English (DARE)* and the *Oxford English Dictionary (OED)* say its original source is the Efik language, spoken in what is now Nigeria, where *mbakára* means "he who surrounds or governs." It is (or was) most common in the United States in Gullah communities in coastal South Carolina and Georgia. It first shows up in the written record in 1782 in the form of "Boccarorra" in Benjamin Franklin's *Information to Those Who Would Remove to America. OED* also notes that it appeared in the patois of Surinam.

bule *n.* (boo-luh). Indonesia. Western or white; a white person. *Orang bule* is "white man" in Bahasa Indonesia.

gabacho *n.* Mexico. an American person; a gringo. As an adjective, American or originating in the United States. This term is especially applied as a mild derogative to someone who is, or pretends to be, Mexican or Hispanic. A much older form of the word—dating as early as 1530—was applied to the French and meant "uncouth person of the mountains" and was applied in Spain to people from the north who badly spoke the Occitan language used in the region where France and Spain share a frontier. Later, it was used to apply to all French persons.

gringo *n.* Originally Mexican, now widespread throughout the Americas (including Portuguese-speaking Brazil) and Spain. A white person, especially an American. Dating from at least as early as 1849, it's a highly successful word. In some uses, this word can be seen as soft teasing; in others, it's a harsh accusation of cultural imperialism.

gwailo *n.* (gwye-low) Less often transliterated as *gweilo*. China, Hong Kong, Singapore. Foreigner; Caucasian. Literally "ghost person," though the usual English translation is "white devil" or "foreign devil," perhaps because it sounds more exotic. From the Cantonese.

haole *n.* Hawaii. A white person. According to the *Hawaiian Dictionary* (2003 University of Hawaii Press), the word also seems to have made it into the Marquesan language, where it appears as *hao'e.*

honky *n.* United States. A white person, dating from at least as early as 1946. Usually derogatory. *DARE, OED,* and the *Historical Dictionary of American Slang (HDAS)* agree that this probably an outgrowth from *hunky*, 'a person of Eastern European ancestry; a manual laborer.' Until the 1960s, the spelling *hunky* was common, but *honky* is now the dominant form. It has also, perhaps, influenced *Hongkie*, a mildly offensive term used mainly by Singaporeans to describe residents of Hong Kong, who are seen as more Western and less Asian.

muzungu *n.* Kenya, Malawi, Rwanda, Uganda, Zambia. Swahili. White man; foreigner. The adventurer Richard Burton encountered this term as early as 1857 in Mombasa, Kenya. A different word, *murunge*, is used in Zimbabwe.

ndlebe zikhany' ilanga *n.* South Africa. White man. Zulu for "he whose ears reflect the sun."

vazaha *n.* Madagascar. In the Malagasy language, a white person; a foreigner. In an English translation of *Black Skin, White Masks* (1952), Francophone writer Frantz Fanon says the word means "honorable stranger."

agbero *n.* a taxi or bus tout; (*hence*) a street thug or small-time extortionist. *Nigeria.*

1965 Wole Soyinka *The Road* in *Collected Plays* (June 1, 1973), p. 224 ▶ Samson Baba Agbero...King of Touts! Champion of motor park! **1995** Niyi Osundare @ Lagos *Newswatch* (Ikeja, Nigeria) (Mar.) "See Lagos and Die" ▶ Lagos is suchlike text, only more baffling, more amorphous.... Where else would you encounter the inventive ribaldry of the agbero (motor park tout)? **2000** Sarah Krose @ Univ. of British Columbia (*Museum of Anthropology*) (B.C., Can.) (July 24) "Principles of Traditional African Art in Yoruba Thorn Wood Carvings: Conversations with Titi Adepitan," p. 100 ▶ The Yoruba word for bus conductor is *agbero*, the one who collects fares from the passengers. We sometimes also call them touts. They are as terrible as you'll ever get. Maybe we have the prime selection of bus conductors and touts anywhere in the world for their cantankerousness. I mean, they're always talking and talking and making trouble. **2002** Anthony Okoro @ Lagos, Nigeria (*All Africa*) (Jan. 17) "Lagos Smoke Shacks" ▶ These smoke joints are said to be responsible for the increasing rate of miscreants popularly called Agbero in the area. **2002** Anthony Okoro @ Lagos, Nigeria (*All Africa*) (July 22) "Agbero, 6 Traffic Management Authority Men in Street Fight" ▶ While the officials were preventing drivers from making unnecessary U-turns, the agbero was said to be encouraging them and even directing them to drive against traffic. The excesses of the miscreant reached such a point that he was stopping vehicles on the middle of the bridge, molesting and extorting money from drivers and conductors, thereby compounding the already chaotic traffic situation. **2005** *Daily Champion* (Lagos, Nigeria) (June 16) "Menace of Touts" (Int.) ▶ Despite the pull and push that has made Lagos a city of first choice for many who seek a good head-start in life, Lagos has its unique draw-backs, one of which is the menace of social miscreants otherwise known as Area Boys and motor park touts called Agberos in local parlance.

air supply *n.* a type of corruption in which money is paid for services not rendered, usually with the agreement of both parties. *Crime & Prisons. Politics. Uganda.*

1988 Mary Battiata @ Kampala, Uganda *San Francisco Chronicle* (Calif.) (July 27) "Graft, Corruption Hobble Uganda's Comeback

Efforts," p. 3/Z6 ▶ Although petty corruption is rampant in the civil service, Ruzindana has focused on the big fish—senior officials motivated less by need than greed. His target is the booming and notorious Ugandan enterprise known here as "air supply." Translation: fraud. "It means you supply nothing, and yet you are paid," said Ruzindana. **1989** Paola Totar *Sydney Morning Herald* (Australia) (July 4) "Regular Shorts," p. 26 ▶ We thought you should be given a quick taste of the fiddles his Ugandan counterpart uncovered. For bagmen, brothels, bookmakers and bribes read "air supply." **1997** *New Vision* (Nov. 24) "Uganda Wildlife Authority Wants Edroma Prosecuted" (in Kampala, Uganda) ▶ Donors and Government funds were diverted. For example $600,000 from reserve funds is unexplained, 500m/= was either diverted or unaccounted for while 136m/= was fraudulently expended. We also discovered anomalies to do with air supply of solar panels and drugs, etc. **2004** Henry Ochieng *Monitor* (Kampala, Uganda) (July 16) "Politics of Graft; Sad Movt Legacy" (Int.) ▶ This growth occurred at a time when "air supply" was introduced into the Ugandan lexicon. People in positions of influence began conniving with government accounting officers to win tenders on which they hardly delivered. The moment the cheque was cashed they would split the money and run.

alambrista *n.* an illegal immigrant who crosses into the United States via its border with Mexico. *Mexico. Spanish. United States.* [Spanish *alambrista* 'tightrope walker' = 'wire crosser']

1950 Bill Dredge *L.A. Times* (May 2) "Thousands of Mexicans Illegally Cross U.S. Border Each Month," p. 12 ▶ The feelings of the line jumpers—the alambristas—are reflected in the words of Julian Terrones Segura, 36, and newly arrived from his native village in Guerrero. **1959** White Masterson *Zanesville Signal* (Ohio) (Sept. 10) "The Dark Fantastic," no. IV, p. 31D ▶ For the Mexican turned out to be merely an alambrista, a poor peon hoping to slip across the line and find work. **1970** *Daily Report* (Ontario, Calif.) (Sept. 13) "No Peace of Mind for the Alambristas" (in Fresno, Calif.), p. A5 ▶ Alambristas, disparagingly known as "wetbacks," are being used here and elsewhere to harvest crops, particularly grapes. **1986** Sheric C. Neville @ Santa Ana, Calif. *Orange County Business Journal* (Calif.) (Feb. 17) "Study Shows Undocumented Workers Don't Steal Jobs," vol. 9, no. 3, p. 11 ▶ For years, he's answered requests by community groups to tell of his early adventures in the 1950s—how he labored, among other things, as a gardener and a trash collector; how he returned to California over and over; and how as an alambrista (wirejumper) he cooperated with the Border Patrol in what he saw as a "game."

Amexica *n.* the zone where the United States and Mexico share a border, culture, language, and economic conditions. *Politics.* The first cite is related only in that it refers to a joint Mexican-American advertising agency.

[**1945** *N.Y. Times* (Oct. 20) "Advertising News," p. 21 ▶ Publicidad Amexica, Avenida Balderas 96, Mexico City, has been formed to act as exclusive associate of Export Advertising Agency, Inc.] [**1995** *Economist* (U.K.) (Oct. 28) "Opportunity Knocks; Amexica the Beautiful" ▶ More than that, they could for the first time aspire to American standards of freedom and well-being without losing the Mexican way of life. Call it "the Amexican dream."] **1995** Robert Mottley *American Shipper* (Dec. 1) "NAFTA's Logistics Challenges," vol. 37, no. 12, p. 69 ▶ Viva Amexica. Well, not just yet. The North American Free Trade Agreement has changed the way shippers in the United States view Mexico, but only a few are responding strategically with logistics plans targeted to the large but volatile Mexican market. **2001** *Time* (June 11) "A Country of 24 Million," vol. 157, no. 23, p. 46 ▶ The united states of "Amexica" share more than a border and a common heritage: both sides welcome the benefits of trade but struggle with the pressures of growth. **2003** Ed Vulliamy *Observer* (U.K.) (Aug. 24) "Farewell America" (Int.) ▶ Poverty and race also define the country I call 'Amexica' that runs along either side of the Mexican border, belonging to both countries and neither. **2004** Samuel P. Huntington *Foreign Policy* (Mar. 1) "The Hispanic Challenge," p. 30 ▶ Charles Truxillo of the University of New Mexico predicts that by 2080 the southwestern states of the United States and the northern states of Mexico will form La Republica del Norte (The Republic of the North). Various writers have referred to the southwestern United States plus northern Mexico as "MexAmerica" or "Amexica" or "Mexifornia." "We are all Mexicans in this valley," a former county commissioner of El Paso, Texas, declared in 2001.

AMW *n.* a (pretty) woman whose career derives in some way from her appearance. *Acronym. Entertainment. Fashion. Slang. United States.* [Initialism for *a*ctress *m*odel *w*hatever]

1988 Jeannine Stein *L.A. Times* (Oct. 24) "Into the Night," p. 2 ▶ Who was there:...assorted AMWs (actress, model, whatever). **1995** Deborah Michel *Buzz Magazine* (Apr.) "The Himbos Are Coming!" (Int.) ▶ Today, hyphenates abound among himbos, many of whom are the male equivalent of AMWs (actress-model-whatevers). **1996** Peter Biskind *Premiere Magazine* (Apr.) "Good Night, Dark Prince" (Int.) ▶ He would rarely sleep with friends or colleagues. He preferred to hit on AMWs (actress-model-whatevers) who would do it for a few lines of blow and a bottle of Cristal, or do a casting-couch number. **2001** [Steve Regan] *Hull Daily Mail* (U.K.) (Jan. 1) "I loathe the sound of breaking glass I DON'T like the sound or sight of breaking glass..." ▶ I don't need the image of an AMW (actress, model, whatever) flashing her thighs and pouting saucily to encourage me. **2004** Xeni Jardin *Boing Boing* (May 5) (Int.) ▶ We stopped to let some AMWs (*actress-model-whatevers*) cross the street from SkyBar toward Chateau Marmont.

area boy *n.* a hoodlum or street thug; AGBERO. *Crime & Prisons. Nigeria.*

1992 Karl Maier @ Lagos, Nigeria (*Africa News Service*) (June 8) "Crisis Rocks Oil Giant" ▶ Sporadic riots continued for several days, especially in the big Idumota market on the central island of Lagos, where local thugs known as "area boys" sought to extort protection money from traders. **1993** (*Inter Press Service*) (July 6) "Nigeria: Army Calls for Calm as Violent Demonstrations Continue" (in Lagos, Nigeria) ▶ Markets, shops, stalls and businesses remained closed in most of the mainland while the densely populated area of the island reported violence, mainly by miscreants known here as "area boys." **1999** *Tempo* (Lagos, Nigeria) (Aug. 18) "Journalists for Cash" ▶ League of Airport and Aviation Correspondents are the denizens of airport journalism— the act of ambushing traveling VIPs for sound bites and money. Yes, money, the way an "area boy" would do it. **2005** *Daily Champion* (Lagos, Nigeria) (June 16) "Menace of Touts" (Int.) ▶ Despite the pull and push that has made Lagos a city of first choice for many who seek a good head-start in life, Lagos has its unique draw-backs, one of which is the menace of social miscreants otherwise known as Area Boys and motor park touts called Agberos in local parlance.

armchair pilot *n.* a person who talks about, studies, or directs airplane flying but is not qualified to, or does not, handle the controls; an aviation enthusiast. *Military.*

1934 *N.Y. Times* (Oct. 7) "Army to Weed Out 'Armchair' Pilots" (in Washington, D.C.), p. 9 ▶ The United States Army is going to weed out its "swivel chair" airplane pilots by making all air corps officers with fifteen or more years' service take tests to determine their flying ability. **1936** *Clearfield Progress* (Pa.) (Aug. 10) (in advert. for Chesterfield cigarettes), p. 2 ▶ One sure way to tell the real thing from an arm-chair pilot...put the stick in his hand and give him a job to do. **1938-39** Individual aviators @ N.Y. *LOTJ* "Aero-Manufacturing and Aviation Slang and Jargon," p. 1 ▶ Armchair pilot. One who talks a good flight while on the ground. **1943** *Chicago Daily Tribune* (July 11)

"Son's Airplane Club Makes His Mother Expert," p. NW8 ► Mrs. Lilly's son, George, and nine of his pals organized an aeronautical club.... These young armchair pilots have taken their club work seriously. **1946** William L. Laurence @ Aboard U.S.S. *Shangri-La,* San Diego, Calif. *N.Y. Times* (May 10) "Bikini Rehearsal Staged by Robots," p. 8 ► Lieut. Comdr. Winfield G. Maurer, USN, was the armchair pilot who took the four drones off the deck of this carrier. **1948** [176-10-6146] *Era* (Bradford, Pa.) (July 21) "Sand Pumpings," p. 14 ► One of the most popular radio shows locally is WESB's "Midnight Clipper."...Former U.S.A.A.F. hot pilot George Ward does the disc-jockey work and sends an armchair pilot's "license" to all the fans who request one. **1986** Rex Redifer *Gettysburg Times* (Pa.) (Feb. 10) "Aviation Enthusiast Collects Memorabilia," p. 14 ► Block is strictly an "armchair pilot." The flights are all in his mind, and probably more vivid than if he had actually experienced them.

Asbo *n.* a court order designed to curtail unwanted public behavior. Also **ASBO.** *Acronym. Crime & Prisons. Politics. United Kingdom.* [*anti-social behaviour order*]

1997 Raymond Duncan *Herald* (Scotland) (Nov. 17) "Minister Seeks Legislation for Stronger Powers Over Anti-Social Tenants," p. 7 ► The move would give Scotland's local authorities, who would be able to apply for Anti-Social Behaviour Orders (Asbos), greater clout in trying to deal with unruly tenants.... It would be unprecedented for the police to apply direct to the civil courts in Scotland, and Mr. McLeish has gone along with this and proposed only council involvement in seeking Asbos. **1999** *Nottingham Evening Post* (U.K.) (July 13) "More 'Noise' Action" ► Individuals who break the conditions will be charged with a criminal offence. But Mr. Coaker revealed that only one ASBO has been issued nationally since the guidelines were introduced in April. **2002** *BBC News* (Apr. 2) "Report Shows Yob Order Gaps" (Int.) ► Anti-social behaviour orders, introduced in 1999, work successfully where they are implemented, according to the new Home Office study.... Known as Asbos, the orders are designed to prevent theft, intimidation, drunkenness, violence and other nuisance behaviour.

Asiental *adj.* Asian of unknown or unspecific nationality. Also *n.* [*Asian* + Ori*ental*]

2001 *Usenet: alt.religion.kibology* (June 20) "Pride in the Name of Ramen" ► The local Carrs Plus/Safeway store, where I shop, has the most wonderful "asiental" aisle with all kinds of goofy stuff in it with pictures of martian fruits and vegetables on the packaging next to bug-eyed cartoon kids (and poki!). ***2002** *The Uvnaut Contingency* "Beware the Yellow Menace!" (Int.) ▶ It is my dream that every Asian/Oriental /Asiental person in the world would own and wear this shirt. **2004** Josh Berthume (beltane) *iamsadred.com* (Oct. 19) "#00003—Metrobution" (Int.) ▶ The people in front of us had some very urgent business that needed immediate attention, and this business had to be discussed in Asiental as loud as possible. The only English I heard was "Call me back in five minutes—the movie is starting." **2005** [Jin] @ Iowa City, Iowa *A Discontent Malcontent* (Seattle, Wash.) (Mar. 3) "Making No Friends in Fourth Grade" (Int.) ▶ I brought Tiger Balm to school for show and tell. I didn't know exactly what it was for but that it looked all asiental and so I thought people would think it was cool. So I passed it around and told everyone to put it under their eyes because Tiger Balm was what made Chinese people so good at math and the violin. They believed me.

asplode *v.* a jocular form of *explode*. Also **a splode.** Often used in representations of uncouth or uneducated speech. Sometimes said to be a representation of a Spanish speaker's pronunciation of the English word, particularly as demonstrated by Cuban actor Desi Arnaz. This term was popularized in 2004 by the character Strong Bad on the Homestar Runner web site homestarrunner .com.

[**1996** *Usenet: alt.fan.letterman* (Dec. 17) "Dave Made Fun of Kid?" ▶ Is it me, or did Dave make fun of the kid's pronunciation and said "Asplode" instead of explode?] **2002** *Usenet: alt.dss.hack* (Mar. 8) "Re: What 222 Was All About—a Scenario" ▶ Oh an I almost fergot that all my heirs fells outsa my hed when I asploded it cause I wuz standin too cloze ta it. **2004** *Homestarrunner.com* (Jan. 12) "Video Games" (Int.) ▶ YOUR HEAD A SPLODE. **2004** [waterlily25] *Raechalsan* (Jan. 15) "Your Head Asplode!" (Int.) (title). **2004** [IBleedPurple11] *Fark* (Jan. 31) "Woman Gives Birth to Her Own Grandchildren, Making the Newborns Their Own Parents" (Int.) ▶ IBleedPurple11: "What's with all the exploding heads? A running joke that I'm missing? And besides, shouldn't it be a'splode?" rancidPlasma: "when i said my 'head exploded,' it was a euphemism for fapping...this story is just too damn erotic for me." **2004** *Usenet: alt.games.mame* (Feb. 28) "Re: My Reply" ▶ I'll buy household items from IKEA and sell them on line...and then I can make a web site wih lots of spelling mistakes, and then also make sure I POST USING JUST CAPITALS...Your head a splode. retard. **2004** [Jorad] *Fark* (Apr. 6) "Photoshop Al Franken Taking a Break from Spreading Liberal Propaganda" (Int.) ▶ Al Franken's Head-A-Splode.

awfulize *v.* to imagine or predict the worst circumstances or outcome. The first cite is an unrelated nonce usage.

[**1974** Arthur Allen Leff *Virginia Law Review* (Mar.) "Commentaries on Richard A. Posner's 'Economic Analysis of Law,'" vol. 60, no. 3, p. 460 ▶ It is a most common experience in law schools to have someone say, of some action or state of events, "how awful," with the clear implication that reversing it will de-awfulize the world to the full extent of the initial awfulness.] **1980** Sharon A. Terry-Haag *Family Relations* (July) "Review: Sex and the Liberated Man," vol. 29, no. 3, p. 417 ▶ He highlights and subsequently shatters a multitude of erroneous myths that are conceived within the particularly large cleavage between what one feels he "should" or "must" do, and what he wants to do or does. His technique? Quite simply, anti-awfulizing—which seems to be proposed as the panacea for everything from impotence to omnipotence. He instructs his reader to focus on pleasuring himself *and* his partner and to learn to accept himself as he is. **1981** Albert B. Crenshaw *Washington Post* (Jan. 11) "Don't Blame Others for Stress You Can Handle," p. B8 ▶ Awfulizing is "terminal pessimism," which turns a half-hour delay into a global crisis. **2005** Kelly Griffith *Orlando Sentinel* (Fla.) (July 3) "Bits and Bytes to Ponder, Even Avoid" (Int.) ▶ Heard a new word recently and decided I like it. *Awfulizing* is the practice of thinking something is so horrible and so awful that there's no other way to feel but depressed, dejected and without hope. Awfulizing drags people into pitiful states of despair—usually needlessly. If you catch yourself awfulizing, stop and ask yourself, "What's *really* the worst thing that can possibly happen here?"

B

babalog *n.* a young, Westernized social group or individual concerned with wealth, pop culture fads, appearance, material goods, or other superficialities; a yuppy or yuppies. Formerly associated with associates of Rajiv Gandhi. Also *attrib. Hindi. India. Urdu.* [< Anglo-Indian 'children' < Hindi *baba* 'father' + *log* 'people, tribe, caste, folk']

1998 Sevanti Ninan *Hindu* (Chennai, India) (July 12) "A Question of Style" ▶ Star News, with its socioeconomic category A and A+ audience firmly in mind, hires the babalog of New Delhi's movers and shakers, the sort of young people who have trouble reading the Devnagri script. **2002** Usenet: *rec.arts.movies.local.indian* (Feb. 7) "Humour: Our Brown Sahebs (Re: Language in Indian Films)" ▶ This is a hilarious article I dug up from an *Illustrated Weekly* dated July 5, 1970..."Our Brown Sahebs—By Bachi N. Kanga...The Brown Sahebs babalog go to public schools where they wear caps and striped ties (the tie is Very important, it is the bond of a lifetime), learn latin, play cricket and eat Irish stew. They get their facts of Indian history from S. Reed Brett Esq., who dwells in great and gory detail over, the Black Hole of Calcutta. Jalianwalla Bagh? Never heard of it." **2003** Usenet: *rec.sport.cricket* (Jan. 14) "Re: Sidhu Road Rage Murderer?" ▶ i'm anyway opposed to this Kakaji (Babalog) culture where these brats are given so many resources and power that they consider themselves much above the lesser mortals. **2004** Shobha De *Times of India* (Feb. 1) "Page 3 Politicians" (Int.) ▶ The Babalog are gearing up for the party ahead (everything's a party, darling, when you get to the bottom of it). Their idea of grass-roots level democracy does not go beyond checking their own manicured lawns for weeds. Don't be surprised if election promises include really, really vital stuff like extending lounge bar timings and doing away with taxes on designer clothes. The party they belong to is the one being hosted by a polo-playing buddy in a sprawling farmhouse. These good-looking leaders will push an agenda that might include the transformation of their shrewdly chosen constituencies into versions of Buddha Bar. **2004** David Orr, David Guttenfelder @ Delhi, India *Scotsman* (Scotland) (May 16) "Triumph of Dynasty's Darling" (Int.) ▶ These are the 'babalog,' the young crowd, or to use the buzzword of the Indian media, the 'GenNext': cyber-savvy, computer-literate, young urban professionals.

babyface turn *n.* in professional wrestling, a change of allegiance or attitude by a wrestler, usually from bad to good. *Entertainment. Jargon. United States.* In professional wrestling, *babyface* equals 'good guy' and *heel* equals 'bad guy.'

1993 *Usenet: rec.sport.pro-wrestling* (Oct. 10) "Eddie Gilbert's Scarlet Letter" ▶ He mentioned then how the actions that occurred after that, including his unscheduled babyface turn at the 9/18 show, cost him his best friend in the business. **1997** *Chicago Sun-Times* (June 15) "Steve 'Mongo' McMichael," p. 35 ▶ Meltzer called McMichael's May PPV tussle with the Packers' Reggie White "easily the worst match of this or many other years." Don't be surprised if a major storyline twist (read babyface turn) occurs soon. **2002** Eric Quinones *Star-Ledger* (Newark, N.J.) (Sept. 26) "Booker T Will Be Main Man Soon" ▶ Booker T languished in mid-card programs—yet gradually began winning over fans with his charisma and humor. After a brief run with the New World Order, he was bounced from the heel group, cementing his babyface turn. [**2003** Classy Freddie Blassie *Legends of Wrestling: "Classy" Freddie Blassie* (May 1), p. 158 ▶ Sometimes, a promoter decides to turn a guy babyface because he's not getting over as a heel. Other times, the fans make the decision for the promotion.] **2004** *Usenet: rec.arts.movies.reviews* (July 14) "Review: King Arthur (2004)" ▶ Merlin (Stephen Dillane) seems to be warring with Arthur's crazy-brave knights, until he pulls a babyface turn (as they call it in wrestling) and decides to join the fight for Britain against the Saxons.

babymoon *n.* a planned period of calm spent together by a just-born baby and its parents; occasionally, time spent by parents without their baby. [Author Sheila Kitzinger claims to have coined the word.]

1993 *Usenet: misc.kids* (Nov. 10) "Re: WAS (Sweet Homebirth Story—1 Year Later) Now: The Milkmoon?" ▶ The Milk Moon is my own twist on the term "baby moon"; the new baby honeymoon. **1995** *Usenet: misc.kids.pregnancy* (Mar. 1) "Re: Family Help After Delivery??" ▶ I think it's great to give yourselves time for a babymoon before sharing your new little one with all of creation. **1996** Sheila Kitzinger *Year After Childbirth* (Sept. 6), p. 203 ▶ The transition to fatherhood is easier when a man can take time off to be with his partner and baby in what I call a "Babymoon." A couple lay in food and other necessities, lock the door, and go to bed with their baby for a few days. **1997** Ian Hargreaves *Guardian* (U.K.) (Feb. 5) "Parents: Nappy Days,"

p. T8 ► This period is the "babymoon," when the parents enjoy a few days inside a bubble before contending with other, more familiar realities. **2004** Lisa Lewis *Athens Banner-Herald* (Ga.) (Dec. 26) "Lewis: You May Be Entitled to a Babymoon" (Int.) ► I have learned a brand-new word—"babymoon."...This is just like taking a honeymoon except you're pregnant. So, in truth, this must be nothing at all like a honeymoon, however, the purpose is to have one last "hurrah" as a couple (whatever that may mean—a solid night's sleep?) before baby arrives.... The originally coined term "babymooning" has an altogether different definition. The babymoon, as childbirth educator and author Sheila Kitzinger described, is the necessary uninterrupted time parents need to bond with their new baby the first days after birth, sans well-intentioned visitors.

backdoor draft *n.* extension of military enlistments through stop-loss orders, which force personnel to involuntarily extend their tours of duty. *Military. Politics. United States.*

1999 *Usenet: alt.military* (Apr. 5) "Re: Recalls Occurring; Seeking More Info" ► One individual advised that he is being involuntarily recalled for placement in the Army Reserve, despite having been out of the Army for over two years. Apparently the referenced action is being taken because of the Army's ongoing manning problems. I'm aware of the continuing liability for recall after separation, but among some of my correspondents the news that this "back door draft" is actually occurring was understandably greeted with surprise and concern. **2003** Carol Lin *CNN Sunday* (Nov. 9) "New Poll Shows Half of Americans Disapprove of Bush's Handling of Iraq" ► [Arnold] Garcia:..."The use of the increasing dependence on the reserve and guard components amounts to, as one of the editorial writers said in a meeting yesterday, a back door draft."...[Carol] Lin: "That's interesting. A back door draft. In a sense even though it's a volunteer army, but these guys didn't sign up with the idea of spending their Christmas in the desert, I [*sic*] sure, certainly under these battle conditions." **2004** Bettijane Levine *Orlando Sentinel* (Fla.) (Nov. 5) "Uncle Sam Still Wants Them" (Int.) ► That's a draft...a backdoor draft. That's compulsory military service...against the individual's will.

backpacker *n.* a fan of hip-hop who is seen as a poser, slummer, faker, or elitist. Also *various adjectival and attributive forms. Derogatory. Hip-Hop. Slang. United States.* This term is usually derogatory.

[**1996** *Usenet: rec.music.hip-hop* (Oct. 30) "Re: Gangsta Rap R.I.P." ► If i came on here talkin bout baggy-jean, stripped-shirt, & beanie hat wearing, backpack toters, aka "hip-hoppers" I would get flamed.]
[**1998** *Usenet: rec.music.hip-hop* (July 9) "Re: Prosylitizing the Under-

ground and Other Lanky Stinky Madness" ▶ I think that's already happening in the form of what Stretch Armstrong disdainfully calls "backpack rap"—emphasis on lyrics and/or bugged production, with head-nodding a low priority. unfortunately, this kind of synthetic genre is almost always defined by target demographic, not internal resemblance.] **1999** *Usenet: rec.music.hip-hop* (Jan. 13) "Re: Last Night's Eminem Show" ▶ Zee must have been mad because em is rollin with dre and will most likely be on a for sure classic Chronic 2000 and zee will still be nothin more than a boring piece of shit backpacker loser bum. **1999** *Usenet: rec.music.hip-hop* (Mar. 1) "Re: Exactly What Is a 'Backpacker'?" ▶ I use the term when describing either a trendy only independent loving hip-hop kid...you usually see them at concerts with backpacks on or the college hip-hop kid who wears a backpack out of necessity...they too often are on the independent/underground tip...these 2 often are one in the same. Another "backpacker" I can think of is the urban youth who are strictly public transportation, sporting the walkman listening to hip-hop. **2000** *Usenet: alt.rap* (May 19) "Re: A Classic Situation" ▶ If you wanna battle, nerdy-ass backpacker style and see who can throw out the most obscure, old-school, underground, unheard of ass joints then step right up son, you will lose quick, fast in a hurry. I know it taxes your underpowered brain to come up with terms like "true head" but that shit is weak...you're trying to make yourself out to be some bad-ass backpacker, 'cuz you can throw out a few names that maybe someone who listens to Master P and Mase hasn't heard of. **2004** Tony Green *MSNBC* (June 22) "South on the Rise in Hip-Hop World" (Int.) ▶ There are a lot of places that we still didn't get to in the video—Arkansas, Kentucky. And there is a big "backpacker" (or alternative) hip-hop scene that we didn't get to. But that doesn't take away from this video. It says exactly what needed to be said exactly when it needed to be said. **2004** Neil Kulkarni *Hip Hop: Bring the Noise* (July 1), p. 33 ▶ Company Flow first crashed into our lives in 1995.... We were dumb enough to think that Rawkus could be bold, new avatars of the hip-hop revolution. The word "backpackers" didn't even have any currency at the time; the reflexive self-hatred and reverse-racial inferiority complexes that would break out like a rash across the avant-garde hip-hop scene hadn't yet gained such an engulfing weight.

bag drag *n.* generally, the transportation of luggage; in air travel, a connecting flight or the act of getting to a flight (with luggage); in the military, a change in deployment, especially a multipart itinerary that includes a change in vehicles, modes of transportation, or gear. *Military.*

1990 Carey French *Globe and Mail* (Toronto, Can.) (Nov. 17) "Airport's Luggage Crisis of More Than 20 Million Bags Yearly Has British Airways

Staff 'on the Brink of a Nervous Breakdown,'" p. F6 ► "Why, if we are incapable of transferring passengers' bags, do we continue to pretend we can." Faced with the anguish of being separated from luggage, the personal "bag drag" would surely be the better way, the staffer suggested. **1994** Vince Kohler *Oregonian* (Portland) (Jan. 29) "Astronaut Makes Rounds in Portland," p. B4 ► Astronauts call it "the bag drag." The name comes from lugging their bags from airport to airport as they make the rounds on behalf of the National Aeronautics and Space Administration. **1994** Laura A. Galloway *L.A. Times* (Mar. 20) "L.A. Speak: Flight Attendants," p. 12 ► *Bag drag*: n. when a flight attendant takes a trip but never even opens her luggage. **1998** Department of the U.S. Air Force @ Rhein-Main Air Base, Germany (*FDCH Regulatory Intelligence Database*) (June 16) "Troops Heading for Bosnia Can Say Goodbye to 'Bag Drag'" ► The service is going one step further and getting rid of the No. 1 irritant for troops deployed to Hungary and the former Yugoslavia: The bag drag they experience when they deploy from their home base. **1998** Ray Johnson *Airman* (Oct. 1) "Over Here, Over There," vol. 42, no. 10, p. 40 ► For almost three years, the bulk of Balkan-peacekeeping troops have served in Croatia, Bosnia-Herzegovina and Hungary. To arrive, most did the infamous "bag drag," hauling mobility gear from airport to airport, often incurring excess-baggage costs, delays and weapons hassles. **2000** Jeanne Claire van Ryzin, Becky Howell *Austin American-Statesman* (Aug. 31) "The Work We Do," p. 26 ► Sometimes if you have a 20 or 30 minute turn in a city, somebody on the crew will make a food run to the terminal. If you're lucky, you stay with one plane all day. If not, you've got a bag drag from one end of the airport to another. **2003** Richard A. Bowen @ Foothill Ranch, Calif. *L.A. Times* (Apr. 6) "If He Has to Fly, He'll Skip the Trip," p. L16 ► As the son of an international airline captain and a pilot in the Marine Corps for 22 years, I have spent a lot of time in the back—and front—of aircraft.... On a recent ski trip to Utah, I did not enjoy doing the "bag drag" to a security checkpoint after standing in line at the main ticket counter. **2004** Dave *Flight Level 390* (Phoenix, Ariz.) (Dec. 5) "Non Directional Beacon" (Int.) ► At Las Vegas we had a bag drag, airline parlance for an aircraft change.

bajet *n.* budget. < *English. Malaysia. Malaysian. Money & Finance. Politics.* [From English *budget.*]

2002 Shamsul Yunos *Malay Mail* (Malaysia) (Sept. 21) "More Breathing Space for SMIs" ► The Prime Minister was hinting at a paradigm shift when he wanted the Budget to be known as "Bajet" and not "Belanjawan" from this year on. **2004** Leslie Lau *Straits Times* (Singapore) (May 4) "Uproar Over Rojak Malay" (Int.) ► This does not explain why the government itself introduced new words like Bajet, for 'Budget,' into the Malay language, when the word Belanjawan was once commonly used.

bakkie *n.* a small pickup truck or van. *Automotive. South Africa.* [The Datsun 680, 1200, and 1400 light trucks were a few of several similar models, made by the now-defunct manufacturer, which took the nickname "bakkie." A similar vehicle is now sold in South Africa by Nissan as the "Nissan 1400 bakkie." It seems the term originated as a nickname, not as a brand name.]

1978 *N.Y. Times* (Jan. 8) "A Walk to Freedom," p. E19 ► Eventually, along came a "bakkie"—a small farm van—and the driver took me to near Sterkspruit. **1986** Michael Parks *L.A. Times* (Oct.2) "Residential Segregation Will Continue, President Botha Vows," p. 5 ► "It is strange that we are prepared to travel in a car with a Colored, and allow him to ride on our bakkie (pickup truck) on the farm," Botha said, "but when he wants to live close to you, then there is trouble." **2002** [David] *Datsun 1200 Club* (Nov. 20) "Datsun 1200 History, Models and Production" (Int.) ► The B140 is still being made in South Africa (the truck is called "Bakkie" in SA). **2003** *Wheels24* (S. Africa) (Dec. 12) "Honda's Double Cab Bakkie" (Int.) ► Honda is going to show an innovative bakkie concept at the Detroit Motor Show in January. This new and innovative pickup concept will provide the world with its first glimpse of the direction Honda will take with a future production sport-utility truck model.

Baltimore wrench *n.* a chisel and hammer. Jocular or lightly derogatory. Besides *Oregon wrench* given in the citations below, *HDAS* records the similar *Canal wrench*, which is a shovel, and there is an unpublished *HDAS* citation for *big red wrench* 'an acetylene cutting torch.' From these we can get a broader definition of *wrench* 'a tool used for a purpose other than for which it was intended, especially when used as an implement of brute force.'

***1938-39** Mendelowitz @ Wisc., Ohio, N.Y., Ind., Mich., Ala. *LOTJ* "Machinists' Slang and Jargon ['add Machinists'])," p. 3 ► Baltimore wrench. Hammer and flat chisel used to remove tight nuts. [**1958** McCulloch *Woods Words,* p. 128 in *HDAS* ► *Oregon wrench*—Cold chisel and hammer.]

bampot *n.* a crazy person; a fool or dolt. *Scotland. Scots.* [Most likely a form of *barmpot*. According to *OED*, *barm*, "the froth that forms on top of fermenting malt liquors; the head of a beer," is used attributively as a formative to indicate a crazy or feebleminded person or idea. This is, obviously, related to *barmy* or *balmy* 'crazy.'

Thanks to Michael Quinion of World Wide Words for the tip on *bampot*'s etymology. Probably not related to the Irish Gaelic *bambairne* 'dolt, stupid person, lout.' In "Some Modern Irish Loanwords Describing People" (*Celtica* vol. 18, p. 53, 1986, School of Celtic Studies, Dublin) Mícheál Ó Siadhail connects *bambairne* to the old Spanish slang *bambarria*, which, according to the *Velasquez Spanish and English Dictionary* (1985, New Win Publishing) means 'a fool; an idiot.' *Bambarria* is glossed as "blockhead" in Carnoy, Albert. "Apophony and Rhyme Words in Vulgar Latin Onomatopoeias." *American Journal of Philology*, vol. 38, no. 3. (1917) 271.]

1988 Sharyn McCrumb *Paying the Piper* (Nov. 13), p. 27 ▶ All the old bampot wanted to do was measure stone circles and to prove his engineering theory. **1990** Andrew Rawnsley *Guardian* (U.K.) (Mar. 29) "The Day in Politics ▶ Border Skirmish Has Sassenachs Out in Force" ▶ Labour's Scots erupted in uproar, shouting "Ye silly bampot" at Mr. Greenway and the old dialect phrase: "goo boil ye heed." **1993** *Usenet: soc.culture.celtic* (July 13) "Re: Help with a Kilt!" ▶ "Bampot," or "bam" for short, means something like "self-important obsessionally deluded fruitcake." **2002** Pamela Stephenson *Billy* (Sept. 11), p. 115 (Int.) in (Dec. 1, 2003) ▶ He was highly embarrassed by his son, the bampot, or crazy, welder with hair like a woman and two earrings. **2003** *One Fine Day in the Middle of the Night* (May 1) "Christopher Brookmyre," p. 50 ▶ Sociopath, psychopath, whatever you like, Matt had always preferred bampot. Not *a* bampot but *the* bampot; the absolute quintessence of bampottery. **2005** Magnus Linklater *Times* (London, Eng.) (Aug. 13) "Labour Party at Prayer Salutes Cook the Atheist" (Int.) ▶ "What a bampot," muttered another (bampot being a peculiarly Scottish word for idiot).

bang *v.* in baseball, to call off a game because of inclement weather. *Sports.* [Perhaps from the notion of a judge banging a gavel, an act of finality comparable to a referee deciding to end a game prematurely.] This verb is usually transitive: **bang a game.**

1986 Dennis Brackin *Star Tribune* (Minneapolis-St. Paul, Minn.) (Mar. 22) "When It Rains It Pours—Twins All Wet Again" ▶ Last year we're down 7-3 in New York and they bang the game after 32 minutes. **1994** Matt Michael *Post-Standard* (Syracuse, N.Y.) (Apr. 13) "Chiefs Slosh Past Ottawa at Big Mac" p. B1 ▶ After an hour-long rain delay, the umpires called the game because the field was a mess.... "Early in the game I thought, 'Yeah, we're going to get banged pretty soon,' but once we got into the fifth, sixth inning and they didn't bang it I said, 'Well, we're going to play right through.'" **1995** [Rob

Mallicoat (mallyman)] *1995 Replacement Diary* (Apr. 7) (Int.) ▶ We were rained on for 6 solid hours and the game was banged by 4:30. **2003** David Andriesen *Seattle Post-Intelligencer* (Wash.) (May 16) "A Win Worth Its Wait; Rain Halts Long Enough for Mariners to Secure Victory," p. D1 ▶ The baseball slang for canceling a game is to "bang it." **2003** John Hoffman *OriolesHangout.com* (July 13) "Orioles Minor League Game Summaries" (Int.) ▶ The game was banged after a 48-minue rain delay, that included 30 minutes of actual rain. **2005** [Marc] *Reds Spring Training* (Cincinnati, Ohio) (Mar. 9) "Wet Wednesday" (Int.) ▶ As of this moment, neither game has been called off—or "banged," in clubhouse parlance—but plenty of the players have their fingers crossed.

Bangalored *adj.* (said of a corporation, project, or employment) having been relocated to India; having lost business or employment due to such a relocation. *Business. Employment. Technology.* Technologically, Bangalore is the Indian equivalent of Silicon Valley in the United States.

2003 *Usenet: comp.os.vms* (Mar. 11) "Re: [OT] After Two Months of SAP Training :-(" ▶ CPQ UK's order management stuff (which I *think* covers Europe) *was* in the process of being Bangalored. **2004** Christopher Farrell *BusinessWeek* (U.S.) (Apr. 9) "A Double Standard on Trade" ▶ I am a software developer who is about to be "Bangalored." **2004** Chidanand Rajghatta @ Washington, D.C. *Times of India* (July 21) "Bangalored! BPO Bashers' War Cry" (Int.) ▶ An online anti-outsourcing web site is marketing a T-shirt with the legend "Don't Get Bangalored," a term suggesting losing one's job to outsourcing.

bang in *v.* to call in sick to work; (*hence*) to take a day off from work under false pretenses. *Slang. United States.* This is probably related to *bang the books* 'to commit time and attendance fraud,' which at least one source indicates is part of FBI jargon.

1982 *N.Y. Times* (Mar. 26) "Jargon of Correction Officers," p. B4 ▶ *Banging in*—When an officer calls in sick. **1987** Mike Barnicle *Boston Globe* (Mar. 20) "On His Route to Happiness," p. 19 ▶ All of us know people who, at one time or another, have banged in sick instead of going to the plant or the office in the morning even though there was nothing physically wrong with them. **1994** Peter J. Howe *Boston Globe* (Feb. 15) "Sick-Day Abuse Abates Since Crackdown by Weld," p. 15 ▶ Gov. Weld, who has had mixed results purging state government of the alleged hacks and layabouts he once called "walruses," has scored a rare success in attacking part of the walrus culture—abuse of sick time. State Revenue Department employees two years ago were the leaders in what Beacon Hill bureaucrats have dubbed "banging in." **1996** *Usenet: ne.general* (Jan. 9) "Re: How Are Big Companies Handling Employee 'Snow Days'?" ▶ I can't speak for THIS company, but the way I think it all works is Non-Exempt (Hourly) people don't get paid and use a finite number of sick days if they do happen to bang in sick on any day, including snow. **1998** *Usenet: alt.snail-mail* (Jan. 13) "Re: Excessive Sick Leave?" ▶ Before I was hired, a few of our city carriers worked nights at Yankee Stadium as ushers. They banged in so that they could work an afternoon game, and wound up on TV. Waved to the camera and everything. They were seen. No discipline. **1998** *Usenet: sci.optics.fiber* (Jan. 18) "Question" ▶ In Boston, when one "Bangs out," it means to call in sick for your shift. Conversely, the police "Bang IN." **2004** [Sullysox] *Sons of Sam Horn: P&G Archives #3* (Mar. 4) "I Banged in Today" (Int.) ▶ I banged in today. I haven't been this hung over since college. I feel kinda guilty about calling in sick. **2004** Bill Tortolini *Dabel Brothers Forums* (June 3) (Int.) ▶ I banged in sick to work for 2 days to finish the last GRRM book! **2004** Sari Horwitz *Washington Post* (Oct. 18) "Police Show Strain from Endless Alerts" (Int.) ▶ By the end of the Columbus Day weekend, more than 70 officers charged with protecting Congress had called in sick. It was the largest number of Capitol Police officers who ever had "banged in." Many of them say they really were sick—an illness brought on by fatigue.

bank *v.* to gang up on (someone); to ambush. *Slang. United States.*

1992 Robin Farmer *Richmond Times-Dispatch* (Va.) (Oct. 11) "New Start Seeks to Change Behavior," p. B1 ▶ Candy, constantly sucking her finger, says she thinks her nose is broken from a recent fight. "Two girls banked me," she explains. **1998** Dawn Fallik @ Baltimore, Md. *Peoria Journal Star* (Feb. 13) "Schoolyard Squabble Ends in Boy's Death," p. C8 ▶ The Bella Vista Boys—named, in a fashion, after the Baltimore neighborhood Belle Vista—didn't just blame Rabb, they "banked" him, or ganged up on him to teach him a lesson. **2004** Adam Billington, Mike Taylor *News Journal* (Wilmington, Del.) (June 13) "An Increase in Girls Fighting Girls" (Int.) ▶ The 16-year-old said she was "banked," a street word meaning she was ganged up on, by East Side girls. She was hit and scratched and her hair weaves were pulled out.

barbecue stopper *n.* a topic of constant and widespread conversation, especially a divisive political or social issue; (*hence*) a social gaffe. *Australia. Politics.*

2001 Jennifer Hewett *Sydney Morning Herald* (Australia) (Oct. 27) "Man on a Mission," p. 29 ▶ That's one reason he will talk about improving the balance between work and family, a topic he describes as a "barbecue stopper" because it engenders so much conversation whenever people get together. **2003** Catherine McGrath *Australian Broadcasting Corporation* (July 29) "Federal Cabinet Discussing the Problem of Housing Affordability" ▶ Is housing affordability the new barbeque stopper? After yesterday's figures confirming that housing prices are getting further and further out of many people's reach, moves are gathering pace to set up an inquiry into the issue. **2003** Luke Morfesse *West Australian* (Dec. 3) "Police Defend Macro" ▶ Although more than seven years have passed since their deaths, the Claremont serial killer case has often been a barbecue stopper. A mixture of fear and fascination fuelled by media updates on any developments in the case has ensured this. **2004** Sarah Wilson *Sunday Herald Sun* (Melbourne, Australia) (Jan. 11) "A Kiss May Tell Far More Than You Think" ▶ Can crazy, aching love stem and sustain itself from one kiss?...This topic became something of a barbecue stopper among my sausage-turning friends this week. The meat of the discussion was: How do you know if you have enough to launch a full-blown romance? **2004** *Usenet: aus.bicycle* (Mar. 1) "Re: Peck Order" ▶ Always amuses me how friends at a BBQ will complain how trucks harass and force them off the road. "Just like riding a bike when you're driving a car," I said on the weekend. "Oh, but I don't do that," she said. Her kid pipes up, "Yes you do, mum. What about that man you almost hit yesterday." "Oh, god I'm sorry," she said. "Don't be sorry to me, just try to avoid having to apologize to that guy's family next time." Now, that's a BBQ-stopper!!! **2004** *Usenet: alt.politics* (May 14) "Re: Kerry's Lead of a Week Ago All Gone Now, Thanks to the Iraq Prisoner Scandal" ▶ Maybe if we're lucky, there will be a religious nut who will stand as an independent and be a BBQ stopper for the Republican party. Nothing would please me more than seeing the Republican party split into factions resulting in around 35% support for GWB. **2005** Mr. Whippy *BBQ Stoppers* (Australia) (Jan. 14) "Why Would You Want to Stop a BBQ?" (Int.) ▶ I should explain exactly just what the phrase "BBQ Stopper" actually means. It's Australian slang for a social incident or inappropriate comment that causes everyone at the BBQ to stop talking and look at you in a half-embarrassed, half-accusing kind of way.

bark mitzvah *n.* a (13th birthday) party held for a dog. *Animals. Religion.* [From *bark* 'the onomatopoeic sound a dog is said to make' + bar *mitzvah*, the Jewish ceremony for a boy's arrival at the age of manhood and religious responsibility, or bat mitzvah, the equivalent ceremony for a girl.] Usually jocular. The events themselves usually have few, if any, serious religious components and are less coyly known simply as *cat mitzvahs* and *dog mitzvahs*. In many cases, the 13th birthday is figured in *dog years,* usually said to be a ratio of seven dog years for every one human year.

1991 Bonnie Miller Rubin, Paul Gapp, Valli Herman *Chicago Tribune* (Dec. 29) "Best of Bad Taste: Our 10 Picks for the Year's Worst Ideas in Home Decor" ▶ What? No Bark Mitzvah? There seems to be a major taste problem when it comes to pet products. Who can forget Jim Bakker's air-conditioned dog house? Yet it's hard to imagine a bigger turkey than a kitty yarmulke. From the Crazy Cat Lady catalog: "For kosher cats who want to impress their friends at temple. For gentile kittens, there are kitty Santa hats." **1992** Kit Boss *Seattle Times* (Wash.) (Feb. 24) "1,700 Hours of TV: What Does It Mean?" p. K7 ▶ Next channel. Talk show host Joan Rivers appears. It's her dog Spike's 13th birthday, his "bark mitzvah." Rivers promises, "We're going to have a gala celebration with lots of four-legged friends and their celebrity owners." **2000** Lucy Broadbent @ L.A. *Mirror* (U.K.) (June 27) "LA Story—The Fairy-Tail Lives of Hollywood's Hounds" ▶ An LA dog can expect no less than lunch in his own restaurant, a pet limousine service to take him there and a "barkmitzvah" party, complete with doggy catering for his friends. **2004** Lily Koppel *N.Y. Times* (Dec. 20) "Today He Is a Dog; Actually, He Always Was" (Int.) ▶ In the long walk of history between man and dog, the bark mitzvah could be seen as an unexpected pit stop. Yet it was celebrated on Saturday night in the Bronx in a traditional way, with a party for family and friends of the 13-year-old that included a chopped-liver sculpture, choruses of "mazel tov!" (or, in this case, "muzzle tov!"), a cantor and gifts.

battle rattle *n.* (protective) military gear worn in combat situations. *Military. Slang.* An identical term dating to at least 1945 and meaning "nervousness in the face of combat" or "combat fatigue" is apparently separately derived. *Battle rattle* also appears in news, prose, and poetry as a literal term.

1995 Indira A.R. Lakshmanan @ Tuzla, Bosnia-Herzegovina *Boston Globe* (Dec. 21) "NATO Brings Fresh Mandate to Bosnia," p. 2 ▶ The main gate, which previously was manned by a Swedish soldier in a ribbed turtleneck, camouflage pants and felt beret, was secured by at least six American paratroopers and military police in full combat regalia, heavy body armor and helmets—battle rattle, as they call it. **2001** Greg Fontenot (July 1) "The Urban Area During Stability Missions Case Study" in *Capital Preservation Russell Glenn,* p. 213 ▶ Maintain the standard for the duration—full battle rattle and alert troops was our standard. **2004** *[Oneguy]* @ *Iraq MREater* (Boise, Idaho) (Oct. 8) "Spinning Up" (Int.) ▶ At 0001 hrs today we started to wear our "battle rattle," or as it's more affectionately known, our crap.

bat wings *n.pl.* flabby undersides of the upper arms; untoned tricep muscles. *Health.*

1993 *Toronto Star* (Can.) (Oct. 25) "'Bat Wing' Procedure Becoming Popular," p. E6 ▶ With so much celebrity flexing and flaunting going on, more women are turning to plastic surgeons to give them shapelier, more sinuous arms, *Harper's Bazaar* reports. The "bat wing procedure" for tightening and defining the triceps has become increasingly popular. **1995** Lisa Garcia *Roanoke Times & World News* (Va.) (Sept. 17) "Arm Yourself for Glamour," p. 12 ▶ You don't want someone to grab the backs of your arms and come up with bat wings. **2004** Lisa Nicita *Arizona Republic* (Phoenix) (Sept. 28) "Toned-Up Triceps Are as Easy as 1-2-3" (Int.) ▶ Women often complain about bat wings, also known as less-than-toned triceps.

bazooty *n.* the buttocks; the *ass.* Also **bazootie.** *Slang.* See **GO BAZOOTIE.**

1991 George Diaz *L.A. Daily News* (May 5) "6 Cities Show Off for NL Miami Is Leader in Expansion Bids," p. SB1 ▶ Barry wrote recently that prospective owner Huizenga has "financial resources out the bazooty." **1992** *Usenet: bit.listserv.fnord-l* (Apr. 10) "Oh What's to Be Done with You, Loren Miller" ▶ Retard! If you can't tell a fake hallucination when you see one, a real one's just gonna go right by yer bazootie. **2001** *Usenet: alt.support.crohns-colitis* (Jan. 20) "Re: Vaginal Swelling" ▶ I've had 8 interns looking up my bazootie at once. **2005** Dave Barry *Ledger-Enquirer* (Columbus, Ohio) (Feb. 27) "Here's a Way to Lick That Hair-Loss Problem" (Int.) ▶ The point is that Refrigerator had all the fur removed from his rear end (or, in medical parlance, his "bazooty").

bed blocker *n.* a patient who will not or cannot be moved to another medical facility, either due to a shortage of beds or because of the patient's refusal. *Australia. Canada. Health. Medical. Slang. United Kingdom.*

1985 Donald Grant *Globe and Mail* (Toronto, Can.) (Feb. 18) "'Bed Blockers' Blamed for Emergency Ward Crunch," p. P16 ▶ "Bed blockers" are patients who had been given acute care in a Metro hospital bed but no longer need that attention. They should be sent to a chronic care hospital but there are no available beds. **1992** Malcolm Dean *Lancet* (U.K.) (Aug. 29) "NHS Withdrawal from Continuing Care," vol. 340, no. 8818, p. 539 ▶ The son said she was not going to be moved. He was happy to pay for chronic care, but not for the six weeks of nursing care that the consultant had deemed necessary for the acute incident.... I can vouch for this story because Biddy is my mother, and I am the son who refused to move her. I confess that I suffered twinges of guilt in my stand. I realised she would be classified as a "bed blocker." [**2004** Chris Moncrieff *Scotsman* (Scotland) (May 10) "Politics Column" (Int.) ▶ Many veteran Conservative MPs who might have been expected to retire from the fray at the next General Election, are obdurately staying put.... Since Tony Blair is unlikely to send them to the House of Lords on retirement, they are opting to stay in the Commons, to while away their twilight years.... They are aptly known as "the bedblockers."] **2004** Kate Legge *Australian* (Apr. 17) "Age and the Long Wait" (Int.) ▶ A former railway worker who paid his taxes and worked hard to put two children through private school, Ray Smith had been languishing in Launceston General Hospital since August, waiting for a bed in a secure dementia facility. Health bureaucrats cursed him as a "bed blocker," which is ironic given Smith's propensity to wander off up the corridor and out the front door.

bed head *n.* a hairstyle in (intentional) disarray. *Fashion.*

1987 John Haslett Cuff *Globe and Mail* (Toronto, Can.) (July 8) "I Couldn't Face Another Year on TV," p. C5 ▶ Richler always looked to be afflicted with a terminal case of "bed head."...His casual apparel and rock locks were sometimes an impediment for The Journal's audience. [**1988** *Washington Post Mag.* (Jan. 31) "Say Wha?" p. 9 ▶ *Bed head* n. A person who looks like he just woke up (Ann Marenick, Woodbridge).] **2001** Christie Ridgway *This Perfect Kiss* (Jan. 1), p. 292 ▶ Morning hair. Really bad bedhead. It's my curse. **2003** Tara Jon Manning *Men in Knits: Sweaters to Knit That He Will Wear* (Oct. 28), p. 6 ▶ He tries very hard to capture that contradictory "I don't care" bedhead look that is also perfectly groomed and precisely put together. This guy rarely tucks in a shirt. **2004** Lisa Scottoline *Killer Smile* (June 1), p. 258 ▶ She looked remarkably corporate in her blue sleeveless dress, but she still had bedhead, her blonde hair going every which way. Mary thought it might be intentional, because nobody but her actually *parted* their hair anymore, especially everybody in whatever generation she was supposed to be in. **2005** Jessica Pressler @ Philadelphia *N.Y. Times* (Aug. 14) "Philadelphia Story: The Next Borough" (Int.) ▶ Ms. Neighbor and Mr. Matz discovered Fishtown, a gentrifying blue-collar neighborhood adjacent to Northern Liberties, where, in the last five years, youthful faces with bed head have made their way among the traditionally Irish Catholic residents.

bent *n.* a recumbent bicycle. *Sports.* [Clipping of recum*bent*.]

1991 *Usenet: rec.bicycles* (Aug. 9) "Recumbent Riding Observations" ▶ On a bent you can just cruise along, if at a high rate of speed, and wave back at the cars. **1996** Stephanie Dunnewind *Columbian* (Vancouver, Wash.) (Oct. 15) "Sit Back & Enjoy the Ride" ▶ Riding a "bent," as they are known, is like pedaling while sitting in your office chair. **1998** Ben Hewitt *Bicycling Magazine's Complete Book of Road Cycling Skills* (Jan. 15), p. 2002 ▶ The Union Cycliste Internationale, the governing body of international racing, banned recumbents after a 'bent rider began winning professional road races and shattering records in the early 1930s. **2005** Sharon Tummins *Daily News* (Galveston County, Tex.) (July 17) "The View from a Different Angle" (Int.) ▶ Last year I converted from a road bike (fondly called a "wedgie") to a recumbent (proudly called a "bent").

beta *n.* in the sport of rock climbing, advice or instruction on the best way to climb a geographic feature. *Sports.* [The term is said to be derived from *Betamax*, the first popular format for recording video.]

1989 John Hanc *Newsday* (Oct. 16) "The Rat Rock Ballet in the Park," p. 2 ▶ Stripping his suit to reveal a pair of bright green lycra tights, the Manhattan businessman lifts himself up onto the east face of the rock to demonstrate "the beta"—that's climbese for the ability to flawlessly execute a sequence of moves. **1990** *Usenet: rec.backcountry* (Feb. 22) "Re: 5.12 Babble" ▶ A flash has come to mean the ascent of a route with no weighting of the rope (falls, hangs, etc.). It also generally connotes no significant pre-inspection, beta, etc. An "a vue" ascent is a flash with *absolutely* no beta or inspection. **1991** *Usenet: rec.climbing* (Apr. 13) "Re: Best Use of *ugh* Climbing Wall" ▶ There are also a bunch of people there who do not climb *real* rock. i was talking with one guy and we were discussing the beta on a 5.11a. i asked him about what kind of stuff he was leading and he said, "leading? like outdoors? oh, i've never done that." **1992** Rick Ansorge *Colorado Springs Gazette Telegraph* (Colo.) (Feb. 15) "It's 'Mutants' Against the 'Rock' at New Indoor Climbing Center," p. B1

▸ *BETA*: A verbal videotape of how to make a particular climb. Example: "Lay off the arete to a mono, cross through left then match on the slope, rock on the high step, set and dyno for the bucks." **1995** Sharon Doyle Driedger *Maclean's* (Can.) (Sept. 18) "Why Indoor Rock Climbing Is the Height of Fashion," p. 50 ▸ *Beta*: Tips, clues or any other information on how to climb a difficult route. **2003** *Milwaukee Journal Sentinel* (Wisc.) (June 6) "David Christopher Gunstone," p. 4B ▸ Gunstone wrote and published "The Traveler's Guide to Washington Rock Climbing" and was widely known as "Beta," a term used by rock climbers to refer to good information on a route. **2005** Brendon Connelly *Slacker Manager* (Apr. 4) "The Rock Climbing/Management Metaphor" (Int.) ▸ When the climber understands that the belayer is truly working for them, then the climber is limited only by their own technical skill and degree of boldness. This is particularly true if the belayer has already experienced the route and can offer genuinely helpful advice (*in the climbing world, such advice is called beta*).

Big Apple *n.* New York City. *NYC. United States.* Although there are many claims about the origin of "The Big Apple" as a nickname for New York City, each of the others lacks crucial supporting evidence or is demonstrably false. Among historians, lexicographers, and researchers it is now widely accepted that newspaperman John J. Fitz Gerald is the popularizer of "The Big Apple" and that he picked it up in the horse-racing industry. There is no evidence that it originated with whores or a brothel, that it entered the American language through jazz, or that it came about via any other mechanism. Unless new evidence comes to light, the citations supporting this entry should henceforth set the record straight. Credit and thanks go to Barry Popik and Gerald Cohen for the research.

1921 John J. Fitz Gerald *Morning Telegraph* (NYC) (May 3) p. 9 (Int.) in *The Big Apple* Barry Popik: J. P. Smith, with Tippity Witchet and others of the L. T. Bauer string, is scheduled to start for "the big apple" to-morrow after a most prosperous Spring campaign at Bowie and Havre de Grace. **1924** John J. Fitz Gerald *Morning Telegraph* (NYC) (Feb. 18) "Around The Big Apple" (Int.) in *The Big Apple* Barry Popik: The Big Apple ▸ The dream of every lad that ever threw a leg over a thoroughbred and the goal of all horsemen. There's only one Big Apple. That's New York. Two dusky stable hands were leading a pair of thoroughbred around the "cooling rings" of adjoining stables at the Fair Grounds in New Orleans and engaging in desultory conversation. "Where y'all goin' from here?" queried one. "From here we're headin' for The Big Apple," proudly replied the other. "Well, you'd better fatten up them skinners or all you'll get from the apple will be the core," was the quick rejoinder. **1926** John J. Fitz Gerald *Morning Telegraph* (NYC) (Dec. 1) "In the Paddock," p. 11 (Int.) in *The Big Apple* Barry Popik ▶ So many people have asked the writer about the derivation of his phrase, "the big apple," that he is forced to make another explanation. New Orleans has called it to his mind again. A number of years back, when racing a few horses at the Fair Grounds with Jake Byer, he was watching a couple of stable hands cool out a pair of "hots" in a circle outside the stable. A boy from an adjoining barn called over. "Where you shipping after the meeting?" To this one of the lads replied, "Why we ain't no bull-ring stable, we's goin' to 'the big apple.'" The reply was bright and snappy. "Boy, I don't know what you're goin' to that apple with those hides for. All you'll get is the rind."

big dance *n.* an important event, especially when the culmination of long preparation or smaller events; (*hence*) in sports, a tournament or championship game. *Sports.* Usually constructed with the definite article: *the big dance.*

1917 *N.Y. Times* (May 12) "Big Offensive Next Spring," p. 6 ▶ In his opinion what may be termed the great allied offensive, or, as he put it, "the big dance," will begin next Spring. **1982** Gordon S. White Jr. *N.Y. Times* (Mar. 7) "Virginia Victor—N. Carolina Wins," p. S1 ▶ [Jim] Valvano was not totally disappointed. "I feel we deserve a spot in the NCAA tournament next week," he said. "I think it would be a shame with 22 victories not to be invited to the big dance." **1984** John Duka *Globe and Mail* (Toronto, Can.) (July 31) "Lookalikes Everywhere," p. F3 ▶ As Geraldine Stutz, the president of Henri Bendel, said, "For us, July has been okay, not spectacular. Let's just say it's the last beat before the big dance begins in the fall." **1986** *Newsday* (NYC) (Feb. 14) "Key Brink's Suspect 'Intelligent' Radical," p. 11 ▶ He has written a forthcoming book entitled "The Big Dance," the gang's code name for the robbery. **2004** Steven Mackay *Birmingham Business Journal* (Ala.) (Sept. 29) "Scrushy's 85-Count Indictment Reduced" (Int.) ▶ Parkman says he is ready "to go the big dance in January," referring to Scrushy's federal trial that begins Jan. 5.

big voice *n.* a public address and siren system used for warnings (of incoming artillery fire, missiles, tornados, etc.) over a large (outdoor) area. *Military.* This is often used as a proper noun and without an article: *Big Voice.* A more common synonym is **giant voice.**

2000 *Atlanta Journal-Constitution* (Ga.) (Feb. 20) "Metro Tornado Defenses Spotty" ▶ Cobb also will install two so-called "big voice" sirens, a combination public address and siren system with a 1.5-mile range. **2002** (*Department of Defense*) (U.S.) (Dec. 18) "UFC 4-021-01: Design and O&M: Mass Notification Systems" (Int.) ▶ *Giant Voice System.* This system is also known as Big Voice. The Giant Voice system is typically installed as a base-wide system to provide a siren signal and pre-recorded and live voice messages. It is most useful for providing mass notification for personnel in outdoor areas, expeditionary structures, and temporary buildings. **2003** Mark Mazzetti, Julian E. Barnes @ Camp Commando, Kuwait *U.S. News & World Report* (Mar. 20) "Saddam's First Shot: Rattling the Marines" ▶ As they filed out of the bunker after the first attack, marines pulled off their gas masks and steadied their nerves with their first few breaths of fresh air. As one marine put it: "You know, I'm pretty p—ed at that Big Voice right now." **2004** Chris Schnaubelt (*National Guard Association of California*) (Jan. 28) "NGAC 1st VP's Update: More News from Baghdad" (Int.) ▶ When there is an attack, a siren goes off that sounds like the air raid sirens in the movies. Then, there a speaker system we call "Big Voice" that directs everyone to "take cover." **2004** Joseph L. Galloway *Sun Herald* (Biloxi, Miss.) (Oct. 5) "A Doctor's List of Memories of Iraq, Good and Bad" ▶ The siren and the inevitable "big voice" yelling at us to take cover. **2005** Oneguy *MREater* (Iraq) (Mar. 8) "Rocketman" (Int.) ▶ I didn't hear an explosion, so I started the engine and prepared to move out. Just then I heard Big Voice announcing "Alarm...Red..."...I shut off the engine and sat there a bit, figuring I was as safe in an up-armored hummer as in a bunker. After a while Big Voice announced "Alarm...Black...," so we could move around guilt free.

biking *n.* an (all-you-can-eat) food buffet or smorgasbord. < *English. Food & Drink. Japan. Japanese.* [From English *Viking,* referring to the Scandinavian origins of the Swedish *smörgåsbord.*] Rendered in Japanese as バイキング and usu. Romanized as *baikingu.*

*2003 Bill Edwards *A Visit with Bill* "Fireflies and Such II" (Int.) ▶ "Whah? The dinner was biking?" We were obviously confused. "Yes, biking style." And it is here that we must explain, dear reader, one of the many things which makes communication with the Japanese difficult. Much like the constant confusion between "l" and "r," there is often no difference between "v" and "b" to the Japanese. So we slowly came to realize that a buffet dinner is considered to be a meal eaten "viking" style. **2004** Seth Rosenblatt *Big in Japan* (Japan) (Apr. 10) "The Truth About 'Biking'" (Int.) ▶ "Biking" is one of many Japanese words that they've taken from English. It means "all-you-can-eat," pretty much the same as "tabehodai," the proper Japanese words for such culinary indulgence. ***2004** Alan R. Miller *Loan Words* (Int.)

▶ Examples are バイキング which sounds like *biking*. However it is from the word Viking and means smorgasbord.

birth control glasses *n.pl.* military-issue eyeglasses; (*hence*) ugly eyewear. Also **BCGs.** *Military. Slang.*

1991 Frank Bruni *Houston Chronicle* (Tex.) (Feb. 24) "Dynamic Duo in Combat Zone/Identical Twin Brothers Share Bond and Serve Together," p. 24 ▶ Right now they're both wearing Army-issue brown heavy plastic frames, which the soldiers call BCGs, birth control glasses, because they're so ugly no woman would want to make a baby with a soldier wearing a pair. **1992** *Usenet: soc.veterans* (Sept. 20) "NamVet Newsletter, vol. 5, no. 2 (2/6)": "VOL. 5, NO. 2" ▶ "Birth Control Glasses," a term used to describe the ugly military-issued eyeglasses. **1993** Poppy Brite *Drawing Blood* (Oct. 1), p. 151 ▶ A skinny, grinning kid with badly cut dark hair and birth-control glasses and ears that stuck out goofily. Looked like a hundred computer geeks Zach had known. **2005** Pam Mellskog @ Firestone *Daily Times-Call* (Longmont, Colo.) (Mar. 24) "Doctor, Soldier" (Int.) ▶ He also wore thick-framed, Army-issue glasses, an object that earned an unofficial acronym, BCGs—"birth control glasses"—for being remarkably unattractive.

blaccent *n.* a mode of speech that is said to imitate African-American vernacular English, especially when used by a white person. Also **blackcent.** *Derogatory.* [*bla*ck + ac*cent*] This term is usually derogatory.

2001 *Usenet: alt.tasteless.jokes* (Dec. 21) "Re: 10 Things a NIGGER Would Never Say" ▶ I like ur "blaCkcent"...*sniCker*. **2002** *Usenet: alt.fan.conan-obrien* (Sept. 7) "List for September 3-6 / 02" ▶ Janeane Garofalo, after ranting about folks like Justin Timberlake and Christina Aguilera copying the "blaccent," "I mean, did you guys come up the hard way through the Mickey Mouse club?" **2002** Desson Howe *Washington Post* (Nov. 8) "Eminem Wins by a 'Mile,'" p. T37 ▶ To some, he's the anti-Vanilla Ice, white with a blackcent. **2004** [Stumps McGurk (whiskeyblood)] *Tons of T&A* (Pittsburgh, Pa.) (Feb. 3) "Pant Pant Pant Pant" (Int.) ▶ I'm slowly being adopted as the new favorite employee of the crazy black girl in my department. I've been there two days. I think it's because I told her that her weave must be in too tight if she thought I was ready to start taking calls. Ooops. Sometimes the blaccent just blasts out and there's nothing for it. **2005** Des *Life in text Format* (Detroit, Mich.) (Mar. 7) "Things I Hate About Work" (Int.) ▶ Even if some of the whites put on a phony "blaccent" and try to be down so to speak. Just cause you pushing a couple biracial babies, got a few black friends—one of whom might be with you, like to fuck black dudes, listen to rap, etc., don't mean we'll automatically connect, *remember that*!

BlackBerry prayer *n.* the posture taken by users of the Black-Berry-brand personal digital assistant manufactured by RIM. *Technology.*

2000 Steven Chase *Globe and Mail* (Toronto, Can.) (Dec. 14) "Black-Berry Season RIM's Wireless E-mail Device Generates Its Own Vocabulary as Road Warriors Get Hooked on Its Addictive Simplicity," p. T1 ▶ The device has also generated an odd new social ritual that sees BlackBerry users discreetly operate their devices at meetings behind cupped hands with heads intently bowed toward its tiny screen. The position makes one look as if they are seeking help from a higher power—giving rise to the expression "BlackBerry prayer." [**2002** Joan O'C. Hamilton *BusinessWeek Asia* (Feb. 18) "Hooked on Black-Berry" (Int.) ▶ I'm told many users now call the increasingly familiar BlackBerry posture of head down, hands in the lap under the conference table, the "BlackBerry prayer." **2002** Erika Engle *Honolulu Star-Bulletin* (Hawaii) (Mar. 10) "Wireless World at Their Fingertips" (Int.) ▶ More common to daily life, users are seen engaged in "PDA prayer," which Ogasawara describes as occurring regularly at boring meetings. The device is held low, just below desk level with the user looking down, presumably at folded hands.] **2005** Renee Montagne (*NPR*) (Jan. 12) "Morning Edition: Increasing Use of BlackBerrys and Similar Devices in the Workplace" ▶ Heavy BlackBerry users call themselves CrackBerry addicts, referring to the highly addictive form of cocaine. Bow your head to check the device for e-mail during a meeting? That's a BlackBerry prayer.

bleeding deacon *n.* a person who believes himself indispensable to a group, especially a person who becomes so over-involved in a group's internal management, policies, or politics as to lose sight of its larger goals; (*hence*) a person with a negative, moralizing character, who acts like the sole source of wisdom. *Slang. United States.* Most cites are connected to Alcoholics Anonymous or to similar 12-step programs. The historical information in the 1998 and 1999 cites is not verified.

1988 *N.Y. Times* (Feb. 21) "The Changing World of Alcoholics Anonymous," p. 6-40 ▶ "If anything is going to destroy A.A.," says Dr. John Norris, a nonalcoholic physician, friend of Bill Wilson's and for many years chairman of A.A.'s board of trustees, "it will be what I call the 'tradition lawyers.' They find it easier to live with black and white than they do with gray. These 'bleeding deacons'—these fundamentalists—are afraid of and fight any change." **1990** Vernon E. Johnson

I'll Quit Tomorrow: A Practical Guide to Alcoholism Treatment, p. 92
► Even in aftercare or AA, if this quality of rigidity continues, it can reach a point where patients are no longer viewed by their peers in recovery as a zealot for the program but as "bleeding deacons" who insist loudly that "my way is the only way to make the program." **1997** *Pittsburgh Post-Gazette* (Feb. 20) "Gambling's Not the Answer," p. A14 ► Our town is going nuts with gambling. I don't have a conversation with my friends when we're not talking about off-track betting, the Meadows, the Lotto or poker machines. I am not a Bible-thumper or bleeding deacon, but I'm really ticked off! **1998** *alt.recovery.catholicism* (Oct. 4) "Re: Former RC/Padre_Andre vs. 'John M'" ► The term Bleeding Deacon is a corruption of an old New England term from the 18th or 19th century. The original term was Bleating Deacon, evoking a farmer's image of an old goat in the pulpit. **1999** *alt.recovery.aa* (Dec. 9) "Re: In and Out—Is AA for Me?" ► When the term was first applied it was intended for those people who have a set of cries such as "it will never work" or "if it ain't broke, then don't fix it." The actual term used was "bleating beacon" [*sic*] (as in sheep). The GV even ran a series titled "The Bleating Deacon's Corner." I prefer the term "bleeding deacon." Truth is that I used to be one but I ran out of blood. ***2004** Gregg Easterbrook *Beliefnet* "A.A.: America's Stealth Religion" (Int.) ► There is also no professional clergy, but true-believing Program old-timers are often referred to, more or less affectionately, as "bleeding deacons."

blocktimer *n.* an independent journalist or producer who buys airtime in order to broadcast programs on radio or television. *Media. Philippines. Television.*

1985 David Briscoe (*AP*) (Aug. 4) "More Than Dozen Journalists Killed in Philippines in Year" ► Abangan is a "blocktimer," radio announcers who pay for their own time on the air and sell advertising time. **1996** Anna Leah Sarabia @ Philippines *Contemporary Women's Issues* (68) "Women's Experiences in Media" ► Those independent producers who are now thriving are directly the same people who already had control of media outlets under the Marcos government, or are allied by kinship or partnership to network owners, advertising agencies, government agencies or powerful religious organizations. Even available airtime is controlled by a kind of "blocktimers mafia." **2003** Mars W. Mosqueda Jr. *Manila Bulletin* (Philippines) (June 14) "Task Force Formed to Probe Shooting of Cebu Broadcaster" ► Greg Sanchez pledged assistance to Cortes, even as he clarified the broadcaster is not a regular employe[e] of the station but a blocktimer, who buys airtime. **2004** Nonie C. Dolor *Manila Times* (Philippines) (Aug. 21) "Why They Kill Local Journalists" (Int.) ► Most of these hard-hitting journalists—print or broadcast—are independent, free-lancers, or in our broadcast parlance, "blocktimers."

blow-in *n.* an outsider; a carpetbagger. *Politics.*

1995 Yvonne Preston *The Age* (Australia) (May 11) "Medical Mystery" ▶ On Saturday, Bradfield's 190 pre-selectors will declare the result of this young bull/old bull stoush between the 36-year-old blow-in from Hobart, and the white-haired David Connolly, who is nearing the end of his political career after 21 years on a margin which rarely slipped below 23 per cent. **1998** Alan Ramsey *Sydney Morning Herald* (Australia) (Oct. 31) "Poll Proves High Profiles Count" ▶ The Government hypes the professed wisdom that Kernot was a high-profile "blow-in" who almost failed because the voters of Dickson, in Brisbane's southern suburbs, wouldn't accept a political carpetbagger. **1999** Joe Carroll *Irish Times* (Dublin, Ireland) (July 10) "Hillary Attracts Media Circus on Her Upstate 'Listening Tour,' Leaving Bill Down on an Indian Reservation" ▶ Rudy Giuliani has been plugging away at the carpetbagger charge and plans his own fundraiser in Arkansas to highlight her New York "blow-in" status. **2004** Dale Russakoff @ Boston, Mass. *Washington Post* (July 25) "Discipline and Ambition Overcame First Defeat" (Int.) ▶ Kerry swept the district's upscale suburbs, but not the mill towns, where unemployment was rising as jobs fled. There, locals tagged Kerry with their own slang for carpetbagger: "blow-in."

blue angel *n.* an ignited burst of flatus. *Slang.*

1994 *Usenet: alt.folklore.urban* (Jan. 18) "Sparks from Lifesavers Candy in Your Mouth (& Exploding Blue Angels)" ▶ You must all know about blue angels, where you hold a lighter/match very close to your jeans/butt and fart. It makes a blue flame. **1996** Alexandra Paul *Winnipeg Free Press* (Manitoba, Can.) (Feb. 29) "It's a Gas, and on the Rise!," p. A9 ▶ Then there are the blue angels that were famous in the youth culture of the 1950s and 1960s. Blue angels was a nickname given to bluish flames teenagers created by blowing wind and igniting it with a flame to create special visual effects with flatus. [**2003** Robert Buckman *Human Wildlife* (Feb. 15), p. 115 ▶ There is a fraternity at a college in the Midwest where the initiation rite is lighting a fart, and the frat members are known colloquially as "The Blue Angels."]

blue light bandit *n.* a person with criminal intentions who impersonates a police officer in a patrol car. *Crime & Prisons. Police.*

1986 Margaret L. Knox @ Savannah *Altanta Journal-Constitution* (Ga.) (Jan. 24) "Chatham Jury Convicts Alleged 'Blue Light Bandit,'" p. A11

▶ After nearly deadlocking Thursday, a Chatham County Superior Court jury returned Friday and delivered a guilty verdict against one of Savannah's alleged "blue light bandits." Jimmy Bradford, 20, was sentenced to 15 years in prison on an armed robbery charge stemming from an incident on March 14, 1984, in which robbers used a flashing light and posed as law officers to stop and frisk a motorist. **1991** *Herald* (Rock Hill, S.C.) (Oct. 11) "Police Have Arrested Two Men They Say Were Selling Crack Cocaine," p. 8A ▶ A 53-year-old Monroe High School teacher refused to stop her car Thursday after being followed by a suspect flashing a blue police-style light on his pickup truck. Reports of a blue-light bandit who stopped women using such lights have been filed in Mecklenburg and several surrounding counties in the past year. **2005** Fred Kelly *Charlotte Observer* (N.C.) (May 29) "Attack by Fake Officer Reported" (Int.) ▶ Impersonating police officers has become so common that law enforcement officials refer to them as "blue light bandits."

blue-sky *v.* to imagine or propose unreasonable or as-yet unfeasible ideas.

1964 Aileen Snoddy *Edwardsville Intelligencer* (Ill.) (Nov. 16) "Blue Skying for the Future Home," p. 4 (title). **1975** Jack Anderson, Les Whitten *News* (Frederick, Md.) (June 11) "The Washington Merry-Go-Round," p. A4 ▶ He insisted he was merely "blue skying" the idea. He swore he had never used the report, which he had promoted while at NIAAA, to solicit loans from banks to build a private treatment center. **1982** Richard S. Rosenbloom, Alan M. Kantrow *Harvard Business Review* (Feb. 1) "Nurturing of Corporate Research," p. 115 ▶ They couldn't understand why we would pour money into such "harebrained blue-skying" instead of giving it to them to design yet another model of their ill-fated line of processors. **1984** Michael Harris *Globe and Mail* (Toronto, Can.) (Nov. 5) "NDP's Leader Knows the Score in N.S. Election," p. P5 ▶ At a time when North Americans are romancing the political right, however, the woman who once took Tommy Douglas sailing and grew up in a household where M. J. Coldwell was a frequent visitor is not "blue-skying" her party's chances on election night. **2004** Paul Harris *Vive le Canada* (Aug. 17) "Healthcare: The Truth About Your Government" (Int.) ▶ Can't you just hear some government official blue-skying and saying the system would be so much more affordable if all those pesky old people would just die?

blute *n.* a newspaper. *Media.* This is a nice confirmation of a term that has repeatedly been taken (as in the 2002 cite) from David

Maurer's *The Big Con* (1940). One of his original sources for the term is mentioned in the 1982 *American Speech* cite below.

1937 Individuals; Wayne Walden @ NYC *LOTJ* (Dec. 6) "Slang of Newspaper and Mail Delivery (Rewrite Canny)" ► Blutes—Papers in general, as "what time does the next blutes come?" **1982** Raven I. McDavid, Jr. *American Speech* (Winter) "David Maurer (1905-1981): A Memoir," vol. 57, no. 4, pp. 278-79 ► What impressed me about the meeting was Dave's discussion of *The Johnson Family Blute*, a newspaper even more restricted in its circulation than the *White House Press Digest,* for there was only one copy of each issue, that intended for Dave. He had met members of the Johnson mob some years earlier, and they had taken such an interest in his work that they developed the habit of communicating with him regularly, to bring him up to date on changes in the lingo.... After a long run the *Blute* expired when the family broke up during the dispersal of the mobs during World War II. **2002** Duane Swierczynski *Complete Idiot's Guide to Frauds, Scams, and Cons* (Dec. 17) "Con Man Glossary," p. 241 ► *Blute.* Fake clippings from a newspaper, used in big con games.

boi *n.* a feminine male homosexual or a masculine lesbian. *Gay. Sexuality.*

1997 Usenet: *rec.music.industrial* (Aug. 14) "Re: Industrial Web Pages! Labels!" ► You want to become a bigamist? And a gay one?! Well, you look feminine enough in that Goth Boi Babe picture. **1999** Deana Finley *Plain Dealer* (Cleveland, Ohio) (Feb. 17) "Rave Review for Rave Scene," p. 1G ► A cute raver boi (a male raver, pronounced like "boy") in a T-shirt that read "I Love Ghetto" carried a bag of Blow Pops (along with one in his mouth) and handed them out. **2003** Sandra McLean *Courier-Mail* (Brisbane, Australia) (June 7) "It's a Boi Thing" ► Some of these women are getting physical. They bind their breasts to erase any hint of a cleavage, others are "packing," which is boy (oops, boi) poseur talk for stuffing socks, a dildo or whatever down their designer duds to help them pass the he-man test. **2004** *GO NYC* (NYC) (Feb. 3) "Gloss Celebrates Four Years," p. 39 ► Girlie girls are dressed to impress and bois, butches, andros, trannies and all the in-betweens flirt, dance and drink until the wee hours. **2004** Rona Marech *San Francisco Chronicle* (Calif.) (Feb. 8) "Nuances of Gay Identities Reflected in New Language," p. A1 ► A "boi" describes a boyish gay guy or a biological female with a male presentation.... Justin, who is 19 and didn't want to use his last name because he's not out to his family as transgender, calls himself a "boi"—with an "i"— because he feels like a boy—with a "y"—but "I don't have the boy parts, as much as I wish I did." **2005** Jennifer Vanasco *Southern Voice* (Atlanta, Ga.) (May 27) "The Death of Femme" (Int.) ► Young women who once called themselves butch now call themselves tranny bois, and these tranny bois are mostly dating each other.

bomber *n.* an old, dilapidated automobile; (*hence*) a class of such automobiles used with few or no modifications in stock car racing. *Automotive. Sports.* [This is directly related to the term *bomb* 'an old, dilapidated car,' which goes back to at least the 1950s. There is also a now out-of-fashion sense of *bomb* 'a hot-rod or fast car.']

1981 Jonathan Mann *Globe and Mail* (Toronto, Can.) (Aug. 14) "Follow the Leader Tactics Change in 6-Hour Event," p. P49 ▶ The limited sportsman division, with cars of up to 255 cubic inches, the mini-modified division, with cars up to 2,200 cubic centimetres, and the bomber division, with six-cylinder street-stock cars, will round out the card. **1994** James Dempsey *Telegram & Gazette* (Worcester, Mass.) (May 4) "Hot Rod Is Epitome of Cool," p. B1 ▶ It's not that the Old Bomber is on its last legs, you understand. Everything still works fine. Properly nurtured, this '85 Chevy could probably go another hundred thou before giving up the ghost. But the old dear wouldn't win any beauty contests. **1996** Perri O'Shaughnessy *Invasion of Privacy* (July 1), p. 370 ▶ I took him out to his car and made it up to him. It was our first time. He wasn't very good. I got out and got in my old bomber of a car and went home. **1997** Jo Ann Shroyer *Secret Mesa* (Oct. 10), p. 74 ▶ Mercer-Smith tore into the parking lot in a rusty yellow 1970s vintage LTD, a boatlike bomber of a car. **2002** John Case *Eight Day* (Nov. 26), p. 43 ▶ It didn't seem like a good idea to arrive at Adele Slivinski's office in the Bomber—it was a car that tended to make people skeptical of the driver. **2005** Stacy Ervin *West Liberty Index* (Iowa) (Apr. 5) "Racing: Kile Family Races Together, Stays Together" (Int.) ▶ When Kurt was 15, his parents bought him a "bomber" car, a vehicle which resembles some street cars and is also known as hobby stock.

bonk *n.* a sound made by a handheld radio, indicating a transmission cannot be made, characteristic of digital trunk radio systems typically used by fire and police departments. Also **bonking.** *Technology.*

1999 Hector L. Torres @ Baltimore, Md. *Fire Chief* (June 1) "Cooperative Communications" (Int.) ▶ Unlike our former system, the new system emits a "bonking" tone when a transmission doesn't go through, so a user can then move to try to establish a better connection.

2004 *Marquette County Firefighters Home Page* (Detroit, Mich.) (Jan. 5) "Detroit Fire Dept. Message Board" (Int.) ▶ You find that the digital signal can't get thru the concrete and steel so you get the "out of range" bonking noise—which means you have to go over to a window so you can lean out to get a repeater to receive your signal. **2004** *CapeCodFD.com* (Cape Cod, Mass.) (July 2) "Communications System Fails" (Int.) ▶ Several "symptomatic" problems followed over the following days with a static sound trailing transmissions for a brief period and a number of "bonk" situations, where the ability to transmit was prevented for some reason. **2004** Jennifer Lin *Philadelphia Inquirer* (Pa.) (Oct. 1) "Council Hears of Radio Glitches at Fire" (Int.) ▶ Ayers testified that on the night of the row house fire, firefighters at the scene complained of an excessive level of blocked calls—or "bonking," as they call it, for the busy signal the radios make when a call cannot be completed. ***2004** *Channels Close Up* (Oct. 1) "Kansas City Upgrades and Training Win Praises," vol. 2, no. 1 (Int.) ▶ A simple anecdote was told about how one of the city's firefighters was concerned that the "NC bonk"—a feature designed to alert him when the radio was out of signal range—had not activated recently and thus was broken.

bonk *v.* in bicycling, to become exhausted. Also **bonk out** and **bonking**, *n. Sports.*

1979 J.A. Cuddon *Macmillan Dictionary of Sports and Games,* p. 119, in *HDAS* (1994) J.E. Lighter ▶ *Bonk*...A state of extreme fatigue caused by overexertion and lack of blood sugar. **1983** *Usenet: net.bicycle* (June 27) "Joe Bike Reports from GEAR South" ▶ As we took off to follow Scott back, we noticed we had dropped Walter and the aforementioned bikie who bonked on the hill. **1984** Suzanne Charle *N.Y. Times* (Sept. 23) "'Go for It': Making Your Way in a Triathlon" ▶ But there is also the flip side, when fatigue hits all sets of muscles at once. If you've been riding hard and then start running, often it feels as if your thigh bones are no longer attached to your shinbones. Experienced athletes call this "cross-bonk." **1986** James McNamara *Washington Post* (Aug. 15) "Cyclist's Challenge: Turning 100" ▶ This is because such exercise will quickly deplete the body's reserves, causing severe fatigue (in running this is called hitting the wall, in cycling it's known as the bonk, which is the sound you make when you hit the wall). **1990** *Usenet: rec.bicycles* (Jan. 26) "Primer for Getting Started in Bike Racing" ▶ Even if you have a teamate in the break, chase it down. You never know when the guy could bonk and get dropped. **1990** *Usenet: rec.bicycles* (Apr. 25) "Cadence Matters" ▶ My goal is to be able to increase my efficiency at the higher cadences so I can spin without "blowing up" (in a crit) or "bonking" (in a long road race). **2005** *Ventura County Star* (Calif.) (July 4) "Cycling Through the Lingo" (Int.) ▶ *Bonk:* Term used to describe running out of energy when riding.

boo-boo face *n.* a pout or pouty facial expression; moue; **boo-boo lip**, an out-thrust lip. Probably from the facial expression children make when they have a *boo-boo* 'minor injury.'

1991 *Usenet: soc.singles* (Mar. 13) "Re: Sexual Fantasies" ▶ Michel, I'm soooo jealous....)-; (Best boo-boo face on the net....) **1993** *Usenet: alt.sexual.abuse.recovery* (Dec. 8) "ED ED ED" ▶ But I caaaaaaaaaan't telnet, only send mail (big whine)!! Can you please show me the way? Boo-boo lip sticking out bigtime. **1994** Stan Savran *Pittsburgh Post-Gazette* (Pa.) (June 11) "Mother of All Strikes Premature End to Season Could Help Baseball in Long Run," p. D6 ▶ You'll stomp your feet and put on your best boo-boo face and spew forth about how you're not coming back, and that this time you really mean it. But you'll come back. You always have. **1994** C. Johnston *Courier-Mail* (Australia) (July 25) "Annalise's Exit a Crying Shame" ▶ Drawing on the heaviest weapon from her considerable thespian arsenal, she makes a boo-boo face. As the tears stream down her cheeks, it is apparent to all but southern TV critics that Annalise has firmed in the betting for next year's Gold Logie. I'll go out on a limb here and state that no soap star makes boo-boo face like Annalise.... He said he was bloody upset too, and promised at the next premiers' conference to put up for debate the question of whether watching Annalise make boo-boo face deserves to be included in the Medicare schedule. **2000** Tina Wainscott *A Trick of the Light* (Mar. 1), p. 29 ▶ "She's so banged up," Marilee wailed. "Bruised, a gash on her lip, a scrape on her cheek, those beautiful curls all matted with blood. Girls, she has her boo-boo face on." **2003** *St. Petersburg Times* (Fla.) (Nov. 9) "Sapp Should Chase QBs, Not Spotlight," p. 13C ▶ It is such a refreshing sight to see Warren the Sapp standing on the sideline with his boo-boo lip hanging out, looking "dumb"-founded, with nothing to say. **2004** Ian Demsky *Tennessean* (Nashville) (May 1) "Police Chief Encourages Letter Writers," p. 8 ▶ "We're not going to boo-boo lip," he said. "I'm not going to come here and tell you what we can't do. I'm not going to tell you what we don't have. I'm not going to tell you all the reasons in the world you shouldn't hold us accountable."

boondocking *n.* living without conveniences such as municipal electricity or water, indoor plumbing, or grocery stores, especially when camping with a recreational vehicle; *roughing it.* [From *the boondocks*, a wild or unpopulated area, from the Tagalog *bundoc* or *bondoc* 'a mountain.'] Variations on **to boondock**, according to the *Historical Dictionary of American Slang*, are the military sense of 'to go into or through boondocks; to march through boondocks as punishment or training'; the youth or student sense of 'to go with a date into a wooded or isolated area for the purpose of love-making'; and the trucking sense of 'to travel on back roads.' The 1963 citation probably belongs to the latter sense.

1951 Quentin Pope @ Guam, Mariana Islands *Chicago Daily Tribune* (Dec. 29) "Bungling by U.S. Found in Trust Isles of Pacific," p. 2 ▶ The trust territories administration is ordering officials to live as if in a desert island economy. "Boondocking"—raiding of available supplies from wherever they can be held—has official blessing. **1961** *Monroe County News* (Albia, Iowa) (Mar. 20) "Facts for Hunters," p. 4 ▶ The store of outdoor wisdom gathered over 25 years of boondocking and chore-dodging falls into four broad categories. **1962** Bill Dredge *L.A. Times* (Jan. 14) "Mexican Joy Ride by Camper Unit," p. 17 ▶ Time was, not many years ago, when a motorist, bound for boondocking in the wilds of Baja California, said good-buy [*sic*] to his wife, hugged all the children and plopped a bedroll in the back seat of a war surplus command car. [**1963** *Deming Headlight* (N.M.) (Oct. 31) "Formal Opening of the Lonnie Beyer Jeep Sales & Service" (in advert.), p. 5 ▶ New Willys models provide a dual-purpose vehicle suitable for family or business use, as well as "boondocking."] **1983** Judy Fossett *Sunday Oklahoman* (Oklahoma City, Okla.) (Oct. 16) "Mother Left with Pain, Hate" ▶ They were friends, and on the night she was killed, Paula, Brett Harris and Karen Winfield went "boondocking" along the river in Harris' Toyota Land Cruiser. **1995** Bill Moeller *RVing Basics* (Jan. 1), p. 11 ▶ Staying in a place with no hookups is known as *boondocking*, *primitive camping*, or *dry camping*. **2005** Bill Draper @ Emporia, Kan. *Kansas City Star* (May 21) "RVers Taking Scenic Route All the Way to Wal-Mart," (Int.) ▶ "Boondocking," also known as primitive camping, is the RVer term for camping without the use of such conveniences as electricity and water. The subject, especially as it pertains to Wal-Mart lots, is a favorite topic among Internet-savvy travelers on such sites as freecamping.com, fulltimerver.com and Woodbury's rvtravel.com.

booster bag *n.* a bag, sack, pouch, purse, or box used by a shoplifter to conceal or disguise merchandise. *Crime & Prisons.* [*to boost* 'to steal; to shoplift' + *bag*]

1927 *L.A. Times* (May 21) "Mother Faces Burglary Trial with Daughter," p. A5 ▶ Friday the 13th was unlucky for the mother-and-daughter team, according to arresting officers, who said they followed the two on that day in a downtown department store and watched them take...goods. All was stuck in a booster-bag, the officers said, and later wrapped into parcels in the ladies' rest room and placed in a shopping bag. **1954** Grace Lewis *Post-Standard* (Syracuse, N.Y.)

(Aug. 5) "Shoplifting Constant Threat to Stores But Detectives Must Be Very Sure!" p. 1 ▶ Fact is, she may pick up 12 or 15 different articles and put them in her shopping bag or umbrella or her booster bag on one floor and then go on to the next. A booster bag is a store-label dress or suit box with a panel or slot cut in the side. Cotton batten is put in the bottom, just in case the lifter picks up something heavy. It won't make a clunk when it drops in. **1984** Ferdie J. Deering *Daily Oklahoman* (Oklahoma City) (Apr. 16) "Harvesting Fruits of New Morality" ▶ Such activities are no more right than the robber with a gun, a shoplifter with a "booster bag," or a crook making purchases by using other people's credit cards. **1989** Henry Stancu *Toronto Star* (Can.) (July 12) "39 Arrested in Joint Probe of Inter-City Theft Ring," p. A7 ▶ During the raids, police seized booster bags worn under women's dresses to conceal goods shoplifted from stores. "They could get articles as large as fur coats, video recorders, computers, fax machines, 20-piece bone china sets—right under the skirt and out the door." **2004** Jay Warren *WCPO-TV* (Cincinatti, Ohio) (Nov. 30) "Mall Security Boosted for Holiday Shopping Season" (Int.) ▶ "One thing that I look for when I come out here—people coming in with bags, empty bags, almost empty bags, refer to it as a booster bag which is a lining inside the bag but open to guard against the metal detectors," said Detective "X."

booth capturing *n.* the act of seizing and controlling a polling station so that many fraudulent votes may be cast there. *India. Politics.*

1983 *N.Y. Times* (June 10) "Gandhi Party Demands New Voting in Kashmir," p. A5 ▶ The general secretary of the Congress Party, Malik Mohiuddin, said the National Conference Party had destroyed "the very fiber of the democratic system in the country by its alleged large-scale rigging and booth capturing." **1984** *Washington Post* (Dec. 25) "Heavy Voting and Violence Mark Indian Elections" ▶ Police said that the deaths and injuries occurred during clashes between rival parties, police gunfire to break up disturbances and incidents of "booth capturing," a uniquely South Asian election phenomenon in which armed partisan gangs raid a polling station where an election is closely contested and shoot it out until one party takes command of the election boxes. **2004** Davie Rohde *N.Y. Times* (Apr. 27) "On New Voting Machine, the Same Old Fraud" (Int.) ▶ The men had carried out a new version of a storied Indian electoral trick: "booth capturing," in which armed thugs hired by political parties seize control of a polling place and stuff ballot boxes.

bootleg *adj.* inferior, unappealing, worthless. *Slang.*

2001 [Libby] (*Musselman Library*) (Gettysburg College, Pa.) (Jan. 25) (Int.) ▶ "You guys need to get new headphones. Most of them are so bootleg! They don't work and kill my ears. Please."..."Libby admits that until hearing from you, she'd never used a pair of headphones in the library. Yuck. We'll replace them. Libby was also puzzled by your choice of words, and had to ask for help with the phrase 'so bootleg.' Libby, being a tad on the old-fashioned side, associates bootleg with illegal liquor or Chinese knock-off CDs. She never considered bootleg headphones. So for all of you really un-hip readers, Libby asked a very with-it librarian for help. She defined bootleg as 'totally skanky.'" **2001** [Rajan] *Blag Job* (July 29) "I'm in Control, Just" (Int.) ▶ I need to figure out what I want, achieve it, and be satisfied with it—for once. If it happens before the end of August, I won't end this chapter thinking this was one bootleg summer. **2003** [Jonathan] *Wonder Jonathan* (June 17) "Major Bitch" (Int.) ▶ I just checked out that Friendster web site that Oz makes reference to, and I thoroughly don't understand it. To be able to actually see others' profiles, you have to invite people who in turn invite other people. Then to actually see anyone else other than yourself, people you invite have to actually join the site themselves. Sorry Oz...that's bootleg. **2003** [kozmo] *Kardoi* (Sept. 18) (Int.) ▶ Erik the winner of the Go Cart racing. and ummmm i forgot who had the slowest car...i think it was Ivan haha the birthday boy got the bootleg car. **2004** [Gangstah_giggles (Giana)] *Xanga* (Mar. 16) "The Perfect Guy. (Not Really)" (Int.) ▶ what kind of car does he drive?—whatever just as long as we not rollin in some jacked up ugly ass "bootleg car." y'enoe it gotta have the sound system and the wheels and errrythang. **2004** [Grady] *Grady Rocks* (Sept. 20) "Yup, I'm Still Lazy" (Int.) ▶ The whole joke is the yin-yang twins and the fact that they're 100% bootleg. For those of you who don't know, bootleg is the new word that the cool kids use to describe some that is ghetto in a bad way. For example, a 1986 ford tempo with three rims and a homemade spoiler is bootleg.

boot party *n.* the kicking and stomping of a person.

1989 John Snell *Oregonian* (Nov. 12) "Year Later, Skinhead Still Clings to Beliefs," p. 1 ▶ "He hit the ground immediately. After that, we had a little boot party." A boot party is the term Skinheads use to describe an attack in which a victim is encircled and kicked repeatedly. [**1991** *Usenet: alt.skinheads* (Sept. 25) "Chicago Rally" ▶ The latest issue of Boot Party Skinzine is out.] **1995** *Street Gangs* (Jan.), p. 40 ▶ Casual talk of a "boot party" refers to the fact that the members have attacked someone and used their boots in the assault.... As a Skinhead's primary weapon, the boots play an important role in this as well as most other assaults. **2005** John Bowers *Salt Lake City Weekly* (Utah) (Apr. 28) "Cell Survivor" (Int.) ▶ Inmates throughout the BOP suffer boot-parties on an alarming scale because of this "trick bag."...A few lumps on my head and a paint job on my eyes is far better than what could happen if I didn't immediately fight—a boot party from my own people.

boots on the ground *n.pl.* personnel deployed under military command. *Jargon. Military. United States. Boot* dates to before World War II as indicating a military recruit or a green enlisted man.

1980 John K. Coole *Christian Science Monitor* (Boston, Mass.) (Apr. 11) "US Rapid Strike Force: How to Get There First with the Most," p. 7 ▶ Many American strategists now argue that even light, token US land forces—"getting US combat boots on the ground," as General Warner puts it—would signal to an enemy that the US is physically guarding the area and can only be dislodged at the risk of war. **1996** Dennis J. Reimer @ Washington, D.C. (*Congressional Testimony*) (Mar. 13) "FY 97 Defense Authorization" ▶ Our cooperation with "boots on the ground" helps assure their future military and political cooperation while increasing United States influence worldwide. **2004** Judith Scherr *Berkeley Daily Planet* (Calif.) (Nov. 30) "Berkeley Author Investigates Iraq War Profiteers" (Int.) ▶ "In the first Gulf War one in 100 'boots on the ground,' as they call it, was a private contractor." When the U.S. invaded and occupied Iraq in 2003, one in 10 was a private contractor. "Today, as we speak and the U.S. is launching a war in Falluja, one in four 'boots on the ground' is a private contractor."

botnet *n.* a collection of automated scripts, or bots, that create a small chat-based network; (*hence*) such a collection intended for malicious or surreptitious uses. *Jargon. Technology.*

1994 *Usenet: alt.irc* (Dec. 26) "Re: The No Lag + No Split Alternative" ▶ There are many files available from the bots on the botnet which can be reached even if the bot is on another network. **2002** [Curve] *DALnet* (Jan. 2003) "Just What Is a Botnet?" (Int.) ▶ The major difference between a bot in a botnet and your common eggdrop or IRC client script bot in a channel is that the botnet variety has been created with a trojan and, almost always, without the knowledge of the person whose computer they are running from. **2004** John Leyden *Register* (U.K.) (Apr. 30) "The Illicit Trade in Compromised PCs" (Int.) ▶ In February German magazine c't reported how it was able to buy access to infected machines—commonly described in the parlance of spammers as "BotNets"—from virus writers.

bougie *n.* in volleyball, a hit on the head by the ball. *French. Sports.* [See the 2001 citation. This entry is unrelated to senses of *bougie* well-covered elsewhere, such as 'n., (a contemptuous name for) a black person,' 'adj., bourgeois (middle class), especially as an accusation between black Americans,' the latter having various spellings including *bourgie*, *boojie*, and *boojy*.]

2001 *Usenet: rec.sport.volleyball* (Mar. 27) "Re: 16.2.3 Clarification Requested" ► Even a very good "candle hit" as we say in french ("une bougie" = "a candle" is a spike which hits an opponents directly in his head...just like gently blowing a candle.... :-)). **2004** Glen Dawkins *Winnipeg Sun* (Manitoba, Can.) (July 2) "Digging Up Support" (Int.) ► The band was originally called Bougie after the slang term for getting popped in the head with a volleyball which gives some idea of their commitment to musical excellence.

bouma shape *n.* a word's silhouette, recognizable form, or visual impression. Also **bouma.** *Jargon. Science. Technology.*

1992 A.W. Senior (*Cambridge University Engineering Dept.*) (Dec.) "Off-Line Handwriting Recognition: A Review and Experiments" (Int.) ► Taylor & Taylor used these Bouma shapes for a study on the text of their own book and found that the Bouma shape uniquely specified 6953 out of 7848 words in the sample. **1999** Steven Killings *Connect: Information Technology at NYU* (NYC) (Feb. 12) "Optical Character Recognition" (Int.) ► In visual terms, a word is distinguished by its characters' relation to the white space surrounding it and the nature of its letter face (for instance, small thin strokes are common to handwriting, and thick short strokes are common to non-serifed print fonts). Psychologists describe this as its "Bouma-shape" (after Dutch psychologist Herman Bouma) in cognition studies. **2001** M. Michele Mulchahey *Canadian Journal of History* (Aug. 1) "Space Between Words: The Origins of Silent Reading," vol. 36, no. 2, p. 323 ► Nor have the palaeographers and codicologists ever noted one of the most important lexical consequences of the adoption of minuscule, as opposed to majuscule, as a book script is that it contributed, in conjunction with word separation, to giving each word a distinct image, which modern psychologists call the "Bouma shape," peculiar to Western writing and a significant aid to silent visual processing. **2002** Hrant H. Papazian *Typophile Forums* (Sept. 25) "Bouma" (Int.) ► I didn't really invent the term "bouma": it's adapted from the term "Bouma-shape" used by Saenger in his "Space between words"; he in turn claims to have taken it from the work of Taylor & Taylor (although I myself have yet to find any such term used by them), and is based on the Dutch psychologist Herman Bouma who formalized empirical research into word-shape-based reading. Professor Bouma himself had never heard of the term (a friend of mine asked him). The only things I can take credit for is making it convenient (a single lc word), and spreading it. **2004** Kevin Larson *Microsoft* (July) "The Science of Word Recognition" (Int.) ▶ Some have used the term bouma as a synonym for word shape, though I was unfamiliar with the term. The term bouma appears in Paul Saenger's 1997 book *Space Between Words: The Origins of Silent Reading*. There I learned to my chagrin that we recognize words from their word shape and that "Modern psychologists call this image the 'Bouma shape.'"

boy beater *n.* a ribbed white cotton tank top; a **wife beater.** *Fashion. Slang. United States.* [Parallel to the masculine garment, a *wife beater*.]

2000 Usenet: uk.gay-lesbian-bi (July 7) "Join Today!" ▶ Perhaps you are butch and just like to sit around in a boy-beater all day drinking beer. **2002** *Wearables Business* (July 1) "New Products," p. 74 ▶ Women's tank. Just in time for Summer, American Apparel has added four new colors to its ribbed tank style 3308, the Boy Beater. **2004** Bronwyn Jones *blogging.la* (May 3) "Have It Made" (Int.) ▶ If you're in the market for a boy beater (in the parlance of our times) that says "OUTLAW," I guess you could do worse than Bad Kitty Clothing.

break off *v. phr.* to freely or gratuitously give something (to someone), especially money or something highly prized; in the form *break (someone) off a piece*, to give or receive sexual favors. *Black English. Hip-Hop. Slang.* [Perhaps originating from or reinforced by advertising for the Kit-Kat chocolate candy, which for many years used as a marketing jingle "Break me off a piece of that Kit-Kat bar."] Usually constructed as a transitive with an indirect object, "break someone off something," although there exists also the form "break me off" with an unspoken but understood direct object. Occasionally, it is followed by the preposition "with," perhaps by parallel construction to "hook me up with" 'to grant me access to (something); to get for me (something difficult to acquire).'

1993 Ice Cube, K-Dee, QDIII *Lethal Injection* (song) (Dec. 7) "Make It Ruff, Make It Smooth" ▶ I gots to make a livin', I'm out to get mo/money, and got mo nuts for yo honey/so come and break me off, this nigga's walkin' soft. **1996** Usenet: alt.rap (Feb. 18) "Snoop's Trial" ▶ Can anybody break me off with some news on Snoopy's Murder? **1996** Edward Humes *No Matter How Loud I Shout: A Year in the Life of*

Juvenile Court (Mar. 5), p. 59 ▶ "I told them I just reached down and picked up some of the money sitting there on the floor of the van and said, 'Break me off.'...What's wrong with that? Wouldn't you want to break off some of the money for yourself, too?"..."You think the judge is going to believe anything you say now? Break me off. He's gonna break you off, all right. Break you right off into prison." **1997** *Jim Rome Show* (Jan. 15) "Huge Fax of the Day" in *Usenet: rec.collecting .cards.discuss* (Apr. 29, 1999) *"Why Stuart Scott Sucks"* ▶ Tell me the scores, don't break me off a little sumpin, sumpin. Give me information, don't "bust out with the 411." **1997** *Usenet: rec.gambling .blackjack* (Mar. 21) "Guaranteed 1 Million in Blackjack!" ▶ Don't forget when you hit that million bucks to break me off 5 grand. **1998** *Usenet: alt.rock-n-roll.metal.death* (Oct. 19) "Deadeyesunder Seeks Artist" ▶ We need someone with some artistic abilities to break us off a nice brutal-ass evil/dark looking death metal logo. none of thise 45 Photoshop filters stuff. **1999** *Usenet: ucd.life* (Apr. 18) "Re: Battle of the MCs 2000" ▶ I won't disgrace myself with my white-boy rhyming skillz, but I think Ola should definetly break us off sumthin. **1999** *Usenet: 3dfx.products.voodoo3* (Apr. 21) "Re: John Reynolds, DUDE!" ▶ Ill trade your ass for a pack of smokes bitch. now break me off a piece of dat ass, bitch! **1999** *Usenet: alt.tv.star-trek.voyager* (May 21) "Re: This Is Who They Are!" ▶ Hey Fiver, break me off with a copy of that pic. **1999** *Usenet: alt.sports.basketball.nba.hou-rockets* (June 28) "Re: Rice or Bread?" ▶ Do you look at your posts before sending them? Perhaps an extra moment or two for proofreading would help you appear more intelligent. Although pushing for Knight is crazy no matter how well you craft your text. Just break us off some punctuation, "G." **2001** *Usenet: alt.seduction.fast* (Sept. 6) "MuLtlpLe ChOiCe TeSt" ▶ At a nightspot, you offer an arousing female a drink and she accepts. You would ideally like to end up having this girl "break you off a piece." **2003** Franklin White *Money for Good* (Nov. 15), p. 17 ▶ I'm going to find Rossi before the weekend is over and see if he'll break me off.... Ain't no way I'm gonna let that easy money get away. **2004** Lori Bryant-Woolridge *Hitts & Mrs.* (Jan. 1), p. 110 ▶ You're not drawn to him at all? Not one little iota of I'd-like-to-break-me-off-a-piece-of-that buzzing around your head or other, more pertinent parts? **2005** Rob Harvilla *East Bay Express* (Calif.) (June 1) "Scions of Scion" (Int.) ▶ I've seen DJs roll around in those things, and I think what they do, if you're willin', they'll hook you up on some sort of artist payment plan.... It's funny; a lot of people figure, "It's a fuckin' car company, break us off." But those are $20,000 cars.

breastaurant *n.* a restaurant that features scantily clad or sexually appealing waitresses. *Food & Drink. United States.* This term
usually refers to the restaurant chain Hooters.

1987 James Hagy *Florida Trend* (Sept. 1) "How Big Can Hooters Get?"
vol. 30, no. 5, p. 80 ▶ The concept has become so popular that Hooters has spawned a number of restaurants with similar cheesecake formats. Most, like Hooters, can be recognized by their locker room
names, such as Knockers and Melons. But none of them has perfected
the breastaurant formula like Hooters. **1990** Curtis Krueger *St. Petersburg Times* (Fla.) (Sept. 30) "Hooters Chain Goes for National Appeal,"
p. 1B ▶ Despite their efforts to attract families, not everyone wants to
eat in a "breastaurant." **2004** Walter Olson *Overlawyered* (Nov. 23)
"Hooters Sues Its Competition" (Int.) ▶ Trial began last week in a lawsuit filed by Hooters of America against a rival "breastaurant" operator named WingHouse, which also relies on curvy waitresses to sell
sports-bar food and drink to a clientele of young men.

brekko *n.* breakfast. *Australia. Food & Drink. United Kingdom.* This
is a newer version of an old form: **brekker** or **brekkers** in the
U.K. and **brekkie** in Australia.

1991 B. Dickins *Herald Sun* (Australia) (June 22) "Give Me Some Real
Tennis" ▶ What Boris Becker had for brekko, for instance. **1992**
Andrew Loudon *Daily Mail* (London, Eng.) (Aug. 24) "Cola Wars Put
Fizz Back in Eldorado," p. 19 ▶ If you use fictitious names like Brekko
Flakes on a packet of cereal it just doesn't look right. **1993** R. Gibson
Sunday Mail (Australia) (Mar. 21) ▶ Radio B-105 is turning on a free
brekko for any secretary worth her spiral pad at the Brisbane City
Travelodge. **1999** *Usenet: alt.religion.christian.roman-catholic* (Sept. 7)
"Re: Florida Supreme Court Questions Admissibility of Electric Chair"
▶ "Confused? You won't be after you've had your brekko." "More por-
ridge I am afraid." "You're serving porridge AGAIN?" **2002** *Derby
Evening Telegraph* (U.K.) (Oct. 28) "Counting Cars, Sheep and Bats,"
p. 21 ▶ After this grueling Nazi-like torture, came back, had brekko,
then got on the bus and did another day's work. **2004**
[Muckspreader] *Natives.co.uk* (Jan. 7) "Marmotte Times Issue Five"
(Int.) ▶ If you're late for work you have to do a whole week of early
brekko shifts. **2004** James Kelman *You Have to Be Careful in the Land
of the Free* (May 1), p. 49 ▶ Naybody gies ye a fucking el brekko. Ye
have to grab this world by the coat-tails. **2004** [Lucy&Luke Relph]
BBC: Get Writing: A Forum Conversation (U.K.) (June 13) "De ladding"
(Int.) ▶ Am going for brekko. Back in half an hour.

brownfield *n.* an industrial site, esp. when contaminated; a vacated building lot that has not reverted to a green state. *Architecture. Environment. Jargon.*

1984 Constance Holden *Science* (July 13) "Environmentalists Produce National Economic Agenda," vol. 225, p. 150 ▶ The report supports modernization of smokestack industries and urges that those that are relocated be kept in "brownfield" areas where they will do less environmental damage and supply jobs in already industrialized regions. **2000** Daniel E. Johnson *California Construction Link* (Aug. 1) "Brownfield Development: Cleanup of Urban Areas for Re-Use; More Than 5,000 Sites Exist in California; EPA Loans and Grants May Assist Property Owners," p. 28 ▶ Known as brownfields, these areas are defined by the USEPA as "abandoned, idled, or under-used industrial and commercial facilities where expansion or redevelopment is complicated by real or perceived environmental contamination." **2004** Jennifer Clare *North Brooklyn Community News Greenline* (Brooklyn, N.Y.) (Apr. 8-30) "Turning Brownfields Green," vol. XXIX, p. 3 ▶ The legislation offers incentives for the public and private redevelopment of former industrial sites (some are contaminated—also known as brownfields) into new housing and economic development opportunities.

buckaloose *adj.* unhinged, crazy, out of control, erratic; (of a woman) loose, easy. *Colloquial. English-based Creole. Hawaii. United States.*

2002 [Alfred Pennyworth] *Ultrablognetic* (Sept. 22) (Int.) ▶ da internet is running so slow cuz, it's makin me all buckaloose. I mean fa real kine I'm gonna break yo face. **2003** Jena Osman *Chain 10: translucinacion* (Sept. 1), p. 245 ▶ Wen look like everyting boing come all buckaloose and maybe going get war, ees up to da bruddahs and sistahs who get da cool head, dey da ones gotta say someting for protess da crime and da outrage das going be perpetuated on top a-dem. **2004** [Emily]*...a beautiful distraction* (June 3) (Int.) ▶ our hawaiian native is teaching us some of their, as she calls it, "pidgeon slang." like "i'm bow with my reading." or "that girl is buckaloose."

buckle bunny *n.* a female groupie of rodeo cowboys. *Slang. Sports. United States.* This term is similar to PUCK BUNNY.

1978 Roger Kahn @ Cody, Wyo. *N.Y. Times* (July 24) "The Sport of Cowboys," p. C4 ▶ "Are there girls," I said, "who follow rodeo cowboys?" Sundown grinned. "We call them buckle bunnies." **1988** Sally Jenkins *Washington Post* (Feb. 23) "Of Prairie Fires and Cowgirl's Kisses," p. E4 ▶ If you don't know how to do the two-step, a Buckle Bunny (cowboy groupie) will be happy to help you. **2004** Jeannine

Crooks *Milford Daily News* (Mass.) (June 10) "Pick Up Lingo to Rope in Good Time" (Int.) ▶ Buckle bunnies: Rodeo's version of groupies, women who love to be around rodeo cowboys.

budget dust *n.* money said to be insignificant when compared to other (planned) expenditures. *Money & Finance.*

1990 Gene Pentecost @ Franklin, Tenn. *USA Today* (July 6) "Are You Angry About the Savings and Loan Bailout?" p. 10A ▶ The regulators should help pay the price by going to jail, having their salaries reduced, or both. This is another burden on the taxpayer. Everybody in Washington is to blame. This isn't just budget dust, this is big bucks. **1991** Cathy Taylor *Orange County Register* (Calif.) (Mar. 12) "A Lesson in Budget Dust and Burn Rate," p. D1 ▶ *Budget dust.* A small cash amount relative to the company's total dollar budget. Many managers are being told to spend less, but if you want to arm wrestle, try this: "Why boss, that program accounts for just budget dust; let's keep it in." **1997** Rhonda L. Wickham *Cellular Business* (Nov. 30) "Budget Dust or Bust" ▶ During the heat of the bidding process, a few wannabe licensees obviously felt as though their high-dollar bids for spectrum would be justified and add up to mere "budget dust" in the long-term. **2002** Rebecca Cook @ Olympia, Wash. (*AP*) (Dec. 29) "In State Spending, Hot-Button Items Amount to Mere 'Budget Dust'" ▶ It seems strange to talk about $30 million here and there as mere budget dust—as the budget writers call it. But in the state's $23 billion budget, $30 million is a bit like the loose change you find under your sofa cushions. **2005** Lisa Mascaro @ L.A. *Orange County Register* (Calif.) (June 5) "Despite Budget Woes, MTA Board Dines Well" (Int.) ▶ Some of the items certainly appear to be extravagant in light of the fact that the agency has consistently run a deficit. And although the relatively small amount may, in the grand scheme of things, be no more than what we refer to as budget dust, it is both symbolic and reflective of what they bring to the table. They're not very cost-conscious.

buffet flat *n.* a speakeasy or other unregulated or illegal entertainment establishment that sells alcohol, usually located in an apartment or home. *Crime & Prisons. Food & Drink. Slang. United States.*

1911 *Chicago Daily Tribune* (Jan. 24) "Veteran Gambler Says Vice Grows with Police Aid," p. 1 ▶ From Twenty-second street south in Michigan avenue, Wabash avenue, State street, and the cross streets as far south as Thirty-first street is a rich district of the so-called buffet flats. There, too, can be found hundreds of handbooks, gaming houses, and all night saloons of the most vicious character. **1911** Gene Morgan *Chicago Daily Tribune* (Feb. 19) "It Takes an Out-of-Town

Minister Really to See Chicago Vice," p. 11 ► The "buffet flat" is thus termed because it is possible to buy all kinds of liquor in these places at all hours—and for all prices. **1916** *Lincoln Daily News* (Neb.) (Sept. 8), p. 3 ► The Buffet Flat and Wine Room, Recruiting Stations for White Slavers, Exposed. **1927** Harvey Anderson @ NYC *Port Arthur News* (Tex.) (Jan. 9) "Buffet Flat Solves Many of High Society's Drinking Problems," p. 3 ► The casual, migratory and unskilled drinkers of the world, along with a scattering of habitual, non-migratory and skilful [*sic*] drinkers, have found a new haven. It is the buffet flat and the New York police are authority for the statement that there are now about 10,000 of these sheltered retreats in Manhattan and Brooklyn and they are diverting streams of "sucker" money from the night clubs and they constitute a new and baffling factor in the problem of liquor law enforcement. **1933** *Nevada State Journal* (Reno) (Dec. 17) "Emperor Jones Is Coming," p. 7 ► Have you ever been to a buffet flat? It's neither a lunchroom nor a variation of a western plain. It's peculiar to Harlem, yet few white visitors to that Negro haven in New York City ever hear of it, and practically none get into one. In "Emperor Jones," a picturization of Eugene O'Neill's famous play...a buffet flat is shown in all its colorful detail. A buffet flat is simply a Harlem apartment to which people come to sit around, eat, drink, talk, sing and dance.

bug *n.* an illegal lottery; the numbers game. *Gambling. Georgia.* This term appears to be most common in Georgia and Alabama. It often takes the definite article: **the bug.**

1936 Joseph Ator *Chicago Tribune* (Oct. 25) "We Bet Five Billion," p. E10 ► The lottery is a poor man's game. Its operators are the slummers of the gambling industry. There are, of course, exceptions. Society women play the "bug," as the numbers game is called in Atlanta.... Atlanta arrests an average of a hundred "bug" agents a month. **1940** Carson McCullers *The Heart Is a Lonely Hunter* (May 18, 1993) ► Father, that is sure one bad, wicked place. They got a man sells tickets on the bug. [**1946** *Cullman Banner* (Ala.) (Mar. 7) "Buettners Hold Annual Teachers Banquet," p. 7 ► In the "Bug" game, Mrs. Donahoo won first and Mrs. Willoughby took second prize.] **1949** *Dothan Eagle* (Ala.) (May 21) "31 Persons Arrested by Authorities Here," p. 2 ► Pleading guilty to a lottery charge today was Pency Capane, Dothan Negress. The woman was arrested Saturday, along with another Negro on whom police said they found bug tickets. **1950** Ernest E. Blanche *Annals of the American Academy of Political and Social Science* (May) "Lotteries Yesterday, Today, and Tomorrow," vol. 269, p. 74 ► The numbers game (known also as *policy, clearing house, the bug, butter and eggs* and other names) operates every day except Sunday throughout the year, players wagering anything from a penny upward on a three-digit number (000-999). **1951** Jim Thomasson @ Phenix City, Ala. *Ironwood Daily Globe* (Ironwood, Mich.) (May 17) "Alabama City Tames Down," p. 11 ▶ Dice tables are covered in this robust Chattahoochee river town. Slot machines have disappeared. And if any bug tickets—lottery slips—are written, they are passed under the counter. **1959** Pharr (*Stubblefield v. the State 38210*) (Fulton Co., Ga.) (Dec. 17) "101 Ga. App. 481; 114 SE2d 221" (Int.) ▶ If you believe beyond a reasonable doubt that the defendant did possess "bug" or lottery tickets, and that they were a part of the paraphernalia of the lottery known as the "bug" or numbers game, and the defendant thus aided, assisted and participated in the carrying on of the lottery, if one was carried on, you would be authorized to convict the defendant of this charge. **1993** Charles Walston *Atlanta Constitution* (Ga.) (Aug. 8) "Experts Say State Lotteries Compete with Illegal Numbers Games in Cities," p. D5 ▶ Three-digit lottery games with daily drawings, such as the one that starts Tuesday in Georgia, are virtually identical in format to longtime illegal games—the "Bug" in Atlanta, the "Numbers" up north, and the "Bolita" among the Hispanic communities of South Florida. **1995** Bill Montgomery *Atlanta Journal-Constitution* (Nov. 29) "'The Bug': Shadow of Former Self Numbers Racket Survives, But Lottery Has Cost It Players," p. B1 ▶ The illegal numbers racket known as "the bug" lives on after the murder this week of one of its one-time kingpins.

Bugs Bunny changeup *n.* in baseball, a slow pitch disguised as a fast ball that seems to stop in front of the plate. *Sports. United States.*

[**1993** Javier Morales *Arizona Daily Star* (June 30) "Barrett's 'Super Slow Ball' Baffles Edmonton," p. 5D ▶ I perplexed them with my super slow ball.... I think I remember Bugs Bunny saying that once.] **1997** John Henderson *Denver Post* (Colo.) (May 5) "Schilling Might Have Looked Nice in Purple" ▶ Catcher Jeff Reed calls the superb changeup by Philadelphia's Mark Portugal a "Bugs Bunny changeup." Why? "Because it just stops right there," Reed said. **2004** Mark Whicker @ Omaha, Neb. *Mercury News* (San Jose, Calif.) (June 25) "Fullerton's Sarver an Unlikely Story" (Int.) ▶ The newest entry into the baseball vernacular is "Bugs Bunny changeup." Translation: It rushes up to the plate and then suddenly stops. Sarver fed the Gamecocks carrots and lettuce all night.

bukateria *n.* a cafeteria, canteen, or simple eating-place. Also **buka.** *Food & Drink. Nigeria.* [< ? *buka* + cafe*teria*] The etymological information in the second 2002 cite has not been verified.

1999 Bamidele Adebayo @ Lagos, Nigeria *All Africa* (July 18) "Campus of Deaths" ▶ In 1996, a lecturer in the department of food, science and technology and the proprietor of A la-carte, a restaurant in the new bukateria of the university, was gunned down by people suspected to be secret cult members. **2002** Ian R. Young @ Ibadan, Nigeria *CASLIS Atlantic Newsletter* (Can.) (Apr.) "'Ile-Ikawe' Means 'House of Readers' or 'Library' in Yoruba," vol. 9, no. 3 (Int.) ▶ A typical nutritious "chop house" or "bukateria" meal of pounded yam, melon seed and palm oil stew, accompanied by a couple pieces of beef—all eaten with one's bare hand—plus a Coke costs N60, or about US$0.50. **2002** Molara Ogundipe *A Sunday Afternoon with Ayi Kwei Armah* (Aug.) (Int.) ▶ From this restaurant of the people or *bukateria* (from the Hausa word, buka, for eating house) as we would say in Nigeria, simple and pleasing in its decor, everywhere you looked you saw the sea. **2002** Victor Akobundu (*All Africa*) (Nigeria) (Aug. 30) "Season of the Wonder Crop" ▶ Meanwhile, those who ran the bukateria, an eating place for the common man, have introduced the corn meal or corn vita (Tuwo Masara). **2004** Sam Umukoro, Dafe Ivwurie *Vanguard* (Apapa, Nigeria) (May 23) "Ozekhome: A Generalissimo in Whom 72 Kings Are Well Pleased" (Int.) ▶ We asked the chief who hails from Iviukwe in Etsako East Local Government Area of Edo State if he visits these eateries popularly called "mama put" in Nigerian parlance. His words: "Yes, even now I like eating in the bukateria. I like this mama put system where you go to the pot and point out the orisirisi (assortment of meat), the edo (liver), the saki, the ponmo and the rest."

bullets and beans *n.pl.* the weapons, munitions, equipment, and supplies of a military; material. *Military.* See the cites for variations, which are usually alliterative.

1950 *Washington Post* (Nov. 19) "Korea Airlift Carried 100,000 Passengers" (in Feaf Combat Cargo Command, Japan), p. M2 ▶ The commander said the airlift carried more than 63,000 tons of bullets and beans and 100,000 passengers in that period. **1978** Ruth S. Knowles *The Greatest Gamblers,* 2 ed., p. 284 in (Aug. 1, 1980) ▶ Like the first war, World War II was—in Admiral Nimitz' words—"a matter of oil, bullets and beans." **1989** Charles W. Koburger *The Cyrano Fleet* (Mar. 7), p. 111 ▶ As far as the officers of the fleet went, they had still to be fully involved with the day-to-day running of their departments, and with their ships. Their problems revolved around "bullets, beans, and black oil." **1994** Merrill B. Twining *No Bended*

Knee (June 1), p. 40 (Mar. 30, 2004) ▶ General Vandegrift's order was brief: "Take only that with is necessary to fight and live." This meant bullets, beans, and blankets. **2001** John Bowe *Gig* (Aug. 21), p. 570 ▶ I have to oversee all the maintenance of the airplanes as well as make sure we've got all the bombs and bullets and beans we're supposed to have everywhere. **2003** Chuck Pfarrer *Warrior Soul* (Dec. 30), p. 172 (Dec. 28, 2004) ▶ Daily, landing craft disgorged trucks, jeeps, and trailers onto the piers, supplying the troops with bullets, beans, and butt wipe. **2005** Scott Gold, Rone Tempest *KTLA-TV* (L.A.) (July 27) "Army Probes Guard Unit" (Int.) ▶ The first sergeant holds an important position of authority in a company and is largely responsible for overseeing the preparedness and welfare of the soldiers in the unit—"bullets and beans," in the vernacular of the Army.

bull tailing *n.* a sport in which mounted riders take down bulls by the tail. Also **steer tailing.** *Animals. Mexico. Sports. United States.* Known in Venezuela as **toros coleados**; in Mexico as **las colas** or **colas en el lienzo**.

1880 *Chester Daily Times* (Pa.) (Mar. 13) "All Sorts," p. 2 ▶ General Grant did not like bull tailing in Mexico, a sort of substitute for the scarcely more barbarous bull fight. When one bull was thrown and had his leg broken, and another bayoneted, General Grant abru[p]tly retired. "I never saw this sport before, and I shall never see it again," he remarked on the way back. **1985** Ramon Bracamontes *Dallas Morning News* (Dec. 22) "'Charro' Life Full of Danger; Mexican-Style Rodeos Attract El Paso Riders," p. 73A ▶ The nine events in the overall competition are horse showmanship, horse roping, bull tailing, bull riding, rope showmanship, bronco riding, foot roping, horse roping and the pass of death. **2004** *WKMG-TV* (Tallahassee, Fla.) (Apr. 24) "Senate Passes Ban on 'Bull Tailing'" (Int.) ▶ The rodeo-like sport of bull tailing, or Toros Coleados, which Venezuelan immigrants have brought to South Florida, involves cowboys on horseback who grab a running bull by the tail and pull it down. There's a similar event in Mexico, known as colas.

burner *n.* a gun, especially a handgun. *Slang. United States.*

1988 Sari Horwitz *Washington Post* (Apr. 24) "A Drug-Selling Machine That Was All Business," p. A1 ▶ In another seizure, police recovered a crude, handwritten drug-trade manual from a PCP ring.... It listed the "workers" and the "deliverers," assigning beepers, walkie-talkies, police scanners and "burners" (guns) to them. **1989** Bill Nichols, Mike McQueen *USA Today* (1A) (Apr. 25) "D.C. Crack Street Fights to Survive" ▶ *Burner* A gun, usually a handgun. **1992** Sue Anne Pressley, Keith Harriston *Washington Post* (Feb. 2) "A Crazed Fascination with Guns," p. A1 ► The inmates talked about their crimes in a generally easy manner, some with a lingo that focused on "beefs," or disputes, and then getting "a burner," or gun, to settle the score. **2004** Alex Wood *Journal Inquirer* (Manchester, Conn.) (Dec. 11) "Man Who Shot at Cops Says He Was Scared" (Int.) ► He said he had had an altercation on Zion Street the previous morning with a man who had threatened him, saying, "You better keep your burner on you tonight." "Burner" is a slang expression for a gun. **2005** Curtis Johnson *Herald-Dispatch* (Huntington, W.Va.) (Apr. 21) "Witness Points Finger at Fields" (Int.) ► "He asked Justin to get him his burner, because he was going to murk that bitch," White said. In testimony, White said "burner" was a word meaning "pistol, gun" and "murk" meant to "murder, kill."

burn off *v.* in entertainment television, to broadcast un-aired episodes of a canceled program. *Entertainment. Jargon. Media.* **1986** Ed Bark *Dallas Morning News* (Tex.) (May 31) "'Dallas' Gets New Time Slot for Summer," p. 1F ► The summer season, used primarily to burn off reruns, failed series pilots and documentaries, is becoming more important as a possible springboard for freshman series that had modest ratings in the regular season. **1992** Greg Dawson *Chicago Tribune* (Dec. 11) "Hopes Ride on 'Burn Off' Viewers," p. 8 ► VQT pins its slender hopes on seven unseen episodes of "Brooklyn Bridge" that CBS plans to air ("burn off" in TV lingo) sometime after the first of the year. **1996** Lon Grahnke *Chicago Sun-Times* (June 5) "Networks 'Burn Off' 5 Canceled Series," p. 53 ► In TV lingo, networks "burn off" episodes of rejected series after the official prime-time season ends in May.... The burnoff season also provides a bonus for viewers, giving them a fresh alternative to the nightly diet of reruns. Sometimes the final burned-off episodes of a high-quality, low-rated series. **2005** Joanne Ostrow *Denver Post* (Colo.) (Feb. 14) "Listening in on the Moguls" (Int.) ► Burn-Off Theater...the presentation of shelved losers and leftovers, ie. making use of pilots that didn't go. Fox president G. Berman: "Summer isn't just for Burn-Off Theater anymore."

buscon *n.* In the Dominican Republic, a facilitator for legal or bureaucratic matters, such as a job recruiter for organizations in the United States or a baseball scout. Also **buscone.** *Dominican Republic. Spanish. Sports. United States.* [From the Spanish **buscón** 'rogue,' 'cheat,' 'pettifogger,' with the etymological connection to *buscar* 'to search' probably also coming into play.] The form *buscone* is an Anglophone back-formation from the Spanish plural *buscones.* The bracketed items in the 1996 citation are found in the original text.

1991 Gregory Katz @ Bon Repos Repatriation Center, Haiti *Dallas Morning News* (Oct. 25) "Haitians Feel Oppression from Dominican Bias," p. 1A ▶ The new system calls for Dominican and Haitian buscones, or recruiters, to go to Haiti and promise workers easy money, good housing and soft jobs. **1996** Bill Chastain *Tampa Tribune* (Fla.) (Jan. 28) "Dominican Connections Benefit Rays" ▶ "Whenever you sign one of their players you have to pay [the buscone] $500 or $1,000. Either that or they will take it off [the prospect's] bonus." **1998** Gordon Edes @ San Pedro de Macoris, Dominican Republic *Boston Globe* (Mar. 27) "Red Sox Are Digging Deeply into One of the Richest Troves of Talent Anywhere," p. F3 ▶ "But now if you don't sign a player on the day he tries out, the buscon will take him to another team," Norman said. "And now, some buscones are going to agents instead." **2002** Jim Salisbury *Philadelphia Inquirer* (Pa.) (July 23) "Search for Dominican Talent No Longer a Hit-or-Miss Affair" ▶ Throw a scout, an agent, a coach and an entrepreneur into a blender, then mix, and you have a buscone (boo-SCONE-ay). **2003** (*Efe News Services*) (Sept. 18) "La Ligas Mayores quieren poner control sobre agentes dominicanos" (in Washington, D.C.) ▶ La proliferacion de "buscones," refleja el crecimiento de la actividad de los cazatalentos en la Republica Dominicana, de donde salen al menos una cuarta parte de los peloteros que juegan bajo contrato en equipos de las Grandes Ligas. **2004** Ed Price *Baseball America ESPN* (May 8) "Rosario Signing Raises Red Flag" (Int.) ▶ They paid $100,000 to Ivan Noboa—a "buscone," or independent developer of talent in the Dominican—and gave Rosario a $400,000 bonus. **2004** German Marte *Hoy* (Santo Domingo, Dom. Rep.) (July 17) "Denuncian anomalías obtener documentos" (Int.) ▶ Obtener una acta de nacimiento én la Oficialía Civil de la Segunda Circunscripción del Distrito Nacional es una verdadera odisea para cualquiera, "a menos que usted se cantee con RD$350 y le pague a un buscón," denunciaron ayer varias personas. **2004** Matt Lockhart *Charleston Daily Mail* (W.Va.) (July 21) "Some Alley Cats Still Learning to Talk the Talk" (Int.) ▶ Signing is also a major issue currently in the Dominican Republic. Talent hunters, buscones as they call them, journey the streets and fields for ambitious ball players. Buscones promise a chance at professional baseball, but it comes at a price. While agents in the United States charge around five percent of a client's signing bonus and salary, buscones have been known to demand more than 35 percent. ***2004** U.S. State Dept. (*U.S. Embassy, Dom. Rep.*) (Aug. 4) "Cuidado con los Buscones"

(Int.) ▶ Estamos seguros de que no tiene dinero para desperdiciar, y nosotros en la Sección Consular no queremos que usted se convierta en víctima de los buscones y tigueres que hacen promesas que no pueden cumplir.

bustdown *n.* a promiscuous or undesirable woman; a *ho*; a *bitch.* Also **bust down, busdown.** *Black English. Chicago. Hip-Hop. Slang. United States.* This term appears to be common in Chicago.

2003 [Ana] *The Java Arcade* (Mar. 2) "Hoe He Don't Want u trick" (Int.) ▶ Bowwow is mine the real Shad Moss A.K.A. Bowwow right here bitch you busdown ass hoe. **2003** Diplomats *Diplomatic Immunity* (song) (Mar. 25) "Dipset Anthem" ▶ I'm on the westside of Chicago, lookin' for a bust down/And make me put my two arms up, Touchdown! **2003** LaShaunna Watkins *Northern Star* (Dekalb, Ill.) (Nov. 11) "E.B.O.N.Y. Confronts 'Bust Downs'" (Int.) ▶ Nekika Skinner, president of E.B.O.N.Y. Women, said a "bust down" is a girl who sleeps with numerous people without any discretion and also carries herself in a bad manner. [**2004** Steven G. Fullwood *Stevengfullwood.org* (NYC) (Feb. 27) "My Friend, the Pimp" (Int.) ▶ One day while working at a hair salon that he owns, Jeff explains to me that he was constantly being asked by the young black women who frequented the shop to bring a bunch of "ballers" (men with money who enjoy flossing) together and host a party so that they could make some money by performing sexual acts. The name of such an event is called a bust-down.] ***2004** Judy Howell *Foster and Adoptive Care Association of Minnesota* (Mar. 11) "When Will I Be Loved?" (Int.) ▶ She is no longer a ho or a busdown or a bitch as she had been told day-in and day-out by her birth mother. **2004** [loserpunk17] *carMen's Journal* (Calumet City, Ill.) (Apr. 16) (Int.) ▶ "im ₁gettting low with some bitches and some hoes, what? getting low? like a busdown?" "steven is mad? ok i got to bust down tonite" we are bust downs! **2004** [G.O.D.] *SOHH.com* (May 9) "Women Enjoy Sex Just as Much as Men" (Int.) ▶ Man...this chic let me fukk the first night...she's a busdown...i'm gonna have fun with her for a couple months than skate. **2004** [mzcurtisjacksonnigga] @ Chicago, Ill. *G-Unit Board* (May 10) "Sexy Niggas Need a Hardcore Rated-X Bitch!!" (Int.) ▶ U nasty as hell u shouldnt put yo self out there like that its makes u look like a busdown, a ho, a infected ass female and shit jus plain nasty. **2004** [HipHopGenius] *Eminem Forum* (May 12) "$tinger vs. Hiphopgenius (5-3)" (Int.) ▶ He so ugly he paid a busdown just to give him a kiss. **2004** *Iconator* (Aug. 13) "Paris Hilton No Marts634" (Int.) ▶ Paris is a busdown yo and has a crow nose because shes so friggin rich she a spoiled brat. **2004** [I'm Deon] @ Detroit, Mich. *411Hype.com* (Aug. 16) "Love Ain't" (Int.) ▶ She went from boo to busdown?...rofl. **2004** [Jasmine] *Right On! Magazine* (Oct. 9) "Guest-book" (Int.) ▸ Hold up wait a minute mz b weezy dan came up in it. Holl aback i love bow wow and 50 cent also but bow is my # 1 boo forever and always so all yall little busdown wannabes need to back dat azz away fa you get merked. [**2005** nbamami @ Va. *Blackfolk* (Jan. 9) "WOW: I Found This Small Gossip at groovevolt.com's Guess What Section" (Int.) ▸ Bentley is a bust down, he's an ugly dude. It sounds like fake groupie stories.] **2005** [Christopher] *Christopher's Windy City Weblog* (Chicago, Ill.) (Feb. 21) "Teaching on the South Side: Language" (Int.) ▸ A "bust-down" (pronounced "busdown," and sometimes abbreviated as "bussy" or "busser") is a woman of loose morals (although my students would define it by using graphic examples of what such a woman does). ***2005** [Baby2Phat] @ Chicago, Ill. *BlackPlanet.com* (Feb. 21) "Baby2Phat's BlackPlanet.com Personal Page" (Int.) ▸ She a pimp but when it comes down to it so dont treat her like no busdown. ***2005** Quient (Q-Dogg) @ Chicago, Ill. *Black-Planet.com* (Feb. 21) "25Gee-Q's BlackPlanet.com Personal Page" (Int.) ▸ When I look 4 a woman I don't look 4 a busdown, a party, a motor-head, golddigger, or a girl that is just not right to herself. ***2005** [Smoke] *Mixedrace.com* (Feb. 21) "lil_smoke2004" (Int.) ▸ What I'm NOT lookin for in a girl...a neighborhood ho...a busdown. ***2005** [D.J. Rader] @ Chicago *BlackPlanet.com* (Feb. 21) "Djrader's BlackPlanet.com Personal Page" (Int.) ▸ A head strong woman that knows what she want in life and has goals for herself. An educated woman not a dumb @$$ busdown.

C

C4ISR *n.* the integration of intelligence and communications functions (of a military group). *Acronym. Jargon. Military. United States.*

1995 *Defense News* (Dec. 18) "Information Laboratory Would Link C4 Efforts US Defense Officials Want to Invest More Than $1 Bil to Establish C4ISR Decision Support Center" ▶ C4ISR stands for command, control, communications, computers, intelligence, surveillance and reconnaissance systems needed for effective battle. **1996** Jim Mannion (*Agence France-Presse*) (July 25) "Today's Terrorist Threats Among Pentagon's Military Research Priorities" ▶ The programs generally eschew big new weapon systems, focusing instead on developing software to pull together all the strands of military intelligence gathering and communications into manageable formats. In US military parlance, this is "C4ISR." **2004** Stephen Blank *Asia Times* (Hong Kong) (May 5) "Spinning the Nuclear Missile Wheel" (Int.) ▶ China is building more missiles and also appears to be focusing on depriving either side's defenses from finding its missiles and thus concentrates on attacking their command, control, communications, intelligence, surveillance and reconnaissance capabilities (C4ISR in military parlance) while also moving to join the other two governments in weaponizing space.

caging *n.* the processing of responses to a fund-raising or marketing campaign, especially when concerning money. *Advertising. Jargon.* [Perhaps related to a *teller's cage*.]

1981 Morton Mintz *Washington Post* (Feb. 7) "Outsider Money Inside a California District," p. A3 ▶ The contribution checks went to a Viguerie "caging function" here for processing. Peck protested, charging that Dornan's campaign was "run out of Falls Church." Recognizing that "Peck's got a point," Steinberg said he had felt that the return envelopes should have been pre-addressed to a Post Office box in the district. He prevailed early this year, and the caging chore was moved to Santa Monica. **1984** Jay Mathews @ Sacramento, Calif. *Washington Post* (July 3) "'Booming Enterprise' New Forces Take Political Initiative" ▶ Computer Caging (caging is the direct-mail industry term for collecting money) had raised money for Gann's fight to preserve Proposition 13 from a legal counter-attack. **1989** *Fund Raising Management* (Jan. 1) "How to Cut Costs on Gift Processing," vol. 19, no. 11, p. 35 ▶ Many people use many terms for this service. Some of them are:

lock box operation, cashiering, scanning operation, caging operation, cash management, and OCR operation. **1990** Susan Hovey *Folio: The Magazine for Magazine Management* (Nov. 1) "Playing It Smart: Going Global Means Finding Readers, Managing Editorial, Delivering the Goods, and Getting Paid in Currency You Can Use," p. 148 ▶ Clients saw a 14 percent increase in subscribers in 1988 from use of KLM's caging/cashiering service, compared to a 3 percent rise in those countries where subscribers had to send a U.S. money order. **1995** Denison Hatch *Target Marketing* (Oct. 1) "Suspect Until Proven Otherwise," vol. 18, no. 10, p. 66 ▶ Caging is the receipt of mail to locked cages where clerks extract and count money. **2003** Assoc. of Fundraising Professionals *AFP Fundraising Dictionary* (June 9), p. 18 (Int.) ▶ *caging,—noun Informal.* the process or act of collecting donations by an entity other than the not-for-profit organization for which they were solicited. **2003** Richard W. Stevenson *N.Y. Times* (Oct. 22) "Bush Spending for '04 Tops Any Rival's," p. A19 ▶ When the checks come in, they are subject to one of the strangest entries on the campaign's expense ledger: "batching and caging," or opening the envelopes, sorting the checks and keeping them secure. **2004** Greg Palast *Baltimore Chronicle* (Md.) (Nov. 2) "An Election Spoiled Rotten" (Int.) ▶ The GOP's announced plan to block 35,000 voters in Ohio ran up against the wrath of federal judges; so, in Florida, what appear to be similar plans had been kept under wraps until the discovery of documents called "caging" lists.

Califunny *n.* a jocular or derisive name for California. *California. United States.*

1991 *Usenet: alt.sex.bondage* (Sept. 10) "Re: Incest" ▶ I have known of three sets of siblings who had sex with one another (no, I don't peek in windows and ask leading questions). Two, some time ago back in redneckland and one in sometime free and easy Marin County Califunny. **1994** *Usenet: comp.org.eff.talk* (Feb. 25) "Re: Over 10,000 Have Signed Petition to Oppose Clipper" ▶ Does he use a bed_of_nails keyboard so it REALLY feels good when he's replying? Well, no surprise really. He _is_ after all, posting from Southern Califunny. All that smog, for all those years. **2004** [Vee Koz] *My Never-Neverland* (Sept. 27) "I Did It" (Int.) ▶ I voted once for a governor, with Boucher's help, when I was living in Califunny. Alas, Arnold won.

Canada point *n.* a place away from a city's center where newspapers are distributed to newsboys and news agents. *Media. NYC.* [Probably by comparison of the remote locations of such centers of distribution to the vast expanses of Canada, although it is possibly influenced by the common use of crosstown streets in New York City as landmarks or reference points, which is similar to the use of geographic latitudes, or parallels, to refer to places and distances in Canada.] Now historical. This term appears to have been used only in Boston and New York City.

1906 *Washington Post* (Sept. 18) "A.F.L. Council Will Frame Political Plan," p. 4 ▶ A committee...appeared, claiming jurisdiction over those boys working at "Canada" points, that is, the wholesale and retail distribution of newspapers at several points in large cities. **1906** *Washington Post* (Sept. 20) "Abolition of Child Labor Asked by A.F.L.," p. 2 ▶ It was decided to sustain Newsboys' Union of Boston by ruling "that the the [*sic*] wholesaling and retailing of newspapers at the so-called 'Canada Points' is comprehended in the charter and jurisdiction of the Newsboys' Protective Union." **1937** Canny; Rosenberg *LOTJ* (Nov. 29) "Newspaper Deliverers Jargon" ▶ Canada-point man. Distributes to newsboys from truck at certain sections. **1937** Individuals; Wayne Walden @ NYC *LOTJ* (Dec. 6) "Slang of Newspaper and Mail Delivery (Rewrite Canny)" ▶ Canada points—Points such as at 42, 125, Streets, Union Sq. etc. where newspapers dealers may obtain supplies from a seller stations at points. **1938-39** Individual delivery workers at Park Row, New York City @ NYC *LOTJ* "Mail and Newspaper Delivery Workers' Slang and Jargon" ▶ Canada-point man. Man who makes deliveries to dealers and newsboys at points far up-town. **1972** *N.Y. Times* (July 12) "Lauren D. Lyman, 81, Won Pulitzer Prize" (in Bridgeport, Conn.), p. C8 ▶ The newspaper was aware that the competition sent copy boys to Times Square, the first delivery point, to check for stories and so the edition with the Lindbergh exclusive was dispatched to so-called "Canada points," or outlying districts first.

Canadian Ballet *n.* exotic dancing; a strip club; collectively, strip clubs in Canada. *Canada. Slang.*

1993 *Usenet: rec.sport.football.pro* (Oct. 4) "Kelly Out Drinking Before Miami Game" ▶ When asked what he had been doing in Canada, he responded that he had been bar-hopping. Undoubtedly going to the girlie bars to watch the Canadian Ballet. **1995** Nicole Peradotto *Buffalo News* (Aug. 13) "Strippers Take a Stand Against Lap Dancing," p. E1 ▶ "Do you wanna dance?" The question, when posed at the Canadian Ballet—the euphemism used to describe the north-of-the-border strip clubs so popular with Western New Yorkers—usually refers to a tangle instead of a tango. **1998** *Usenet: soc.subculture .bondage-bdsm* (Apr. 16) "Re: Survey: For Doms, Regarding Obese Subs" ▶ As for most of the strip clubs in my area, which includes Western New York and lower Ontario, Canada, they are relatively clean as are the clientele.... North of the border, these establishments are referred to as the Canadian Ballet. **2004** Josh Fruhlinger *Comics Curmudgeon* (Baltimore, Md.) (Sept. 4) "Oh, Canada!" (Int.) ► Dozens of strip clubs line the streets of the Canadian towns just across the Niagara River from Buffalo. (These clubs were collectively known as "the Canadian ballet," a euphemism I find terrifically amusing to this day.)

canine freestyle *n.* a competitive sport in which a dog obeys a handler's commands in a routine set to music. *Animals. Sports.*
1995 Dan Rodricks *Baltimore Sun* (Md.) (Mar. 15) "Hint to Thief: Don't Try to Palm Off a Stolen Plant on Its Owner," p. 1B ► Coming up this Saturday...Joan Tennille on "canine freestyle dancing." There will also be a pet fashion show. I am not making this up! **1998** Stephanie J. Taunton *The Trick Is in the Training* (Mar. 1), p. 50 ► There is a new sport called Canine Freestyle, in which handler and dog perform a routine of their own devising to music. **2004** Kathleen Fordyce *Miami Herald* (Dec. 4) "Pooches Dazzle on Dance Floor—Even with Their Two Left Feet" (Int.) ► Dancing with dogs—or canine freestyle, as aficionados call it—is an emerging sport in the dog world.

cannonball Sunday *n.* a sparsely attended church service, especially immediately following a Christian holiday. *Religion.*
2003 John W. Wurster (*First Presbyterian Church*) (Findlay, Ohio) (Dec. 28) "Ode to Christmas" (Int.) ► 'Tis three days after Christmas/And I don't know what to say./No one really wants to preach/On a Cannonball Sunday. **2004** J. Dale Suggs *Torrey Pines Christian Church* (La Jolla, Calif.) (Feb. 22) "Enough Is Enough" (Int.) ► I'm amazed that anybody is here this morning. I advertised for weeks that today we were going to talk about giving generously. Stewardship sermons have a way of creating what we call in the business "cannonball Sunday." **2004** Stephen Van Etten *Hunterdon County Democrat* (N.J.) (Dec. 22) "Area's Churches Have Open Arms, Full Pews" (Int.) ► Attendance at his church picks up slightly for Christmas, but he calls the following week's service "Cannonball Sunday." **2004** Alan Kimber *RecordNet* (Stockton, Calif.) (Dec. 25) "Spirited Words" (Int.) ► On these great festivals of the Christian faith, churches are crowded, often to overflowing while on some other Sundays the exact opposite is true. In fact, the Sundays after these great festivals are sometimes referred to as "cannonball Sundays," meaning you can fire a cannon through the congregation and probably not hit anyone.

cardinal *n.* a chairman of any subcommittee of the U.S. House of Representatives Appropriations Committee. *Politics. United States.*

[Probably from the similarity to the College of Cardinals at the Vatican, a body of men who collectively wield great power and influence.]

1989 Dan Morgan *Washington Post* (June 30) "In College of 'Cardinals,' a Summer of Frustration," p. A1 ▶ This is turning into a difficult summer for the 13 chairmen of the House Appropriations subcommittees, the powerful legislators known reverentially on Capitol Hill as "the cardinals." **1995** James V. Grimaldi *Orange County Register* (Calif.) (Dec. 12) "Packard Now Backs Bosnia Plan," p. A1 ▶ As a so-called "cardinal," or appropriations subcommittee chairman, Packard will influence the debate. **1997** Peter Hardin *Richmond Times-Dispatch* (Va.) (Jan. 8) "'Safe' Wolf Was 'Present,'" p. A8 ▶ The 57-year-old Wolf is a so-called cardinal on Capitol Hill, the term for chairmen of subcommittees of the House Appropriations Committee. **2001** Jim Myers *Tulsa World* (Okla.) (May 16) "Istook Says No to Run for Governor," p. 7 ▶ Istook gained even more influence after being named a so-called "cardinal," the moniker given to those who chair an appropriations subcommittee. **2002** Abner J. Mikva *Chicago Tribune* (Mar. 14) "Kaszak Support," p. 18 ▶ The editorial mentioned that the district encompasses a good part of the old district of Sidney Yates, and talked about him as a so-called "cardinal" (a chairman of a House appropriations subcommittee). **2005** Bob Kemper @ Washington, D.C. *Atlanta Journal-Constitution* (Ga.) (Feb. 10) "Kingston's Panel Axed in Changes" (Int.) ▶ Subcommittee chairmen are sometimes referred to as "cardinals" on Capitol Hill, for the influence they wield.

care leaver *n.* a person who has been a ward of the state but no longer qualifies for or receives any government assistance. *Australia. Health. Jargon. United Kingdom.*

1989 Tim Lunn *Guardian* (U.K.) (Mar. 22) "A Package Pressed for Time" ▶ The list of young people, like care leavers and abuse victims, who can claim benefit because they live away from home is being extended to include young people who are—in the words of the DSS—"genuinely estranged from their parents." **1995** *COI's Hermes* (U.K.) (Mar. 7) "Department of Health–John Bowis Addresses Leaving Care Conference" ▶ Leaving care arrangements must be evolutionary over a period often of many years and links should remain for as long as a young care leaver needs them. **2004** Claire Halliday *The Age* (Melbourne, Australia) (July 4) "Who Cares?" (Int.) ▶ Wards of the state are officially referred to as Care Leavers but the people who have been brought up this way don't like that title. They would argue that no care was given to them at all.

carpet-crossing *n.* the act of joining an opposition (political party) or conceding to its policies. Also sometimes called **crosstitution.** *Politics.*

1993 (*Inter Press Services*) (Jan. 26) "Opposition Parties Showing Their True Colours" (in Dakar, Senegal) ▶ Political observers here view the opposition carpet-crossing as an attempt to secure ministerial posts if, as is widely expected, Diouf wins a third term in office. **2000** Alan Kachamazov *Izvestia* (Russia) (June 27), p. 3 in *Defense & Security* (June 30, 2000) A. Ignatkin *"First Success"* ▶ Presidential Advisor Sergei Yastrzhembsky views the commanders' carpet-crossing to the side of the federal troops as a significant success for Akhmed Kadyrov. **2004** Thomas Imonikhe *Daily Champion* (Lagos, Nigeria) (Aug. 16) "Why Indiscipline Thrives in Parties" (Int.) ▶ Indiscipline among politicians took various forms including working against the overall interest of one's party and dumping it for another after an election. This decampment, was also known as "carpet crossing" while such anti-party activities were usually visited with stiff penalties.

cashish *n.* money. *Money & Finance.* [From *cash* 'money in the form of bills or coins.' Imitative of *hashish* 'a hallucinogenic resinous extract of the hemp plant,' which also lends a connotation of illicitness or addiction.]

1989 *Usenet: comp.sys.mac.digest* (Apr. 4) "Info-Mac Digest V7 #63" ▶ Thanks to everyone who has sent the life-giving cashish through. It keeps me posting. **1992** *Usenet: rec.music.phish* (Nov. 2) "Columbus, OH, Show" ▶ Drinks at the Newport are heavy on the wallet...mucho cashish. **1999** Isobel Kennedy @ NYC *Market News International* (Oct. 18) "Talk from Trenches—US Stocks, CPI Will Tell It All" ▶ If you started out Sept. with $50,000 in a 401k plan, you would now have only $46,150. And that is a lot of "cashish-ola" even if it's only on paper. **2000** J.J. Connolly *Layer Cake* (Apr. 6), p. 15 ▶ After a few false starts and offers of hare-brained, get-rich-quick schemes that would only get me put away for stretches, I started moving bits and pieces around town just to keep my hand in really and to top up my dwindling cashish reserve. **2005** [theperfectcrime] *Ask Metafilter* (June 10) "My Debit Card Was Lost/Stolen and Fraudulently Misused" (Int.) ▶ The system told me that my balance was several hundred dollars overdrawn, and when I checked the most recently posted transactions, the amounts ($50-75) did not immediately ring a bell. I also knew that my shit was not fucked up to the tune of (at least quite) that much cashish.

cat face *n.* aberrant surface features or an irregular appearance on fruit, vegetables, or trees, especially when caused by healthy tissue growing over damage. Also *v., adj., attrib. Food & Drink.*

1890 Montgomery M. Folsom *Atlanta Constitution* (Ga.) (Mar. 9) "My Blue-Eyed Babies," p. 13 ▶ I mentioned to her the fact that there was a bumble bee's nest in the big cat-faced pine just over the branch. **1905** *Washington Post* (Mar. 26) "Their Speech Is Vivid," p. F1 ▶ You may hear that...much of the timber is "cat-faced"...that "cat face" is a scar made by a fire in a tree. **1934** Frank Ridgway *Chicago Daily Tribune* (Aug. 24) "Roasts, Canned Goodes, and Fruit Cheap This Week," p. 17 ▶ Wholesale vegetable men are commenting upon the excess waste in some of the tomatoes they are handling at low prices. Many show cracks from alternate drought and rain and the fruit blotches referred to by the trade as "cat faces." **1955** George Abraham *Chronicle-Telegram* (Elyria, Ohio) (May 13) "Green Thumb Queries," p. 27 ▶ When you pick up a gnarly apple or peach, or a misshapened strawberry...the cause of this damage has been attributed to cold weather, frost, lack of pollination, disease, etc., but in most instances you can put the finger of guilt on a group of "cat-facing" insects.... Although the healthy tissue around the injured spot grows, a scar is formed over the damaged spot and normal development is slowed down at this point. When this happens...you get a "cat-faced" or deformed fruit hardly fit to eat. **1987** Peter Korn @ Ore. *Chicago Tribune* (Nov. 15) "Hotshots on the Line Battling a Forest Fire," p. 12 ▶ Salladay's greatest fear is of cat-faced timber—a tree burned out at the base by fire, leaving what appears to be a solid tree but is now just a shell with no support inside. This tree is dangerous to fell but too dangerous to let stand. **1988** Melissa Balmain Weiner *Orange County Register* (Jan. 14) "Irvine Farmers Examine Effects of Chill on Strawberries," p. 1 ▶ Temperatures dipped to about 30 degrees Fahrenheit the last week of December, not quite low enough to kill entire plants, they said. Winds at times were strong enough to dent, or "cat-face" fruit. **1988** Jeff Barnard *L.A. Times* (May 15) "Some Species Need Forest Fires to Survive Plants Sprouting in Charred Oregon Woodland," p. 4 ▶ The cat face is a ring of bulging bark that has grown to heal a scar left by a fire. Because the healing bark is loaded with pitch, it tends to burn more intensely each time fire sweeps past, and the cat face grows. **2001** C.L. Chia, Richard M. Manshardt @ College of Tropical Agriculture & Human Resources *Fruit and Nuts* (Manoa, Hawaii) (Oct.) "Why Some Papaya Plants Fail to Fruit," no. 5, p. 1 (Int.) ▶ Cool winter weather or high soil moisture can lead to a shift toward femaleness, where the stamens fuse to the carpals or ovary wall. The resulting fruits become severely ridged (carpelloid, or "cat-faced") and hence are deformed and unmarketable. **2004** Florence Fabricant *N.Y. Times* (Dec. 21) "Forget About Taste, Florida Says, These Tomatoes Are Just Too Ugly to Ship" (Int.) ▶ Unlike the smooth, round baseball-size tomatoes usually shipped from Florida from mid-October through mid-April, the lush, vine-ripened UglyRipes have what the industry calls a "cat face," full of uneven crevices and ridges.

cereal test *n.* the judgment of an editor or a producer as to whether (news) material is appropriate to publish or broadcast. Also **breakfast test, Wheaties test.** *Media.*

1987 Lou Gelfand *Star Tribune* (Minneapolis-St. Paul, Minn.) (Feb. 8) "Editors Were Wise to Withhold Photographs of Aborted Fetuses," p. 31A ▶ Fleming said those pictures "surely pass the 'Wheaties' test," meaning that one could look at them while eating breakfast.
1991 Mark Guidera *Baltimore Sun* (Md.) (June 21) "Nudes at 11 Is No News in This Bureau," p. 10 ▶ Running such pictures would not pass that unshakable tenet of the newspaper business: The Breakfast Test.
1991 Mike Foley *St. Petersburg Times* (Fla.) (July 21) "Demi Moore Cover Photo Had People Talking," p. 3D ▶ Editors apply what is generically referred to in the newsroom as the "cereal test." Photos that might upset a reader over breakfast are screened very carefully, and are used only if the subject matter or news value warrants it.
1996 Geneva Overholser *Washington Post* (July 21) "Ombudsman: Policing the Issue Ads," p. C6 ▶ Rosenberg applies what he calls "the breakfast-table test" to any gruesome picture, titillating image or vulgar word. He doesn't want to make people sick over their cornflakes.
2005 Ryan Pitts *Mail Tribune* (Jackson County, Ore.) (Jan. 23) "Graphic Images: Too Much?" (Int.) ▶ Many journalists invoked the so-called "cereal test," newsroom slang for a simple question: Would I want my family to see this photo at the breakfast table tomorrow morning?

chalk *n.* the personnel and equipment that make up the load of an aircraft. *Jargon. Military.* Almost certainly an extension of a *chalk* as a record-keeping mark, which dates at least 400 years.

1993 Dept. of the Army *Field Manual 55-9: Unit Air Movement Planning* (Apr. 5) "Glossary" (Int.) ▶ *Chalk*—Designated troops, equipment, and/or cargo that constitute a complete aircraft load.
1999 Dept. of Army *101st Airborne Division (Air Assault) Gold Book* (Fort Campbell, Ky.) (Feb. 4) (Int.) ▶ The following information is placed on a 3x5 inch index card and handed to the pilot by the chalk leader. This serves as a contract between the pilot and the chalk of

soldiers to ensure coordination of LZ data. In case the chalk lands in a different LZ, the pilot will write the grid of the new LZ and hand the 3x5 card back to the chalk leader before the soldiers exit the helicopter. **2004** Joseph M. Bossi *Screaming Eagle Veterans Web site* (Jan. 25) "327th Infantry and Other Units Come Home!" (Int.) ▶ Included in this Chalk was also most of Abu Company members and other attachments from the 101st Airborne Division.
2005 [majorsamuel] *The Kosovo Kronichles* (Jan. 17) "Out of Washington" (Int.) ▶ The evening before the flight I was informed, joy of joys, that I would be the movement commander for one plane load of soldiers (in military parlance a "chalk"). ***2005** Dennis J. Reimer *Filipino Airsoft* (Feb. 1) "Glossary" (Int.) ▶ *Chalk*—A squad of soldiers, usually about a dozen, assigned to a helicopter.

chamcha *n.* a sycophant, toady, or hanger-on. *Hindi. India. Pakistan. Politics. Urdu.* [From the Hindi and Urdu word for 'spoon.']

1989 Stuart Auerbach *Washington Post* (Mar. 26) "Nehru and His Nation" ▶ Akbar has been called a chamcha (which means spoon in the Hindi language and has become a slang word for sycophant) to the Gandhi family. **1994** William Dalrymple *City of Djinns: A Year in Delhi* (Dec. 1) "Glossary," p. 340 ▶ *Chamcha* Sycophant (lit. 'spoon'). **1997** Ghulam Nabi Azad *India Today* (June 23) p. 13 ▶ I have my own standing in the party. I cannot be anybody's chamcha (stooge). **1997** Sudhir Vaishnav *Times of India* (Aug. 24) "A Very Political Exercise" ▶ Several hangers-on. They are available aplenty everywhere in the country and are often known in the local market as Chamcha. **1998** P.S. Sharma *Times of India* (Jan. 17) "In Praise of Chamchagiri" ▶ No doubt, the British also had their sycophants—toadys, bachhas, jholichuks and hukkabardars—but chamchas of the modern vintage they had none. Chamchas are a breed apart. A chamcha verily is more than a favourite. He is a catalytic agent to activate the Sahib's ego and cloud and obfuscate his thinking. **2004** Krishnakumar *Mid Day* (Mumbai, India) (Sept. 21) "Leaders' Chamchas Get Lucky" (Int.) ▶ All three have pulled strings in their respective parties to get Assembly poll tickets for their puppets and close confidants, better known in political parlance as chamchas. **2004** [Ambar] *rvinst* (Bangalore, India) (Oct. 2) "Advanced Kannada Slang" (Int.) ▶ *Chamcha*: A person who uses lot of "Maska" to promote his self interest. The villain in old kannada movies, nowadays portrayed as a statesman. **2005** Asra Nomani *American Prospect* (Mar. 5) "Pulpit Bullies" (Int.) ▶ Speaking in Urdu, the language of South-Asian Muslims, local Muslims who opposed the posse had taken to calling its members chumcha, or "spoons," a cultural concept akin to being a lackey.

cheese cutter *n.* especially among motorcyclists, a roadway guard rail made of cable, rope, or high-tension wire. *Automotive. Slang.*

1996 *Usenet: uk.transport* (Sept. 22) "Re: Stick & Rope Crash Barriers" ▶ In view of the poor reputation which I recall for the two wire system from the 1960s, I suspect this has more to do with the improved quality of protection in modern cars.... Most modern cars have a passenger cage, which should resist the cheese cutter effect much better. **1999** Brent Davison *Newcastle Herald* (Australia) (Jan. 2) "Winners & Losers," p. 29 ▶ The NSW State Government for installing motorcycle rider-unfriendly "cheese cutter" wire cable fencing on our highways. **2002** *Motorcycle Riders Foundation* (Washington, D.C.) (Feb.) "Making Crash Barriers and Road Maintenance Practices Motorcycle-Friendly" (Int.) ▶ Study existing crash barrier designs in the United States to identify those most hazardous to motorcyclists (e.g., "cheese cutter" cable runs) to prioritize those systems for replacement. **2002** Steve Sellers @ South Arm *Hobart Mercury* (Australia) (Feb. 21) "Wire barriers," p. 18 ▶ Your recent photo of the vehicle that mounted the dividing strip and wire-rope barriers...is a graphic demonstration of the incorrect and dangerous practices that Transport Tasmania follows when installing these controversial cheap "cheese cutter" barriers. **2003** *Irish Times* (Dublin, Ireland) (Dec. 17) "By-Pass Risk to Bikers," p. 50 ▶ This type of barrier is known as a human scale "cheese cutter" and has been identified...as the worst possible choice from a motorcyclist's perspective. **2005** Pierrette J. Shields *Daily Times-Call* (Longmont, Colo.) (June 12) "Road to Safety" (Int.) ▶ Some motorcyclists are wary of the tensioned wires in the new guardrails. "In the motorcycle world, in our vernacular, we call those cheese cutters.... They could have a guillotine effect on a motorcyclist's body."

chevrolegs *n.pl.* a jocular reference to one's legs, particularly by comparison to an automobile. *Automotive. Colloquial. United States.* [Automobile brand *Chevro*let + *legs*]

1994 *Usenet: misc.writing* (Nov. 17) "Re: Bumper Stickers?" ▶ "My Other Car Is My Feet." "Which model? Chevrolegs or Toyotoes?" **1999** *Usenet: alt.cellular.sprintpcs* (Aug. 4) "Re: Shipping/Handling— Where Do YOU Work?" ▶ When gas is $1.35 around here (which it hasn't been in years), I just use my Chevro-Legs a little more often. [**2000** Preston Williams *Washington Post* (July 2) "Long Journey Behind Him, Reliever Marr Still Has Sights on Moving Up," p. V10 ▶ Cannons reliever Jason Marr was so upset that he walked from Pfitzner Stadium to his home, a trip that took nearly as long as the game. This season, Marr has not had reason to "Chevroleg it," as he calls it.] **2001** *Usenet: rec.models.rockets* (Oct. 12) "Re: [ANN] Rocket

City Blast Off Scheduled for Oct 27/28" ► Lemme just throw on my shoedabakers and start my chevrolegs and truck on down there. **2004** [Daddy Rich] *RapTalk.net* (Jan. 21) (Int.) ► My 5 point toes my chevrolegs I aint got shit right now but I use to have 2 72 chevelles but I got my L'S revoked. **2004** *Usenet: rec.sport.pro-wrestling* (Feb. 14) "Re: (Poll) The Official RSPW Poll" ► "What do you drive?" "Chevrolegs. Can't afford a car."

chicane *n.* a barricaded, tightly curved, or zig-zagged roadway that forces traffic to slow while still permitting it to pass; the series of structures that form such a roadway. *Architecture. Automotive. Jargon.*

1956 Frank M. Blunk *N.Y. Times* (Aug. 10) "New Auto Racing Era," p. 14 ► They will spend Saturday, Aug. 18, practicing on the course, which will have the usual "chicane" and the usual quota of sharp turns. **1960** *Palladium-Times* (Oswego, N.Y.) (Oct. 8) "Crack Drivers Race Sunday at Watkins Glen" (in Watkins Glen, N.Y.), p. 9 ► Race officials have bypassed the abrupt chicane curve at the southern end of the 2.3-mile closed course to speed lap times. **1977** Barry Lorge @ Monte Carlo *Washington Post* (May 22) "Checkered Flag for Ambience," p. C1 ► The course is filled with curves and straight ways, hairpins and chicanes that are familiar to racing buffs around the world. **1984** *Washington Post* (Sept. 22) "Criticism of Security at Embassy Rises" ► A maze-like series of four concrete barriers known as a chicane was constructed at the head of the street where the building was located. The suicide van managed to get through that series of barriers. **2004** *Centre Daily* (State College, Pa.) (May 24) "Glossary of Terms" (Int.) ► *Chicane*: A series of curving curb extensions that alternate from one side of the road to the other.

chi chi man *n.* a homosexual. *Derogatory. English-based Creole. Gay. Jamaica. Sexuality.* The second 2001 cite contains lyrics from the song whose title is mentioned in the 2000 cite; the release date for the album lagged behind the song's success in the dancehalls of Jamaica.

2000 *Usenet: rec.music.reggae* (Nov. 26) "Playlist DANCEHALL VIBES October 7, 2000" ► 20. T.O.K. - Chi chi man. **2001** Nicole White *Miami Herald* (Fla.) (Aug. 5) "Rhythm of Hatred: Anti-Gay Lyrics Reflect an Island's Intolerance," p. 9M ► Being gay or lesbian—a "chi-chi" man/gyal or a "battyman"—is the ultimate sin in Jamaica, an island paradise so steeped in religion that it holds the Guinness Book of World Records title of having the most churches per square mile and where it is still legal to arrest two men caught having sex. **2001** T.O.K. *My Crew My Dawgs* (Oct. 1) "Chi Chi Man" (Int.) ► From dem a par inna chi chi man car/Blaze di fire mek we bun dem!!!! (Bun dem!!!!)/From dem a drink inna chi chi man bar/Blaze di fire mek we dun dem!!!! (Dun dem!!!!) **2004** Peter Moore *365gay.com* (June 25) "Concert Cancelled After Complaints of Homophobia" (Int.) ▶ In Jamaican patois slang, "batty man" and "chi chi man" are the equivalent of "poof" and "faggot."

chili-dip *v.* when swinging a club in golf, to hit the ground before hitting the ball. *Jargon. Sports.*

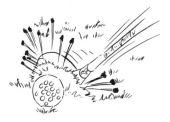

1967 Jim Murray *L.A. Times* (July 5) "When It Comes to Golf, TV 'Tells It Like It Ain't,'" p. B1 ▶ Encourage these guys to chili-dip shots to get on camera. **1978** Ben Gieser *Washington Post* (May 11) "Hollenbeck, Looney Lead," p. D8 ▶ Looney double-bogeyed the 390 yard, par-four finishing hole when she "chili-dipped" a chip shot and three-putted after hitting two fine shots to be close to the final green. **2001** Bob Rotella *Putting Out of Your Mind* (June 5), p. 159 ▶ Many amateurs, I know, worry about skulling or chili-dipping their short shots, particularly from tight lies.

chillax *v.* to relax, take it easy, chill out. *Slang. United States.* [*chill* + re*lax*]

1994 *Usenet: bit.listserv.cinema-l* (Dec. 6) "Re: Devil Worshipping Mom Beaters" ▶ Chillax my friend.... This juvenile form of attacking others who don't share your opinion isn't going to help you win anyone over to your side. **1998** *Usenet: uk.music.rave* (Sept. 8) "Re: Hello from a 1st Timer" ▶ yo wut up, home slice! welcome to our crib. we're usually just kickin back and chillaxin, ya know wut i'm sayin. **2004** Lim View *jigsaw jazz & the get-fresh flow* (Singapore) (May 19) "My Nose & I (We Have a Love-Hate Relationship)" (Int.) ▶ Okay, the few things I can look forward to, over the coming few months:...chillaxin' (new word I picked up) with friends.

chippy *adj.* irritable, temperamental, or fractious. *Colloquial. Sports. Oxford English Dictionary* cites this meaning as early as 1885 as a colloquial form of 'given to chipping, ready to chip.' In recent decades in North America it has become most commonly, though not exclusively, used in connection to sports play, especially hockey, where it is perhaps reinforced by the idea of rough play causing the ice to chip.

1959 Don Maclean *Lethbridge Herald* (Alberta, Can.) (Nov. 26) "Native Sons Gain Entry in Five-Team Hockey Loop," p. 10 ▶ The game was wide open with end-to-end rushes and very little chippy stuff and few penalties. **1978** Allen Abel *Globe and Mail* (Toronto, Can.) (Apr. 24) "Spare Us the Tales of Hockey Heroics," p. S1 ▶ Tonight's game was a little chippy, conceded Roger Neilson. We're trying to play as rough as we can. **1985** Chet Kaufman *Baton Rouge State Times* (La.) (Aug. 2) "North Looks Toward Gold in Ice Hockey," p. 3-Spec. ▶ "The boys did get a little chippy" in Thursday night's game, said North head coach Frank Anzalone. "We just don't want to see the boys dropping our gloves and fighting and an American sports festival. There is no fighting here. We don't tolerate it." **1988** *Globe and Mail* (Toronto, Can.) (June 4) "Wheels Within Wheels," p. D6 ▶ Out of a somewhat chippy summit meeting in Moscow, the superpower leaders have agreed through gritted teeth that each side has a lot to learn about the other. **2003** *NFL.com* (Nov. 13) "Del Rio Excited About New Acquisition" (Int.) ▶ Speaking of Tennessee, things have gotten a touch shall we say "chippy" between your team and the Tennessee Titans, with whom there's been a little bit of a verbal jousting going on this week. **2004** Christian Aagaard *Kitchener-Waterloo Record* (Ontario, Can.) (Aug. 25) "Special-Ed Spending Spree Bites Hand That Feeds System," p. B1 ▶ Because the current relationship the board has with the top politician running the Ministry of Education—the hand that feeds—has, shall we say, been somewhat chippy of late.... **2004** Patrick Reusse *Star Tribune* (Minneapolis-St. Paul, Minn.) (Oct. 24) "Patrick Reusse: The Baseball Gods Must Be Angry" (Int.) ▶ The non-sensical night was not restricted to the ballplayers. Francona was wrapping up his interview session when a radio guy who had seen too many Patriots games asked: "Coach, do you think the long playoffs these two teams were in caused it to be chippy tonight?"

chocolate foot *n.* the foot favored to use or to start with when running, biking, or kicking; one's dominant foot. *Sports.* [Perhaps a calque from the German *Schokoladenbein* 'favored leg' (literally 'chocolate leg'). A similar German word is *Schokoladenseite* 'attractive side' (literally 'chocolate side').]

1996 Hans Rey, Scott Martin *Mountain Bike Magazine's Complete Guide to Mountain Biking Skills* (Feb. 15), p. 116 ▶ Keep your pedals horizontal, with your "chocolate foot" (your strongest foot) forward. **1999** *Scottish Daily Record* (Sept. 20) "Roddy Gets It Right with a Bit of Luck" ▶ I turned inside a defender, created a bit of space and hit a shot with my chocolate foot, my right, and luckily it went in. **2002** *Usenet: rec.games.roguelike.adom* (Dec. 29) "Re: Left-Orium" ▶ "There's even something like a 'dominant leg'! You automatically try to take off from that one if attempting to jump. Try. You'd be amazed. There's a phrase for that in German: 'Schokoladenbein.'" "Chocolate leg? I'm going to assume that something was lost in the translation here." **2004** Leonard Zinn *Zinn's Cycling Primer* (June 1), p. 34 ▶ The first thing you must know before hucking yourself off a drop-off is which foot is your "chocolate foot," as Hans "No Way" Rey calls it. Your chocolate foot is your favorite foot, the one you always keep forward when standing on the pedals.

cho-mo *n.* a child molester. *Crime & Prisons. Sexuality. United States.* [*ch*ild + [*o*] + *mo*lester]

1997 Steve Fisher *TriQuarterly* (Evanston, Ill.) (Mar. 22) "Windy Gray," p. 169 ▶ "Dude's a fuckin' cho-mo," said the other. "Or he's a reverse cho-mo, what the hell, it's almost worse than a child molester. Look at him!" **1998** Brian Smith *Phoenix New Times* (Ariz.) (Dec. 3) "Night in the City" (Int.) ▶ If you prove to me that someone is a cho-mo (child molester) around here, or stole from one of us, I'll go get him for ya. **2004** Jon Hanian *KBCI-TV* (Boise, Idaho) (June 28) "'Internet Crimes Against Children' Unit Racking Successes" (Int.) ▶ Because they are talking about "cho-mo" which is prison slang language for child molester.

chones *n.pl.* underwear, especially undershorts or panties. Also **chonies, choners.** *Mexico. Slang. Spanish. United States.* [(Mexican) Spanish slang *chones*, perhaps from the Mexican Spanish **calzones** 'underwear' or less probably from the English **long johns.** The *Oxford English Dictionary* includes a 1717 first citation for *poncho* from Frezier's *Voyage to the South Sea* in which *Chony* appears; however, it may be unrelated: "The Spaniards have taken up the Use of the Chony, or Poncho...to ride in, because the Poncho keeps out the Rain."] Despite its proximity to a mention of lingerie, *chonies* in the 1928 citation is probably a typographical error for *chorines*.

[**1928** Gilbert Swan *Zanesville Signal* (Ohio) (Feb. 2) "See-Sawing on Broadway," p. 3 ▶ These are the days when the buyers come to town in droves and herds; when the lingerie shows go merrily on in hotel and office building display rooms.... Those alluring photos of chonies in ticket brokerage windows.] **1972** Oscar Zeta Acosta *Autobiography of a Brown Buffalo* in *Race-ing Masculinity* (July 2, 2002) John Christopher Cunningham, p. 78 ▶ She asked if I wanted to see what was under her panties. To be quite honest I had never seen even the underskirts of my various cousins' chones, so she lifted up her little red dress. **1984** Ema Yanes, Angel Arista @ Mexico, D.F. *Revista Nexos* (Aug. 1) "Un año despues" ▶ Me sali con un fondo y unos chones gratis: me los lleve puestos. **1992** Louis Owens *The Sharpest Sight* (Feb. 1), p. 178 (Sept. 1, 1995) ▶ How can I shoot hoops while my pants are drying in here?...It wouldn't look good, the deputy sheriff bouncing a ball around in his choners. **1994** *Usenet: soc.culture.asian .american* (Mar. 9) "Re: Singapore Airline Girls" ▶ My disclaimer here is that netters are an unrepresentative lot, so don't getcher chonies in a knot, 'kay? **1994** Robert Kowalski *Denver Post* (Colo.) (Aug. 21) "Forgotten Firefighters," p. A1 ▶ *Chonies*—Underwear, as in "You had better change those chonies." **1994** Terri de la Peña *Latin Satins* (Sept. 1), p. 67 ▶ Dígame, Jess. When did Chic decide to take care of the itch in Rita's chones? **1994** Dennis Romero *L.A. Times* (Dec. 20) "More to Love; His Bod's Larger, His Mane's Tamer," p. 1 ▶ They give me $150 an hour, tell me to strip down to my "chones," and take pictures of me. **1996** *Usenet: alt.punk* (July 26) "Re: The Infections and Other Rip-Off Items" ▶ Chones means "dirty underwear" in Spanish. **1996** Gabriela Martinez @ Mexico, D.F. *El Nuevo Inversionista* (Nov. 1) "Glamour Lingerie: Con los calzones bien puestos" ▶ Con sus "chones" a otra parte Ante la tormenta, Glamour Lingerie por fin tuvo que reconocer que ya no existian mas las condiciones para que saliera a flote su producto, y no solo por la adversa situacion del mercado, sino porque entre las mujeres mexicanas no existe una cultura del uso de lenceria fina. **1998** Richard Montoya *Culture Clash: Life, Death and Revolutionary Comedy* (May 1), p. 12 ▶ Thousands of tourists lose their collective chonies there each year in the barrio streets of their mind. **2000** Cathalena E. Burch *Arizona Daily Star* (Tucson) (May 17) "Inside the Tucson Enchilada," p. E1 ▶ Amy Blodgett, who runs a screenprinting business in Tempe and an Internet T-shirt business, concedes her "Keep It Underwear" line of chones won't stop kids from having sex. **2002** Rick Redding *Reno Gazette-Journal* (Nev.) (Mar. 16) "This Kid's a Marvel," p. 1 ▶ He speaks some Spanish, excitedly describing the cartoon characters dotting his blue "chonies"—underwear—to his visitors. **2004** James E. Rogan *Rough Edges* (July 1), p. 111 ▶ If they put on his socks and shoes, they probably put on his *choners*, too!

choosing money *n.* a fee paid as a demonstration of earning power by a prostitute to a pimp with whom she chooses to affiliate herself. *Money & Finance.*

1986 Helen Reynolds *Economics of Prostitution* (Feb. 1), p. 31 ▶ The process of "choosing" involves a woman deciding if she wants to affiliate herself with a pimp.... A woman who is attracted to a pimp may find that he woos her initially and then requires her to produce some money for him. Successful completion of the task of earning the "choosing money" means that a woman is "qualified" to work for the pimp. **2001** John S. Dickson *Rosebudd the American Pimp* (Oct. 3), p. 303 ▶ She had said the right things to let me know she wasn't bullshittin', which is the purpose of choosing money.... If she chooses, out of spite or anger, and a pimp didn't get any money, the pimp looks stupid. So for the protection of his pimpin' image and to make sure of the ho's intentions, he demands a choosing fee. **2005** Courtney Hambright *New Times Broward-Palm Beach* (Ft. Lauderdale, Fla.) (June 23) "Big Pimpin' FLA" (Int.) ▶ Blue, whose real name is Robert Kramer, tells me this story to explain the concept of "choosing money"; it's basically a dowry that whores give to a pimp when they want to join his "stable" of girls, he says.

chope *v.* to reserve (a place, a seat, etc.). *Singapore.*

1992 Marie Rose Glasmier *Straits Times* (Singapore) (May 25) "A Little Extra Learning," p. L2-1 ▶ She did not think her children needed tuition, but five years ago, a colleague persuaded her to chope (book) a tutor who was a former secondary school mathematics teacher. "It all started when a colleague said: 'I will chope a tutor for you.' I said: "But my daughter is only in Secondary 2, she doesn't need a tutor!' My colleague said the tutor had taught her three sons and she is choped a year ahead—she has a long waiting list." **1995** *Straits Times* (Singapore) (May 4) "Digital Kopitiam" ▶ The dictionary, called Ah Kow's Ingglish Dicksonairy, carries explanations for words such as "chim," meaning difficult to understand, and "chope," to reserve something. **1997** *Usenet: soc.culture.singapore* (Apr. 2) "I'm a Failure" ▶ i see all the Very Beautiful Girls all kena choped by all the Very Rich Guys in their Very Posh Sportscars. me—nothing. nothing. nothing. **2004** Hwee Ling *verbiage or garbage?:O* (Singapore) (May 18) "Of Nude Bodies and Tissue Chopes" (Int.) ▶ Here's an evidence of tissue choping i witnessed at Ikea yesterday while I was there for kopi...*chope*—(verb) local slang meaning "to reserve." Example: It's free seating at the concert, we need to get there early to chope seats for our group.

churched *adj.* having attended (Christian) religious services. *Religion.*

1950 *Berkshire Evening Eagle* (Pittsfield, Mass.) (Dec. 11) "Youth Church Proposed by Local Pastor," p. 4 ▶ Mr. Kibby estimated that "hundreds of thinking, 'un-churched' teen-agers would welcome the opportunity of being part of such an organization." **1978** *Washington Post* (June 16) "Book Indicates 'Unchurched' More Permissive," p. A30 ▶ The 7,000 Americans interviewed for the book were grouped in five categories—churched and unchurched Protestants, churched and unchurched Catholics and "those who have no religious identification." The affiliated who attend church once a year or less were considered unchurched. **2000** Young-gi Hong *International Review of Mission* (Apr. 1) "Revisiting Church Growth in Korean Protestantism: A

Theological Reflection," vol. 89, no. 353, p. 190 ▶ This forces us to face the question whether the growth patterns of certain "successful" churches mainly represent their increased share of the churchgoing population, or whether they are attracting significant numbers of the formerly-churched and never-churched individuals to replace those being lost to the world. **2004** Heather Regan *Southwest Daily News* (La.) (June 9) "Faith Community Growing" (Int.) ▶ Pastor LaFleur said that communities can be broken into three groups—people who attend church regularly, those who don't now but once did and those never "churched."

circuit bending *n.* the manipulation or modification of electronics or electronic instruments, via chance short-circuiting, to create sounds or (experimental) music. *Music. Technology.* [The term was coined by Qubais Reed Ghazala.] Reed Ghazala writes in a private note, "The addition of 'chance' to the definition is the key factor dividing bending from the more theory-true hacking. Bending is like Calder's mobiles or Japanese suminagashi: dependent upon chance for its configurations."

1997 Qubais Reed Ghazala *Gravikords, Whirlies & Pyrophones: Experimental Musical Instruments* (Jan. 29) in *Washington Post* (Jan. 29, 1997) Richard Harrington "Just Playing Around; Experimental Instruments Tickle the Ears," p. D1 ▶ While, in an attempt to confront reality, current "fuzzy logic" technologies confront chaos, the reverse-image clear illogic technology of circuit-bending, in looking at the other side of that same reality, implements chaos. Perhaps the much-lamented lack of human spirit within computers could be addressed through circuit-bending's personalized electronic systems of organic eccentricity, a very human trait. **2002** Natasha Kassulke *Wisconsin State Journal* (Madison) (Feb. 14) "Biff in Bloom; Musician Making a Name for Himself," p. 3 ▶ [Biff Uranus Blumfumgagne has] invented a few instruments, including the Bat-tar (a heavy bat-shaped electric guitar), the Therolin (a five-string electric violin with a theremin hiding inside), and the Mando-synth (an electric five-string mandolin with a synth pickup and a whammy bar). "I enjoy circuit bending and experimental musical instruments." **2003** Qubais Reed Ghazala *Electronic Musician* (Jan. 1) "The Art of the Creative Short Circuit," vol. 19, no. 1, p. 86 ▶ The creative short circuit, or the technique that I call circuit bending, is a form of hardware hacking or modding, but with two important differences. First, whereas hackers usually know something about electronics, you don't need any real knowledge of electronics to circuit-bend. Second, while most people hack an instrument with a particular goal in mind—such as increased frequency range or cleaner outputs—the circuit bender works improvisationally and has no idea where the trail will lead. In circuit bending, the instrument shapes itself by telling the bender what it can do. **2004** Marc Weidenbaum *Disquiet* "Sacto Instruments" (Int.) ▶ Circuit-bending reinforces the unique characteristics of physical instrumentation, without which discourse among electronic musicians might end up becoming little more than the sharing of home-coded subroutines (or "plug-ins") for commercial software programs. Circuit-benders, hackers by nature, thrive on the quirks of the devices they choose to retrofit, bypassing owners manuals in favor of experimentation.

clean-skin *n.* a person without a police record; someone who does not trigger suspicions; (*hence*) an unimpeachable person; a LILY-WHITE. *Crime & Prisons. Police.* This term is more common in Australia, where it dates to at least as early as 1941.

1986 Jenni Hewett *Australian Financial Review* (Aug. 29) "Punch-Ups and Paranoia in the West," p. 1 ▶ One of Simpson's most important credentials as a candidate was his "cleanskin" image as a retired businessman with no involvement in the party's bloody inner politics. **2000** John Sweeney *Observer* (U.K.) (July 9) "Menace of 'Clean-Skin' Drug Dealers," p. 16 ▶ They use public transport, not Ferraris, pay their rent and council tax on time, hold down a boring job and never get in trouble with the law. These are the "clean skins" or "lilywhites"—the new drugs traffickers who dwarf the activities of the old English crime "families." **2005** *TodayOnline* (Singapore) (July 14) "Model Citizens, Ruthless Killers" (in London, England) (Int.) ▶ The Times said that at least two of the men had just returned from Pakistan, but none were on the files of security services. This meant they were "cleanskins"—intelligence parlance for terrorists with no previously known link to suspicious groups, and thus incredibly hard to track down before they strike.

Clydesdale *n.* in running or road-racing sports, a heavyweight classification for (male) participants weighing more than 200 pounds; a runner in that weight class. Also *attrib. Sports.* [From the breed of large draft horse of the same name, via the Clydesdale Runners Association, which lobbied for weight division awards in running sports.] The upper limit for the classification can vary. A similar category called *Athena* is for women weighing more than 155 pounds.

1990 Craig Smith *Seattle Times* (Wash.) (Feb. 9) "The Weigh to Go—Clydesdales Starting to Leave

Their Hoofprints on Racing," p. D8 ▶ The Clydesdale Runners Association has been founded to lobby for the weight-division awards...[Joe] Law said the name Clydesdale was a natural because of its connotation of "strength and power." He said before the name was adopted, people turned up their noses when he approached them about creating "heavyweight divisions.... They thought I was just talking about overweight people." **1990** *Usenet: rec.running* (Nov. 14) "Hubba-Bubba" ▶ Equivalent times for runners of different weights. Based on results from races which have included "Clydesdale" weight divisions in their competition. **1996** *Usenet: rec.sport.triathlon* (Aug. 28) "More on Santa Barbara County Tri" ▶ Even though this is one of only 4 races this season with a Clydesdale/Athena division, don't worry about placing, just enjoy the race. **2004** [Burns] *First Day of the Rest of My Life* (Nov. 12) "The New Me" (Int.) ▶ Being the big guy that I was, I was basically happy with that and quickly becoming one of the faster guys in my area over 200 pounds ("Clydesdales" in racing parlance).

CODEL *n.* a congressional *del*egation; a junket or fact-finding mission undertaken by members of Congress. *Politics. United States.*

1962 Drew Pearson *Manitowoc Herald-Times* (Wisc.) (Sept. 4) "Washington Merry-Go-Round," p. 2T ▶ "Paris—Codel (congressional delegation) desires use of U.S. Army car and chauffeur. Reserve three for first show and dinner best table Lido 8-16." The Lido is the Paris night club famous for its undraped girlies. **1978** Donald P. Baker @ Lisbon, Portugal *Washington Post* (Mar. 30) "Logistics, Cost of Trip Staggering," p. A1 ▶ The embassy responded by assigning 22 employees to operation CODEL (congressional delegation) IPU. **1987** Mark Nelson @ Kiev, U.S.S.R. *Dallas Morning News* (June 7) "The Road to Moscow: If It's Monday, This Must be Kiev," p. 14 ▶ What follows is a brief diary of CODEL (congressional delegation) Wright, the official name for the trip the Fort Worth Democrat led to Madrid, Kiev, Moscow and Berlin. **2005** Cragg Hines *Houston Chronicle* (Tex.) (July 2) "Do You Know Where Your Rep Is—and Who's Paying?" (Int.) ▶ There are few more terrifying terms than "codel," bureaucratese for "congressional delegation."

Collyer *n.* an apartment excessively packed with junk, trash, or belongings. *Eponym. NYC. United States.* [After the Collyer brothers, who were discovered dead in their junk-packed apartment at 2078 Fifth Avenue and 128th Street, March 21, 1947. The two were hermits for decades. Homer was blind and bed-ridden; Langley took care of him. A booby-trap set for intruders trapped and eventually killed Langley; without care, Homer starved to death in his bed. About 140 tons of debris were removed from their home, including a Model T and at least 10 pianos.]

1995 Matthew Fleischer *Village Voice* (Jan. 31) "Burning Down the Squat," p. 15 ▶ A veteran firefighter called the job a "Collyer mansion"—packed and crowded with junk and debris like the old upper Fifth Avenue spread. **2003** Jeff Pearlman *Newsday* (Nov. 3) "Hoarding Hermits? A Typist's True Tale," p. B3 ▶ Still today, New York City firefighters call junk-jammed apartments "Collyers." **2004** Zoe Heller *Daily Telegraph* (U.K.) (Jan. 24) "Hoarding Drives My Boyfriend Mad," p. 24 ▶ When firemen are called out to jobs at run-down, junk-filled houses, they call it "doing a Collyer." **2004** Steven Schnaudt @ Washington Township, Mercer City, N.J. *Firehouse.com* (June 2) "New Jersey Firefighters Battle Two Alarm House Fire" (Int.) ▶ Engine 402 arrived on scene at 1:21 P.M. and crews entered the home with a 1 3/4 inch attack line. Crews were severely hampered by extreme "Collyers Mansion" conditions throughout the home.

colorway *n.* a color scheme in which a pattern or style (of fabric, apparel, furnishings, wallpaper, etc.) is available. *Arts. Fashion. Jargon.*

1949 Mary Roche *N.Y. Times Mag.* (Apr. 10) "New Ideas and Inventions," p. 48 ▶ The second collection of Liebes-weave designs has appeared on the market, somewhat more intricate than the first, larger in scale, and in some colorways more suitable for big, bold decorative panels rather than retiring backgrounds. **1959** Kay Sherwood *Times-Mirror* (Warren, Pa.) (June 4) "Color Sets a Cool Scene for Summer," p. 7 ▶ Five color-coordinated fabrics in almost three-dozen different colorways (combinations) are inspired by the South Seas colors. **1980** *N.Y. Times* (Aug. 14) "Where to Find Reproduction Patterns," p. C8 ▶ Scalamandre Silks, 950 Third Avenue (361-8500), has specialized in reproductions and adaptations of antique wallpaper and fabric patterns for the past 50 years. Its collections include an estimated 2,500 different colorways (as opposed to patterns). **2004** Doug Rutsch *Sacramento Bee* (Calif.) (Dec. 3) "Taking a Shine to Shoes" (Int.) ▶ Lam doesn't mind dropping $180 for new Jordan 5s with a white-black-and-red color scheme ("colorways" in shoehead parlance).

conehead *n.* a scientist; a brainy person. Also **cone.** *Science.* Probably influenced by *pointy-head* 'a brainy or intellectual person.'

Despite what the 1997 citation says, this term is probably also influenced by a series of skits and a movie about the Coneheads, hyper-literal and unemotional space aliens played by Jane Curtin and Dan Aykroyd, which first aired in 1976 on the sketch comedy show "Saturday Night Live." *Cone* meaning 'the head' dates to at least as early as 1870.

1986 Clifford Terry *Chicago Tribune* (July 25) "No Apologies Needed for This HBO Movie," p. C5 ▶ The U.S. government's CIA-like "Office of Investigations"...proceeds to form the elite but unorthodox C.A.T. (Counter Assault Tactical) Squad, rather than going with the usual operatives ("a bunch of Ivy League coneheads spinning their wheels all over the world"). **1997** Tom Sharpe *Albuquerque Journal* (N.Mex.) (Jan. 10) "The New Mexican Lexicon," p. 1 ▶ *Conehead.* This has nothing to do with the space-alien routine made famous on "Saturday Night Live." In Los Alamos, it means scientist, stemming from the unflattering "pointy-headed"—meaning too intellectual. Somehow, the folks at the lab have turned it into a badge of honor. They might say of someone whose intellect is in doubt, "His cone isn't all that sharp." **1999** Martin Forstenzer *Ski* (Feb. 1) "Remember Los Alamos," vol. 63, no. 6, p. 58 ▶ People joke about the lab guys being coneheads—people who are all brains and live with a computer and that's it. **2004** *Santa Fe New Mexican* (Dec. 20) "Getting a Glimpse at Lanl's Challenges," p. A7 ▶ Many Northern New Mexicans hired to do the construction and upkeep have tales about "coneheads" keeping 'em at bay when they show up to perform carpentry, plumbing or electrification jobs. **2005** *CBSNews.com* (Aug. 7) "Los Alamos' Future Up in the Air" (in Los Alamos, N.Mex.) (Int.) ▶ Where scientists are never addressed as doctor because everyone has a Ph.D.; instead they're affectionately known as "cones" as in cone heads.

cookie *n.* a screen, board, card, or cloth, cut with shapes or holes, used to throw a light pattern when shooting film or television; the light pattern thrown by such a device. Also **cucoloris, cucolorus, cucaloris, kukaloris, kookaloris, cuke, coo-koo, kook, dapple sheet, ulcer, gobo.** *Entertainment. Slang. United States.* [A claimed etymology is that *kukaloris* is Greek for "breaking of light," but there seems to be no evidence to support this, nor can the etymological claims in the 2001 cite below be verified. Another claim is that it is named after its inventor, a Mr. Cucoloris; however, this, too, lacks supporting evidence.]

1994 Steven Bernstein *Film Production* (July 19) 2nd ed., p. 206 ▶ *Ulcers* or *cucalorises* (*cookies*) can also be used on faces to create dramatic mood. **1997** Gerald Millerson *TV Scenic Design* (July 3), p.

96 ▶ An all-purpose shadow device, known variously as *cookie*, *cuke*, *cucoloris*, or *dapple sheet*, has found regular use in all types of programs. **2001** Ivan Curry *Directing & Producing for Television* (Nov. 29) 2nd ed., p. 28 ▶ *Cookies*. Also called coo-koos, or cucaloris, these metal or wood templates are placed in front of instruments to create shadow patterns, often of clouds or leaves. The word "cucaloris" comes from the Greek for shadow play. **2004** Johnny North (*personal e-mail*) (NYC) (May 4) "Re: Punishing the Light" ▶ The effect, he explains, though is what we would refer to as "modeling" the light, which involves taking it away in certain spots to create shadows and add mystery. One way to achieve this effect, and what I think he is referring to specifically, is by using a cucoloris, or a "cookie." A cookie is a frame, usually made of wood that has a pattern of amorphous blobs cut out (sort if like camouflage) that gets rigged in front of a light source creating random pools of light and a lot of shadows.

Corrupticut *n.* a derisive or derogatory name for the state of Connecticut. *Connecticut. Crime & Prisons. Derogatory.* [The name stems from a series of corruption scandals, including one involving the state's governor.]

2003 Paul von Zielbauer *N.Y. Times* (Mar. 28) "The Nutmeg State Battles the Stigma of Corrupticut," p. 1 ▶ Nowadays, from Storrs to Stamford, there are jokes about living in Corrupticut, Connection-icut or, the new favorite, Criminalicut. **2003** *Connecticut Post* (Bridgeport, Conn.) (July 1) "Ganim Gets 9 Years" (in New Haven) ▶ "Connecticut is now derisively referred to as Corrupticut," he said. "Bridgeport has earned a reputation as a place where politicians can be bought." **2005** Carole Bass *New Haven Advocate* (Conn.) (Feb. 24) "Busted! Lennie Grimaldi" (Int.) ▶ Of all the fish in the Corrupticut Sea, the federal dragnet snags only a few.

counter-recruiter *n.* a person who, as a practice of belief or profession, tries to counteract enlistment efforts of the military. *Military.*

1991 Beth Shuster *L.A. Daily News* (N1) (Jan. 23) "School Board Votes to Stop Selling Names to Recruiters" ▶ The board's action was praised by a counter-recruiter for the American Friends Service Committee, a Quaker organization. **2004** Leslie Fulbright *Seattle Times* (June 3) "Eastside Group Warns Parents of Military Recruiting in Schools," p. B1 ▶ The Bellevue father and some other Eastside parents are working to get the word out about recruiting activities in schools at a time they feel the armed forces are aggressively targeting their children. The parents are among a growing number of "counter-recruiters" nationwide. **2005** David Shrauger *Living Iraq Journal* (May 30) "Memories"

(Int.) ▶ When I read about "Counter recruiters" hovering outside their offices trying to talk kids out of it I get frustrated.

crime scene sex *n.* sexual intercourse with a woman who is menstruating. *Sexuality. Slang.*

2001 [asteve5] *Stern Fan Network* (Nov. 20) "WOW. What a weekend!!!" (Int.) ▶ I saw more blood than I have ever seen in my life. Even more blood than my "crime scene" sex situations!!! **2002** *Usenet: alt.sport.lasertag* (Dec. 5) "Re: Dictionary of Bizarre Sexual Practices" ▶ Crime Scene Sex: Having sex while a woman is having her period. **2002** *Usenet: alt.tasteless* (Dec. 26) "Re: Dogs Die to Teach Peru's Soldiers How to Kill" ▶ I read on the web site for my IUD that bleeding can occur for the first few weeks after insertion. Well, I've been bleeding now for 13 days. Geesh. I hope it stops soon. If not by this time next week, I'll go get checked out. Mal's getting tired of crime scene sex. **2004** [SG in ATL] @ Atlanta, Ga. *Baseball Think Factory* (June 15) "New York Yankees (40-21) at Arizona Diamondbacks (26-37) 9:35 P.M. EDT" (Int.) ▶ I've heard "crime scene sex," which if you perform will earn you your red wings. **2005** Lisa Feuer (mysticchyna) *With Camera in Hand* (Md.) (Mar. 2) "I'm Getting Too Old" (Int.) ▶ "What in the HELL is crime scene sex?" "Sex when a woman has her period."

cross-decking *n.* in a navy, the sharing of resources between two or more vessels, especially in an impromptu or ad hoc manner. *Jargon. Military.*

1972 Drew Middleton *N.Y. Times* (Sept. 23) "NATO War Games End in 'Victory,' But Norway Defense Problem Stays," p. 2 ▶ Cooperation was evident at sea during the exercise both in simulated air strikes and anti-submarine warfare. The Kennedy and Ark Royal participated as a team with their planes "cross-decking"—landing and refueling on each other's flight decks. **1986** Tim Carrington *Wall Street Journal* (Apr. 21) "U.S. Raid on Libya, Called Military Success, Heartens the Pentagon" ▶ Neither did, a Navy officer said, adding that five years ago these ships were "cross-decking" vital equipment, or trading it back and forth, because there weren't sufficient supplies for both. **1998** Dennis J. Reimer (*Political Transcripts by Federal Document Clearing House*) (Mar. 12) "House Committee on National Security Holds Hearing on FY 99 National Defense Authorization Budget Request" ▶ Cross decking is for...when you have an officer and enlisted who possesses a specialty that is so unique and so low in numbers that when you're operating at the type of tempo we're operating sometimes that individual's value is such that you will literally cross deck him or her from one ship to another.

crunk *adj.* good, fine, phat. *Black English. Hip-Hop. Slang. United States.* The *crunk* in the first citation is probably a typographical error for "drunk."

1995 *Usenet: rec.music.country.western* (Jan. 5) "Re: Garth Gone Over the Edge?" ▶ The majority of Garth's songs are not about getting crunk, or losing your girlfriend, like most country (especially, the so called classics).] **1995** *Usenet: rec.music.hip-hop* (Dec. 1) "Totally Unofficial Rap-Dictionary (Bi-weekly Posting, part 1/2)" ▶ *crunk* (adj.) Hype, phat. "Tonight is going to be crunk"—??. [**1996** Sonia Murray *Atlanta Journal and Constitution* (Aug. 21) "Local Rappers Spelling Out Atlanta's New Moniker," p. D1 ▶ On that same MTV broadcast, TLC's Tionne "T-Boz" Watkins introduced another addition to the Southern lingo list, "crunk"—as in "really good." Or the way Watkins put it: "That video was crunk." **2004** [Amy Seefeldt] *Poor Mouth* (Ga.) (May 4) (Int.) ▶ He looks around the classroom and a wide smile breaks across his face. He starts enthusiastically bobbing his head and out comes, "Dang, this class is crunk!" I think what he was trying to say was that he was excited to be interested in what he was learning.

crypsis *n.* the camouflage or protective appearance of an insect or animal. *Biology.* Crypsis includes the stripes of a zebra that permit individuals to blend with a herd, moths that take on bark-like coloring so they are indistinguishable on trees, non-venomous snakes evolved to look like venomous species, insects that look like twigs or leaves, and brightly colored frogs that falsely indicate to predators that they are poisonous.

1956 H.B.D. Kettlewell (*Proceedings of the Royal Society of London. Series B, Biological Sciences*) (July 24) "A Resume of Investigations on the Evolution of Melanism in the Lepidoptera," vol. 145, no. 920, p. 297 ▶ In those insects which gain protection from mechanisms other than crypsis (warning, threat and flash coloration), or even in those cryptic moths which benefit from resembling dead leaves, the melanics are rare, recessive, sub-lethal and are probably retained by recurrent mutation. **1983** Craig Packer *Science* (Sept. 16) "Sexual Dimorphism: The Horns of African Antelopes," vol. 221, p. 1191 ▶ The correlation between body weight and the presence of horns in females may be a consequence of the relation between body weight and antipredator behavior in antelopes: smaller species rely on crypsis or flight while large species often show direct defense against predators. **2005** Tim Cam *RedNova* (Feb. 23) "The Adaptive Significance of Coloration in Mammals" (Int.) ▶ Animals can remain concealed when their overall coloration (box 1) resembles or matches the natural background of their environment (Endler 1978). This phenomenon, also known as general color resemblance, includes crypsis (a type of camouflage), in which overall body color resembles the general color of the habitat, or pattern blending, in which color patterns on the body match patterns of light and dark in the environment.

cuddie *n.* used vocatively, friend or pal; **homie, cuz.** *California. Hip-Hop. Slang. United States.* [The etymological information in the June 2004 cite is unverified, though it is plausible. The term probably is not related to the Scots-English *cuddie* 'donkey, ass, or small horse,' though the latter term is sometimes used as a term of coarse affection to mean 'a person who is stubborn or obstinate.'] This term appears to originate in Vallejo, California, and is closely associated with the performers Mac Mall and Mac Dre.

[**2001** *Usenet: rec.music.hip-hop* (July 7) "Re: The All Ugly Team of Rap Music" ▶ "Many times here, what I've considered to be thoughtful commentary based off Hip Hop history and the mores therein has been twisted to mean that I'm hating on something. Hmmmm..." "Not by me cuddy. though I disagree with you from time to time."] **2001** *Usenet: fr.rec.arts.musique.hip-hop* (Dec. 4) "1 ptit cours?? lol...just 4 introducing myself...a joke" ▶ *Cuddie*: Un pote de toujours. Cf interview de Mac Mall dans The Source n80. **2004** Eric K. Arnold *East Bay Express* (Calif.) (June 30) "The Politics of 'Hyphy'" ▶ *Cuddie* (n.): A close friend or relative, derived from "Cousin"; anyone from Vallejo's Crestside neighborhood (cf. Mac Mall, Illegal Business? 1993). **2004** Eric K. Arnold *East Bay Express* (Calif.) (Nov. 10) "Requiem for a Mac" (Int.) ▶ [Mac] Dre was riding shotgun in a white van driven by Dubee, his longtime cuddie (that's Crestside, Vallejo, parlance for "close homie"). ***2004** [Christopher Abad] *Ambient Empire* (Calif.) (Nov. 11) "Bay Area Slang" (Int.) ▶ *cuddie* n.—Don't ever say nigga, it's just retarded if you're not of the right race to use that word even if you think you know the right context. So take it from the Crestside peeps and use this word to identify your friends. Go get keyed with your cuddies. ***2004** *LyricSeek* (Nov. 11) "PSD Tang & O.J. Lyrics" (Int.) ▶ Called up my cuddie for the spark/And he told me Gully Barbecue later on at the Crest Park.

cuff and stuff *v.* to (physically) place someone under arrest. *Crime & Prisons. Police. United States.*

[**1991** Lily Eng *L.A. Times* (Jan. 18) "Complaints Prompted Sweeps, Officer Testifies," p. 16 ▶ The homeless were cuffed and stuffed into patrol

cars.... Not one of them were charged with property crimes.] **1991** Howard Sinker *Star Tribune* (Minneapolis-St. Paul, Minn.) (May 3) "Club Owner's Sense of Something Off-Key Led to the Arrest of Rock-Star Imposter," p. 1A ► We're a white-collar unit—paper crimes, fraud, embezzlement. The old cuffing-and-stuffing routine doesn't come to us very much. **1992** Maureen Harrington *Denver Post* (Colo.) (Mar. 11) "Junk Cars, Trashed Yards Their Prey," p. 1F ► Last year, with the help of police, Turner got an incorrigible trash dumper "cuffed and stuffed." **1992** Wil Haygood @ Mogadishu, Somalia *Boston Globe* (Dec. 25) "On a Rooftop in Somalia, Dreams of New England," p. 1 ► Both Somalis are handcuffed and taken away. "Cuffed and stuffed" as one of the Marines says. **1993** Carol Rust *Houston Chronicle* (Tex.) (July 23) "'Cruising for Crooks' Cops Nail Big Time with Capers," p. 6 ► They are "cruising for crooks," or "fishing for felons." Suspects are "hooked and crooked," "cuffed and stuffed," "nailed and jailed," and they "ride like they hide." **1998** *Palm Beach Post* (Fla.) (May 23) "DARE Lessons Worth It; Kids Remember," p. 13A ► The days of cuffing and stuffing criminals in jail are long gone. The role of police officers has been broadened to include the title of educator. **2004** *August Free Press* (Waynesboro, Va.) (Dec. 14) "It Needs to Be Said" (Int.) ► Why she was then cuffed and stuffed, to borrow from the vernacular, is still up for discussion. School officials are saying that they were following state law by calling the police, who are themselves saying that they were following procedure by handcuffing her and taking her downtown.

curbstoning *n.* **1.** the conducting of (streetside) business without a license, especially automobile sales and formerly real estate; **2.** among census-takers, falsifying information about a household. *Business. Crime & Prisons.* [Both senses of *curbstoning* come from the notion that the activity is performed on the street, at the curb.]

[**1893** *Washington Post* (Aug. 10) "After Curbstone Brokers," p. 7 ► The regular dealers pay $50 a year license and complain that they daily encounter persons who pay no license, but watch for opportunities to make sales and frequently cause the regular brokers trouble by stepping in when sales are partly completed and claiming a part of the commission. As a first step to check this curbstone business, as it is called, the following letter was yesterday sent to the District Commissioners.] **1913** *Modesto Evening News* (Calif.) (Mar. 27) "Worth Realty Measure," p. 4 ► The measure regulates realty dealers by prohibiting any one from selling land as agents for another without securing a certificate of license.... The passage of this act would effectually abolish "curbstoning," and much of the unreliable tactics employed by irresponsible real estate sharks. **1980** Robert McG.

Thomas Jr. *N.Y. Times* (B3) (Nov. 13) "Commerce Secretary Is Told to Testify on Census Count" ► One, Steven P. Glusman, a former enumerator and crew chief in Harlem, told of occupied buildings misclassified as vacant and of "curbstoning," the practice of filling out forms without conducting the required interviews. **1988** Mark Albright *St. Petersburg Times* (Fla.) (Feb. 8) "Going for Good Deals on Wheels," p. 15E ► Wholesalers prefer the state would turn its effort instead to putting so-called "curbstoners" out of business. Those are unlicensed hobbyists who park collections of used cars in vacant lots along the roadside and sell them in defiance of the law. **1990** Richard Levine *N.Y. Times* (Sept. 22) "Can Heads Be Counted in a Dynamic City?" p. 25 ► There are follow-up visits to housing units where residents did not send in forms or mailed back incomplete ones and field inspections of addresses declared vacant or listed as having only one occupant, a danger signal that a "curbstoning" census worker may not have taken the trouble to look inside. **2004** Stephanie Hanes *Baltimore Sun* (Md.) (Nov. 20) "Time on the Run, Then Time to Pay" (Int.) ► Schecter had learned how to "curbstone." That was the street term for buying cars at auctions and from wholesalers, rolling back the odometers and then placing ads in newspapers, pretending to be the original owner.

cut heads *v.* to compare musical skill in an informal competition; to hold a jam session. *Music.* This is directly related to *to cut* 'to hold an (informal) musical competition,' which dates to at least the 1930s and possibly to the 1920s. The competition is sometimes called a *cutting contest.*

1977 Melvin Moore in *The World of Count Basie* (1980) Stanley Dance, p. 340 ► He and Charlie used to cut heads. The guy that taught Charlie everything on guitar was Chuck Richardson. **1985** Gus Johnson (Oct. 1) in *Swing to Bop: An Oral History of the Transition in Jazz in the 1940s* Ira Gitler, p. 24 ► We'd have jam sessions, "head-cutting" sessions.... The first thing the drummer said was he was there to "cut heads" on drums. Jesse Price, he was nowhere to be found. He was a "head cutter" around at the time. So, I was down there, and we went in a little place down there, and everybody said, "Come on. Play. Come on. Play." I wouldn't play until after he got drunk. After he got drunk, then I'd cut his head. **1991** Dave Tianen *Milwaukee Sentinel* (Wisc.) (Oct. 30) "Blues Guitarist Rogers Masterful, Imaginative," p. 6B ► When it comes to slide guitar, he can cut heads with any guitarslinger on the range. **2005** *[Al] Diary of Guitar Guy Al* (Jan. 19) "Bands I've Been in Part 5: The First and Second Gig" (Int.) ► I still long to be in a band that plays just good, old, classic rock and roll music. After playing that song, Phil asked me if I wanted to "cut heads" which is blues slang for friendly competition of dueling guitar solos.

cutie *n.* a boxer willing to take, and capable of withstanding, a lot of blows; an unrefined or unorthodox boxer who relies on tricks. *Sports.* [Perhaps from the idea of a "good chin," meaning the boxer can take a beating to the face without being knocked out. **Cute** has a long-standing meaning of 'clever,' though less common now.]

1936 Bill McCormick *Washington Post* (Mar. 22) "Around the Ring," p. X4 ▶ Prize-ring cuties are boxers who pay far less attention to inflicting damage on their opponents than to protecting themselves. Some of our most successful fisticuffians have been cuties, cuties who have outfumbled good opponent after good opponent, advancing relentlessly toward the top—and leaving every arena in which they appeared badly in need of fumigation. **1940** Jack Cuddy *Sheboygan Press* (Wisc.) (Mar. 21) "Louis Trains Seriously for Paychek Fight on March 29," p. 26 ▶ After Louis' pathetic showing against Arturo Godoy on Feb. 9, the elderly negro with the razor tatting on his face is taking no chances against Paychek whom he described as "a cutie who ought to make Joe look pow'ful silly if he gits discautious." **1956** Jack Hand @ NYC *Reno Evening Gazette* (Nev.) (Jan. 7) "Savage Draws with Lausse in Tight Bout," p. 17 ▶ Eduardo Lausse, the darling of Argentina, knows today why they call Milo Savage a "cutie." The handsome South American had to get off the floor and close with a rush to get a draw. **1970** Jake La Motta *Raging Bull: My Story,* p. 113 ▶ I would have to say that Robinson was the best I fought—a cutie, fast, with all the tricks, but he could also take a punch and he could throw one. **1977** Dave Brady *Washington Post* (May 8) "Bobick Still Thinks of Stevenson as He Prepares for Norton Bout," p. D4 ▶ Futch was reminded that Norton has other skills than being a fighter and, if he is not quite a cutie, he can box. **1986** Jack Fiske *San Francisco Chronicle* (Feb. 15) "Tossup Fight for Lightweight Title Tomorrow," p. 42 ▶ Crawley is a cutie, a side-to-side boxer who will stick and move, just like Anthony Fletcher, a southpaw, who holds the only win over Bramble. **1988** Michael Wilbon *Washington Post* (E5) (Sept. 16) "U.S. Is Uncertain If '88 Can Bring Stars in the Ring" ▶ Guys all want to be punchers now, not boxers. People are calling them cutie-pies, and it's because they're emulating guys they see in the ring as pros.... I've been on them not to go into the middle of the ring doing those jive gestures. I told them, "When you do that, the referee already considers you a cutie-pie and is going to rule accordingly." **1989** Lowell Cohn *San Francisco Chronicle* (Feb. 21) "Tyson Must Be Tested to Be

Great," p. D1 ▶ Both are characterized by a brutal brawling style, although Tyson, who is no cutie, is slightly more polished. **1990** Jon Saraceno *USA Today* (Mar. 16) "Fans the Real Winners in Taylor-Chavez Bout," p. 12C ▶ Chavez is no defensive cutie, but he does have a terrific chin. **2002** Russell Sullivan *Rocky Marciano: The Rock of His Times* (Aug. 1), p. 83 ▶ Walcott's fighting style also presented a target. He was commonly known as a "cutie."...Some sportswriters...cast him as a stereotypical figure looking to sneak through life. Franklin Lewis, for instance, claimed that Walcott "is in the main a trickster." Likewise, C.M. Gibbs of the Baltimore Sun maintained that he possessed "a gift of cuteness by nature." **2005** Sean Newman *RingSideReport .com* (Feb. 23) "Boxing: Final Bell Tolls for Jimmy Young" (Int.) ▶ He was, in boxing parlance, a "cutie," and used this style to his advantage in gaining wins over the likes of Ron Lyle and Foreman.

D

dago T *n.* a ribbed, white cotton tank-style undershirt; a **wife-beater**; a **boy beater**. *Fashion.* A synonym is *guinea T.*

1980 *English Journal* (Mar.) "Revision: Yes, They Do It. Yes, You Can Teach It," vol. 69, no. 3, p. 44 ▶ He lived in the ghetto in an all Italian neighborhood.... You can still picture him sort of short, stocky build, hair greased back, dago-t-shirt tattoo of a heart and an old girl friend's name, he is always dirty. **1993** *Usenet: alt.sex.stories* (June 11) "Story: Family Fun 1/3" ▶ She was also dressed in shorts and a white dago-T. **1993** Lisa Scottoline *Everywhere That Mary Went* (Nov. 1), p. 36 ▶ It's almost transparent, made from some obscure synthetic fiber, and he's got the dago T-shirt on underneath. **1996** James Grippando *Informant* (Sept. 1), p. 25 ▶ A statuesque brunette clad in a strategically ripped dago-T scurried toward the Ford Agency. **2000** Peter Torbay *Creation Myth* (Feb. 1), p. 166 ▶ The two girl cooks made the rounds of the boat pack, looking for a bunk mate or threesome, and Look had a chance to dance belly-to-belly with one, a skinny shag blonde in torn-off parachute pants and a dago-T top. **2002** Richard Roeper *Chicago Sun-Times* (July 2) "Attention-Cravers Flourish as Summertime Sets In," p. 11 ▶ Not to mention...the guys who wear "Dago T's" so everyone can see the 47 tattoos covering their arms and shoulders.

dead wagon *n.* a vehicle used as part of a protection racket in which uncooperative distributors of milk, soda fountain syrups, or other products are forced out of business by undercutting their prices and other tactics. *NYC.* This term is now historical, as is the once more common meaning of *dead wagon*, a vehicle used as an ambulance or to transport corpses.

1909 *Nebraska State Journal* (Lincoln) (Dec. 26) "Milk Trust Gets Airing" (in NYC), p. 3 ▶ The "dead wagon" was put on the Harlem company's trade. This wagon is run by the protective association nominally to collect milk cans, witnesses testified, but its real value lies in the canvassing of every customer of a dealer marked for destruction. His price is cut and milk is offered even below cost price to win away his customers. **1910** *N.Y. Times* (Jan. 8) "Fixing Milk Prices" ▶ Mr. Herkstroter said that he "had heard" there was sort of agreement among the milk dealers of the city not to undersell each other and that the "dead wagon" was run against offenders. **1929** *N.Y. Times* (Oct. 25) "Threats on His Life Disclosed by Groat," p. 23 ► Allis, who said he had been without a business for the past seven months, told how he had received an offer of $100 a week from Fay to ride a "dead wagon," distributing cheap milk to grocers served by recalcitrant dealers. **1931** *N.Y. Times* (Aug. 7) "Swear Syrup Ring Boasted City 'Pull,'" p. 6 ► He said he was told he was "in a bottle already," and in two weeks three-fourths of his customers, from 300 to 400, were taken away from him by the organization underselling with the "dead wagons." **2004** Andrew Coe *Gastronomica* (Summer) "The Egg Cream Racket" (Int.) ► Harry Dolowich's plans crystallized when Larry Fay hit the headlines in mid-1929.... About one hundred independent milk dealers paid thousands apiece for membership in the Milk Chain; in return Fay guaranteed to keep the price of milk high. Those who couldn't afford the dues, or attempted to sell for less, found that wholesalers wouldn't supply them, health inspectors would harass them, and their customers would receive visits from the "dead wagons." These were association trucks that undersold recalcitrant dealers, causing retailers to drop their regular suppliers. After a few weeks of dead wagons, the holdouts usually had to shut their doors.

death cross *n.* in financial markets, a situation where long-term and short-term averages converge, seen as evidence that values will decline. *Business. Jargon. Money & Finance. United States.*

1994 (*Reuters*) (Dec. 5) "Silver Prices Tumble on Fund Sales, Chart Factors" ► A Death Cross happens when the 50-day moving average (price) turns down to cross the 200-day moving average from above. **2004** David Berman *National Post* (Ontario, Can.) (July 28) "Markets Fine, Except for 'Death Cross'" (Int.) ► You probably won't take any comfort in learning that a technical indicator for the Dow Jones industrial average is pointing to a so-called "death cross." The nasty-sounding indicator pops up when an index's 50-day moving average (or intermediate-term trend) dips below its 200-day moving average (or long-term trend). As the name suggests, it is often considered among technical analysts to be a bearish signal for stocks. **2005** Tomi Kilgore *MarketWatch* (Mar. 21) "Can Chips Help Cushion the Nasdaq?" (Int.) ► In addition to all the support, the 50-day SMA crossed above the 200-day earlier last the week. This pattern is referred to as a "golden cross" and is viewed by many as a long-term buy signal (a downside crossover is known as a "dead cross" and is a sell signal).

decleat *v.* in American football, to knock an opponent off his feet. Also *n.,* **decleater.** *Sports. United States.*

1986 Mal Florence *L.A. Times* (Sept. 19) "USC's 248-Pound Todd Steele Is a Real Blockbuster," p. 7 ► Todd Steele earned the team's award as decleater of the week for his blocking. A decleater is knocking an opponent off his feet. He buried some Illinois defensive backs last week. **1986** Mal Florence *L.A. Times* (Oct. 31) "At USC, the Big Bully on the Block Is Jeff Bregel," p. 2 ▶ "You run at them with the pitch and power plays and, although you might not get the yards at first, they'll be worn down in the third and fourth quarters to the point that they don't feel like coming off blocks and you can decleat them." The decleater, in USC parlance, is knocking a defensive player off his feet and onto his backside. **1991** Natalie Meisler *Denver Post* (Colo.) (Jan. 8) "W. Ridge's Hammond Picks CU," p. 1D ▶ He took a 190-pound kid who lowered his shoulder on Rick and decleated him. **2004** Bill Coats *St. Louis Post-Dispatch* (Mo.) (Oct. 6) "Trev Faulk Makes Impact in Return to Action" (Int.) ▶ Faulk charged downfield, upended a would-be blocker—a "decleating," in NFL parlance—and dropped Jamal Robertson "like nobody else was on the field," coach Mike Martz said.

dementia Americana *n.* a (supposed) form of insanity, leading to violence, that comes over a man who believes his home or family has been violated. *Crime & Prisons. Health. Law. United States.*
1907 *Chicago Daily Tribune* (Apr. 10) "Unwritten Law Thaw's Last Hope" (in NYC), p. 1 ▶ "Ah, gentlemen," said Mr. Delmas, dramatically, turning to the alienists who testified for the prosecution, "if you desire a name for this species of insanity let me suggest it—call it dementia Americana. That is the species of insanity which makes every American man believe his home to be sacred; that is the species of insanity which makes him believe the honor of his daughter is sacred; that is the species of insanity which makes him believe the honor of his wife is sacred; that is the species of insanity which makes him believe that whosoever invades his home, that whosoever stains the virtue of this threshold, has violated the highest of human laws and must appeal to the mercy of God, if mercy there be for him anywhere in the universe." **1908** *Wayne County Journal* (Mo.) (Jan. 30) "Local Happenings" (Int.) in *MOWAYNE-L* (June 22, 2004) Sharon *"Local Happenings—Thursday, January 30, 1908 Wayne County Journal"* ▶ The County court met Monday to pass on the sanity of Tony Hood. In the court's opinion the case was found to be a bona fide case of insanity, unalloyed with "Dementia Americana" exaggerated ego or any other newfangled phase of insanity, and the boy was ordered to the Farmington asylum. Sheriff Barrow accompanying him to that place Tuesday morning. **2002** *Film Quarterly* (Summer) "Headline Hollywood" (Int.) ▶ When Thaw's attorney made the case that his client had been acting out of a condition he termed dementia Americana—a legitimate rage triggered by the desecration of a man's home—a powerful nexus of concerns with national identity, patri-

archy, class, and the public sphere emerged. Meanwhile (and most interestingly), Evelyn Nesbit Thaw became "the first person to capitalize on a scandal to become a film star."

derecho *n.* a type of strong, ground-level prairie wind caused by rapidly descending cold air and characterized by a straight, horizontal advance. *Science. Spanish. United States.*

1890 *Chicago Daily Tribune* (Mar. 30) "Predictions of Tornadoes," p. 12 ► If genuine tornadoes were not developed, there were violent squalls or the peculiar storm styled by Prof. Hinrichs the "derecho," or straight-blow. **1893** Mark W. Harrington *L.A. Times* (Apr. 16) "Tornadoes: What They Are; Where and When They Occur," p. 18 ► The third form appears rather as horizontal than as vertical whirls. They appear to be what Dr. Hinrichs has called derechoes (from *derecho*, straight) and advance in the form of a horizontal roll of dust. The front extends in length as they advance, so that the territory they pass over is fan-shaped, instead of the strap-shaped area of the tornado proper. **1993** Chris Burbach *Omaha World-Herald* (Neb.) (July 16) "Errant Weather Systems Make Misery" ► On the evening of July 8, cool air made heavy by rain crashed earthward at tremendous speed in central Nebraska, said Pollack, the weather service meteorologist. The descending air touched off a weather phenomenon known as a derecho, he said. The cool air caused the big winds, Pollack said. After it hit the ground, the air spread out, blowing wind in front of the thunderstorms and causing more thunderstorms. **2004** Hayli Fellwock *Bowling Green Daily News* (Ky.) (July 14) "Storms, Damage Return" (Int.) ► Tuesday night's storm was called a "derecho," the Spanish word for huge wind event, according to Benjamin Schott, meteorologist for the National Weather Service in Louisville. The winds ranged between 60 to 80 mph, Schott said.

descanso *n.* a roadside marker or memorial to a victim of an automobile accident. *Religion. Spanish. United States.* [From Spanish *descanso* 'resting place (of a dead person),' from the verb *descansar* 'to (have a) rest.']

1994 Kelly Garbus *Kansas City Star Magazine* (Kan., Mo.) (Sept. 4) "Roadside Reminders," p. 8 ► The practice of erecting memorials may have its origins in Mexico. Roadside memorials there are called descanso, which means resting place. **1999** Rod Allee *Record* (N.J.) (June 18) "Tenuous Bond Links Two Memorials" ► Alongside Interstate 80 in Knowlton Township is something called a descanso, a Spanish word that means a roadside memorial. It is for State Trooper Philip Lamonaco. **2000** Steve Shoup *Albuquerque Journal* (N.Mex.) (Aug. 23) "Fiery Crash on I-25 Kills One," p. A1 ► Williams said one of the cars came to rest against a descanso, or roadside cross often put up by family and friends to mark where someone died, usually in a traffic accident. **2002** Elda Silva *San Antonio Express-News* (Tex.) (Nov. 3) "Americans Find Room for Descansos," p. 1J ▶ While a gravesite marks the resting place of physical remains, a descanso is intended to mark the place where the spirit left the body. **2004** Forrest Valdiviez *Island Packet* (Bluffton, S.C.) (Oct. 17) "Signs of the Cross" (Int.) ▶ In the Southwest, the markers are called descansos, which comes from the Spanish word for resting. The practice comes from a Spanish tradition of placing stones where pallbearers rested between the church and the cemetery. Later the stones became crosses.... Some states don't think roadside memorials are sacred. **2005** Rachel Ray *Albuquerque Journal* (N.Mex.) (June 12) "Historian, Photographer Track New Mexico's Tradition of Roadside Crosses" (Int.) ▶ [Kathleen] McRee and oral historian Troy Fernandez, both Santa Feans, have spent years researching, photographing and interviewing people about the roadside crosses known variously around New Mexico as descansos, crucitas or memorias.

deve *n.* a coerced payment; "protection" money. *Crime & Prisons. Money & Finance. Nigeria. Slang.* [*develop*ment levy.] Jocular reference to actual levies made by the government for growth and development.

2003 (*All Africa*) (Aug. 19) "Displaced Residents Flee Warri" (in Warri, Nigeria) ▶ Motorists, shop owners and commuters were subjected to varied harrowing experiences during which victims lost money, wares to youths who terrorised the area, demanding all manner of fees tagged development levy, otherwise called "deve." **2003** Onyema Ugochukwu @ Nigeria (*All Africa*) (Sept. 29) "NDDC Is Reconstructing the Destruction of 50 Years—Chairman" ▶ There is something now, they call it "deve," that is development levy. It has become so bad these days they even charge on the basis of blocks and that is what we face. (That is, if a construction is to be embarked upon, the people would, in a manner of quantity surveying, collect commission per number of blocks to be used for the project.) **2003** Barry Morgan @ Port Harcourt, Nigeria (*Upstream*) (Oct. 17) "Oil Stoking Fires of Ethnic Rivalry" ▶ Onyema Ugochukwu says that after 33 months of operation, 405 projects have been completed despite the emergence of what is dubbed "deve"—an unofficial development levy charged on-site by local communities on contractor's construction materials even though projects are meant for their benefit. **2004** Bobson Gbinije *Daily Champion* (Lagos, Nigeria) (May 20) "Killing the Renaissance in Delta State" (Int.) ▶ The word deve is a neologistic infusion and shortened form of "Development Levy."

D-girl *n.* a (junior) film industry executive who considers scripts for further development into funded movie productions. *Entertainment.*

1987 Anna McDonnell *L.A. Times* (Aug. 23) "D-Girls: The Women Behind the Scripts," p. 18 ▶ "D-girl" is the movie industry sobriquet for a woman who works in the murky world of "development." Men dominate most of the power jobs in the industry—directing, producing, running studios—but women reign supreme in the Big D, development.... There are probably about 100 D-girls in Hollywood. Perhaps a fourth are really young men, but women are so prevalent in development that even the men often are referred to as "D-girls"— and even appear that way on many agency lists. **1995** *Usenet: alt.showbiz.gossip* (Jan. 6) "Re: Liking Demi Moore" ▶ Demi's "production company" is simply a vanity shell deal at Columbia Pictures. All the above-the-title actors have them to soothe their egos. Essentially, the studio gives them a few hundred thou to pay a D-girl or D-boy to "develop" scripts for them. **2004** Ms. Gonick *San Francisco Chronicle* (Calif.) (Sept. 3) "Running Down Lunacy Lane with a D-Girl" (Int.) ▶ The idea came from Kitty, a D-girl (or, in wicked Hooeywood parlance, "Development Slut") from the TV division of Genius Nerd Films.

dhimmi *n.* a non-Muslim living with limited rights under Muslim rule. *Arabic. Religion.*

1929 C.H. Kraeling *Journal of the American Oriental Society* "The Origin and Antiquity of the Mandeans," vol. 49, p. 199 (Int.) ▶ The Moslem rulers classed the Mandeans with those called "dhimmi," *i.e.*, the ones with whom a compact for religious toleration had been made.... The Koran mentions three groups of *dhimmi*, the Jews, the Christians and the Sabiun or the Sabeans, not to be confused with the Sabean family of the Semitic peoples. **1942** Arthur Jeffery *Journal of Near Eastern Studies* (Oct.) "The Political Importance of Islam," vol. 1, no. 4, p. 388 (Int.) ▶ The offer of Islam or *Dhimmi* status must be made before the attack is launched. **1955** *N.Y. Times* (Dec. 30) "Equality Promised North Africa Jews," p. 14 ▶ Jews had held the status of "dhimmis" since the twelfth century. "Dhimmi" means a protected person without the rights of a citizen. He could not vote, get a passport or have his oath accepted in a Moroccan law court. **1982** David B. Ottaway @ Kfar Matta, Lebanon *Washington Post* (Nov. 29) "Uneasy Peace Prevails in Village for Lebanese Christians, Druze," p. A18 ▶ Lebanese Forces officials say they are only trying to establish a balance of power between Christians and Druze and end what they allege is the Christian status as dhimmi, second-class citizens, in the Chouf. **1996** Bernard Lewis *The Middle East*, p. 210 ▶ Tolerated unbelievers were called *dhimmi*, or *ahl al-dhimma*, "the people of the pact." This was a legal term for the tolerated and protected non-Muslim subjects of the Muslim state.... The *dhimma*, which determined their status, was conceived as a pact between the Muslim ruler and the non-Muslim communities and was thus essentially a contract. The basis of this contract was the recognition by the *dhimmis* of the supremacy of Islam and the dominance of the Muslim state, and their acceptance of a position of subordination, symbolized by certain social restrictions and by the payment of a poll tax (*jizya*) to which Muslims were not subject. In return, they were granted security of life and property, protection against external enemies, freedom of worship, and a very large measure of internal autonomy in the conduct of their affairs. **2004** Val McQueen *Tech Central Station* (Washington, D.C.) (Oct. 12) "You Only Die Once" (Int.) ▶ Even the colorless—and clueless—dhimmi-in-chief also known as British Foreign Minister Jack Straw raced off to visit the family—to what purpose, who knows?

ding-ding *n.* a streetcar or trolley. *Hong Kong.* [Imitative of the sound of a bell.] Although this term is specific to Hong Kong, in Japan streetcars are sometimes called *chin chin densha*, meaning 'ding ding trains.'

2001 Verna Yu *Townsville Bulletin/Townsville Sun* (Australia) (Jan. 27) "Ding-Dings Face the Chop," p. 55 ▶ The wooden double-decker "ding-ding," so nicknamed for its clanging bell, is to make way for a new generation of streamlined aluminum models, which Hongkong Tramways Ltd says will be safer, faster and more comfortable. **2005** Bianca Tong @ Hong Kong *Imprint* (Univ. of Waterloo, Can.) (July 15) "Luxury, Rain and Ding-Dings in Hong Kong" (Int.) ▶ Serviced by an amazingly efficient public transportation system, people have access to streetcars (affectionately called "ding-dings"), subways, trains, buses, and ferries.

dipping *n.* rocking or bouncing a vehicle by alternately hitting the gas and brakes or by quickly adjusting a hydraulic suspension. *Automotive.*

1995 *Usenet: rec.music.hip-hop* (Sept. 14) "Totally Unofficial Rap-Dictionary (Bi-weekly Posting, Part 1/2)" ▶ Dipping is what a car with a hydraulic suspension does. **2004** Shaheem Reid *MTVNews.com* (Nov. 8) "Hyphy: Crunk, Northern-California Style" (Int.) ▶ One popular example of kids acting hyphy or "going dumb" is "gas-brake dippin'." In the Bay, they pile into their cars and, instead of driving normally, they'll hit the gas, then quickly hit the brake; hit the gas, hit the brake; hit the gas, hit the brake. And when they really want to get into it, they open all the doors on the vehicle, turn the music to its loudest possible volume and.... You guessed it: Hit the gas, hit the brake. **2005 Harry Harris, Laura Casey** *Oakland Tribune* **(Calif.) (Feb. 7) "Future Father Is Shot to Death" (Int.)** ▶ According to Green, some of Baeza's passengers said the other van was "dipping," a street term meaning the driver would "hit the gas, then brake, then swerve to make it rock." **2005 Louis Sahagun @ Oakland, Calif.** *L.A. Times* **(Mar. 7) "Deadly Swerves and Spins" (Int.)** ▶ Maneuvers include *sidin'*—another term for doughnuts—and *dippin'*, in which a driver hits the brakes and the gas to make a car rock back and forth in time to, say, Tupac Shakur's "Starin' in My Rearview" or Mac Dre's "Thizzelle Dance," a slang reference to Ecstasy. **2005 Harry Harris, Laura Casey @ Oakland** *Argus* **(Calif.) (Aug. 9) "Man Captured, Admits Killing Father-to-Be in February" (Int.)** ▶ Baeza's passengers said Gonzalez's van, which was alongside theirs, was "dipping," a street term for a driver hitting the gas then braking and swerving to make it rock.

dirty dirty *n.* the southern United States; the South. Also **durrty durrty.** *Hip-Hop. Music. United States.* [From "Dirty Dirty South," heavily influenced by a trend of southern hip-hop music called "Dirty South." The spelling *durrty* is closely associated with hip-hop music.] Usually used with the definite article: **the dirty dirty.** Capitalization is inconsistent.

1999 Rob Sheffield @ Charlottesville, Va. *Village Voice* **(NYC) (Mar. 2) "Top 10 Plus," p. 82** ▶ OutKast are so weird I gave up on getting a handle on Aquemini, which is when it started bubbling in my brain. I love how they represent the dirty-dirty with more juice than Zeus, rocking the ill mbira and letting Erykah Badu shake that load off with trunkloads of booty-club bass. **1999 Usenet:** *alt.rap* **(Apr. 9) "Betta Who? Betta Wha?"** ▶ Banned in 47 Countries baby from the Dirty Dirty, to your Uranus. **2001** *Business Wire* **(Oct. 11) "Loud Records Gears Up for Southern Compilation" (in NYC)** ▶ Loud Records will be releasing Hypnotize Minds Presents...The Dirty Dirty Volume 1 January 15, 2002, a compilation of some of the South's hottest records. **2003 Liz Balmaseda** *Miami Herald* **(Fla.) (Feb. 9) "A New Breed: Miami Rapper Pitbull Has All of South Florida Barking About His Skills," p. F1** ▶ "I'm from the Dirty Dirty...," goes one of Pitbull's most contagious raps, "Dirty." **2004 Ace Atkins** *Dirty South* **(Mar. 2), p. 227** ▶ "People like to talk and divide us. People like to break us apart. But we all the Dirty South." "Dirty, dirty." ***2004 [Marvulus]** *Trickology* **(Oct. 10) "The Reunion: Where Do You Live?" (Int.)** ▶ New

York, cuz while I'd love to hit up the durrty durrty, I won't be able to...depends when I guess.

discordant couple *n.* a pair of long-term sexual partners, such as a married couple, in which one is infected with a sexually transmitted disease and the other is not. *Health. Jargon. Medical.*

1990 (*USA Today/Gannett Nat. Info. Network*) (Apr. 22) "Morbidity and Mortality Weekly Report" in *Usenet: sci.med.aids* (Apr. 24, 1990) (David Canzi) *"HICN 314 News—Excerpts"* ▶ The physician who performed the inseminations reported that in January 1990 a second HIV-1-discordant couple (i.e., seropositive husband with hemophilia, seronegative wife) underwent one insemination using the same density gradient centrifugation procedure. Nine weeks after the insemination, the woman was negative for HIV-1 antibody by EIA and Western blot and for proviral HIV-1 DNA by polymerase chain reaction. **1990** Kay Longcope *Boston Globe* (Mass.) (Aug. 23) "AIDS Threat to Women Increasing" ▶ Jim, 31, says he and his wife, June, are "a discordant couple," meaning that one is infected with the AIDS virus and the other isn't. **2004** [Big Issue Writer] *East African Standard* (Nairobi, Kenya) (July 26) "Aids Spread Relief" (Int.) ▶ In the discordant couple phenomenon, one partner is HIV-positive, while the other remains negative, even as they continue to live together as man and wife or simply maintain a long-term relations.

DNF *adj.* **1.** *d*id *n*ot *f*inish, in course-based sporting events, such as boating, auto-racing, and horse racing. **2.** *d*id *n*ot *f*ind, in geocaching. *Acronym. Jargon. Sports.*

1943 James Robbins *N.Y. Times* (July 29) "Race Week Starts at Larchmont Y.C.," p. 15 ▶ [boat-racing scores:] D.G. Millar, d.n.f. **1978** *Globe and Mail* (Toronto, Can.) (Aug. 30) "Winds Helpful to U.S. Sailor in CORK Event," p. P31 ▶ The worst finish has been dropped in computing the standing in classes that have completed five or more races: dns—did not start; pms—premature start; dnc—did not compete; dnf—did not finish. **2004** Parker Morse *Flashes of Panic* (May 2) "Community Watch" (Int.) ▶ There is—or was—a cache there called "Valley View Too" which hadn't been found since last May, though with only one "Did Not Find" logged since then. (Curiously, the caching slang for a failed search, "DNF," is the same as the runners' slang for a failed race, where it indicates "Did Not Finish.")

dog *n.* in horse racing, a cone or barrier for delimiting a path. *Sports. United States.*

1962 Walter Haight *Washington Post, Times Herald* (Nov. 15) "About Horses and People...," p. D12 ▶ Race track "dogs" (or the equivalent thereof) could have been a factor in the International victory of France's Match II.... They're in the category of the carpenter's "Horse."...A few feet of two-by-four with four legs attached.... The removal of two legs, from one end, turns a horse into a dog. The wooden dogs, often seen in guarding a street excavation and holding a red light at night, once were stock equipment at all race tracks.... Most have been replaced by the inverted yellow traffic cones. Dogs or cones are placed several feet out from the inside rail at times when a track is wet, so that this part of the racing strip will be protected during morning workout hours. **1986** Bob Schwarzmann @ Renton *Seattle Times* (Wash.) (May 4) "If Problems Surface, Coffey Can Help Smooth Them Out," p. C11 ▶ Coffey said Coble had been reluctant to use "dogs" because he felt the horsemen would not accept them. "Dogs" are barriers—flame-orange traffic cones in this case—to keep the hoofs away from an area of concern. **2004** David Grening @ Elmont, N.Y. *MSNBC* (Oct. 15) "Badge of Silver Debuts for Frankel" (Int.) ▶ Exercise rider Emanuel Davy never asked her for anything during the work, conducted around a triple set of orange traffic cones, commonly referred to as dogs.

dog-whistle politics *n.* a concealed, coded, or unstated idea, usually divisive or politically dangerous, nevertheless understood by the intended voters. Also **dog whistle issue.** *Australia. New Zealand. Politics. United Kingdom.* [Despite the information in the first 2000 citation, this term probably originated in Australia or New Zealand, though it could be derived from the *dog whistle effect* in American polling, which is the ability of survey participants to distinguish a difference in questions where a pollster may not have intended one. The credit for the coinage in the 2005 cite is unproven though possible, since Lynton Crosby ran four election campaigns for Australian Prime Minister John Howard; Crosby certainly introduced the term in the U.K.] A *dog whistle* is often used as a figurative device for something that cannot be heard or understood by everyone, or that surreptitiously compels people to come along.

1997 *Dominion* (New Zealand) (Dec. 16) "Election Fight on Race Issue," p. 8 ▶ Labor's spokesman on aboriginal affairs has already accused Mr. Howard of "dog-whistle politics"—in rejecting a race election, he actually sent a high-pitched signal to those attuned to hear it. **2000** Tony Wright *The Age* (Australia) (Apr. 8) "The Dog Whistler" ▶ The Americans call this "dog-whistle politics." Blow a dog whistle, and you won't hear much to get excited about. But the target of the whistle...the dogs—will detect a sound beyond the audible range of the rest of us, and will react to it. Two quite different messages are contained within the one action of blowing the whistle: the one benign, the other designed to be heard and heeded only by the ears tuned to it. **2000** Dennis Atkins *Courier Mail* (Brisbane, Australia) (Apr. 10) "Driving a Wedge to Win," p. 13 ▶ A simple statement such as "I don't like political correctness" might not sound too threatening but there are some who hear something quite different, such as "It's okay to be racist." When the politician who used the original words is challenged for inciting racism, he or she is able to say, "No, all I said was I'm against political correctness, what's wrong with that?" A number of people last week hotly disputed that wedge and dog-whistle politics are played in Australia. Don't believe them. That's just spin. **2002** Shaun Carney *The Age* (7) (Nov. 2) "Closer to Asia Than You Think" ▶ The message from the Howard Government in its early days was that Australia was not part of Asia and never would be. To a considerable degree, it was part of a dog-whistle campaign by the Coalition. At a time when rural voters and elements of blue-collar Australia were rallying around Pauline Hanson's simplified nostrums for dealing with what she portrayed as the Asianisation of the nation (and the featherbedding of Aborigines), Howard was, with some fanfare, cutting back immigration numbers. **2005** Jonathan Freedland *Guardian* (U.K.) (Apr. 12) "Beware the Nasty Nudge and Wink" (Int.) ▶ Every election introduces a new phrase into the political lexicon and the "dog-whistle issue" is 2005's early contribution. Coined by Lynton Crosby, the strategic guru imported from Australia by Michael Howard, it refers to those policies that summon back voters who have gone astray.

doji *n.* a stock-trading session in which the opening and closing prices are (nearly) the same. *Japanese. Jargon. Money & Finance.* [From the Japanese *doji* どじ 'a blunder; a blunderer; a fool or foolish thing.'] The plural is also *doji*.

1993 David Toole *Toronto Star* (Can.) (Mar. 21) "Technical Analysis Within Reach of Average Investor," p. H3 ▶ In no time you'll be looking at your candlestick charts (which are based on an ancient Japanese system developed to analyze rice contracts) and looking for exotic price patterns like "morning star," "dark cloud cover" and "dragon-fly doji." **1994** Nigel Cope *Independent* (U.K.) (Jan. 4) "Pembroke: Careless Underground Leak Blows Murdoch's Cover" ▶ Instead, it concerns an arcane 17th-century Japanese method of mastering the markets via a system of "harmi line patterns," "doji line candles" and "dark cloud corners." **2004** Rick Pendergraft *Schaeffer's Research* (Dec. 6) "Shooting Stars Are Not Always Lucky" (Int.) ▶ When a stock's opening price and closing price are virtually the same, it is called a "doji" in candlestick parlance. The third stock formed what is known as a "gravestone doji," which is a type of shooting star.

dollar van *n.* In New York City and Long Island, privately owned multipassenger vehicles that operate along regular routes. *Automotive. NYC.* In manner of operation, dollar vans are similar to **por puestos** in South America, TAP-TAP in Haiti, **chapas** in Mozambique, and **matatus** in Kenya, Tanzania, and Uganda. Dollar vans sometimes charge more than a dollar. Though once illegal, many are now licensed by the city.

[**1993** *Newsday* (Long Island, N.Y.) (Mar. 15) "Cops, Sanit Worker Rescue 18 from Sinking Vehicles," p. 18 ▶ In all, 13 commuters were pulled from the rented Dollar van—12 passengers between the ages of 15 and 65 years and a 7-month-old girl.] **1993** Russell Ben-Ali *Newsday* (Long Island, N.Y.) (Dec. 20) "Van Hits Queens Boy Leaving Church," p. 32 ▶ "Witnesses told us it was a dollar van," said one officer, referring to one of the privately owned livery vans that carry passengers along Linden Boulevard for a $1 fare. **1995** Gary Dauphin *Village Voice* (NYC) (Nov. 21) "The Show: Sometimes the Audience Produces More Entertainment Than the Plot Line," p. 10 ▶ You really did have to drive, and so although it was certainly always possible to go to Sunrise via bus, train, or dollar-van, the thought that one might actually take those public transportations to get there was usually the first and last thought before announcing "fuck it" and "I'm not going." **2002** Jaira Placide *Fresh Girl* (Jan. 8), p. 162 ▶ We ask directions from a man with a long beard who's selling oils and incense. He tells us the dollar vans would be the fastest way. The van we get is packed with four rows of people and their bags of presents. **2004** Sewell Chan @ NYC *N.Y. Times* (Dec. 21) "City Sets Talks After Strike Is Approved at 2 Private Bus Lines" (Int.) ▶ Officials have arranged for licensed commuter vans, also known as dollar vans, to operate limited service along the affected routes if a strike occurs.

do-me queen *n.* a selfish, submissive sexual partner, especially in a male homosexual relationship. *Sexuality. Slang.*

1994 *Usenet: alt.sex.bondage* (Oct. 25) "Re: *** The End of Alt.Sex .Bondage?" ▶ That would be as rude and abusive as if i had followed up your post asking why rob didn't go create alt.sex.bondage—only for you to go play in and called you a lazy, snide, self-centered do-me queen bottom. **1996** W.A. Henkin *Consensual Sadomasochism* (Sept. 1), p. 65 ▶ *Do-me queen*—a *bottom* whose sole interest is in receiving physical, sexual, and/or emotional attention, and does not give back to the *Top*. **2003** [Puppy Sharon] *The Puppy Papers: A*

Woman's Life and Journey into BDSM (Nov. 30) p. 45 ► Steven,...While i won't deny that i intensely enjoy the "do-me-queen" aspect, it is the pleasing & serving that I enjoy more.... sharon.

doona day *n.* a day taken off from work for relaxation or idleness. *Australia.* [*Doona* is a trademarked brand in Australia now well on its way to becoming a generic term there for any duvet or down quilt.] As indicated in the citations, synonyms include **mental health day, duvet day, sickie** (in Australia), and the uncommon *eiderdown day.*

2001 David Wilkes *Courier Mail* (Queensland, Australia) (Jan. 9) "Doona Day, the Official 'Sickie,'" p. 8 ► After a heavy night out, or if you just can't face getting out of bed, you would be allowed to call in to say you were taking a Doona Day. **2004** Robyn Pearce *Getting a Grip on Leadership* (Aug. 31), p. 250 ► What about giving yourself a duvet day, eiderdown day, doona day, mental health day...—a delicious and luxurious day in bed, reading, resting by yourself. **2005** Christina Larmer *Sunday Telegraph* (Australia) (May 8) "Doona Days" (Int.) ► You can dress it up however you like—sick leave, mental health day or, as it's known in particularly innovative companies, doona day—but a growing band of organisational experts say taking regular time off makes for a happy, healthy and productive worker.

door buster *n.* a discounted item of limited quantity intended to bring customers into a store; a sale of such items; a **loss-leader.** Also *attrib. Advertising. Business.*

1935 *Hammond Times* (Ind.) (Aug. 14), p. 9 ► This is the final cleanup of $4, $5 and $6 dresses, including many dark shades for fall wear. A real door buster. We warn you, come at 9:30! **1958** *Syracuse Herald Journal* (N.Y.) (Apr. 18), p. 13 ► Door Buster. Sale! Bamboo cafe curtains! 88¢ pr. **1986** (*PR Newswire*) (Sept. 2) "Chrysler's 2.4% Loan Program a 'Real Blockbuster'" (in Detroit, Mich.) ► Chrysler Motors' 2.4 annual percentage rate financing is a REAL blockbuster. And it's a door buster, too, according to reports from Chrysler/Plymouth and Dodge dealers nationwide. "We almost couldn't handle the traffic," said one dealer from Houston. "We had the highest traffic counts in months." **1992** *Usenet: rec.scuba* (Dec. 11) "Re: Need Tanks" ► A shop here in SLO had some for $250 new, but I think that was some sort of "door buster" special. **2004** Lauren Foster @ NYC *Financial Times* (U.K.) (Nov. 27) "Stores Open Doors to Bargain Hunters" (Int.) ► Retailers such as Wal-Mart and Sears, Roebuck opened at 6am yesterday to promote their "early bird" specials, also known as "door-buster" sales.

door prize *n.* a collision between a bicyclist and a suddenly opened vehicle door. This term seems to be particularly common in Toronto.

1991 *Seattle Times* (Nov. 5) "Sharing the Road—Bicycle Commuters Are Here to Stay," p. A21 ▶ There are reasons why a cyclist might ride "in the middle of the road." Cyclists don't always ride right next to the edge of the road for several reasons: a) glass, gravel, potholes, sewer grates, etc., on the side of the road, b) cars nosing out of blind driveways, c) parked cars along the side of the road (it's no fun to be somebody's door prize). **1994** Margot Gibb-Clark *Globe and Mail* (Toronto, Can.) (May 10) "Middle Kingdom Basics Training: Riding Out the Blacktop Jungle" ▶ Ride one metre out from the sidewalk or parked cars, not only to avoid road debris or someone suddenly opening a car door ("the door prize"), but because you'll be better able to manoeuvre to the right in a tight situation. **2005** [transient0] @ Toronto, Can. *Kuro5hin* (Mar. 19) "A Coder in Courierland" (Int.) ▶ I was knocked from my bike. My front wheel and shocks were damaged, but i wasn't. The second time was a door prize. As i rode north up Yonge, someone opened the door of their parked car directly into my path.

doosra *n.* a cricket delivery bowled in such a way as to spin away from right-handed batsmen. *Hindi. India. Pakistan. Slang. Sports. Urdu.* [< Hin./Urd. *doosra* 'second, other, another']

1999 (*Agence France-Presse*) (Nov. 16) "Saqlain Puts Faith in God's Gift" (in Hobart, Australia) ▶ Saqlain [Mushtaq], 22, who flicks his thumb and index finger across the seam while keeping his wrist action almost identical to his stock off break, has revolutionised his art with his "doosra."...) "The Urdu word for it is doosra, first is off spin and second is 'doosra' bowl. It's the same grip but I just use my finger, the same spinning finger and my thumb." **2003** Michael Atherton *Sunday Telegraph* (U.K.) (Dec. 7) "Murali a Law unto Himself in Throwing Controversy," p. 9 ▶ It is his new delivery, his version of the "doosra," the one that spits and spins away from the right-hander like a leg-break that has aroused suspicion. **2004** *That's Cricket* (India) (May 15) "Howard Feels the Heat of Murali 'Deliveries'" (in Bulawayo, Zimbabwe) (Int.) ▶ Perth-based biomechanics experts subsequently tested him and initially found he straightened his bent arm by 14 percent in bowling a delivery tagged the "doosra." The doosra is a delivery which spins away from right-handers instead of coming into them like a normal off-break. **2004** Khaled Ahmed *Daily Times* (Lahore, Pakistan) (May 30) "Muralitharan and 'Doosra'" (Int.) ▶ Moin Khan shouted doosra because he wanted Saqlain to deliver his disguised leg spin. When he said doosra he used the Urdu word for the other one. The purpose was to hide the instruction from the non-Urdu-speaking batsman.... Doosra in Urdu-Hindi means the other or second. It comes from doh meaning two.

dosia *n.* marijuana. *Drugs. Slang. United States.* There appears to be no connection to the detergent of the same name, nor to the Indian food dish, which is usually spelled *dosai*.

1995 Luniz *Operation Stackola* (song) (July 3) "I Got 5 on It" ▶ I'm da roller/that's quick to fold a blunt out of a buncha sticky dosia/hold up, suck up my weed is all you do. **1999** Usenet: *alt.games.cheats* (Nov. 26) "Look at the Golf Ball and Grin!" ▶ If we could all take the time to educate our children, to avoid smokin' the dosia, and to better ourselves, this world would be hundreds of times better than it is now. **2000** Usenet: *rec.music.hip-hop* (Feb. 16) "Dinky (Some L.A. Street Knowledge...)" ▶ What, you think 'Rips just roll through 'Ru or Blood hoods and get out they cars, fuck with blood females, hit up, drink, and hit dosia on Damu blocks and Bloods dont react? ***2004** [Christopher Abad] *Ambient Empire* (Calif.) (Nov. 11) "Bay Area Slang" (Int.) ▶ *Dosia* n.—The marijuana, the weed, the pot or the hut. So no matter what you call it, grab those zig-zags and roller-up a twamp sack of that dosia.

Dover test *n.* a determination of what level of military losses, esp. war dead, will be tolerated by voters. *Military. Politics. United States.*

1994 Michael Ross *L.A. Times* (Sept. 24) "Pre-Election Battle Over Haiti Shaping Up in Congress Politics," p. 4 ▶ As it stands, congressional support for the Haiti mission is too thin "to pass the Dover test," said Sen. John Glenn (D-Ohio), referring to the Dover, Del., Air Force base where the bodies of any U.S. soldiers killed in Haiti will be flown. **2004** Chris Hall *American Narcolepsy* (Apr. 26) "A Quick Note on Opinion" (Int.) ▶ Since Vietnam, you may or may not have heard about the "Dover test," which a military official coined as the threshold for what Americans could take as acceptable losses to the country, to people, and to the psyche in times of war. Dover Air Force Base in Delaware is the official entry point for America's war dead. In the first Iraq War, the government banned media outlets from showing any returning deceased at Dover.

drab *adj.* wearing men's clothing; *dressed as a boy.* Also *n. Acronym. Fashion. Sexuality.* This term can apply to women, but it applies especially to cross-dressing or transvestite men who see traditional male clothing as *drab*, 'charmless; boring.' The common explanation of *drag* in the 1996 citation is a backronym, a fanciful initialism made after the word *drag* 'feminine attire worn by a man' already existed.

1994 *Usenet: alt.transgendered* (Mar. 3) "Re: Just Some Observations" ▶ I have worn nothing *but* switchable clothing when out and about in drab for the past 6 months, with no notice. I wear either oxford-cut blouses or women's turtlenecks, along with slim-fit lady's Levis and Reebok Princess sneakers. In fact, this has been so successful that part of this weekend's planned activities is a trip to the Goodwill dropoff place to give away all of my 'boy' clothing. **1996** *Usenet: rec.org.mensa* (Jan. 20) "Re: Reverse Discrimination—No Education for Men" ▶ "No men at RPI? They must be women in drag then."...) "That's 'drab.'" drag: DRessed As a Girl. drab: DRessed As a Boy. **2004** [androgy8] *Curiosity Killed the Cat* (Calif.) (Dec. 15) "Second Meaning for the Word 'Drab'" (Int.) ▶ I learned a new word just now: drab. Dressed As a Boy.

Driving While Teen *n.* an offense said to be committed by teenaged automobile drivers who are pulled over by police for (ostensibly) no reason at all. Also **DWT**. *Automotive.* This, like the similar term *DWB* 'driving while black,' is probably a play on *DWI* 'driving while intoxicated.' Another similar term, *DWO* 'driving while Oriental' is a derogatory description of the supposed bad driving habits of Asians.

1998 *Usenet: rec.autos.tech* (June 12) "Re: Drunken-Driving Penalties" ▶ "The driver has to drive in a fashion that would cause him to be stopped, intoxicated or not." "For instance: Scrupulously observing the speed limit. Driving While Teenaged. Driving While Black. Driving While Hispanic." **1999** G.D. Gearino @ Raleigh, N.C. *News & Observer* (E1) (Mar. 23) "Why Are Dads Like a Police State?" ▶ In fact, my daughter is convinced there's a traffic offense called DWT: driving while teen. **2000** *Usenet: alt.business.multi-level* (Jan. 7) "Why You Don't Need..." ▶ Ever heard of DWF or DWT? Driving while Female. Driving while a Teenager. Are you aware that these two "minority" groups are more likely to be stopped than are adult white males? **2000** Samantha Morin *San Diego Union-Tribune* (Calif.) (Mar. 17) "Teenagers: The Discounted Majority," p. B7 ▶ How many times have we been stopped on the road for DWT (Driving While Teen-aged)? No matter what guise it appears under, the prevalent message is that teen-agers can't be trusted. **2003** *Reno Gazette-Journal* (Nev.) (Feb. 6) "Editorials," p. 9 ▶ Is there something else that would make an officer suspicious—"driving while black," "driving while Hispanic" or even "driving while teenage"? **2005** Ben Westhoff *Riverfront Times* (St. Louis, Mo.) (Jan. 5) "Christopher Young Gives 'Loop Rats' Legal Advice—at a Deep Discount" (Int.) ▶ "That's the beauty of being seventeen," explains Young, who coined the acronym DWT, or Driving While Teen. "You're allowed to screw up, and you still get second chances."

drown night *n.* an event offering unlimited alcoholic drinks for a set fee; an all-you-can-drink happy hour. Also **drink and drown night.** *Food & Drink.*

1974 *Chronicle-Telegram* (Elyria, Ohio) (Dec. 26) "Big Dick Raps" (in advert.), p. H-3 ▶ On Sunday my deal is draft beer drink and drown night. My prices are the best in town. **1975** *Chronicle-Telegram* (Elyria, Ohio) (Feb. 14) "Big Dick Raps" (in advert.), p. 22 ▶ Every Sun. my special no rip off deal is 22¢ drink & drown night. **1976** *Color Country Spectrum* (Saint George, Utah) (Dec. 18) (in advert.), p. 3 ▶ Thursday Night Drink or Drown Night. 1 Price Covers It All: *Admission* Disco Dancing. All Draft Beer or Mix You Can Drink. **1985** Leo C. Wolinsky *L.A. Times* (Mar. 7) "Part of Crackdown on Drunk Driving Measure Takes Sober Aim at 'Happy Hours,'" p. 3 ▶ They were motivated to act, they said, in part by the kinds of promotions offered by some bars. Among those, Russell said, was a "drink and drown" night staged by one tavern and another that advertised its happy hour with the slogan, "Come in a car, leave in a coma." **1989** Ellen Miller @ Woodland Park, Colo. (*AP*) (Oct. 10) "Flash Cadillac Still Majors in Fun" ▶ Tulagi's, a saloon of some note in those years, initially booked Flash Cadillac for a "drown night," allowing students to drink unlimited amounts of beer for $1.75. **2001** Barbara Allen *Tulsa World* (Okla.) (Jan. 28) "Are You Ready for Some Football?" p. 1 ▶ The post-game show will feature karaoke and a drown night—$7 for all you can drink. **2005** *KAUZ-TV* (Wichita Falls, Tex.) (May 9) "Oklahoma Senate to Vote to Ban So-Called 'Drown Nights'" (Int.) ▶ A bill to ban so-called "drown nights" at beer bars is up for final approval this afternoon in the state Senate. The bill would stop promotions when unlimited amounts of beer are sold at a flat rate.

dry drunk *n.* a sober person who behaves as if drunk, esp. a recovering alcoholic who displays bad judgment; such behavior. *Jargon. United States.*

1891 *Arizona Republic* (Phoenix) (Nov. 17) "A Secret Way of Getting Drunk," p. 3 ▶ He has hit upon the "dry drunk" scheme as a way to indulge his appetite without hurting his conscience. He is employed as a porter, and every night before he quits work he takes particular pains in cleaning up the wine cellar. He devotes about twenty minutes to smelling the bunghole of a barrel containing a particularly strong brand of cognac, after which he staggers homeward with all the symptoms of a regular "howling jag." **1957** Morris Kaplan *N.Y. Times* (Feb. 24) "Addictions Study Cites 'Dry Drunk,'" p. 58 ▶ A non-alcoholic drunk—a person intoxicated with his own abstinence—was described here yesterday at a medical meeting.—Dr. Curtis T. Prout labeled such a person a "dry drunk."—The "dry drunk" was found to have grown almost obsessed with his changed existence. The maintenances of abstinence was associated frequently with a disturbed mind. Dr. Prout pointed out that addiction was characterized by a desire "toward an object and away from it." **2002** Katherine van Wormer *Counterpunch* (Oct. 11) "Addiction, Brain Damage and the President" (Int.) ▶ *Dry drunk* is a slang term used by members and supporters of Alcoholics Anonymous and substance abuse counselors to describe the recovering alcoholic who is no longer drinking, one who is dry, but whose thinking is clouded. Such an individual is said to be dry but not truly sober. Such an individual tends to go to extremes.

drylabbing *n.* the faking of laboratory test results, especially when the test has not been conducted. *Science.*

1986 William H. Meyers *N.Y. Times* (Dec. 7) "Miracle Merchant" ▶ University doctors have been known to blackmail drug companies, demanding payoffs for favorable test results. Sometimes they don't even conduct the tests they have been paid to perform—a process known in the trade as "dry labbing." **1993** Ullica Segerstrale *Contemporary Sociology* (July) "Judging the Fudging," vol. 22, no. 4, p. 498 ▶ This, arguably, begs the question and therefore may be seen by some as defending such practices as "trimming" (moving extreme data points closer to the mean) and "cooking" (selecting the best data), and who knows what other practices, stopping short of total "drylabbing." **2005** Ralph Blumenthal @ Houston, Tex. *N.Y. Times* (July 1) "Officials Ignored Houston Lab's Troubles, Report Finds" (Int.) ▶ For years, while rain from a leaky roof contaminated evidence in the Houston Police Crime Laboratory.... Officials even failed to take proper action when two laboratory analysts were cited for four instances of fabricating scientific evidence, or drylabbing.

dub *n.* an automobile wheel measuring twenty inches in diameter. *Automotive. Slang. Sports.*

[**1999** *Usenet: alt.auto.mercedes* (Dec. 3) "SV: E300D Mysterious Dash Light, Etc." ▶ I have Good Year Ultra Grip 400, with dubs, as my winter-wheels. Good tires, but i'm not sure you can get these in the US.]

2000 *Usenet: alt.autos.corvette* (Sept. 26) "Re: Bigger Wheels on a C5" ▶ "I was wondering how my c5 would look with 20″ wheels on the back and 19″ on the front (as appose to 18 in back and 17 in front)." "You're gonna put your vette on dubs, huh? Cool." **2004** Denny Lee *N.Y. Times* (Apr. 23) "The Dub Generation: Gearheads Go Hip-Hop" (Int.) ▶ Dub, a niche car magazine,...took its name from street slang for 20—as in a double-dime bag of marijuana—because when it was founded most oversize wheels were 20 inches in diameter.... G.M. became the first big carmaker to cross the 20-inch wheel threshold by unveiling its own line of dub-size rims. **2004** Mike Bresnahan *L.A. Times* (May 29) "The Art of the Wheel" (Int.) ▶ They have no function other than to look hip, their constant-motion appearance helping teens and early 20-somethings achieve status at a time where "dub-deuces" (22-inch wheels) and sparkling, showy rims are part of urban chic.

dub-dub *n.* a restaurant server or waiter. *Food & Drink. United States.* [Clipped pronunciation of first letters of *w*aiter and *w*aitress] Possibly specific to the TGI Friday's restaurant chain.

2000 @ Pittsburgh *Usenet: pgh.food* (Apr. 22) "Re: Monterey Bay, General Ranting" ▶ After the classroom training, you followed a "top ten" waiter/waitress (w/w—pronounced dub-dub) around for a week before you could even wait a table yourself. ***2004** *TGI Friday's* (Watford, U.K.) (Int.) ▶ Arzu is a "dub-dub" at TGI Friday's. Derived from the abbreviation for waiter/waitress—"W/W"—"dub-dub." **2004** *INQ7.net* (Makati City, Philippines) (May 22) "Minding the (Bar) Business" (Int.) ▶ Thus when a slot was opened at Alabang where he was a dub-dub (or server in Friday's lingo), he grabbed the opportunity.

dugout *n.* a beach-side shelter for surfers. *Sports.*

2003 *Desert Sun* (Palm Springs, Calif.) (Aug. 10) "Surfers Allowed to Participate in X Games for the First Time" (in Huntington Beach, Calif.) (Int.) ▶ Coaches swapped riders from a beach tent "dugout." Normally chill Florida surfers talked trash with Southern California rivals during lulls in the action. **2004** Mark Conley *Santa Cruz Sentinel* (Calif.) (May 15) "The Waiting Game: Lousy Surf Greets Team Surfing in Santa Cruz" (Int.) ▶ "I wish it were better," said Santa Cruz team member Omar Etcheverry as he pow-wowed with teammates in the so-called "dugout," a group of chairs perched atop a small scaffolding on the cliffs overlooking the break.

dump truck *n.* a lawyer seen as too willing to plead cases, especially a public defender. *Derogatory. Law. Slang.*

1984-1988 Debra S. Emmelman @ Calif. *Law & Society Review* "Trial by Plea Bargain: Case Settlement as a Product of Recursive Decision-making," vol. 30, no. 2, p. 351 ▶ Once they realize you're not resisting their demand to go to trial and their demand that they pay you some attention...then they will drop their resistance to a plea bargain based specifically on you as the dump truck who doesn't care about them. **1991** Paul M. Barrett *Wall Street Journal* (A1) (July 26) "Drug Lawyer Offers Feds a Sweet Deal: Crooks Who'll Fink—One After Another After Another; Then One Client Halts the Ponzi Scheme" ▶ Mr. Minkin is what some drug lawyers deride as a "dump truck," an attorney whose clients plead guilty and cooperate. Indeed, the 59-year-old Mr. Minkin says he is "second to none in...knowing how to make deals." **1993** Clayton Ruby *Globe and Mail* (Toronto, Can.) (Mar. 23) "Fifth Column; Law and Society," p. A22 ▶ *dump truck* (dump truk) *n.* Slang. A criminal lawyer who seldom fights a case, but who plea-bargains his way to a fast guilty plea. **1995** Tracey Tyler *Toronto Star* (Oct. 1) "High-Volume Lawyer Dodges 'Dumptruck' Tag," p. SU2/A1 ▶ Some lawyers contend that a handful of high-volume practitioners like Stern have bled the Ontario Legal Aid Plan dry by setting up veritable plea factories. They've even given them a name: "dumptrucks." **2001** Bryan A. Garner *Dictionary of Modern Legal Usage* (Mar. 1) ▶ Clients often refer to their public defenders as "dump trucks," a term that apparently derives from the defendants' belief that defenders are not interested in giving a vigorous defense, but rather seek only to "dump" them as quickly as possible. **2005** Deborah Sontag *N.Y. Times* (Mar. 20) "Inside Courts, Threats Become an Alarming Part of the Fabric" (Int.) ▶ "One of the cruel ironies is that on the tier in any prison, the person most inmates name as responsible for them being there is 'the dump truck P.D.,'" said David Coleman, the public defender in Contra Costa County, Calif. "Thus, the razor or weapon used against a public defender is all too common." ***2005** *Law Office of David Alan Darby* (Tucson, Ariz.) (Mar. 20) "Arizona DUI" (Int.) ▶ "Dump truck" is what attorneys call other attorneys who mostly just plead their clients guilty, instead of trying cases.

duster *n.* a dry, non-producing oil-prospecting hole. *Jargon.*
1881 *Democrat* (Olean, N.Y.) (Aug. 4) "Allegany Field," p. 1 ▶ Wells, rigs, drilling and dusters all appear in greater force than they did in the proceeding [*sic*] month. The latter class however are not in quite as strong force as the public outside of this field evidently anticipated. Four so-called dusters are paying producers, two of the same being wells of a superior grade, while the two remaining ones will pay a handsome interest on the investment and possibly enable the investort [*sic*] to lay by something against the proverbial rainy day besides. That this field has been presistantly [*sic*] discriminated against and the character of its wells purposely misrepresented by the cowardice

or jealously of outside capital, either or both, cannot be denied. **1906** *Times-Democrat* (Lima, Ohio) (Sept. 10) "Running River of Oil Fills Ohio Ditches," p. 3 ► The Ohio Oil company has drilled in a duster in a test on the M. Colter farm, section 35. **1954** *Great Bend Daily Tribune* (Kan.) (June 20) "Operators End Week with 88 Completions from as Many Starts," p. 2 ► Stafford County had one pool start, one wildcat duster, a pool completion and a duster in a pool start. **1982** Midge Richards *Sunday Oklahoman* (June 13) "Legendary Wildcatters Turned Oil Fever into Fortunes" ► These are some of the legendary wildcatters who drilled many a duster and brought in countless great gushers during Oklahoma's first historic oil boom. **2005** Matt Jenkins *Vail Trail* (Colo.) (Jan. 13) "The BLM Wields Fork and Spatula Over the West's Wildlands" (Int.) ► El Paso Corp. drilled another dry hole— which the industry calls a "duster"—just 200 feet from the six-year old Amoco hole.

DYKWIA *n.* an abbreviation of *"do you know who I am?"* said to be used by celebrities or others seeking special privileges. Also *attrib. Acronym.*

1997 Alan Mcmillan *Scottish Daily Record & Sunday Mail* (Glasgow, Scotland) (Apr. 21) "A Dutch Out of Order" ► I'm told Ally had lost his voice and was ordering drinks by sign. L for lager, ML for more lager and DYKWIA for do you know who I am? This came in handy if lager was ever refused. And if he was really bad come closing time, he had DYKWIL—do you know where I live? **2000** *Usenet: alt.tv.polincorrect* (Oct. 8) "Re: Step on the Scale, Bill..." ► "Bill probably gave the cop the old 'don't you know who I am' routine and pissed him/her off." "I don't know how ya'll respond to DYKWIA in California, but in Nashville, nothing will get you nowhere quicker than that phrase." **2004** Mike Murdock *Reverend Mike's House of Homilectic Hash* (Mar. 9) "Attitude Is Everything" (Int.) ► I'm only speculating here, but given everything else I've ever read about Martha, I wonder if she fell victim to DYKWIA Syndrome—"Do you know who I am?" I have relatives in law enforcement, and I could easily imagine their response to such an attitude—"Why, yes I do know who you are, prisoner number 26845."

E

eat up the camera *v. phr.* in movies, to be appealing or engaging on screen. *Entertainment.* This term is distinct from *eat the camera*, which is sometimes said of an actor whose face fills the screen.

1998 Esther Hecht *Jerusalem Post* (Israel) (Aug. 14) "A Model Child?" p. 18 ► Beyond looks, a child has to exude personality and a passion for the camera, she says. "They have to eat up the camera." **2003** Angela Mulholland *CTV.ca* (Can.) (Nov. 25) "Jim Sheridan Gets Personal 'In America'" (Int.) ► The girls rewarded him with their tremendous talent. They practically eat up the camera when they're on screen. **2005** Dutch Boyd *Because Everybody Pays Their Own Way* (Fresno, Calif.) (Apr. 24) "Smoking Cigarettes and Watching Captain Kangaroo" (Int.) ► Both of those guys are great characters and eat up the camera. **2005** *Yahoo! News* (Apr. 25) "Malik Makes His Screen Debut" (in India) (Int.) ► Vipul told me that he liked my confidence in Indian Idol, and the way I speak, and the way I eat up the camera. **2005** *Native American Times* (May 3) "Producers Seeking Some Good-Looking Natives" (in Hollywood, Calif.) (Int.) ► Thunder Mountain media is currently conducting a talent search for Native American men and women between the ages of 18 and 50 that, as they say in Hollywood, "eat up the camera." The producers say they are looking for people who are photogenic.

eco-roof *n.* a roof planted with vegetation. *Environment. Jargon.*

1996 *Building* (Oct. 18) "It's Turf at the Top," p. 71 ► Hines argues that there are sound technical reasons to use an eco-roof. "A grass roof protects the roof membrane on flat roofs from extremes of temperature and also blocks ultra-violet light, which helps the membrane last longer," he says. **2004** Art Chenoweth *Daily Vanguard* (Portland State Univ. [Ore.]) (Apr. 27) "'Sustainability' Is the Key" (Int.) ► The eco-roof is a roof that is planted in cactus and other water-retaining vegetation.

ecotone *n.* an area where two ecologies meet or overlap. *Environment. Jargon. Science.*

1906 H.L. Shantz *Botanical Gazette* (Sept.) "A Study of the Vegetation of the Mesa Region East of Pikes Peak: The Bouteloua Formation. II. Development of the Formation," vol. 42, no. 3, p. 179 (Int.) ▶ In most places under natural conditions there seems to be an ecotone, a place of equal aggressiveness, between this formation and the Bouteloua formation. **1982** Ian Mulgrew *Globe and Mail* (Toronto, Can.) (Feb. 16) "Seattle Suggests Deal with B.C. Over Flooding of Skagit Valley," p. P11 ▶ The Skagit Valley is hailed as a unique ecotone, an area of 1,000-year-old forests where two climatic zones overlap. As a result, plant and animal hybrids are common, all of which would be wiped out by the flooding. ***2003** *Ecotone: Writing About Place* (Int.) ▶ An ecotone is a term from the field of ecology. It is a place where landscapes meet—like field with forest, or grassland with desert. The ecotone is an area of increased richness and diversity where the two communities commingle. Here too are creatures unique to the ecotone...the so-called "edge effect."

Ecozoic *n.* an (imaginary) era in the future when humans live in harmony with nature and the Earth. Also *adj. Environment.* [This term was popularized and probably coined by Thomas Berry. From Greek *oikos* 'house' + *zoikos* 'of animals.']

1991 Thomas J. Billitteri @ Saint Leo *St. Petersburg Times* (Fla.) (May 18) "Defenders of Nature" ▶ In [Rev. Thomas] Berry's view, the planet is moving out of the 65-million-year Cenozoic era, during which the major developments of life occurred, into a new uncertain age he calls the Ecozoic. "The major developments of the Cenozoic took place entirely apart from any human intervention," he says. "In the Ecozoic the human will have a comprehensive influence on almost everything that happens." **1992** Thomas Berry *Art Journal* (Summer) "Art in the Ecozoic Era," vol. 51, no. 2, p. 46 (Int.) ▶ To reestablish the Earth in a viable situation requires a transition from the terminal Cenozoic era to what might be called the Ecozoic era. **2001** Rich Heffern *National Catholic Reporter* (Mar. 16) "Spinners Weave Wisdom Ways," vol. 37, no. 20, p. 16 ▶ In Vermont, Sr. Gail Worcelo and lay associate Bernadette Bostwick, together with their community of Passionist nuns, are starting an Ecozoic Monastery in the Green mountains. They hope to soon found the first Catholic community of nuns in the world dedicated to healing the Earth. ***2004** *Center for Ecozoic Studies* (Nov. 7) "Ecozoic Era" (Int.) ▶ The term the "Ecozoic Era" refers to the promise of a coming era when humans live in a mutually enhancing relationship with the larger community of life systems. The Ecozoic Era could also be called the "ecological age."

ecuavolley *n.* a form of volleyball with a high net, three players per side, and permissive ball-handling rules. *Ecuador. Spanish. Sports.* [*Ecua*dor + *volley*ball] This game originated in Ecuador but is increasingly visible in other countries.

1990 Phyllis White; Robert White *St. Petersburg Times* (Fla.) (Jan. 7) "Ecuador: A Blanket Bargain," p. 1E ▶ There's also a court where the local game, played fiercely here, is "Ecuavolley," a version of volleyball with a high net and only three players on each side. Any gringo not used to exercising at this altitude will last about the first 10 minutes. **1999** Rudi Colloredo-Mansfeld *Native Leisure Class* (Nov. 1), p. 22 ▶ Aside from water taps and electric poles, Ariasucu's only public infrastructure is a concrete volleyball court. Beginning around three o'clock in the afternoon, men of any age gather to play three-a-side "Ecuavolley," betting the equivalent of a day's wages on the outcome. **2000** Wilma Roos *In Focus Ecuador* (Oct. 1), p. 66 ▶ The other favorite is the more obviously named *ecua-volley*, a game played between two teams of three. According to ecuavolley rules, the net hangs at a height of at least six feet and players are allowed almost to catch the ball before throwing it over the net, a skill disallowed by orthodox volleyball. **2005** Nathan Thornburgh @ Danbury, Conn. *Time* (Aug. 1) "Serving Up a Conflict" (Int.) ▶ What's to blame for the moral rot? It's not drug dealing or gang wars. In Danbury the vice, according to local officials and longtime residents, is volleyball. Specifically, "ecuavolley," a form of the game so beloved in Ecuador that when Ecuadorians began migrating en masse to this small working-class New England city, they built backyard courts all over town, some big enough to accommodate up to 150 fans and players.

Ediacaran *adj.* having characteristics of, belonging to, or designating the Precambrian geological period of the Neoproterozoic Era, 600 to 542 million years ago. Also **Ediacarian, Vendian, Neoproterozoic III.** *Science.* [< Ediacara Hills of South Australia]

1983 H.J. Hofmann, W.H. Fritz, G.M. Narbonne *Science* (July 29) "Ediacaran (Precambrian) Fossils from the Wernecke Mountains, Northwestern Canada," vol. 221, p. 455 ▶ The term "Ediacaran fauna" refers to a Late Precambrian assemblage of fossils of soft-bodied animals, mainly coelenterates and annelids, first discovered in the Ediacara Hills of South Australia.... Sparse but nevertheless worldwide finds of the Ediacaran fauna have prompted a call for an Ediacaran (or Ediacarian) Period and system (1–3). **2004** *BBC* (U.K.) (May 17) "Geological Time Gets a New Period" (Int.) ▶ Geologists have added a new period to their official calendar of Earth's history—the first in 120 years. The Ediacaran Period covers some 50 million years of ancient time on our planet from 600 million years ago to about 542 million years ago. It officially becomes part of the Neoproterozoic, when multi-celled life forms started to take hold on Earth.

ego ramp *n.* a proscenium, catwalk, runway, or stage spur that extends into or over an audience. *Entertainment.*

1992 Jon Bream *Star Tribune* (Minneapolis-St. Paul, Minn.) (Aug. 4) "Guns N' Roses and Metallica Bring Different Worldviews to Their Monstrous Summer Tour," p. 1E ▶ We've got an oval thrust stage, and there's people [fans] inside it in a type of pit. Then when Guns goes on, they cover it up and he [Rose] has got his ego ramp to go out on. So it worked out pretty good. **1995** *Charleston Gazette* (W.Va.) (Feb. 22) "Boyz II Men Lays Claim to Spotlight," p. P3D ▶ Even the gimmicks—a for-real rain shower in "Water Runs Dry" and a hanging "ego ramp" that allowed for a romp deep into the crowd on "Motownphilly"—were tastefully applied. **2001** *Usenet: alt.music.u2* (Jan. 14) "Re: Golden Circle Seats...How Good Are They?" ▶ If you want to be anywhere near the very front of the stage, the "ego ramp" or "catwalk" (whatever you want to call 'em) you would want the General Admission Floor. **2004** Clay Robison *Houston Chronicle* (Tex.) (Sept. 1) "President to Deliver Address on Special Stage" (Int.) ▶ A 10-hour construction project had begun to erect a new, island-like stage from which President Bush will deliver his acceptance speech tonight surrounded by delegates. It will be the first such use of an island or arena stage—also known as an ego ramp—at a national political convention.

elephant *n.* a site containing very large mineral or petroleum deposits. *Jargon.*

1979 *Wall Street Journal* (Aug. 27) "Hottest U.S. Hydrocarbon Hunt Is in Western Rock Formation" ▶ Though more than a thousand discoveries are made in the U.S. yearly, "elephant fields"—those containing proven recoverable reserves of 100 million barrels of oil, one trillion cubic feet of gas, or the equivalent in mixed reserves—are rare. **1985** James Cook *Forbes* (June 17) "Armand's New Elephant," p. 66 ▶ It is sitting on what looks like the biggest new oilfield since the North Sea and Mexico offshore: a giant, by oil industry standards, if not yet exactly an elephant—Cano Limon, in Oxy's 2.7 million-acre contract in Colombia. **2003** Brent Jang *Globe and Mail* (Toronto, Can.)

(Nov. 25) "Penn West Prefers to Play at Home," p. B15 (Int.)
► Squeezing out the last drop from existing energy plays makes sense when so many rivals are going overseas to hunt for "elephants"—industry jargon for huge conventional reserves. **2004** *Bloomberg.com* (Oct. 27) "Ivanhoe Seeks Riches Selling Output of Mongolian Mine to China" (Int.) ► Vale threw a party in Ulan Bator with samba dancers flown in from Brazil to mark the company's arrival in Mongolia to search for another "elephant"—mining parlance for a big discovery.

en chinga *adv.* fast, hurriedly, quickly. *Colloquial. Mexico. Spanish. United States.* [From the Spanish *chingar* 'to copulate; to screw.']

1997 *Usenet: alt.california* (Apr. 3) "Mexi-Threats in So. Cal." ► This means that we are heading into an economic depression, pero en chinga. Jobs will be no more and the peso will be worth more than the dollar. **1999** *Usenet: soc.culture.mexican.american* (Oct. 1) "Re: David Gleaser Donde Esta" ► Stoy aqui pero ando en chinga. Right now I'm cranking out the implementation of a Framework Based Software Synthesis system based on the Uniform Modeling Language. **2004** *Daily Texican* (Dallas, Tex.) (Aug. 11) "Cholo Word of the Day—En Chinga" (Int.) ► Well, I'm not sure if this is necessarily a "cholo" word, but it's pretty damn close. I have to post "en chinga."...Meaning According To DT: haste, fast, freakin' quick, in a hurry (might be considered a curse word, depending on who you're talking to).

endo *n.* **1.** a bicycling accident in which the rider is thrown forward over the handlebars. **2.** an intentional bicycle stunt that lifts the bike's rear tire off the ground. *Jargon. Sports.* [Perhaps from *end-over-end.*]

1987 Ray Hosler *San Francisco Chronicle* (Dec. 7) "Turning Sharp Corners Can Be a Balancing Act," p. E4 ► Going over the bars is known as an "endo" in bike jargon, and is one of cycling's more hazardous maneuvers. **1990** *Usenet: rec.bicycles* (Feb. 13) "Re: Brake Positions" ► This is so that when you are dismounting and have both legs on the left side of the bike, and your right hand is on the top tube or seat—you can still brake (hard) with your left hand without endo-ing. **1990** *Usenet: rec.bicycles* (July 2) "Re: Drop Bars for Mtn Bikes (LONG)" ► If you're down low in the drops, I think it would be impossible to jump over the bars during an endo. **2003** [eclipse2000] *Beyond.ca* (July 3) "Bike Tricks" (Int.) ► To pull an endo get going a little bit and then slam on your front brakes and lean forward, but not too hard or you will flip. **2004** Mark Davis *Pioneer Press* (St. Paul, Minn.) (May 2) "'Downhill' Follows Peaks and Valleys of a Mountain-Bike Legend" (Int.) ► Her life turned upside down, an "endo" in biking parlance. Her brother and best friend, Mark, died in a tragic accident overseas. **2004** [Mat] *BMX Wastelands* (May 6) "Re: Some Flatland Tricks" (Int.) ▶ hey im gona tell you how to do an endo. there is many ways to do an endo but this is my favorite go at a slow speed then quickly shove your foot in the front tire and lean forward be careful not to flip it now it seems like a basic trick but once you can do it really good it will improve your bunny hop.

estacode *n.* funds intended to cover traveling costs (of an athlete, politician, etc.). *Money & Finance. Nigeria.* [Perhaps from the non-public *Estacode*, the unofficial rules of British civil service (covering all matters of conduct and discipline, including conflicts of interest and political activities) that eventually became the Civil Service Management Code. The Estacode began about 1944.] The term is usually a collective noun but is sometimes also used as a count noun.

[**1993** David McKie *Guardian* (U.K.) (Feb. 4) "The Fall of the Houses of Poulson," p. 2 ▶ What there wasn't was any attention to the Estacode which governs the lives of senior civil servants and says you must never accept gifts from those with whom you have official connections.] **1994** James Jukwey @ Lagos, Nigeria (*Reuters*) (Jan. 21) "Nigerian Money Changers—Illegal But Flourishing" ▶ Many people did, including military and other government officials who exchanged estacode, foreign exchange given to them for overseas trips, on the black market rather than in banks. **1994** Utibe Ukim *Newswatch* (Lagos, Nigeria) (Oct. 24) "Where Is the Money?" ▶ An NNPC official told Newswatch last week that the corporation had become the source of free fund for government. "The practice is that the ministry passes over some expenditures to the corporation to pay and debit it later. But the refund is hardly made by the ministry." He cited the case of payment of estacodes to ministry officials by the corporation. As at June, the corporation had paid N140 million to the ministry as estacode allowance. **2000** *Post Express* (Lagos, Nigeria) (Oct. 13) "The Rise and Rise of Cameroon Sydney 2000 Fall-Out" ▶ No fewer than eight Ministers accompanied the team to USA and were drawing heavy chunks from the scarce estacode, leaving the players to scrounge. **2005** Bisi Lawrence *Vanguard* (Lagos, Nigeria) (Jan. 27) "Waiting for the Repeal" (Int.) ▶ Overseas travel allowances, also known as "estacode," provides a rich source of money for those who are billed to travel with the national teams or other teams engaged in international competitions.

Eurabia *n.* the (perceived) political alliance of Europe and Arab nations (against Israel and Jews); a name for Europe if its Muslim or Arab immigrants become a large or powerful minority. *Jar-*

gon. Politics. [*Euro*pe + A*rabia*. Bat Ye'or is usually given credit for this term, although citations earlier than her claimed first usage exist.]

2001 *Usenet: nl.politick* (Nov. 17) "Nieuwe naam voor Europa" ▶ Net tegengekomen op een Berber-forum. Eurabia...Tja, wat niet is kan zeker nog komen. **2002** Sam Orbaum *Jerusalem Post* (Israel) (Apr. 26) "Resentment and Revenge," p. 31 ▶ Within 50 years those poor anti-Semitic Christian Europeans will be overwhelmed by a Crusade in reverse, in a veritable Eurabia. **2002** Bat Yeor *National Review* (Oct. 9) "Eurabia" ▶ The ministers and intellectuals who have created Eurabia deny the current wave of criminal attacks against European Jews, which they, themselves, have inspired. **2004** Niall Ferguson *N.Y. Times* (Apr. 4) "Eurabia?" sect. 6, p. 13 (Int.) ▶ The Egyptian-born writer Bat Yeor has for some years referred to the rise of a new "Eurabia" that is hostile in equal measure to the United States and Israel. **2004** Alessandra Rizzo @ Rome, Italy (*AP*) (Apr. 5) "Fallaci's New Book Hits Bookstores in Italy" ▶ Describing Europe as "Eurabia"—a mix of Europe and Arabia—Fallaci said the continent "has sold itself and sells itself to the enemy like a prostitute."

eveninger *n.* a newspaper published for evening distribution, or an edition of such a newspaper. *Media.* This term is now common only in Anglophone Asia.

1944 AP @ Madrid, Spain *Chicago Daily Tribune* (Mar. 5) "Germans Dry Up a Golden Oasis in Monte Carlo," p. 4 ▶ Here is what the Eveninger Madrid's correspondent reports of the gloomy last night of Monte Carlo. **1965** AP @ Budapest, Hungary *Post-Standard* (Syracuse, N.Y.) (Dec. 9) "Hungary Exports Cowboy Blue Jeans," p. 20 ▶ The Budapest Eveninger Esti Hirlap said the last consignment of an important order from Lebanon had just been routed to Szeged, a south Hungarian town. **1982** *Xinhua* (China) (Jan. 12) "Iranian Deputy Industrial Minister Shot Wounded" (in Tehran, Iran) ▶ Hojjatoleslam Hassan Monfared, deputy industrial minister of Iran, was the target of a new assassination attempt and narrowly escaped here yesterday, according to eveningers here today. **1996** *Business Today* (India) (July 22) "Credibility Crisis," p. 130 ▶ That was the day when the managing director of Coltex India, a subsidiary of the New York-based Coltex Inc., had picked up the copy of Mumbai's leading eveninger kept in his car to read on his way home from work—as had been his practice for years—with the screaming headline: Bis Ordered to Probe Ingredients Used by Cleentooth. **2005** Meghdoot Sharon @ Ahmedabad *Business Standard* (India) (Feb. 24) "Sambhaav to Hit City Stands in Tabloid Avataar on March 12" (Int.) ▶ Two vernacular eveningers in the form of broadsheet, Western Times and Aajkal are already existing in the Ahmedabad market and Aajkal reportedly has a wider circulation than Western Times.

eve-teasing *n.* harassment of, or sexually aggressive behavior toward, women or girls. *India. Pakistan. Sexuality.* [The term most likely references the biblical Eve, the supposed first woman.]
1960 *Times* (London, Eng.) (Apr. 22) "Protection for Indian Girl Students" (in Delhi, India), p. 9 ▶ One aspect of the problem of student indiscipline which is plaguing university authorities in India has been the bullying and harassment of girl students in the few coeducational institutions—a pastime so common that it has been given the name of "Eve-teasing."…"Eve-teasing" is not, apparently, just the oafish high spirits or ill will of a handful of male students but is rather a symptom of the strong resentment which many students feel against women in the universities. **1963** Selig S. Harrison *Washington Post, Times Herald* (D.C.) (Oct. 26) "The Sad State of India's Youth," p. A8 ▶ Police officials have been discovering that the collegiate enthusiasts who prowl streets in Indian cities are not content to watch the girls go by. Indian newspapers have carried accounts of police roundups in Srinagar, Dehra Dun and other centers for indecent advances at bus stands and traffic intersections…. Happy headline writers have dubbed the new offense "Eve-teasing." **1974** T.K. Oommen *Asian Survey* (Sept.) "Student Politics in India: The Case of Delhi University," vol. 14, no. 9, p. 787 (Int.) ▶ Goondaism refers to anti-social behavior of persons who generally indulge in violent and other "illegitimate means" to get things done…. While their student friends go to the classes, they sit in coffee houses or on lawns of the University and indulge in "eve-teasing." **1978** Ursula M. Sharma *Man* (June) "Women and Their Affines: The Veil as a Symbol of Separation," vol. 13, no. 2, p. 232 (Int.) ▶ To snatch a girl's *dupatta* is one of the forms of "eve-teasing" which occurs on many a school bus. **1984** *Guardian* (U.K.) (Oct. 2) "When the Teasing Had to Stop" (in New Delhi) ▶ Buses in Delhi are notoriously the worst place for "Eve-teasing"—the Indian term which covers everything from sexual harassment, pestering, groping, whispered obscenities as well as light-hearted cat calls and equivalents of "hello darling." **1986** *Houston Chronicle* (Tex.) (May 4) "Girl-Watching Violates Islamic Dictates in Pakistan" (in Islamabad, Pakistan), p. 15 ▶ Eve teasing or "Eve watching" is watching or trying to meet women, and both are illegal in Pakistan. **2005** *Times of India* (Apr. 25) "Men at Work" (Int.) ▶ "Eve-teasing," a peculiarly Indian euphemism for lewd taunting, was one indignity visited on women on the streets.

Eye-wreck *n.* a jocular name for Iraq. *Iraq.*

2001 *Usenet: soc.history.what-if* (Oct. 16) "Re: WI the Terrorists Win?" ▶ If we are ever attacked with Ebola or Plague you will see some major league dying. Of course if that happens the U.S. was go on a rampage. Allah help Afghanistan and Iraq (which will soon become eye-wreck). **2004** [John Koch] *Just World News* (July 21) "Ground-Level Reports from Inside Iraq" (Int.) ▶ None of the "that stuff in Eye-Wreck" news will fit the American categories of perception and discourse. Hostile Iraqis, Abu Ghraib, gesticulating clerics, robed jihadist, incessant street bombings—none of these things fit the script. **2004** [Tickyul] *Drudge Retort* (Dec. 25) "GOP May Challenge Wash. Governor Recount" (Int.) ▶ After 9-11 one of the first things we should have done was secure the borders of this country, not go to trashcanistan and meddle with a bunch of savages. Look at eye-wreck, what a fucken mess.

F

fairy ring *n.* a naturally occurring ground circle caused by fungi or other biological agents; figuratively, a fanciful ring or circle of mystical or unusual behavior or action. *Biology. Environment.*

1844 *Ohio Repository* (Canton, Ohio) (Jan. 11) "The Paradise of Contentment," p. 1 ▶ The rosy horizon beyond which youth cannot see—the gay rainbow that overarches fancy's landscape—the halo that genius spreads around the barren pathway of existence—the green and fairy ring encircling over the beloved! **1855** *N.Y. Daily Times* (2) (Oct. 25) "The Newcombes" ▶ Our poor friend the Colonel, disappointed in his first scheme, hopefully blesses the union, and prays once more for that domestic happiness which he fondly believes can only be found within the fairy ring of home. **1872** *N.Y. Times* (Mar. 3) "Fairy Rings," p. 2 ▶ Everyone who is accustomed to the country knows a "fairy ring" when he sees it. Each ring is only a belt of grass of a much darker green than that surrounding it.... If the grass of these "fairy rings" be examined in the Spring and early Summer, it will be found to conceal a number of agarics or "toadstools." **1984** Richard A. Kerr *Science* (Feb. 10) "Why Are There Any Nodules at All?" vol. 233, p. 577 ▶ Some sediment dweller has built its mound hard against a nodule. And on the left is a "fairy ring" of unknown origin that seems to be slipping and perhaps rolling nodules into its moat. **1984** *Globe and Mail* (Toronto, Can.) (May 26) "The Price of Success in the Lawn Care Trade" (in Plainview, N.Y.) ▶ Property values, neighborhood competition and the challenge of nature aside, the suburban psyche will not rest while the hairy chinch bug and the fairy ring fungus are at work. **1990** Leo Schofield *Sydney Morning Herald* (Australia) (May 22) "Cholesterol People, Beware," p. 3 ▶ For a minute there we thought some radical new accompaniment might break the spell of this fairy ring of cloned presentations. **2004** Joe Rigney *Santa Cruz Sentinel* (Calif.) (July 22) "Redwood's Amazing Biology Makes Them Survivors" (Int.) ▶ Evidence of logging is best visualized by the way redwoods grow in rings, sometimes referred to as "fairy rings." These are caused by the resprouts that grow around a stump. You can get a sense of how big the original tree was by measuring the inside of the fairy ring.

fan service *n.* a feature, inside joke, or obscure reference included in entertainment primarily to please a core fan group, or a work of entertainment expressly created for that purpose; (*hence*) in anime and manga, visuals that include nude or semi-nude figures. *Entertainment. Sexuality.*

1991 *Usenet: rec.arts.anime* (Nov. 15) "Re: Silent Mobius" ▶ I think the movie was made for fan service and/or to investigate the potential market for bigger project. **2000** *Usenet: rec.arts.anime.misc* (Dec. 1) "Re: What's a Fan Service?" ▶ Fan service is anything in media that is there because the creators think it will please the fans, not because it advances plot, theme, character, or any other overall value of the work. **2003** Judith S. Juntilla *BusinessWorld* (Philippines) (May 16) "The Matrix Reloads—Where's That Damn Spoon," p. 38 ▶ Now we come to The Matrix. Fans of this movie are a different lot. Not only do you have to satisfy their craving for gee-whiz visual effects, you also have to live up to their lofty expectations of what has been called "The Thinking Man's Action Movie." These are Star Wars fans all grown up; they've been betrayed by George Lucas who churned out prequels that were no more than fan service. **2004** Susan J. Napier *Japan Spotlight* (Japan) (Mar. 1) "Why Anime?" ▶ That these themes are presented in a package of giant robots, monsters and "utterly puerile fan service" components of adolescent sexuality and humor make it a truly unique experience.

fantouche *adj.* fancy, extravagant, frivolous. Also **fantoosh.** *Scotland. Scots.*

1947 *Dictionary of the Scots Language* (Int.) ▶ There are quite a number who consider it more fantoosh to do their shopping in Perth. **1996** *Usenet: soc.culture.celtic* (May 25) "Re: Cernunous" ▶ It seems to me very like the situation in England; Scots is closer to the short-word phase, having lost all its fantoosh expressions when it lost its Court and fashionable people in the 1600s. **2000** *Usenet: alt.tv.x-files* (Aug. 10) "Re: News from Locarno?" ▶ We'll watch some Mitch and later, I'll try out my sister-in-law's fantouche recipe on you. ***2003** Simon Taylor *Scottish Place-Name Society* (Scotland) (Aug. 5) "About the Scottish Place-Name Society" (Int.) ▶ Onomastics is the "leirit or fantouche" word for the study of names of all kinds, especially personal and place-names.

feather lift *n.* a delicate method of cosmetic surgery involving implanted cords that lift and pull. *Health. Medical.*

2002 Carla Wheeler *Press-Enterprise* (Riverside, Calif.) (June 25) "Light Like a Feather," p. E1 ▶ Barnes recently underwent a Feather Lift, a new cosmetic procedure imported from Russia that employs a tailor's tools and works by implanting a small, surgical nylon thread under the skin to lift sagging skin in the chin, cheek, eyebrow, jaw or neck areas. **2004** *Fashion Week Daily* (June 4) "How L.A. Fashionistas Spend Their Summers" (Int.) ▶ Checking out the new "Feather Lift." The secret password of this L.A. summer. Some plastic surgeons are already experimenting in the hottest new development in plastic surgery in years: doing less invasive (and quick healing) surgeries with lifting skin with cords attached from one internal area of the face to another.

Fedders house *n.* a cheaply made apartment building, specifically those featuring highly visible window air conditioner sleeves bearing the brand name "Fedders." *Architecture. NYC.* This term is specific to New York City and is usually plural, *Fedders houses*, in an echo of naming terminology for government-sponsored apartment complexes, such as *Walt Whitman Houses*. It was coined by Victoria Hofmo, a community activist from Bay Ridge, Brooklyn.

2004 Paul Berger *Gotham Gazette: Community Gazette for District 43* (NYC) (Feb. 7) "Bay Ridge: Fighting the Fedders Houses" (Int.) ▶ Last year, a group took to the streets to protest the loss of their homes to condominiums and co-ops—buildings they have labeled "Fedders houses" after the air-conditioning units that protrude from the outside walls. **2004** *NYC Department of Urban Planning* (NYC) (Oct. 18) "City Planning Certifies Zoning Proposal to Preserve Character of Bay Ridge, Brooklyn" (Int.) ▶ The recent proliferation on detached house blocks of multi-family housing, characterized by some as "Fedders buildings" for the name on the air-conditioning sleeves, prompted local officials to request that Department of City Planning (DCP) study the area. **2005** Greg Mango *Brooklyn Papers* (NYC) (Mar. 12) "In Bay Ridge, Fedders Doesn't Mean Cool" (Int.) ▶ Perhaps most vocal among the complainants decrying the development of "Fedders houses," as they have come to be known, are residents of Bay Ridge, whose neighborhood awaits city approval of a rezoning measure that would bar such housing developments. So ugly and bland are those buildings, say some, that their most striking architectural trait may well be the air conditioner sleeve itself.... "I would hope the houses are as well built and as high quality as the air conditioners they're named after." The colloquialism, while originating by most accounts in Bay Ridge several years ago, has spread to all corners of the city in recent months.... Bloomberg has used the term "Fedders houses" on numerous occasions and, said Coffey, uses it when referring to zoning measures in other neighborhoods and boroughs.

feederism *n.* a fetish in which pleasure or sexual gratification is taken from the overfeeding or intentional fattening of one's self or one's partners. *Food & Drink. Health. Sexuality.*

1995 *Usenet: alt.sex.fat* (Feb. 22) "Re: Now I'm REALLY Confused—" ▶ Ok, but you're grouping and therefore comparing feederism with violent, aggressive, pain-oriented pastimes, which is a big-time misrepresentation. **2003** Theodora Sutcliffe *Mirror* (U.K.) (Mar. 1) "Relationships—Having It Large," p. 8 ▶ It might sound like an unusual thing to have a fetish about but, thanks to the Internet, feederism is on the increase. By surfing the web, feeders and feedees can put a name to their "preference" and find a host of cyber-friends to discuss the joys of feeding with—and even a partner. **2004** *(National Assoc. to Advance Fat Acceptance)* (Apr. 29) "Against Feederism" (Int.) ▶ The practice of feederism is defined as the promotion of intentional weight gain for the sexual pleasure of oneself or another person. People engaging in the active practice of feederism are referred to as feeders and feedees. Feederism is also known as "encouraging," and its participants as "encouragers" and "gainers."

femtosecond *n.* 10 to the −15th power or 0.000000000000001 second, equaling a quadrillionth of a second or 0.3 light microns. *Science. Technology.* [Danish or Norwegian *femt*, from *femten* "fifteen" + *-o*. *Femto* was established as a standard prefix equaling 10 to the −15th power by the International Union of Pure and Applied Physics in 1961.] Commonly used in measurement of light in laser or light-related technologies.

1997 Katie Walter *Science & Technology* (Livermore, Calif.) (Oct.) "A New Precision Cutting Tool: The Femtosecond Laser" (Int.) ▶ Other major U.S. manufacturers are looking into incorporating femtosecond machining systems into their production lines. In manufacturing, new materials are constantly appearing, and the features on all kinds of devices are becoming smaller and smaller. **2001** *Physics Web* (Bristol, U.K.) (Feb. 21) "Beating the Femtosecond Limit" (Int.) ▶ The shortest visible and infrared laser pulses are typically just a few femtoseconds...in duration and contain just a few cycles of the laser field.

ferret legging *n.* an endurance test or stunt in which ferrets are trapped in pants worn by a participant. *Animals. Entertainment. Sports.*

1986 Diane Petzke *Wall Street Journal* (Apr. 4) "The Pet of the Year Isn't a Pinup or a Pup But It Is Just as Cute—It Is the Mischievous Ferret, Furred in Designer Colors" ▶ For many years, Englishmen have competed at something called "ferret-legging"—dropping ferrets down their trousers as a sort of endurance sport. **1993** *Usenet: alt.sports.darts* (Feb. 4) "Re: Darts???" ▶ I've got the perfect self-indulgent sport for this...get. Ferret Legging. First, one puts on a pair of woolen trousers. Underwear is illegal. Second, rope is secured around the cuffs at the ankle. Third, two hungry ferrets are dropped down the top of the trousers. Fourth, a belt is pulled tight to seal the waist. Fifth, the happy contestant has to stand there and see how long he can take it. **2004** Skot *Izzle Pfaff* (Aug. 11) "So Very Special" (Int.) ▶ Of the four people who actually showed up, three were betting on ferret legging, and the other one was, horribly, actually doing work.

fiending *n.* craving, desiring, wanting, obsessing (over or about). *Hip-Hop. United States.* This term originally referred to drug addicts but is now trivialized and generified. It acts primarily as a verbal noun. *Feenin* is a very common alternate spelling popularized by the song of the same name by the hip-hop artist Jodeci on the 1993 album *Diary of a Mad Band.*

1988 Don Terry *N.Y. Times* (Sept. 4) "'Everybody Is Crying and Sad': Slain Ice Cream Vendor Is Mourned," p. 42 ▶ "Whoever did it," the man said, "must have been fiending for drugs, that's all they do around here. They tried to rob an ice cream truck. I mean how much money is on an ice cream truck. That's stupid." **1989** Paul Vitello *Newsday* (Long Island, N.Y.) (Jan. 22) "Day of Promise, Night of Waste," p. 6 ▶ He was afraid the crack house would sell out. This happens. Cops call it the "fiending" frenzy. **1990** James Kindall *Newsday* (Long Island, N.Y.) (Jan. 21) "On Streets to Nowhere," p. 10 ▶ Almost all can tell tales of confrontations with irate Johns or fellow street people who began "fiending" (striking out in a furious need for more drugs). **1992** *Usenet: alt.rodney-king* (May 5) "Rhyme" ▶ You've seen it, they mean it, now I'm fiending for a bum rush. **1994** *Usenet: alt.rap* (Apr. 1) "Re: What Does Feenin' Mean???" ▶ "Feenin'" = "fiending." you know like wanting. a crack fiend, a microphone fiend. **1995** Jacinda Abcarian @ Berkeley, Calif. (*NPR*) (Dec. 27) "Youths Give Perspective on Tobacco Controversy Segment Number: 13 Show Number: 2074" ▶ Throughout high school, I watched as many of my friends tried to balance going to class and fiending for the next hit. "Fiending" is just an expression my friends and I use to describe how crazed smokers get when they're looking for a cigarette. **2000** *Usenet: alt.consumers.free-stuff* (Feb. 1) "Re: Sparks.com $10 Off No Min.... Free Shipping" ▶ Sheesh, me and my chocolate feenin!!! lmao! **2004** Gail Mitchell *Billboard* (U.S.) (Sept. 4) "LaBelle Ringing," vol. 116, no. 36, p. 19 ▶ "People are fiending for real R&B again," he says. "All the

sampling has brought people's minds and ears back to real music."
2004 [Laurabee] *Tell Laura I Lo-ve Her* (Sept. 26) (Int.) ▶ Feenin.
Yeah. As in I was feenin for a night on the town with a side of partay.
Feenin as in "he was feenin for her something bad." Feenin as in "you
got me feenin."

fifi *n.* a masturbatory substitute for a vagina. Also **fifi bag, fifi
towel.** *Crime & Prisons. Sexuality. Cassell's Dictionary of Slang,*
edited by Jonathan Green, dates the term *fifi bag* to the 1960s
and connects it to the adjective *fifi* 'effeminate,' giving both terms
a U.S. designation. A similar term is *muff bag.*

1998 *Usenet: alt.anger* (June 9) "Re: What the Hell Happened?"
▶ Actually, the instructions for such an organic liaison originate with
the invention of the famous "fifi bag," used since the first horny prisoner in some long ago jail cell discovered that a rubber glove, or bag-
gie, or sheep's bladder, or anything else that would hold intact some
substance such as raw liver, or hand lotion, or even some nice, warm
oatmeal would be, with just a dash of imagination, a better-than-
nothing replacement for the warm, slick inner walls of one's favorite
orifice. This discovery led to the realization that a great many of our
little green and yellow buddies (as zappa called them) could be used
in much the same way. **2000** *Usenet: alt.music.stone-temple* (Apr. 7)
"Re: Irving Plaza" ▶ Scott even asked people who listened to Howard's
show if they tried his Fifi (sock, rubber glove, Vaseline) contraption.
Someone also told me that KROCK aired parts of the concert on the
radio. **2002** Jeffrey Ian Ross, Stephen C. Richards *Behind Bars: Surviving Prison* (May 7), p. 186 ▶ *Fifi.* Artificial vagina; sex toy. **2003**
Noah Levine *Dharma Punx* (June 1), p. 45 ▶ One day in the shower he
explained to us how to make a Fifi—a prisoner's pocket pussy. **2003**
Gavin McInnes *Vice Guide to Sex and Drugs and Rock and Roll* (Sept.),
p. 190 ▶ A Fifi towel is a homemade vagina. Simply take a small
towel, fold it in half, and roll it into a tight cylinder. Then keep it that
way using elastic bands. To make the vagina realistic, inmates insert a
rubber glove into one of the ends. The wrist of the glove is folded
over the edge of the towel and tucked under the elastic bands. After it
is secure, the glove is filled with Vaseline and then inserted into the
first glove and tucked under the same elastic. The hot water melts the
Vaseline and makes it feel warm and soft. Like a woman. **2005**
[spawnsong] @ Montreal, Can. *Make Your Sister Think I Love Her*
(May 11) "The Road to Hell Is Paved with...Socks" (Int.) ▶ Actually, in
Juvie, they used to call it a Fifi and it was a rubber glove instead of a
sock.

filthy stuff *n.* in baseball, good pitching. *Sports. United States. Stuff as a term for a pitcher's ball delivery has a long history in baseball, dating to at least as early as 1905. Filthy stuff is also a euphemism for money.*

[**1997** Tom Krasovic *Sporting News* (St. Louis, Mo.) (Sept. 1) "Me and My Shadow," p. 30 ▶ I don't know how the hell Ashby gave up five runs.... His stuff was so filthy.] **1997** Gordon Edes @ Toronto, Can. *Boston Globe* (Sept. 26) "It's the Crowning Blow," p. D5 ▶ It's a lot more fun catching Clemens than it is hitting against him. Roger was nasty. He had filthy stuff. **2003** Dan Mcgrath *Chicago Tribune* (Sept. 7) "The Arm and the Man," p. 13 ▶ Clemens, from the Houston suburb of Katy, is his acknowledged heir with 300 wins, 4,000 strike-outs and a nasty disposition, still dealing "filthy" stuff and still intimidating hitters at age 41. **2004** John Crowley *San Francisco Examiner* (June 23) "Giants Take Over1st" (Int.) ▶ Other than a pitcher with "filthy stuff," as they say in dugout parlance, nothing can kill a hitting streak like over-analysis.

Finnegan pin *n.* a nonexistent part or tool; a thing whose name is forgotten or unknown; a **doo-dad** or **thingamajig**.

***1938-39** A.T. Rosen @ Brooklyn, N.Y. *LOTJ* "Gas Station Slang" ▶ Finnegan pin...[*struck*] a vague expression to cover the fact that something in the car in [*sic*] wrong but not yet exactly known, a who-sis, etc. Its [*sic*] akin to the slang expression, a paper-stretcher, or left-handed pencil. [*end struck text*] Nonexistent auto part which mechanic blames for trouble he cannot locate. **1941** *L.A. Times* (Jan. 13) "Psst...Here's That Man Again" (in advert.), p. A12 ▶ It seems they wanted to remove my carbon and install new Finnegan pins all around and now I'm so healthy I've got Johnny Weissmuller scared striped about his Tarzan work. **1968** In *DARE* (1991) Frederic Cassidy, Joan Houston Hall, et al., pp. 420-21 ▶ Finnegan pin...A nonexistent object used as the basis of practical jokes.... A finnegan pin in the muffler gear. **1998** Merton R. Hubbard *Choosing a Quality Control System* (Dec. 9), p. 75 ▶ Don't pay any attention to any of that *fun* stuff. We're here to make Finnegan Pins; if they want fun, they can do it on their own time. **1999** Denis Hamill *N.Y. Daily News* (June 29) "Nuts Over Assembly Instructions at My House," p. 5 ▶ To put the fan together, first you must hacksaw through the bolts of an overhead grate, crawl through the 18-inch rat-infested duct, attach the back fan guard to the steel Finnegan pin, descend a six-story greased drain-pipe, outrun six Rottweilers.

flash-bang *n.* an explosive device that emits noise and light but is not intended to cause damage. *Military. Police.* **Flash-bang grenade** is the full, more-common, form.

1985 *L.A. Times* (Jan. 26) (in San Diego), pp. 2-8 ► Police officers shot a "flash-bang" grenade into an Ocean Beach apartment late Thursday, then burst through the doors and arrested three men on narcotics charges. **1985** Patricia Klein, Stephanie Chavez *L.A. Times* (Feb. 9) "Pacoima Leaders Protest Police Use of Motorized Ram" ► Police Capt. Cunningham cited a December drug raid in which a woman was killed when a police diversionary explosive device, commonly known as a "flash bang," was hurled into a rock house. Other officers, however, said a "flash bang" device was also used in Wednesday's raid. **2005** Stephanie Heinatz *Virginian Pilot* (Norfolk, Va.) (Aug. 4) "State Trooper Is Injured by Flash-Bang Grenade" (Int.) ► While the flash-bang, as they are called in the trade, looks, operates and explodes much like a grenade, it's meant to cause shock, not damage, police said.

flavor saver *n.* facial hair, specifically a beard tuft beneath the lower lip.

[**1986** *Usenet: soc.singles* (Sept. 25) "Lynn Gold Wants to Know 'Why Oral Sex...'" ► I have a tube of toothpaste to clean up with a little later...and a bar of soap to clean up the flavor saver—er—beard and moustache. **1996** *Usenet: rec.music.gdead* (May 15) "Re: Did Jerry Prefer Hostess or Drake's?" ► My housemate calls those little, tiny, under the lip pieces of beard (a la grunge musicians) a "flavor saver." **1997** Bernie Lincicome *Chicago Tribune* (Oct. 5) "Bickering Bulls Will Be the Life of The NBA," p. 1 ► And before we forget it, just what is that growth of hair under Jackson's lip, anyhow? "Jud Buechler calls it a flavor saver," Jackson said. "It's my Frank Zappa look." **1999** Jean Patteson *Orlando Sentinel* (Apr. 30) "Little Bit o' Soul the Soul Patch—Barely There Facial Hair—Grows Popular," p. E1 ► Of all Piazza's assets, the one most easily shared by other cool guys is that close-cropped triangle of chin hair known as a soul patch, flavor saver or cookie duster. **2000** Colin Devenish *Limp Bizkit* (Oct.), p. 163 ► Fred's belief is that *Nature's Cure* will be the vehicle that drives him to become the only movie mogul with a backward hat and a flavor-saver. **2003** Andy Lochrie *Fish Lips* (Nov.), p. 163 ► That triangle of hair below my lower lip is called a flavor saver, soul patch, or nub buffer.

flip *v.* to force oneself to vomit, esp. among horse-racing jockeys. *Slang. Sports.*

1985 Wayne Johnson *Seattle Times* (July 19) "Life on the Fast Track—Each Day, a Jockey Must Wage a Tough Struggled to Keep Ahead of the Rest," p. C1 ▶ Not even high-fashion models watch their weight closer than jockeys do. Ideally, a jockey should weigh 112 or less. "A lot of jocks eat, eat, eat and then puke, puke, puke. It becomes habitual with them. We call 'em flippers, because they'll stuff down a shake and french fries and then go flip it all up." (In the toilet area of the jocks' room, there's a hand-lettered sign: "No flipping in first two stalls.") **1991** Joe Sierra *Washington Post* (Apr. 28) "Pound for Pound, a Most Dangerous Sport; Bulimia Common Among Jockeys," p. D1 ▶ Bulimia is prevalent enough that jockeys casually refer to it as flipping, or heaving. **2004** Sherry Ross *N.Y. Daily News* (Apr. 28) "Weigh in on Riders" (Int.) ▶ "It's hard for me to feel sorry for guys that are driving three Mercedes and living in million-dollar homes and worrying about six or seven pounds because they have to 'flip,'" Lukas said. (Flipping is racetrack parlance for self-induced vomiting.)

FLOHPA *n.* collectively, the states of Florida, Ohio, and Pennsylvania, said to be important in the 2004 United States presidential election. *Acronym. Jargon. Politics. United States.* [From the postal codes for the three states: Florida, *FL*; Ohio, *OH*; Pennsylvania, *PA*.] **2004** Ben Elberger (*Dem Swingers*) (May 2) "Florida, Ohio, and Pennsylvania (FLOHPA) Voter Registration Info" (title). **2004** [Eric] *ToughEnough.org* (July 9) "FLOHPA vs. The Edwards Strategy" (Int.) ▶ Setting all else aside, most experts would agree, whoever goes two for three in the states of Ohio, Pennsylvania and Florida (FLOHPA) wins the election. **2004** [mapantsula] *Daily Kos* (Oct. 22) "FLOHPA" (Int.) (title). **2004** John Mercurio, Molly Levinson *CNN* (Oct. 28) "Eight States Too Close to Call" (Int.) ▶ If Kerry wins Florida, Ohio and Pennsylvania—the battleground trifecta being referred to as "FLOHPA"—Bush would need to hold all of his red states and win two Democratic-leaning states. **2004** *Hotline* (Washington, D.C.) (Oct. 28) "The State of Flohpa" ▶ While it's perfectly logical for one to assume that the candidate who wins a majority of FL, OH and PA (or "flowpa" as we call this 68 EV-heavy virtual state), nothing should be assumed conventional.—With Bush renewing his focus on MI and continuing intensity in NH and MN, one can get Bush to 270 without ANY of the FLOHPA states.

flyero *n.* a person who distributes handbills or fliers, usually a Spanish-speaker. *California. Spanglish. United States.* This term appears to be specific to Santa Ana, Calif. **1994** Agustin Gurza *Orange County Register* (Calif.) (Feb. 6) "Are Fliers Handed Out on Fourth St. a Boon or Bane?" p. B1 ▶ They call themselves Los Flyeros—The Flier People—and they say it with a certain esprit de corps. They stand on street corners and in doorways along Fourth Street, swooping into the path of passing pedestrians, offering fliers for everything from bridal gowns to abortions, palm readings to tax returns. **2004** Jennifer Mena *L.A. Times* (May 2) "To Some, the Best Remedy" (Int.) ▶ Clinic owners—usually private-practice doctors—hire *flyeros*, as they are known in Spanglish, to distribute fliers in the 4th Street shopping district in Santa Ana, a city where 74% of the population speaks Spanish.

flying fox *n.* a hand-grip or riding car suspended by pulley from a cable along which one can roll above the ground; a zip line. *Australia. Canada. New Zealand. United Kingdom.*

1989 Tim Treadgold *Business Review Weekly* (Australia) (Nov. 3) "The Escape and the Challenge of Adventure," p. 108 ▶ Afternoon activities might include a paddle on Merribrook's trout-filled lake, a bushwalk, bike ride or, to cater for those over-active kids again, a trip down what is billed as the world's longest flying fox, a 400-metre "zipwire" journey across a grassy valley. **1997** *Evening Post* (N.Z.) (Dec. 16) "Pools Make a Holiday Splash" ▶ New at Naenae Pool will be the Zipline, a 40-metre flying fox with a drop of five metres. **2004** Peter Kuitenbrouwer *National Post* (Ontario, Can.) (June 4) "Dundas Square Finally Makes Sense" (Int.) ▶ At another spot, visitors grab a "flying fox," also known as a zip line, and fly through the air 8.9 metres over a sand pit, the long jump Olympic record Bob Beamon set in 1968.

fobbit *n.* a soldier or other person stationed at a secure forward operating base; (*hence*) someone who seeks the security and comfort of a well-protected military base. *Iraq. Military.* [forward operating base + hob*bit*]

2004 Steve Smith @ FOB Bernstein, Iraq *ArmySteve* (Nov. 12) "Fob-bits and Other Iraqi Critters" (Int.) ▶ Those of us who conduct missions "outside the wire" on a regular basis have come up with a variety of terms to refer to those who remain safe and comfortable on base. The most common one lately has been "Fobbit," referring to those short, fat, hairy creatures that live in little holes and rarely venture out into the world (see Tolkien for more info). I've also seen some units refer to them as FOB Dwellers, with one platoon of Bradleys stenciling the letters FUFD on their back hatches (FU FOB Dweller). Prior to deploying, non-combat troops were usually referred to as REMFs, where RE stood for Rear Echelon (and MF you can guess), but that term seems to have been replaced by Fobbit here. **2005** David Zucchino *L.A. Times* (Mar. 27) "Comforts of Home Amid Perils of Iraq," p. A1 ▶ Administrative specialists who never leave the fob are known, with some condescension, as fobbits. Like every soldier here, a fobbit could be killed at any time by a random rocket or mortar round. But on most days the greatest danger to a fobbit's health are the three heaping, deep-fried daily portions of mess hall food. **2005** Anna Badkhen *San Francisco Chronicle* (June 6) "Appointment in Samarra" ▶ According to soldiers at Patrol Base Uvanni in central Samarra...everyone at Brassfield-Mora, or any other FOB, is a Fobbit. But...1st Lt. Jason Scott...narrows down the definition: a Fobbit is someone who never goes out of a FOB except to go to another FOB. Sgt. Christopher Caulk, 37, from Hawaii, a medic at Brassfield-Mora, is more specific.... "If a mortar round hits your FOB and you can't hear it because your FOB is so big, you're a Fobbit. If you have more knives than you have hands and you act like John Wayne, you're a Fobbit.... If you're out in a Bradley (fighting vehicle) and you close the hatch when you receive small-arms fire, while the gunner at the Humvee is fighting back with his 50-cal (machine gun), you're a Displaced Fobbit. You're out on the front line, but you belong on a FOB." **2005** Edward Lee Pitts (*AP*) (July 9) "Stories from Embedded Journalists with U.S. Units in Iraq" ▶ If you think leaving "the wire" might be a fun adventure, you might be a fobbit, and if the second time you'll be off the FOB is on leave, you might be a fobbit. **2005** Sri Lausier @ Camp Liberty, Iraq *MaineToday.com* (July 18) "Living in Iraq" (Int.) ▶ I am a sentry in our FOB (forward operating base). I am what people call a Fobbit, because I never leave the "wire."

Foblish *n.* stilted or incorrect English spoken or written by a non-native speaker. *Acronym. Derogatory. Slang.* [From *FOB* "fresh off *b*oat" + Eng*lish*.]

2002 [Vy Ngoc Khanh Vo] @ Montebello, California *s.u.r.r.e.a.l. e.x.i.s.t.a.n.c.e.* (Feb. 6) "My Day in Review" (Int.) ▶ Albie and I went to the SG Soopa-See-tore (NO, it's not Latin—that's just Foblish) where she bought some paper. **2002** *T Today* (Taipei, Taiwan) (Oct. 2) (Int.) ▶ Or you are just speaking "foblish." Foblish = Fob's English. Fob = L.A. people's term for new immigrants that can't speak English correctly. **2002** [School (Skewl)] *School's Blog* (Oct. 24) "It Begins..." (Int.) ▶ My head's been out of whack for the past 2 weeks, anybody who has talked to me during that time probably knows what i'm talking aboot (misspelling, breaking/dropping crap in chem lab, speakee in foblish, etc.) otherwise not being my normal, grammatically-perfect, smooth self. **2002** [FariMaMa] @ Florida *Islamica Community Forums* (Nov. 8) "The SAMAR Thread" (Int.) ▶ Cuz she dont speak foblish and you do. **2003** [kw0n] @ Japan *descend from grace* (Dec. 18) "[Janelle in Japan IV] End of JSP" (Int.) ▶ Your English hasn't gone downhill, you've just learned to speak some fabulous foblish! **2004**

[jkan2001] *Club RSX Message Board* (Mar. 19) "Spec-V Drove an RSX-S Again Today—Comparison of Sorts" (Int.) ▶ Your foblish command of the English language might have been a problem. **2004** Min Jung Kim *BrainDump* (July 23) "Sure Thing" (Int.) ▶ I wind up speaking pidgin Foblish to poppa.

fooding *n.* a restauranting trend that emphasizes food as a style choice, usually via new or fusion cuisines in combination with factors not related to food, such as a unique or trendy atmosphere. < *English. Food & Drink. France. French.* [The term is usually said to be a combination of English *food* and feel*ing*.] In French, it takes the masculine article: *le fooding.*

2000 *Le Figaro* (Paris) (Apr. 5) "La note, s'il vous plaît..." ▶ O. P. A. Ni tout à fait club ni vraiment resto, un bon spécimen du «Fooding» que ce loft arbitrant «groove», bar et nourritures mouvance à un public «glamorama». **2000** Sara Saez *El Mundo* (Spain) (June 12) "El fooding (del inglés food, comida), la última pasión por experimentar con la cocina" ▶ Es el nuevo «deporte» de mesa: la de la típica casa de comidas con menú del día o la del restaurante más sofisticada. Una moda para paladares inquietos con sus propias tendencias. No hay soirée que se precie que no comience por una buena cena ni negocio bien cerrado que no se haya firmado sobre un mantel. Así reza el primer mandamiento del fooding (del inglés food, comida), la última pasión por experimentar con la cocina que viene pegando fuerte desde Londres y París. **2000** Guillaume B. Decherf *Libération* (Paris) (Dec. 2) "Le fooding, du flan pour la crème ▶ Le fooding veut marier food (nourriture) et feeling (sentiment): soit l'art d'ingérer des nourritures terrestres avec spiritualité sur un fond musical planant. **2004** Fay Maschler *Evening Standard* (U.K.) (July 21) ▶ It was difficult to gauge whether this microcosm of ultra-modern Japanese fooding—as the French call the combination of eating and lifestyle—will give the area a different buzz, magnifying the quiet hum already emanating from the Spanish Fino. **2004** Jennifer Paull *Fodor's Blog* (Aug. 24) "Free Fooding in Paris" (Int.) ▶ One of my favorite bits of franglais is the word le fooding. The meaning of this contraction of "food" and "feeling" is slippery, but it relates to a trend of fresh, original cooking that's taking hold in France. **2004** Alison Tyler *Evening Standard* (U.K.) (Oct. 8) "Sexe Et La Citè...The £1,000 Paris Weekender" ▶ Go "fooding." No, it's not a typo, but a new Parisian word to describe the concept of food as a fashion lifestyle choice. Le fooding is as much about the ambience and style of the restaurant as the food on your plate.

food insecurity *n.* the state of, or risk of, being unable to provide food (for oneself, a family, a nation, etc.). *Food & Drink. Health. Jargon.*

1983 *Globe and Mail* (Toronto, Can.) (Oct. 20) "Food Prospects Are Bleak, Club of Rome Leader Warns," p. P11 ► In the past, the concept of food security could never become a cultural value, because food insecurity was then the norm. Only more recently, since it has been shown that enough food could be produced to satisfy all human needs, has food security become a moral and humanitarian issue. **2004** Sharon Emery *Grand Rapids Press* (Mich.) (Apr. 21) "Economy Dishes Up Hunger Pains" (Int.) ► Driving the "food insecurity" numbers—a term coined by the federal government to measure hunger—is Michigan's stubborn unemployment rate, the anti-hunger research and policy group said. **2004** *Workers World* (NYC) (Apr. 1) "Is the Glass Half Empty or Half Full?" (Int.) ► There was a 15 percent increase between 1999 and 2002 in the number of U.S. households facing "food insecurity"—1.5 million families. Overall, this translates into more than 12 million families not knowing where their next meal will come from due to layoffs and low-wage jobs with no benefits.

foot facelift *n.* surgical or cosmetic enhancement of the feet. *Fashion. Medical.*

1997 Paul McInerney *Illawarra Mercury* (Australia) (July 16) "Raffle Rigmarole a Riotous Laugh," p. 11 ► During a pedicure (that's a foot facelift) this week, the beautician explained she was using a paddle-like instrument that used to be known as a pedi-file. Since the Wood Royal Commission hearings, they have been known as pedi-paddles! **2003** Sarah Baxter *Times* (London, Eng.) (Aug. 10) "Women Cut Off Toes to Wear Stilettos," p. E2 ► Dr. Suzanne Levine, who operated on Richards, is known as the "foot facelift doctor." She performs about 300 foot operations a year, a phenomenon she ascribes to the reluctance of women to accept middle age. **2004** Jane Common *Daily Star* (U.K.) (Apr. 18) "Steps to Heaven," p. 11 ► The latest craze to hit Britain from New York is the foot facelift. Originating with catwalk models, it involves Restylane being injected into the balls of the feet to give them extra padding and make wearing high heels more comfortable. **2005** Laila Weir *East Bay Express* (Calif.) (Jan. 5) "The Designer Foot" (Int.) ► Dr. Oliver Zong is a New York podiatrist who has built his career around cosmetic foot surgery. He offers "toe tucks" to slim the pinky toe and "foot facelifts" to narrow and beautify the whole foot.

foot fault *n.* in jurisprudence, a minor criminal or procedural violation; a legal misstep. *Jargon. Law.* [This is a direct borrowing from net-based sports, such as tennis, badminton, and volleyball, where a *foot fault* is the placement of a foot outside the baseline when serving.]

1997 Coffey Eschbach, Diane P. Wood @ Ill. *FindLaw* (June 9) "U.S. Court of Appeals for the Seventh Circuit: No. 96-3406" (Int.) ▶ This argument rests on a procedural foot fault that our circuit has held should not defeat jurisdiction where the district court asserts its jurisdiction by directing proceedings even in the absence of a formal grant of leave to appeal. **2000** John M. Allinotte, Glen S. Pye, David V. Daubaras, David M. Penney, et al. *Tax Executive* (Jan. 1) "Misrepresentation of a Tax Matter by a Third Party," vol. 52, no. 1, pp. 64-70 ▶ TEI is highly concerned that even the slightest misstep—a mere foot fault—by a corporate employee could lead to Draconian personal penalties. **2001** John Gilmour *Sydney Morning Herald* (Australia) (Mar. 17) "How the Big End of Town Makes Its Own Rules," p. 48 ▶ Telstra suffered a judicial humiliation when it was constrained from making false and misleading statements about charges for its services and in what might be regarded as another foot fault, it was forced to give refunds to customers who were overcharged. Some little mistake that. Just $45 million. **2003** Dahlia Lithwick *Slate* (Dec. 3) "The Wing Nut's Revenge" (Int.) ▶ [Antonin] Scalia, the only justice on Favish's side today, puts it bluntly to him: "We have relatives here who will be very much harmed. You've demonstrated some foot faults, the investigators made mistakes. Who cares?" **2004** Bill Barnhart *WGN-TV* (Chicago) (June 13) "Wall Street vs. A State That Cries Foul: Watch This Trial" (Int.) ▶ But if the jury finds against Forstmann, a cascade of copycat litigation and reform proposals could erupt. "We will all examine every inch of what occurred and find out if there was a foot fault that was justifiable."

fourth point of contact *n.* especially among Airborne personnel, a euphemistic term for the rump, buttocks, or anus; by extension, one's body, person, or self. *Military. Slang.* [The information in the 2002 citation probably refers to the correct origin of the term.]

1992 *Usenet: rec.sport.football.pro* (Oct. 15) "Yes! The Football Gods Have Answered!" ▶ Let's hope that the Bills coaches get their heads out of their fourth point of contact for tomorrow night's game. **1997** *Usenet: rec.games.mecha* (Jan. 21) "Re: WoB" ▶ His opponent had his head so far up his fourth point of contact he practically served the level III to the SCol on a platter. **2000** Geoff Metcalf

SaveOurGuns.com (Aug. 14) "Do What You Gotta Do" (Int.) ▶ If I have a choice between supporting a whoosy Republican intent on pressing for enforcement of unconstitutional bad law or a blue dog Democrat who is a 2nd Amendment absolutist, the collaborating Republican can kiss my Airborne fourth point of contact. **2001** Robert Bateman *Armor* (Jan. 1) "An Infantryman's Thoughts on Armor," vol. 110, no. 1, pp. 11-12 ▶ You can bitch and whine all you want that armor "shouldn't be used in cities," but you know what?...if they put my "fourth point of contact" in a city, you can bet I am personally going to be screaming for armored support. **2002** Richard R. Burns *Pathfinder: First In, Last Out* (Feb. 26), p. 6 ▶ I had no problem climbing onto the bed of the truck, since I was ten pounds lighter in my fourth point of contact.... p. 394: The fourth point of contact when performing a parachute landing fall is the buttocks. **2004** Luis Canales @ Seale, Ala. *Columbus Ledger-Enquirer* (Ga.) (Mar. 16) "Sorry Veteran" ▶ I am sorry I was in the 1/27th Infantry freezing my "fourth point of contact" on the Big Island when the veterans were in Grenada and Lebanon. **2005** David Shrauger *Living Iraq Journal* (Jan. 16) "When I Say Mission..." (Int.) ▶ This is aside from the normal everyday Military jargon such as a "fourth point of contact" (Posterior region).

fourwalling *n.* in the movie industry, directly renting theaters to show a film rather than selling the distribution rights to a third party. *Entertainment. Jargon. United States.*

1974 Stephen Farber @ Los Angeles *N.Y. Times* (Feb. 24) "So You Make a Movie—Will the Public Ever See It?" p. 105 ▶ The example of "Billy Jack" is being studied by everyone in the industry. Tom Laughlin, the producer, director and star of the 1971 film, was dissatisfied with Warners' distribution of the film, so he went out and dealt directly with the exhibitors. Under his careful strategy, the film was recently re-released by Warners to astonishing business.... John Rubel, vice president of Billy Jack Productions, explains Laughlin's "fourwalling" scheme that proved so successful on re-release: "Instead of the usual percentage deal, we rent the theater for a week so that we become in effect the exhibitor of the film." **1974** Charles Foley *News Journal* (Mansfield, Ohio) (Oct. 27) "'Four-Walling' Hikes Movie Profits," p. 3 ▶ How, in these inflationary times, do you persuade the public to pay $23 million to watch your old home movies, mixed in with some stock wildlife footage? Answer: You call the confection the "Great American Something," or simply the "American Something"— and you four-wall it.... This new marketing technique, so-called because the film-maker literally rents the theater's four walls himself, has already made fortunes.... Dub's astonishing success is due almost

entirely to his adroit use of four-walling. **2003** Joe Bob Briggs *Reason* (L.A.) (Nov.) "Kroger Babb's Roadshow" (Int.) ▶ Kroger Babb, who billed himself as "America's Fearless Young Showman," ruled over a vast army of Mom and Dad "roadshow units" from his headquarters in Worthington, Ohio. He used a form of exhibition that has all but disappeared today, called "fourwalling." Instead of booking his film into theaters for a percentage of the box office, he would simply rent the theater outright and take it over for the week or, in smaller markets, just one or two days. He would pay for all advertising and promotion, put his own banners and marquees out front, and turn the theater into a midway attraction, complete with lobby curiosities designed to lure customers.

fragged *adj.* planned; outlined in a fragmentary order, or FRAGO. *Jargon. Military. United States.*

1995 @ Natal, Brazil *Air Force News Service* (Oct. 26) "AF Deploys to Brazil for First Time Since WW II" in *Usenet: sci.military.moderated* (Oct. 31, 2004) Sysop Afpan "Air Force News Service 26oct95" ▶ "We have flown everything as fragged," Cantres said. "Today was the first day of flying and the box score reads 12 scored, 12 flown, 9.7 flying hours." **2002** Pete Wilkie *Flying Safety* (U.S.) (Oct.) "Situational Awareness [Lucky or Good?]" ▶ Without both preparation and experience, tactical lessons and execution fall short of ideal. The mission may come off "as fragged," but the learning curve remains stagnant. **2004** Rahul Singh @ Ambala, Haryana *Times of India* (Aug. 20) "IAF Marathon Flyers Outpace the Best" (Int.) ▶ They didn't understand that when the Americans said "as fragged" they meant "as planned," the Indian parallel for "hack" was "time-check" or that the US pilots called "fess up" to own up a mistake.

FRAGO *n.* In the military, a (hasty or sudden) change or amendment to a previous operational order; a *frag*mentary order. Also **frago, frag.** *Acronym. Military. United States.*

1998 Wayne Barefoot *Military Intelligence Professional Bulletin* (Jan. 1) "Keys to S2 Success at JRTC," vol. 24, no. 1, p. 48 ▶ Targeting meetings should result in a fragmentary order (FRAGO) to subordinate units. **2002** *Usenet: comp.sys.ibm.pc.games.strategic* (Oct. 27) "TacOps Gazette 02.02" ▶ Could call this a "FRAGO" style exercise. When the players first assemble online they have no choices with regard to the initial tactical disposition nor organization of their unit markers. They get a simple frag order and one hour to cross the line of departure. **2003** Steven Lee Myers @ Baghdad, Iraq *Washington Post* (Apr. 13) "Discovering Doubt and Death on Drive Toward Baghdad," p. A1 ▶ The Army has lots of acronyms. One is Frago, short for fragmentary order, or a change in the main attack plan. **2004** (*NPR*) (May 24) "More Troops for Iraq?" (Int.) ▶ When they get their FRA-GOs as they call it, their fragmentary orders, they're very focused on how to carry that out the following day.

frankenbite *n.* in the making of reality television shows, several recorded clips edited seamlessly together. *Entertainment. Television.* [*Franken*stein's monster + sound *bite*. *Franken* is a classic portmanteau word that, no matter where it is attached, connotes something unholy patched together from many sources.]

2004 William Booth @ L.A. *Washington Post* (Aug. 10) "Reality Is Only an Illusion, Writers Say," p. C1 ▶ The reality stories have a beginning and middle and end, shaped by writers who are called not writers but "story editors" or "segment producers," who use the expression "frankenbites" (after Dr. Frankenstein's monster) to describe the art of switching around contestant sound bites recorded at different times and patched together to create what appears to be a seamless narrative. **2004** Kevin Arnovitz *National Post* (Can.) (Oct. 16) "Realityspeak: Reality Television Has Developed a Nomenclature All Its Own," p. SP5 ▶ Frankenbite...An edited reality show snippet, most often found in contestant testimonials, that splices together several disparate strands of an interview, or even multiple interviews, into a single clip. A frankenbite allows editors to manufacture "story"...efficiently and dramatically by extracting the salient elements of a lengthy, nuanced interview or exchange into a seemingly blunt, revealing confession or argument. While the frankenbite's origins certainly don't reside in reality TV, this is a reality show editor's most potent tool for manipulating viewer perception of a contestant. **2005** Richard Verrier *L.A. Times* (June 21) "Reality Show Writers Seek Representation" (Int.) ▶ Writers also splice together comments to create story lines and manufacture drama. In industry parlance, it's an editing process known as "Frankenbite."

fratmosphere *n.* an environment resembling or affiliated with a college fraternity.

1997 Shannon Wells *Charleston Gazette* (W.Va.) (Apr. 10) "Michigan's the Verve Pipe Prepped for Success," p. P1D ▶ Though Brown, at 35, is the oldest member in a band with an average age of 30, all of the guys in the verve pipe plan to remain settled in the East Lansing area, where the "fratmosphere" of Michigan State University gave the band its initial boost. **1999** *Usenet: alt.non.sequitur* (May 1) "Re: White Salve Triad to Be Held at Dale's House?" ▶ Thinking strikes you as humorless, intelligence destroys your fratmosphere of innuendo and mooning the dean. **2005** (*PR Newswire*) (June 13) "Zagat Releases

2005/06 NYC Nightlife Survey" (in NYC) (Int.) ▶ There's a brand-new word coined by a Zagat surveyor—"Fratmosphere"—describing nightspots reminiscent of a fraternity house.

freeball *v.* to not wear underpants (beneath clothing); **to go commando.** *Fashion. Sexuality. Slang.* Although this term usually applies to men, as you can see by the 2002 citation, it is sometimes applied to women.

1990 *Usenet: alt.sex* (Nov. 30) "Re: No Underwear" ▶ I have gone "free-balling" [as I heard it called]. One just has to be more conscious and slower when zipping, ouch %-{ It was comfortable. **1993** *Usenet: alt.tasteless* (Nov. 7) "Re: Cats Bloody Cats" ▶ This same friend free-balled one day...and was forced to wear his denim jeans while running the 440 meter in his gym class. **2002** Rebekah Gleaves *Memphis Flyer* (Tenn.) (June 26) "Uncle Sam's Men Think Undies Aren't Necessary; Why Should Civilians?" p. 23 ▶ Call it free-balling, California casual, alfresco, or the much-preferred "going commando." Unless that sundress is super susceptible to breeze, super short, or you're super drunk, no one will know the difference. **2003** Robin Troy *Missoula Independent* (Mont.) (Oct. 2) "Balls, Boobs and Beer, Oh My!" p. 6 ▶ A fight broke out, sending a free-balling man sailing onto the chest of another who was fully clothed. **2004** *Mimi Smartypants* (Chicago) (Nov. 15) (Int.) ▶ Cyril Freeballs It! Cyril's Unclad Squirrel Scrotum Now Haunts My Dreams!

freeco *n.* a cost-free service, item, or performance; a freebie; a handout; a *comp. Guyana. Trinidad & Tobago.* Given the constant and common cultural exchange between Caribbean nations, this term also may be in use on other Anglophone West Indian islands.

1992 *Usenet: soc.culture.caribbean* (Feb. 20) "Trini Words for the WEEK" ▶ *Freeco*—A free event. As impoverished struggling students, I know this is usually our first question when going somewhere. eg. T&T) IS AH FREECO FETE OR WHAT? NO, DEN WHAT IS DE DAMAGE? QE) Is there a cover charge for the party? No, well then how much? **1992** *Usenet: soc.culture.caribbean* (Feb. 25) "Re: Mother's Day Concert" ▶ "Where we getting de free co tic." "This reminds me of the Tradewinds song 'It's Traditional.' '... And if somebody put on a dance, or a big show or a movie, West Indians believe they have a duty, to try and get in free They gon scale the walls, bruise up they hand and knee, Oh yes, it's traditional.'—Dave Martin." **1996** *Usenet: soc.culture.caribbean* (Mar. 20) "Calling Guyanese on the Net" ▶ It's all a FREECO (yuh know how Guyanese like freeness). **2001** Terry Joseph *Trinicenter.com* (Trinidad & Tobago) (June 20) "Land of the Free" (Int.) ▶ Now, no one asks a neurosurgeon for a "freeco" or even a discount, perhaps out of respect for that particular type of profession, or concern that the doctor might perform a job precisely equal to the amount tendered. **2002** Sadiq Baksh (*Parliament of the Republic of Trinidad and Tobago Hansard Debates*) (Trinidad & Tobago) (Dec. 10) "Rent Restriction (Re-Enactment and Validation) Bill," p. 548 ▶ In 1981, as an election gimmick—part of its "freeco" for the 1981 election—the Rent Restriction Act came into being in a refined way. What it did was freeze rents for some people from then until now. What it seeks to do is to continue to provide those people with "freeco." Do you know why? We saw why on television last night. That is why. Before the election the PNM gave "freeco" to all its supporters; those that promised to vote and those they expected to vote for them. **2003** *Trinidiary* (Trinidad & Tobago) (Oct. 28) "Tantie Talk" (Int.) ▶ Now dat ent to say yuh cyant have a big bram concert, but dat bong to mus' be a one time/grand finale ting even a open air lie dong on de grass all day picnic kinda ting dat could be a freeco, because yuh done make yuh money wid de small sessions. **2004** Kevin Baldeosingh *Kevin Baldeosingh—Caribbean Writer, Author, Journalist, Trinidad and Tobago* (Trinidad & Tobago) (Jan. 9) "Female Facts" (Int.) ▶ As an adult, thanks mostly to my being a writer, I've had the opportunity to travel freeco to India, Ghana, Germany, America and, within the Caribbean, Jamaica and Barbados. **2004** Stephen Kangal @ Caroni *Trinidad Guardian* (Nov. 14) "Manning's Integration for Small Island Votes" (Int.) ▶ Since I cannot quantify the scope of the "freeco" that the Caricom Santa Claus dispensed at the November feeding frenzy, our Parliament must be engaged because too many politically-partisan decisions have been made in giving away unconditionally part of our crown jewels. **2005** [Queen Macoomeh] *Commess University* (Jan. 1) "Caribbean Book Reviews!" (Int.) ▶ All yuh fowl teef who feel de internet is a free-co have some respeck. **2005** Terry Josephs *Trinidad & Tobago Express* (Jan. 21) "The Gathering Stormers" (Int.) ▶ So entrenched has the attitude become, we have developed a special Lexicon for begging. At first it was a "freeco," then a request to "run something." Lately there has been an adoption of the Americanism "free stuff," as a way of softening the exchange, replacing "comps" which, by reduction to the level of pet-name, already made asking for complimentary admission more target-friendly.

freedom lawn *n.* residential land permitted to or designed to contain a variety of plants other than manicured grass, especially when containing plant life that occurs without cultivation, chemicals, or cutting. *Environment.*

1993 Peter Pringle @ U.S. *Independent* (U.K.) (June 21) "Suburbia Spurns the Lawn Police" ▶ These figures are published in a new book,

Redesigning the American Lawn, by three concerned environmentalists from Yale University, Herbert Bormann, Diana Balmori and Gordon Geballe. They propose "freedom lawns," allowing natural and unrestricted growth of grasses, clover, wild flowers and other broad-leafed plants that lawn-obsessed people regard as weeds. **1999** Thomas G. Barnes *Gardening*  *for the Birds* (Feb. 1), p. 16 ► Sherri Evans...recommends planting "prairie patches and woodland niches" in addition to perennial ground covers to create a "freedom lawn"—a new landscape notion that is more environmentally friendly and views the lawn as a green space in an interconnected ecological system. **2005** Laura Wexler *Charlotte Observer* (N.C.) (Apr. 24) "Many Denizens Roam the Backyard Jungle" (Int.) ► She is against cultivating a green shag rug through the aid of chemicals, advocating instead something the lawn industry calls a Freedom Lawn: "a delicately balanced mixture of whatever can grow in any particular spot and doesn't mind getting whacked by the mower every couple of weeks."

freeter *n.* a person who takes a series of temporary jobs; a job-hopper, temp worker, or freelancer. Also **freeta.** < *English. Business. Employment. German. Japan. Japanese. Korean. South Korea.* [*free* + Ger. arbe*it* 'work']

1989 Minoru Koshida @ Tokyo (*Reuters*) (Sept. 22) "More Japan College Graduates Rebel Against Jobs for Life" ► Kato worked for a trading firm for about two years after he graduated from college with a major in law in 1982, but decided to quit when he realised he could take time off anytime he wanted and have larger pay cheques if he became what is known in Japan as a "freeter." "Freeter" is a combination of the English word "free" and the Japanese word "arubaito" meaning part-time, casual or temporary work. **1999** Tim Larimer et al. *Time Asia* (May 3) "From We to Me," vol. 153, no. 17, p. 18 ► If he can't find what he's looking for, he's happy to take a part-time job and join the growing ranks of freetas. **2001** *N.Y. Times* (Oct. 16) "Young Japanese Breaking Old Salaryman's Bonds" (in Tokyo), p. A3 ► The advantage of being a "freeter" is that if you missed the shift, the responsibility falls on the person who hired you. **2004** *JoonAng Daily* (Seoul, S. Korea) (June 4) "They Pay You to Do What?" (Int.) ► Some young people choose to live on a series of part-time jobs rather than look for a permanent one. In the local vernacular, they're called "freeters," a combination of "free" and "arbeiter," which is German for "worker." **2005** Deirdre Van Dyk *Time* (U.S.) (Jan. 24) "Parlez-Vous Twixter?" (Int.) ► Japan: *Freeter* The term, a combination of free and arbeiter, the German word for worker, describes an unmarried young adult who job hops and lives at home. The trend has even been debated in Parliament.

French hours *n.* a workday that begins at noon; a precisely timed workday, usually without breaks. *Business. Entertainment.*

1956 Gene Moskowitz @ Paris, France *N.Y. Times* (Nov. 11) "Production Views Along the Seine," p. 145 ► [Billy Wilder] also likes the French hours—noon to 7:30 P.M. "In Hollywood, with the five-day week and early hours, one can make fifty silly errors before one begins to work." **1986** William Hall *L.A. Times* (Mar. 9) "'A Man and a Woman' Redux: Trying to Rekindle the Ashes," p. 3 ► Up at 6 to get ready for the day's shoot (civilized French hours of noon to 8 p.m.), in bed some time after 1 a.m. **1986** Carol Burton Terry *Melville, Newsday* (Long Island, N.Y.) (Oct. 26) "Off Camera," p. 66 ► He works two days a week, commuting from Palm Springs to Toronto, where the Grosso-Jacobson series is produced. "We work French hours up there," he said. "You go to work in the afternoon and work through eight hours." **2003** Johanna Schneller *Globe and Mail* (Toronto, Can.) (Apr. 4) "How Many Directors Can You Fit in a Phone Booth?" p. R1 ► We would get there at 6 a.m. and roll by 6:45. We did "French hours." You don't break for lunch, you just keep passing food all day. Colin's confession at the end, that's the ninth day of shooting—it's the first take and the only take. He was exhausted and you can see it. **2004** [Ross] *Strategize* (July 21) "French Hours" (Int.) ► During *Phone Booth*, no lunch breaks were taken because all of the staff agreed not to take lunch breaks (food was simply available for crew to grab and eat when they could) versus normal movies where there are very specifically set times or hour metrics that determine exactly when each meal must occur and the entire production stops while the crew eats. In short, French Hours mean moving more quickly and more efficiently while still retaining the same quality.

frogspawn *n.* jocularly, tapioca or similar starchy pudding. *Food & Drink. United Kingdom.* The appearance of tapioca does very much resemble egg masses laid by amphibians.

1991 Jonathan Meades *Times* (London, Eng.) (Apr. 13) "Artificial Colouring" ► A sago pudding served with palm sugar. This last item combined school-lunch frog's spawn with school-treat Callard & Bowser molasses flavour. **1992** *Usenet: soc.culture.celtic* (Dec. 19) "Re: What Is Sago?" ► Sago—vulgar form "frogs' spawn"—is one of those nice glutinous round pellets which comes as a dried little nodule and cooks into stuff that, well, looks like frogs' spawn. **1994** Hattie Ellis *Times* (London, Eng.) (Feb. 26) "In Praise of Tasty Tarts" ▶ When Alfred Bird created his famous powder in 1846 (because his wife was allergic to the eggs found in real custard), he started a tidal wave of packet custard which, for some, is a childhood trauma on a par with tapioca frogspawn. **1995** Alex Berlyne *Jerusalem Post Mag.* (Israel) (Sept. 22) "Toad-Hair Vetoed 'Brekekekex-Coax-Coax,'" p. 31 ▶ The nearest I ever came to the subject was to shudder whenever my schoolmates ate their tapioca pudding, usually referred to as frogspawn. **2005** *Express & Star* (Wolverhampton, U.K.) (Aug. 2) "Back to School for the Dinner Ladies" (Int.) ▶ Anyone who remembers dry faggots with brown mushy peas, rock hard treacle tart or a mushy tapioca commonly known as "frogspawn" will be in for a shock.

—fu *suffix* indicating mastery or expertise. Also **foo.** [Probably from kung *fu*, a Chinese martial art, and probably not related to the *foobar*, *fubar*, or the *foo* often used by programmers.] Film critic Joe Bob Briggs, who tends to sprinkle the suffix throughout his reviews, is often credited with popularizing it.

[**1986** *Usenet: net.movies* (Mar. 14) "Re: UFOria" ▶ Anyway, it's shy on monsters and breasts, but great religion-fu.] **1998** *Usenet: comp.graphics.apps.gimp* (Oct. 14) "Hello!" ▶ The purpose is to make a button generator accessible from the web where users can create their sets of images. I do this with the Perl-Fu. **1999** *Usenet: alt.callahans* (Oct. 9) "Re: Toast: Blue Thing!!!" ▶ Master of DejaNews Search-Fu. **2002** [Trip] *Trip's Brain-Sucking Web Site* (Jan. 26) (Int.) ▶ She didn't win, but it was pretty clear she was there not to demonstrate her superior cooking fu but to spread the word of Thai food to Japan. **2003** Juha Saarinen *OCTools* (Dec. 8) "Highpoint e.SATA RAID Kit: Installation and Setup" (Int.) ▶ This is the typical approach for low-end RAID adapters, and it isn't necessarily bad—it does require good driver-writing-fu though. **2004** *alt.ph.uk* (Aug. 11) "Your Call Cannot Be Completed as Dialed" ▶ I am *so* sure I have read something about this recently, but I'm damned if I can find it again, my google foo is weak today.

fukubukuro *n.* a gift bag or package containing unknown and varied merchandise, sold at the New Year for a large discount. *Japan. Japanese.* [From Japanese 福 *fuku* 'good fortune; luck' + 袋 *fukuro* 'bag']

1988 *Japan Economic Journal* (Jan. 2) "Town Scenes: Y15 Mil. 'Fuku-bukuro' Up for Grabs," p. 11 ▶ Grab bags, known as fukubukuro (lucky bags), are popular items in almost every store during the New

Year holiday season in Japan. Some are especially large, such as one selling for Y15 million by the Takashimaya & Co. department store in Tokyo. That bag contains Y27 million worth of clothing, jewelry, a suitcase, a video camera and two round-trip tickets to Hawaii on the luxurious *Queen Elizabeth II* ocean liner. Fukubukuro are usually sold for price less than their contents as a New Year attraction. **1990** Yumiko Ono *Wall Street Journal* (Jan. 5) "Too Bad Wobbly S&Ls Can't Fit Real Estate into a Pretty Pouch," p. B1 ▶ The bargains come in grab bags, called fukubukuro, or sacks of fortune. The bags used to be a traditional way for stores to unload unwanted merchandise. But now that more Japanese have money to burn, department stores are turning fukubukuro into a lavish New Year's event. **2004** *Honolulu Star-Bulletin* (Hawaii) (Dec. 30) "Style File" (Int.) ▶ Fukubukuro, practiced by Japanese merchants, is one way for retailers to say thanks to their customers, and Ala Moana Center will start 2005 with the tradition. Fukubukuro literally means "surprise bag" and is a grab bag with mystery contents priced at least 50 percent off the retail value of the merchandise inside.

full boat *n.* a full price or total amount of money; generally, all of something; as an *adj.*, having many or elaborate features, options, or functions. *Food & Drink.* [Perhaps influenced by a *full boat* 'full house' in poker, representing three of one kind and two of another.] Often constructed as **to pay full boat** or with the definite article: **the full boat.** In yoga and exercise there is a pose also called the *full boat*, which is probably unrelated.

1985 Ken Castle *San Francisco Chronicle* (Calif.) (Oct. 14) "Ski Wars: The Price Is Right to Buy Equipment," p. 75 ▶ Even the Bay Area's most upscale ski specialist, Any Mountain, has been forced to lower prices on items it would have sold at full boat during previous years. **1995** Jerry Eichenberger *Business & Commercial Aviation* (Nov. 1) "Flying for Fun," vol. 77, no. 5, p. 90 ▶ Paying the full-boat premium for coverage while exercising ATP privileges is still a bargain. **1997** William Diehl *Reign in Hell* (Sept. 23), p. 430 ▶ You'll do five to ten which means if you're a good boy, you should be out in three to four years. And then we'll put you in witness protection. Think about it. Which is it? The full boat? Or a chance to resume your life less than five years from now? **1997** Jon Kosmoski *How to: Custom Paint & Graphics* (Oct. 1), p. 15 ▶ A scanner makes it easy to take a sketch or photo and use that as the basis for a design. Like everything else these come in everything from the four-cylinder econo-box model to the full-boat Cadillac version with air conditioning and 10-speaker stereo. **2001** Jim Sterne *World Wide Web Marketing* (June 4), p. 260 ▶ The Affiliate Program on Steroids. HP created a full-boat, e-commerce

site filled with all their products and handed it to its resellers. **2002**
Darwin Holmstrom *Harley-Davidson Century* (Sept. 1), p. 370
▶ Another was a full-boat tour with the FLT fairing. **2003** Stephen J.
Cannell *Runaway Heart* (July 11), p. 22 ▶ He picked one, wondering at
the stupidity of having full-boat security and leaving such easy access
through system defects. **2005** Melanie Asmar *Concord Monitor* (N.H.)
(May 8) "Hospitals Challenged Over Billing" (Int.) ▶ "These hospitals
call themselves non-profit, but here they are charging people who can
least afford it the full boat," Grant said. "That doesn't sound very
charitable to me."

full-gorilla *adv.* in baseball, aggressively or with the utmost force,
especially in the phrase **to go full gorilla**. Also *n. Sports.*

1994 Michael Murphy *Houston Chronicle* (Tex.) (July 4) "Huisman
Closes Book on Past," p. 5 ▶ He was always the type of pitcher who
went full-gorilla all the time.... He was always aggressive and went
right after us. **2004** Ross Newman *L.A. Times* (Sept. 12) "Angels'
Rodriguez Is an Animated Special," p. D4 ▶ In only his second full
season in the majors, with a better concept of location and selection
but still basically what pitching coach Bud Black calls "full gorilla" on
every pitch, Rodriguez has set a club record for strikeouts by a
reliever. **2005** Elliott Teaford *Daily Breeze* (Torrange, Calif.) (Aug. 5)
"Angels Notebook: Washburn Placed on the 15-Day DL" (Int.) ▶ "He
felt better but is not at a level where we can just turn him loose on
Saturday," Manager Mike Scioscia said of Washburn, who threw off a
bullpen mound and said he felt only slight discomfort while going
"full gorilla," as he termed it.

fumblerooski *n.* in American football, a play in which the quarterback pretends to fumble and a teammate picks up the ball.
Sports. United States.

1984 Michael Wilbon @ Miami, Fla. *Washington Post* (D1) (Jan. 3)
"Nebraska Falls, 31-30, on Day of Upsets" ▶ The play is called the
"fumblerooski." Steinkuhler picked up a deliberate fumble by Gill and
ran around left end for the score that made it 17–7 with a minute still
to play in the first quarter. **1988** Bruce Lowitt *St. Petersburg Times*
(Fla.) (Jan. 2) "It's Hurricanes' Season," p. 1C ▶ Oklahoma's second
TD was a trick play—a "fumblerooski." Quarterback Charles Thompson laid the ball on the ground and All-America guard Mark Hutson
picked it up and ran 29 yards for the score. **2004** Bruce Hooley *Cleveland Plain Dealer* (Ohio) (Nov. 20) "Gold Standard" (Int.) ▶ In more
common parlance, the play was a "fumblerooski," designed for center
Joe Dooley to place the ball on the ground after touching it to quarterback Mike Tomczak's hands.

fundagelical *n.* a fundamentalist or evangelical Christian; a person who evangelizes or espouses fundamentalist beliefs for any cause. Also *adj. Derogatory. Religion. United States.* [*funda*mentalist + evan*gelical*] Usually derogatory.

1990 *Usenet: soc.motss* (Feb. 20) "Re: Queers and Jungle Coons" ▶ Actually, after the quake I kinda figured that the Christian Fundagelicals would jump all over this point. **1990** *Usenet: soc.motss* (Sept. 20) "How Can We Trust the Christians?" ▶ I have come to the point, based on reports such as the one above, from regularly reading the postings in talk.religion.christian and talk.religion.miscellaneous as well as from watching the fundagelical programs on television that for me it is no longer possible to just oppose specific noxious positions taken by groups of Christians. **1999** *Usenet: comp.lang.perl.misc* (Mar. 29) "Re: Why Do We Like Perl?" ▶ Plus the attitude of many of the regulars in this group is very "fundagelical"—anyone who doesn't accept that perl is the one true language is a heretic, and you should never use anything other than perl regardless of the application. **2003** Brian Heath *heathbar66.livejournal.com* (Akron, Ohio) (Dec. 13) "Saturday Morning Thoughts..." (Int.) ▶ I was channel-surfing past some religious shows on TV today—and I realize that a lot of fundagelical preachers love to use the Book of Revelation as a tool to try scaring people.

futsal *n.* an organized form of indoor soccer. *Spanish. Sports.* [Spanish *fút*bol 'football; soccer' (or Portuguese *fute*bol) + *sala* '(large) room' (or Portuguese *sala*̃o)]

1987 Johnny Warren *Sun Herald* (Australia) (Sept. 20) "'Pay-Up' Blitz on NSL Clubs," p. 83 ▶ Like most South Americans, the Uruguayan midfield genius played Futsal (or Indoor Soccer) ONLY until the age of 17. **1991** *Usenet: rec.sport.soccer* (June 21) "World Cup of FUT-SAL (Minisoccer)" ▶ Portugal is the new World Champion of Fut-Sal (minisoccer). **2004** Christopher L. Gasper @ Middleton, Mass. *Boston Globe* (Dec. 12) "Turning Soccer Inside Out" (Int.) ▶ Short for *futbol sala*—loosely translated as indoor soccer—futsal is played in soccer-crazed countries all over the world. It is hailed as a teaching tool that develops players' technical and tactical abilities by forcing them to maneuver and make decisions in confined space.

G

gamer *n.* in sports, a committed or exceptional player. *Sports. United States.* [Probably from *adj.* form of *game,* 'willing; committed (to an undertaking or idea).'] This is a different sense from *gamer* 'a person who plays (video) games' and the much older and perhaps archaic sense 'a person who participates in sports.'

1978 Thomas Boswell @ Philadelphia, Pa. *Washington Post* (Aug. 20) "Joyful Blue Humining, Eyes 2nd Young Award," p. D1 ▶ "Blue's such a damn good battler, the way he puts his heart and soul into it, that he really impresses me," said Philadelphia slugger Mike Schmidt. "He's a gamer," Schmidt added. **1982** Joe Goddard *Oklahoma City Times* (Jan. 8) "Bowa Trade Rumors Include Former 89ers" ▶ Sure, I'd take Larry in a minute. He's a gamer, a winner. **2001** Tom Shael *Omaha World-Herald* (Neb.) (Oct. 29) "Solich, Huskers Really Special," p. 1C ▶ He runs. He throws. He catches. What Crouch showed them is that he's a gamer, and maybe this is the year a gamer wins. **2004** Kelly Candaele *N.Y. Times* (Oct. 17) "Caminiti Was a Gamer Who Played Hard Even When Hurt" (Int.) ▶ Ken Caminiti's fellow players called him a gamer. In professional baseball parlance, that is someone who plays through pain when injured, someone who is willing to do whatever it takes to win.

gank *v.* to rob, rip off, or con (someone). *Crime & Prisons. Drugs. Slang. United States.*

1989 Karen Dillon *Chicago Tribune* (July 19) "Youths Get 79 Years for Beating Elderly," p. C10 ▶ In their confession to police, the two youths said they would go "make a run" or "gank an o.g.," which means they would drive around until they spotted an elderly woman, usually at a bank or shopping center or near a school. **1990** Alan Gottlieb *Denver Post* (Colo.) (July 8) "One Sibling Resists Entangling Net, Sets Eyes on College, Future," p. 13A ▶ "Base had just ganked a tweaker," James said—conned a crack addict out of her money. **1991** John M. McGuire *St. Louis Post-Dispatch Everyday Magazine* (Mo.) (July 8) "The New Breed Young St. Louis Cops Look for Seasoning, Respect—and Yogurt," p. 1D ▶ "Don't gank me," Kelly says. As a verb, Kelly later explains, "gank" means "to chump you, or play you for a fool." **1991** Ken Kolker *Grand Rapids Press* (Mich.) (Nov. 27) "Hickman Tells of Plan to Sell Fake Cocaine to Undercover Agent" ▶ Hickman said he and Maurice Pointer planned to "gank"—the street term for rob—the undercover agent, posing as a customer, by selling him fake cocaine for $28,000 on April 8 on the MSU campus in East Lansing. **1994** Ron Stallworth (*Congressional Testimony*) (Feb. 23) "Influence of Lyrics on Children" ► Let him think he's gettin' over while I gank him for his riches robbin', stealin', killin' at will—. **1994** Mary Carole McCauley *Milwaukee Journal* (Wisc.) (June 24) "Petition Sheds Light on Events of Slaying, But Motive Is Murky," p. B3 ► One told the others, "Let's gank him," which the 17-year-old understood to mean that he wanted to rob Eshman.

gank *n.* fake illegal drugs sold as real. *Crime & Prisons. Drugs. Slang. United States.*

1996 Regina Akers *Kansas City Star* (Kan., Mo.) (Jan. 19) "Drug Dens Are Closed in KCK," p. C2 ► Some involved retaliation for previous killings, others involved dealers seeking revenge on customers who did not pay, and some were reprisals from customers who purchased "gank," a slang term for fake drugs. **1997** Joy Powell *World-Herald* (Omaha, Neb.) (July 27) "Big Plans, No Patience James Burnett Let Ambition Turn to Greed" ► Distributors became upset at him for selling "gank"—bad crack. **2004** Tim Hahn *Erie Times-News* (Pa.) (Apr. 16) "Police Arrest 10 in Neighborhood Sweep" (Int.) ► Duane Beason, 35, of the 200 block of West 18th Street, was charged after police accused him of trying to sell undercover officers "gank," a street term for something that looks like drugs but isn't, at the intersection of East Seventh and Wallace streets.

ganny *n.* marijuana from Afghanistan. *Drugs. Slang.*

1999 [hikchik@bellsouth.com] *Stoner's Pot Palace* (Sept. 2) "Guestbook" (Int.) ► Favourite Strain (of weed?): ganny. ***1999** [sous420@hotmail.com] *The SouS Spot* (N.H.) (Dec. 19) "Prices in Your Area" (Int.) ► If you have a price for weed in your area send it to me and I will post it here.... Ganny: 30/60. **2002** *Usenet: rec.music .artists.kings-x* (June 7) "Re: Rush" ► On side 2 the song TRAIN TO BANGKOK he speaks about the sweet Jamaican pipe dreams, golden Acapulco nights and the fragrance of Afghanistan (we now call "skunk" we once called "ganny" short for Afghanistan). What a cool song. **2003** [oxsan] *Asylum* (July 1) "Asylum Forums: Oxsan's Word Fun" (Int.) ► According to Dr. [Ebenezer Cobham] Brewer a "ganny" is a portion of cannabis from Afghanistan. **2005** [stutteringgypsy] *AstutteringGypsy* (Tallahassee, Fla.) (Feb. 12) "Hell Week" (Int.) ► We all have heard the slang terms for pot or whatever but we had never heard of "ganny." ***2005** *Probert Encyclopedia* (Feb. 14) (Int.) ► Ganny is British slang for Afghani cannabis.

gap out *v.* to become distracted; to *space out*. [Likely directly related to *to gape* 'to stare at with the mouth open.']

1997 *Usenet: rec.aquaria.freshwater.goldfish* (Sept. 11) "Re: GF: Gill Mites-Reply" ▶ "Also can't find much on gill mites in my books = what exactly are they?" "There is no such thing, that is why you can't find it. I'm sure the store owner just gapped out for a second when telling about gill mites as well*probably meaning to say flukes." **1997** Dave Perkins @ Halifax, N.S. *Toronto Star* (C8) (Nov. 9) "Skate Results Show Perfection Needed to Win at Nagano" ▶ Look at Kwan last night. She is as wonderful an athlete as it gets, but she had a so-so (for her) performance, gapping out and falling down in the final 10 seconds. **1998** *Usenet: alt.folklore.ghost-stories* (Nov. 12) "Re: Very Strange" ▶ I've gone back and there is no way to get to that other road from the road that I was on. So, it wasn't really that I just gapped out and was down the street past my exit. I was actually on another road parallel to the one I was on. I don't know how to describe how strange it was. [**1999** *Usenet: alt.thanatos* (June 8) "Re: Part 2—Wanna Look at the Boat?" ▶ I was drunk enough that time was "gapping out" on me: I'd come to and not remember what had happened for the last ten minutes or so.] **1999** *Usenet: alt.drugs.pot* (Oct. 13) "Fucking Cops" ▶ Steve (my friend) rolled up the joint while I was on look-out, and doing a rather half assed job because I was gapping out all the time. **2004** Murray Waldren, Douglas Coupland *Australian* (Sydney) (Dec. 4) "Doug Day Afternoon" (Int.) ▶ As for his latest book, he mentions casually, "for better or worse I've done so little press on it so far that I don't have any script prepared, so when I gap out, it's a real gap out...." I hope this is merely a "random thread," as he calls it when a thought-line peters out—and which, as the dusk slowly darkens into night, become more and more prevalent.

gasser *n.* a sprint, usually run in series as a form of athletic conditioning. *Sports.*

1973 *Chicago Tribune* (C2) (July 24) "Csonka Says He'll Be Ready" (in Miami, Fla.) ▶ After testing his pulled thigh muscle in a morning workout and running the gassers [a series of all-out 40-yard sprints] that conclude each morning's chores in the home of the World Champions, Csonka told a writer: "I'll play in the All-Star game." **1987** Tommy C. Simmons *Baton Rouge State Times* (La.) (Aug. 24) "What Good Is Football? Moms Share Their Views," p. 1C ▶ "Gassers, what's a gasser?" the football player's Mom asked her son. "Oh, don't worry about it, Mom. It's just part of conditioning—some sprint work we have to do." **1995** Madeleine Blais *In These Girls, Hope Is a Muscle* (Jan. 1), p. 100 (Jan. 1, 1996) ▶ Coach Moyer planned to run a tight ship this year. Dire visions of "suicides," also known as "gassers" and "back-and-downs," sprang up in the heads of the Hurricane hopefuls. **2005** Andrew Mikula @ Palm Coast *News-Journal* (Daytona Beach, Fla.) (Aug. 3) "Start of Season Brings Rigors, Benefits of Two-a-Day Practices for Bulldogs" (Int.) ▶ Campana and the other assistant coaches are running the 40-yard wind sprints, not-so-affectionately known as "gassers" among the players.... Players have to run 10 times for 40 yards at full sprint and woe to the player who holds his head down or puts his hands on his hips during the momentary periods of rest between the sprints.

gay church *n.* jocularly, a gym. *Gay.* Popularized by, if not originated by, the American television sitcom "Will & Grace." Occasionally, in various nonce uses as in the 2004 citation, the term is applied to other places or activities stereotypically associated with homosexuals.

2001 James Burrows *"Will & Grace"* (television series) (Dec. 6) "Stakin' Care of Business" ▶ Don't lie. Not here. This is a gym. This is—this is gay church. **2001** *Usenet: misc.writing* (Dec. 11) "Re: Ok, Hugh. You Asked for It. Guns" ▶ The other night on "Will & Grace" a guy chastised another guy for acting up in the gym. He told him "You can't do that at a gym. Gym is like gay church." [**2004** *Traveling Spotlight* (Cleveland, Ohio) (June 14) "I've Been Bad...Very Bad!" (Int.) ▶ But instead of going to Catholic church, I attend the gay church, the hair salon. Hell hath no fury like a hairdresser.] **2005** [Christian] *Lesbian, Gay, Bisexual and Trans Association* (Univ. of Nottingham, U.K.) (Feb. 21) "Sport?" (Int.) ▶ Worry not, after all they do call gyms "gay church." **2005** Christopher Stone *AfterElton.com* (July 11) "30 Days: A Straight Man Visits the Castro" (Int.) ▶ Ryan's first full day starts with a visit to the gym, or "gay church," as he calls it.

gbege *n.* an act of (vengeful) violence. *Crime & Prisons. Nigeria.*
2004 *FACTNet Message Board* (May 1) "Religious Cults and Sects: Nigerian Student Cults: PC Will Forever Reign" (Int.) ▶ any gbege na yawago bring out blud, like they say odas is odas, blud 4 blud [laugh],...we go strikewith tha might of korofo. **2004** Bobson Gbinije *Daily Champion* (Lagos, Nigeria) (May 20) "Killing the Renaissance in Delta State" (Int.) ▶ The word gbege is a neologism for violent response. When Uvwie youths go out to collect development levies and you refuse to pay they resort to violence (gbege).

gedunk *n.* ice cream, a dessert, a snack, or any easy-to-consume food; a store, mess hall, or other place where such treats are bought or eaten. Also **geedunk, gedonk, geedonk.** *Food & Drink. Military.* In the 1925 citation *to gedunk*, meaning 'to dunk (food),' is just one of many uses of the term in a regular reader-con-tributed humorous column, where it was something of a running gag. It is contemporary with and probably related to the *gedunk sundaes* that appeared in the comic strip "Harold Teen" by Carl Ed, who, in turn, is probably the popularizer of *gedunk*. The later uses of this term are strongly associated with the Navy.

1925 *Chicago Daily Tribune* (Jan. 21) "A Line o' Type or Two," p. 8 ▶ Not once did the gedunked part sever its connection with the unge-dunked part and fall geplatsch into the coffee. **1926** E.A. Edmonds *Chicago Daily Tribune* (Mar. 10) "Gedunk Sundaes," p. 8 ▶ You possess one comic feature that is changing the habits of the nation. I refer to Harold Teen and his Gedunk sundae. I have two children, a boy and a girl, now of high school age, and I have spent many a painstaking hour teaching them correct table manners. Their conduct was above reproach until the notorious Gedunk sundae made its appearance. **1982** Richard Harrington *Washington Post* (Apr. 8) "Circus!," p. B1 ▶ You could pack any doubts about the wonderfulness of the Ringling Bros. and Barnum & Bailey Circus into a toy poodle's knapsack and still have plenty of room for cotton candy and other spectator gee-dunks. **1984** *Omaha World-Herald* (Neb.) (Feb. 15) "Memories Kin-dled by Ship's Rebirth" (in Iowa) ▶ We had about four barber chairs, a clothing store, a "Geedunk," that's an ice-cream store, our own laun-dry and water system. **1993** Lewis Shiner *Glimpses: A Novel* (July 1), p. 47 ▶ The rest of the day I just hung around the geedunk, you know, the PX. **1996** James Patterson *The Thomas Berryman Number* (Apr. 1), p. 33 ▶ I put cream and raw sugar in my coffee. All motions. I wasn't going to drink the muddy geedunk. It reminded me of the Mississippi River. **1996** Ben Bradlee *A Good Life* (Sept. 11), p. 65 ▶ Then we would ask the carrier to send over all the geedunk (ice cream) they had. **2000** Sean Clancy, Barbara D. Livingston *Saratoga Days* (Aug. 15), p. 182 ▶ A geedunk stand (that's a term my father uses for quick food stores). **2001** Joy Waldron Jasper, James P. Del-gado, Jim Adams *USS Arizona* (Nov. 15), p. 54 ▶ It depended on where you were and what your uniform was, what you could do. It wasn't too bad a life. We'd go down to the ice cream parlor and get a gee-dunk—a pint of ice cream—and go to the movies. **2003** Robert McKenna *Dictionary of Nautical Literacy* (June 23), p. 136 ▶ *geedunk*, naval term for dessert, candy, junk food, or a place to buy same. **2004** Jim Kinney *Saratogian* (Saratoga Springs, N.Y.) (Sept. 16) "Sub Grub Was Never Gourmet" (Int.) ▶ Ron Phelix, a sub vet from the Malone area, raved about the food on the USS *Skipjack* from 1960 to

'64. He said they had "geedunks," a slang term for doughnuts and cinnamon buns, each night at midnight.

Generation E *n.* a comparatively younger generation to which certain traits are attributed. [*generation* + entitlement, entitled, or electronic]

1996 John Rosemund *Buffalo News* (N.Y.) (Dec. 15) "Yes—Hurt Your Child's Feelings" ▶ Jurists tell me that all too often today's young people think breaking the law is a big deal only if they lack the money to hire the best attorneys. This isn't Generation X. This is Generation E, for entitled. **2000** Shabnam Minwalla @ Mumbai, India *Times of India* (Sept. 10) "Tomorrow's Technology—Honey, I Shrunk the PC" ▶ While members of Generation E may take these gizmos for granted, anybody who has been acquainted with the mammoth mainframes of yore is bound to be rattled by such relentless miniaturization. **2004** *Federal Information & News Dispatch* (Washington, D.C.) (May 19) "Voice of America Press Releases and Documents" ▶ Some people call these Internet do-it-yourselfers Generation C, for the creative content they put on the Net. Or citizen media, meaning they're average people offering their work to the world. Another name is Generation E for entitled, because these folks feel they have just as much right as established writers or musicians or filmmakers to be heard. **2004** Jill Matthews @ Montgomery, N.J. *Princeton Packet* (N.J.) (June 22) "Montgomery Graduates Bid Adieu to the 'Wonder Years' They've Shared" (Int.) ▶ "It is disturbing to me that you are sometimes referred to as Generation E—Entitlement," said Linda Romano. "While you are always, always loved, you are never entitled."

get brain *v.* to receive fellatio. *Sexuality. Slang.*

1998 The LOX *Money, Power & Respect* (song) (Jan. 13) "Get This $" (Int.) ▶ Hotter in the club getting brain from a diva. **1999** *Usenet: alt.rap* (Apr. 2) "Re: Getting Brain" ▶ G'tting' brain is getting your dick sucked. **1999** *Usenet: rec.music.hip-hop* (Apr. 4) "Re: Getting Brain" ▶ If you get brain that means a female is sucking your penis. **2000** *Usenet: rec.music.hip-hop* (Oct. 18) "Re: How Come?" ▶ I've found that on some high school shit, it was much easier to fuck than to get brain.... I'm telling you, I've had broads...give me quality, 4 mic brain surgery. **2004** *N.Y. Daily News* (Nov. 5) "Bus Ban on Sex Ads" (Int.) ▶ Kids say "get brain" does not mean smarts. It's slang for oral sex.

ghetto pass *n.* figurative or literal approval from black Americans or the hip-hop music community (of a non-black person or a now-successful black person); the *street cred* of someone known for *keeping it real. Hip-Hop. United States.* [This term was popularized by, if not coined in, the song "True to the Game" from the 1991 album *Death Certificate* by the hip-hop performer Ice Cube.]

1991 Ice Cube *Death Certificate* (song) (Nov. 5) "True to the Game" ▶ House nigga scum/Give something back to the place where you made it from/Before you end up broke/Fuck around and get your ghetto pass revoked. **1993** Vahe Gregorian *St. Louis Post-Dispatch* (Mo.) (June 14) "Open-Field Hits: Cox Tackles Tough Subjects," p. 3C ▶ It's like Ice Cube says: "You're going to get your ghetto pass revoked." **1994** Paul Beatty *Next: Young American Writers on the New Generation* (May 1), p. 48 ▶ Born and raised in the 'hood, Todd didn't need a Ghetto Pass or a black Family Circle Seal of Approval. **1995** Rebecca Edby Walker *To Be Real* (Oct. 1), p. 128 ▶ The first time I saw Latifah in person, I left my feminism and classical political theory class early so that I could hear her speak over the electric fence between a (white) feminism that many Harvard students and faculty wanted to hear her advocate, and a (black) womanism that the nebulous B-Boy council and many black students needed her to defend so that she could retain her ghetto pass. **1997** *Usenet: rec.music.hip-hop* (Mar. 11) ▶ I never thought Ice Cube would give up his Ghetto Pass. **2004** Brian Smith *Metro Times* (Detroit, Mich.) (Dec. 12) "Champ's Town" (Int.) ▶ We gave Kid Rock his ghetto pass. We're black, all about the love.

ghost soldier *n.* a soldier who is enlisted or placed on active duty but does not serve; a fake name listed as an active-duty soldier. *Military.*

1926 *Helena Independent* (Mont.) (Apr. 21) "Convicted But Not Dishonored," p. 4 ▶ Butler is not out of the army officially, but he is morally and mentally. He is a thing apart. He will be a "ghost" soldier, more dead in army circles than any who fell in Flanders field. **1972** Fox Butterfield @ Datdo, South Vietnam *N.Y. Times* (June 112) "Battle for Datdo Tests Local Vietnamese Leadership" ▶ There were no regular South Vietnamese Army units station in Phuoctuy, and the province grew rich on "ghost soldiers," phony names on the military roster. **2004** Michael Gilbert *News Tribune* (Tacoma, Wash.) (June 19) "Troops Bask in Bush's Praise" (Int.) ▶ The phrase "ghost soldiers" has a negative connotation in Army parlance—a reference to the administrative practice of filling units with names on paper, but not actual able-bodied soldiers.

gleek *v.* squirting liquid (including saliva) through the teeth or from under the tongue; less commonly, squirting saliva directly from the saliva glands or expelling liquid through the sinuses. This is not the same as the Shakespearean *gleek,* which means 'to trick; to make a gibe or jest (at a person).' There is a similar word, *gleet,* 'to discharge pus (from the body); to ooze.' But it is not in current usage and there appears to be no provable connection with *gleek.*

1988 James. E. Van Horn *Gettysburg Times* (Pa.) (Feb. 3) "Early Teen Years Can Be Difficult," p. 5B ▶ "Gleeking" is the act of making saliva shoot through the space between the two front teeth. You're "gleeked" if you get hit!...Boys, I'm told, partake in this wintertime sport, but not many girls. While older youth can partake, most gleeking is done by 12- to 14-year-olds. **1993** *Herald-Journal* (Syracuse, N.Y.) (Feb. 15) "Principal Cracks Down on Spitting" (in Burrillville, R.I.), p. B2 ▶ He has also felt the gleekers' wrath.... Gleeking is a style of spitting that has captured the imagination of many boys at the 713-student school. **1995** *Usenet: talk.bizarre* (Feb. 7) "Wason" ▶ Some people can gleek at will, that little trick of spraying saliva out of your pores with your mouth open. **1995** *Usenet: rec.martial-arts* (May 23) "Re: Finger in the Eyes?" ▶ I saw a guy on David Letterman snort milk up his nose and squirt it out his tear ducts. Given the fact that most kids have access to milk at the age when they like to gross people out it should be common to see kids gleeking milk out their eye sockets according to the above logic, but to date I've only witnessed this one instance of elactulation. **2000** [Martin] *Robot Lounge* (Nov. 14) "Pen Flicking" (Int.) ▶ Where I come from, gleeking was called glicking. Maybe the SoCal dialect? No, I never mastered the art, but I didn't try that hard, either. **2004** Paul Davidson *Words for My Enjoyment* (Mar. 11) "Throat Scratching and Gleek" (Int.) ▶ What is gleeking? It is when you can spray a stream of liquid from underneath your tongue. Sometimes, you may have done it by accident while eating a sour candy—liquid does a quick spray from underneath your tongue. But I can do it on command. And the stream goes as high as 4 feet over my head, as far as 10 feet. **2004** Lori Bradley *A.D.D. (Another Dissertation Distraction)* (Oct. 20) "I'd Like to Teach the World to Gleek...in Perfect...Harmony? Blech." (Int.) ▶ You CAN shoot pure saliva...from under your tongues. Keep at it and one day all your snargling (gleeking/lurching) dreams will come true.

global gag rule *n.* a restriction that forbids U.S. government funds being given to organizations or countries that recommend, permit, or perform abortions. *Health. Politics. Sexuality. United States.*

1995 *Contemporary Women's Issues* "Cairo +5–Assessing U.S. Support for Reproductive Health at Home and Abroad," p. 1 ▶ The latest reincarnation of the Mexico City Policy, termed the "Global Gag Rule" by women's advocates, including Secretary of State Madeleine Albright, would go far beyond the current legal prohibitions on abortion. It also would bar organizations in U.S. aid recipient countries from receiving population assistance if they use their own non-U.S. funds to provide legal abortion services. The proposed restriction would also deny funding if such non-U.S. organizations participated—consistent with their own laws—in efforts to alter laws or governmental policies with any connection to abortion. This proposed limitation would include not only overt lobbying, but also sponsoring conferences, distributing materials and disseminating public statements. **1997** *Abortion Report* (June 6) "Int'l Family Planning: Smith Tries Again" ▶ Denying U.S. aid to family planning organizations and imposing a global gag rule will only increase the need for abortion. **2004** (*U.S. Newswire*) (June 2) "Transcript of Opening Keynote Address by Nils Daulaire" (in Washington, D.C.) (Int.) ▶ This clique condemns these organizations because one has not been willing to agree to the so-called Mexico City Policy—also known as the Global Gag Rule—and the other continues to work with humane health programs in China, despite the Chinese government's lamentable policies.

G-machine *n.* an automobile capable of withstanding one *g* of extra gravitational force due to braking and turning at high speeds; (*hence*) any fast vehicle, such as an automobile or boat. *Automotive. Jargon. Sports.* [*G-* < 'gravity' + *machine*]

[**1994** *Usenet: rec. models.rc* (June 6) "Re: (CAR) G MACHINE 2*Untweakable!*" (title).] **1995** Don Sherman *Popular Science* (Oct. 1) "A Sustained Blast. (1996 Porsche 911 Turbo) (Evaluation)," vol. 247, no. 4, p. 38 ▶ The 911 eclipses the mile-a-minute mark in 3.9 seconds, having used less than 200 feet of roadway to do so. In short, Porsche's turbo thruster is the most efficient g-machine *Popular Science* has ever tested. **1996** *Usenet: rec.autos.makers.honda* (Sept. 9) "Cheap Tires for My Civic" ▶ I didn't expect them to transform the Civic into a balls out G-machine, but all in all I'm happy with 'em. **1998** Ron Eldridge *Trailer Boats* (Sept. 1) "G Machine," vol. 27, no. 9, p. 34 ▶ This G Machine can carve 'em up with the hottest performance boats, and manages to do so with safety, comfort and panache. **2003** [Mad'lac] *CadillacForums.com* (Jan. 7) "Jeff Schwartz' Caddy Modifications" (Int.) ▶ I like some of the ideas you have on the caddy. But I don't think I am going to make it a G-machine though. I would like to set up my caddy for long haul and road trips. That's why I am leaning toward a 350. ***2003** Robert Bilicki (Stonybrook State Univ. of N.Y.) (July 24) "The Bilicki Zone" (Int.) ▶ This is my attempt at building a G-machine. All the term G-machine means is a car that has enough modification to pull 1 G in acceleration, braking, and turning. ***2004** Chris Endres *Popular Hotrodding* "Course Correction" (Int.) ▶ Knowing that every g-machine is based on a solid suspension and chassis combination, Huntimer got the project under way by addressing these areas. ***2004** Chris Endres *GM High Tech Performance* "G-Whiz!" (Int.) ▶ With the ever-growing g-machine movement, building an open-road racing style car presents a fresh chance to build a car with a look all its own.

goat grab *n.* at gatherings or celebrations in the Middle East, a communal self-served meal of meat and vegetables eaten with the hands. *Food & Drink. Iraq.*

1981 *Economist* (Feb. 28) "Kuwait: Bedouin Eatanswill" (in Kuwait), p. 45 ▶ The electors munched their way to and from the polling booths, helping themselves to platters of mansef (impolitely described as "the goat grab") and heaving hillocks of that favourite Kuwaiti sweet, jello. **1990** Margaret Gillerman *St. Louis Post-Dispatch* (Aug. 19) "Desert Sprint Missourian Tells of Race Through Sand, Darkness, Tanks, Soldiers to Freedom," p. 1A ▶ The Saudi soldiers feted the Americans, offering them juice, tea and platters of lamb and rice. Diemler explained it was "goat-grab," where "you tear off a piece of meat with your hands, mix it with rice and get it into a ball and pop it in." **2004** David J. Morris *Storm on the Horizon* (Feb. 3), p. 189 ▶ The enlisted men were subjected to a daily routine of whole boiled goat or chicken served up on a large metal platter. Mixed in the gruel were all the entrails, including beaks, hoofs, feet, and eyeballs.... Chowtime soon became known as "The Goat Grab." **2004** Robin Moore *Hunting Down Saddam* (Mar. 18), p. 82 ▶ A goat grab is basically a local tradition of having a big long table where they put out platters of rice, vegetables, and literally hunks of sheep that have been on a spit, roasting and so forth. You just dig in; you grab sheep or lamb, or fish, or what have you. **2005** Matt Misterek @ Mosul, Iraq *News Tribune* (Tacoma, Wash.) (June 18) "Deuce Four's Many Hats" (Int.) ▶ They call it a "goat grab," a night of traditional feasting to celebrate the bonds between American and Iraqi soldiers.

goat-rope *n.* a messy or disorganized situation. Also **goat roping, goat rodeo.**

[**1951** Albert E. Barrantine @ Korea *Bridgeport Sunday Post* (Conn.) (July 1) "Bridgeport Office Lauds Buddy Who 'Fires' Artillery by Radio," p. C12 ▶ I've been to two world fairs, goat roping in Idaho and cut off at Unsan, but I've never seen anything like this.] **1987** Randy Galloway *Dallas Morning News* (Jan. 25) "Giants to Beat Broncos: Simms Is Pressure-Proof," p. 4B ▶ Any team good enough to get this far comes in fully aware that for several morning hours every day you will have to endure a media goat rope. **1990** *Usenet: sci.space* (Apr. 18) "Re: Pegasus Launch from Valkyrie" ▶ In fact, it sounds a lot like what is called in the oilfield a "goat-roping exercise." **1992** *Usenet: alt.music.alternative* (Aug. 4) "Dallas Indie Music Festival (Re: The Buck Pets)" ▶ In a moment of temporary insanity, I volunteered to be some kind of stage manager for this goat-rope! Can you imagine getting fifteen bands on and off a stage—most of them don't even have roadie. **1993** *Usenet: alt.president.clinton* (May 18) "Re: Laser Focus on Economy" ▶ It remains to be seen if this will be a real investigation, or just a C.Y.A. goat-rope. **2004** Mark Davis *Atlanta Journal-Constitution* (Ga.) (Sept. 3) "Developer Files Suit Against Snellville" ▶ The article derided the proposed annexation and rezoning as a "goat roping." **2004** John Battelle *Searchblog* (Dec. 22) "A Look Ahead" (Int.) ▶ We will have a goat rodeo of sorts in the blogging/micropublishing/RSS world as commercial interests push into what many consider a "pure medium."

go bare *v.* to be uninsured. *Jargon.*

1976 *Washington Post* (Jan. 26) "Some Practicing with No Policies" (in L.A.), p. A12 ▶ Dr. Edwin Colbern is "going bare"—that is, he is practicing medicine without malpractice insurance coverage. **1978** Nancy L. Ross *Washington Post* (Feb. 18) "Suits Against Architects Rise by 20%," p. E17 ▶ As a result, the American Institute of Architects says a growing number of professionals are following the example of their medical colleagues and "going bare," or doing without liability insurance except where government contracts require it. **1992** Bruce Hight *Austin American-Statesman* (Tex.) (Jan. 26) "Uninsured Employer Takes Risk by 'Going Bare,'" p. A12 ▶ Going bare means going without workers' compensation insurance. **1998** *St. Petersburg Times* (Fla.) (Apr. 29) "'Bare' in Plain Sight," p. 10A ▶ Other doctors drop malpractice insurance because they have been sued so many times they cannot afford it. In either case, patients have the right to know when a doctor is uninsured or "going bare," as the practice is called. **2005** Don Doggett *Houston Chronicle* (Tex.) (Jan. 8) "Workers' Comp Gives

Protection" (Int.) ► Employers who choose not to carry workers' comp, sometimes referred to as going bare, face unlimited liability if an injured employee can show the employer was negligent.

go bazootie *v. phr.* to go crazy. *Slang.* This term is not common. It is probably a form of *go berserk* 'to become frenzied; to go crazy' and related to the also uncommon **go bazonkers.** Also see **BAZOOTY.**

1988 Carol Gentry *St. Petersburg Times* (July 10) "Trauma Care in State a Patchwork System," p. 1A ► Several states have assumed the role of anointing hospitals as trauma centers in areas that need them and have none. But when someone suggested a similar plan for Florida, said Alexander, the Florida Hospital Association "absolutely went bazootie." **1992** Michael Gee *Boston Herald* (July 20) "Rog's Right, But Not Bright Reaction Overshadows a Very Legitimate Gripe," p. 78 ► I think there's a major difference between criticizing a public figure for actions taken in public, like going bazootie on the mound during a playoff game..., and criticizing a public figure on one person's unsupported account of a long ago private moment. **1999** Christopher Sandford *Springsteen: Point Blank* (Sept. 1), p. 169 ► The total bill came to $500,000. CBS's Walter Yetnikoff "went bazootie" when he got it.

godunk *n.* a person who solicits free airplane trips or rides.

1938-39 Individual aviators @ N.Y. *LOTJ* "Aero-Manufacturing and Aviation Slang and Jargon," p. 6 ► Godunk. Aerial hitch hiker. **1946** ["Slick" Hightower] *Port Arthur News* (Tex.) (Sept. 28) "At the Airports," p. 16 ► Godunk or chisel rider—One who hangs around an airport begging for free rides.

go north with the club *v.* in baseball, to join a major league team (from a farm team or the minor leagues). Also **go north with the team.** *Canada. Jargon. Sports. United States.* [Baseball spring training is held in warm southern states, so to join the team as a regular player is almost always to literally go north to the team's home city.]

[**1903** *Decatur Review* (Ill.) (June 2), p. 3 ► Pitcher Eul, the Peoria man who has been dickering with McFarland, got in time to go north with the team and John Mertens was left at home.] **1942** *Syracuse Herald-Journal* (N.Y.) (Apr. 6) "Skidding the Sport Field with 'Skid,'" p. 14 ► Vance will probably go North with the club and if he does it means that infield practice will be well worth watching because his rifle-like arm is the big feature of Syracuse warmups.

1952 Jack Hand *Joplin Globe* (Mo.) (Mar. 21) "BoSox Will Go with Oldsters as Long as They Keep in Race," p. 7B ▶ Eight survivors of the six-week training school at Sarasota are due to go north with the club. **1983** *N.Y. Times* (Feb. 28) "Strawberry Draws Attention" (in St. Petersburg, Fla.), p. C6 ▶ "He's such a good young player," Manager George Bamberger said, "that there's absolutely no point in rushing him. In my mind, I don't think he'll go north with the club. But we expect him to make it before long, and to stay a long time." **1987** Dave Perkins @ Dunedin, Fla. *Toronto Star* (Can.) (Feb. 25) "Caudill's Forkball a 'Slice,'" p. C1 ▶ Despite his luscious contract—Caudill made $1,233,000 for his lost season in 1986 and is signed for three more years—he needs to beat people out to go north with the team. **2004** Allen Ariza *NYFansOnly.com* (Nov. 21) "CD's Phuture Phillie Phenoms...North Philly 40" (Int.) ▶ A player told that he has made the team is referred to as "going north with the club."

goon *v.* to act like a goon; to attack (someone) with undue or unprovoked violence. Also *n.,* **gooning.** *Canada. Sports. United States.*

1978 Allen Abel @ Uniondale, N.Y. *Globe and Mail* (Toronto, Can.) (May 1) "Leafs Muscle Beats Talent, Downcast Islanders Agree" ▶ In the playoffs, intimidation, gooning it up, being as vicious as you can be is a big part of hockey. **1986** Jerry Zgoda *Star Tribune* (Minneapolis-St. Paul, Minn.) (Mar. 2) "St. Louis Owner Singles Out Hospodar for Gooning" ▶ He criticized the NHL for allowing too much gooning. **1994** *Worker's Vanguard* (NYC) (July 8) "Reformists Cover for Teamster Bureaucracy" in *Usenet: misc.headlines* (July 13, 1994) (PNEWS) "[WV] 603 Teamsters Article" ▶ He got his group off the ground by gooning leftists and militant workers on behalf of the San Francisco labor tops during the 1983 Greyhound strike. **1994** Adrian Dater @ Lakewood, Colo. *Denver Post* (Colo.) (Sept. 4) "Green Mountain Stuns Thornton" ▶ Thornton coach Nate Leaf said his team played almost as well and was the victim of some rough Rams play, particularly on star halfback John Carroll. "They were 'gooning' him," Leaf said. **2004** Jeff Coen, Glenn Jeffer *Chicago Tribune* (Aug. 5) "Teenager Held in Fatal 'Gooning'" (Int.) ▶ The group of teenagers called it "gooning," authorities say, slang for the beating in the street of unsuspecting people they perceived to be drunk or elderly or otherwise defenseless.

goonda tax *n.* money extorted as 'protection' or to permit passage on public thoroughfares, or paid as a simple bribe. *Crime & Prisons. India. Money & Finance. Pakistan.* [The Hindi and Urdu term *goonda* can be translated as *rascal* or *ruffian* and even as *goon,* but there is no evidence to indicate that the English *goon* comes from *goonda* or vice versa.]

1996 @ Sialkot *Dawn* (Karachi, Pakistan) (Sept. 10) "Police-Outlaws Battle Near Sialkot Continues" in *Usenet: soc.culture.pakistan* (Sept. 10, 1996) Hassan Naqvi "Muqabla Continues with Terrorists of Punjab" ▶ All the murders committed by the duo are reported to have been linked with their activities of collecting "goonda tax" at the general bus stands of Narowal district. **1999** *Times of India* (Mar. 19) "Man Accused in Magarasa Homicide Arrested" (in Kanpur) ▶ The man accused in the Magarasa massacre was arrested by the police on Wednesday morning from the same locality while he was engaged in extorting goonda tax from shopkeepers. **2002** Jatinder Sharma @ Rohtak *Tribune* (Chandigarh, India) (Feb. 13) "Mining Mafia: Ex-CM Seeks Probe" (Int.) ▶ Addressing newsmen here today, Mr. Bansi Lal described the extortions as "goonda-tax." **2004** *Times of India* (Oct. 7) "Cops Net Ranchi Don in City Hotel" (in Kolkata) (Int.) ▶ A notorious criminal based in Ranchi, he patronised the word "goonda tax" (or GT in police parlance) to a good extent in the city, having collected Rs 2 crore over the past six months.

gorilla dust *n.* bluffing, posturing, or making hollow attempts at intimidation. *Animals. Politics.* [The 1998 quote accurately describes the origins of the term.]

1986 Warren Brown *Washington Post* (Dec. 9) "Smith, Perot All Smiles at Encounter," p. D1 ▶ More than 7,000 people showed up here today to witness what one business publication billed as a "clash of titans." But the actual event amounted to little more than a cloud of what one of the combatants called "gorilla dust." **1998** *Hinduism Today* (Kapaa, Hawaii) (Aug.) "Is India's Nuclear Threat Mere Gorilla Dust?" (Int.) ▶ When two male gorillas confront each other, they're too canny most of the time to actually fight, so they resort to the tried-and-true political tactic of intimidation. Both scurry about in a frenzy, grimacing menacingly, beating their chests and tossing clouds of dirt into the air. It's a serious encounter, full of powerful and primitive energies, a test of testosterone. Soon one becomes convinced that the other could win the threatened physical engagement, and retreats. It's called gorilla dust, and nations stir it up all the time. **2003** Zig Ziglar *Ziglar on Selling* (July 31), p. 205 ▶ The sales professional recognizes false objections as "gorilla dust."

grandmother cell *n.* a neuron that is said to fire when a person recognizes a single individual. *Biology. Science.* [Jerome Lettvin is often credit with coining this term, but that has not been verified.]

This term is directly tied to a theory of neurology that posits that individual brain cells contain individual memories, as opposed to each memory being stored across a matrix of cells.

1975 Gunther S. Stent *Science* (Mar. 21) "Limits to the Scientific Understanding of Man," vol. 187, no. 4181, p. 1056 ▶ The Grandmother cell.... Should one suppose that the cellular abstraction process goes so far that there exists for every meaningful structure of whose specific recognition a person is capable (for example, "my grandmother") at least one particular nerve cell in the brain that responds if and only if the light and dark pattern from which that structure is abstracted appears in its visual space...? **1983** Robert Walgate, Wallace Immen *Globe and Mail* (Toronto, Can.) (Apr. 1) "Stripes of the Auditory Cortex Register Tones Somewhat Like Keys on a Piano Brain 'Hears' Stereo Sound," p. E10 ▶ In vision, the search for a "granny cell"—a cell that fired only when you saw granny (or some other such complex object)—proved fruitless, so we are probably not going to detect a "Bach cell" or a "Stravinsky cell" in the auditory cortex. **2005** Roxanne Khamsi *Nature.com* (June 22) "Jennifer Aniston Strikes a Nerve" (Int.) ▶ The brain would contain a separate neuron to recognize each and every object in the world. Neurobiologist Jerome Lettvin coined the term "grandmother cell" to parody this view, as it would mean that the brain contains a specific cell to recognize one's own grandmother.

granny flat *n.* a separate apartment built on a lot already containing a home. *Architecture. Colloquial. United States.*

1978 Robert Sheppard *Globe and Mail* (Toronto, Can.) (Jan. 23) "House Leaps Three Centuries and an Ocean," p. P25 ▶ One of the two barn-like structures that until recently still stood in the English countryside now forms a four-car garage with upstairs servants' quarters, guest house or teen room. (The builders also suggest it would make an ideal granny flat.) **1987** Sandy Rovner *Washington Post* (Apr. 14) "Age-Speak 101: How to Tell a NORC from a DRG," p. Z25 ▶ *Granny Flat*: A separate, self-contained unit designed for temporary installation on the side or in the backyard of an adult child's home. **2005** Kellie Schmitt, Dan Stober *Mercury News* (San Jose, Calif.) (Mar. 27) "P.A. Considers Allowing More 'Granny' Units" (Int.) ▶ As part of sweeping zoning changes, the city council will decide next month whether to increase the number of homesites that could add garage apartments or cottages, commonly referred to as granny or in-law units.

grayshirt *v.* to not participate in a college sport (for a season) while still retaining eligibility. *Sports. United States.* A similar—but not identical—term is *redshirt*. The differences depend on the sport and the league.

[**1992** Jorge Valencia, Maureen Delany *Press-Enterprise* (Riverside, Calif.) (Oct. 1) "Poly Star Plays Bigger Than He Looks," p. C8 ▶ But he injured his left knee and took a grayshirt year (going to school part time without losing a year of eligibility).] **1993** Carl Sawyer *Orange County Register* (Calif.) (Dec. 4) "Bowl Games a Feast for Scouts," p. C12 ▶ Even before deciding on Orange Coast, I knew I was going to grayshirt. I have dyslexia (a reading-learning disability), and I felt that I needed to take some classes and learn what college is all about before I tried playing ball. **2005** Gentry Estes *Ledger-Enquirer* (Columbus, Ga.) (Jan. 9) "Tide Builds to 85 Scholarships" (Int.) ▶ Three players off the Crimson Tide's 2004 signing class were forced to grayshirt this season, meaning they could enroll in school, but there simply wasn't enough room to officially add them to the team until 2005.

green GDP *n.* a reconciliation of a nation's economic record with its environmental record. *Environment. Money & Finance.* [GDP = *G*ross *D*omestic *P*roduct.]

1990 Michael McCarthy *Times* (London, Eng.) (Apr. 30) "Government May Have to Make 'Green' Reports to the United Nations" ▶ The commitments...include environmental systems of national accounting to show "green GDP" as well as the merely financial balance sheet, a determined campaign on energy efficiency, and a public commitment to "reduce the harmful effects of the transport sector." **1994** J. Steven Landefeld, Carol S. Carson *Survey of Current Business* (Apr. 1) "Integrated Economic and Environmental Satellite Accounts," p. 33 ▶ Work on the natural resources satellite accounts was given added impetus and extended in scope in 1993 when President Clinton, as part of his April 21 Earth Day address, gave high priority to the development of "Green GDP measures [that] would incorporate changes in the natural environment into the calculations of national income and wealth." **2004** *Xinhuanet* (China) (Apr. 2) "China's 'Green GDP' Index Facing Technology Problem, Local Protectionism" (Int.) ▶ The "green" GDP, considered an echo of China's newly raised "scientific concept of development," requires adjusting the traditional national GDP to account for the degradation of both natural resources and environment.

griefer *n.* an online game player who willfully and habitually disrupts game play. *Entertainment. Technology.*

2000 *Usenet: rec.games.computer.ultima.online* (Aug. 14) "Re: Scamming" ▶ Being your standard UO griefer, he laughed at us and refused to return it, and there was quite a long standoff. Fortunately, this was a newbie griefer, and said he would sell me the 1600 wood back for 500 gold. Of course, upon handing over the 500, he wouldn't drop the wood, so several people paged GMs. About a minute later *poof* someone appears asking where the scammer is. Of course by then we had told him that we had paged the GMs, so the griefer handed over the wood. **2001** *Usenet: alt.games.everquest* (Nov. 19) "Re: Is DAOC Really THAT Good?" ► If someone as generally mild-mannered...as me could grief with such ease, imagine what dedicated griefers could do.... To the true griefer, time wasted is irrelevant. They are preventing you from doing what YOU want to do—that's satisfaction enough. **2002** Alex Pham *L.A. Times* (Sept. 2) "Bullies Give Grief to Gamers Internet," p. A1 ► Frerichs is what the online world calls a griefer—someone who plays to make others cry. They stalk, hurl insults, extort, form gangs, kill and loot. Although a tiny percentage of the millions who play online games, griefers are prolific in sowing distress and driving away thousands of paying customers. **2004** David Becker *CNET* (Dec. 13) "Inflicting Pain on 'Griefers'" (Int.) ► As online-game companies court new and wider audiences, many are running into an old problem: "griefers," a small but seemingly irradicable set of players who want nothing more than to murder, loot and otherwise frustrate the heck out of everyone else.

Gringolandia *n.* the United States of America. *Mexico. Spanish. United States.* [Mexican Spanish *gringo* 'Yankee; English-speaking North American' + *landia* (suffix indicating 'place')]

1953 Fisgona *El Informador* (Guadalajara, Mexico) (Mar. 8) "Indiscretas," p. 6 ► Ruth Román, la luminaria yanki que filma en nuestros estudios, al lado de otros astros del cielo fílmico de Gringolandia, perdió su bolso en los estudios Churubusco. **1969** Robert Berrellez *Daily Times* (Salisbury, Md.) (May 2) "U.S. Tied Closely with Problems Facing Mexico," p. 27 ► Many Mexicans believe their country has become, in the age of decolonization, a colony of the United States. Some call it Gringolandia. **2004** Dane Schiller *Express-News* (San Antonio, Tex.) (Nov. 21) "If Called a 'Gringo,' See If It's Said with a Smile" (Int.) ► Even in worst-case scenarios, it is a few notches less antagonizing than other words for people from the United States, known as gringolandia, or gringo land.

gronk *n.* a general term of derogation for a man, especially one considered weak, stupid, or brutish. *Australia. Derogatory. Slang.*

1987 R. Gibson *Courier-Mail* (Australia) (June 17) "Nine Double-Header on Crime and Corruption" ► They talk about the "gronks"— those prisoners who don't shower or carry any personal dignity. **1987**

Michael Cordell, Bernard Lagan *Sydney Morning Herald* (Australia) (Nov. 21) "Inside Our Jails" ► Alexander was labeled a "gronk"— young, slow, and an easy target for sex. According to Steve, a 30-year-old who served four years in jail for more than 10 bank robberies, "a gronk is someone who can't flow with the normal stretch, they're a bit slow on it or whatever." **1999** John Stapleton *Australian* (Mar. 24) "Where the Final Price Is High Indeed," p. 14 ► Those were the days when myth said heroin was just another drug, a creative juice, before methadone and dereliction, before decent people turned into evil little gronks, before so many talented people died. **1999** Adele Horin *Sydney Morning Herald* (Apr. 21) "Giving It the Hard Cell," p. 17 ► In a letter Armytage later wrote to the then Minister for Juvenile Justice, Faye Lo Po, he listed examples of the racial abuse the youths alleged they had been subjected to. "You black c—, you got no ticker." "Come on, you black gronk, hit me." And "Shut up, you black mutt." **2002** *MX* (Melbourne, Australia) (July 2) "Language Grows as Teens Go Sik," p. 9 ► Today, anything that is cool is sik while a gronk is someone who might previously have been called an idiot. **2002** Peter Brala @ West Pennant Hills *Daily Telegraph* (Sydney, Australia) (July 4) "Teenage Vernacular," p. 28 ► The work "gronk" does not have its genesis in ethnic youth. I first encountered this term while working as a psychologist in the NSW prison system in the mid-1980s. This term has gained a more widespread usage since then. **2004** The_Brick *Wanna Be Big Bodybuilding and Weightlifting Forums* (Mar. 1) "Gronk in the Gym Rant" (Int.) ► In Australia the term "gronk" was originally used to describe prison inmates. Now the term is used to describe wannabe mama's boy thugs, derelicts and general idiocy in people. Anyway I was at the gym which I have been a member of since it opened, where I know almost every hardcore trainer including the manager and staff when this gronk tried to "own" me. **2004** Niyi Awofeso *Journal of Mundane Behavior* (Millersville, Pa.) (June) "Prison Argot and Penal Discipline" (Int.) ► Not unexpectedly therefore, most argot terms relating to prison health workers had unflattering connotations. For instance, the argot term "gronk" is remains [*sic*] in current use in Australian prisons in describing health workers perceived as insensitive to prisoners' health and welfare interests. **2004** Lara Zamiatin *Sydney Morning Herald* (Australia) (Oct. 31) "The House of Gronk" (Int.) ► Delaveris was immediately hooked on prison lingo— and particularly taken with one word, "gronk," which has myriad meanings. In prison parlance, it's a derogatory term for inmates used by prison guards. Linguists, however, are divided. Some suggest it means "sex slave"; others say that it refers to a Neanderthal or a brutish person with limited intellect.

GUBU *adj. g*rotesque, *u*nbelievable, *b*izarre, *u*nprecedented; (*hence*) disreputable or scandalous. Also *n.* and *attrib. Acronym. Ireland. Politics. United Kingdom.* [The acronym was coined in 1983, based on words spoken by Irish Prime Minister Charles Haughey in 1982, by journalist Conor Cruise O'Brien, who also spared little effort in popularizing it. Originally referring to scandals related to the Haughey government, it has since—much like the American Watergate—become a more general term for scandal or political disrepute.]

1987 Hugh Carney *Financial Times* (Jan. 26) "Unsinkable Haughey Has Power in His Sights," p. 2 ▶ Sometimes labelled the "GUBU" Government, for "grotesque, unbelievable, bizarre, unprecedented" after words Mr. Haughey himself used about one incident, the events were remarkable by any standard. **1989** Conor Cruise O'Brien *Times* (London, Eng.) (May 30) "Power That Must Be Denied" ▶ Gubu happens to be my personal contribution to the political lexicon of the contemporary Republic. **1992** Maol Muire Tynan *Irish Times* (Dublin, Ireland) (July 18) "Reynolds Sends the Message by Carr," p. 5 ▶ In the GUBU days of Fianna Fail, however the company was called upon once more and Mr. Savage subsequently made contact with Albert Reynolds and Padraig Flynn. **1996** Rory Godson, John Burns *Sunday Times* (London, Eng.) (Dec. 8) "The Dunne Thing" ▶ It was always unlikely that Haughey, who survived the arms trial, allegations about land deals in north Dublin and the GUBU saga, was going to be tripped up at the age of 71. **1999** David Quinn *Sunday Times* (Dec. 5) "The Last Thing Mothers Need Are Lord Kitchener's Marching Orders" ▶ Everyone from hardline feminists to dyed-in-the-wool conservatives hate what he has done. He has achieved a double distinction by producing an unpopular budget on the back of an enormous budget surplus. Why does the word Gubu spring to mind? **2003** John Mulcahy *Irish Times* (Dublin, Ireland) (July 17) "Nation of Property Addicts Who Just Want More and More," p. 52 ▶ Irish people have a confused, contradictory, even GUBU attitude to property. **2003** Denis Coghlan *Irish Times* (Dublin, Ireland) (Oct. 25) "An Irishman's Diary," p. 15 ▶ My youth was spent in an English hospital, receiving treatment for scoliosis, which also caused spinal curvature. So we were both, as far as Haughey hard-liners were concerned, twisted. But to suggest this was a voluntary effort on my part was a GUBU notion in keeping with the times. **2003** *Irish Times* (Dublin, Ireland) (Oct. 25) "A Sinking Feeling as North Deal Falls at the Final Fence," p. 13 ▶ It has been an annus horribilis for the Prime Minister. The combination of an unpopular war in Iraq, which split his cabinet and his party, and the GUBU nature of the David Kelly affair, not to mention the Hutton

Inquiry exposures, have taken their toll on his trademark bounce.
2004 Willie Kealy, Jim Cusack *Sunday Independent* (Ireland) (July 18)
"No More Politics in Garda Jobs" ▶ The systemic problems in the
Garda management were not confined to its operations in Donegal,
Mr. McDowell said, reiterating his GUBU-esque description of recent
events as: "Frightening, unprecedented, egregious and devastating."
2004 Tommy Conlon *Sunday Independent* (Ireland) (Nov. 7) "A Heist,
a Con-Job and Conspiracy Theories Galore" ▶ The story took another
twist and headed straight for GUBU country. Between 6 p.m. Monday
night and 7.15 a.m. Tuesday morning someone broke into the offices
of the Equestrian Federation of Ireland and stole a file on O'Connor's
number two horse.

güey *n.* a dude, guy, buddy, buster, *cabrón, cuate; orig.* chump,
punk, idiot, fool. *Derogatory. Mexico. Slang. Spanish. United States.*
This term is usually said to be a form of *buey* 'ox' or, in Mexico,
'idiot.' Often used vocatively as a salutation or interjection. Like
cabrón, usually used only among friends, but not between men
and women or strangers. Unlike *cabrón*, it also is used among
women. It is pronounced similar to *way* or *hoo-way*. It is sometimes spelled *wey* or *way* in English or in informal Spanish.
1940 R. García (Austin, Tex.) "A Medias Copas" (Int.) in *Philadelphia
Papers on Linguistic Anthropology* (Dec. 2, 1998) Peter C. Haney "'En
un clavo están colgadas.' History, Parody, and Identity Formation in the
Mexican American Carpa," p. 3 ▶ Que mi vieja me hizo güey. That my
vieja made me a *güey* (lit. "ox" / fig. "impotent fool"). **2000** Anthony
Bourdain *Kitchen Confidential* (May 22) p. 221 ▶ *Pinche wey* means
"fucking guy" but can also mean "you adorable scamp" or "pal."
2003 Leslie Salzinger *Genders in Production* (Apr. 1), p. 191 ▶ *Guey* is
a slang form of the word *buey*, meaning "ox" (beast of burden), and
is used in conversation the way "man" is in English. **2003** [Mirasol]
Flowerpop (Tucson, Ariz.) (June 18) (Int.) ▶ It comes with the service,
so everyone in the city walks around with their phones blabbering
away on the radio while every innocent bystander must be subjected
to hearing, "que paso anoche guey." Then *beep* "pos nada guey, fui
a Chamucos con Kike y Pepe." *beep* "Bueno pues, soy a la puente.
Hablame manana, vas a jugar el futbol?" *beep* "Si guey, quiere ir?"
beep "Pos hablame cabron." *beep* ***2004** Roxana Fitch *Jergas de
habla Hispana* "Jerga de México" (Int.) ▶ *buey*: (m.) (pronunciado
güey) idiota. También se usa como término informal entre amigos.
2004 [Fluken] *Redota* (Jan. 11) "Güey" (Int.) ▶ Contrariamente a lo
que se pueda pensar en México Güey en la mayoría de los casos no es
una ofensa. Significa amigo, camarada o compañero. Ejem: ¿Qué
onda güey? = ¿Qué hay de nuevo amigo? Estás re-güey = Eres muy

tonto (en esta frase, el güey es un poco despectivo pero a la vez pater-
nal).... El güey se utiliza unicamente con personas con las que se tiene
cierta confianza. Es un poco ofensivo usarlo con personas mayores o
con mujeres, aunque algunas mujeres también lo utilizan entre ellas.
2004 Maria Cortés Gonzalez *El Paso Times* (Tex.) (May 8) "Coors Ad
Makes Many Question" (Int.). ▶ For many young adults along the border, "güey" is a simple slang greeting among friends. For others, it's a
crude insult that's not used in polite company.

gun-grabber *n.* a person who advocates gun control. *Derogatory.*
United States. This term is common in the United States among
members of the National Rifle Association.

1978 Bob Levey *Washington Post* (Aug. 10) "Moonshine Buster Remi-
nisces," p. 6 ▶ Davis, 54, got a TNT-like retirement gift from one
right-wing newspaper. Atop a story announcing that Davis was going,
the paper's headline cried, with utmost objectivity: "Chief Gun-Grabber Retires." **1995** *Proponent* (Columbus, Ohio) (Sept.) "The Third
Option," vol. 7, no. 9, in *Usenet: alt.current-events.clinton.whitewater*
(Sept. 12, 1995) Dennis P. Carney *"PROponent—September 1995—PRO
Newsletter"* ▶ In a perfect world the NRA wouldn't have to be spending so much of your money to hold the pack of rabid gun-grabbers at
bay. **1996** Victor Milan *Libertarian Enterprise* (Dec. 1) "Letter to a
Gun-Grabber: The Wrath to Come" (Int.) **2004** Jeremy Rich *Daily
Oklahoman* (Oklahoma City) (Oct. 29) "Your Views: Presidential Cam-
paign; How Is America Safer Now?" p. 17A ▶ I read in the paper that
John Kerry was out goose hunting trying to convince gun owners he
isn't a gun grabber. If Americans fall for that lie, our goose is cooked.
Kerry has never had a positive vote for America's gun owners or the
Second Amendment.

gurgitator *n.* a person who participates in
eating competitions. *Food & Drink. Sports.*
This term was popularized by, if not coined
by, the International Federation of Competitive Eating, a marketing and promotions organization that has a newsletter called "The
Gurgitator."

2002 Jennifer Harper *Washington Times*
(Feb. 18) "Fox's 'Glutton Bowl' Lures 'Gurgita-
tors' with $25k Prize," p. A9 ▶ Chicken wings,
matzo balls, pickled quail eggs, cannoli, hot dogs, jalapenos, sushi,
pancakes, oysters, mince pie—it's all fair game to competitive eaters
who have their own federation, regulations, world records and yes,
competitive eat meets where less is definitely not more and the best

professional gurgitator wins. **2003** Jim Auchmutey *Atlanta Journal-Constitution* (Jan. 26) "The Amazing, Incredible, Record-Setting Big Mouth Dale Boone Is Making a Name for Himself on the Competitive Eating Circuit," p. LS1 ▶ The two-time defending Coney Island champion, Takeru "The Tsunami" Kobayashi, weighs barely 120 pounds and looks more like a gymnast than a gurgitator. **2005** Cheryl Rosenberg Neubert *Kansas City Star* (Kan., Mo.) (Mar. 7) "Competitive Eaters' Looks Can Be Deceiving" (Int.) ▶ Jed Donahue is a professional competitive eater, or gurgitator as they're called in the biz.

H

haji *n.* an Iraqi; any Muslim, Arab, or native of the Middle East. Also **hadji;** *attrib. Iraq. Military. Slang. United States.* [< Arabic *haji* 'pilgrim.']

2003 @ Tampa Bay, Fla. *Usenet: soc.culture.iraq* (Mar. 30) "Re: Americans, You Idiot" ▸ Learn to type correctly Hadji—we will conduct the war on OUR terms not yours. You are obviously one of the terrorists. **2003** *American Enterprise* (June 1) "Dust and Stars: An Iraq War Journal" (in Tallil Air Base, South-Central Iraq), vol. 14, no. 4, pp. 18-55 ▸ If nature calls, don't go out far or you could be mistaken for a haji. **2003** Andrew England @ Baghdad, Iraq (*AP*) (Sept. 9) "Iraqis Say It Will Take More Than Words and International Troops to Solve Their Problems" ▸ Some have grown to despise Iraqis, whom they call "Hajis," scowling rather than waving as they pass locals along highways and dirt roads. **2004** *Usenet: us.military.army* (May 25) "Re: Crocodile Tears (was Re: Gotta Find a Scapegoat to Keep the Ragheads Happy)" ▸ To me, the ordinary Iraqi people count as "people" the thugs trying to set themselves up as warlords are "Hadji" or "enemy." **2004** Douglas Jehl, Andrea Elliott @ Afghanistan *N.Y. Times* (May 29) "Cuba Base Sent Its Interrogators to Iraqi Prison," p. 1 ▸ We were pretty much told that they were nobodies, that they were just enemy combatants. I think that giving them the distinction of soldier would have changed our attitudes toward them. A lot of it was based on racism, really. We called them hajis, and that psychology was really important. **2004** John Koopman @ Ramadi, Iraq *San Francisco Chronicle* (Calif.) (July 9) "Trolling for Bombs" (Int.) ▸ The explosive had been placed inside a tiny roadside market—a "haji stand" in GI parlance—which was closed when the bomb went off. **2004** Jimmy Schaffer @ Taji, Iraq *Uncool Adventures* (Derby, Kan.) (July 11) "Every Day's a Holiday" (Int.) ▸ *Hadji*—A term used for any local national, primarily those that are dumber than a box of rocks. **2004** Gordon Lubold @ Camp Hurricane Point, Iraq *Marine Times* (July 17) "Marines in Iraq: Reporter's Notebook; But It's a Dry Heat" (Int.) ▸ It's SO hot that if I wash my clothes in the Haji washing machine. (That's shorthand for anything bought locally, and by the way, "Haji," Lloyd tells me, is not a pejorative term since it means "wise man." Marines use the term as a prefix for anything. "Haji-movies," "hajified," you name it.) **2004** Steve Smith @ FOB Bernstein, Iraq *ArmySteve* (Nov. 12) "Fobbits and Other Iraqi Critters" (Int.) ▶ Many haji shops have signs out front of them that read "hajee shop" so it seems at least these proprietors don't mind the term. **2004** *WorldNetDaily* (U.S.) (Nov. 27) "Combat in Iraq: A Ground-Level View" (in Iraq) (Int.) ▶ I can recognize a Sadiqqi (Arabic for friend) from a Haji (Arabic word for someone who has made the pilgrimage to Mecca, but our word for a bad guy). **2005** Paul Rockwell *Online Journal* (Apr. 1) "Army Reservist Witnesses War Crimes" (Int.) ▶ "Hajji" is the new slur, the new ethnic slur for Arabs and Muslims. It is used extensively in the military.... It is used in the military with the same kind of connotation as "gook," "Charlie," or the n-word. Official Army documents now use it in reference to Iraqis or Arabs. It's real common. There was really a thick aura of racism. **2005** Grace Leonhart *Hope Star* (Ark.) (July 6) "Driver Sees All Sides of Humanity in Iraq" (Int.) ▶ I saw Haji (another name for Iraqis) successfully load two full-grown camels in a Ranger pickup without sideboards.

haji mart *n.* among American military in Iraq and Afghanistan, a flea market, bazaar, or roadside vendor. *Arabic. Military.* [**HAJI** 'an Iraqi or Afghani local; a Muslim' + *mart* 'market.'] Often capitalized as if it is a proper noun, probably by comparison to American retail chains "Wal-Mart" and "K-Mart." Usually derisive or jocular.

2003 Zaheera Wahid *Orange County Register* (Calif.) (Dec. 13) "Wounded Soldier Diane Gilliam Will Cherish Time with Her Family in O.C.," p. 1 ▶ She arrived with two black footlockers packed with her belongings and Christmas presents she'd bought at the Hajji Mart, an Afghan bazaar. **2003** Charles Clover, Peter Spiegel *Financial Times* (U.K.) (Dec. 22) "Name Game," p. 18 ▶ A "Hadjimart" is a roadside kiosk; a "Hadjimobile" is a minibus. **2004** John Koopman @ Ramadi, Iraq *San Francisco Chronicle* (July 9) "Trolling for Bombs," p. A1 ▶ "We should just clear out all these haji marts," one said. "Bring in a bulldozer." **2004** Edmund Sanders @ Baghdad, Iraq *L.A. Times* (Oct. 15) "Suicide Blasts Kill 6 Inside Iraq Safe Area," p. A1 ▶ After the bomb was found last week in the restaurant, the U.S. Embassy issued a security advisory to Green Zone residents, urging them to avoid the restaurant and the bazaar, known in the compound as Haji Mart. **2004** Brita Brundage *Fairfield County Weekly* (Conn.) (Dec. 2) "Commando Correspondents" (Int.) ▶ Outside the base, soldiers freely shopped at a marketplace set up by Iraqis (derisively called "Haji Marts" by soldiers) that sold everything from alcohol to bootleg DVDs to bayonets.

half-past-six *adj.* bad; shoddy, slipshod. *Singapore.*

1992 Jenny Lam *Straits Times* (Singapore) (July 18) "The Shrimp People" ▶ The fairer elite (those who are descended from Europeans) are known as "the upper 10." At the other extreme are the Portuguese-Eurasians with Malaccan roots who belong to the "half-past six" or "lower-10" strata. **1997** *Edge* (Singapore) (Sept. 29) "Anticipating Corporatisation" ▶ We can live with our competitors. If you provide good service, patients will come to you but if you do half-past-six jobs, you may not be so lucky. **1998** *Malay Mail* (Malaysia) (Oct. 13) "Duh...We Have a National Team Again—Honest" ▶ More Malaysian soccer fans support any number of foreign teams, even a half-past six side like Manchester United, rather than a local team. **2003** Tan Shzr Ee *Straits Times* (Singapore) (Dec. 3) "SSO Exec Is Moving On" ▶ My Chinese is "half-past-six" and I must brush it up. **2005** Denyse Tessensohn *Today* (Singapore) (May 26) "Save Our Shiok!" (Int.) ▶ *Half-past-six*: (Original Singapore coinage) Slipshod.

haltura *n.* secondary work about which one is not serious or to which one is not fully committed; hackwork, moonlighting, free-lancing. Also *attrib. Business. Entertainment. Hebrew. Israel. Russia. Russian.* In Hebrew, חרוטלה. In Russian, халтуры.

1923 Nikita Balieff *N.Y. Times Mag.* (June 24) "Off Stage and Us Again," p. 9 ▶ "Haltura" is a word which has been used frequently by the Russian actor during Bolshevism and signifies an extra job on the outside of his own theatre. The "haltura" apparitions are staged without any artistic aims, and interest the actor only as a means by which he can earn an extra few million rubles. **1991** Mikhail Bulgakov *Washington Post* (Nov. 17) "The Devil Comes to Moscow," p. X5 ▶ This last depicts a theater troupe's desperate attempts to take a draft of a new play and, with only 20 minutes preparation, present it to the government censor for approval. As it happens, this drama about a revolution on a tropical island is perfectly awful, phony art of the kind called haltura in Russian. **1993** Michael Ajzenstadt *Jerusalem Post* (Israel) (Aug. 2) "IPO Says Farewell to Mehta's Arms: Back Again in '94" ▶ I'm not going away from Israel to do "halturas" (free-lance jobs) with other orchestras. It's basically going to be an opera season for me. **1998** Yosef Goell *Jerusalem Post* (Israel) (Sept. 28) "Wanted: A Foreign Minister," p. 8 ▶ He is treating the Foreign Ministry portfolio as a haltura (a side job), which has left the Foreign Ministry and all its accumulated expertise in a shambles. **2002** Galya Kolosova *Theatre for Young Audiences Around the World* (July) "Children's Theatre in Russia," p. 43 (Int.) ▶ There is a very good word in Russian which is impossible to translate into English—"HALTURA."—It means money made on the side with help of cheap art. This kind of activities always existed and was always considered shameful. Actors used to conceal it from everybody. They visited faraway towns and played their thrash shows for local public who was captured and raptured to see famous actors alive. **2002** [BadaBing!] *Gonzo Engaged* (Dec. 23) "Time Persons of the Year. What the Fuck?" (Int.) ► Haltura is when you are pretending to do a good job, pretending to be a professional, expert with a diploma and you are supposed to know what to do but you know you are just fucking around. **2004** Mark Heinrich @ Tel Aviv, Israel (*Reuters*) (June 27) "Culture of Improvisation Buoys, Bogs Down Israelis" (Int.) ► Israelis call it "haltura," slang for a cross between make-do ingenuity, shoddy amateurism and moonlighting, with a dash of disdain for the letter of the law thrown in.

hammerhead *n.* a committed bicyclist; an aggressive or adventurous cyclist. *Slang. Sports.*

1989 Lee Feinswog *Baton Rouge Sunday Advocate* (La.) (July 2) "Ripple Leaving Big Wake in Triathlon Series," p. 4C ► It's expected that Jan is expected to lead on the bike. And that's a lot of pressure. Some of the girls are starting to call me Hammerhead. It's pressure. **1993** Tom Steadman *Greensboro News & Record* (N.C.) (May 9) "Even You Can Learn the Lingo!," p. C11 ► Hammerhead—A Road Rider. **1993** *Usenet: rec.bicycles.rides* (July 22) "Re: Death Ride, or 'Where I Died on My Summer Vacation'" ► We both got called hammerheads for plowing up one of the hairpins as we passed a big pack. "Hammerhead back!... Another hammerhead back!" **1995** Brian Swartz *Bangor Daily News* (Maine) (June 15) "Mountain bikers are taking the plunge in the Carrabassett Valley" ► National competitions have developed since the first "hammerhead," a self-descriptive term used among hardcore bikers, plunged downhill on a ski slope. **2004** Jessica M. McRorie *Daily Local* (West Chester, Pa.) (June 27) "Bike & Brew" (Int.) ► The club also provides for all levels of riders, starting with the "A" group, or the "hammer heads," which is cyclist slang for fast and aggressive riders.

hamster care *n.* high-volume health care in which patients are not given specialized attention. Also **hamster health care.** *Health. Jargon. Medical.*

1999 (*Federal News Service*) (July 14) "National Press Club Newsmaker Luncheon with Dr. David Lawrence, CEO, Kaiser Permanente" ► Ian Morrison...has coined a phrase. I think it's going to appear in "Modern Health Care," actually. He calls it "hamster care," where people are just churning like mad to keep up with the demand. **2000** Richard Smith *British Medical Journal* (Dec. 23) "Hamster Health Care: Time to Stop Running Faster and Redesign Health Care" (Int.)

▸ Perhaps the purest examples of hamster care are in Canada and Germany. In these countries there is a fixed budget for all services provided by doctors and a standardised schedule of fixed fees. Doctors try to earn their target income by providing more and more services. But as the number of services provided by all doctors rises and exceeds set total budgets, so the fee for each service goes down. Like frantic hamsters the doctors run ever faster—but to no avail. **2004** Nancy Luna @ Santa Ana, Calif. *Orange County Register* (Calif.) (Jan. 12) ▸ "The average doctor is seeing thousands of patients a year to survive, and the result is hamster care, or treadmill medicine," said Dr. Jack Lewin, chief executive officer of the California Medical Association. **2004** Arthur Caplan *Wichita Eagle* (Kan.) (July 7) "Good Health Care Should Not Be Only for Wealthy" (Int.) ▸ One might wonder why it is necessary to pay a bounty to get a doctor to call you back. The answer is that under the watchful eye of managed care and insurance companies, the quality of care has gotten so awful that doctors refer to it as "hamster care." Only those patients who pay more are going to get treated by the "concierge" doctors who get off the daily treadmill and practice good medicine.

handbags at ten paces *n.* a verbal spat, usually between athletes on the field of play. *Sports. United Kingdom.* Also **handbags**. Probably related to any number of Monty Python sketches that have the actors dressed in drag, battling each other with handbags, such as in Series 1, Episode 11, "Battle of Pearl Harbor." **1991** Neil Robinson *Guardian* (U.K.) (Oct. 21) "Griffin Park Statisticians Sad to Find That You Cannot Keep a Goodman Down" ▸ Then a scuffle broke out between Brentford's Bates and Albion's Bradley. "Handbags at 10 paces," said Bobby Gould, Albion's manager, with a glint in his eye. **1996** *Times* (London, Eng.) (Mar. 23) "The Times Match-By-Match Guide to the Premiership This Weekend—Football—Preview." ▸ Undignified scenes at Highbury the last time these teams met, in the Coca-Cola Cup quarter-finals in January, with Bruce Rioch and Terry McDermott indulging in handbags at ten paces after Ginola had been sent off. **2003** Paul "Deacon" Mirengoff *Power Line* (Bethesda, Md.) (Oct. 27) "Handbags" (Int.) ▸ One of the joys of following English soccer is learning some of its delightful jargon. My favorite bit, perhaps because it is so politically incorrect, is the phrase applied to second-rate soccer fights—"handbags at ten paces," or "handbags" for short. **2004** Iain Aitch *Guardian* (U.K.) (June 24) "Are We Dead Yet?" (Int.) ▸ We point, shout and indulge ourselves in what football commentators usually dub "handbags at 10 paces."

hang-up *n.* in prison, a suicide by hanging. *Crime & Prisons. NYC.*

1982 *N.Y. Times* (Mar. 26) "Jargon of Correction Officers," p. B4
▶ *Hangups*—Suicides. [**1999** Bill Tuttle @ Queens *Newsday* (Long Island, N.Y.) (Dec. 23) "Nun Helps Inmates Beat the Holiday Blues," p. A43 ▶ One New Year's Eve nine years ago, four inmates told her they were going to "hang up"—jailspeak for committing suicide by hanging.] **2005** Paul von Zielbauer *N.Y. Times* (Feb. 28) "In City's Jails, Missed Signals Open Way to Season of Suicides" (Int.) ▶ Suicides—"hang-ups" in the cold vernacular of the cellblock—have always been a jailhouse reality.

hapa *adj.* racially mixed, esp. with an Asian racial background. *Hawaii. United States.* [Hawaiian *hapa* 'half.'] This is "Asian" in the North American sense, where it usually refers to East Asians from China, Japan, Vietnam, and Korea.

1989 *Usenet: soc.culture.asian.american* (July 28) "Re: Truth and Beauty Re: Inter-Racial Dating" ▶ As far as a hapa person sharing my experience, of course there are going to be some things that we both understand, and some that only one of us understands. For example, I couldn't understand the extent to which a hapa person might experience an identity crisis in terms of having parents of 2 different colors. But that doesn't keep me from trying to understand, and listening to whatever they have to say. **1989** Felicity Barringer *N.Y. Times* (Sept. 24) "Mixed-Race Generation Emerges But Is Not Sure Where It Fits," p. 22 ▶ Faced with a similar question, 5-year-old Gabriella Grosz says, "I'm black and white." And Cindie Nakashima, a 22-year-old graduate student who once called herself "half-Japanese and half-white," now uses the Hawaiian word for "half," saying simply, "I'm hapa." **1991** Elizabeth Atkins *St. Louis Post-Dispatch* (Mo.) (June 25) "Students of Mixed Race Form Bond," p. 1D ▶ At Stanford last year, a group of women who are Asian and white and were in classes together formed HAPA, the Half Asian People's Association. "Hapa" is Hawaiian for half Asian. **2005** *Picolute* (Seattle, Wash.) (Feb. 7) "More About Hapa" (Int.) ▶ Sometime during my sophomore year I stumbled upon MiXeD at UW which lead me to my exploration of Mavin Foundation. I was incredibly excited to hear that there's a magazine on multiracial backgrounds. I have a vague memory when I was about 10 years old and imagined what it would be like to have a country dedicated to all of us hapa kids. I discovered that Hawaii is as close as it gets.

Harvard death *n.* a death that occurs despite all symptoms being treated successfully or all medical test results appearing normal.

Medical. This term is often explained to mean "the operation was successful but the patient died."

1985 Dena Kleiman *N.Y. Times* (July 15) "Doctors Ask, Who Lives? When to Die?" p. B1 ▶ He spoke about how some doctors make a game of resuscitation; how the challenge for some young doctors becomes having patients die a so-called "Harvard" death, in which their blood gas numbers perfectly match those given in textbooks. **1989** Anne Burson-Tolpin *Medical Anthropology Quarterly* (Sept.) "Fracturing the Language of Biomedicine: The Speech Play of U.S. Physicians," vol. 3, no. 3, p. 287 ▶ To die "a Harvard death" (meaning the physicians have managed to normalize the laboratory test values but failed to help the patient). **1998** C.J. Peters *Virus Hunter* (Apr. 13), p. 284 ▶ When I was an intern, we used to refer to this as a "Harvard Death": you kept pumping meds until all the cultures were negative and test results were normal but the patient still succumbed. **2005** Perri Klass *N.Y. Times* (Apr. 5) "In a Pile of Papers, the Ghost of a Once-Healthy Child" (Int.) ▶ I thought about that bitter medical student joke, the "Harvard death," in which all the lab results are perfect, all the electrolytes and body chemistry numbers "in the boxes"—as the patient dies.

hawasim *n.* a looter or thief. *Arabic. Crime & Prisons. Iraq. Slang.*

2003 [A.Y.S.] *Iraq at a Glance* (Baghdad, Iraq) (Nov. 1) "Freedom Is a Responsibility" (Int.) ▶ I said, "Do you have a car?!" He said, "Yes, doctor," at once I concluded that he was a thief (in slang known as Hawasim, a name derived from Saddam's description of the coming war at that time as Al-hawasim, which means The Decisive War, after the end of the war, everyone seen in the loot and robbery is called 'Hawasim'!!). **2004** Mushriq Abbas, Nasir al-Ali *Al-Nahdah* (Iraq) (Mar. 15), p. 1 in BBC Monitoring Middle East (Mar. 19, 2004) "Iraqi Report on Smuggling of Saddam Era Tanks, Heavy Arms to Iran" ▶ According to residents of the area, hundreds of tanks have been purchased from civilians, Al-Hawasim gangs [a term used by Iraqis to refer to the thieves well-nourished during and after the last war, which was named Al-Hawasim by the former regime], or the foreign forces. [**2004** Patrick Graham @ Iraq *Harper's* (June 1) "Beyond Fallujah," vol. 308, no. 1849, p. 37 ▶ Saddam had called this war the Harb Al Hawasim, the Final War, and Iraqis immediately renamed looted goods in Iraq Hawasim.] **2004** Peter Y. Hong @ Baghdad, Iraq *L.A. Times* (July 19) "Baghdad Real Estate Sizzles Amid Chaos," p. A1 ▶ Some of his customers, he said, are hawasim, looters who took part in the rampant plundering of government buildings, banks, Iraqi army bases and businesses after the war.

heartsink *n.* a feeling of dismay or disappointment; in medical use, **heartsink patient,** a patient that is difficult or impossible to help. *Medical.*

1937 Jimmy Fiddler *Washington Post* (Mar. 10) "In Hollywood," p. 13 ▶ Imagine the heart-sink that comes to an adult star when he receives the script and finds himself teamed for scene after scene with Deanna Durgin or Freddie Bartholomew. **1974** Lewis Thomas *The Lives of a Cell* (May 31), p. 58 in (Jan. 1, 1995) ▶ The less immense, more finite items, of a size allowing the mind to get a handhold, like nations, or space technology, or New York, are hard to think about without drifting toward heartsink. **1989** Marilyn Dunlop *Toronto Star* (Dec. 30) "'Heartsink' Patients Overwhelm Doctors," p. F2 ▶ Heartsink patients may fit into four categories, the editorial says. Dependent clingers, entitled demanders, manipulative help-rejecters and self-destructive deniers. They can overwhelm and exasperate their doctors by their behavior. **1992** Cormac McCarthy *Blood Meridian* (May 5), p. 98 ▶ The woman looked up. Neither courage nor heartsink in those old eyes. **1995** Jenny Tabakoff *Sydney Morning Herald* (Australia) (Sept. 18) "Beware of Heartsinkers, Even If They Do Have One Useful Function," p. 13 ▶ There are any number of heartsink words and phrases in the English language, and they are proliferating. Words such as "forum," "convention" and "summit" send a signal to most people's brains: Turn off now. **2000** Seau-Tak Cheung @ Dundee, Australia *sBMJ* (London, Eng.) (Apr.) "Maybe There Are Also Heartsink Doctors" (Int.) ▶ There is no doubt that heartsink patients are a great source of stress for their doctors, but at the same there must exist "heartsink doctors"—doctors that patients dread seeing, not because of what they may tell them, but because of the doctor's personal characteristics. **2001** Nick Hornby *How to Be Good* (Aug. 1), p. 128 ▶ The patients that dismay me the most are the ones I see a lot whom I can't help. We call them heartsink patients, for obvious reasons, and someone once reckoned that most partners in practice have about fifty heartsinks on their books. **2002** Robert Ashton *This Is Heroin* (Oct. 1), p. 105 ▶ I knew then, with total heartsink, that he was on heroin, because that's what heroin addicts have to do—steal from anyone or anywhere for cash to buy their stuff.

heater *n.* a crime or criminal case that attracts a lot of (media) attention. *Crime & Prisons. Media. Police.*

1986 Tom Fitzpatrick *Chicago Sun-Times* (July 24) "Echeles Is Up to Elbows in Case of Fugitive Killer," p. 7 ▶ "The thing that I'm concerned about," Echeles said, "is that this was the first 'heater' case for Judge Themis Karnezis...." "What do you mean by a 'heater' case?" I asked. Echeles sighed at my lack of knowledge. "A heater case is one that brings a lot of press coverage, like the Marquette 10 or any Greylord case." **1987** Mary Durusau *Baton Rouge Sunday Advocate Mag.* (La.) (Jan. 18) "Unholy Matrimony," p. 4 ▶ In 1974, John Dillmann was a 27-year-old detective on the New Orleans Police Department's homicide unit and hungry for his first "heater" case—a big publicity case that would earn him status on the force. He didn't know how soon that case would come. **1993** Anne Keegan *Chicago Tribune* (Dec. 22) "Chicago Speak," p. 1 ▶ *Heater case*: A crime that's getting a lot of publicity. It means the pressure is on to solve it immediately, a k a "front burner." **1996** James Varney *Times-Picayune* (New Orleans, La.) (Jan. 27) "Teen Guilty of Murder Outside Quarter Lounge," p. A1 ▶ Hill pointed out police had called Superintendent Richard Pennington within a half-hour of the shooting, calling it evidence that "this case was a heater from the beginning." **2005** David Heinzmann, Jeff Coen *Chicago Tribune* (Jan. 4) "Rapes in Poor Areas Rarely Get Spotlight" (Int.) ▶ Bernie Murray, head of the Felony Trial Division in the Cook County state's attorney's office, said that though the office handles more sexual assaults in economically depressed areas of the city, he understands when some cases become "heaters." "In deference to (the media), if there's a neighborhood where there is not a lot of crime, and then you have a situation where there's a serial rapist in the area, that's news," Murray said.

heatiness *n.* a characteristic of certain foods or stimulants said to cause emotional or physical reactions associated with temper, fever, passion, excess, or true heat. *China. Food & Drink. Health. Hong Kong. Malaysia. Singapore.* From Chinese culture and medicine.

1993 Teh Hooi Ling *Business Times Singapore* (May 26) "Herbal Jelly Maker Goes Global with Help from Sisir" ▶ The company was started two years ago to produce the jelly—which many Chinese believe can relieve "heatiness"—from about 20 types of herbs. **1994** James Chadwick *South China Morning Post* (Hong Kong) (Aug. 2) "Understanding the Key to Tapping the Mainland," p. 3 ▶ The heart of the matter is the intricate philosophy of "heatiness and cooliness"—a traditional Chinese belief in the balance between hot and cold air within the body. "To understand the market, you must understand the myths. Cognac is perceived as being 'heaty'—it encourages sexual activity. Whisky and menthol cigarettes are 'cooling,'" Ms. So said. "The marketing strategists have to understand these things—they have to overcome deep-rooted perceptions." **1996** Kieran Cooke *Financial Times* (U.K.) (Feb. 17) "Dispatches: Irish Year of the Rat" ▶ The other ailment Doris waxes lyrical about is a peculiar affliction called heatiness. This, according to Chinese culinary traditionalists, is caused by eating the wrong combinations of foods or downing too much strong alcohol, thus provoking a fire inside. **2001** *Usenet: soc.culture.thai* (Oct. 21) **"Re: What Does 'Ron Nai' Translate to"** ▶ Ron-Nai is what the Chinese call "re-qi" which is roughly translated as "heatiness" which is a term widely used by Malaysian and Singaporean Chinese.... Food that is typically known as "heaty" will include fried food, food high in fat content and certain fruits such as Jack-fruit. Heatiness will cover a whole spectrum of symptoms from indigestion, mouth ulcers and feeling febrile. It may also cause halithosis. The opposite spectrum is "cooling" food which includes fruits such as watermelon and a variety of herbs to counter heatiness such as Chrysantemum tea, etc. Too much cooling food may cause cough and abdominal pain. **2004** Teo Pau Lin *Straits Times* (Singapore) (June 13) **"Prickly Heat"** (Int.) ▶ Eating mangosteens can counter the "heatiness" of durians. Fact: Once again, Dr. Zainal said there is no scientific evidence to support this.

hecka *adv.* very; *hella. Slang.* [A milder form of *hella.*] This term, like *hella*, probably comes from California.

[**1985** Tony Cooper *L.A. Times* (Feb. 28) **"2-A Boys Defense Does It for Oceanside,"** p. 15 ▶ "We had a hecka season," Seaman said. "No Mission Bay team has ever been to the CIF finals. Our kids don't have anything to be ashamed of."] **1992** Shann Nix *San Francisco Chronicle* (Nov. 17) **"How to Talk Like a Kid,"** p. A9 ▶ For an all-purpose superlative, use "hella" as in "He's hella fine," (he's good-looking) or "that test was hella-hard." For prudes or freshman girls, "hella" may be replaced by "hecka." **1992** *Usenet: alt.fan.rush-limbaugh* (Nov. 22) **"Re: Here Are the Undeniable Truths of Life"** ▶ Gee, was this more of your hecka-subtle irony? Whoosh, it went right over my head. **1995** Peggy Orenstein *Schoolgirls* (Sept. 5), p. 201 ▶ She told me shyly that she dreamed of becoming a lawyer. "It would be hecka fresh," she said at the time, "because you get to defend people who are really innocent and help them." *****2004** Crispin Boyer, Dan Hsu, Parker Ames *1Up.com* (Dec.) **"Child's Play II"** (Int.) ▶ These controls are hecka hard.

helitack *n.* firefighting that uses helicopters (to deploy firefighters, gear, water, etc.). Also *adj. Firefighting. Jargon.* [*heli*copter + at*tack*]

1956 *L.A. Times* (Calif.) (June 10) **"Fire-Fighting Copter Tests Start in Forest"** (in San Bernardino), p. A23 ▶ First of a series of tests—tabbed the Helitack Program—on the use of helicopters in firefighting will start next week in the San Bernardino National Forest. **1979** Victor Malarek @ Dryden *Globe and Mail* (Toronto, Can.) (July 24) **"Fighting Modern-Day Forest Fires Like a 'War Without the Casualties,'"** p. P9 ▶ The helitack was advised by the regional control centre about the fire being bombed by the Canso. The initial attack crew squeezed into the helicopter and were off within three minutes. **2004** Gregory Alan Gross *San Diego Union-Tribune* (Calif.) (Nov. 16) "Elite, Mobile Fire Crew Might Soon Be Permanent Here" (Int.) ▶ They are the fire service's shock troops, and they soon might be a year-round fixture in San Diego County. Officially, they are known simply as "helitack."

heresthetics *n.* the framing of a debate or issue so that one is on the superior or winning side, or so that one's choices are better-received by others. Also **heresthetic.** *Politics.* [The term was coined by William Riker (1920-1993).]

1984 William H. Riker *American Political Science Review* (Mar.) "The Heresthetics of Constitution-Making: The Presidency in 1787, with Comments on Determinism and Rational Choice," vol. 78, no. 1, p. 8 (Int.) ▶ In this connection the distinction between rhetoric and heresthetic is that rhetoric involves converting others by persuasive argument, whereas heresthetic involves structuring the situation so that others accept it willingly. **1990** Bernard M. Bass *Bass and Stogdill's Handbook of Leadership* (July 1), 3rd ed., p. 137 ▶ *Heresthetics.* For Riker (1986), leadership, as practiced by successful politicians, is primarily political manipulation. According to this view, leadership is evident when a politician is able to change an issue in the minds of constituents and legislators, so the minority support for older framing of the issue swells to a majority because of the politician's new interpretation of the issue. **1992** John M. Bryson, Barbara C. Crosby *Leadership for the Common Good* (Nov. 4), p. 259 ▶ Even if problems, solutions, and politics are coupled, it is still possible to lose during formal adoption sessions to shrewd opponents who find ways to split the coalition or to use the formal decision-making rules of the relevant arena to defeat what otherwise would be a "sure" winner. This is where a knowledge of "heresthetics"—the name Riker (1996) gives to "the art of political manipulation"—is essential. **1996** *Usenet: talk.politics.guns* (Oct. 29) "Re: John Johnson Calls NRA a Liar" ▶ "Either way I win." "Gee, what a virtuoso grasp of heresthetics!!!" **1998** *Boston Globe* (July 17) "Leadership Seminar Set at Dartmouth," p. 12 ▶ "Heresthetics and Rhetoric and the Spatial Model," by William Riker, Rochester University political science professor. **2004** Andrew R. Cline *Rhetorica* (May 14) "Campaign Maneuvers..." (Int.) ▶ John Kerry's suggestion that he might delay acceptance of his nomination and the Republican response to that suggestion, are excellent examples of heresthetics—structuring the world so you can win.

hikikomori *n.* a state of social withdrawal or willful anomie. *Japan. Japanese.*

2000 Ryu Murakami *Time International* (Asia) (May 1) "Japan's Lost Generation," vol. 155, no. 17, p. 49 ▶ Hikikomori has become a major issue in Japan. Loosely translated as "social withdrawal," hikikomori refers to the state of anomie into which an increasing number of young Japanese seem to fall these days. Socially withdrawn kids typically lock themselves in their bedrooms and refuse to have any contact with the outside world. They live in reverse: they sleep all day, wake up in the evening and stay up all night watching television or playing video games. Some own computers or mobile phones, but most have few or no friends. Their funk can last for months, even years in extreme cases. **2000** Mark Goldsmith *Daily Yomiuri* (Tokyo) (May 13) "Locked Inside: Cases of Hikikomori, or Social Withdrawal, on the Rise," p. 7 ▶ Hikikomori is not a disease. For reasons ranging from bullying to exam failure, some young people are shutting themselves away in their rooms and having as little direct contact with the outside world as possible. Many are suicidal but lack the will to make good their morbid fantasies. It is not clear at what point someone crosses the line into hikikomori. But after a month of seclusion it would not be too soon to seek treatment, psychiatrists say. Machizawa knows one person who shunned professional help for 20 years. **2004** Paul Wiseman *USA Today* (June 2) "No Sex Please—We're Japanese" (Int.) ▶ In fact, as many as a million young men—mostly teenagers, but increasingly older men as well—suffer from what is known here as *hikikomori*. It's a condition in which they seclude themselves in their rooms for weeks at a time (though the causes seem to go well beyond fear of women to traumatic experiences from the past, such as being bullied at school).

hillbilly armor *n.* scavenged materials used by soldiers for improvised bulletproofing and vehicle hardening, esp. in Iraq. *Iraq. Military. United States.*

2004 Deena Winter *Bismarck Tribune* (N.Dak.) (Aug. 30) "Chaplain Brings Message Back Home to Congregation," p. 1A ▶ Millican only briefly spoke of the "horrible sand," unrelenting heat, "hillbilly armor" they initially wore and camel spiders as big as a Frisbee. **2004** Stephanie Heinatz @ Camp Arifjan, Kuwait *Daily Press* (Hampton Roads, Va.) (Sept. 11) "Truck Drivers Recount the Road to Baghdad," p. A4 ▶ "We call it 'hillbilly armor' because all we did was cut out thick steel and put it on our doors," Jackson said. "We have a really good welder who worked really hard on that to give us the extra protection." **2004** Thom Shanker, Eric Schmitt *N.Y. Times* (Dec. 10) "Armor Scarce for Big Trucks Transporting Cargo in Iraq" (Int.) ▶ Continuing shortages have prompted soldiers going to Iraq to scrounge for steel and ballistic glass, improvising shields that have come to be called hillbilly armor. **2005** David Shrauger *Living Iraq Journal* (Jan. 16) "Victory Is Mine" (Int.) ▶ We were able to install ballistic windows (that we will have to take off and put on another truck when it is their turn to convoy) and put these strange flexible kevlar sleeves over our plastic doors to go along with the particle board "hillbilly" armor built around the back of our gun truck.

hiplife *n.* a musical genre from Ghana that combines elements of American-style hip-hop and the Ghanaian pop genre known as *highlife. Entertainment. Ghana. Hip-Hop. Music.*

1999 Elena Oumano *Billboard* (Mar. 6) "Fusion-Based Hiplife Genre Invigorates Ghana" ▶ In hiplife, hip-hop beats fuse with raps in any of Ghana's many languages or English-language raps ride beats that incorporate elements of highlife, Ghana's indigenous pop style. **1999** Joyce Mensah @ Accra *Ghanaian Chronicle* (Oct. 22) "Hip-Life Music Awards" ▶ Hip-life music has been the main dominant rhythm in our music industry; hardly a day passes by without radio stations blaring them on air. This is because the "westernised" youth who form the majority of our population are madly in love with it since it presents them freestyle and a break. This has indirectly led to the proliferation of hip-life music youth groups like Buk-Bak, Nananom, VIP, Sas Squard, and individuals, such as Reggie Rockstone, Nana King, Ex-Doe, are "idolised' by the youth. **2004** Omar Dubois *Ghana Music.com* (July 26) "Hiplife: A New Dawn; A New Day" (Int.) ▶ Hiplife was almost solely the brainchild of Reginald "Reggie Rockstone" Osei. Memory lane: Whilst we were both in Accra from London on Christmas holidays in 1994, I vividly recollect meeting Reggie at a friend's place and hearing him rap in Twi. I was quite taken aback, for I'd never heard it done before—and it was effortlessly good. "I'm not new to this rap thing," hiplife's founding father—who also coined the genre's name—tells me almost nine years later.

hit the deuces *v. phr.* in a penitentiary or prison, to summon help. *Crime & Prisons.* [This appears to derive from the radio code "222" used by prison guards to call for assistance. The term may be specific to Federal prisons.]

*1999 Tom Manning *Tom Manning—Poetry—Big House* (Leavenworth, Kan.) (Aug. 30) "Another Day in the Big House" (Int.) ▶ Jarred awake—screws screaming/Hit the deuces (222) back to your cells/Lock-in, fist fight/Shattered teeth—splattered blood. **2002**

[Fee-X] @ Texas *Prison Talk Online* (June 11) "Dirty Little Drinker" (Int.) ▶ The other CO up in the unit hit the deuces when he flew off the ladder, just because it scared her so bad. **2003** [Spikeman] @ Dallas-Fort Worth, Texas *Prison Talk Online* (Apr. 23) "Is Everything Cop-Esthetic?" (Int.) ▶ Pretty soon Pavlov is running for his life being chased by a drag queen inmate with a midget broom. Did I mention that Sheila was wearing panties and a homemade bra? The entire unit watched in awe as this went on for 15 minutes or so. It took poor Pavlov that long to remember to hit the deuces and summon help. **2004** Seth M. Ferranti @ Glenville, W. Va. *HoopsHype* (Nov. 27) "No Love for Ron" (Int.) ▶ Man, I seen the guard looking all scared and shit.... Ready to hit the deuces. He didn't know what the fuck was going on. **2005** John Bowers *Salt Lake City Weekly* (Utah) (Apr. 28) "Cell Survivor" (Int.) ▶ An officer "hits the deuces"—a button on his hand-held radio—which summons a hundred guards like ants to a picnic.

HNWI *n. h*igh *n*et *w*orth *i*ndividual. *Acronym. Jargon. Money & Finance. United States.*

1989 Robert Gottliebsen *Business Review Week* (Jan. 27) "Equicorpse," p. 22 ▶ With that equity base and his own maverick image, Hawkins began lending to develop the Equiticorp finance company—just as he had done with CBA Finance. However, instead of rural loans Hawkins chased HNWI's—high-net-worth individuals. **2003** Sam Ali *Seattle Times* (Aug. 10) "The Wealthy Way to Investing in Volatile Times," p. E1 (Int.) ▶ Indeed, the ranks of the world's HNWIs—financial parlance for "high-net-worth individuals," with investable assets of $1 million or more—increased in 2002 by 2.1 percent to 7.3 million, according to the World Wealth Report.

hocker *n.* a person who harangues, beseeches, or talks persuasively; a person who trades in information, gossip, or personal connections; someone who is (obnoxiously) ambitious. *Derogatory. Yiddish.* [< *hock* 'to nag, criticize' (According to Leo Rosten, perhaps shortened from *Hok mir nit kayn chainik* 'don't knock me a teapot' = 'don't harangue me; stop nagging, annoying, or pestering me') < Yiddish *hock, hok,* or *hakn* 'to chop, strike, knock' < German *hack* 'to cut, chop, or strike (with a blow)'; High German *hock* 'to hit, chop.'] *Hocker* is common and well-known to yeshiva students in New York City. Related etymologically to, but not derived from, *hawk* 'to embarrass, annoy, or disconcert,' which, according to the *Dictionary of American Regional English* (*DARE*), is used in Mid-Atlantic states such as North Carolina and Virginia as a synonym for *hack*, more commonly found in the

American South and South Midlands. The noun variant of *hack* means "a state of embarrassment, confusion, or defeat." The adjective *hacked* means "embarrassed, annoyed, cowed, flustered" and dates as far back as 1892. It's also, therefore, related to *to hack off* 'to annoy.' A Jewish correspondent from Boston also reports using *huck* to mean "to nag," probably just a pronunciation and spelling variant of the Yiddish *hock*.

1996 Nancy K. Miller *Bequest and Betrayal: Memoirs of a Parent's Death* (Oct. 1), p. 32 (Mar. 1, 2000) ▶ The father's self-representation as Hocker confirms the son's characterization of him, in which an authorial Roth reaches for a recognizable, if not entirely appealing, type glossed for the goyim. The writer supplies the dictionary entry in parenthesis: "Hock: a Yiddishism that in this context means to badger, to bludgeon, to hammer with warnings and edicts and pleas—in short, to drill a hole in somebody's head with words." **1999** Howard Pollack *Aaron Copland* (Mar. 1), p. 377 in (Apr. 1, 2000) ▶ Morros and Finston, he afterward wrote Copland, were "political hockers—and the atmosphere they gave off is not fragrant. (But I'm afraid that is 95% of Hollywood.)" **2000** *Usenet: alt.humor.jewish* (May 11) "Boro Park Millionaire" ▶ We only have 5 contestants because the other 5 got stuck in Boro Park traffic behind some hocker who triple-parked his Lexus on 13th Avenue. **2003** [Yuda] *Welcome to the yudaSphere* (N.Y.) (June 3) "Finalizing..." (Int.) ▶ At Binyomin's, when Senior came over to visit, he said in response to my schmoozing, "My, my, you are such a hocker!" So I flashed a smile at him and said, "How true! I have a question, though. What is a hocker?" With some deliberation, he answered me, "A hocker is...the same as a *tutzuch*." **2003** Rachel Horn *Yeshiva University Observer* (NYC) (Nov. 4) "From the Editors Desk" (Int.) ▶ "Hocker" has since seeped into our lingo. The catch phrase has come to connote the student in the know, who rubs elbows with the higher-ups at Yeshiva, often organizing Yeshiva events and programs. The proverbial hocker at Yeshiva seems to know and be known by virtually every student. This personality type is often innocuous. Students immersed in "the hock" must be constantly aware of the fine line that distinguishes the cream of the crop from the social elite. **2004** [Nicht] *The House of Hock* (June 2) "Rabbis & Journalists II" (Int.) ▶ Some reporters are hockers, which may be true. However, once they begin publishing what they hock, Rabbis may be reticent to speak to them.... Of course, there are Hockers which have poor information & hockers with better information.... **2004** Steven I. Weiss *Fiddish* (NYC) (June 3) (Int.) ▶ Sem wonders if skeptical rabbis mean that the press can't do its job, and that therefore "hockers" are the best sources of information for what the rabbis think.... When it comes to the "hock" associated with those rabbis, a journalist who has a similar relationship is just as valuable as the hocker, perhaps even better in some cases I've been involved with, because the rabbi knows that the journalist isn't just looking for the latest *lashon hara.*

hog-dogging *n.* **1.** a (blood) sport in which trained dogs corner (wild) pigs; **2.** showing off; *hot-dogging. Animals. Sports. United States.* [The two 1995 citations (from the same journalist) and the second 1999 citation probably illustrate a form of *hot-dog* 'to show off; to make ostentatious displays of behavior' and have no relation to the sport *hog-dogging.*] Though both are often called *hog-dogging,* some participants make a distinction between *hog-baying,* in which the dogs are only permitted to howl, bark, and bay to keep the hogs in check, and *hog-dogging,* in which the dogs are permitted to fight and bite the hogs. The former activity is usually part of a *hog dog rodeo* and the latter is not.

1994 Ron Wiggins *Palm Beach Post* (Fla.) (May 19) "Hog Hunting Rodeos Are for the Dogs," p. 1D ▶ Now I have, second hand, a story on people who sic dogs on captured wild hogs, chasing them around a pasture and biting them into submission. This is no joke. Hog dogging rodeos are for real and they're happening throughout rural Florida. **1995** Bill Connors *Tulsa World* (Okla.) (Mar. 2) "Bud's Favorites at Moment of Truth," p. S1 ▶ Richardson's previous group of outstanding players who inspired this hostility might have responded more to Richardson's liking than his current players. Oliver Miller and Todd Day, with blatant taunting and hog-dogging, made it easy for opposing fans to dislike Arkansas. They reveled and played lights out when confronted with such hostility. **1995** Bill Connors *Tulsa World* (Okla.) (July 25) "Skill, Passion Make Irvin Leader at Dallas," p. S1 ▶ Michael Irvin was being Michael Irvin. That is, hog-dogging, charming, leading. **1999** John W. Gonzalez *Houston Chronicle* (Tex.) (May 11) "Time Runs Out for Hundreds of Bills Left Pending in House Committees," p. 1 ▶ Among the dead and dying ideas are a lower sales tax rate, approval for state-run casinos, a ban of hog-dogging and the option for juries to sentence a murderer to life without parole. [**1999** *Usenet: alt.sports.football.pro.sf-49ers* (Nov. 28) "Re: Team of the Nineties" ▶ Big eared, hog-dogging, high-stepping, arrogant, overrated cornerbacks need not apply.] **2000** Robert Anderson *Ice Age* (Oct. 20), p. 90 ▶ He was the only one who ever spoke to her—the others hovered with crossed arms and chain gold hogdogging the available light. **2004** Manuel Roig-Franzia *Washington Post* (Mar. 29) "A Squealing Time Hog-Dogging at Uncle Earl's; At La. Event and Others Across South, It's Hounds Against Boars," p. A3 ▶ A hog-dogging event seemed like a natural, and the inaugural Uncle Earl's in 1995 coincided with a burst of hog-dog trials across the South, a phenomenon that has grown into a circuit of bawling hounds. **2004** *Arizona Republic* (Dec. 17) "Husband and Wife Busted in Bloody Sport Involving Dogs, Hogs" (Int.) ▶ Authorities arrested a Cave Creek couple Friday on animal-abuse charges over a bloody sport known as "hog dogging," in which bull terriers are released in an arena area to chase down wild boars.

hogger *n.* a machine used to compact or shred waste materials.
1986 Roselle M. Lewis *L.A. Times* (Feb. 13) "Southland Sees Recycling as Good Turn," p. 10 ▶ This firm uses a Hogger shredder for processing paper. **1991** Bela G. Liptak *Municipal Waste Disposal in the 1990s* (Sept. 15), p. 357 ▶ Depending on their applications, shredders are also referred to as crushers, pulverizers, hammer mills, hoggers, grinders, and ball mills. **1992** *Encyclopedia of Environmental Science and Engineering* 3 ed., p. 350 ▶ Shredders, hoggers, and chippers are devices which reduce refuse, bulky items, and other solid wastes to a manageable size. **2005** Sam Bond *Edie News Centre* (U.K.) (June 17) "Manslaughter Charge for Recycling Firm After Paper Shredder Death" (Int.) ▶ The charge followed the death of Kevin Arnup, a foreman at the firm, in December 2003 as an industrial paper shredder, or hogger, restarted as he tried to clear a blockage.

hokey Dinah *other* an exclamation of surprise or marvel. [Probably a form of the slightly more common *holy Dinah*.]
2000 Usenet: *rec.outdoors.fishing.bass* (Jan. 15) "Re: Jet Skiers" ▶ Hokey Dinah!!...I can see a new newsgroup on the horizon! **2003** *Weddingbells.ca* (Can.) (July 23) "Re: Next GTA Get Together" (Int.) ▶ Hokey Dinah, why didn't I read this thread earlier? I'm in! **2004** [Joanne] *Ioan Gruffudd Community* (Aug. 31) "Hello Monthly Poll" (Int.) ▶ Great support! Lovely! Hokey Dinah! **2005** [twistedhip] *twistedhip* (Toronto, Can.) (Jan. 24) "Airlift My Loaf" (Int.) ▶ "Hokey Dynah!"...The person who uses this phrase just got finished using "pritneer" in a sentence, and something has just startled him.

hollow army *n.* an understaffed, underfunded, or outdated military. *Military.*
1980 George C. Wilson *Washington Post* (May 30) "Joint Chiefs of Staff Break with Carter on Budget Planning for Defense Needs," p. A1 ▶ "Right now, we have a hollow Army," responded Gen. E. C. Meyer, Army chief of staff, in what turned out to be the bluntest response. "I don't believe the current budget responds to the Army's needs for the 1980s," said Meyer of Carter's fiscal 1981 defense budget. "There's a tremendous shortfall in the ability to modernize quickly"

in response to the Soviet threat. **2005** Charles A. Krohn *Washington Post* (June 24) "Finding Our Next Army" (Int.) ▶ Will quantity in recruiting become a silent substitute for quality, leading to what is often referred to as a "hollow army"?

Hollywood no *n.* a lack of response (to a proposal, phone call, message, etc.). *Entertainment.*

1992 Connie Benesch *L.A. Times* (Aug. 16) "Proper Etiquette—What a High Concept!," p. 19 ▶ Confused because the production executive hot in pursuit of your screenplay last week isn't returning your calls this week? Well, meet the Hollywood "no." **1992** Jason E. Squire *The Movie Business Book* (Nov. 1) 2 ed., p. 176 ▶ Nothing is more frustrating for a filmmaker than the "Hollywood No," which is silence. It is debilitating and insensitive. **2004** Jordan Rosenfeld *Jordan's World* (Sept. 18) (Int.) ▶ I'm tired of the "Hollywood no" as he calls it (they don't get back to you).

homegoing *n.* a death; a funeral. *United States.*

1874 Benjamin B. Bausman *Herald and Torch Light* (Hagerstown, Md.) (Apr. 29) "Reminiscences of the War" ▶ If the dead have died in Christ, then dying is a home going. **1918** (Greene) *Iowa Recorder* (June 12) "Bristow," p. 2 ▶ Mr. C.V. Surfus who passed out of this life...was born in De Kalb County, Ind., November 25, 1837 and at the time of his homegoing was 80 years, 6 months, 7 days. **1983** *Daily Oklahoman* (Oklahoma City) (Feb. 14) "Izora Clark Rogers" ▶ She leaves to mourn her home going, 1 son. **2004** John M. Broder *N.Y. Times* (June 19) "In a Sprawling Memoir, Clinton Cites Storms and Settles Scores" (Int.) ▶ He said that in the many black churches he had visited he had heard funerals referred to as "homegoings."

honey dip *n.* a desirable girl or woman; a term of affection for a girl or woman. *Black English.* Perhaps after the sweetness and color of honey-dipped doughnuts.

1950 *The Cap-Tans* (Sept.) "Crazy 'Bout My Honey Dip" (in song title). **1994** *Usenet: alt.rap* (Feb. 15) "Re: Lyrics: 93 'til Infinity" ▶ It's dip...you know like kickin' game to a honeydip. Get it? **1998** Ta-Nehisi Coates (Feb. 1) "Alice Flips the Script" in *Catch the Fire!* Derrick I. M. Gilbert, p. 174 ▶ She is not another bourgeoise honey-dip./Sister is deep like sinkholes./Hollow like them too. [**2001** Carol Taylor *Brown Sugar* (Jan. 1), p. 185 ▶ The clip's concept is a sex subway filled with scantily clad ho's in various buck-wild positions—sliding down poles, gyrating their hips, swinging their phat honey dips.] **2005** *Veronica Chambers Miss Black America* (June 14), p. 11 ▶ He'd be calling Mommy "Miss Black America" and his "brown sugar honey dip" as soon as she got home. **2005** Kristie Rieken @ *Houston Star-Telegram* (Dallas-Fort Worth, Tex.) (July 2) "Texan Paul Wall Shines in Sea of Rappers" (Int.) ▶ The rapper, whose real last name is Slayton, relies on a dizzying array of local vernacular to describe everything from attractive females (honey dips) to rims (swangaz) and tires (vogues).

horse blanket *n.* a large, complex, or comprehensive report or chart. *Jargon. Military. United States.* [Probably derives from a size comparison of sheets of chart paper to actual horse blankets.]
1998 William Hartzog (*Federal Document Clearing House*) (June 9) "General William Hartzog Holds News Briefing to Discuss Changes in the Army's Division Structure" ▶ There is a facing-page discussion of each in your handouts. There are some other materials that we've given you in terms of some articles that have been written lately about this particular division design—a full horse blanket, if you will, that's got numbers and specifics in it. ***2000** David L. Lawrence, John C. White (*Aviation Operations at the Joint Readiness Training Center*) (Fort Leavenworth, Kan.) (Apr. 18) "Ch. 3: Light-Army Aviation at the JRTC: Do We Perform Search and Attack?" no. 5, (Int.) ▶ At JRTC most light infantry task forces conduct platoon- and squad-sized search and attack in specified areas dividing the battalion sector. They often resemble an artillery "horse-blanket" graphic used to support quick clearance of fires on a non-linear battlefield.... A "horse-blanket" graphic might be employed by the infantry battalion in search and attack. **2002** *Standard Army Training System E-Newsletter for Unit Leaders & Trainers* (Fort Eustis, Va.) (Spring-Summer) "Horse Blanket Report for SATS Users" (in U.S. Army Training Support Center), vol. 6, no. 1 (Int.) ▶ This tool is planned to replace the current cumbersome manual Horse-blanket, 5 year, "canned" and other ad-hoc reports currently manually developed using normal operating system commercial software. **2003** Jeanne Cummings @ Washington, D.C. *Wall Street Journal* (Apr. 11) "Afghanistan Aid Sets Bad Example—Bush Doesn't Want Infrastructure Delays Repeated in Iraq," p. A4 ▶ An oversized chart—nicknamed the "horse blanket" because of its size—was created to display the postwar targets for one month, six months and a year out. **2004** U.S. Army *Action Officer Guide to the Force Design Update* (Fort Monroe, Va.) (Nov. 5) (Int.) ▶ FDD prepares an executive-level briefing chart that condenses each of the issues into a single briefing slide for presentation to the Dir RI. The briefing chart, also known as the horse blanket, is forwarded to the Dir RI. ***2004** U.S. Army *ST7000, Action Officer Development Course* (Dec. 6) "Appendix A—Informal Staff Language" (Int.) ▶ *Horse blanket* Very large sheet of paper pasted on a wall and used to brief complex data or diagrams.

2005 Peter Guinta *St. Augustine Record* (Fla.) (June 6) "Soldiers' Lingo Gives Everyday Language an Added Flair" (Int.) ► O.C.T. is an acronym for observer-controller-trainer. These are usually Iraq veterans certified to act as teachers on immersion battlefields. OCTs use a "horse blanket," or a large board listing all the training phases and the week they are supposed to be held.

hotbox *v.* **1.** to smoke marijuana in an enclosed space so that it becomes filled with smoke; **2.** to take a long drag or a quick series of drags on a joint or cigarette. *Drugs. Slang.*

1994 *Usenet: alt.drugs* (Feb. 18) "Re: Smoking in Dorm Room" ► "I feel sorry for you, just try to find a safe place outside that you can go and smoke"..."try hot boxing a car :) it works...although you have to be careful, and out on some old gravel road." **1995** *Usenet: alt.drugs* (Mar. 3) "Cats' Reaction to Mary Jane" ► "My cat loves getting stoned too, but I'm concerned for her health as well. Do you think I'm wrong to let her passive smoke my weed?" "Ditto...my roommates love to hotbox a room, and usually invite my cat in to join them." **1996** George P. Pelecanos *The Big Blowdown* (June 1), p. 161 (Sept. 24, 1999) ► Karras took a drag off the Lucky, hotboxed it with a tandem draw, pitched it away. **1998** *Usenet: alt.drugs.pot* (Aug. 20) "Re: MJ Vocabulary" ► In CA it's not a clambake but a hotbox.... You can hotbox a car or a room etc. **1999** *Usenet: alt.drugs.pot* (Feb. 8) "Re: Holding Your Smoke In?" ► Have you ever hotboxed a car, closet, room before. It's the same principal as a madhatter, or breathing into a bag. **2004** *Sheilnak.com* (Sept. 24) "Word Up, It's a Ghetto Dictionary" (Int.) ► Hotbox—to smoke marijuana in a confined space so that the smoke remains in circulation. "We hotboxed the car." **2004** Peter Plate *Angels of Catastrophe* (Dec. 10) in *Outlaw Bible of American Literature* Alan Kaufman, p. 456 ► Lonely Boy hotboxed the cigarette and exhaled three perfectly symmetrical smoke rings, working his jaw like a locomotive to execute the trick.

hot desk *v.* to share a desk, office, or other work space between employees on different shifts or schedules. *Business. Jargon.*

1991 Godfrey Golzen *Times* (London, Eng.) (May 5) "Cut the Office in Half Without Tears" ► The new trend, "hot desking," is that desks are shared between several people who use them at different times. This has been made possible because more people are now working from home or with the customer. **2004** Robert Watts *Telegraph* (U.K.) (June 27) "Civil Servants Will 'Hot Desk' to Cut Costs" (Int.) ► In a scheme that could be rapidly rolled out across Whitehall, all civil servants at the Department of Trade and Industry are to "hot desk," a process beloved of management consultants, which will see mandarins of all ranks move from desk to desk throughout the department.

hotel journalism *n.* cursory, nonexpert, or secondhand reporting from a sheltered location or perspective (in an otherwise unsafe place). Also **hotel reporting.** *Media.* The first citation is probably unrelated to the current usage.

[**1916** George Ade *N.Y. Times Mag.* (Jan. 2) "George Ade Is Reminiscent About Celebrities," p. 14 ▶ They set him to do hotel reporting. He was a failure as a hotel reporter because the young man employed by The Herald and the young man employed by The Times secured interviews every day with interesting visitors whom he was never able to find. He could not find them because these interesting personages did not exist.... The visitor who told the wondrous tales invariably left on the afternoon train for New York, but his name was on the hotel register as a corroborative detail intended to give verisimilitude to an otherwise bald and unconvincing narrative.] **1987** T.E. Bell *Houston Chronicle* (Tex.) (June 14) "What's Really Happening in Nicaragua: A Film Maker's View," p. 20 ▶ The jacket tout compares "Where is Nicaragua?" to Joan Didion's " Salvador," a condescending and superficial bit of hotel journalism published a few years ago. That is unfortunate. Didion's slim volume was full of holes you could drive a tank through, and was shot through with faulty political and cultural judgments about El Salvador and Central America based on a three-week visit in 1981. **1989** Howard Rosenberg *L.A. Times* (Dec. 21) "A View from the Hotel: Reporting the Panama Conflict," p. 1 ▶ ABC's Peter Jennings called it "hotel reporting." We got it from China last June when many Western journalists, their freedom of movement severely restricted in Beijing, were forced to observe the crackdown of pro-reform dissidents from their hotel rooms overlooking Tian An Men Square. **2005** *ChannelNewsAsia.com* (Jan. 12) "European Press Pulls in Horns in Face of Iraqi Terror" (in Paris, France) (Int.) ▶ Leonard Doyle, foreign editor of The Independent in London, said, "We make a big effort not to do what you might call 'hotel journalism,' and we make a very big effort not to sub-contract work to local Iraqi journalists—we think that's basically unfair. It's a risk to them. We carry the same risk." **2005** Robert Fisk *Independent* (U.K.) (Jan. 17) "Hotel Journalism Gives American Troops a Free Hand as the Press Shelters Indoors," p. 22 ▶ "Hotel journalism" is the only phrase for it. More and more Western reporters in Baghdad are reporting from their hotels rather than the streets of Iraq's towns and cities.

hot shoe *n.* a reckless or unnecessarily fast race-car driver; (*hence*) a winning driver. Also **hotshoe.** *Automotive. Slang. Sports.*

1988 Tom Jones *St. Petersburg Times* (Fla.) (Oct. 20) "The Hotshoe Flipped at the Chicane: What? Series: GRAND PRIX 88," p. 6E ▶ Anyone who gets behind the wheel of a race car is taking a risk, but a "hotshoe" is someone who travels at higher-than-usual speeds and takes unusually risky chances. **1989** *USA Today* (Mar. 13) "Track Secret in Water," p. 10C ▶ The long chutes and wide sweeping turns of this fabulous clay oval will give these drivers ample room to enjoy life in the fast line as they battle for the checkered flag.... Now let's find out who's got the hot shoe tonight. **1993** Brian Moore *Toronto Star* (Can.) (Aug. 28) "Hot Shoes Battle for Supremacy in F2000 Series," p. H9 (title). **2004** Bill Whitehead *Commercial Appeal* (Memphis, Tenn.) "Virginia Is for Lovers—Fans Can't Help But Adore Martinsville," p. C10 ▶ The Hendrick Motorsports camp hopes rookie Brian Vickers can be the next hotshoe at the slightly-banked bullring.

hot wash *n.* a performance review, particularly after a training exercise or combat operation. *Military.* This term appears to be migrating out of the military, where it originated.

1991 John M. Broder @ Washington, D.C. *L.A. Times* (Mar. 3) "In the Wake of the 'Storm' U.S. Sees Glitches in War Machine," p. 1 ▶ The day the fighting ended, senior Army aides presented to Army Chief of Staff Carl E. Vuono their first observations on the operation. Such an initial review of a just-concluded operation is called a "hot wash." **1997** Philip D. Chinnery *Air Commando: Inside the Air Force Special Operations Command* (Jan. 15), p. 292 ▶ Before he could make his drop, his aircraft was hit with small-arms fire and he elected to call "NO DROP." During the hot wash [after-action meetings], he explained his decision not to drop. **2000** David H. Freedman *Corps Business: The 30 Management Principles of the U.S. Marines* (Jan. 1), p. 187 ▶ During the hot-wash a Coyote major diplomatically asks LeSavage, Davis's executive officer, whether he feels that the MAGTF's actions against the enemy's main body were completely effective. **2000** Robert L Cross *Strategic Learning in a Knowledge Economy* (Mar. 2), p. 196 ▶ The U.S. Army has the most experience with the After Action Review, having done them for ten years. Everyone is used to taking time quickly out of action to do a "hot wash" which happens in the action or a "cold wash" after the action is completed. **2001** Peter H. Zipfel *Modeling and Simulation of Aerospace Vehicle Dynamics* (Jan. 1), p. 510 ▶ After the play the training audience gets a good night's rest while the control cell burns the midnight oil analyzing the data and composing the debrief. This *hot wash* is given the next day. It summarizes the events from an overall perspective and provides red and blue with the rationale behind all the important decisions. **2003** Joseph A. Barbera *Jane's Mass Casualty Handbook: Hospital* (July), p. 312 ▶ A "hot wash" critique by key personnel should take place immediately following the exercise. **2004** Madanmohan Rao *Knowledge Management Tools and Techniques* (Sept. 23), p. 20 ▶ The consortium uses expertise yellow pages, a consulting knowledge base, and after-action reviews called "hot washes." **2005** Peter Guinta *St. Augustine Record* (Fla.) (June 6) "Soldiers' Lingo Gives Everyday Language an Added Flair" (Int.) ▶ At Camp Shelby, troops who complete a training operation are often given a "hot wash," or a critique of what they did and how they did it. Personalities are put aside and the objective is better performance.

ho-wop *n.* a form of music that combines the sensibilities of hip-hop and doo-wop genres. *Entertainment. Music.* [Probably coined by music artist Eamon, from Staten Island, N.Y.]

2004 Scott Mervis *Pittsburgh Post-Gazette* (Feb. 20) "For the Record," p. W31 ▶ On "My Baby's Lost," [Eamon] even sounds like a potty-mouthed Frankie Vali. The New York crooner claims to have masterminded a new genre he calls "ho-wop": "raw hip- hop and smooth doo-wop." **2004** Jill Alphonso *Straits Times* (Singapore) (July 14) "S'cuse Me, Are You a Man-ho?" (Int.) ▶ Called ho-wop, the vocals are crooning and the beats smooth but the lyrics will not win any decency awards. Arguably the first song of its kind is Eamon Doyle's F*** It (I Don't Want You Back), a harsh break-up song liberally studded with swear words.

HoYay *n.* originally an interjection (of approval) used when encountering accidental or actual homoeroticism in television or movies; now the homoeroticism itself. *Media. Sexuality.* [This term originated in the discussion forums of the web site Mighty Big TV, now called Television Without Pity.]

2001 *Usenet: alt.tv.buffy-v-slayer.creative* (May 27) "Re: Call Waiting 6" ▶ "He's a complicated man And no one understands him but his Wesley...CHARLES GUNN! Bwa-hahaha!" "The Ho-Yay! thread's corrupted you too!" **2001** *Usenet: alt.tv.buffy-v-slayer* (June 28) "Re: New Writer Joins BUFFY Staff" ▶ This should really help the HoYay! quotient on BtVS, which was largely lacking in S5, Willow and Tara notwithstanding (it's not as much fun if it's *text*). **2002** Cary Darling *Miami Herald* (Dec. 9) "New Superhero RAGEs Out of the Closet" ▶ The TV-fan site http://www.televisionwithoutpity.com, on its Smallville pages, even casts a rainbow spotlight on Superman's youth with a board devoted to the show's alleged gay undertones or "HoYay!," shorthand for "homoeroticism, yay!" **2004** Usenet: alt.tv.er (Oct. 16) "Re: Night of the Crazy Interns" ▶ Either that, or she'd simply start having sex with Neela. (Hey, the Ho!Yay! was already out there on the table...I can hardly be blamed for taking a bite out of it.) **2005** Ramin Setoodeh Newsweek/MSNBC (Jan. 20) "Television: Having a Gay Old Time" (Int.) ▶ A phrase has even sprung up in the blogosphere—"HoYay!" meaning "Homoeroticism Yay!"—to describe awkward glances or sexually ambiguous dialogue between guys. "The director sets up a soap opera—two male characters clenching their jaws—and you're totally thinking to yourself, 'Just kiss already!'" says Sarah Bunting of TelevisionWithoutPity.com. "It's almost funnier when the writers aren't aware."

huck v. to throw, to toss, to short-arm; in disc-based sports, to throw for distance; in cycling, kayaking, snowboarding, and similar sports, to ride over a drop-off. This term is probably related to chuck 'to throw with a short arm motion.' There is a sense of hawk 'to let fly' with a single citation in the Oxford English Dictionary.

1989 Virginia Myers Kelly Washington Post (Aug. 11) "Disk Drive," p. N7 ▶ It means you've just "hucked" (thrown long) to the perfect spot. **1990** Usenet: alt.boomerang (Nov. 11) "Still Waiting..." ▶ I have to confess to having also experienced the thrill and Zen-like experience of hucking some handcrafted cellulosian creation aloft. **1992** Martha Brooks Two Moons in August (Jan. 1), p. 32 ▶ "Don't count on it. Think fast, Stafford," cackled the idiot, hucking an eraser at him. **1996** James Campion Deep Tank Jersey (July 3), p. 356 ▶ A dark, thin, pre-teen hucking an old amplifier up the metal stairs of a neighbor's pool deck. **1997** Michael O'Brien Strangers and Sojourners (Apr. 1), p. 174 ▶ She walked and talked early and was shamelessly domestic but just as at home in the barn hucking manure as her brother. **2002** Sean Cliver Jackass (Oct.), p. 137 ▶ He joined Tremaine in hucking oranges at Steve-O's bobbing head. **2003** Gloria Beim Female Athlete's Body Book (Apr. 2), p. 83 ▶ They try to take big air off cliffs and sometimes land against immovable objects, such as trees. The snowboarders call this "hucking carcass." Hucking carcass means they find the steepest drop and the biggest cliff to take the biggest air. I call it taking hospital air. **2003** Todd Richards P3: Pipes, Parks, and Powder (Dec. 1), p. 4 ▶ Sometimes, I'd turn into the six-million-dollar runt, running through the shallow water, bending seaweed as if it were steel, and hucking the cooler all over the beach. **2004** Tim McHugh Poet Chronicles (May), p. 254 ▶ He swings it several times before hucking it toward the stage. **2004** Tyler Williams

Whitewater Classics (May), p. 171 ▶ Her descent of 78-foot Sahalie Falls in Oregon was a world record until waterfall hucking came into vogue in the months following her run. **2004** Leonard Zinn *Zinn's Cycling Primer* (June 1), p. 34 ▶ The first thing you must know before hucking yourself off a drop-off is which foot is your "chocolate foot."

hudda *n.* a police officer. *California. Slang. United States.*

1993 Jeff Schnaufer *L.A. Times* (May 13) "Police See Deadly Message in T-Shirt," p. 3 ▶ While the literal translation of the shirt is the police code for homicide ("187") followed by gang slang for police ("hudda"), many Valley police, school officials and gang experts see it another way: "Murder a Cop."

Hurban *n.* a commercial radio programming format made of music intended to be popular with black and Spanish-speaking city-dwellers. *Media. Music.* [*H*ispanic + *urban* 'a broad genre that includes music made by and for black Americans.'] The format usually emphasizes reggaeton, dancehall, and English- and Spanish-language hip-hop, but also includes pop music in both languages, as well as merengue, salsa, and R&B.

1997 Yolanda Rodriguez *Sarasota Herald-Tribune* (Fla.) (Oct. 3) "Mega Fest Features Grupos Latinos" ▶ The programming format is dubbed "hurban" (Hispanic urban) and mirrors radio formats in Los Angeles, New York, Philadelphia and other cities. **2000** (*NPR*) (June 26) "Morning Edition; Profile: Spanish-Language Radio Stations Growing in Number and in Audience Size" ▶ A decade ago, Boston didn't have the audience for a single large Spanish-language station much less two. Now whether your style is romantic or the Hispanic urban sound known as Hurban(ph), whether your favorite Iglesias is velvet-voiced Julio or his son Enrique, there's a station for you. **2005** Tom Jicha *Bradenton Herald* (Fla.) (Feb. 13) "Out with the Hard Rock, in with the 'Hurban'" (Int.) ▶ The new sounds, dubbed "Hurban"—a melding of Hispanic and urban—will blend Reggaeton, Spanish hip-hop and dance music.

hype man *n.* a hip-hop performer responsible for backup rapping and singing, and increasing an audience's excitement with call-and-response chants. *Hip-Hop. Slang. United States.*

1988 Lee Hildebrand *San Francisco Chronicle* (Apr. 3) "M.C. Hammer Nails Down a Royal Reputation," p. 42 ▶ Hammer and the Posse, a group consisting of four dancers, two DJs and one "hype man" ("He's the guy who pumps the crowd up," Hammer explained), hope to win over rap fans. **1995** *Usenet: rec.music.hip-hop* (Aug. 30) "Re: Suge Vs Puffy" ▶ Puff is up on stage with Biggie rappin' almost as much as

Biggie. He's not just the "hype man" on stage goin' Yea Yea, he's rappin' whole verses. **2004** Jordan Harper *Riverfront Times* (St. Louis, Mo.) (May 26) "I Love a Parade: Radar Station Hitches a Ride with Great Big Rappers" (Int.) ▶ Hype-men, for those of you unfamiliar with the lingo, are the fellas you see at rap shows who stand next to MCs and bellow certain words along with the rap to add emphasis.

hypersigil *n.* a creative work that via the medium of its artificial universe changes its creator, its observers, the real world, or other things. *Arts.* [*hyper* 'over, beyond, or above' + *sigil* 'a seal or sign claimed to have occult or mystical properties.' Coined by Grant Morrison in relation to his multipart comic series "The Invisibles."]

[**1999** *Usenet: pl.rec.gry.rpg* (Nov. 8) "Re: Nie Tylko Deadlands (Was: deadlands)" ▶ To moze...hyper-sigil ktory zmieni rzeczywistosc.] **2003** *Usenet: alt.fan.rawilson* (Jan. 15) "Grant Morrison Working on Book with Disinfo Founder" ▶ According to today's Disinfo e-newsletter, Invisibles author Grant Morrison is working on a book with Disinfo founder Richard Metzger. This should be interesting, since Morrison has talked about Invisibles as a "hypersigil" and Metzger has described Disinfo as a sigil. **2003** Grant Morrison *The Book of Lies* (Oct. 1) ▶ The "hypersigil" or "supersigil" develops the sigil concept beyond the static image and incorporates elements such as characterization, drama, and plot. The hypersigil is a sigil extended through the fourth dimension.... The hypersigil is an immensely powerful and sometimes dangerous method for actually altering reality in accordance with intent. Results can be remarkable and shocking.... The hypersigil can take the form of a poem, a story, a song, a dance or any other extended artistic activity you wish to try. **2004** [sine] *Barbelith Underground* (Mar. 18) "Tulpa Creation Through RPG Hypersigil" (Int.) ▶ My idea is simple: I want to attempt tulpa creation through an RPG hypersigil. **2004** [William] *Spiritkin Forums* (Apr. 13) "Grant Morrison's The Invisibles as a Hypersigil" (Int.) ▶ According to Morrison it is part of his 3-part (using 3 entirely different comic franchises) Hypersigil, which is apparently intended to bring about some sort of "Revival" or large growth in interest in the Occult/Bring about a greater desire for free will.

hyzer *n.* in disc golf or other disc-related sports, a backhanded throw that curves in a direction opposite of the arm used to throw. *Sports. United States.*

1991 *Usenet: rec.sport.disc* (June 7) "Re: Hyzer (was: Re: Forehand Throw Technique)" ▶ The "angle of hyzer" refers to the angle the "side" of the disc (9 o'clock for throwing from the left side of the body, or 3 o'clock for throwing from the right side) makes with the ground. A disc which is held flat has no hyzer. **1993** David Oberhelman *Chicago Tribune* (Aug. 20) "Disc Golf Tries to Put a Spin on Leisure Time," p. 4 ▶ As precision and confidence increase, expand your arsenal to discs that angle right (in the lingo, a "hyzer" for a right-handed thrower) and left, and a putter. **2004** *News-Herald* (Southgate, Mich.) (Aug. 4) "Spin: Learn the Lingo" (Int.) ▶ *Hyzer*: When using a backhand throw, the disc's flight arc, which causes it to fall in the direction opposite of the throwing arm. For a right-handed player a backhand hyzer shot fades to the left, a sidearm shot fades right.

IDP *n.* a person who is a refugee or (forced) migrant within his or her own nation (or region). *Acronym. Jargon. Politics.* [internally displaced person(s) or people]

1994 Mark Dodd (*Reuters*) (May 4) "Cambodian Fighting Closes in on Key Northwestern Town" ▶ There's 30 to 40,000 internally displaced in Battambang—it's the largest IDP (internally displaced people) problem since 1989. **2004** Davin A. Hutchins *Egypt Today* (Cairo) (May) "The Art of Flight" (Int.) ▶ Many scrape by in Jabal Ulia, Jabaronna or Wad Al-Bashir—government-run camps for internally displaced persons—IDPs, in refugee argot—on the outskirts of Khartoum.

i18n *n.* internationalization. *Technology.* [The "18" replaces the middle 18 letters in the word *internationalization*.] This term usually is used in the localization of software, in which all text is translated into other foreign languages. It is sometimes written as *il8n*, where the second letter is a lowercase *L*, rather than a numeral 1. It is usually not capitalized to avoid confusion between an uppercase *I* and the second letter. A similar word is *l10n* 'localization.'

1991 *Usenet: rec.guns* (May 7) "Buy American?" [in "from" field] ▶ I've got an I18N hat on this week. **1998** Karl Mamer *Toronto Sun* (Can.) (Mar. 1) "Unicode Brings Together World's Alphabets" ▶ A big part of i18n is incorporating a new character code that can comfortably represent every alphabet in the world. **2005** [cobrabyte] *Slashdot* (June 23) "How Are You Accomplishing Your i18n?" (Int.) ▶ My team has recently been given the task of implementing internationalization (i18n) in our MySQL databases (PHP-interfaced).

I love me wall *n.* a public display of awards, certificates, plaques, and photographs with or from celebrities, etc.; a *brag wall.* Also **me wall, love me wall.**

1989 Tom Clancy *Clear and Present Danger* (Aug. 1), p. 112 ▶ The wall on the left was liberally covered with plaques of the ships he'd served on, and enough signed photographs for a Hollywood agent's office. Naval officers call this phenomenon the I LOVE ME! wall, and while most of them have one, they usually keep it at home. **1991** Mary G. Gotschall @ Beverly Hills, Calif. *Regardie's* (Washington, D.C.) (Jan. 1) "The Machine Behind Michael Milken," vol. 11, no. 5, p. 58 ▶ His office boasts a "me wall" that would be the envy of any Washington lobbyist; it's full of autographed photos of himself with Ronnie and Nancy and George and Barbara. It spells access. **1992** Ted Bryant *Oregonian* (Portland) (Apr. 23) "From Russia, with Love," p. 1 ▶ Citations and certificates filled what he smiling calls "my Wonderful-Me wall." **1994** Raymond Smith *Press-Enterprise* (Riverside, Calif.) (Feb. 24) "Firefighter's Enthusiasm Is Unquenchable," p. B1 ▶ Then there is what Hendershot calls the "I Love Me Wall." A dozen plaques from over the years attest to his and his wife's community service. **1995** Ron Dalrymple *The Feeding* (Jan. 1), pp. 74-75 ▶ Schizm's office was posh, with glass bookcases, photographs of the great man receiving awards, and an array of degrees and fellowships on the walls. O'Murphy said, "That's a great I LOVE ME WALL." **2005** Alexandra Jacobs *N.Y. Times* (June 26) "'The Washingtonienne': D.C. Horizontal" (Int.) ▶ It's amusing to see Washington fixed by such a vodka-gimlet eye; we can all recognize the type of government geek who refuses to remove his security badge—"how canine," sniffs Jackie—or posts photos of himself taken with famous politicians on a "Me Wall."

impact incarceration *n.* jail or prison time structured with discipline and drills similar to a military boot camp. Also **high-impact incarceration.** *Crime & Prisons. Jargon. United States.*

1990 Charles N. Wheeler III @ Springfield, Ill. *Chicago Sun-Times* (Apr. 7) "Boot Camp Proposed for Youthful Offenders," p. 1 ▶ A prison work camp in southern Illinois will be turned into a military-style boot camp designed to shock youthful offenders out of a life of crime, Gov. Thompson announced Friday. The planned "impact incarceration" program could open this fall. **1990** James Barron *N.Y. Times* (Aug. 2) "Boot-Camp Jail to Begin in Fall at Rikers Island," p. B2 ▶ The New York City Correction Commissioner said yesterday that a "high impact incarceration plan"—similar in some ways to the state's boot-camp program for prisoners—would begin at Rikers Island in September. **2004** James Washburn *Lincoln Courier* (Ill.) (June 19) "Guilty Plea Lets Lincoln Man, 25, Avoid Lengthy Prison Term" (Int.) ▶ A 25-year-old Lincoln man pleaded guilty Friday to unlawful criminal drug conspiracy, a Class II felony, and was sentenced to four years in prison with a recommendation for impact incarceration, also known as boot camp.

interview without coffee *n.* a formal disciplinary meeting or official reprimand; a dressing-down. *Military. United Kingdom.*
1990 John Goodbody *Times* (London, Eng.) (Apr. 2) "Greater Communication Urged to Fight Drugs" ▶ Mahony said that the final interview by the IOC Medical Commission "was one of the most unpleasant, intimidating experiences of my life. After two carefree days, with a medal burning a hole in my pocket, it was an interview without coffee. It was not a pleasant experience." **1999** *Usenet: uk.people.exforces* (Apr. 30) "Re: Off Topic Fried Bread" ▶ "'Stern' warning, does that mean 'Off Caps' at Defaulters on the QD?" "An interview without coffee?" **2000** *Belfast News Letter* (Ireland) (Sept. 16) "RIR Officer 'Reprimand'" ▶ The first step will be a formal reprimand by a senior officer, who could even be the Commander-in-Chief of UK Land Command, General Sir Mike Jackson. The procedure is known in the Army as "an interview without coffee." The outcome will be reflected in his service record. **2000** *Usenet: alt.military.army-cadet* (Jan. 27) "Re: What Would You Do?" ▶ A definite Commandant's "IWOC" (as we used to say in the Regulars...an "Interview without Coffee") and serious disciplinary sanction. (Demotion? Transfer?) **2001** Matthew Hickley *Hobart Mercury* (Australia) (Dec. 1) "Daring Raid Fails to Nab bin Laden" ▶ Eighteen Taliban were killed and dozens wounded and taken prisoner. I imagine they will be given a fair but tough interrogation—what the lads call interview without coffee. **2004** Robert Fox *Evening Standard* (U.K.) (Jan. 19) "Troops Face an Unacceptable Level of Risk," p. 2 ▶ The meeting between Geoff Hoon and Samantha, the widow of Sergeant Steve Roberts, shot after he had handed back his body armour in Iraq, will be something of an interview without coffee—military jargon for a commander's dressing-down of a subordinate. **2004** James Kirkup, Gethin Chamberlain *Scotsman* (July 22) "Commanders Warn All Ranks to Silence Dissent in Public," p. 2 ▶ Punishments could include "administrative action and a nasty letter or interview without coffee," a reference to a formal disciplinary meeting with superior officers. **2005** *Ireland On-Line* (Jan. 21) "Officer Not Punished over Iraqi Crackdown Order" (Int.) ▶ The order by Major Dan Taylor breached the Geneva Convention and the crackdown which followed at an aid camp near Basra led to three soldiers being charged with abusing civilians. But Maj. Taylor was only dealt with at "summary level," which means he was spoken to by senior officers—a process known in Army slang as "interview without coffee." The officers concluded that he was guilty of no more than "misguided zeal," the court heard today.

iron ride *n.* a roller coaster or similar rail- or track-based amusement. *Entertainment.*

1972 Horace Sutton *Washington Post, Times Herald* (July 16) "Coney Island of the West," p. K5 ▶ Some of the old iron rides in new dress, of course, have been revived. Perhaps they are even more devilish than they were in the old days. A twin-track roller coaster has been built and two sets of cars soar down the speedways racing each other at 60 miles an hour. **1986** Bruce Horovitz *L.A. Times* (Mar. 25) "Two New Disneyland Attractions Will Be Months Late," p. 7 ▶ Industry officials say this type of entertainment attraction—with video screens, flashing lights and popular rock music—is quickly replacing costly iron and steel rides. "They can get more bang for their buck with things like these," said Harmon, the consultant. "I'm not sure the big iron ride makes sense anymore." **1990** Pam Sherbourne et al. *Amusement Business* (Mar. 26) "Texas: An Amusement Business Special Section," p. 17 ▶ Attraction to state's traditional iron ride parks not fading.... Where the Texas pride shines the brightest is in the state's outdoor, traditional iron ride parks. The Iron Parks. With an attendance in excess of 2.5 million, Six Flags Over Texas, Arlington, leads all Texas parks in attendance. **2001** Harold Goldberg *CNN.com* (July 31) "Roller Coaster Designers Exploit Gravity" (Int.) ▶ Iron rides continue to chug along stronger than ever, bringing in more visitors and more money. "A new coaster can add up to 11 percent to a park's revenue." **2005** Richard Ruelas *Arizona Republic* (Phoenix) (Mar. 21) "Legend City Offers Lessons for New Amusement Park" (Int.) ▶ They brought in more "iron rides," industry parlance for roller coasters and Ferris wheels.

isht *n.* a euphemistic misspelling of *shit*, with the same uses and meanings. Also **ish.** *Hip-Hop.* This term is also a part of spoken language and in both written and oral cases a form of taboo-avoidance. An unreliable source reports this term originated in the obscuring of obscenities in hip-hop recordings by rearranging their syllables. In American communities with Scandinavian heritage (mainly in Minnesota and Wisconsin), the unrelated interjection *ish*, indicating disgust or dislike, can be found. According to the *Dictionary of American Regional English*, it derives from the Norwegian *isj* and the Danish and Swedish *isch*.

1994 *Usenet: alt.rap* (Oct. 30) "Re: DP Blowout Comb Question" ▶ It didn't seem like he did much on the last album, but he could still cut that isht up in concert. **1995** *Usenet: alt.rap* (Feb. 22) "Re: Scared the #@%$ Outta Me!" ▶ On Public Enemy's Muse Sick in Hour Mess Age (the CD), if you reverse past the first track (about 1:25), there is Chuck D on the mike talking isht. **1995** *Usenet: alt.rap* (Mar. 21) "Biz, the Roots, O.C., and Group Home" ▸ While waiting for PR & CL they shot the isht around freestyle like behind the curtain. **1999** *Usenet: rec.sport.pro-wrestling.fantasy* (July 25) "Re: RSPWF Reeks of Shit" ▸ You're full of ish, you ish head. Incidentally, I have a strange question: are you aware that "ish" is the term used instead of "shit" in many rap songs so they can be played on the radio, etc.? **2000** *Usenet: alt.religion.christian.adventist* (Mar. 16) "Re: How Do You Join the Church" ▸ I don't give a "ish" what you think of the SDA church. God saved my old man's life. **2005** Des *Life in Text Format* (Detroit, Mich.) (Mar. 7) "Things I Hate About Work" (Int.) ▸ Got they're hair and nails did while the kids lookin' bombed out—running through the store tearing ish up & acting a fool.... A lot of these chicks see me as a potential implant in a ready made family. They kids lookin' at me 'n ish like "Are you gonna be our new daddy?"...If I take her to dinner, she wanna take a doggybag home to them and all that other ish. **2005** [babigirllena (Salena)] *Tha Lyfe of That One Babi Girl* (Mass.) (Mar. 9) "Driving" (Int.) ▸ Now imagine me on tha road. holy isht. havin mad cars around me waitin for me to do this, to do that.

item girl *n.* in Indian cinema, a woman who appears in an *item song*; (*hence*) a female actress, singer, or dancer, esp. one who is poised to become a star. *Entertainment. India. Music.* An *item song* or *item number* is a musical performance that has little do with the film in which it appears, but is presented mainly to showcase beautiful dancing women, to promote a song, or to lend marketability to a film. Item numbers often have a life on stage long after a movie has left theaters. There appears to be some confluence with the term *"it" girl*, to signify someone who is much talked about or sought after.

2000 Lata Khubchandani *Times of India* (Oct. 29) "I Was Almost Finished" ▸ Shilpa Shetty tells Lata Khubchandani that she's happy to have abandoned her "item song" reputation and rebuilt her career from scratch. The one-time "item" girl has suddenly become one of the most sought after actresses in Bollywood. **2002** *Indian Express* (India) (Oct. 6) "Are You Mad About Antara Mali?" ▸ For instance, it is believed Varma is yet to recover from Bollywood's applause for the bestowal from his stable—the redesigned Matondkar to item-girl Isha. **2004** *Kerala News* (India) (Oct. 4) "Bollywood Starlets Head for Nepal to Chill Out" (in Kathmandu, Nepal) (Int.) ▸ Upcoming performers who start their careers in the Hindi film industry by doing dance numbers in films or music videos—"item girls" in Bollywood parlance—are now becoming part of Kathmandu's entertainment scenario as well. **2005** Jhumari Nigam *Times of India* (June 27) "Straight Answers" (Int.) ▶ We don't have just "item girls" but "item boys" as well. And why not? After all, a star is a commodity that helps to sell a film.

J

jackass *v.* to do something by brute force or by human power; to travel a circuitous route or itinerary.

1930 Ralph J. Fairbanks *Touring Topics* (June) "My 73 Years on Southwestern Deserts," no. 22, pp. 24-25 in *Death Valley & the Amargosa* (1986) Richard E. Lingenfelter, p. 409 ▶ In 1916 I made the strike that I'd been jack-assing for thirty-five years trying to locate.
*1938-39 R. Pecheur, machinist, 147 Grand St.; Fearing *LOTJ* "Machinists" ▶ Jackass, jackassing—to move by manpower a tool ordinarily machine-powered. Manpower in general. **1939** Maddin Malone *L.A. Times* (June 25) "The Drummer Still Drums in Los Angeles," p. H19 ▶ Mr. Brooker is such a good drummer that he doesn't have to go "jackassing." "Jackassing" is the trade term for taking samples to customers instead of having the customers come to the hotel to see the samples. **1955** John Hart *Carpenter* (Sept.) "All About Francis," no. 75, pp. 29 31 in *Calf's Head & Union Tale* (Oct. 1, 1996) Archie Green, p. 134 ▶ Davis and Francis were jackassing the chute into place when in walks the architect. **1993** Carol Higgins Clark *Decked* (Aug. 1), p. 6 ▶ Mrs. Watkin's eyes grew heavy as Gavin helped her stagger to her penthouse. I've got some job, he thought wistfully, jackassing people around the ship. **1999** Rob Kean *The Pledge* (Aug. 1), p. 544 ▶ He knew enough about killing to know that it should be carried out quickly and cleanly or not carried out at all, and that jackassing all over campus in search of his target was just plain foolish. **2003** William J. Veigele *Sea Bag of Memories* (May 15), p. 15 ▶ There was a time when everything you owned had to fit in your Sea Bag.... You warped your spine jackassing the goofy thing through a bus or train station. **2005** Linda Fairstein *Entombed* (Jan. 4), p. 276 ▶ We've been jackassing all over the place since we left Manhattan.

janky *adj.* inferior, bad, weird. Also **jinky, jainky, jankie, jankey.** *Slang. United States.* The connection between *janky* and *jinky* is uncertain, but as their usage seems interchangeable, I am defining them as a single term.

1993 *Usenet: soc.culture.iranian* (Apr. 19) "Leave My Login Alone!" ▶ You understand what I am saying? Stupid and your shers are very janky, just like you. **1994** *Usenet: soc.penpals* (Apr. 10) "4 All U Guys Out There" ▶ For those of you who get off on posting weird or Jinky letters go ahead do It. **1995** *Usenet: rec.games.miniatures* (Feb. 2) "Re: GW: Paints" ▶ Yep, wade in amongst the tired looking housewives wearing those janky looking jumpsuits buying neat little craft crap for christmas presents. **1995** *Usenet: alt.society.generation-x* (Feb. 4) "Re: Repubs 0, Demos 0—EVERYBODY Gets a Big Fat Zero..." ▶ When society gets really jinky about some stupid "claim," I think it is entirely proper for individuals to kick society in the pants rather than give in. **1996** *Usenet: alt.rap* (Apr. 16) "Re: White Rappers" ▶ Jankie has two meanings. In most areas, jankie means flawed, bad, "booty" as you put it. :) In Southern Cali, it does mean dope. **1997** *Usenet: alt.fan.tank-girl* (Mar. 6) "Re: TG Look...What Do YOU Do?" ▶ I posted a note that was witty and cute and informative in response to this posting. However, it got lost when my fucking server went jinky. **1997** *Usenet:rec.games.trading-cards.magic.misc* (Aug. 2) "Re: Whatever Happened to the Slang Dictionary" ▶ I believed it got 187ed when john tried to get al fruity-assed with weedwhacker. Kinda jankey if you ask me. **1997** *Usenet: alt.comp.sys.palmtops.pilot* (Sept. 10) "Re: Reseating Stylus in PalmPro Turns It Off" ▶ I got this yesterday, I thought it was just me. Except that the screen went all jinky and I had to do a soft reset. Very strange. **2000** Cintra Wilson *A Massive Swelling* (July 13), p. 101 ▶ Twenty-eight girls, most of whom were nervous and janky and fell down once or twice, slunk off to joylessly watch their bad numbers roll up on the screen. **2000** William Shaw *Westside: Young Men and Hip Hop in L.A.* (Apr. 12), p. 322 ▶ "That janky-ass bitch?" *Janky* is Rah's favorite word these days. Anything below par is janky. **2003** Bill Fitzhugh *Heart Seizure* (Mar. 4), p. 217 ▶ That janky-ass cameo boy got some shit on the side of my ride? **2003** Jen Loy *Kitchen Sink* (Oakland, Calif.) (Oct. 31) "There Goes the Neighborhood," vol. 2, no. 1, p. 72 ▶ The two artists wear white, "janky-ass Tyvek" painter's suits; they move quickly, transferring wooden panels and cement legs to the curb beneath the AC Transit sign. Within minutes, they are assembling the bench. **2003** [Zachary James] *The Mofluff Confessional* (Dec. 16) "To His Coy Mistress" (Int.) ▶ Nine more of these jainky little definitions and I'm home free.

Ja well no fine *other* a noncommittal expression of unconcern, indifference, apathy, or ambivalence. *Colloquial. South Africa.*

1991 John MacLennan *Sunday Star* (Johannesburg, S. Africa) (July 7) "The ANC Could Take a Tip or Two from the NP," p. 14 ▶ The question was put directly to new secretary-general Cyril Ramaphosa this week and his inconclusive reply can best be described as a diplomatic "Ja, well, no fine." **1994** James Flannery @ Johannesburg, South Africa (*Reuters*) (Apr. 14) "Paradoxes Abound in S. Africa's March to Democracy" ▶ A casual conversation includes the benediction: "Ja well, no fine," meaning: "How interesting, do go on" or "I've had enough, go away." **2000** Kurt Shillinger @ Johannesburg, South Africa *Boston Globe* (Oct. 22) "Letter from South Africa: Blend of Languages Hard to Digest," p. A17 ▶ Consider the local expression, "Ja, well, no fine."...Is it one word? Does it have commas? Even the Dictionary of South African English stumbles: "to explain this to a non-South African is a challenge." A few years ago, the former radio broadcaster RJB Wilson, who coined the expression back in 1978, tried to explain it. "My youngest brother," he wrote, "was in the habit of saying 'no fine' to everything that really required a 'c'est la vie' or 'that's the way the cookie crumbles.' It had a nice South African feel to it. I added 'Ja, well...' to it to reinforce the South Africanism." **2002** Jean-Marie Dru *Beyond Disruption: Changing the Rules in the Marketplace* (Apr. 12), p. 93 ▶ Because "ja well no fine" makes sense to us. **2004** [Marcia Klein] *Sunday Times* (S. Africa) (May 2) "Grapevine: Casualties of Jargon" (Int.) ▶ The blurb reads: "The intention is to pilot various healthcare models to focus on cost-effective and quality healthcare delivery that is comprehensively measured by clinical outcomes." Ja-well-no-fine.

Jesus year *n.* a person's 33rd year of life. [From the age that Jesus is said to have been when he died] A similar term is *Elvis year* 'a person's 42nd year of life; the year at which a person or thing peaks in popularity.'

1995 *Usenet: rec.music.ambient* (June 8) "Old Gits" ▶ Greetings from another oldster! Just hitting my Jesus year (33). **1996** Dave Hoekstra *Chicago Sun-Times* (Feb. 28) "For Morris, the Beat Influence Goes On," p. 30 ▶ Especially in Nashville, I don't talk about it. I will say I've done my Jesus year (he's past 33, but he has yet to hit his Elvis year, 42). **2005** Hank Stuever @ L.A. *Washington Post* (Mar. 14) "Late Night Raises the Burr" (Int.) ▶ The show leaps at you—at 12:35 a.m., an ungodly hour for anyone past their Jesus year, age 33.

jitterbug *n.* a gang member; a juvenile delinquent. *Crime & Prisons. Slang. United States.*

[**1941** Bosley Growther *N.Y. Times* (Jan. 25) "'High Sierra' at the Strand, Considers the Tragic Plight of the Last Gangster," p. 11 ▶ The big holdup job gets messed up by a couple of "jitterbugs" who are assisting on it, the girl turns out a great disappointment, the gunman is rendered a fugitive with a moll and a dog who love him.] [**1963** Russell Baker *N.Y. Times* (Dec. 29) "Observer," p. 106 ▶ Edward G. Robinson, Humphrey Bogar and James Cagney in the movies, "Gangbusters" on radio, bubblegum "war cards" depicting atrocities, and "zoot suit" riots among the jitterbug set were widely deplored as symptoms of national sickness.] **1993** Renee Graham *Boston Globe*

(Dec. 12) "On the Edge of Oblivion: The Forecast for the Nation's Poor Black Children," p. B36 ▶ "Bojack" started robbing parking meters as a 10-year-old; by age 16, he was "a bona-fide 'jitterbug'—the first lieutenant and known warlord of a very large gang." **1999** Simon Reynolds *Generation Ecstasy* (July), p. 107 ▶ The clubs started putting the phrase "no jits" on the flyers—"jit" being short for "jitterbug," Detroit slang for gangsta. **2000** *Usenet: triangle.general* (May 4) "Re: Unspoken Media Truths..." ▶ I'm sure every woman brutalized by some jitterbug incited by gangsta rap is happy to learn that the issue there is fantasy. **2001** Marian Elaine *And I Cry* (Aug.), p. 70 ▶ I see you one of those hard ass jitterbugs, huh? **2002** Paula L. Woods *Stormy Weather* (July 30), p. 118 ▶ A third group nearby argued that the NAACP's more recent threats of boycott probably wouldn't increase the number of minority production executives or result in even *one* black person who could greenlight a film. "Man, it's gonna be the same thugs, slugs, and jitterbugs as usual." **2004** Susan Spencer-Wendel *Palm Beach Post* (Fla.) (May 30) "Judge Lupo's Legacy More Than Just One High-Profile Trial" (Int.) ▶ "Idiot! You're an idiot!" she started in, grilling him about why he started crack at age 47, about flushing his life down the toilet, about how now, at his age, he would join the idle, young black males in jail. "Jitterbugs," Lupo called them, using street lingo.

JND *n.* in psychophysics, the minimum difference between two inputs that is detectable by a human. *Jargon. Science.* [*just* notice-able *d*ifference]

1956 R. Duncan Luce *Econometrica* (Apr.) "Semiorders and a Theory of Utility Discrimination," vol. 24, no. 2, p. 181 (Int.) ▶ The two j.n.d. functions of the induced semiorder are two of the given functions. **1986** *Usenet: sci.med* (Nov. 12) "Re: Tone Deafness?" ▶ With this method, the "just-noticeable-difference," (jnd) can be calculated. **2004** Mike McClintock *Washington Post* (July 8) "Home Sense" (Int.) ▶ Many people can detect a change of only one dB, which in engineering parlance goes by an interestingly nonjargon, nontechnical term called the JND, or Just Noticeable Difference.

jointery *n.* command shared between two or more branches of military; (*hence*) military command shared between two or more nations. *Jargon. Military. United Kingdom.*

[**1989** Chris Moncrieff (*Press Association*) (U.K.) (Sept. 8) "Owen 'Clanger' Cost Us Votes, Says Steel" ▶ All through the previous parliament David had dragged his feet on joint selection of candidates, joint parliamentary meetings, joint everything and even now when "jointery" had proved wanting here, he was putting up more obstacles to unity.] **1994** Bruce Clark, Roland Rudd *Financial Times* (U.K.) (July 15)

"'Tri-Service' Plan Triumphs over Tough Vested Interests," p. 10 ▶ Under the new principle—referred by the ugly new word "jointery"—there is to be a tri-service hospital and a tri-service staff college. Joint arrangements will be promoted in areas such as flying instruction, music lessons and veterinary care. **1994** Donald Anderson *Commons Hansard* (U.K.) (Oct. 18) "House of Commons Hansard Debates," vol. 248, p. 168 (Int.) ▶ Peacekeeping will have major procurement implications: there will be an emphasis on flexibility and amphibiosity and the marines will have a new significance. There are implications for heavy transport and training and for "jointery," one of the themes of the defence costs study, and there will be renewed emphasis on the interoperability of equipment. **1998** Douglas Barrie *Flight International* (U.K.) (July 15) "Rhetoric or Reality?" ▶ The Government, however, now has to turn the rhetoric of the SDR into reality—in particular, what Johns describes as the key theme of "jointery," of tri-service commands—known as Purple commands in the U.K. **2004** *SpaceWar* (Oct. 22) "US Command of British Troops in Iraq 'Business as Usual'" (in London, Eng.) (Int.) ▶ Multinational command—known in military parlance as "jointery"—was a vital component of modern warfare.

Jorge Arbusto *n.* George H. W. Bush or George W. Bush. *Brazil. Mexico. Politics. Portuguese. Spain. Spanish.* [*Jorge* 'George' + *arbusto* 'bush'] Often jocular or mocking.

1992 *Usenet: soc.culture.mexican* (Aug. 12) "Re: NAFTA" ▶ Escuche hoy en la man~ana que el sen~or Jorge Arbusto firmo esta man~ana el tratado en la casa blanca. **1997** *Usenet: soc.culture.spain* (June 12) "Re: Si el toreo es arte, el canibalismo es gastronomia" ▶ Los nombres de ciudades, paises, etc se pueden traducir. Los nombres de personas no se traducen. A caso dices Jorge Arbusto en lugar de George Bush? Si haces ese tipo de traducciones, ya no se clasificaria como horterismo sino como pura ignorancia. **2003** Richard Adams *Guardian* (U.K.) (Jan. 29) "American Presidents All Mixed Up" ▶ Of course it also means Brazil ends up with George Bush. But then Jorge Arbusto, as he would be known, might quite enjoy life up the rugged Amazon. **2003** [Enrique] @ London, U.K. *Enfermero español en Londres* (Aug. 31) (Int.) ▶ En fin, que sigan las vacaciones, y que como mi amiguete Jorge Arbusto dice, que el CO2 no tiene nada que ver con estos calores, que es que cada poquito estamos algo mas cerca del Sol, y que total, tanto quejarse de frio en Diciembre, y ahora que no nos hace falta el paraguas, pues eso, que somos unos desagradecidos. **2004** [Single White Male] *Single White Male* (June 3) "Jorge Arbusto" (Int.) ▶ A Mãe Natureza dá uma mãozinha e ajuda a ridicularizar (ainda mais) o presidente Jorge Arbusto. Thank you Mother Nature. **2004** César Fernando Zapata *La Crónica* (Mexico D.F.) (July 10) "Sorry, yo no spekeo español, ni english. Spanglish, for plis" (Int.) ▶ Aunque George Bush—Jorge Arbusto, como también se autonombra—sea el primer presidente americano que promueve abierta, aunque involutariamente, la causa del spanglish. Como todo texano.

journalists' colony *n.* government-subsidized housing or land intended for citizens employed in the media. *India. Media. Pakistan.* Such developments are often seen as attempts to soften media criticism of the government or ruling parties.

1988 K.K. Sharma @ New Delhi *Financial Times* (U.K.) (Aug. 23) "Housing Shortage That Can Destroy Friendships," p. 3 ▶ Mr. Saeed Naqvi is a prominent editor in New Delhi whose wife insisted 12 years ago that he build a low-cost house on a cheap 500 sq m plot he had acquired under a scheme for a journalists' colony. **1998** G.S. Bhargava *Times of India* (Feb. 4) "Seeing Red" ▶ Over 20 years ago when Gulmohar Park came up as a journalists' "colony," it had neither Gulmohars nor any VIPs. It was as barren as most areas in Delhi, though some founding fathers of the "colony" wanted it to be named "Bottle Nagar" after the journalists' deference to the Bacchus. **2003** Edgar Martins *Gaonet Email List* (Aug. 18) "Re: Fred's Delayed Response" (Int.) ▶ The Indian Government like most Governments specially the US, is very sensitive to Journalists exposing in the media their corrupt practices. As per the Australian Broadcasting Corp., they have created Journalist Colonies all over India to cater to the comforts of those who could stir up public sentiments. **2005** *Business Recorder* (Karachi, Pakistan) (Jan. 16) "Five Foreign Investors Teams Due on January 18" ▶ The minister further said that Chief Minister Punjab had sanctioned a journalists' colony for each district to provide shelter to homeless journalists. **2005** Phillip Knightley @ London, England *Sydney Morning Herald* (Australia) (Aug. 12) "Restoring Citizens' Respect for Journalism: We Are Not Without Power" (Int.) ▶ There are other ways of managing the media without using the "risk to national security" approach. The government of India adopts a carrot and stick tactic. The carrot can include subsidised housing in so-called "journalists' colonies."

jubu *n.* a Jewish person who maintains Buddhist beliefs or practices. *Religion.* This term was popularized by Rodger Kamenetz through his 1994 book *A Jew in the Lotus: A Poet's Rediscovery of Jewish Identity*.

1994 Verlyn Klinkenborg *N.Y. Times Book Review* (July 24) "Going to See the Lama," p. 10 ▶ In autumn 1990, a Jewish Buddhist, a poet and eight distinguished Jews traveled to Dharamsala, India, for a four-day exchange of views...with the Dalai Lama.... The Jewish Buddhist (or JUBU, as some say) was Marc Lieberman, a San Francisco oph-thalmologist. **1995** Noachman Spiegel *Jerusalem Post* (Feb. 10) "A Dharma Zionist?" p. 19 ▶ Kamenetz wanted to learn what it was about Buddhism that lured many Jews to embrace the tenets of the Buddha and become "JUBUs." **1999** Luisa Yanez *Sun-Sentinel* (Ft. Lauderdale, Fla.) (Apr. 15) "Ties That Bind: The Shared Pain of Persecution Led Many South Florida Jews and Cuban Exiles to Tibetan Buddhism and the Dalai Lama" ▶ "It's sort of a Jewish phenomenon that so many of us turned to Buddhism," Katz said. "There's even a name for Jews who switch. It's 'JUBU.'" **2005** Don Lattin *San Francisco Chronicle* (Jan. 23) "Bridging Eastern and Western Buddhism" (Int.) ▶ They pre-fer "Christian with a Buddhist practice," or "Ju-Bu," a term coined to describe American Jews who embrace Buddhist meditation.

Judas window *n.* an aperture or glass pane that permits safe or surreptitious observation through a door or wall. This is a varia-tion on *Judas hole*, *Judas trap*, or just *Judas*.

1874 *N.Y. Times* (Aug. 23) "Through a Judas Window," p. 2 ▶ In addi-tion to a door of communication, there was a contrivance for the effectual protection of privacy, consisting of a sheet of glass in a hinged frame let into the wall.... By means of this honestly-avowed peephole, he could at all times command a view off the outer office.... I could see through the Judas window in the wall, which I have described, but without moving from their respective places they could not see me. **1949** Virginia Teale *Sedalia Democrat* (Mo.) (Nov. 1) "The Cameo," p. 2 ▶ A small Judas window in the top section of the door was opened cautiously. **1954** *Nevada State Journal* (Reno) (July 2) "Estate Repayment Ordered by Court" (in San Francisco) ▶ This was about three months after Belote, admittedly her lover, was convicted of killing Allen B. Friedman by shooting him through the Judas win-dow of the front door of his home. **1985** Stanton Delaplane *San Francisco Chronicle* (Jan. 24) "Chicken Soup in the Medical Bag," p. 55 ▶ I went over to the school and peeked at him through the classroom judas window. He wasn't over-active. **2005** Hugh Reilly *Scotsman* (Scotland) (Mar. 9) "Yes, Head Boys Must Have the Latest Toys" (Int.) ▶ Classroom surveillance is nothing new. Most classroom doors have a glass section—a Judas window in chalkie parlance—allowing man-agement to surreptitiously spy on Sir's lesson.

jugaad *n.* an improvised or jury-rigged solution; inventiveness, inge-nuity, cleverness. *Hindi. India.* [< Hindi.]

1995 Barun S. Mitra *Asian Wall Street Journal* (Jan. 26) "India's 'Infor-mal' Car," p. 10 ▶ If one drives out of Delhi in any direction one is likely to encounter these hybrid vehicles within an hour. Known as

"Jugaads," which means roughly to provide or arrange, they have become a mainstay of rural transportation. **2002** *Straits Times* (Singapore) (Sept. 29) "What's Culture Got to Do with IT?" ► New Delhi-based IT entrepreneur Karan Vir Singh, managing director of Voxtron Dezign Lab, called it the "jugaad" factor—the improvised quick fix. "It's like putting two spoons of turmeric powder into your radiator if you spring a small leak," he said. "It works, it will seal the leak. In Punjab, I have seen villagers buying an agricultural water pump at government subsidised rates, cannibalising some other parts from here and there, and turning it into a vehicle." **2004** Sudip Talukdar *Times of India* (Jan. 1) "Makeshift Miracles: The Indian Genius for Jugaad" (Int.) ► The operative world of jugaad, implying alternatives, substitutes, improvisations and make-dos, is spurred by a native inventiveness steeped in a culture of scarcity and survival. **2004** John W. Fox *Press & Sun-Bulletin* (Binghamton, N.Y.) (July 16) "Chopra Master of the Improbable" (Int.) ► Daniel Chopra, who learned his golf in India, "seems to have plenty of the typical Indian quality of jugaad."…A reporter who had peeked translated it as "finding alternative ways of doing improbable things...creative improvisation." **2005** Vaibhav Varma *Channel NewsAsia* (Singapore) (Mar. 20) "Ingenious 'Jugaad' Vehicles Are an Integral Part of Rural Indian Economy" (Int.) ► In India, one vehicle is called the "jugaad" which literally translates as a "put-together contraption that moves."

juice bar *n.* a methadone clinic, especially one that is seen to encourage addiction rather than cure it. *Drugs. Slang.*

1997 (*AP*) (Jan. 22) "Three Methadone Clinics to Close" (in Portland, Ore.) ► Toni Phipps, interim director of the state's Office of Alcohol and Drug Abuse Programs, said clinic operators "were basically running a juice bar," doling out methadone while providing little or no treatment. **2001** Mark Shanahan *Portland Press Herald* (Apr. 28) "Portland Getting Clinic for Addicts," p. 1A ► The methadone-only approach, sometimes called a "juice bar," would not be awarded the state's $100,000 contract, she said. **2002** Bill Radford *Gazette* (Colorado Springs, Colo.) (Aug. 31) "Critics Fear Decline in Service if County Halts Methadone Care" ► Steve Gilbertson, deputy director of substance-abuse programs for Connect Care, said he has ruled out some clinics that simply would have been "a juice bar" handing out methadone and sending people on their way. **2005** Chen Chekki *Chronicle-Journal* (Thunder Bay, Ontario, Can.) (Feb. 17) "Meth Clinic Opens" (Int.) ► The clinics are often referred to as "juice bars," a place where some people believe they can get an easy fix of methadone.

jukebox musical *n.* a theater show built around popular songs. *Entertainment. Music.*

1993 D. Partridge *Courier-Mail* (Australia) (Feb. 1) "Enthusiasm Can't Save This Musical" ▶ Another jukebox musical—revive someone else's plot (in this case Shakespeare's Tempest and a forgotten MGM sci-fi movie of the 1950s), punctuate it with feel-good songs from the 1960s, and disguise the thin idea. **1995** Bill Morrison @ Fayetteville *News & Observer* (Raleigh, N.C.) (May 29) "'Five Guys' Swings on Jordan's Star" ▶ Right now they're putting on the ultimate jukebox musical, Louis Jordan's "Five Guys Named Moe," and swinging everybody into bad health. **2005** Jesse McKinley *N.Y. Times* (Feb. 14) "You Can Name the Tune, But Does It Fit the Plot?" (Int.) ▶ It highlights the challenges faced by writers of so-called catalog, or jukebox, musicals, an increasingly popular form of show in which a new story is woven around existing hit songs.... In particular, the problem for "Good Vibrations," and other jukebox shows, is that the song lyrics cannot be altered to fit the sentiments of the characters who sing them.

jump-out *n.* an arrest made (suddenly) by undercover police using unmarked vehicles; a police officer or detective who makes such an arrest. Also **jump-out boys, jump-out gang.** *Crime & Prisons. Police.*

1986 Nancy Lewis *Washington Post* (Oct. 31) "U.S. Judge Seals Parts of Clean Sweep Manual," p. B7 ▶ U.S. District Court Gerhard A. Gesell agreed to seal parts of the 11-page typewritten manual that contained specific instructions, such as how many uniformed officers should be present as a backup and how many officers should be used in a "jump-out" squad. Earlier this month Assistant Police Chief Isaac Fulwood Jr. began an investigation of the "jump-out" tactic, which was being used by police to search large groups of people without probable cause. **1987** Kent Jenkins, Jr. *Washington Post* (Sept. 14) "Caught in Drug Cross Fire," p. A1 ▶ The department's tactical unit, known as the "jump-out boys," has met with flying debris when officers swoop in. **1988** Rene Sanchez *Washington Post* (June 5) "Learning to Play the Drug Game; District Youngsters Emulating Adults in Make-Believe Deals," p. A1 ▶ "When they play the games, it's 'We'll be the hustlers, you be the jump-outs.'" **1988** Jeffrey Good *St. Petersburg Times* (Dec. 23) "Death Puts Heat on Tough Cops in a Rough City," p. 1B ▶ Miami police could point with pride to the success of their undercover anti-drug team. Its 15-member squad, dubbed the "Jump Out Gang" for the way officers sprang at unsuspecting criminals, helped account for roughly 6,000 drug-related arrests since 1986.

1989 Jon Jeter *Star Tribune* (Minneapolis-St. Paul, Minn.) (July 14) "Police Pursue 'Crack' Dealers into the Streets," p. 1A ► Since May, undercover officers have targeted street-level dealers, buying packets of crack at a street corner, then moving in with vehicles full of police who "jump out" and make arrests. First conducted in Florida, the "jump-outs" have drawn mixed reviews from other agencies that have duplicated them. **2001** Lara Becker *Democrat and Chronicle* (Rochester, N.Y.) (Aug. 12) "Battfield on Beat 252" (Int.) ► One week after Tyshaun's slaying, narcotics officers made a bust at a house across the street. As officers approached, the three children left unattended there shouted a warning to their mother: "The jump-outs are here." **2003** American Friends Service Committee-Middle Atlantic Region *MARStar* (Summer) "Teens Learn Their Rights in an Advanced HIPP Session," vol. 11, no. 2 (Int.) ► The young Nebraskans were particularly fascinated and curious about the "jump-outs" that DC police conduct twice each week, in which undercover officers attempt to buy drugs from young people who fit the profile of a drug dealer. **2004** *Y&B.net* (Chicago) "Y & B's Chicago Slang Dictionary" (Int.) ► *Jump Outs*: Phrase used for Detectives who are known for quickly stopping their vehicles, jumping out and conducting arrests. (Jump out boys) ex: We was chillin & all of a sudden the JUMP OUTS rolled up and kilt the whole demo. **2004** Anthony J. Pinizzotto, Edward F. Davis, Charles E. Miller *American Psychological Association* (May 24) "Intuitive Policing: Emotional/Rational Decision Making in Law Enforcement," p. 2 (Int.) ► When the unmarked units approached the street corner, the crowd of individuals immediately began dispersing upon observing the presence of the "jump outs." **2004** City Council *City of Asheville* (Asheville, N.C.) (June 8) "Council Minutes" (Int.) ► Mr. Iver Thomas said that the drug program can be solved by tough police action; however, he is not in favor of the jump-outs by the police officers. He would prefer to see a reverse sting where the customers are arrested. **2005** Francisco Alvarado *Miami New Times* (Jan. 27) "Crack Kills" (Int.) ► He emerges from a wood-frame house and quickly rides off, watching vigilantly for Miami police cruisers and "them Jump Out Boys," the undercover vice cops rolling in unmarked rental cars.... "It's kind of weird how every dope fiend in this neighborhood knows Tuesdays and Thursdays the Jump Out Boys are coming. Yet a lot of them get busted anyway. What the fuck is wrong with that picture? If you know there is a good probability the Jump Outs are going to be at the dope hole, it just doesn't make sense to go there."

junk *n.* the genitals or genital area. *Sexuality. Slang.* Often used with the definite article: **the junk.**

1996 *Usenet: rec.sport.pro-wrestling* (Dec. 3) "Re: Poll: What Moments in Wrestling Made You Laugh Hysterically?" ▶ Jacque picks up one of the New Zealanders for a bodyslam and not only grabs his junk, but gives him a pretty good rubdown. The camera gives a perfect angle. Next time you watch it, don't fast forward this match...look for the junk grab!!! [**1999** *Usenet: alt.music.spice-girls* (Oct. 31) "Re: Help! Schoolie in Distress" ▶ I'm gonna kick her in the junk.] **2000** *Usenet: rec.music.phish* (June 20) "Re: Any Good Tricks Getting Your Stash Past Security This Summer?" ▶ I have been with a guy who stashed stuff in his pants only to have the male security guy actually grab his junk and bust him. **2002** [Dylan M.] *Saint Paul Blog* (Minn.) (June 29) "What a Drag It Is Getting Old" (Int.) ▶ Please contact your editor, and kick him/her in the junk for not deleting that. **2002** *Usenet: alt.fan.robert-jordan* (Sept. 10) "From Your Sex Instructor: Vocabulary, Part II" ▶ *Finch*—When the guy tucks his junk between his legs and gets head from behind. **2003** *Electronic Gaming Monthly* (May 1) "MLB SlugFest 20-04 (PS2)," no. 166 ▶ In my first game, I punch Todd Helton in the face, then knee him in the junk. **2003** [Kitten-Walk (Amber)] @ Vancouver, B.C. *bcpsportsbikes.com* (Can.) (Aug. 26) (Int.) ▶ "Just because you're somewhat hot, you shouldn't sit on other people's bikes without their permission. If your cleavage hadn't distracted me, I would have kicked you in the junk!"..."You should have kicked her in the junk anyways...cutie pie." **2004** Joe Rybicki *PlayStation Magazine* (July 1) "Psi-Ops: The Mindgate Conspiracy; Mind over Matter," p. 88 ▶ The resoundingly mediocre story and writing give this otherwise superlative game a vicious kick in the junk. **2004** *Craigslist* (Oct. 14) "I'm Becoming a Llama" (in San Francisco) (Int.) ▶ I'm a llama. Maybe I can start spitting on people and kicking them in the junk. **2004** *Usenet: alt.support.stop-smoking* (Oct. 27) "Re: Patches Not Sticking" ▶ See the story of the guy in Singapore (I think) who was cheating on his gf and she Ripped His Junk Completely Off?!! That'd make John cringe.

KAGOY *n.* a marketing concept based on the idea that children participate in pop culture or desire material goods intended for older consumers. *Acronym. Advertising.* [*k*ids *a*re *g*etting *o*lder *y*ounger]

1998 Leonie Wood *The Age* (Dec. 12) "Make or Break Time in Toyland," p. 1 ▶ Kids are getting older younger—known as KAGOY within Mattel. Children are becoming more sophisticated faster than previous generations and are increasingly savvy about the world around them. **1999** Donna Leccese *Playthings* (Oct. 1) "Baby Steps," vol. 97, no. 10, p. 28 ▶ Younger children want the same kinds of products as their older siblings.... With the KAGOY philosophy, there are more opportunities to broaden our product range. **2003** Anne Sutherland *Kidfluence* (July 21), p. 40 ▶ KAGOY actually begins much sooner than that and in a more altruistic form. Parents, in the hopes of giving their child a head start in life, are now reading and playing music to their unborn babies. **2005** Chuck Salter *FC Now* (Feb. 23) "Adult Toys—No, Not That Kind" (Int.) ▶ Another problem facing the industry is "kagoy." Translation: "Kids are getting older, younger." As early as 8, they're putting down traditional toys and turning to video games and the Internet.

kalo-kalo *n.* a slot machine or casino; (*hence*) a jocular reference to the financial affairs of Nigeria. Also **kalokalo.** *Gambling. Money & Finance. Nigeria. Slang.*

1996 *Usenet: soc.culture.nigeria* (1996) "Re: Beemers and Big Cars" ▶ One of my brother's friend's...is a Nissan salesman (notice how he dropped the Maxima into the conversation), he referred to your car as a "kalo kalo" (fruit machine) for gas. And all the gadgets on it, I wish my brother had seen it, he loves stuff like that. **2001** [Babawilly] *Babawilly's Dictionary of Pidgin English Words and Phrases* (Nigeria) (Int.) ▶ *Kalo-kalo*: 1. One armed bandit. 2. Amusement arcade game machines. **2002** Mike Ikhariale *Niger Delta Congress* (Nigeria) (Aug.) "Buhari's Polemical Marksmanship" (Int.) ▶ So the Buhari that is likely to register in the minds of many Nigerians today, depending on where you belong and from where you are looking at him, is...the man who attempted to liberate the Nigerian economy from the clutches of corruption and its kalo-kalo fiscal idiosyncrasy. **2002** By Tunji Bello

THISDAY (Nigeria) (Oct. 30) "Were You Better Off Under IBB?" (Int.) ▶ No wonder scores of kalo-kalo banks sprang up overnight as beneficiaries of rentier era. **2003** Kingsley Osadolor *Naija-news* (June 18) "Y'Hello, Network Busy!" (Int.) ▶ It is like you are using slot machines, the so-called kalokalo. **2003** Louis Odion *Lagosforum* (Lagos, Nigeria) (Nov. 24) "The Truth Okonjo-Iweala Didn't Tell About Naira" (Int.) ▶ The finest hour for those who have always likened the management of Nigeria's economy to Kalokalo (casino), it appears, is here. Put roughly, Kalokalo refers to the inclination to enter an economic river without a compass.

katastroika *n.* In the former Soviet republics, a disastrous government reform or change, esp. the *perestroika* movement of the 1990s and the collapse of the Soviet Union. Also **catastroika.** *Derogatory. Russia. Russian.*

1989 Richard I. Kirkland Jr. *Fortune* (NYC) (June 19) "How China's Chaos Affects the West," p. 77 ▶ While Gorbachev's political reforms are breathtaking, his economic perestroika appears overly cautious and utterly ineffectual. French scholar Jacques Rupnik has suggested a new label: catastroika. The sprawling Soviet empire—full of fractious Ukrainians, Armenians, Tatars, and other nationalities—constantly threatens to come apart at the seams. **1990** Jonathon Steele *Guardian* (U.K.) (Mar. 9) "Five Years of Gorbachev: Soviet Fears of Katastroika" ▶ In the first phase of Mr. Gorbachev's rule, some Russians thought that glasnost was just a trick to get the reformers to stick their heads above the parapet and identify themselves. "Perestrelka," said the satirists, meaning a general shoot-up. Now the joke is at the expense of the economic collapse: "katastroika." **1991** Desmond Christy *Guardian* (U.K.) (Oct. 18) "Europe: Light at the Opera—Gazetta" ▶ *Catastroika*. A mixture of catastrophe and perestroika, it is used by Alexander Sinoviev in the title of a satirical novel he wrote in 1989. **2004** Mark G. Field *New England Journal of Medicine* (July 8) "HIV and AIDS in the Former Soviet Bloc," vol. 351, no. 2, p. 120 (Int.) ▶ The threats in the region from AIDS and other epidemics are potentially dire. Prophecies are always hazardous, but in the former Soviet Bloc, the outlook for the next few decades is perhaps best characterized by a Russian neologism invented to describe the adverse effects of the disintegration of the Soviet system: "katastroika."

kayfabe *n.* the showbiz and stagecraft of professional wrestling, including the ring personas of professional wrestlers, especially when maintained in public; insider knowledge of professional wrestling. Also **keyfabe.** *Entertainment.* [Probably from a Pig Latin form of *fake*.] The historical information in the 1998 citation is unverified.

1990 *Usenet: rec.sport.pro-wrestling* (Apr. 5) "Re: The Future Is Now" ▶ It would not be voted the #1 organization by any group of smart fans or any of the kayfabe sheets. This seems to bother you and I can't figure out why. **1996** *Usenet: rec.sport.pro-wrestling* (June 19) "Re: [INFO] Hack Notes—12 June 1996" ▶ HHH lost his push, and was pulled out of all the WWF's summer PPV's because of the infamous event at the Garden, i.e. the breaking of keyfabe. **1997** John Kelso *Austin American-Statesman* (Tex.) (May 12) "Cult Songs, Wrestling and Deer, Oh My," p. B1 ▶ Joe's interview with you is called a kayfabe interview in the trade. Kayfabe is the wrestling pig-Latin term for fake. As in he kayfabed you about wrestling. **1998** Sharon Mazer *Professional Wrestling: Sport and Spectacle* (Feb. 1), pp. 22-23 ▶ All participants, including fans, present others with at least a bit of a "kayfabe," a term which is taken from nineteenth-century carnival, medicine show, and sideshow practice and simply refers to a con or deception. Kayfabe can also, less pejoratively, refer to participants' self-promotional, rhetorically inflated, and somewhat truth-obfuscating patter that resembles that of the talkers at the traditional sideshow. A kayfabian, then, is a con artist; most wrestlers are proud to be called kayfabians because it means they're in on the (con) game. **2002** Bobby Heenan, Steve Anderson *Bobby the Brain: Wrestling's Bad Boy Tells All* (Aug. 1), p. 33 ▶ The babyfaces hung around together and the heels stayed with each other as well. That's the way it was in those "kayfabe" days. ("Kayfabe" is wrestling slang that refers to protecting the business. To "kayfabe" basically means that the wrestler keeps the inner workings of the business to himself and doesn't share them with the fans. Sort of like a magician doesn't reveal his tricks.) **2005** Jimmy Van *Pro Wrestling Insider* (Apr. 20) "Former WWE Diva Amy Weber Discusses Why She Walked Away from WWE in Detail" (Int.) ▶ Did you hear any of the old schoolers throw around the word "kayfabe"? Amy said she did and she knows exactly what kayfabe is. JV mentions that kayfabe has sort of died off due to the Internet, but some performers like Ric Flair are still protective.

kegler *n.* a bowler. *Sports. United States.* [< German *Kegler*, a player of a form of ninepins, in which a wooden disk or ball is thrown.]
1923 *Sheboygan Press-Telegram* (Wisc.) (Apr. 10) "Rotarians Not at Their Best in Wire Tourney," p. 3 ▶ DeWitt Riess, another good kegler, was not up to standard. His three-game score of 455 was not anywhere near what he is capable of doing. **2004** Rick McCorkle *Daily News* (Longview, Wash.) (June 25) "Longview-Kelso Teams Fair Well in All-Stars Tournament" (Int.) ▶ Hayden, Idaho, kegler Gaylah Spackman

won the all-events with a tournament-record 2150, a 238.9 average for nine games.

kick flick *n.* a martial arts movie. *Entertainment. Media.*
1984 *Washington Post* (Nov. 2) "Films," p. W37 ► Ninja III: The Domination...—Lucinda Dickey liberates kung fu as the first woman ever to star in a kick flick. **2005** Tony Mochama *Society* (Nairobi, Kenya) (June 19) "Mitumba Country" (Int.) ► At the Ronald Ngala Street, people stop to peer through the shop windows at videos— mostly cheap Chinese kick-flicks or weird Nigerian productions—that play in silent mode.

king *v.* among graffiti artists, to (pervasively) paint one's name or symbol (throughout an area); to *own* an area through *tagging* or *bombing*. *Arts. Slang. United States.* [The verb probably derives from the noun *king* 'chief or principal person; the best or top person.' This is supported by some of the cites included below.]
1996 *Usenet: alt.graffiti* (Jan. 27) "Re: ORFN (S.F.)" ► As far as tightest bay area taggers go i've gotta say Kose and Ceav are the best...most up anyhow...definatley kose...he's the king of the bay, has been since like 93, and before that he was kinging shit with his old name...RDS.
[**1996** *Usenet: alt.graffiti* (July 24) "Re: Supreme Cold Crusherz" ► Dont read subway art, it missinforms you, and corrupts your language with words like "toy" and "king."] **1997** *Usenet: alt.graffiti* (July 18) "Re: Tyke+Kaws= Kawn" ► Ive met hiphop heads in graff, ive met dirtty hippies heads in graff, that could probably king all of us, graff isnt a culture by itself, its a big melting pot full of every culture.
1997 *Usenet: alt.graffiti* (Aug. 11) "Re: Honet Rules!!!" ► Xplicit grafx gives you a wrong insight of paris train scene cause its run by ***-crew and so it makes you believe this xxx-crew is kinging paris trains.
[**1999** *Usenet: fido7.mo.graffiti* (Jan. 10) "Dict" ► Crew names are usually three letters, many times ending with "K," which stands for "kings" or "kills" in most cases. Some crew names are just two letters, some are four, it all depends.... For example, "He's the king of insides" would mean he's really up on the insides.... *King.* The best with the most. Some people refer to different writers as kings of different areas. King of throwups, king of style, king of a certain line, etc.]
[**1999** *Usenet: alt.graffiti* (Feb. 28) "Re: World Famous Wake Up Show" ► There is ALOT of crap also...and people who think that just tagging constitutes being king.] **2002** *Usenet: alt.gossip.celebrities* (Feb. 3) "Re: WEHT That So-called Celebrity Quality-Of-Life Offender?" ► Not to mention that you got busted by the cops in every single solitary town that you attempted to king. [**2004** Jane Ganahl *San Francisco Chronicle* (Calif.) (Nov. 9) "In a Low-Budget, Spontaneous Movie About the

Mission, Its Walls, and Its Artists, Speak About Life on the Streets"
(Int.) ► It was designed loosely on Picasso's "Burial of Casagemas"
painting, but I put a crown on the body, since in graffiti parlance, a
"king" is an artist.]

KKN *n.* corruption, collusion, and nepotism. < *English. Acronym.
Business. Crime & Prisons. Indonesia. Politics.* [Initialism of the
Bahasa Indonesia words *k*orupsi, *k*olusi and *n*epotisme, which are
probably derived from English.]

1998 *Usenet: soc.culture.singapore* (Mar. 17) "Harry Lee, Is There Corruption Involved in the Small Arms Industry?" ► Could the kkn
(korupsi, kolusi dan nepotisme) plague thrive in HDB-land after all?
1998 *Bisnis Indonesia* (May 22) "Habibie Must Show Anti-KKN
Stance." ► A number of public figures expect President BJ Habibie to
come up with a cabinet that is free from practices that reek of collusion, corruption and nepotism (otherwise known here as KKN) in
order to gain public and international trust. **2004** *Jakarta Post*
(Indonesia) (Oct. 20) "People Have Their Say on Susilo" (Int.) ► He
will have to deal with KKN (the Indonesian acronym for corruption,
collusion and nepotism).

KLPD *n.* sexual frustration; *blue balls*; unfulfilled (sexual) desire or
an unfulfilled promise; (*hence*) a letdown, a disappointment. Also
KLD. *Acronym. India. Pakistan.* [From Hindi and Urdu, variously
transcribed as (*Khadi* | *Kade* | *Khade* | *Kheray* | *Khari*) (*Lun* | *Lund*
| *Land*) (*Par* | *Pe* | *Par*) (*Dhokha* | *Dhoka*), meaning, roughly, "trick
or betrayal of an erect penis."]

1992 *Usenet: soc.culture.pakistan* (May 15) "Re: Population Explosion"
► The problem with deliberately arousing one sexually and then refusing to have sex (what a friend of mine used to refer to as KLPD) is
not like showing $1000 bills. There is an emotional cycle that is
started in the process, that should normally end in an intercourse.
1993 *Usenet: soc.culture.indian* (July 28) "KLPD" ► KLPD: All the net-
langots on the net, standing and cheering the imminent demise of
PVNR (the government I mean) and the imminent Snagh-Parivar-
Ram-Rajya. A sad case of deflation. Perhaps one could call it Khade
lang(ot) per Dhoka? eh? **1995** *Usenet: rec.sport.cricket* (Apr. 3) "Re:
1st Test WI AUS" ► Judging from the WIndies record, the Australian
fans shouldn't be celebrating yet. Otherwise, they will be setting
themselves up for one long, big and painful KLPD. **1999** Vandana
Aggarwal *JaaL* (India) (Mar. 1) "Are Indian Women Frigid?" (Int.)
► "This guy Raju rescues this woman from a sadistic husband,

restores her confidence in her art, makes her a star...and what does he get in return? Ruin and death. That's the classic Indian woman, frigid and prude. It was the ultimate example of KLPD." "What's KLPD?" "Khari L.... Par Dhoka!" "What's L.... ?"...(I couldn't see the connection. That's why I'm convinced that the brains of the Indian males lie mostly in their L...s.) **2000** Usenet: rec.arts.movies.local.indian (Aug. 6) "Review of Refugee from Gandmasti.Com + a Request..." ▶ He falls in luv with Karona and goes Crowna...Crowna...Crowna till he realises it is a major one way traffic for him. Crowna has given him KLD (Khade L*nd pe Dhoka). **2000** Usenet: soc.culture.indian (Nov. 18) "Re: Gore Gored: Judge Terry Lewis Supports Harris" ▶ "What is KLPD?" "Kade lund pe dhokha. It was slang in IITK— dunno if it was more universal." **2000** Amit Goel Amit Goel (India) (Dec.) "The Big Island, Hawaii" (Int.) ▶ Kahuna Falls were a major KLPD! ***2002** B.R. Gurunandan Cybersteering.com (India) (Apr. 16) "Zen & the Info for Bullet Maintenance: Part 2" (Int.) ▶ I hate a KLPD as much as you do, but heck, nothing worthwhile comes in an instant.... So let us go the systematic route, by listing some more helpful ideas & things before we get oil on our hands.... Whoever says India does not protect Intellectual Property, curb piracy, etc must try to get the workshop manual or a spare copy of the owner's manual!...When you finally manage to get it, THEN you know what a KLPD REALLY is!...They haven't been seriously updated in donkey's years. They are often misleading. **2002** Usenet: soc.culture.indian.delh (July 2) "Re: Query–klpd Means What?" ▶ One may say "klpd ho gaya" when one is frustrated in reaching a much anticipated and sought after goal. For instance, you wanted desperately to go see a certain show and you had even found tickets to the best seats in the house—only due to some problem, the show is cancelled at the last moment. It could be "a major klpd" as you may explain to your friend later. **2002** Vikas Kamat Kamat's Potpourri (Nov. 11) "Monsoon Wedding, Good" (Int.) ▶ When Aditi's brother whispers "KLPD." This was quite a popular slang during my time. The movie translated KLPD as "betrayal of the erect penis," but the slang has a far more hilarious connotation. BTW, in my time, there was even more hilarious slang KLPR (khade lund pe Rakhi). ***2005** [Vikram] DesiFantasy.com (India) (Mar. 4) "A Long Long Time Ago" (Int.) ▶ We reached the climax, and I see that it's time and held by the hips while she was bent and pressed fully into her arse and grabbed her tits. She reacted and said stop. I will complain etc—I stopped, and she left with a remark "bathroom mein maza kar lena." I said that what a klpd, and said maybe I went too far.

knot *n.* a roll of paper currency, esp. many small-denomination bills wrapped in a higher-value note. Also **Michigan roll, Missouri roll.** *Hip-Hop. Slang. United States.*

1998 DMX, The L.O.X., Mace *Woo* (May 5) "Niggas Dun Started Sumthin'" Soundtrack (Int.) ▶ Yo Mase and The Lox we taking knots from the outta state spots/Any nigga make it hot get found in vacant lot. **1999** Eminem, Dr. Dre *Slim Shady* (Feb. 23) "If I Had" ▶ I'm tired of faking knots with a stack of ones/Having a lack of funds and resorting back to guns.

L

land of fruits and nuts *n.* California. *California. Derogatory.* A reference to both the agricultural bounty of California and the stereotypical image of Californians as being other than normal, *fruit* n., 'a crazy person' and *nuts adj.,* 'crazy.' Usually jocular but sometimes derogatory.

1970 Terry Galanoy *Chicago Tribune* (Aug. 30) "Ted Liss—Talent Polisher," p. 42 ▶ You can make book on some of the people who were there. That is, if you get a chance to see them perform before some midnight rider from the William Morris Agency makes off with them to the land of fruits and nuts. **1982** Al Strachan *Globe and Mail* (Toronto, Can.) (Sept. 7) "NFC West Holds Surprises Falcons Should Soar; 49ers Must Dig Deep," p. P61 ▶ Last year, San Francisco 49ers came out of the land of fruits and nuts to surprise almost everyone and become NFL champions. **1990** Ronald Reagan *An American Life* (Nov. 15), p. 201 (Oct. 1, 1999) ▶ In the presidential race, I knew we'd have to confront a different stereotype: the bias many Northeasterns held against Californians—the one that says since California is a land of fruit and nuts, it's a great place if you're an orange. **2003** Mary Starrett *NewsWithViews.com* (May 14) "You Can't Make This Stuff Up" (Int.) ▶ From the land of fruit and nuts comes word of the Oreo lawsuit. A San Francisco lawyer has sued Kraft foods because the popular cookies contain "trans fats."

learning cottage *n.* a residential trailer (British 'caravan'; American 'mobile home') used as a temporary or portable classroom. *Education. United States.*

1996 Mark Schultz *Chapel Hill Herald* (Durham, N.C.) (July 10) "Trailers Still Needed Despite New School," p. 1 ▶ "The big joke around here is we call them 'learning cottages,'" said Joines, who taught in the same trailer last year, her first in the system. **1999** Victoria Benning *Washington Post* (May 6) "Learning on the Run: Trailer Classrooms Are a Way of Life at Centre Ridge Elementary, Which Makes Getting to Class—and to the Bathroom—a Negotiation," p. B1 ▶ Eight of the trailers—or "learning cottages," as Fairfax parents and staff jokingly call them—house fourth-grade classes, four are third-grade classrooms, and the remaining ones are used for music and classes for gifted and disabled students. **2000** Mary MacDonald *Atlanta Journal-Constitution* (Ga.) (Nov. 4) "Marietta Schools Fight Battle of Bulge; 'Retreat' Today to Discuss Influx," p. G6 ▶ Photo Fifth-graders in Erica Allen's class at Lockheed Elementary School place their book bags into plastic bins outside their "trailer," which has been dubbed a "learning cottage." **2004** Meredith Byrne *B9_Learning* (Atlanta, Ga.) (Dec. 9) "A Little TinTin-Nabulation: Trailer Trainin' (Web Hook-Up)!" (Int.) ▶ Somehow, trailer (be it on a farm, or in a public school parking lot) just seems to lack esteemable associations. So now they've coined the term "learning cottage" to soften up the blow...at the same time I can't help but to think "learning cell."

leitkultur *n.* mainstream or guiding culture. *German. Germany.* [German *leit* 'leading (adj.)*; leader' + *kultur* 'culture.'] **1995** Stephan Speicher *Frankfurter Allgemeine Zeitung* (Mar. 8) "Europa ist nicht Biarritz," p. 39 ▶ Immer noch befassten sich Buerger und Medien lieber mit der (nationalen) Innenpolitik, als mit aussen- oder europapolitischen Fragen. So komme es darauf an, ein Bewusst-sein der gemeinsamen europaeischen Kultur zu entwickeln. Dass eine Leitkultur, wie es die franzoesische ueber Jahrhunderte war, nicht mehr anerkannt wird, soll dabei nicht stoeren; vielmehr zur Anerken-nung des Reichtums fuehren. **2000** Erik Kirschbaum @ Berlin, Germany (*Reuters*) (Oct. 25) "German Conservatives Push for Immigration Controls" ▶ Merz, CDU parliamentary floor leader, has been criticised for saying foreigners had no choice but to accept German as the "dominant culture," using the term German "Leitkultur" that raised memories of terms used by the Nazis. **2001** Imre Karacs @ Berlin, Germany *Independent* (U.K.) (Apr. 12) "'Stress Society' Makes More Time for Fun," p. 15 ▶ There has been much talk in recent months of the emerging Spasskultur—roughly translatable as "fun ethos," and not to be confused with Leitkultur. The latter is an undefined mish-mash of traditional German values with which, according to some conservative politicians, immigrants should be force-fed. **2004** *Frank-furter Allgemeine Zeitung* (Germany) (Nov. 22) (Int.) in BBC News "European Press Review" ▶ "This debate," it adds, "must not omit the issue of a (German) 'Leitkultur' (guiding culture), nor the commit-ments which a self-confident society...not ashamed of its Christian foundations may require of those who live in its midst."

lesbian bed death *n.* the decline of sexual relations between a committed lesbian couple. *Sexuality.* **1992** *Usenet: rec.music.video* (Oct. 6) "Re: The Girls of Music Video" ▶ Railing against lesbian bed death, she vows to marry a real man,

like a college sophomore in Computer Science. **1995** John Haslett
Cuff *Globe and Mail* (Toronto, Can.) (Nov. 29) "Hutton Has Brains 'n'
Beauty," p. C1 ▶ The talk I heard was exclusively about relationships
and careers, subjects ranging from lesbian "bed death" (translation:
domestic sexual ennui) and "toxic men," mostly those who have never
been married or ever had a long, serious relationship with a woman.
2000 D. Merilee Clunis, G. Dorsey Green *Lesbian Couples* (Aug. 1)
3 ed., p. 104 ▶ Greta is more interested in sex than her partner, Jen.
If the frequency or intensity of their sex life slips a bit, Greta is convinced it is the beginning of "lesbian bed death."

levanton *n.* a lift or boost; a kidnapping; a ride (in a vehicle);
euphoria or an emotional lift. *Mexico. Spanish. United States.* [From
the Spanish *levantar* 'to lift, raise, pick up.' In Spanish the word is
accented: *levantón*.]

1990 Patrick McDonnell *L.A. Times* (Sept. 2) "The Lethal Path to the
North Popular Alien Route Crosses, Crisscrosses Perilous Freeways,"
p. 1 ▶ The smugglers, mostly men in their 20s, station themselves at
strategic spots—along the roadway shoulders, medians and in adjoining brush-offering levantones ("lifts," or "rides")..."Levanton! Levanton!" the smugglers advertise as each new group arrives alongside the
edge of I-5. **1996** Ana Luisa Ochoa @ Mexico, D.F. *Mundo Ejecutivo*
(July 1) "Industria hotelera Definiendo estrategias" ▶ Para que Mexico
de el verdadero levanton en la industria turistica y, por consiguiente,
en la hoteleria, se debe concientizar a los servidores y funcionarios
publicos de la importancia del turismo. **1996** Jorge Ernesto Witker @
Mexico, D.F. *Crónica* (Nov. 16) "Entrenador nuevo, filosofia vieja"
▶ Con la llegada de Carlos Miloc, la inyeccion de momentaneo animo
produjo el acostumbrado levanton del debut. **2002** (*AP*) (Dec. 10)
"DEP FUT Mexico Semifinales" (in Torreon, Mexico) ▶ Por su parte el
entrenador del Santos, Luis Fernando Tena, senalo que su equipo tuvo
"un levanton" en buena momento, por lo que espera que sus
jugadores sigan poniendo su "maxima entrega." **2004** Mark Getty @
Ciudad Juárez *Frontera NorteSur* (N.Mex.) (Jan.-Feb.) "Mexico's Forgotten Disappeared: The Victims of the Border Narco Bloodbath" (Int.)
▶ During the last 10 years, hundreds of people from Tijuana to Mata-
moros have been forcibly carted off by heavily armed men sometimes
sporting police insignias and uniforms. They are the victims of a style
of violence known in border lingo as the "levantón," which could be
literally translated as the "lift" or "pickup." Occasionally the "levanta-
dos" turn up murdered bearing signs of torture but frequently they
are transformed into memories of agony for distraught relatives.
2004 Minerva Canto @ Ciudad Juarez, Mexico *Orange County Register*
(Calif.) (June 15) "Sure Her Husband Is Innocent, Miriam Garcia Won't
Turn Her Back on Him," p. 1 ▶ Miriam fears her husband is the victim

of a levanton, one of the kidnappings that plague this border city as the drug trade spreads its ugly claws. **2004** Aline Corpus, Tim Gaynor @ Tijuana and Nuevo Laredo, Mexico (*Reuters*) (Sept. 15) "'Disappearance' New Weapon in Mexico Drug Wars" (Int.) ▶ The incident is one of a rising number of forcible abductions in crime-ridden towns and cities flanking the 2,000-mile (3,200-km) U.S. border. They have become so common that local residents have coined a name for the phenomenon: the "levanton" or "big pickup." ***2004** State of Calif. (*California Highway Patrol*) (Sept. 16) "Child Booster Seats" (Int.) ▶ Give 'Em a Boost!...Déles Un Levantón! ***2004** [Tony] *Chalino Sanchez Site* (Sept. 17) "The Truth Is Out There...This May Be It." (Int.) ▶ Chalino having grown up in Sinaloa, being in the mob himself, could have spotted a "levanton" miles away. Chalino had to have known that if you get pulled over at 3 am by federales your chances of living are zero.

LGBTQ *adj.* having a sexual orientation other than heterosexual. *Acronym. Gay. Sexuality. United States.* [*L*esbian, *g*ay, *b*isexual, *t*ransgender/*t*ranssexual/*t*wo-spirited, *q*ueer/*q*uestioning.]

1991 Val Codd, Rebecca Myers-Spiers *Off Our Backs* (Aug. 1) "Young Queers Unite," vol. 29, no. 8, p. 4 ▶ Many participants voiced concern that although the Castro, the city's premier gay neighborhood, is a safe space for all lgbtq people, it is primarily a gay male middle-class enclave, and is not always a safe space for queer homeless youth. **1998** Daphne Scholinski *The Last Time I Wore a Dress* (Oct. 1), p. 209 ▶ National coalition of organizations and agencies serving LGBTQ youth. **2004** Sheila Mullowney *Newport Daily News* (R.I.) (May 17) "'Queer' Label Still Raises Questions" (Int.) ▶ It can be used to describe both gender identity and sexual orientation and increasingly is being used in a new, wide-ranging alphabet soup—LGBTQQ, for lesbian, gay, bisexual, transgender, queer and questioning in Youth Pride's case, or in the case of the Rhode Island Foundation's "Meet the Neighbors" report released last year, LGBTQ, for lesbian, gay, bisexual, transgender, transsexual, two-spirited (a Native American reference), queer and questioning.

libero *n.* in volleyball, a restricted, roaming back row player. *Italian. Sports.* [From Italian adj. *libero* 'free,' a shortened form of *battitore libero* 'free beater,' a similar position in soccer that originated with a Milanese team in the late 1960s.]

1996 *Usenet: rec.sport.volleyball* (Feb. 27) "Atuacao do Libero" ▶ Gostaria de saber como sera a atuacao do libero numa equipe de volley diante da possibilidade dessa alteracao na regra. **1996** *Usenet: rec.sport.volleyball* (Mar. 20) "Bonus Point Scoring Info Web Site"

▶ The better defence is perhaps true in lower level of playing, where the attack is not so strong. My prognosis is also that the new "libero" concept, approved recently in FIVB to be tested after Atlanta, will give similar results. **1996** *AFP* (July 18) "Volleyball Is to Bring in Softer Balls" ▶ The International Volleyball Federation (FIVB) has decided to reduce the pressure of balls for the men's game by a quarter to give defences a better chance. The libero system—where a designated player can be sent in and out of court by coaches for backcourt play—will be tested at the Grand Prix series this year. **1998** *AFP* (Apr. 20) "Championships" (in Tokyo) ▶ According to the new rules, each team can register one specialised defensive player "libero," who is restricted to performing as a back row player, not hitting an attack, serving, blocking or attempting to block. **2004** Dave Campbell *News-Sentinel* (Fort Wayne, Ind.) (Dec. 15) "Gophers, Gentil Geared Up for Another Final Four" (Int.) ▶ One of the additions was the libero. It's an Italian word meaning "free"...can come in at any time in the back row without counting against the team's substitution limit.

lily pad *n.* an outpost, advance camp, foreign base, or staging area. *Military. United States.*

1998 Robert Goodrich *St. Louis Post-Dispatch* (Mo.) (Nov. 13) "Buildup Order Kicks Air Base Into High Gear," p. A7 ▶ McPhillips described the operation as "building an air bridge" to the Mideast, with stops at "lily pads along the way" in addition to aerial refueling. **2001** (*M2 Presswire*) (Nov. 27) "DoD News Briefing" ▶ Mr. Secretary, can you tell us, do you envision the force of Marines as the vanguard in the battle against terrorism in Afghanistan? Do you see them being used to seek out and destroy al Qaeda networks, or are they setting up a lily pad of sorts, for other units that will follow on? **2001** Hilary Mackenzie @ Washington, D.C. *Ottawa Citizen* (Can.) (Dec. 1) "Rebels Close in on Last Taliban Stronghold" ▶ Terrorist Osama bin Laden had a different agenda, he said. "He uses Afghanistan as a lily pad, a place to be, a place to go out and kill other people around the world." **2002** Dennis Blair (*Federal Document Clearing House*) (Mar. 7) "House Committee on Appropriations: Subcommittee on Military Construction Holds a Hearing on FY 2003 Pacific Command Appropriations" ▶ We went too deep in Guam with our closures. It's the last piece of land in the west that we own. It's United States owned. It's going to be a lily pad for moving out. **2002** William Safire @ Washington, D.C. *Times Union* (Albany, N.Y.) (Sept. 19) "Germany No Longer Necessary," p. A15 ▶ We are already "reconfiguring our footprint"—that is, reviewing deployment of our troops globally to make us capable of applying mobile force anywhere rather than to sit in place to meet any specific threat. That's part of the "lily pad concept," on the analogy of frogs hopping around a number of forward bases.... Saudi threats to restrict our use of bases there caused us to build a Qatar lily pad. Would Germany also prove unreliable as a jumping-off point in a crisis? **2004** *MSNBC* (Sept. 22) "U.S. Expands Military Outposts Worldwide" (in Washington, D.C.) (Int.) ▶ Among the places the military already has placed or hopes to base such new "lily pads" or jumping off points: the eastern European nations of Bulgaria and Romania; a pier in Singapore; and a tiny island off the oil-rich coast of West Africa.

lilywhite *n.* a person without a police record; someone who does not trigger suspicions; a CLEAN-SKIN. This is a more specific sense of the adjectival form of *lily-white* 'lacking faults or imperfections; beyond reproach.'

1992 Richard Ford, Stewart Tendler *Times* (London, Eng.) (Apr. 23) "RUC Is Strongest Thread in Web Spun to Destroy the IRA" ▶ Ever-tighter IRA internal security and the organisation's use of "lily whites," activists with little or no known history of involvement in violence who keep their distance from the Irish community in Britain, have been given as reasons for the recent successes of the IRA's mainland campaign. **1993** Stewart Tendler *Times* (London, Eng.) (Feb. 11) "Hidden Camera Recorded Invisible Quartermaster" ▶ He epitomised the new breed of undercover operator, dubbed "lilywhites" because they have no criminal record linking them to terrorism, and who rouse little suspicion. **2000** John Sweeney *Observer* (U.K.) (July 9) "Menace of 'Clean-Skin' Drug Dealers," p. 16 ▶ They use public transport, not Ferraris, pay their rent and council tax on time, hold down a boring job and never get in trouble with the law. These are the "clean skins" or "lilywhites"—the new drugs traffickers who dwarf the activities of the old English crime "families." **2004** Robert S. Leiken @ Committee on House International Relations Subcommittee on International Terrorism, Nonproliferation and Human Rights (*Congressional Testimony by Federal Document Clearing House*) (June 16) "Visa Waiver Program and Terrorist Screening" ▶ We should make no mistake: the recruitment of women, converts, lily-whites and other Western faces is aimed at the United States. **2005** Daniel McGrory *Australian* (July 14) "The Call That Cracked the Case" (Int.) ▶ What became quickly obvious was that neither MI5 nor MI6 knew anything about these four. They were, in the vernacular of counter-terror officers, "lilywhites."

limb hanger *n.* a male turkey with long heel spurs. *Animals. Sports. United States.* [See the last 2004 cite.] Long spurs on a jake are correlated with the maturity and size of the bird.

[**1995** *Usenet: rec.hunting* (Mar. 29) "Re: Which Turkey Calls Are Best?" ▶ The Primos Limb Hanger is nice too, but difficult to call softly on.] **2002** Richard P. Combs *Advanced Turkey Hunting* (Feb. 1), p. 49 ▶ The real limb-hangers are four or five years old or more, and chances are most of them get whipped regularly by two- and three-year-old birds. **2002** *Montreal Gazette* (Can.) (Nov. 25) "Bash Planned to Mark Wild Turkey Resurgence" (in Ottawa), p. A10 ▶ "What we're trying to do is enhance the population by sort of speeding it up, by bringing birds in and releasing them in the area," said Dave Arbour, a member of Limb Hangers, a NWTF chapter named after the way the birds perch on tree limbs at night. ***2004** Gary Caughman *Tomturkey's Web Page* (Union County, S.C.) (Int.) ▶ I didn't even have to move the gun, just knocked it off safe and dropped him in his tracks. He scored 18 lbs, 10" beard, and 1 1/2" spurs. A real limb hanger!!! **2004** Bob Gwizdz *Kalamazoo Gazette* (Mich.) (May 29) "Lt. Gov. Cherry Lends Hand on Turkey Hunt" (Int.) ▶ The Lenawee Limb Hangers (turkey-hunting parlance for a bird with large enough spurs you could push them into a branch to hang the bird) won the drawing and selected Ellis.

lindy bomb *v. phr.* to swing dance as a group in a place where it is not normally done. *Entertainment.*

2002 Clark Breyman *SFSWING (Mailing List)* (San Francisco) (July 5) "Any Lindy Bombing the Fillmore Jazz Fest?" (Int.) ▶ I'm not familiar with any of these acts? Are any of these bombable? **2004** [E:go] *Buzz-life Message Board* (Mar. 20) "Demographics Follow-Up Poll, Take 2" (Int.) ▶ There's nothing better than lindy-bombing the techno scene! (God I love that swing dancing works with EDM!) **2004** Florida Swing Dancing Club *SWINGUF-L (Mailing List)* (Fla.) (July 1) "Lindy Bomb at Turlington" (Int.) ▶ To get some exposure and let everyone know about Friday's dance, we will be lindy bombing turlington plaza on thursday from noon till whenever everyone's too tired to dance. **2004** [Nightowl] *23 Skidoo* (Denver, Colo.) (Nov. 19) "Dan and Tiffiny Class FAQ" (Int.) ▶ What is a Lindy Bomb? When dancers converge on one non-swing location with some sort of portable music source to dance, exposing the public to the dance. Another version is to go to hip hop/seventies club etc and dance swing. This was all the rage for a while until it was discovered that the actual effect was opposite of the

intended effect (to get people to want to dance). **2005**
[JesusWithShoes] *Swing Society* (Champaign, Ill.) (Mar. 28) "Lindy
Bombs!" (Int.) ► Who wants to lindy bomb the mall? Who has a
boombox for lindybombing use?

listicle *n.* a (newspaper, magazine, web site, etc.) article consisting primarily of a list. *Media. United States.* [*list* + ar*ticle*] This term is often used in a deprecating way, to describe an article or news story that required very little effort to produce.

*2001 John Davin *John Davin's Web site* (Pittsburgh, Pa.) (July 14)
"My Comments and News" (Int.) ► Added an article to the listicle to
the lists section. **2003** Elizabeth Spiers *Gawker* (NYC) (July 31) "The
Daily Listicle: Corn, Castro & Che" (Int.) ► I've decided to default to
one of the magazine world's last great lame clichés—lists. Lists as articles. Listicles. (I feel dirty even saying it.) Consider this my homage to
sappy service journalism. **2003** [Joey] *Tale of Two Cities* (NYC)
(Nov. 13) "Our Mutual Friends" (Int.) ► It's called "Out Mutual
Friends," and it's an alphabetical rundown of things we like, hate,
think are cool, think suck, are funny, are not funny, etc. Yes, a "listicle" if you will, of things that are currently impacting the zeitgeist.
2004 Anil Dash *Anil Dash* (Oct. 6) "Best of Best of" (Int.) ► People
who haven't worked in the publishing industry (or haven't worked at
the Voice) don't necessarily know that "best of" issues are generally a
chance for the editorial staff to phone it in. Inside jokes, lazy writing,
and the triumph of the listicle; it's everything I love in a paper that's
mainly funded by ads from whores. I say that because I love my Voice
friends!

Lochnerism *n.* generally, a form of judicial activism in which court decisions are made based upon presumed rights not specifically addressed by existing (constitutional) law, especially when influenced by political or personal beliefs. *Eponym. Law. Politics.* [From *Lochner v. New York*, 198 U.S. 45 (1905), a U.S. Supreme Court case that declared unconstitutional a law that limited bakers to a maximum 10-hour workday and 60-hour workweek.]

1978 John Hart Ely *Harvard Law Review* (Nov.) "The Supreme Court,
1977 Term," vol. 92, no. 1, p. 97 ► Even if the Court extends this
mode of scrutiny to review social and enactments generally, it does
not seem necessary to wave the bloody shirt of Lochnerism. **1990**
Henry J. Abraham *The Constitutional Bases of Political and Social
Change in the United States* (Apr. 23) "Of Courts, Judicial Tools, and
Equal Protections," p. 324 ► The Court's meddlesome approach
towards state economic-proprietarian legislation, often under the

guise of substantive due process, ended—only to be replaced by the still more meddlesome spirit of the double standard, largely fueled under the guise of the new equal protection. A new "Lochnerism" had come of age. **1996** Roberto Mangabeira Unger *Modern Law Review* (Jan. 1) "Legal Analysis as Institutional Imagination," vol. 59, no. 1, p. 14 ▶ American legal theory regularly congratulates itself on its rejection of "Lochnerism," the fetishistic acceptance and constitutional entrenchment of a particular private rights-system against all efforts to redistribute rights and resources and to regulate economic activity. **2003** Douglas T. Kendall, Timothy J. Dowling *Washington Post* (Sept. 19) "Judicial Throwback," p. A25 ▶ She has written that she "initially accepted the conventional wisdom" that the doctrine used in Lochner was "a myth invented by judicial activists that were up to no good," and that "Lochnerism is the strongest pejorative known to American law." Brown now rejects that conventional wisdom, however, and she chides conservatives for their "dread" of judicial activism. In her words, it "dawned on me that the problem may not be judicial activism. The problem may be the world view—amounting to altered political and social consciousness—out of which judges now fashion their judicial decisions." **2005** Stuart Taylor, Jr. *National Journal* (May 2) "Does the President Agree with This Nominee?" (Int.) ▶ What lawyers call "Lochnerism" was the basis for dozens of decisions striking down minimum-wage, maximum-hours, and other worker-protection laws as infringing "freedom of contract"—a right that, as Bork has put it, can be found "nowhere in the Constitution." Almost all modern constitutional scholars have rejected Lochnerism as "the quintessence of judicial usurpation of power," in Bork's words.

lolicom *n. Loli*ta *com*plex, the attraction of older men to girls or very young women. < *English. Entertainment. Japan. Japanese. Sexuality.*

1993 *Usenet: rec.arts.manga* (Dec. 19) "Re: The Shoujo Myth" ▶ It seems that the path of yaoi growth is exactly the same as that of lolicom thing: from doujinshi to anthologies and magazines. **1997** Stuart Young (*Reuters*) (Feb. 13) "Japanese Seek to Shed Child Porn Tag" ▶ The reports have said that one of the most disturbing features of the teenage prostitution phenomenon is the premium younger girls fetch from "lolicom" clients—older men with "Lolita complexes" for little girls. **2005** Ines Cho *JoongAng Daily* (Seoul, S. Korea) (Jan. 18) "The Words of a New Generation" (Int.) ▶ *Lolicom* "Lolita" + "complex." When a man is infatuated with pretty young girls. Example: He's married to an older woman, but he has a Lolicom online.

looping *n.* in the American education system, the practice of a teacher staying with the same students through more than one school year, as opposed to the usual method of a different teacher each year. *Education.*

1994 Meredith Carlson *Hartford Courant* (Conn.) (Mar. 3) "'Looping' Could Provide Pupils with More Continuity," p. C5 ▶ School administrators are likely to implement "looping" next year. Teachers would flip-flop grades so that one teacher would move up with youngsters while the other teacher moved down a grade. **1994** Ruth Yodaiken *Washington Post* (Sept. 15) "Non-Graded School Brings Innovation, Optimism," p. J3 ▶ Another feature of the Nongraded School is "looping." Students will spend up to two years in the same class before they "loop" to another level. **1997** Jim Grant *Looping Q & A* (Sept. 1), p. 12 ▶ Looping is a practice which allows single-grade teachers to remain with the same class for a period of two or more years. **1999** Martha Kaufeldt *Begin with the Brain* (Apr. 1), p. 17 ▶ In a multiage (two or three grade levels mixed together) or looping classroom (single graded, but teacher moves with entire class up to next grade), students may stay with the same teacher for two or three years. **2005** Alan Finder @ Ardsley, N.Y. *N.Y. Times* (July 11) "Goodbye, Class. See You in the Fall" (Int.) ▶ Having a teacher stay with a class for more than a year—or looping, as it is known—is on the rise.

lose the dressing room *v.* of a sports team manager or coach, to not have the respect of the players. *Sports. United Kingdom.*

1993 Glenn Gibbons *Observer* (U.K.) (Oct. 10) "Can Macari Be Kellys' Hero?" ▶ The Irishman's placidness was also perceived as a handicap in a job which requires infectious animation and this was confirmed by a player who said Brady had "lost the dressing room and when that goes, everything goes." **1996** Charlie Nicolas *Sunday Mirror* (U.K.) (Aug. 18) "Arsene About!" ▶ When a manager loses the dressing room, he loses everything. **2004** Stuart Cosgrove *Daily Record* (Glasgow, Scotland) (Aug. 19) "Scots Bosses Must Look Out for Each Other" (Int.) ▶ The biggest favourite for the tintack is Southampton boss Paul Sturrock, who in football parlance has "lost" the dressing room.

love-cum-arranged marriage *n.* matrimony between a mutually acceptable and consenting couple that has been facilitated by the couple's parents. *India.* [*Cum* is Latin for "with" or "together with."]

1994 *Usenet: soc.culture.tamil* (Jan. 29) "Re: Matrimony—FAQ&A—Tip 1:2" ▶ Provided your mAmA's (or any suitable relative's) ward is an acceptable spouse for you. Slowly make your parents sort-of-choose him/her for you. This is a type of "Love-cum-Arranged marriage"—as you should fall in love with your would-be-partner. Warning: Considered the fashion, but still works out greater than many of those "Love Marriages" and pure "Arranged Marriages." **1997** Anupama Chopra *India Today* (July 28) "Govinda: The Lovable Hero," p. 76 ▶ "I came home one day from shooting and my mother said it's high time I got married. Sunita and I were married the next morning at 4.30 a.m." Govinda describes it as a "love cum arranged marriage." **1999** Susan C. Seymour *Women, Family, and Child Care in India* (Jan. 28), p. 213 ▶ "Instead of seeking extensively for a bride,...consulting lots of people and taking much time, I suggested to him a girl he had known for some years. I would not have proceeded had my son not agreed. I would never force him into such a decision." Another member of the family referred to this as a "love-cum-arranged marriage." **2005** Shambhu Sahu *Times of India* (Aug. 11) "What's the Right Choice Baby?" (Int.) ▶ So we have the bold, the beautiful and the handsome asserting that a love-cum-arranged marriage is more stable than an arranged one.

L's *n.* In the United States, a driver's license. *Acronym. Automotive. Slang. United States.* In Australia, *L's* is widespread and refers to the learner's "L-plates" and learner's driving license, precursors to the driver's permit—one's *P's*—which grants full driving privileges. In the United States, the learner's permit is not issued with special plates. These citations encompass only the American *L's*, which refers to the full driver's license and likely originated independently and more recently.

2002 *Usenet: rec.music.hip-hop* (Apr. 7) "Let Me Help Build Mr. Rick Up" ▶ On tops of all that my L's been suspended & my car got impounded like 3 times since Sept. **2004** [Daddy Rich] @ San Francisco Bay area, Calif. *RapTalk.Net* (Jan. 21) "(What Yall Smobbin)?" (Int.) ▶ My 5 point toes my chevrolegs I aint got shit right now but I use to have 2 72 chevelles but I got my L'S revoked real quick. **2004** *Cannabis Edge* (Feb. 19) "Have Cops Ever Helped?" (Int.) ▶ He woke up from a drug induced coma cuffed to a hospital bed with a leo standing over him...gets more time than the driver, who was driving on a suspended L's for dui. **2004** [ototpnoy4o8] @ Sacramento, Calif. *Xanga.com* (Mar. 17) (Int.) ▶ I found out AK got locked up...at least that's what DT told me...he got caught ridin in his scraper i guess and he didnt have his "L's." **2004** [C.U.D.D.I.E. Tha Mouthpiece] @ Bay Area, Calif. *RapTalk.Net* (Apr. 8) "Savage C..." (Int.) ▶ It's hard to connect when we live in dff cities, me with no L's.

lumberjill *n.* a female lumberjack.

1937 Alice Hughes *Washington Post* (Sept. 11) "A Woman's New York," p. 13 ▶ The vogue for bright plaid sport coats is going to brighten up the stands to no end.... Topping the ensemble...will be a gay beret to match; the whole effect being that of a fancy lumber-jill in technicolor! **1940** *Clearfield Progress* (Pa.) (Aug. 24) "'Lumberjill' Does Her Bit," p. 3 ▶ Handling tree trunks like this is as easy as falling off a log for this sturdy British "lumberjill."...She's doing her bit for Britain's defense by taking over a lumberjack's job. **1984** Ira Berkow *N.Y. Times* (Nov. 23) "The Gobblers' Last Stand," p. D15 ▶ At Northland College in Wisconsin, the teams are known as the Lumberjacks and the Lumberjills. **2005** Molly Gilmore-Baldwin *Olympian* (Olympia, Wash.) (June 2) "Forest Festival Shows Off Skills" (Int.) ▶ The lumberjacks—and, as they are called, lumberjills—will compete in events including cross-cut sawing.

lung-opener *n.* a sporting event that begins a series of contests or a season. *India. Ireland. Sports. United Kingdom.*

1993 Christopher Dodd *Guardian* (U.K.) (Mar. 25) "Rowing: Lightly Forceful" ▶ Oxford reached a rating of 45 in a 25-stroke lung-opener to the scratch's 42 and continued to pull out leads in their subsequent work. **1999** Brandon D'Souza *Times of India* (Sept. 15) "Exciting Golfing Season in the Offing" ▶ In the season's lung opener Cosmo-Hindu Open, Vijay Kumar winner of the Order of Merit for last two years, was a picture of excellence. **2004** Khalid A-H Ansari *Mid-Day* (Mumbai, India) (July 17) "Thank the Lucky Stars" (Int.) ▶ To that extent, the lung opener, to borrow an expression from horse racing lexicon, was useful in fine-tuning the team for the stern tests ahead, starting with the clash against Sri Lanka at Dambulla tomorrow.

M

maconha *n.* marijuana or hemp. *Brazil. Drugs. Portugal. Portuguese.*
1951 Roberval Cordeiro de Farias (*United Nations Office on Drugs and Crime*) (Jan. 1) "Use of Maconha (Cannabis sativa L.) in Brazil" (Int.) ▶ Maconha is true hemp—*Cannabis sativa* L.—which has become acclimatized in Brazil under a wealth of popular names, being variously known in different areas as *diamba, pango, liamba, dirijo, birra, elva, fininha* and *fumo de Angola.* **1995** *Rosângela Petta* (Aug.) "Quando a Maconha Cura" (Int.) ▶ Está provado. Os efeitos medicinais da maconha beneficiam pacientes de câncer, Aids, glaucoma e esclerose múltipla. Mas os médicos do mundo inteiro se vêem num dilema crucial. **2004** *Love in Rio* (Brazil) (Apr. 25) "Brazil, Legalize Drugs, Now!" (Int.) ▶ Amidst the fray, no one dared whisper an obvious option: complete legalization of pot (maconha, in local parlance) and cocaine.

Madibaland *n.* South Africa. *Politics. South Africa.* [*Madiba* is the name of the Xhosa clan to which Nelson Mandela belongs, and it is applied to him by transference as a familiar title.]
1998 Denis Beckett *Madibaland* (S. Africa) (title). [**1999** Stephen Smith *Libération* (Paris, France) (June 17) "Nelson Mandela, le crépuscule du père de la nation arc-en-ciel" ▶ A Qunu, son village natal au fin fond du Transkei, Mandela a par ailleurs fait construire un véritable Madibaland. Au coeur du complexe, qui intègre une ferme, se trouve la réplique de sa dernière prison, la cage dorée (une villa de trois pièces avec accès, de plain-pied, à une piscine) mise à sa disposition en 1986 dans le périmètre du centre pénitentiaire de Paarl, près du Cap.] [**2004** Roger Gbégnonvi *La Nouvelle Tribune* (Benin) (Feb. 26) (Int.) in *Le Bulletin des OSCB* (Nov. 25, 2004) Gbaguidi Akpovi Olivier *"La Revision De La Constitution A L'ordre Du Jour!"* ▶ Les révisionnistes auront ensuite à cœur d'adopter très rapidement la nouvelle division du pays que viennent de concocter sept sages pour qu'on en finisse avec les promiscuités indignes, honteuses et dangereuses: Madibaland, plus réduit, ira des Collines à l'océan Atlantique.] **2004** [danhyk] *Kick Off* (Cape Town, S. Africa) (May 25) "FNB to Be Renamed After Madiba?" ▶ As much as I admire Madiba, I think to call every building after him is taking it too much.... But I must admit I like the Madibaland suggestion for our country.

2004 Matome Sebelebele *BuaNews* (Pretoria, S. Africa) (Nov. 23) "Why Sell SA Short? Tutu Asks" (Int.) ▶ Archbishop Tutu affirmed that the country, which he coined "Madibaland," had come a long way and was now reaping socio-economic and political fruits, producing more heroes and heroines every day.

magalog *n.* a catalog-like magazine with an exceptional amount of advertising or product-focused articles. *Entertainment. Media.* [*maga*zine + cata*log*]

1970 Jo Moreland *Walla Wall Union-Bulletin* (Wash.) (Apr. 3) "Feminists Taking to the Warpath," p. 4 ▶ The 75-page "magalog" features models in very little lingerie designed "for girls who don't like to wear underthings" and a mod boudoir scene with a young couple preparing for bed—sans wedding bands. **1983** Beverly Bowen *Globe and Mail* (Toronto, Can.) (Apr. 14) "Fashion," p. P17 ▶ The people at Simpsons have dubbed their new concept—a cross between a catalogue and a magazine—a "magalog." **2004** Lisa Keys *Jewsweek* (May 2) "Crazy like a Foxman" (Int.) ▶ As editor in chief of Condé Nast's latest venture, Cargo, a shopping magazine—or, as some cynics prefer, "magalog"—for men, the younger Foxman told the Forward he's out to empower men.

mahoff *n.* a person of importance; a *big shot*. *Slang.* This term is associated with Philadelphia.

1951 William Moore @ Washington, D.C. *Chicago Daily Tribune* (Feb. 20) "'Big Shot' Tells of Gifts to Cop in Philadelphia," p. 15 ▶ The man known as "the big mahoff" of Philadelphia gambling told the Kefauver senate crime committee today that he...denied cash payoffs to Richardson for protection.... Rosen and Weisberg, both Russian born, came to the hearing together.... Weisberg explained that "the big mahoff" means "the big shot," but denied he had ever heard Rosen called that. **1990** Carmen Brutto *Harrisburg Patriot* (Pa.) (Dec. 17) "'It's Not Who's Pro Tem, It's Who Has Votes,' Pardee Hack Says," p. A11 ▶ The pro tem is the big mahoff in the Senate, the guy with the title and the money and the power. **1991** *Toronto Star* (Can.) (Aug. 29) "Come Peer into Future of Baseball," p. C2 ▶ A number of other baseball people—including big mahoffs from the Expos, Pirates, Brewers, Braves and the brand-new Florida Marlins—are on record as viewing at least some of these giant steps as not only good, but necessary to keep baseball afloat. **1996** Carrie Rickey *Gazette* (Montreal, Can.) (Jan. 21) "How the Golden Globes Went Legit," p. F3 ▶ Hollywood mahoffs and celebs, those very people who make fun of the event, have helped transform the Golden Globes ceremony...into what more than one studio honcho calls "the second-most-important awards event in the entertainment industry." **2002** Bill Kent *Street Money* (Oct. 10), p. 300 ▶ Nobody ever raided this place, as long as it was in the family. Not when my grandfather, not when my father owned it. Too many big shots ate here. Mahoffs. What they want with a raid? **2004** [Al Beer] *Padraigin Creen '04* (May 9) "Bio" (Int.) ▶ Our immediate office consists of an Assistant General Counsel for Legislative and Regulatory Affairs (the big "mahoff"—i.e., the "BOSS").

mahogany reef *n.* a place where alcoholic drinks are served, especially in a seaside community. This is a jocular expression associated with sailing and fishing. It is sometimes used as the name of an actual drinking establishment, but it is often capitalized even when it is not. A similar term in skiing is *mahogany ridge* 'the last ski run of the day,' which is also often used as the name of drinking establishments. Another nautical variant is **rum squall,** a euphemism for a session of alcohol drinking after a fanciful weather formation said to prevent a quick return to shore.

1986 Bob Wacker *Newsday* (Long Island, N.Y.) (May 25) "The Executive Went Fishing," p. 29 ▶ If you've got $550 to spend on a day's sport, he'll meet you at a Lake Montauk bar he calls The Mahogany Reef and take you to some of the finest fishing you'll ever enjoy. **1994** Dick Gillespie *Denver Post* (Colo.) (Jan. 19) "It's No Fish Story: Yacht Sales Brisk in Landlocked Yuma," p. 10C ▶ Old-time sailors with hangovers explained away their misery by saying they had been caught in a rum front and hung up on a mahogany reef (a bar). **1996** Noel Peattie *Typhooner* (Winters, Calif.) (June), p. 2 (Int.) ▶ We were glad when the club opened its doors, "Mahogany Reef" (a.k.a. the bar) was ready for business, and we all sat down to a very good dinner. **2004** Phil Downing *Royal Natal Yacht Club Home Page* (Kwa-zulu Natal, S. Africa) (Oct. 21) "Words from Our Rear Commodore" (Int.) ▶ Brian Miller who positioned himself at the Mahogany Reef in our celebrating went to inspect the Flying Fifteens and was struck down by a mysterious force. Brian tells me that he was staring at one of the Fifteens and all of a sudden his legs were taken from him. **2004** *Trazz's Home Page* (Cape Town, S. Africa) (Dec. 8) "Race Reports/Voyages 2004 Summer Season" (Int.) ▶ The South-Easter was honking up to 40+ knots and only four boats crossed the start line, which meant I was forced to abandon the race as there were no valid minimum class entries. Most skippers sensibly remained at their moorings or at the "mahogany reef." **2005** Tom Gogola *Fairfield County Weekly* (Conn.) (Apr. 7) "As the Anchor Drags" (Int.) ▶ Jake was watching with owl-like contempt from the sundeck, and his classic line, oft-repeated at the "mahogany reef" (slang for "bar") when I repeatedly failed to gaff a bass was, "Well, he managed to beat one into submission."

make (one's) bones *v.* to kill a person as requirement for membership in a criminal gang, especially if it is one's first murder; to become a *made* man; *(hence)* to earn a reputation. *Crime & Prisons.* This term is associated with organized crime, especially the Mafia or the mob.

1969 Geoffrey Wolff *N.Y. Times* (Mar. 8) "Persuasive Picture of Crime's World," p. C4 ▶ Business, for Puzo's characters, is almost everything. Vito Corleone "made his bones" (first killing) in cold blood for dollars. **1984** William Diehl *Hooligans* (June 1), p. 46 ▶ The story goes that Chevos killed his own brother to make his bones for Skeet. **1986** Timothy Harper *Dallas Morning News* (Tex.) (Feb. 24) "Murdoch Challenging British Unions," p. 1D ▶ Shah is a 41-year-old publisher of small provincial newspapers who made his bones after winning a bitter strike against the unions that tried to shut down his northern England operation. **1986** Laura Nicholson *Newsday* (Long Island, N.Y.) (Oct. 20) "The Race to Be 2nd—in Command Kavanagh—that's Michael," p. 7 ▶ After he suggested that Cuomo "made his political bones in Queens," which has been rocked with scandal, he said he should have known it would set off opponents. Cuomo aides complained it was an ethnic slur, since "made his bones" is an expression usually connected with the Mafia. **1988** Larry Margasak (*AP*) (Apr. 22) "FBI Agent Nearly Was Inducted into Mafia" ▶ They have reinstituted the requirement that before someone is made a soldier, he will have to "make his bones." That is, he will have to kill someone. **1990** Patricia Hurtado *Newsday* (May 8) "Jury Considers Fama's Fate as Judge Denies Defense Bid," p. 5 ▶ He was not only going to teach Gina [Feliciano] a lesson, Mr. Fama was going to make his bones that night.... He was going to shoot someone. **2005** Doug Ireland *Common Dreams* (Jan. 12) "Mike Chertoff's Dirty Little Secrets" (Int.) ▶ There's a problem for Chertoff with conservative Republicans—he happens to be pro-choice. So, taking the DHS job is Chertoff's way to "make his bones," as they say in Jersey, and grab headlines as a hard-line persecutor of "the towel-heads" to please the right and neutralize his abortion stance.

mama put *n.* a small food stand or restaurant. *Food & Drink. Nigeria.* The etymological information in the 2001 cite is not verified.

1998 *Usenet: soc.culture.nigeria* (Nov. 25) "Nweke Ntioba" ▶ He complained to everyone in the village...how the "mama-put" ladies failed to understand his refusal to pay for a not-too-hot soup. ***2001** [Babawilly] *Babawilly's Dictionary of Pidgin English Words and Phrases* (Nigeria) (Int.) ▶ *Mama-put*: Road side food seller so called because customers frequently beg for extra helpings by saying "*Mama* abeg *put* more now." **2002** *All Africa* (Feb. 15) "150 Years On—Memories of Slavery Re-Echoed in Breadfruit, Lagos" ▶ All around the adjoining streets...market officials, colonial clerks gather in twos and threes savouring local delicacies at mama put joints littering the streets. **2004** Sam Umukoro, Dafe Ivwurie *Vanguard* (Apapa, Nigeria) (May 23) "Ozekhome: A Generalissimo in Whom 72 Kings Are Well Pleased" (Int.) ▶ We asked the chief...if he visits these eateries popularly called "mama put" in Nigerian parlance. His words: "Yes, even now I like eating in the bukateria. I like this mama put system where you go to the pot and point out the orisirisi (assortment of meat), the edo (liver) the saki, the ponmo and the rest."

marbit *n.* a *mar*shmallow *bit* found in processed breakfast cereal. *Food & Drink.*

1990 Marty Primeau *Dallas Morning News* (Tex.) (Apr. 18) "Low-Fiber, High-Sugar Kid's Cereals Are Well-Advertised," p. 4F ▶ While cereals aimed at health-conscious adults are packed with whole grains and fiber, cereals for their children contain things called "marbits" (bits of marshmallows), malt syrup, corn syrup, brown sugar, honey and other sugar products. **1999** T.L. Stanley *Brandweek* (June 28) "Scooby Dooby Two—Halloween Promotion from Time Warner" (Int.) ▶ General Mills will put Scooby imagery on 4 million Count Chocula cereal boxes, and will include Scooby, Mystery Machine, Shaggy and other character "marbits" in the product. **1999** Karen Wright *Discover* (August) "A Charm's Life" (Int.) ▶ She's brought along a box of Lucky Charms featuring the cereal's latest permutation: tiny marbit charms in saturated colors and substandard sizes that the company launched last March. **2004** Richard Hartel, AnnaKate Hartel *Capital Times, Wisconsin State Journal* (Madison, Wisc.) (Oct. 5) "Mystery of Circus Peanuts," p. 5D ▶ Circus Peanuts, and the marshmallow bits (called marbits) in Lucky Charms, are denser, grained marshmallows with some of the sugar in crystal form.

matchbook college *n.* a (real or figurative) school of higher learning with low academic standards. Also **matchbook university.** *Derogatory. Education. United States.* [From the supposed tendency of such a school to advertise on matchbook covers. Sometimes capitalized as if it were a proper noun.]

1995 *Usenet: rec.arts.tv.soaps.abc* (June 4) "Re: GH: Bobbie's (Jackie's) Acting" ▶ Also Zeman is the new Sally Struthers for a "matchbook

college," so we know that school is for FULL FIGURED women.
1997 Greg Lucas @ Sacramento *San Francisco Chronicle* (Calif.)
(Apr. 6) "Enunciations of S.F.'s Most Abstruse Solon" ▶ Modern American politics are dominated by cheesy, simplistic sound bites. Political consultants and some politicians must believe all voters are graduates of Matchbook University's course on Simple Minds and Short-Attention Spans. **1997** Porter Bibb *Ted Turner: It Ain't as Easy as It Looks* (Sept. 1), p. 240 ▶ I can get an honorary degree from some matchbook college anytime I want. **2002** Roy Bragg *San Antonio Express-News* (Tex.) (Sept. 3) "PETA Isn't Pleased, But a Millionaire's Project to Clone Dogs and Other Pets Is Already Doing Big Business," p. 1A ▶ The school, because it was a private venture and not affiliated with any established universities, was criticized by academics as a "diploma mill" and a "matchbook college." **2004** Carol Thompson *Valley News* (Fulton, N.Y.) (Nov. 20) "Taxpayers Foot Tuition Bills for County Employees" ▶ County funds have also paid for "internet campuses" that offer learning programs to "fit your learning style and budget" as well as online multiple choice exams that lead to a college degree. They are also referred to as "matchbook colleges."

mayor's cell *n.* a military unit, akin to the mayoralty of a small town, that handles facilities and infrastructure at a (temporary) base. Also **mayor cell**. *Military.*

1999 *Usenet: alt.folklore.military* (June 23) "Gate Guards" ▶ The guard duty was run by the mayor's cell on a DA6. **2000** *Usenet: alt.folklore.military* (May 26) "Crashing the Party" ▶ The mayor's cell served kind of as "camp counselor," handing out keys to rooms and making sure chow was served on time. My BC turned out to be the mayor...the mayor's cell had to deal pretty closely with the units coming in and out of theater, so that they could be sure they would have enough rooms and such.... Units would come in, and the mayor's cell would bounce it off their schedule of arrivals. **2001** *Army News Service* (Aug. 14) "Area Support Group Activated in Bosnia" (in Tuzla, Bosnia and Herzegovina) ▶ The IC will assign and maintain billets, he said, just as the Mayor's Cell did. **2003** Charlie Brennan *Rocky Mountain News* (Colo.) (Mar. 14) "9,000 Battle-Ready Soldiers Are Wards of Camp Virginia 'Mayor,'" p. 33A ▶ The establishment of the mayor's cell (under Putko) has improved the organization and overall quality of life in Camp Virginia, despite the recent massive influx of soldiers. **2004** Joe *Operation Sandbox* (Sept. 30) "The Wall Shook" (Int.) ▶ On Sunday night I had some extra duty called, "Mayor Cell Duty." See our camp has a mayor. And so a group of about 20 of us had duties related to public works item. **2005** David Shrauger *Living Iraq Journal* (Jan. 16) "When I Say Mission..." (Int.) ▶ The next thing I knew a civilian contractor showed up from the Mayor Cell (the guys who make sure that our living areas are...well...livable).

mean-mugging *n.* Also *v.* staring in an aggressive or threatening manner. *Hip-Hop. Slang. United States.* [From *mug* 'to pout, grow sullen, mope; to make a face.']

1991 *Usenet: rec.music.funky* (Dec. 29) "Interview with Del, the Funkee Homo Sapien" ▶ Why would you want to mean-mug niggas from your car like you want to get out and beat them down? **1994** Lewis W. Diuguid *Kansas City Star* (C2) (July 13) "Our $6 Million Bodies Are Losing Value on Deadly Streets" ▶ One of the three persons charged in the homicide said he gunned down McKay because "he was mean-mugging me." **1996** *Usenet: alt.rap* (Apr. 29) "Re: Chino" ▶ Chino plays the part of the chump with "a complex" getting played because he thinks he's the man. How many videos have that plot? In the other scenes, it's dark and Chino is just flippin' his hands and mean-mugging while flowing. **2004** John Fall *San Francisco Chronicle* (Calif.) (Aug. 15) "Decaying Park Reflects Oakland's Problems" (Int.) ▶ Oakland is a town where "mean mugging," the slang expression for looking at someone the wrong way, results in lethal exchanges of gunfire.

megarexia *n.* a mental condition in which one perceives one's body as too thin and desires to be ever larger. Also **megorexia.** *Health.* The condition is also called **bigorexia.**

1998 Simon J. Williams *The Lived Body: Sociological Themes, Embodied Issues* (June 1), p. 76 ▶ There are also more general risks and dangers involved in body building, not least of which is the emergence of "megarexia," a new condition in which the individual becomes obsessed with increasing the sheer muscular bulk of the body—the very antithesis of the anorexic body. **1999** Kenneth R. Servis, Jr. *Business and Management Practices* (Nov.) "On the Labor Front: Glory at a Price? Labor Takes a Stand On Steroids," vol. 29, no. 6, p. 36 ▶ Steroid abuse can give rise to a condition called megorexia, which is a desire to get and maintain a muscular body and is characterized by over-eating and a distorted body image. **2000** Rachel Solotti *Waikato Times* (New Zealand) (Aug. 3) "Striking a Blow for Your Average Woman" ▶ Men are now going to have plastic surgery, more of them are working out, there's increasing steroid abuse, there's megarexia (where men body build excessively). **2001** Lynette Ng *Pharmvision.com* (July 19) "Dangers of Over-Exercising" (Int.) ▶ Over-exercising...may also be due to other psychological disorders (e.g. obsessive-compulsive disorder) or to megarexia (also referred to as "bigarexia" or "muscle dysmorphia"). Megarexia is characterised by a constant preoccupation with body size and a rigid exercise routine, resulting in compulsive exercising and weight training even when injuries are present. **2001** Liam Rudden *Evening News* (Scotland) (Nov. 5) "Dangers in Weight of Expectation," p. 20 ▶ A member of the body dysmorphic disorders family, muscle dysmorphia is known by many names—barbell blues, bigorexia and megarexia are all commonly used to describe a condition referred to as "inverted anorexia nervosa." **2002** Lynne Luciano *Looking Good: Male Body Image in Modern America* (Jan. 9), p. 229 ▶ Reverse anorexia was first diagnosed in the early 1990s by Dr. Harrison Pope, a Harvard psychiatrist and a bodybuilder. In addition to Pope's research, Dr. William N. Taylor, an expert on anabolic steroids, found that steroid users also develop distorted body images so that they perceive their reflections in the mirror as smaller than they actually are; Taylor called his discovery megarexia.

merk *v.* **1.** to kill (someone); to verbally or physically attack someone; to defeat, to overcome someone or something, to do well; **2.** to depart; to travel (to a place). Also **murk, mirk.** *Hip-Hop. Slang.*

[***1996** Nas @ song *It Was Written* (July 2) "Suspect" ▶ His moms had a stare I wouldn't dare second look when I merk.] **1999** *Usenet: rec.music.hip-hop* (Feb. 17) "This Big-L Thing" ▶ The sad thing is, if Big-L wasn't a rapper then niggas wouldn't even care that he got merked. There's hundreds of kids every day that get slain just like that in ghettos across the country. **2000** *Usenet: rec.music.hip-hop* (Apr. 28) "yo! peep dis battle and vote" ▶ I jump at da opportunity to ruin thee/truthfully you aint got a chance, i merk you brutally/have you in ICU and the cops persuin me. **2001** David Weiss *Wilkes-Barre Times Leader* (Pa.) (Sept. 14) "Wilkes-Barre Man Charged in Killing," p. 21A ▶ "That's when I did him," Yenglee told a witness, according to arrest papers. "I merked (murdered) him." **2002** Bang&Olufsen DK *Acura Legend & Acura RL Community* (Apr. 16) "What Did She Say?!?!?!?!" (Int.) ▶ Idda just merkd out just like Thai said. "No convertible?" "B*ch get yo ass out" skuuuurrrrrrrrrrrrrrrrrrrrrr-rrrr. **2003** *Fulton County Daily Report* (Atlanta, Ga.) (Feb. 7) "Roebuck v. The State," vol. 2, no. 7 ▶ Codefendant Gray told him that the foursome invaded the trailer to steal money and had "merked [i.e., killed] a couple of Mexicans." **2004** [veryunlucky13] *veryunlucky13* (Blacklick, Ohio) (Nov. 2) "Halo Comp Update" (Int.) ▶ I had schooled a kid with the sword winning 6-0. Merked a few others, and was down to Zach Myself left as unbeaten. **2004** David Weber *Boston Herald* (Mass.) (Apr. 22) "Suspect: I Stood Like 'Dummy' as Pal Stabbed Pleading Girl," p. 18 ▶ "I merked that bitch," Bryant quoted Hampton as saying, using a slang word for "killed." **2004** [Jasmine]

Right On! Magazine (Oct. 9) "Guestbook" (Int.) ► Bow is my # 1 boo forever and always so all yall little busdown wannabes need to back dat azz away fa you get merked. **2004** [Jennifer Michele (jennieboo103)] *Dance Like Nobody's Watching* (Rush, N.Y.) (Oct. 12) (Int.) ► Then I merked home and fell asleep. **2004** [mjvirly] *Randomness* (Oct. 22) "Here's Wassup with Me" (Int.) ► I got hurted on pretty fuckin bad...i have the bruised rib cage to prove it...but dont worry i didnt get merked. **2004** [slitsthatdenote (Jimmy)] *And I Know That You Say, This Is What You Get...Love Is the Answer?* (Virginia Beach, Va.) (Nov. 2) "Update..." (Int.) ► The whole party bounced to Eric's crib and it pissed his mom off so we merked to Sals. **2004** [abuakzabu] *StraighT LiFe* (Ontario, Can.) (Nov. 14) "EiD MuBaRaK" (Int.) ► We played em for a buck a ball...n we got merked on purpose for de first game...LOLZ...n they won 15 buckz of us. **2004** [Jacob Wright] *ilXor.com* (Nov. 24) "The Thread That's Totally and Completely on Trim's Dick" (Int.) ► I've spent the last month listening non-stop to both sides of the Trim Taliban white—Boogeyman, and the one over fire hydrant that's just him methodically and comprehensively merking people. **2004** [mizraepyatt24] *i <33 yOu dAnNy* (Niagara Falls, N.Y.) (Dec. 9) "*22 wEekS*" (Int.) ► Danny and I were watchin Maury and this guy had a fear of clowns...And when the clowns came out he started to cry and he def. merked!...I never ever seen a grown man run that fast in my life! **2004** [feed_the_fire_1] *H* (Pennsauken, N.J.) (Dec. 10) "All You Need Is, All You Want Is, All You Need Is Loooooooveee" (Int.) ► I merked my speech the other day, got a 95 on my persuasive speech. **2004** [ticketshomer] *ticketshomer* (Dec. 12) "First Day of Finals" (Int.) ► I had two finals today...I merked the Music one, Chem ehhh not so much. **2005** [Andrew (Majkut; xmajkutdiesx)] *Majkuticus* (Virginia Beach, Va.) (Jan. 17) "Whatchu Know About the Maj-cook?" (Int.) ► Will and I merked to Brinn's at like 10ish and I spent the night. **2005** royaljoe33 *Joes page* (Clifton Heights, Pa.) (Jan. 24) "NFC Champs!!" (Int.) ► Then of course T.O. was HUGE to get not only for his on field merking of people such as ricky manning jr. **2005** [Matt (jesus_is_a_cunt)] *LiveJournal for Matt* (Newport News, Va.) (Jan. 30) "People Are Crazy" (Int.) ► But the girl who had invited me was the one screaming and telling everyone to get the fuck out. At that point, I'd had enough bullshit for one night. So...Me, Daniel and Perm merked. I went to Chenellos to help Chris close. **2005** Curtis Johnson *Herald-Dispatch* (Huntington, W.Va.) (Apr. 21) "Witness Points Finger at Fields" (Int.) ► "He asked Justin to get him his burner, because he was going to murk that bitch," White said. In testimony, White said "burner" was a word meaning "pistol, gun" and "murk" meant to "murder, kill."

met *n.* cancer that has spread beyond its point of origin. *Medical.* [Clipping of *metastasis* 'a change in a location (in a body) of a disease; a disease that has made such a change' or *metastases*, the plural form.] The plural form, **mets,** is sometimes used in the singular, perhaps because of a mistaken reinterpretation of *mets* as a clipping of the singular *metastasis*.

1990 *Usenet: sci.med* (Sept. 1) "Re: Calcium in Blood" ▶ Malignancy with bone mets (breast ca, myeloma, lymphoma). **1991** *Usenet: sci.med* (Aug. 18) "Prostatic Cancer (Again)" ▶ Is it likely that I have micro-mets that are simply too small to show up on the scans? **1999** Cathy Gordon *Houston Chronicle* (Tex.) (Aug. 1) "When the Doctor Is the Patient," p. 8 ▶ I have mets...it has metastasized to my lungs. Don't pay for that trip to France. **1999** *Usenet: sci.med.diseases .cancer* (Oct. 29) "Lung Cancer Symptoms?" ▶ A friend of mine who has unclear chest x-ray and feels a pain in his chest feels strongly that it may be a "mets" from his primary cancer. **2000** Tara McParland *Florida Times-Union* (Jacksonville) (Sept. 12) "The Gift of Small Victories," p. C1 ▶ The CT scan showed mets to the lungs and the liver. **2005** Deborah Hutton *Guardian* (U.K.) (July 3) "Do Mention the 'C' Word" (Int.) ▶ There is no stage V. It was the worst of all news—"as bad as it can get," confirmed the nurse at the Middlesex Hospital who rang to inform me that the CT scan had revealed mets (metastases, or spread) in my liver.

metric buttload *n.* a large but indeterminate quantity. Also **metric ass-load, metric fuck-load, metric shit-load.** *Slang.*

1991 *Usenet: rec.games.trivia* (Aug. 10) "Happy Wombat Double Video Quiz Update" ▶ After a metric buttload of responses (and it isn't even due yet. Sheesh...), I thought I'd up the ante a bit. **1993** *Usenet: alt.peeves* (Feb. 18) "Yet *More* Meeting Peeves" ▶ Not only was his style as lively as a rotting elephant, but he could always be counted on to bring along a metric fuckload of slides to show on the overhead projector. **1993** *Usenet: alt.sex.bondage* (Dec. 21) "My Darling Hypnotist" ▶ Flora had a metric butt-load of gear she wanted to put on me. **1997** *Usenet: rec.sport.pro-wrestling* (Aug. 30) "Death Valley Driver Video Review #48" ▶ It's been a long couple of weeks since the last time I spoke with you gentle readers and I've watched a metric assload of tapes. **1999** Philip Greenspun *Philip & Alex's Guide to Web Publishing* (Apr.), p. 267 ▶ You can collect a metric buttload of data about user activity on your site without too much effort. **2000** *Usenet: alt.guitar.amps* (Jan. 9) "Re: Short Lord Valve (Willie) Story" ▶ I have bought a metric shitload (LV terminology) of stuff from LV over that past year and a half (at least a lot for me). **2003** David

Klinghoffer *Publisher's Weekly* (Mar. 24) "Friction in the Family," p. S11 ▶ "It was embarrassing for some customers to see a naked woman on the cover wrapped in a talis [prayer shawl], and you can see her nipple really clearly," says Alle Hall, marketing manager of Seattle's Tree of Life Judaica, who carried the book but felt it would be most appropriate not to display it face-out. Nevertheless, "We sold a metric buttload of those books." **2004** *Computer Gaming World* (U.S.) (May 1) "Civilization III: Conquests; Queen Tom Versus El Bruce," no. 238 ▶ It may be the late 15th century, but the Spanish have a ton of street cred. They are also going to have a metric buttload of treasure, because Hispaniola is founded right on a tobacco resource and adjacent to some gems. At the end of the game, I'll have my jewelers make me a fancy victory ring. **2004** Merlin Mann *5ives* (Sept. 14) "Five Ass-Related Words I Think I Use a Lot" (Int.) ▶ *metric assload* n.—a lot. **2004** Matt Haughey *A Whole Lotta Nothing* (Oct. 10) "A Metric Assload of Journey Tunes" (Int.) (title). **2004** Maureen Johnson *Bermudez Triangle* (Oct. 12). p. 334 ▶ I got a credit card and bought a metric shitload of DVDs so that she could pick the one she wanted to watch.

microaggression *n.* subtle forms of racism or bias. *Jargon.*

1970 Chester M. Pierce *The Black Seventies* "Offensive Mechanisms," p. 282 (Int.) in *Journal of Negro Education* (1976) LeRoi R. Ray, Jr. "Black Studies: A Discussion of Evaluation," vol. 45, no. 4, p. 391 ▶ Chester M. Pierce says that the society is unrelenting in teaching its white youth how to maximize the advantages of being on the offense toward Blacks. He further advances the notion that offensive mechanisms, "the small, continuous bombardments of micro-aggression by whites to blacks is the essential ingredient in race relations and race interactions." **1992** *USA Today* (May 6) "Anti-Violence Public Policies Urged," p. 7D ▶ Repeated "micro-aggression and micro-insults" wear down blacks, said Bell. When a white child and a black child enter a store, guards follow the black, when a black sits in first-class, flight attendants ask if he's in the right place. **2001** Richard Delgado, Jean Stefancic *Critical Race Theory* (May 1) (Int.) ▶ Social scientists call the event a "microaggression," by which they mean one of those many sudden, stunning, or dispiriting transactions that mar the days of women and folks of color. Like water dripping on sandstone, they can be thought of as small acts of racism.

migra *n.* the border patrol at the shared U.S. boundary with Mexico. *Mexico. Slang. Spanish. United States.* [Clipped form of Spanish *migra*ción 'migration.'] Used by Spanish-speaking undocumented immigrants as **la migra.** The border patrol, originally part of the U.S. Immigration and Naturalization Service, is now a part of the U.S. Customs and Border Protection within the Department of Homeland Security.

1950 Bill Dredge *L.A. Times* (May 2) "Thousands of Mexicans Illegally Cross U.S. Border Each Month," p. 12 ▶ Maybe my water bottle will last and I will come to some place like San Bernardino, or to Los Angeles, and become lost there, from la migra—that is our name for the immigration. **1984** Ivor Davis @ San Ysidro, Calif. *Globe and Mail* (Toronto, Can.) (Mar. 31) "Nightly Ritual: Checker Game on U.S. Border with People as the Pieces," p. P9 ▶ The Border Patrol, la migra to the aliens, is desperately seeking to boost its $533-million budget by $41 million. **2004** Ben Fox, Michelle Morgante @ Ontario, Calif. *Kansas City Star* (Kan., Mo.) (June 18) "Border Patrol Makes In-Country Sweep" (Int.) ▶ Alerts, often false, about "la migra" checkpoints (Spanish slang for immigration officials) have become as common as traffic reports on Spanish-language radio.

moded *adj.* tricked, trumped, or beaten (at a contest of wills or skill). Also **moated.** *California. Slang.* This term appears to have originated in, and is especially common in, California.

1988 Angie Cannon *San Francisco Chronicle* (Calif.) (Nov. 25) "Teachers in S.F. Grab Rap Music as Educational Aid," p. B13 ▶ When people try to bother you,/Don't play their game./Just think twice before you've exploded./Let the other guy be the one who's moded! **1992** Kathleen Moloney, Mary McNamara *L.A. Times* (Apr. 26) "L.A. Speak," p. 10 ▶ *moated* v. to trump someone, get the final word, get them in trouble. "I got Priscilla moated for capping on me." **1992** Alfee Enciso *L.A. Times* (Dec. 28) "Community Essay Living Under 'a Veil of Denial' Bias," p. 5 ▶ I asked the males in my class, "What's the first thing you guys do when you're together discussing a 'freak' or a 'fox'? You ask, 'Hey, what she look like?...Oh, man! She's real fine, man. She's light-skinned,'" at which the class got quiet and smiled. Then a young girl said, "He's right..." while the rest of the students giggled, easing the embarrassment of being "moded." **2004** *Official U.S. Playstation* (July 1) "They Fought the Law, and the Law Won," no. 82 ▶ Getting moded by the FBI: priceless. **2005** Ava Swartz @ San Francisco University High School *SFUHS Update* (Calif.) (Mar.-Apr.) "Sweet, Tight and Hella Stupid" p. 2 ▶ *moded*—beaten.

molecular gastronomy *n.* in cooking, the study and application of chemistry, physics, and other scientific principles on its processes, preparation, and materials. *Food & Drink. Science.* Hervé

This writes to say, "It's not my friend Peter Barham who gave the name 'Molecular Gastronomy,' but Nicholas Kurti and I, in 1988." **1993** *Hobart Mercury* (Australia) (Dec. 24) "Cooking Up Christmas Storm with Science" (in London) ▶ A scientific experiment will take place in millions of homes on Christmas Day in research that has been dubbed "molecular gastronomy" by Dr. Peter Barham. Dr. Barham, a physicist at Bristol University, became so disenchanted with conventional recipe books that he decided to show that cooking is more than "household alchemy"—it is the application of proven principles of chemistry and physics. **2000** Mark Henderson, Adam Sage @ Paris *Ottawa Citizen* (Can.) (Dec. 18) "Haute Cuisine Turns to Science to Unlock Gastronomical Secrets: Chemist to Research Smell of Coffee," p. A2 ▶ One of France's most prestigious academic institutions has founded a laboratory devoted to the study of "molecular gastronomy." The new unit at the College de France in Paris will be headed by Dr. Herve This, a research chemist.... His first new experiment will be to determine whether coffee smells different when sugar is added. He will also study the scientific principles behind the work of Michelin-starred chefs to devise better ways to prepare top-class dishes. **2004** Émilie Boyer King @ Paris *Christian Science Monitor* (Boston, Mass.) (Feb. 18) "Food: His Passion, His Science" (Int.) ▶ Should jam be cooked in a copper pan? When gnocchi come floating to the surface of boiling water, does that mean they are cooked? Molecular gastronomy—a branch of food science that focuses on cooking and food preparation (rather than on the chemical makeup of food, as traditional food science tends to do)—has the answers. **2004** Jaime Ee *Business Times* (Singapore) (May 15) "Adding Some Weird Science as a Cooking Ingredient" (Int.) ▶ The cool thing about molecular gastronomy is that when you understand the chemical make-up of certain ingredients, you have a better understanding of what goes well with what.

Monday hammer *n.* jocularly, a (heavy) sledge or hammer (said to be appropriate for use on a Monday).

[**1938-39** *LOTJ* "The Machine Shop" (in Wisc.), p. 4 ▶ "Monday" hammer. Light sledge.] ***1938-39** Workers at 3rd Ave. and 65th St., carbarn @ NYC *LOTJ* "[pencil] Motormen and Conductors" ▶ Monday hammer. A 32-pound sledge hammer; means worker must have day of rest before being able to wield heavy hammer. **1965** Colin Clark *Economic Journal* (U.K.) (Mar.) "Review: Economics and Sociology of Industry. A Realistic Analysis of Development," vol. 75, no. 297, p. 190

▶ Professor Sargant Florence still seems surprised that absenteeism should be at its highest on Mondays.... From its relatively greater incidence among unskilled men, he asks whether it is due to boredom, and does not discuss the possibility that it may be due to sheer physical incapacity (on Clydeside a hammer with a very thick head is known as a "Monday hammer"). **2004** [Learner Turner] *Ask the Trades* (U.K.) (May 19) "Re: Hire or Beg Steal or Borrow..." (Int.) ▶ If they couldn't get it undone with that, we used a flogging spanner and a "Monday" hammer. This was so called because it weighed 28 lbs, and if you used it on a Monday, you were on the sick for the rest of the week! ***2005** *Lutheran Hour Ministries* (St. Louis, Mo.) (Jan. 27) "Daily Devotions: Monday Hammer" (Int.) ▶ Workers at construction sites use a very heavy hammer to break rocks and concrete. They call it a "Monday hammer." Why "Monday hammer"? Because, they say, on Mondays they come to work fresh and strong, having rested over the weekend and therefore are able to wield this heavy hammer.

money *adj.* in baseball, capable of saving a game or season through heroic effort. *Sports. United States.*

1920 Dean Snyder *Iowa City Daily Press* (Sept. 27) "The Money Players! You Tell 'Em," p. 11 ▶ A good ball player is one thing. A money player is something else. There are both money ball clubs and money ball players.... A star performer may carry a high batting average opposite his name. He may have but a few mistakes recorded in his fielding figures. His workmanship, both on the offense and defense, may be spectacular and brilliant, but if he cracks in the critical pinch plays he doesn't qualify for a money ball player.... When a play comes up to them on which rests the outcome of a battle they'll deliver the goods. If a hit is needed to score the winning run they'll crack it out nine times out of ten. If a bit of super-fielding will save a game they rise to the occasion. **1935** Harry Grayson *Zanesville Signal* (Ohio) (Oct. 9) "By Harry Grayson," p. 10 ▶ Money ball players are so called because when there is something at stake, or when they are in a spot where, if they come through, their outfit prevails, and if they fail, their club loses, they usually deliver.... "When the line forms at the counting house, Goslin, Bridges and Cochrane will be at its head," predicted close observers before the World Series. Their uncanny knack of standing up in the clutches meant to their aggregation an individual difference of $2,449.15.

moneyball *n.* a derisive name for a sport (especially baseball) in which skill and fans seem secondary to money, esp. a sport in which teams, hoping to secure winning seasons and the resulting broadcasting and merchandising incomes, negotiate expensive contracts with desirable players. Also **money ball.** *Money & Finance. Sports. United States.*

1977 Gerald Strine *Washington Post* (Apr. 12) "It's a Bullish NBA Play-off; Blanks Seen for Bullets," p. D4 ▶ It remains to be seen whether coach Dick Motta, having put together a stronger bench, can get consistently superior efforts from Elvin Hayes and Phil Chenier now that the name of the game is Money Ball. **1978** Allen Abel @ NYC *Globe and Mail* (Toronto, Can.) (Oct. 9) "Pride + Tradition," p. S3 ▶ "I didn't think we'd catch Boston. I knew we'd make a run at them, but the distance was too great. I didn't think we could win it. Ahh, but they're just money ball players." George [Steinbrenner] ought to know. He's paying them. **1993** Michael Farber *Gazette* (Montreal, Can.) (Apr. 3) "Pools Reflect Our Lost Innocence," p. D1 ▶ While you were still rooting for your team for no reason more profound than it was your team, they changed the rules on you. The Dodgers and Giants split for the Coast, sharpies like George Steinbrenner bought into the game, the players earned free agency, the World Series became a seven-night affair because that's what was best for television sponsors. Baseball became moneyball, and it made perfect sense for fans to get cut into the game. **2004** Bradford Doolittle *Kansas City Star* (Kan., Mo.) (July 6) "Moneyball's True Gist Is Often Overlooked" (Int.) ▶ The word, moneyball, has pried its way into the baseball lexicon. There are moneyball players and moneyball teams. As with any kind of contrived language, the use of the term carries with it the stigma of stereotype, which, like all stereotypes, is based on misinformation and ignorance.

mongo *n.* material or goods salvaged from items intended for disposal. *NYC. Slang. United States.* New evidence from the unpublished *Lexicon of Trade Jargon*, compiled by the Works Progress Administration, has a form of this word from before 1938: *mungo*, referring to the person who salvages discarded items, rather than the things being salvaged. This term appears to be specific to New York City.

1984 James Brooke *N.Y. Times* (Sept. 10) "Sanitation Art Showings Brighten Workers' Image," p. B4 ▶ Other exhibits at the gallery were a 1,500-square-foot transparent map showing the locations of Sanitation Department offices; three piles of televisions on which videotapes of sanitation workers were shown, and an old, department-section office furnished in "mongo," discarded furniture salvaged by sanitation men. **1996** Mierle Laderman Ukeles (Spring) "Interview: Mierle Laderman Ukeles on Maintenance and Sanitation Art," p. 20 (Int.) in *Dialogues in Public Art* (2001) Tom Finkelpearl

▶ Besides furniture and bathroom, I crammed the section with a decor of "Mongo," items workers selected from the waste flow that they refused to put in the truck—art, religious figures, dolls. **2004** Jane and Michael Stern *N.Y. Times* (June 20) "'Mongo': I Love Trash" (Int.) ▶ "Mongo" is slang for garbage salvaged from streets and trash heaps. Any rubbish can qualify, whether it's edible, wearable, useful or indescribable.

monkey board *n.* a small or narrow elevated platform on which a person stands (to operate a vehicle or machinery, or to perform other work). *Jargon.* While early in its history *monkey board* referred to a conductor's place on wheeled vehicles such as buses, trams, and trolleys, it is now in common use on oil-drilling platforms and also appears in other industries. More or less synonymous terms, often used in a nautical context, include **monkey bridge, monkey island, flying bridge,** and **flying gangway.**

1836 *London Times* (Sept. 23) (in Guildhall), p. 4 ▶ He pursued the poling system down Ludgate-hill, and there he came so close that the pole struck complainant's legs, knocked him off the "monkey board," or conductor's stand, and while he was lying on the ground bawled out that it served him right. **1856** James Parton *Parodies and Burlesques* (NYC), p. 487 ▶ Thy driver, like Nimshi's son—/Driveth/Furiously!/And the cad upon the monkey-board/The monkey-board behind/Scorneth the drag—but goes/Downhill like mad. **1871** James Greenwood *N.Y. Times* (Jan. 29) "The London Street Boys" ▶ The eager, quick-eyed, ragged-headed sprite, who, with the agility of a monkey or a London sparrow, skips about stand-still omnibuses, this side, that side, and hopping on and off the step behind, ever in danger of a kick from the conductor on his monkey board. **1898** *Trenton Evening Times* (N.J.) (July 15) "The Good Old Times," p. 7 ▶ "Young man," continued the pompous gentleman, "I have risen from the monkey board. How? By being careful. When I was young, I made money by saving bus fares." **1921** *Wellsboro Gazette* (Pa.) (Jan. 27) "Words Made by Animals," p. 7 ▶ The step of a bus on which the conductor stands is known as the monkey-board. **1945** *Valley Morning Star* (Harlingen, Tex.) (July 24) "Two Men Injured in Oil Field Accident" (in Raymondville), p. 1 ▶ The men were injured when a finger came out of a monkey board knocking both men down and falling across them. **1992** Karl Laiho @ Kuwait *Toronto Star* (Can.) (June 22) "The Tyranny of the Should," p. D3 ▶ Everything was icy and visibility was restricted to the bottom of the derrick—far below the monkey board, the little platform where I was to work. **1992** Leon Hale *Houston Chronicle* (Tex.) (Dec. 1) "C.T. Taught Me How to Feel Sins," p. A13 ▶ I had seen C.T. throw poultry off the windmill before, and although this practice was forbidden by his stern father, C.T. counted it a considerable thrill. Sometimes he caught white leghorn pullets and pitched them off the monkey board just below the mill blades, and they'd fly 200 feet or more. **1993** *Electrical World* (May 1) "Keep Tools, Tasks Straight: Learn the Lingo," vol. 207, no. 5, p. 42 ▶ The following is a sampling of terms from Tampa Electric's slang dictionary.... Monkey board—A non-insulated aerial platform. **2004** Susan Mansfield *Scotsman* (Scotland) (Nov. 16) "Taking Oil Painting to a Whole New Platform" (Int.) ▶ She also started to learn the offshore patois used to describe the different parts of the platform: the dog house, the monkey board, the rat hole, the cat walk.

monkeyfishing *n.* catching fish by first charging water with an electric current, then netting the stunned or panicked fish. *Florida. Sports. United States.* It is possible this term is specific to Florida. This term is apparently unrelated to the monkeyfishing described in a hoax perpetrated on the online magazine *Slate.*

1995 Jovida Fletcher *Orlando Sentinel* (Fla.) (Mar. 19) "Resident Recalls Times of Drunken Hogs, Monkey-Fishing," p. 3 ▶ In those days, he said, before it was outlawed, fishermen "monkey-fished" area lakes, meaning they would shock the fish and collect them as they floated to the top. **2004** *Ledger* (Lakeland, Fla.) (May 29) "Anglers Charged with a Shocking Crime" (in Ocala, Fla.) (Int.) ▶ Once highly popular, a monkeyfishing angler uses a homemade device to send an electrical charge into the water. To escape the shocks, the fish swim to the surface where fishermen scoop the stunned fish out of the water with a long-handled dip net. **2004** J.R. Absher *Sportman's Guide* (June 2) "The Outdoor News Hound—Shock and Awe Fishing" (Int.) ▶ The act of taking game fish through the use of an electro-shocking device is known in some regions as "telephoning," and in others as "monkey-fishing."

monoline *n.* a company specializing in a single type of financial business, such as credit cards, home mortgages, or a sole class of insurance. *Money & Finance.* Monolines are often required by government regulation rather than by market conditions.

1962 *N.Y. Times* (Jan. 8) "Savings Dollar Eagerly Pursued," p. 114 ▶ Health insurance is offered by about 1,300 organizations. Of these, 819 are insurance companies—560 life, 221 casualty and thirty-eight monoline, offering only health insurance. **1985** David LaGesse @ NYC *American Banker* (Feb. 13) "Escrow Losses Could Hamper Private Issuers," p. 1 ▶ Only 13 companies belong to MICA. They are the closely regulated "monoline" mortgage insurance firms that only guarantee mortgage loans, with state laws forbidding them to enter any other insurance business. **2002** *Cards International* (Feb. 8) "The Monoline: Modeled for Performance," p. 9 ▶ The monoline model has succeeded primarily because of its specialisation. Monolines focus their execution on developing specialist skills and lowering operating costs. All are among the best in the world for their risk management, customer service, segmentation and CRM practices. The card business is completely separate from any other profit centre and decisions such as credit granting are made centrally. **2004** *Green Sheet* (Rohnert Park, Calif.) (July 2) "Credit Card Banks Continue to Post Profits" (Int.) ▶ The Fed defines a "large" credit card bank as a federally insured financial institution with assets in excess of $200 million, and the bulk of those assets in consumer lending with at least 90% of loans originated using credit cards or related products. In banking parlance, these institutions are known as "monolines." **2005** James B. Kelleher @ Chicago (*Reuters*) (Aug. 18) "Merger Talk: US Card Issuers Eye Aftermath of Summer of Mergers" (Int.) ▶ Unlike bank-based issuers, which have access to cheap deposits, the three—known in industry parlance as "monolines"—had to borrow from the capital markets at higher rates.

monster *n.* an addiction. *Drugs.*

1991 *Usenet: soc.culture.misc* (May 16) "Who Says I Am an Addict?" ▶ It is an addiction which has within it philosophical, as well as conceptual and behavioral, elements that make it even harder to deal with. Under the shadow of unimportance, indifference, and humor, this monster keeps growing within us. **1993** Glenn E. Rice *Kansas City Star* (Kan., Mo.) (Apr. 11) "Feeding the Monster: Life of a Cocaine Addict" ▶ The $30 worth of hits turned into a $3,000-a-month monster. Now the monster is Irene's top priority. She's been on crack three years. Three times in rehab. Three times a failure. "This is not an addiction that you can click off and on like a light switch," she said. "You gotta set a goal and you work up towards that goal." **1998** *Usenet: alt.support.stop-smoking* (June 29) "6 Days After Surgery, Struggling" ▶ My mother, who i do not smoke around, has been here and she doesn't even know why i am coughing. She found i smoke years ago but she doesn't know the symptoms enough to see the monster in her son. And I dont have that heart to tell her why. She leaves tomorrow. No hospital imprisonment, no parental shame, just me and my monster. **2001** Caroline Graham *Daily Mail* (U.K.) (Oct. 7) "Mick Was a Great Lover" ▶ I truly believe some kids are born with this monster called addiction inside them. I just woke up my monster earlier than most. **2004** Rachel Sixsmith *Bucks Free Press* (Bucks, Eng.) (Aug. 3) "D-Day + Eight" ▶ After six days without a meal, my monster was ravenous but by refusing to feed it, I was making him grow weaker. Eight days without a cigarette and my monster is now very weak and tired. **2004** Tom Mooney *Providence Journal* (R.I.) (Sept. 5) "Managing Her 'Monster'" (Int.) ▶ As a heroin user, she never tracked how much she injected each day or how much money "the monster," as she calls her addiction, demanded she raise.

MOOP *n.* trash; foreign items found where they do not belong. *Acronym.* [*m*atter *o*ut *o*f *p*lace] This term is associated with the Burning Man festival.

2000 *Usenet: talk.environment* (Oct. 30) "Re: Protest Silicon Satan's Attack on Burning Man" ▶ MOOP bags and pick-up-sticks. **2003** [Tamara (tmonsta)] *LiveJournal for Tamara* (Portland, Ore.) (Aug. 8) "Tearing the House Apart" (Int.) ▶ We want to hand out plastic mugs w/ our camp location on them as an invitation for people to come back to drink tea w/ us and hang out. Much better than flyers which are likely to end up as MOOP (Matter Out Of Place) which is an important consideration in a Leave No Trace environment. **2004** [Diane Desenberg] @ Burning Man *South America Journey* (Sept. 6) "Day 8: Burning Man Festival, Black Rock City, Nevada" (Int.) ▶ We packed up and searched for MOOP on our campsite. MOOP is now part of my vocabulary. It stands for Matter Out Of Place. Part of the permitting process with the Bureau of Land Management includes leave-no-trace standards. Burning Man is the largest Leave-No-Trace event in the world, and so it should come as no surprise that new vocabulary has sprung up. To me, MOOP is conceptual and applies outside the Burning Man environment. A gum wrapper dropped unintentionally on the ground is MOOP. But so is a big lush green lawn in the middle of the desert.

Mortaritaville *n.* a military base subject to regular attack. Also **Mortarville.** *Iraq. Military.*

2004 *The Black Foxes Guild* (Feb. 26) "Greetings from Baghdad" ▶ I've finally made it into Baghdad, though I'll be leaving behind our company's awesome barracks (wired up with heat, AC, internet in each room...) to head out to the place they call Mortarville. **2004** Jerry Griffin @ Iraq *DXer* (Menlo Park, Calif.) (Sept.) "News from Jerry, K6MD/YI9MD" (Int.) ▶ A detention facility by the Iranian border lost their doc cuz he had an irregular heart beat & went for eval in germany, so I get to play prison doc for a couple 2-3 weeks, then back to Mosul (mortarville...). **2004** Tom Bowman *Baltimore Sun* (Oct. 11) "Long an Iraqi Target, No U.S. Help in Sight," p. 1A ▶ This sprawling supply base on a dusty stretch about 50 miles northwest of Baghdad is officially known as a "logistical support area." But some of the thousands of soldiers and contractors who suffer daily mortar and rocket attacks have another name for it: "Mortaritaville." **2004** [Carleeann] *New Castle News Discussion Forum* (Pa.) (Oct. 23) "Who Will You Vote For?" (Int.) ▶ On the Front Page of Stars and Stripes (which is free in Iraq) the paper goes on to tell the world that LSA (logistics support area) Anaconda is now nicknamed Mortarville but it's okay they are used to it and will not get more money to be used for base defense. **2004** Tara Shay @ Baghdad, Iraq *TSV's Journal* (Nov. 15) "Welcome to Mortarville" (Int.) (title) **2004** [batterystation] *Candle-Power Forums* (Dec. 31) "Re: Operation Christmas Lights" (Int.) ▶ On behalf of the "Predator" folks, here at Balad Air Base, Iraq (a.k.a. "mortarville"), I wish to convey my thanks and appreciation for "your" continued support. **2005** Todd Mcadam *Press & Sun-Bulletin* (Binghamton, N.Y.) (Feb. 2) "Long Wait Finally Over for 2 Soldiers, Families" (Int.) ▶ The 45-soldier unit has spent the past 14 months guarding Camp Anaconda, the military's largest support facility in Iraq, about 40 miles north of Baghdad. Soldiers call the place "Mortaritaville," for the daily mortar attacks it undergoes.

mother of Satan *n.* the chemical triacetone triperoxide, used in the making of explosives.

2001 Stephen Kurkjian, Ralph Ranalli *Boston Globe* (Dec. 28) "Terrorist Link Seen in Shoe Explosive Probers Try to Determine If Reid Was Part of a Duo," p. A1 ▶ Palestinian radicals who have made TATP their explosive of choice call it the Mother of Satan, not only because of its power but because it can prove as dangerous to the bombers as it is to their targets. **2005** Sasha Shtargot @ London, England *The Age* (Sydney, Australia) (July 16) "Australian Bus Terror Victim Dies" (Int.) ▶ The explosive believed to have been used by the bombers is triacetone triperoxide (TATP), also known as "Mother of Satan" because of its instability and lethality. It can be made from household items.

mouth-breather *n.* a stupid person; a moron, dolt, imbecile. *Pejorative. Slang.* The original definition of *mouth-breather* referred to a person who, due to medical problems (usually with the sinuses or nose), was forced to breath via the mouth. This leaves the jaw hanging open at most times, which has a tendency to make a person look dopey or spacey.

[**1944** Lloyd Lewis @ Chicago *N.Y. Times* (Oct. 8) "Of a Capitulation in Chicago" ▶ Billy, who has grown rich on the rivers, nevertheless approached in the manner of a mouth-breather, hat in hand, toes crossed.] **1978** Cyra McFadden *N.Y. Times*

Mag. (Feb. 5) "Mary Shelley, Mary Shelley," p. 2 ▶ "How can we reach out to the average viewer?" You know...the middle-class mouth-breather with the camper truck and the short attention span. **1985** Allan Fotheringham *Maclean's* (Can.) (June 17) "The Sacking of a Genuine Star" ▶ One wonders, in fact, if some nervous vice-presidents at the CBC are not looking over their shoulders at some of the mouth-breathers and wall-climbers in the new Conservative caucus who always viewed the CBC as a hive of pinkos and weirdos. [**1986** Sandra Earley *Newsday* (N.Y.) (Jan. 16) "South Street Singles," p. 4 ▶ Conversation is also the old familiar college topics with the occasional joke, sometimes racist—these people are very comfortable together—for a guffaw. "They are all stewardesses, and she had blond hair about down to here," says a mouth-breather, also in a standard gray.] **1987** Mike Keefe *Ten Speed Commandments* (Aug. 4), p. 64 ▶ Then there are the mouth-breathers. These folks are usually slack-jawed, thick-tongued individuals who congregate around pornographic movie theaters. It is the latter method that is used in cycling. **1996** Donald E. Westlake *What's the Worst That Could Happen?* (Oct. 1), p. 61 ▶ No matter how many breasts or royals they exposed, they would still be read only by the same four hundred thousand mouthbreathers. **1997** *Usenet: alt.revenge* (Jan. 23) "Re: Need Help from Someone with Win95 Expertise" ▶ Whatta maroon. Not only does this submoronic mouthbreather send an illegal, obscene message in private email, he posts it here publicly, with a header showing that it was also sent privately. **2001** L. Neil Smith *Lever Action: Essays on Liberty* (Apr. 1), p. 301 ▶ Wellywebb and his sniveling gaggle of political mouth-breathers held a highly publicized rally on the Colorado Capitol steps.

MP3Jing *n.* the live mixing or playing of recorded music in a dance club or other public space using a portable digital audio device such as an Apple iPod. *Entertainment. Music. Technology.* [*MP3* 'MPEG audio layer 3, a digital compression format commonly used to store audio' + *J* 'jockeying; the live playing or mixing of recorded music as a public performance.']

2002 *Usenet: cz.comp.lang.perl* (June 15) "[NET.JAM] Audio & Video STREAM Sundays" ▶ SHARE-assemblage of portable computers, data exchange, performances, MP3Jing sunday afternoons 5-9. **2004** Raj Panjwani *Guardian* (U.K.) (Jan. 7) "Clubs: Last Night an MP3J Saved My Life," p. 10 ▶ MP3Jing is just about extending that accessibility. I co-run a night called noWax at a bar in east London, where people DJ with iPods. **2004** [The Angelus] *Aggregate of the Void Generation* (Los Angeles, Calif.) (Aug. 12) "Enjoying the Silence" (Int.) ▶ I need to look into repairing the headphone jack on my laptop. Without it, I can't run monitors out from my MP3Jing software. That means no beat-mixing. **2004** Julie Clothier @ London *CNN* (Dec. 20) "Turning the Digital Tables" (Int.) ► Welcome to No Wax—the UK's first MP3Jing evenings, where ordinary punters get the chance to publicly show off the music stored inside their MP3 players.

MTA *n.* a model who takes up acting; a *model-turned-actress/actor. Acronym. Entertainment.*

1992 Lesley-Ann Jones *Sunday Mail* (Queensland, Australia) (July 26) "Naomi Supermodel Superstar" ► Look at all the models who turn to acting. They call it MTA—model-turned-actress. Like it's something to be ashamed of. Geena Davis, Paulina Porizkova, Jessica Lange, Lauren Hutton. **1993** *Observer* (U.K.) (Nov. 28) "Signs of Life: Cameron Alborzian," p. 24 ► Is it true that you're going the MTA route (model-turned-actor)? **1998** Bruce Westbrook *Houston Chronicle* (July 23) "Gwyneth Paltrow Gives Model Performance, But That's Not Good," p. 19 ► You've seen them in commercials, soap operas, even the movies. They're MTA's—models-turned-actresses. **2004** *Seattle Times* (Aug. 21) "Athens Spotlight Finds Plenty of Women to Shine On" (Int.) ► In the fashion industry, models that aspire to reach the silver screen are referred to as MTAs, or models-turned-actresses.

mugu *n.* a fool; (*hence*) a person who falls for a scam. *Crime & Prisons. Derogatory. Nigeria. Pejorative.* Outside of Nigeria, this term has become associated with the victims of the advance fee, 419, or money-cleaning scams.

1996 *Usenet: soc.culture.nigeria* (Aug. 26) "Re: Commonwealth vs. Nigeria" ► Chai, dey neva see pepper...pompous, ignoramus, bombastic, and oteteristic (dat last one no dey for dictionary) mugus. **1998** *Usenet: soc.culture.nigeria* (Jan. 15) "Re: Newly Discovered Rainbow" ► Some stupid person/company will fall "mugu" to this latest proposition. **1998** *Tempo* (Lagos, Nigeria) (Dec. 16) "Warri's Many Worries" ► A popular slang in Warri is that In Warri you must follow who know road. If you no do am, you go de look like mugu. (You must identify with those who know how to make things happen easily. If you don't do that you may remain a fool). **2000** Kelechi Obasi *The News* (Lagos, Nigeria) (May 17) "More Gullible Businessmen Fall for the Advanced Fee Fraud Scam" ► Latest revelations have shown that, sometimes, even foreign nationals collude with Nigerians to rip-off unsuspecting partners, popularly called mugus. **2002** Paul Legall *Hamilton Spectator* (Ontario, Can.) (Nov. 1) "E-Mail from 'Princess': She Wants Cash," p. A1 ► They'll then press the dupe—or Mugu as he's derisively known in Africa—for more money to buy chemicals that can be obtained only from the American treasury department to wash the rest of the money. **2004** Leonie Lamont *Sydney Morning Herald*

(Australia) (Nov. 9) "Internet Con Man Gets Five Years' Jail" (Int.)
▶ His victims—or "mugus" as he called them in telephone intercepts with his African fellow scammers—included a Saudi Arabian sheik, a Malaysian property developer and ordinary Australians.

muj *n.* among (Anglophone) foreigners in Middle Eastern or Islamic nations, a guerrilla fighter or fighters. *Arabic. Military.* [Clipped form of Persian and Arabic *mujahideen*, plural for *mujahid* 'one who fights in a *jihad* or holy war.'] *Muj* is used both in the singular and plural.

1986 John Gray @ Peshawar, Pakistan *Globe and Mail* (Toronto, Can.) (Nov. 17) "City in Exile: A World of Intrigue, Hope," p. A11 ▶ A Canadian film-maker's neatly pressed grey flannels and tweed jacket contrast with his week's rough growth of beard. "I'm going in a few days," he says, rubbing the beard. "Do you think I look like a Muj?" **1995** *Usenet: misc.activism.militia* (Aug. 18) "Afghanis & Mountain People in General" ▶ The "muj" have three things they know and there are four things that separate them from the heathen: 1) they are Afghani, 2) they are Muslims, 3) they are from here, 4) the Russians (Or Brits, or whomever) are none of the above. **2001** *Usenet: soc .culture.indian* (July 12) "Re: There Is No Solution to Kashmir Problem" ▶ India should accept the Pakistan no war pact. Much of the army can then be removed from the Rajasthan and Punjab borders and sent to the valley to finish off the Muj once and for all. **2004** Steve Coll *Ghost Wars* (Feb. 1), p. 131 ▶ A parade of well-tailored "Gucci muj," as the CIA Near East officers derisively called them, began to fly in from Pakistan and march from office to office in Washington. **2005** *Popbitch* (U.K.) (Jan. 12), no. 240 ▶ US soldiers refer to the insurgents as "Muj." When captured they get the Muj to pose for photos with the phrase, "Say one, two, three—Jihad!"

murderabilia *n.* collectibles from, by, or about murders, murderers, or violent crimes. Also **murderbilia.** *Business. Crime & Prisons.*

1994 Jeff Huebner *Chicago Sun-Times* (Jan. 19) "The Undersee World of Pop Culture," p. 3 ▶ The Chicago Cartoon and Poster Co., 1941 W. North Ave., specializes in limited edition posters, pop culture collectibles, underground publications, adult comics, T-shirts, and "Murderabilia" (like John Wayne Gacy paintings). **2000** Dan Webster *Spokesman Review* (Spokane, Wash.) (Apr. 29) "It's Morbid, Yes, But Fascinating: Serial Killings Appeal to Dark Side of Human Curiosity," p. A1 ▶ Dozens of Web sites offer everything from serial-murder archives to ordering information for such grisly "murderbilia" as serial-killer collector cards, autopsy photos and desk calendars listing murderers' birthdays. **2004** Cindy Horswell *Houston Chronicle* (Tex.)

(Aug. 2) "Victims Advocate Sees a Test Case in Inmate's Artwork" (Int.)
► He wants to use the sales as the first test case of a state law against criminals profiteering from the marketing of personal artifacts, which range from artwork to hair strands. He refers to it such memorabilia as "murderabilia."

Muzzie *n.* a nickname for a Muslim. *Religion.* This word is often, but not always, derogatory. It is not commonly used by North Americans.

1999 *Guardian* (U.K.) (June 4) "Forget the Cricket, All We Need Is a Decent Song," p. 28 ► I've always been a great believer in having the odd Muslim in the side.... With their well-known religious what-have-yous, the Muzzies were put i/c car keys and the lads went through an entire season without one drink-driving conviction. **2000** *Usenet: alt.atheism* (Sept. 22) "Re: Sahih Bukhari" ► No thanks. I have very little respect for any woman who would cling to a belief that restricts herself to being a "2nd class citizen." And I have even less respect for a man that would help them to do so. Eat more pork, you sadistic bastard. Plonk da Muzzie!!! **2003** (*Australian Associated Press*) (Nov. 17) "Muslim Butcher Accused of Murder Was Taunted, Court Told" (in Melbourne) ► Shepparton Magistrates Court today heard Mohammed had been asked about bomb-making and taunted as a "Muzzie" by his co-workers.... Mr. Regan told the court it was the nature of the town to use nicknames and refer to the Halal butchers as "Muzzies." **2004** *Sports Illustrated* (Sept. 27) "The 20 Great Tipping Points," p. 114 ► The morning after he shook up the world, [Muhammad] Ali confirmed his affiliation with the Muzzies, as fight fans were calling them. **2005** Mark McBride *The 6th Estate* (Baton Rouge, La.) (Mar. 4) "Censorship and How New Journalism Can Fight It" (Int.)
► "Muzzie" as I understand it is the English/Aussie/Kiwi slang for Muslim. I've never seen it before or heard it, but I can find (it) now all over the usenet and the Yahoo comment boards.

N

naco *adj.* common, ordinary, plebeian, unfashionable, vulgar. *Mexico. Pejorative. Slang. Spanish. United States.*

1983 Oakland Ross *Globe and Mail* (Toronto, Can.) (Oct. 15) "A Festival Where Symbols of Whiteness Are Over-Rated," p. P9 ▶ Middle-class Mexicans, she said, tend to use a single adjective to dismiss all that is perhaps most real and most wonderful about Mexican culture, simply because it is dark-complexioned and simply because it springs from the poor. The adjective is naco. Basically untranslatable, it means something like "vulgar." **1992** *Usenet: soc.culture.mexican* (May 10) "Re: Racismo" ▶ Esto es muy triste, pues revela un complejo de inferioridad social. La mayoria de los latinoamericanos somos mestizos, pero preferimos a la gente con apariencia sajona. Acaso el desagradable termino peyorativo "naco" no se referia en su acepcion original a la gente de bajos recursos y de piel morena? He escuchado a varias personas hacer comentarios tales como "es bonita, nada mas que es prieta", refiriendose a alguna muchacha, como si ser morena fuera un defecto. **2004** (*NPR*) (July 8) "Day to Day: It's Hip to Be 'Naco'" (Int.) ▶ In Great Britain, they're known as "Kevins." In the U.S., the words "nerd," "redneck" and "cheesy" come to mind. For Mexicans, it's "naco"—a term that covers everything from guys draped in gold chains to people who dance funny. Some Mexicans still find the word offensive. It was initially a derogatory term used to insult indigenous people and the poor. But for many, "naco" has morphed into a term that represents personal style—or lack thereof—rather than class or wealth. **2004** [elenamary] *Daily Texican* (Dallas, Tex.) (Nov. 23) "Cholo Word of the Day—Naco" (Int.) ▶ In México the word "Naco" is a racist term for an "indio," thus not just "indio" but almost like saying "nigger."…. I remember going to see "Y Tu mama tambien" with some Chilango friends of mine. They translated the word "naco" to "White-trash"; my friend brought up and noted that it was actually the opposite of White trash. "Opposite" was the word he used. Opposite because "naco" is someone who is very indigenous and indigenous as if it is a bad thing. My definition could be different in that my Spanish is Southern Mexican Spanish, not cholo Spanish, not Spanglish, and not big-city-pesudo-northern-Mexcio Guadalajara Spanish…. I stand by my comment it is just as bad as the word "nigger," in my Spanish. I did not grow-up in a chicano community nor in northern

Mexico. In the Spanish of Mexico City and to the south of it, "Naco" is a terrible racist term. **2004** [Becky] *Daily Texican* (Dallas, Tex.) (Nov. 23) "Cholo Word of the Day—Naco" (Int.) ▶ In Mexico City, where I grew up, "naco" is not just racist, it's classist and a pretty offensive term. Basically, anybody who is dark-skinned and/or poor may be termed a "naco." I've even heard people refer to things as "nacadas" (i.e., someone who acts rudely does a "nacada," or something that looks tacky is a "nacada"). It's amazing the number of people I've heard use it in front of me when referring to someone else, but not dare use it to the person to whom they were referring. (It's considered that offensive!)

natural capitalism *n.* an economic theory or practice that assigns a financial cost to the use, maintenance, abuse, or depletion of natural resources and ecosystems. *Environment. Money & Finance.*

1996 Robert Frenay *Audubon* (Jan. 11) "Butterflies and the Dismal Science," vol. 98, no. 1, p. 86 ▶ In the effort to create a greener economic system, some theorists—starting with University of Florida zoologist C.S. Holling—are seeking to define an economic value for nature. Costanza describes what he calls natural capitalism, defining capital as "a stock that yields a flow of valuable goods or services into the future." He says the yield of new trees or fish from parent stocks should be counted as "natural income" and the parent stock itself considered "natural capital." **1999** Paul Hawken, Amory Lovins, L. Hunter Lovins *Natural Capitalism: Creating the Next Industrial Revolution* (Sept. 30), p. 3 ▶ Natural capitalism recognizes the critical interdependency between the production and use of human-made capital and the maintenance and supply of natural capital.... Natural capital, made up of resources, living systems, and ecosystem services. **2004** Rona Fried *Tidepool* (June 17) "A Business Built on Biomimicry" (Int.) ▶ Biomimicry and "Natural Capitalism" are other terms that describe a similar approach to creating products that work with nature.

neurodiversity *n.* the whole of human mental or psychological neurological structures or behaviors, seen as not necessarily problematic, but as alternate, acceptable forms of human biology. *Health. Medical.*

1998 Harvey Blume *Atlantic* (NYC) (Sept. 30) "Neurodiversity" (Int.) ▶ Neurodiversity may be every bit as crucial for the human race as biodiversity is for life in general. **1998** Usenet: *alt.support.learning-disab* (Dec. 29) "Neurodiversity Pride" ▶ Any thoughts on the idea of neurodiversity pride: that is, that those who are wired differently from what is considered the norm, are not BAD, or DISABLED and don't need "fixing," but merely...different? **2004** *Coventry Evening Telegraph* (U.K.) (Jan. 14) "Open Meeting," p. 15 ▶ The next meeting of the Coventry and Warwickshire Neurodiversity Group is on January 29 at 7:30pm.... Guest speaker Janet Taylor will talk about dyspraxia, a condition affecting movement and co-ordination. **2004** Amy Harmon *N.Y. Times* (May 9) "Neurodiversity Forever," p. 4-1 ▶ But in a new kind of disabilities movement, many of those who deviate from the shrinking subset of neurologically "normal" want tolerance, not just of their diagnoses, but of their behavioral quirks. They say brain differences, like body differences, should be embraced, and argue for an acceptance of "neurodiversity."

new shooter *n.* a horse entering a race, but one that has not been an active participant in the horse-racing circuit, particularly those races that include or lead up to one of the Triple Crown events; a newcomer or long shot. *Animals. Gambling. Sports.*

1981 Andrew Beyer @ Belmont, N.Y. *Washington Post* (June 6) "Belmont Stakes: The Third Jewel of the Triple Crown," p. D1 ▶ Sometimes, the Triple Crown horses are ambushed by a fresh new shooter in the Belmont. Stage Door Johnny peaked just at the right time to defeat Forward Pass in 1966. Coastal blossomed late and upset Spectacular Bid two years ago. **1997** Jay Privman @ Lexington, Ky. *N.Y. Times* (Apr. 13) "...and His Archrival, Pulpit, Will Be There Waiting," p. 8-2 ▶ It was a new race over a new track, and there were several new shooters trying to knock him off. But none of Pulpit's potential problems materialized. It was as if divine intervention was bestowed upon the colt, who resurrected his standing among the nation's leading 3-year-olds with an emphatic victory today in the Blue Grass Stakes at Keeneland Race Course. **1998** Ron Indrisano @ Baltimore, Md. *Boston Globe* (May 13) "'Charlie'" Is Withdrawn; Lukas Adds a Rabbit to Field," p. D8 ▶ My horse is fine, 100 percent, and he's going to stay fine because I'm going to take care of him. If I had run him one more time, I'd have to turn him out. Now when Real Quiet goes to the shelf for a post-Triple Crown break, I'll have a new shooter. **2004** Bill Christine @ Baltimore *L.A. Times* (May 15) "Spoilers Aren't Just in Rearview" (Int.) ▶ In Preakness parlance, they are the "new shooters"—horses who miss the Kentucky Derby but show up two weeks later at Pimlico, hoping to spoil a Triple Crown bid.

nicca *n.* a black person; an African-American; vocative equivalent to *man, dude, buddy. Black English. Hip-Hop. Slang. United States.* [From the colloquial *nigga, nigger*, probably due to a transition to a more closed velar sound, from *g* to *k*, but also possibly an intentional misspelling intended to foil keyword-based content filters.]

1999 *Usenet: rec.music.hip-hop* (May 20) "Re: The Best in Hip Hop One Hit Wonders..." ▶ Ed is my nicca 4 life i love that critter. **2003** Mr. Oysterhead *totally un-inspired* (Aug. 9) "Oh Siht in the Middle of Bashin Sumone...Well Just See for Yourself" (Int.) ▶ Tell Devon and Bran i say "wut up niccas" and...uhh...yeah that be it. **2004** [gnosis] *UK Urban Music Forum* (Aug. 13) "King of Advanced: Butta v Gnosis" (Int.) ▶ I just hopped on the employment train, so I been a busy ass nicca. **2004** **muah** (Aug. 27) "iF yUh FeEliN' l1kE a PiMp. NiCcA gO n BrUsH yO sHoUlDeRz oFf!!" (Int.) (title).

Nintendo slider *n.* in baseball, a pitch that breaks unexpectedly over the plate, as if remotely controlled. *Slang. Sports. United States.*

1997 David Ginsburg @ Seattle, Wash. (*AP*) (Oct. 1) "Orioles Do a Shuffle for Matchup with Johnson" ▶ He's 6-foot-10, has a 97 mph fastball from the side and has a Nintendo slider. **2002** Jim Cour @ Seattle *Olympian* (Olympia, Wash.) (July 6) "M's Get Slammed" (Int.) ▶ "He's got the Nintendo slider," [Torii] Hunter said of [Jeff] Nelson. "I wasn't trying to swing for the fence. I made contact and the ball went out. I don't know how." [**2003** Patrick Reusse *Star Tribune* (Minneapolis-St. Paul, Minn.) (Apr. 5) "Full House Sees Team Miles Off Its Game," p. 1C ▶ Fiore relieved some of the Dome's congestion by surrendering a three-run homer to Wells in the seventh. It came off Fiore's palm ball. "That's like a Nintendo pitch," Wells said. "He lets it go, and it just stops."] **2004** Scott Merkin *MLB.com* (May 6) "Wunsch Out to Prove His Worth" (Int.) ▶ It makes it a little easier to get right-handers out when you have more velocity, but when the velocity is lower, you throw a little more junk. Right now, my slider is working well. It looked like a Nintendo slider with the way it was breaking Wednesday. **2004** Jim Souhan *Star Tribune* (Minneapolis-St. Paul, Minn.) (Oct. 5) "Pitching: Nathan vs. Santana" (Int.) ▶ In baseball parlance, a "Nintendo slider" is one that breaks as if controlled by a joystick.

ninth island *n.* Las Vegas; (*occas.*) any place outside of Hawaii with a large number of Hawaiians. *Colloquial. Hawaii. Nevada. United States.* [Reference to the large number of Hawaiians who have relocated to Las Vegas. Eight major islands make up the state of Hawaii.]

1996 *Usenet: alt.culture.hawaii* (June 9) "14 More Days!" ► Leaving Santa Cruz (Hawaii's 9th Island) Sat. the 23rd to stay over night near the airport. **2000** Ronelle Botwinik *Las Vegas Review-Journal* (Jan. 27) "Activities and Events in Las Vegas," p. 2E ► A lecture on "Hawaiian Spirituality on the Ninth Island" will be presented from 5 to 9 p.m. Saturday at Spring Valley Library, 4280 S. Jones Blvd. (391-7416). **2000** *Usenet: alt.music.hawaiian* (Mar. 4) "Fiji Ticket Giveaway..." ► Aloha2go.com aims to make Vegas the REAL 9th Island by bringing you the Best bands from back home. **2002** Bruce Dunford @ Honolulu, Hawaii *(AP)* (May 8) "Hawaii Governor Slips Off to Las Vegas to Promote Hawaii Products Expo" ► Gov. Ben Cayetano has slipped off to Las Vegas to participate in the kickoff of the Great Ninth Island Expo, a three-day event to display made-in-Hawaii gifts and products. **2003** Irene Lechowitzky *San Diego Union-Tribune* (Calif.) (Oct. 12) "Hawaiians Flock to California Hotel for Island Comforts in the Desert," p. D1 ► "It's poi," he laughed. This was one of the reasons Bob came to the California Hotel, aka Hawaii's ninth island. "Try some? The saimin noodles are also good." **2004** Ken Ritter @ Las Vegas, Nev. *(AP)* (Nov. 23) "Vegas Becoming Hawaii's 'Ninth Island' " (Int.) ► Joel and Melodi Kekauoha began hearing the term "ninth island" when their flight from Honolulu descended over the Nevada desert toward the lights of the Las Vegas Strip. They learned the meaning later that morning, when they bumped into a neighbor from their hometown of Kaneohe, which is on Oahu, one of Hawaii's eight islands. Suddenly, Las Vegas seemed awfully familiar.

Nollywood *n.* the Nigerian film industry. *Entertainment. Nigeria.* [Patterned after *Hollywood* (the American film industry), *Bollywood* (the Indian film industry), and *Lollywood* (the Pakistani film industry).]

2002 Norimitsu Onishi @ Lagos, Nigeria *N.Y. Times* (Sept. 16) "Step Aside, L.A. and Bombay, for Nollywood," p. 11 (title). **2005** Innocent Nwobodo *Daily Champion* (Lagos, Nigeria) (Mar. 16) "On Nollywood Films in Ghana" (Int.) ► Bad news, in the newsman's parlance, is good news. Not for Nollywood, the alias for Nigeria's home video industry, which was recently hit by bad weather in nearby Ghana.

non-paper *n.* an off-the-record or unofficial presentation of (government) policy. *Jargon. Politics.*

1980 Joseph Joffe @ Hamburg *Christian Science Monitor* (Feb. 28) "Willy Brandt: Go-between in US-Soviet Dispute?" ► The SPD sources also confirmed that Soviet Ambassador Semyonov did deliver a "non-paper" (diplomatic jargon for an unofficial message) in early February that hinted at a message of mediation. **1984** *Times* (London, Eng.) (Mar. 7) "A Two-Day Meeting of EEC Farm Ministers in Brussels Yesterday Failed to Make an Agreement on the Reform of the Common Agricultural Policy," p. 6 ► M. Michel Rocard, the French Minister, yesterday returned to Paris to discuss the summit with President Mitterrand. He will also be opening a "non paper," setting out the position, which will be put to the council. **2004** Rajeev Sharma, Girja Shankar Kaura @ New Delhi *Tribune* (Chandigarh, India) (Sept. 10) "Dixit, Aziz Hold Secret Talks in Delhi" (Int.) ► It is understood that British Foreign Secretary Jack Straw had given a non-paper on Kashmir problem to the Indian and Pakistani leaderships when he visited the subcontinent in the first week of February this year. In diplomatic parlance, a "non-paper" is used when a government is conveying a point to other government/governments or state actors while keeping nothing on record.

noodle *v.* to hunt bare-handed in water for fish or turtles. *Sports. United States.*

1916 *Fort Wayne Daily News* (Ind.) (Aug. 18) "'Noodling' Is the Newest Way to Fish" (in Kansas City, Mo.), p. 21 ► "Noodling" is only possible in rocky streams, where ledges project into the water. **1938** *Progress-Review* (La Porte City, Iowa) (Sept. 8) "Noodling," p. 6 ► Down in Kansas they have "noodlers."...Iowa also agrees that "noodling" is the lowest and most despicable method of fishing. It is prevalent in all parts of the state, particularly during the catfish spawning season. **1968** Hank Kozloski *News Journal* (Mansfield, Ohio) (Jan. 14) "Ohio Scene: There's More Hunting," p. 8 ► For the fishermen, they can whet their fishing appetites watching Frank Davis and son, Jon, catching large catfish and noodling for turtles. **1982** *Daily Oklahoman* (Oklahoma City) (May 11) "Warnings Issued After 3 State Fishermen Drown" ► Sheriff Thomas Johnstone said Hargraves was noodling (attempting to catch fish bare-handed) when he apparently stepped into a deep hole in Salt Fork River. **2004** Patrick Joseph *Kansas City Star* (Kan., Mo.) (Aug. 1) "Some Fishermen Think Outside the Tackle Box" (Int.) ► If blasting away at fish strikes some as crude, it's nothing next to noodling. Variously known as hand grabbing, hogging, grabbling, stumping and dogging (depending on what part of the country you're in), noodling, as they call it in Texas and Oklahoma, does away with all artifice—rod, reel, line and hook—and uses only the bare hand instead. For bait, there is nothing but the noodler's own fingers, which are wagged enticingly in front of promising catfish holes. **2004** Scott Charton @ Columbia, Mo. *Boston.com* (Dec. 28)

"Missouri Approves Fishing with Bare Hands" (Int.) ▶ Known variously as noodling or hogging, handfishing has long been a misdemeanor punishable by fines, because state officials fear it depletes breeding-age catfish.

noofter *n.* a homosexual. *Derogatory. Sexuality. Slang. United Kingdom.* [Popularized by the British television program "Only Fools and Horses," first broadcast in 1981. Possibly a blend of *nance* or *nancy* and *poofter*.]

1992 *Independent* (U.K.) (Dec. 19) "After the Courses, the Horses," p. 14 ▶ For "Only Fools and Horses," John Sullivan replaced the expletives of south London with a rich invented argot. Jason reveled in it, and, in a neat example of reality reflecting art, made words such as dipstick, noofter and lovely jubbly part of a real-life wide boy's vocabulary. **2001** *Usenet: alt.sailing.asa* (June 17) "Re: Unless You Live Aboard" ▶ If I'm a "plonker" then you are a "pukka noofter"! **2001** Frank O'Donnell *Scotsman* (Scotland) (June 21) "Hearts Acts to Have Bigoted Web site Shut" ▶ There was also a section on the web site called Noofters, which was said to stand for "Nasty Odur (sic) Obese Fenian Timmy Eejit Rubbish Scum." **2003** [Jeef] *OfficialSpin.com* (Nov. 13) "Re: Is Prince Charles Gay?" (Int.) ▶ Prince charle is noofter and should not be alowed within a mile of the brittish throne. **2004** Tom Lappin *Scotsman* (Scotland) (Aug. 2) "Getting Old Can Be a Bit of a Drama" (Int.) ▶ Ray asks him pretty soon after they meet whether Jim is a "noofter."...Jim thinks he rather might be, but the writer's deft plot spine concentrates on Ray gradually coming around to the idea that he might be as well. A homosexual affair between a couple of geriatrics across the class barrier isn't entirely easy territory for any dramatist.

nuclear option *n.* especially in politics, an action of last resort; in recent years in the United States, an extreme method of overcoming a filibuster related to the confirmation of judicial nominees. *Politics.* This term was not coined by U.S. Senator Trent Lott. According to William Safire, the term goes at least back to the Richard Nixon presidency, when he heard it for the first time from Nixon's Chief of Staff, Bob Haldeman.

1986 Richard Thomson *Times* (London, Eng.) (Nov. 12) "Collier Case Seen as Shot Across Bows of Would-Be Rule Breakers" ▶ Morgan Grenfell chose the "nuclear option" and asked Mr. Collier to resign. There is, of course, a range of lesser sanctions appropriate to lesser misdemeanors. **1998** Liam Halligan *Financial Times* (U.K.) (Mar. 10) "MPs Propose Abolition of Ancient Commons Rituals," p. 8 ▶ One Conservative MP, fresh from helping to "talk out" a bill to outlaw fox-hunting last Friday, said the convention was only one of a number of ways to "filibuster" legislation. " 'I spy' is the nuclear option," he said. "But members intent on frustrating a bill can still deliberately table numerous amendments, or shuffle extremely slowly through the voting lobbies." **2003** Charles Hurt *Washington Times* (D.C.) (Mar. 28) "Senate Panel OKs Owen for Judgeship," p. A6 ▶ Republicans have hinted ominously to some "nuclear" option for breaking the judicial logjam some time after Easter. **2004** James D. Besser *Jewish Week* (N.Y.) (Dec. 31) "Judicial Wars Redux" (Int.) ▶ The nuclear option is Washington parlance for the threat by Senate Republican leaders to change the rules to prevent filibusters on judicial nominations.

numptorium *n.* the building used by the Scottish Parliament at Holyrood, or by extension, the parliament itself. *Politics. Scotland.* [Scots *numpty* 'a stupid person' + Latin *-orium* 'a building or place where an activity occurs or a (type of) thing is located.']

2004 *Scotsman* (Scotland) (Oct. 18) "Hickey; Hickey," p. 17 ▶ A prize of a year's supply of the full proceedings of the Scottish Parliament is on offer for the best term for the Holyrood Reichstag. So far, I can reveal two short-listed terms "Auld Drearie" and "The Numptorium." My old chum, Sir Taggart Kilbirnie of that Ilk, suggests that the latter would make the present regime a "Numptocracy"! **2004** Jason Allardyce *Sunday Times* (London, Eng.) (Nov. 7) "Holyrood 'Numpties Are Worse Than Cuba,'" p. 13 ▶ A leading British economist has dismissed the Scottish parliament as a glorified town hall that promotes policies which are more zealously socialist than those of the hardline communist government of Cuba. John Blundell, director-general of the Institute of Economic Affairs, says that Holyrood is a "numptorium" that should be converted into a museum. **2005** George Kerevan *Scotsman* (Scotland) (Jan. 1) "Word of the Week" (Int.) ▶ My nomination for new word of 2004 goes to "numptorium," coined by our own Peter Clarke, and meaning "a political assembly or parliament building staffed by politicians of a low average IQ, or possessed of venal interests."

nut up *v.* to become bold, courageous, or forthright; to SACK UP, man up. *Slang.*

1999 *Usenet: alt.tv.angel* (Nov. 25) "Re: Last Night's Ep—Is this Angel or Star Trek?" ▶ Who ripped off who? Did anyone complain? Nut up or shut up. **1999** *Usenet: rec.sport.pro-wrestling* (Nov. 26) "Re: New Here..." ▶ That's quite a while to lurk...why'd you decide to nut up now? **2004** *Craigslist* (Oct. 4) "Warning: This Post Could Piss You Off" (in San Francisco) (Int.) ▶ Children: Nut up, get out on the blacktop, and throw that dodgeball back at that little shit harder than he threw it at you.

olf *n.* a scientific measure of indoor odor intensity. *Science.* [*olfaction unit.* Coined by Danish scientist P.O. Fanger in 1987.]

1991 Jonathan M. Samet *Indoor Air Pollution* (June 1), p. 360 ► Using an odor panel as a subjective instrument, Fanger (1987) defined the olf (abbreviation for olfaction unit) as the emission rate of bioeffluents from a standard sedentary person in thermal comfort. **2002** Jeremy Colls *Air Pollution* (Oct. 1), p. 341 ► A smoker has been reported as being about six olf even when not actually smoking.

on (one's) bicycle *adj.* in boxing, constantly moving around a ring (to avoid an opponent). *Sports.*

1979 *Globe and Mail* (Toronto, Can.) (Nov. 26) "Weaver Defeats LeDoux" (in Bloomington, Minn.), p. S20 ► We came out here (in the 12th) and Weaver was on his bicycle, dancing around. **1996** W.H. Stickney, Jr. *Houston Chronicle* (June 24) "Nunn Takes His Time, Defeats Armenta," p. 11 ► Capitalizing on the expansive 18-foot ring, Sullivan got on her bicycle for the entire fight to avoid the power and hand speed of Zamarron, who trains in the same Austin gym. **2003** Tim Smith *N.Y. Daily News* (Sept. 21) "Win Despite Boo Byrds," p. 81 ► In the 12th round it looked like Oquendo had hit Byrd with a clean right and knocked him to the canvas, but referee Eddie Cotton ruled it a slip. Perhaps thinking he had the bout sewn up, Oquendo got on his bicycle briefly. **2004** Jim Kernaghan *London Free Press* (Ontario, Can.) (Sept. 11) "Lady Boxer Will Hang Up Her Gloves" (Int.) ► She never got on her bicycle, as they say in ring parlance about excessively defensive fighters, during her boxing career.

187 *n.* a homicide. *California. Jargon. Police. Slang. United States.* [From section 187-199 of the California penal code, which relates to murder.] Also *attrib.*

1993 Jeff Schnaufer *L.A. Times* (May 13) "Police See Deadly Message in T-Shirt," p. 3 ► While the literal translation of the shirt is the police code for homicide ("187") followed by gang slang for police ("hudda"), many Valley police, school officials and gang experts see it another way: "Murder a Cop." **2004** Ryan Wolf *KGBT-TV* (Harlingen, Tex.) (Apr. 29) "School Fights Lead to Arrest of Students" (Int.) ► She later added, the students in question write "187" about him. It's street lingo for a homicide. ***2004** Janene Rae *National Alliance of Gang Investigator Associations* "The Newspaper of the Streets" (Int.) ▶ The number 187 is frequently used in gang graffiti around the United States, and represents the number of the California Penal Code for homicide. Graffiti which includes 187 is literally making a death threat. **2005** Kathy Steele *Tampa Tribune* (Fla.) (Jan. 6) "Graffiti Identifies Gang Activity" (Int.) ▶ They use graffiti to mark territory but also to send messages. In some cases, threats are made as when the number "187," a gang's name and an individual's name appear. "That is a call to kill the person," McDaniel said.

open (up) daylight *v. phr.* especially in horse racing, to outdistance a competitor. *Sports.*

1882 *Bismarck Tribune* (Dakota Territory) (July 7) "The Fourth's Furore," p. 2 ▶ Before the Girl got down to business again the Maid opened daylight between them, but losing her grip before reaching the home stretch on the first half mile, the Girl gathered her in and showed her heels to the pacer to the finish. **1936** *Syracuse Herald* (N.Y.) (Jan. 26) "Gratton Colt Is Surprise as He Takes Derby Trial" (in Hialeah Park, Fla.), p. 3 ▶ The speedy Baby Bubble quickly outfoot that gelding and opened up daylight over Grog. **1978** Beverley Smith *Globe and Mail* (Toronto, Can.) (June 20) "Mat Hanover Winner in 2:03 2/5 at Mohawk in First Betting Outing," p. P36 ▶ He quickly opened up daylight on the field, and coasted home by four lengths. **1984** *Globe and Mail* (Sept. 24) "Birdies Win for January" (in Concord, Mass.), p. S10 ▶ Then January opened daylight with birdies on the third, fourth and fifth holes. **1986** Gary Reinmuth *Chicago Tribune* (June 6) "Spence: USFL Rejected Offers," p. C2 ▶ With Boston opening up daylight in the American League East, New York Yankees owner George Steinbrenner now says trading Don Baylor to the Red Sox might have been a mistake. **1993** Peter Byrne @ Bailbao, Spain *Irish Times* (Dublin, Ireland) (Mar. 29) "McKiernan's Silver Lining," p. 1 (suppl) ▶ Strong and composed, she showed no outward sign of weakening under the pressure and when she decided to go for home, 1 190 metres from the finish, she quickly opened up daylight between herself and the Irish girl. **2000** Ed Fountaine *N.Y. Post* (June 9) "Go for the Global Goodie; Long Shot Is Primed for Belmont Stunner," p. 104 ▶ In the last 20 years, just four favorites have won the Belmont Stakes. That trend will continue tomorrow when a big long shot, Globalize, scoots to the lead on the far turn, opens daylight and outlasts the favorite, Aptitude, in the 132nd Test of the Champions. **2005** Kat Thompson *SportsFan Magazine* (Apr. 14) "Ladies and Gentlemen, Start Your Equines" (Int.) ▶ Bellamy Road, who not only opened up daylight (that's equine parlance for "a can of whoop-ass") on his rivals at last weekend's Wood Memorial (huh, you said...Oh, shut it) but also broke a 13-year-old stakes record in the process.

open the kimono *v. phr.* to expose or reveal secrets or proprietary information.

[**1959** U.A. Casal *Folklore Studies* "The Goblin Fox and Badger and Other Witch Animals of Japan," vol. 18, p. 84 ▶ It was believed that the wolf was shameful of sexual things, having no strong sexual instincts. He would never disclose his organ, but hide it behind his hanging tail. Should a person perchance see his sexual act, he or she would have to open the *kimono* and disclose his or her own organ, so as not to shame the wolf.] **1979** Jennifer Clough *Evening Capital* (Annapolis, Md.) (May 9) "Pledged Projects Get Axed," p. 8 ▶ We started four years ago with opening the kimono (budget book) and now we're caught without our underwear. **1999** Paul Freiberger *Fire in the Valley* (Dec. 9), p. 308 ▶ "I went down to Xerox Development Corporation," [Steve] Jobs said,..."and I said, 'Look, I will let you invest a million dollars in Apple if you will sort of open the kimono at Xerox PARC.'" **2005** Scott Adams @ comic *Dilbert* (June 16) (Int.) ▶ Don't open the kimono until you ping the change agent for a brain dump and drill down to your core competencies.

Orange Curtain *n.* the characteristics, real or imagined, that differentiate Orange County from Los Angeles County and the rest of California. *California.*

1984 Reginald Dale, Paul Taylor @ Orange County, Calif. *Financial Times* (U.K.) (Sept. 4) "Reagan Promises Peace from Behind California's Orange Curtain," p. 4 ▶ Roughly halfway between Los Angeles and San Diego, it is a place to which people tired of city life are reputed to retreat—to surround themselves with the locally renowned "Orange Curtain," as if with a security blanket. **1986** Barry Koltnow *Orange County Register* (Calif.) (Oct. 27) "Police vs. Clubs Conflict Closing Curtain on OC Music Scene," p. D1 ▶ They began scheduling concerts and it looked like original music was making a serious comeback behind the Orange Curtain. **1986** Jeannine Stein *L.A. Times* (Oct. 27) "Orange County Opulence at Two Store-Opening Galas," p. 1 ▶ What of the stereotype of the unsophisticated shopper who lives "behind the Orange curtain"? **1990** Mike Davis *City of Quartz: Excavating the Future in Los Angeles* (Nov. 1), p. 139 ▶ Tom Johnson, ironically an L.B.J. protégé, was brought in from a Texas farm team in 1980 to become *Times* publisher with the specific mission of penetrating the Orange curtain. **1991** Ann Rule *If You Really Loved Me* (May 15), p. 5 ▶ Los Angeles County is bigger, glitzier, smoggier, and its meaner streets are statistically more dangerous. The stargazers and the starlets, the baby moguls and the legends, live there, clawing for fame and fortune, at least according to those south of the "Orange Curtain." Conversely, Orange County residents are deemed priggish, plastic, conservative—even "nerdy" by some of the more urbane Los Angelenos. **2003** Paige Penland *Lonely Planet Road Trip California Highway 1* (Oct. 1), p. 51 ▶ Orange County gets no respect. But behind the Orange Curtain lie treasures worth exploring. **2005** *OC Weekly* (Calif.) (Apr. 1) "Can't We All Just Get Along?" (Int.) ▶ We real Orange Countians could pull out those dusty Don't Tread on Me flags we have stowed in the garage.... For one thing, war never solves anything. For another, they outnumber us, 6 to 1. And it'd seem as if we here behind the fabled "Orange Curtain" (coined in LA, no doubt) suffered from a major inferiority complex.

otherkin *n.pl.* people who believe themselves to be, at least in part, something other than human. Also singular. *Animals. Biology.*

1995 *Usenet: alt.vampyres* (Feb. 6) "Re: Vampyr and Elves" ▶ Vampyres quickly learned NOT to sup on most otherkin. Fae blood can do really nasty things to a vampyre. **2001** Nick Mamatas *Village Voice* (NYC) (Feb. 20) "Elven Like Me" ▶ As kids, many say, they felt out of place in this world, even insisting to their parents that they were adopted. By their late teens, most Otherkin were involved in paganism, fantasy fiction, the Internet, or past-life regression. **2003** Lorne L. Dawson *Cults and New Religious Movements* (May 1), p. 290 ▶ The Otherkin believe they are reincarnated elves, dwarfs, and other mythical and mystical creatures. **2004** [Tirl Windtree] *Otherkin.net* (Feb. 5) "What Is an Otherkin?" (Int.) ▶ Otherkin are essentially people who consider themselves to be not entirely (or not at all) human, for some reason.

P

paint *n.* a tattoo or tattoos. *Slang.*

1995 *Usenet: rec.sport.basketball.college* (Mar. 2) "Re: Stackhouse (Murphy)" ▶ What do you like his tattoo or something? Player of the year is not given for some paint on your arm. **1997** *Usenet: rec.music.artists.kiss* (Nov. 19) "Re: Stop the Bullshit on This News Group!!" ▶ I am a KISS fan, the forever lasting paint on my arm tells the story. **2004** Frank Myers *One Soldier's Journal* (Baghdad, Iraq) (Aug. 29) "Week Seven—Iba Sina Hospital (Rated M for Mature)" (Int.) ▶ His exposed upper body showed a muscular man in his mid-twenties, well painted. For the un-hip, paint is a slang word for tattoos.

paleoconservative *n.* a holder of outdated or old-fashioned conservative beliefs; a long-standing conservative. Also *adj. Politics.*

1984 *The Nation* (NYC) (Oct. 20) "Willing Goodness," vol. 239, no. 12, p. 396 ▶ A few paleoconservative economists in academia have made careers in this numbers racket. **1987** Tim Appelo *Seattle Times* (Wash.) (Sept. 11) "Historical Musical Captures the Sense of the Moment," p. 7 ▶ Scenes like the "High Society Cake Walk" production number and FDR's spat with his haughty paleoconservative mother after his conversion to Eleanor's liberal way of thinking provoked spontaneous applause. **2004** Robin Abcarian *Baltimore Sun* (Md.) (May 30) "Conservative Pundits Can't Agree on Iraq War" (Int.) ▶ "Paleoconservatives," as he calls them—along with libertarians and such anti-interventionists as Patrick Buchanan—have opposed the invasion of Iraq since the beginning.

paper airplane *n.* in aeronautics and aerospace, a flying machine that is strictly theoretical. *Jargon.* The adjectival form *paper*, referring to something that exists only in print or writing but not as a physical object, is fairly common. Here it connotes an actual toy-sized folded paper plane, carrying with it derogatory and jocular undertones.

1981 Eric Pace *N.Y. Times* (July 19) "Jostling to Power Up the Next Jets," p. 3-1 ▶ The jetliner makers are just "throwing paper airplanes at each other," Wolfgang H. Demisch, aerospace analyst at Morgan Stanley, said last week. He suggested that none of the proposed aircraft may reach the market because "the airlines currently have difficulty getting two nickels to rub together." **1981** Richard Halloran *N.Y. Times* (July 23) "Air Force Chief Calls the Stealth a 'Paper Plane' Far from Reality," p. 1 ▶ The Secretary of the Air Force, Verne Orr, has asserted that the Stealth plane, which Secretary of Defense Caspar W. Weinberger is seriously considering as the nation's next long-range bomber, is "a paper airplane" that is far from development. **1985** Lawrence Ingrassia @ London, England *Wall Street Journal* (July 10) "Airbus Buoyed by Hefty Order Book for New Passenger Plane" ▶ Airbus so far has failed to win over British Airways, a loyal Boeing customer. BA declined to place an order for A-320s two years ago, saying it didn't want to order a "paper" airplane. **1999** (*M2 Presswire*) (Nov. 8) "X-43 Hypersonic Flight Research Vehicle Delivered" ▶ The world's first hypersonic air-breathing free-flight vehicle is no longer just a paper airplane. **2000** James Wallace *Seattle Post-Intelligencer* (Jan. 10) "Boeing, Airbus Battling Over Biggest Commercial Jet Ever," p. C1 ▶ So far, it's only a paper airplane. But the Airbus A3XX has already generated a war of words commensurate with its size on both sides of the Atlantic between Boeing and its archrival. **2004** Bob Cox *Fort Worth Star-Telegram* (Tex.) (July 21) "Boeing Officials Report Solid Base of Commitments to Launch 7E7 Dreamliner" ▶ The much-touted Boeing 7E7 Dreamliner is still just a paper airplane, but that's likely to change soon. **2005** Dave Brooks *Nashua Telegraph* (N.H.) (Apr. 6) "Founder of Firm Creating 'Cheap' Jet to Speak at DWC" (Int.) ▶ Aviation has a long history of what people call "paper airplanes"—some guy comes along who's going to build a new plane that goes 1,000 miles an hour and only costs $200 to fly, and he raises money and is never heard from again.

papi store *n.* especially in urban areas with a large Latino population, a small market; a *bodega. Slang. Spanish. United States.* [Perhaps from the Spanish *"mami y papi* store" 'mom and pop store.']

1999 Originoo Gun Clapaz *M-Pire Shrikez Back* (Aug. 17) "Boot Camp MFC Eastern Conference" ▶ I was throw in papi store down wit the tape duct gat. **2004** [Yigga] @ Atlanta, Ga. *Pikhasso.com* (Sept. 23) "Why I'm the Way I Am...My Random Thoughts" (Int.) ▶ In the souf you cant just sit on the poach or go to the corner or slang roks on da blok or go to papi store. **2005** Michael Hinkelman *Philadelphia Daily News* (Pa.) (Apr. 4) "Trapped in a Cycle of Poverty" (Int.) ▶ Since moving into the neighborhood in 2002, Candi Brown said she's noticed a lot more "poppy stores"—street slang for bodegas—have turned up on street corners. Some of these stores attract unsavory types. "You see guys hanging out on the corner all the time, drug dealers, guys trying to recruit kids," she said.

past-poster *n.* a gambler who places a (surreptitious or illegal) bet on a game or race after its outcome has been determined. *Crime & Prisons. Gambling.*

[**1947** Lawrence J. Skiddy *Syracuse Herald-Journal* (N.Y.) (Jan. 30) "Two Stories as Regards Horse Rooms," p. 36 ▶ The judge's story is that Alvin Kaiser, Houma third baseman, admitted he had clipped the bookie for $185 through the ruse of the past posting and the turned back clock. He said he didn't have anything to do with the clock turning, himself.] **1958** *Washington Post, Times Herald* (Apr. 24) "Atlas' Record Aired for PUC," p. A19 ▶ "He (Atlas) is well known in New Jersey as a man who bets with bookmakers after the horse is in the barn," Kitzler testified further. This type of bettor, the detective said, is known as a "past-poster"—a man who bets with unsuspecting bookmakers after he learns the results of a race. **1994** Iver Peterson *N.Y. Times* (May 4) "Cheating 101: Police and Other Officials Learn to Spot Those Who Break the Rules of the Game," p. B1 ▶ At the roulette table the subject is the "team past post," a deft system that accomplices use to slip a huge bet onto the table after the ball has dropped on the winning number. The best past-posters distract the dealers with a clumsy simultaneous attempt that is caught and thrown back. **2004** Richard Marcus *American Roulette* (Nov. 25) "Happy Thanksgiving" (Int.) ▶ The casino industry's first coordinated counterattack aimed at roulette past posters, those plastic cylinders were invented by an ex-cheater working in surveillance for the Sands. Its purpose was to deny past posters access to the winning chips underneath, as well as prevent the laying down of naked cappers.

Patel shot *n.* a candid photograph with a person in the foreground and a place or object of interest (such as a tourist destination or landmark) in the background. *India.* This term appears to be common among Anglophone Indians. The "Patel shot" as characterized in the 2001 and first 2004 citations is used by only a small number of closely associated filmmakers.

1993 *Usenet: soc.culture.indian* (Nov. 24) ":-) Desi Romeo's Guide Book—Fall 1993 Edition" ▶ Carefully documents his summer vacation with the photos taken in front of prominent landmarks, including uncle Chunnibhai's motel in Bakersfield. These photos are commonly referred to as "Patel-Shots." His approach is not "u have to see to believe it," it's more like "look at this foto, yaar, I have been there" showing a patel shot. [**2001** Meena Menon *Business Line* (Sept. 3)

"Breaking a Silence" (Int.) ▶ In a film, "Sangham Shot," featuring the women of Zaheerabad mandal, Narsamma from Pastapur village, explains how in mainstream films, the camera looks down on rural people. She calls this the "Patel Shot."] [**2004** Meenakshi Shedde *Times of India* (Feb. 7) "Dalit Women's Films Bring Drama to Their Lives" ▶ A low angle shot looking up is a "Patel shot."] **2004** Satyen Kale *Satyen Kale @ Princeton U.* (June 14) "San Diego-LA trip 001r" (Int.) ▶ Ok, here's me with the Hollywood sign in the background—a "Patel shot," as Indraneel calls it ;) **2005** Madhu Venkatesan *Me, Myself and Madhu* (Chicago) (Jan. 18) "Patel Shots and the Mystery Around It..." (Int.) ▶ Well here we go i decided to write something about patel shots. Well by definition this means that when you go to a new place you stand right in front of it and take a picture of yourself with "that thing" at the back. by that thing i mean...say you to agra you take a picture of yourself with the taj in the backdrop. It's one of the lamest ever photographs that one can take. Well i guess the word was coined by some english people who observed the patel families of india who did this. **2005** [Sunayana] *TheEnchantedPileOfThatLonely-Bird* (Jan. 27) "Patel Shot" (Int.) ▶ Patel Shot.at Times Square. ***2005** [N. Nachiappan (Nachi)] *Nachi's Home Page* (Feb. 2) "Get-Togethers in US" (Int.) ▶ Stopped in the middle of nowhere to have a photo-session near a lake, there you go, with all the patel shot (single guys looking for photos to send to brides with neat dress, bandha pose near car etc) guys becoming active.

peachalorum *n.* an attractive or excellent person or thing. *United States.* [Perhaps influenced by *cockalorum* 'a self-important little man.'] This word is rare. The second citation is known to have been written by Henry M. Hyde.

1900 George Ade *Washington Post* (Dec. 2) "Modern Fables," p. 33 ▶ If you don't know how to get away with this Job, you ought not to go against it. You are what Charles Francis Adams would call a Peachalorum. **1901** *Chicago Daily Tribune* (June 18) "Confessions of the Reformed Messenger Boy: A Reform that Failed," p. 12 ▶ In comes a regular honeycooler. Say, de minute I git my lamps on her I knows it was all over wid Ag an' all de rest of my daisies. She was one, two, t'ree. De rest of 'em was also rans. "Sally," laughs de old daisy to de peachalorum, "will you loan me a quarter?"

pen down strike *n.* a labor protest in which workers are present at their jobs but do no work. *Employment. India.*

1981 Michael T. Kaufman @ New Delhi, India *N.Y. Times* (Apr. 23) "In India, There's a Demonstration for Any Occasion" ▶ Pen down strike—

In this protest workers come to the office but do nothing. **2005** *News Today* (Chennai, India) (June 29) "Tragically Funny" (Int.) ► Bandhs, hartals, pen-down strike, work-to-rule agitation...the Left has a huge list of euphemisms for simply not working.

perfumed prince *n.* a man who is seen as bureaucratic or careerist; a man who is said to be effete, feminine, ineffectual, vacillating, or cowardly; (*hence*) a member of the U.S. military leadership (at the Pentagon); *top brass. Military. Politics.*

1987 David H. Hackworth *Washington Post* (June 7) "Bring Back Blood-and-Guts Patton!" p. B2 ► He should send the corporate generals and admirals packing quicksmart to industry where their brilliance would be well used, and replace these perfumed princes with colorful, knowledgeable warriors who will return our armed forces to the winner's circle. **1996** David Broder @ Sarajevo, Bosnia *San Antonio Express News* (Tex.) (Jan. 13) "In Bosnia, One Decisive American Leader" ► I'm not sure that his biggest problems here won't be with the politically correct Washington crowd and the top-ranking perfumed princes. **1998** Joe R. Richardson @ Fairview *Cincinnati Post* (Ohio) (Dec. 30) "If You Don't Have Stomach for War, Don't Start One," p. *A ► These Defense Department do-gooders and their Pentagon Perfumed Princes are asking our military personnel to go to war and to kill for their country, but they must do it in a nice way. If they show their warrior spirit in the least, they will be reprimanded and admonished. **1999** *Las Vegas Review-Journal* (Nev.) (July 23) "The Lines Are Drawn," p. 20B ► The only souls who would benefit from their current plans are the Perfumed Princes of the Beltway. Maybe they should call it "The Party of the Bureaucrat." **2002** Robert Coram *Boyd: The Fighter Pilot Who Changed the Art of War* (December), p. 299 ► Boyd was usually late to work, was slovenly, and disobeyed orders. He referred to generals as "perfumed princes" or "weak dicks" who would put their lives on the line for their country but not their jobs. **2003** Charley Reese *Grand Rapids Press* (Mich.) (Sept. 30) "Is Wes Clark Just a Perfumed Prince?" p. A13 ► My friend says that Clark is "the last guy in the world you want to see in the White House." He describes him as a "perfumed prince" who is so conceited he never admits he's wrong and treats subordinates like dirt. **2005** W. Thomas Smith, Jr. *Seattle Post-Intelligencer* (Wash.) (May 12) "David Hackworth: Unforgettable Soldier" (Int.) ► Where Hack and I did—and I still do— agree was in our disdain for ticket-punching senior military officers, who were more concerned about their own careers than they were about the individual soldiers under their commands. Hack referred to them as "perfumed princes," and he wanted them out of the defense establishment just as soon as they showed their cards and before they could make decisions affecting the lives of soldiers, sailors, airmen, Marines and Coast Guardsmen.

phish *v.* to acquire passwords or other private information (of an individual, an account, a web site, software, etc.) via a ruse. *Crime & Prisons. Technology.*

1996 *Usenet: alt.2600* (Jan. 1) "AOL for Free?" ▶ Does anyone know of a way to get an account other than phishing? **1998** *Usenet: news.admin.net-abuse.email* (Feb. 22) "A Day in the Life of a Spammer" ▶ Start up the backbone and phish newbies for passwords. **2004** Timothy C. Barmann *Providence Journal* (R.I.) (Apr. 27) "Fleet Customers Join Preferred Prey of E-Scammers" (Int.) ▶ Phishing attacks are typically sent by e-mail directing the recipients to a phony Web site and asking them to enter private financial information, such as credit card, Social Security and bank account numbers. The information is then used to commit identify theft and credit card fraud.

pipe *v.* to embellish, fabricate, or invent (information for a newspaper article). *Media. Slang.*

1991 Robert Lipsyte *Columbia Journalism Review* (NYC) (Nov. 1) "Damon Runyon," vol. 30, no. 4, p. 83 ▶ Jiggs Bluster may have piped quotes and gilded scum in his time, but in the long run Jimmy Breslin offered this city a gift: he made it clear that the true experts on life are not officials and academics, but those who live it every day. **1998** Claudia Kalb, Richard Turner *Newsweek* (Aug. 17) "What Was He Thinking? Another Boston Columnist Runs into Trouble," p. 57 ▶ He writes in the style of the metro column, a genre that has included some of the best newspaper writing ever, but also its share of "piping," making stuff up in the tradition of Damon Runyon, who wrote fiction. (One columnist calls such fabrications "Danny Boys," as in "Danny Boy, the pipes are calling.") **2004** Howard Raines *The Atlantic* (May) "My Times" (Int.) ▶ Jim Roberts's research also established the likelihood of inaccuracies, plagiarism, piped quotes, and faked datelines in many other Blair stories. **2004** David Kipen *San Francisco Chronicle* (May 11) "In the End, Hollywood Story Works" (Int.) ▶ It anticipated the whole Jayson Blair imbroglio by a good 15 years with a thriller about a reporter who gets burned making up—or "piping," in David Freeman's parlance—a New York magazine article about a pimp.

pipes *n.pl.* the biceps or upper arms, especially large ones. *Slang.* A more common slang synonym is *guns.*

1994 *Usenet: alt.sex.motss* (May 28) "A Guy's Second Erotica Post" ▶ Jeff was the body builder and got a big kick out of showing off his "pipes" to us at school. **1996** Andy Baggot *Wisconsin State Journal*

(Madison) (Nov. 15) "Wiersma Coming on Strong UW Sophomore Builds a More Robust Outlook," p. 1B ▸ Wiersma said she has not given into the temptation to flex her pipes in front of the mirror mainly because there is more to this equation than muscle mass. [**1997** Marty Gallagher *Muscle & Fitness* (Aug. 1) "Designing Delts," vol. 58, no. 8, p. 114 ▸ Over the subsequent years, Melissa started to fill out with lean muscle; her young, male training partners started calling her "Pipes," a begrudgingly respectful nickname that pays homage to her rock-hard guns and true training grit.] **2002** Lara McGlashan *Muscle & Fitness* (Nov. 1) "Best Bi's," vol. 63, no. 11, p. 108-13 ▸ I like to think of hardcore stuff when I'm training biceps, powerful words like "steel" and "iron"! I also like to envision powerful characters when I look at my pipes, like the Hulk and Wolverine. It fires me up! **2005** Robert Trigaux *St. Petersburg Times* (Fla.) (Mar. 30) "H&K's Handling Sets a Troubling Standard" (Int.) ▸ Complaints allege Wright routinely asked some of the firm's young associate women to "feel his pipes" or "feel his guns"—sexually suggestive slang for feeling his biceps.

pirata *n.* an unlicensed taxi; a *gypsy cab. Automotive. California. Mexico. Spanish. United States.* [Spanish *pirata* 'pirate.'] This term is common throughout the Spanish-speaking world but is recorded here because of its entrance into the everyday vernacular of Los Angeles and other communities.

2000 Leo Flores *The News* (Mexico City, D.F.) (Feb. 15) "Media Slant Erodes D.F. Image, the News" ▸ Robles accused the media of siding with pirata drivers and giving the public "the false impression that the D.F. government wants to harm the poor. They (cab drivers) are portrayed as the victims." **2003** Richard Marosi *L.A. Times* (Oct. 16) "For Working Poor, Rides Are a Lifeline," p. B1 ▸ Using a taxi pirata—illegal taxi—is out of the question. The 10-mile ride would cost her more than her daily earnings of $50. **2003** Kenneth Noble *Newsday* (Nov. 9) "Worker Unsolidarity," p. A30 ▸ Some employers have sent minivans to pick up domestics stuck at home or at bus stops. Many bus and rail commuters have turned to taxi pirata. **2004** Caitlin Liu *L.A. Times* (Nov. 22) "Illegal Taxis Keep on Rolling" (Int.) ▸ Also known as bandit taxis, gypsy cabs or piratas—Spanish for "pirates"—they take business away from licensed cabbies, depress bus ridership and pose safety risks for passengers, officials say.

pissdale *n.* on a ship, a scupper for urination; a urinal. Now historical. [The etymological information given in the cite from *The Sailor's Hornbook* is likely correct.]

1707 Ned Ward *Wooden World* in *The Pirate Hunter* (June, 2002) Richard Zacks, p. 25 ▸ Ned Ward in his satiric *Wooden World* described the sailor's morning ritual: "he crawls...to the pissdale where he manages his whipstaff with one hand and scratches his poop with the other." **1778-83** *Encyclopedia Britannica* "Ship," vol. 10, p. 8134 ▶ Explanation of Plate CCLXIV...82, The piss dale. **1799** *A Vocabulary of Sea Phrases and Terms of Art Used in Seamanship and Naval Architecture* (in London), vol. 2, p. 152 ▶ *Piss-dale. f.* Urinoire. **2004** J.E. Fender *Our Lives, Our Fortunes* (Apr. 1), p. 76 ▶ Men selected to follow Frost and Struan Ferguson formed lines at the heads and the lead-lined pissdales amidships to ease bowels and bladders before taking their places in the long boats. **2004** Patrick O'Brian *21: The Final Unfinished Voyage of Jack Aubrey* (Oct. 30), p. 52 ▶ During this anxious night, with so many of his shipmates scouring pissdales or musket-cocks...he sat in the remarkably well-lit space. **2004** David O'Neal *The Sailor's Hornbook* (Nov. 16), p. 78 ▶ *Pissdale.* Compound word for a place on deck where the crew formerly "went"; a special scupper for that purpose. "Piss" is an Old French word, originally not offensive; "dale" is from Old Norse "dael" and means "hole." **2005** Patricia Smith *Daily News* (Jacksonville, N.C.) (May 23) "QAR Dive Produces Interesting Artifacts" (Int.) ▶ It's a pissdale; it's essentially a urinal.

pitching *n.* selling illegal drugs (on the street). *Crime & Prisons. Drugs. United States.* [Directly related to several long-standing meanings of *to pitch*, including 'to place or lay out (wares) in a fixed place for sale' and 'to make a bid or offer for business.'] Transitive and intransitive.

1989 Philippe Bourgois *N.Y. Times Mag.* (Nov. 12) "Just Another Night on Crack Street," p. 53 ▶ Most likely a hail of whistles and shouts will accompany the stroller's arrival as the lookouts warn those "pitching" the drugs that a potential undercover is on the scene. **2001** Kathryn Gordon *Philadelphia Yearly Meeting of the Religious Society of Friends* (Pa.) (Jan. 14) "Independence Mall Vigil for Peace Report #86" (Int.) ▶ The teens who leave, more often than not before they graduate, are like the unsafe factory walls, only instead of demolition the state remedy for them is prison, and instead of stray bricks to walk around on the sidewalks there are young men pitching crack or heroine, and young women selling what they have to sell in order to buy it. **2002** [Gotti Damu] *The Infamous Freestyle Board* (May 9) "B-day!" (Int.) ▶ I'm on da block and I'm constantly pitching/see da jakes and I'm constantly dippin. **2004** Matt Barone *AllHipHop.com* (July) "Tony Yayo: O.G. (Original Guerilla)" (Int.) ▶ All of that in one day, cuz there is no plan B for me man. If this rap s**t don't work, I'm right back on the corner pitching rocks. ***2004** [Siens] *Simplyhood.com* (East Walpole, Mass.) (Aug. 4) "Simply Hood" (Int.) ▶ I'm in the hood, man/pitching and bagging/and burning/exclusive tropic. ***2004** Kash-Murda *Official Site of All Money Is Legal* (Dec. 24) "All Money Is Legal Interview with DOI Questions" (Int.) ▶ If it wasn't for that building out in Queens that had almost all the best eastcoast indy's stars in it...I would probably be working a good job or on the corner pitching to the pot heads! **2004** Ellis Close *Newsweek* (Dec. 27) "Does Cosby Help?" (Int.) ▶ April, a 16-year-old Latina from the Bronx, scoffed at the notion that poor mothers were buying $500 shoes. The only people she knew with such pricey sneakers were those "on the block pitching [dealing drugs]."

plastax *n.* a per-unit fee levied on the use of plastic bags. *Money & Finance. United Kingdom.* [*pla*stic + *tax*]
2002 Chris Parkin *Sunday Mirror* (U.K.) (Mar. 3) "Shoppers Face Taxing Time Over Bag Charge" ▶ Information about the "plastax" has been passed on to the public through a television advertising and billboard campaign. **2005** James Reynolds *Scotsman* (Scotland)· (June 21) "Bid to Bag New Tax from Shoppers" (Int.) ▶ He said there was evidence in Ireland that the "plastax," as it is known, has led to a 90 per cent reduction in plastic-bag use, significantly benefiting landfill sites, where the bags take up to 100 years to break down.

plusing *n.* the act of continuously improving something; adding detail and tweaks to something already satisfactory. Also **plus-ing, plussing.** *Jargon. United States.*
1987 Leonard Berry *American Banker* (Jan. 21) "Top US Retailers Stay That Way by Stressing Customer Service," vol. 151, no. 14, p. 4 ▶ Mr. Vernon refers to these and myriad other actions as "plussing the business." No one has ever been more successful than Mr. Vernon in giving a food store the ambiance of an upscale department store. **1990** Jim Smiley @ Council Bluffs, Iowa *Omaha World-Herald* (Neb.) (Sept. 27) "We'll Be Nation's Best by 2001, ISU Extension Director Promises" ▶ The agency will be marked, he said, "by what Disney called 'plusing.' When a client comes to us he will have certain expectations. If we 'plus' that, when he leaves he will say, 'Boy, I got more from that than I thought I would.' That's plusing." **2001** Jim Poisant *Creating and Sustaining a Superior Customer Service Organization* (Oct. 30), pp. 92-93 ▶ *Plusing the Show:* The term refers to simply making something better than it is. I have a vivid memory of "Plusing the Show" at Disney. My peers would give me their recommendations as to how they could improve my presentations.... After every presentation, no matter how successful, I would review my performance (the show) to see how I could "plus it." **2004** Austin Bunn *Wired* (June) "Welcome to Planet Pixar" (Int.) ▶ Everything after the story reel is

just plus-ing, like the clever labels added to cereal boxes in Wazowski's apartment in Monsters.

Plyboo *n.* a layered building material made of bamboo. *Architecture.* [*ply*wood + bam*boo*] This word is a trade name of a product manufactured by Smith & Fong; however, it appears to be quickly becoming generified.

1995 Timothy O. Bakke *Home Mechanix* (July 1) "Walking on Bamboo; Interior Storm Windows," vol. 91, no. 797, p. 80 ▶ Smith & Fong, a California-based company, has developed a tongue-and-groove flooring product made from bamboo. Called Plyboo ($5 per sq. ft.), the flooring is attractive, wears well and can be sanded and refinished. **1996** Tom Neven *Washington Post* (Apr. 4) "For a Hardwood Floor, Plyboo Is One Tough Grass," p. T5 ▶ The bamboo used to make plyboo is grown in managed forests in China, so there is no impact on wild stands used by pandas as food. **2004** David Lidsky *Fast Company* (Nov.) "Fast Forward 2005," no. 88, p. 69 (Int.) ▶ Based on a steel frame, her homes use plyboo (a bamboo product) and plastic instead of plywood and glass.

plyometrics *n.* a type of fast exercise in which the muscles are not allowed to fully contract after being extended, typically involving jumping and bouncing. *Health. Sports.*

1982 Michael Wilbon *Washington Post* (Aug. 14) "It's All New Under Maryland Sun," p. D1 ▶ He set up the entire workout for the football team before the summer, introducing the players to plyometrics, a weight-training concept he learned from the Soviets that emphasizes muscle speed and quickness. **1985** Connie Yori *Omaha World-Herald* (Neb.) (June 21) "Power Called the Key Quality for Athlete" ▶ Coaches are taught how to make the most out of an athlete through the development of speed, correct weight lifting techniques, nutrition, and plyometrics, a bounding technique to increase speed and power, he said. **2004** Brady Aymond *Advertiser* (Lafayette, La.) (June 27) "How I Spent My Summer Vacation" (Int.) ▶ Plyometrics found its way into the American vernacular in the late 80s when it was discovered that it was the secret to the Russians' success in the Olympics.

pocho *n.* an Americanized person or thing of Mexican origin, including Americanized Mexican Spanish. Also *adj. Mexico. Slang. Spanglish. Spanish. United States.*

[**1946** William E. Wilson *Modern Language Journal* (Oct.) "A Note on 'Pochismo,'" vol. 30, no. 6, p. 345 ▶ *Pochismo*, derived from *pocho*, an adjective which originally meant discolored, has now come to mean a type of popular slang in Mexico. In the evergrowing list of *pocho* expressions are many hybrid words, artificial combinations of English and Spanish.] **1970** *Mansfield Journal* (Ohio) (Oct. 30) "'Name of Game' Episode Set in Cuba" ▶ Hey, Gringo—Hey, Pocho...Tonight, it's Nielsen's scenes with Ricardo Montalban...playing a Mexican-American actor. **1985** Frank del Olmo *Newsweek* (Nov. 7) "Two Men Who Were More Than Hyphens in a Hyphenated Melting Pot," p. 7 ▶ Pocho is a derogatory term that Mexicans use to denigrate Mexican-Americans who put on gringo airs, and the article described the cultural trauma that Lopez faced as a young man when he tried to return to Mexico after attending Harvard Law School. **2004** Rachel Uranga *Albuquerque Tribune* (Ariz.) (Apr. 26) "Spanish-Speaking Politicians Find Favor" (Int.) ▶ His Spanish is admittedly a work in progress—or, as he calls it, "pocho," referring to the hybrid Spanglish developed by second- and third-generation Hispanics.

politicide *n. political suicide. politi + suicide. Politics.*

1972 S. Abdullah Schleifer *Journal of Palestine Studies* (Winter) "Fedayeen Through Israeli Eyes," vol. 1, no. 2, p. 99 (Int.) ▶ The insistence by the guerrillas that they are struggling to destroy the Zionist state and the Zionist-structured society that generates such a state is turned by Harkabi into a concept of "politicide" (an impressive-sounding concept applicable to the aims of any valid liberation movement, e.g. against Rhodesia and South Africa). **1975** Irving Spiegel *N.Y. Times* (Oct. 20) "Criticism in U.S.," p. 6 ▶ Rabbi Alexand M. Schindler...said that the Arab and third-world nations voting for the resolution "made a fateful and ominous decision to take the road of rhetoric, politicide and bigotry rather than the road of needed economic and social change which can come only through consensus, cooperation and decency." **2004** Lindsay Talmud *openDemocracy* (Apr. 27) "From the Sublime to the Ridiculous" (Int.) ▶ The overall plan—now the most fundamental element in Israeli government policy and viewed by many Israelis as a legitimate attempt by their government to reconcile the irreconcilable demands of security, the settlers and democracy—is perceived by the Palestinians as "politicide"—a term Baruch Kimmerling coined to describe "a gradual but systematic attempt to cause their annihilation as an independent political and social entity." It is bound to be resisted, fiercely.

po-po *n. the police. Also* **po-poo, po.** *Hip-Hop. Police. Slang.*

1990 *Usenet: soc.college* (Apr. 29) "Poly Royal" ▶ Mr. Po-po decided that they were not going to be stationary targets for these idiots and

decided to mobilize. Right towards the bottle-throwing dickheads. At a run. You've probably seen film clips of cops beating the shit out of people. [**1990** Candace Sutton *Sun Herald* (Australia) (Dec. 30) "Back Page," p. 100 ▶ A disillusioned member of the State's thin blue line has written to police journal Police News suggesting a new name for officers who think they have been unfairly treated when promotions crop up. "PO-PO. Passed Over, Pissed Off," the unhappy walloper wrote.] **1993** *Usenet: alt.rap* (May 12) "Lyrics: Raw Fusion: Throw Yo Hands in the Air!" ▶ i guess i couldn't hear the sirens yeah it was po-po an that's oh pee dee for those who don't know. **2001** *Usenet: rec.audio.car* (May 10) "Re: OT Kinda: Experience with Window Tinting?" ▶ One wonders if an ignorant po-po [police officer] wielding a razor blade could damage one's windows themselves trying to be smug and strip the tint off.... **2001** *Usenet: alt.rap* (July 5) "MidWest/Philly...Confessions 2001 *rane of terror & redemption*" ▶ Guess I got knocked for what slipped past the cop's vision/whenever I felt like po would throw on the bracelet/I thought, damn, they already let me go on probation. **2001** *Usenet: rec.music.hip-hop* (Nov. 28) "Re: It's a Pig. Strat Peep My Story" ▶ all of a sudden the po poo came thru and my boy twan was like "dam...there go officer woopty woop." **2004** *Usenet: alt.drugs.ecstasy* (Aug. 3) "Re: Mixing Ecstasy with Antipsychotics" ▶ If your son has a little problems with common sense and self-control, then he isn't exactly Mr. Right for MDMA. Or if he can't hide his use from the po-po (police, if you didn't know) or law. **2004** *Boing Boing* (Aug. 22) "Constitutional Rights for RNC Protesters Fact Sheet" (Int.) ▶ At her site, lawcollective.org, there's the pamphlet and tons of other info about how to not lose your rights when dealing with the po. **2004** Eric K. Arnold *East Bay Express* (Calif.) (Nov. 10) "Requiem for a Mac" (Int.) ▶ His notoriety meant he was constantly sweated by the V-town po-pos. **2005** [Tree Herder (treeherder)] *Welcome to My Nightmare* (Crawfordsville, Ind.) (Jan. 10) "...and It's Been a While..." (Int.) ▶ Oh yea, that's right, karate. it'll help out tons when i get to be a po-po, to use the parlance of our times, and it will give me a lot of confidence and keep me in shape and disciplined.

potato *n.* in professional wrestling, a real hit that injures, as opposed to an orchestrated, harmless one. Also *attrib. v. Entertainment. Slang. Sports. United States.*

1990 *Usenet: rec.sport.pro-wrestling* (July 17) "Wrestling Glossary" ▶ *potato* v.t. To injure or knock another wrestler unconscious by hitting him on the head. **1992** *Usenet: rec.sport.pro-wrestling* (May 12) "Japanese TV" ▶ Stan Hansen pinned Kenta Kobashi in a stiff brawl that appeared to have a potato bust open Kobashi's nose. **1992** *Usenet: rec.sport.pro-wrestling* (Oct. 5) "[AAA] Triple-A Report 10/5" ▶

Fishman took what looked like a potato chair shot from Santos (right on the skull, with nothing intervening). **1992** *Usenet: rec.sport.pro-wrestling* (Oct. 27) "Re: WCW/WWF Happenings" ▶ Flair received the injury after UW hit him with a potato shot in a match a couple weeks ago. **1993** Chris Dufresne *L.A. Times* (Feb. 22) "Requiem for a Giant: There Was No One Bigger in Wrestling Than Andre Rousimoff," p. 1 ▶ Funk, who estimates he wrestled him 15 times, said Andre could hurt you without trying. Wrestlers were grateful that The Giant was graceful enough to land very few accidental "potato" punches. **1997** John Kelso *Austin American-Statesman* (Tex.) (May 12) "Cult Songs, Wrestling and Deer, Oh My," p. B1 ▶ If a wrestler is accidentally injured in a match due to a blow that was ill-timed, he was potatoed. **2000** Terry Gross *Fresh Air* (NPR) (Apr. 24) "Interview with Bret Hart" ▶ In wrestling, there's a thing called—they're referred to as potatoes, is when you accidentally hurt somebody for real. And, you know, it—one potato's OK, two potatoes is crossing the line, and the third one, you usually give what they call a receipt, which is you give one right back. **2000** *New Straits Times* (Malaysia) (July 2) "Chyna—The Ninth Wonder of the World," p. 74 ▶ *Potato*—To injure a wrestler by hitting him on the head or causing him to hit his head on something.

potpourri fishing *n.* a type of fishing that offers a variety of (in-season) species or in which more than one method can be used. *Sports.*

1997 John Adams *Press Democrat* (Santa Rosa, Calif.) (Sept. 11) "Cruising Exotic Species Caught Off Pacific Waters," p. C7 ▶ At Fort Bragg, Martin Scribner at the North Coast Angler says marlin have been hooked and lost. Bottom fishing is great on non-windy days. The albacore bite is picking up again after three windy days. And a commercial boat took 45 salmon Tuesday trolling deep. Is this potpourri fishing or what? **2004** Ned Kehde *Topeka Capital-Journal* (Kan.) (May 2) "April Anglers Enjoy Potpourri Fishing" (Int.) ▶ Potpourri time is a colloquialism for the great and enchanting spell when anglers can tangle with vast numbers of fish and a variety of species by plying the many miles of rock-laden shorelines that grace Coffey, Melvern and Milford lakes. **2004** Ken Jones @ Crescent City, Calif. *Pierfishing.com* "Pier Fishing in California" (Int.) ▶ One night I visited the pier for a little potpourri fishing and was startled to see crab pots tied every 7-10 feet around the entire end of the pier.

power hour *n.* celebratory or recreational drinking in which a shot of alcohol is taken each minute for 60 minutes. *Food & Drink.*

1991 Ellen Uzelac, Joel McCord *Baltimore Sun* (Md.) (Aug. 18) "Alcohol's Escape, Thrills Snaring Younger Teens: Heavy Drinking Starts as

Early as 9 or 10," p. 1A ► Frequently, party entertainment includes games such as "power hour," in which players drink a shot of beer every minute for an hour. **1998** *Usenet: alt.beer* (Aug. 6) "Re: Power Hour" ► I used to do power hour every nite in college. It's not that hard. Can u reach the century club? thats 100 shots in hundred minutes. I puked on the 100th shot. **1998** Alan Scher Zagier *News & Observer* (Raleigh, N.C.) (Dec. 13) "Binge Drinking: On Campus, Why Does One Drink Lead to Another...and Another?" p. A25 ► Games like "hall crawl," where partygoers sample a different drink in each room of a dorm or fraternity house. Or "power hour," which requires ingesting a shot of beer each minute for 60 minutes. **2005** Kate Zernike @ Fargo, N.D. *N.Y. Times* (Mar. 12) "Drinking Game Can Be a Deadly Rite of Passage" (Int.) ► The tradition is "power hour," or "21 for 21," as it is known in some other places across the country: 21-year-olds go to a bar at midnight on their birthdays, flash newly legal identification and then try to down 21 shots in the hour or so before the bar closes, or as fast as possible.

pow-pow *n.* powder snow. *Sports.*

1990 *Usenet: rec.skiing* (Dec. 11) "Re: Help!! Which Is the 'Better' Ski??" ► They make great pow pow skis, cut up the Mt. Hood mash potatoes (wet heavy deep) and are more enjoyable on the pack. **2002** *Usenet: rec.skiing.snowboard* (July 1) "Re: Where to Go in October?" ► The only powder to get high on, falls from the sky.... Snowboarding the world's pow pow. **2004** *Sacramento Bee* (Calif.) (Dec. 30) "The Terms of Terrainment" (Int.) ► *Pow-pow*: Deep, fresh powder, also known as freshies.

praise sandwich *n.* criticism prefaced by and followed by compliments.

1987 Julia Duin *Houston Chronicle* (Tex.) (Sept. 21) "Distractions Often Obscured Purpose of Papal Visit," p. 9 ► He may not have cracked the whip this time. Rather he pulled on the reins. He came up with a "praise sandwich," criticism buffered by layers of affirmation. **2000** Rick Wolff *Coaching Kids for Dummies* (Mar. 7), p. 46 ► A slice of praise.... A slice of constructive criticism.... Note that even the criticism is still covered in praise. You want the youngster to really absorb what you have just said.... The final bit of praise.... And that's the praise sandwich. **2005** Max Mignon *Tricks of the Trade* (Jan. 24) "Corporate Middle Manager" (Int.) ► When giving constructive criticism to an employee, open with some comments about something the employee has done well recently. Then address the bad stuff, but make it quick and to the point, like a shot. Close with another positive item. The employee leaves feeling better about the meeting than if you just gave them the criticism, and you've done your job of being the benevolent task master. In the trade, this is known as a "praise sandwich."

pre-sick *adj.* having behaviors or characteristics that could lead to disease or illness. Also *n. Jargon. Medical.*

1985 Clement G. Martin *Low Blood Sugar* (Apr. 1), p. 104 ▶ Throughout Europe, many countries are sponsoring regular physical fitness programs for all of their "healthy inhabitants" because too many of them are "pre-sick" due to the current living habits we all have. **1996** Abigail Trafford *Washington Post* (Apr. 16) "Ethics and Genetics," p. Z06 ▶ The line between having a bad gene and having a bad disease is blurred. Even though you have no symptoms of illness, you may be treated by your health insurance company as though you do. In short, you are genetically "pre-sick." **2002** Fitzhugh Mullan *Big Doctoring in America* (Oct. 7), p. 71 ▶ Wellness care means dealing with the "pre-sick" who have yet-to-be-determined diseases. **2005** John Dorschner *Miami Herald* (Fla.) (May 26) "UM, Humana to Test 'Pre-sick'" (Int.) ▶ The underlying concept is that once patients have chronic conditions and enter disease management programs, they are already quite sick and inevitably will be costly patients. Better to identify and help the "pre-sick" patient before they have chronic problems.

princess disease *n.* said of a woman, one or more characteristics ascribed to a princess, such as having a high opinion of one's self, imperious or haughty behavior, eating disorders, or, in South Korea, a desire for wealth, material goods, or a financially secure marriage. This term is often jocular or derogatory and is reminiscent of *Jewish American princess.* The term *prince disease* is also sometimes used, but it is less common.

1998 *Usenet: soc.culture.korean* (Feb. 10) "Re: Are There Any Good Korean Girls Out There?" ▶ The yoohaksaeng girls have this Princess Disease about graduating from a Western college and going back to Korea to meet rich successful Korean businessmen whose family may be impressed enough with her education to allow their son to marry her (a sort of "I'm as powerful as my husband" mentality). **1999** *Usenet: rec.sport.pro-wrestling.moderated* (Feb. 11) "[WWF] The Netcop RAW Rant for Feb. 9 /99" ▶ Some real backstage heat between the two, mainly over Sunny's "Princess disease" (as people would say here in Korea ie. gongjoo-byung for those of you who speak Korean). **2003** Lara Mills *Ottawa Citizen* (Can.) (Feb. 8) "Princess Bride" ▶ In the end, we knew it was not to be, and realized that the sight of me in that dress had left us both in full grip of the princess disease. The result was an ache that only Belgian waffles with whipped cream and

strawberries could dull. **2003** *emi3680's Home Page* (Japan)
(Feb. 15) "Freakin' Aye" (Int.) ▶ Princess Disease: I'm the best If you
don't understand my feelings, you are simply a cocky person and plus
ur selfish. Listen to meeh and only meeh Lick my toes (yuck!) I am
the rule-book. **2004** [cl0serr (terro)] *cl0serr* (Dec. 8) (Int.) ▶ Girls
who think the world owes them something (princess disease). **2005**
Sandra Richardson *Taos Daily & Horse Fly* (N.Mex.) (Jan. 15) "Taos
Style: Artful Eccentricity" (Int.) ▶ Inger feels the media brainwashing
leads to "the insanity of being unacceptable," which can manifest in
overeating or more serious problems, like the Princess Disease
(bulimia) and the Secret Disease (anorexia). **2005** *El Diario Montañés*
(Cantabria, Spain) (Mar. 3) "Letizia y 'el mal de las princesas'" (Int.)
▶ Cronistas y periodistas del corazón han acuñado recientemente el
término "mal de las princesas" para referirse a la anorexia.

protein spill *n.* vomit or the act of vomiting.

1985 John Masters *Toronto Star* (Can.) (Dec. 21) "Look! Up in the
Sky! Is It a Bird? a Plane? No, It's Skytrain, and What a Way to Go!,"
p. G3 ▶ At other amusement parks they would simply throw up, but
not at Expo. Here, the staff are learning how to respond to "protein
spills." **1990** *Usenet: rec.humor* (Feb. 25) "How About Some Puke
Synonyms?" ▶ I wrote last year, asking people to write any puke synonyms they've heard of lately...protein spill. **1997** Bill Hybels *Fit to Be
Tied* (July 13), p. 47 ▶ I noticed some of the guys were looking a little
green.... All I can say is that they both experienced "unplanned protein spills." **2003** Jeffrey Epstein *Queens in the Kingdom* (Apr. 15), p.
73 ▶ It's only a rumor, but we hear that Disney had to install a floor
that it could "power clean" because they anticipate the zero-gravity
simulation may cause some people to produce, uh, protein spills.
2005 Mike Schneider @ Lake Buena Vista *Bradenton Herald* (Fla.)
(Apr. 18) "Chinese Workers Learn Disney Lingo" (Int.) ▶ Virginia Li
Yuk Wing, 24, a college graduate in marketing who is working as a
custodian at Disney-MGM Studios before moving to the Hong Kong
park, learned the euphemism for the mess created by queasy visitors
after an intense ride: protein spill.

puck bunny *n.* a female fan of hockey or hockey players; a hockey
groupie, especially one who has casual sexual relations with players. *Sports.* This term is sometimes derogatory. It is similar to
BUCKLE BUNNY.

1992 Linda Yglesias *Sunday Patriot-News* (Harrisburg, Pa.) (Jan. 26)
"After the Game: Even as AIDS Rages, Athlete-Groupie Subculture
Flourishes" ▶ The groupie subculture has an argot of its own. There
are "hockey whores" and "puck bunnies." **1998** Celia Brackenridge

Gender and Sport: A Reader "Men Loving Me Hating Women: The Crisis of Masculinity and Violence to Women in Sport," p. 262 ▶ In the rape culture of the [ice] hockey locker room,...females are referred to as "groupies," "puck bunnies," "pucks" and "dirties" among the players. **2005** Jon Tevlin *Star Tribune* (Minneapolis-St. Paul, Minn.) (Mar. 20) "Unchecked Passion for Hockey Leads Fan on Lively Trek to Sweden" (Int.) ▶ Coaxed by Swedish hockey fans on Internet chat boards, the Minnesota Wild fanatic followed her favorite player, Manny Fernandez, to the small city of Luleå, Sweden, where he was tending goal during the NHL lockout.... She acknowledges that such dedication could have been seen as odd, but Pergakis insists she's no "puck bunny."

pudding ring *n.* facial hair made up of a moustache and a goatee. *Slang. United States.*

2003 [Jacob] *Fujichia* (Worcester, Mass.) (Nov. 10) (Int.) ▶ My beard, now a week and a day old, is very heavy in the pudding ring area, weak on the left side, and weaker on the right, and approximately ⅜ of an inch long. **2004** *Bad News Hughes* (Fla.) (July 5) "Independence Day Fun" (Int.) ▶ He was also rocking a swank "pudding ring" (moustache-goatee combo) back then, and looked like a hip cross between the dude from Soundgarden and Cousin It.

puffer *n.* an automobile left unattended and running in cold weather. *Automotive. Colorado. Police.* This term appears to be specific to Colorado.

2000 Kevin Vaughan *Rocky Mountain News* (Denver, Colo.) (Dec. 19) "Cars Left Running Easy Prey for Thieves: Police Say Don't Leave Keys in Car's Ignition," p. 5A ▶ The youngsters, a 15-year-old boy and a 13-year-old girl, were arrested Friday in a traffic stop and accused of stealing a "puffer"—a car left running on a cold morning to warm up. **2001** Kieran Nicholson *Denver Post* (Colo.) (Dec. 23) "Jefferson County Bulletin," p. B2 ▶ "Puffer" is the term police use to describe cars that are left running and unattended to warm up during cold weather. **2004** Sean Kelly, Ann Schrader *Denver Post* (Colo.) (Nov. 30) "Commuters Contend with Storm's Icy Aftermath," p. B1 ▶ Police Chief Gerry Whitman said officers also will be on the lookout for "puffers"—unattended cars puffing exhaust while warming up. The cars often are stolen for joy rides or wind up being used in crimes. Anyone who leaves a car running unattended faces a traffic citation and a fine. Ironically, on the same day Denver police issued the puffer warning to motorists, an unmarked police car was stolen while warming up. **2005** Amanda C. Sutterer *Broomfield Enterprise* (Colo.) (Jan. 19) "Puff and It's Gone: Running Cars Equal Trouble" (Int.) ▶ The police call them "puffers," most likely because the little clouds of exhaust they exude during the cold, wintry months resemble puffs of smoke. The police term refers to cars left running while owners wipe off snow, scrape frost and head back inside for one last cup of coffee before heading to work.

pump head *n.* a loss of mental acuity after surgery. *Health. Medical.*

1999 Jerome Groopman *New Yorker* (Jan. 11) "Heart Surgery, Unplugged: Coronary Bypass Without Stopping the Heart," p. 43 (Int.) ▶ From thirty to fifty per cent of patients will experience a syndrome Cohn calls "pump head," in which they suffer significant cognitive deficits: memory loss, inability to concentrate, difficulties in recognizing patterns, and an inability to perform basic calculations. **2000** Sandeep Jauhar *N.Y. Times* (Sept. 19) "Saving the Heart Can Sometimes Mean Losing the Memory," p. F1 ▶ The syndrome is so pervasive that heart surgeons and cardiologists have coined a term for it: pump head. Some even go so far as to encourage some patients to seek other remedies for their heart disease. **2004** *L.A. Times* (Oct. 4) "Heal the Heart, Hurt the Mind?" (Int.) ▶ Clinton stands a good chance of fully rebounding from the bypass surgery, in which doctors replace clogged arteries to the heart with veins and arteries taken from elsewhere in the body. But many people who undergo the procedure...find that their brains don't function as well as they did before.... In the medical world, this effect is commonly referred to as "pump head," reflecting the widespread, though unproven, belief that the condition is caused by the heart-lung machine.

punch list *n.* a to-do list (of items requiring immediate attention); any list of significance. *Architecture.* This term is strongly associated with building construction.

1961 Goodman A. Sarachan *N.Y. Times* (June 30) "Text of Statement on School-Construction Hearings," p. 15 ▶ The innumerable reports, punch lists and letters of complaint written by principals, custodians and teachers taken from board files and introduced here serve to emphasize that most of these problems were brought to the attention of board officials over and over again without effective response or correction. **1965** *Press-Gazette* (Hillsboro, Ohio) (Nov. 5) "School Board Gets Report on Construction," p. 1 ▶ Architects met with the board to go over what they term "punch-list items," the checking and double-checking of numerous interior details. **1978** Peter G. Miller

Washington Post (Mar. 11) "Tips for New Home Buyers," p. E6 ► Find out what obligations a builder has to complete work listed on the pre-inspection (punch) list. **1984** Darrel Rippeteau *Washington Post* (Nov. 8) "Working with an Architect" ► This is the stage of the project called "substantial completion"; the architect makes his final list of corrections, or "punch list," which the contractor must satisfy before receiving final payment. **1991** David Ferrell *L.A. Times* (Sept. 30) "Gag Man Tosses Schtick by Fax," p. 1 ► Shipper faxes it to New York along with a "punch list"—a checklist of news stories and other topics to be talked about during the four-hour show. **2004** *Chattanoogan* (Tenn.) (Sept. 9) "Weekly Road Construction Report" (Int.) ► This project is complete pending the contractor addressing the final punch list items. **2004** Lynn Stanton (*Telecommunications Reports*) (Sept. 15) "Lawmak-ers See Problems in Justice's Request for FCC to Ensure Electronic Wiretap Capabilities" ► It has run into problems with some companies that have not developed the "punch list" of digital-age surveillance capabilities requested by law enforcement approved by the FCC under CALEA.

purple *adj.* associated with or concerning all branches of the mil-itary. *Military. Purple* is often used in the names of joint or inter-service exercises or task forces. A *purple-suiter* is someone who works on behalf of a joint service operation or task force.

1967 *L.A. Times* (July 16) "Defense News Policy Passes on Unmourned," p. F7 ► The Pentagon nickname for the new breed is "purple-suiter," indicating an officer wears no particular uniform's bias. **1986** Charles Stafford *St. Petersburg Times* (Fla.) (Sept. 18) "Congress Gives Final Approval to Pentagon's Reorganization," p. 3A ► If you combine the colors of the uniforms of the four services, you come up with the color purple. Thus officers who do joint duty, working on projects that cross service lines, are called purple-suiters. **1993** Jeff Gauger *Omaha World-Herald* (June 9) "Navy, Air Force Set Aside Rivalry to Run StratCom," p. 1 ► Behind his desk at U.S. Strate-gic Command, Rear Adm. Ralph Tindal keeps a purple military hat. On the front of the hat is a patch of Velcro, where the service emblem normally would be. Tindal has Navy and Air Force emblems, and he can attach one or both. In the past, purple was bad news to military people. It represented a blending of the four services and the loss of identity for each. **1998** Alexander J. Hindle Jr. (*United States Naval Institute: Proceedings*) (Dec. 1) "Coast Guard Is Joint," vol. 124, no. 12, p. 30 ► It must accept the idea that a cost of jointness is the assign-ment of personnel to action-officer status who will do "purple work" that may have no direct connection to day-to-day Coast Guard busi-ness. **2001** Maryann Lawlor *Signal* (Apr. 1) "Using Information Mandates a Military on One," vol. 55, no. 8, pp. 19-21 ▶ Information does not distinguish between military uniforms or service ranks. It is not limited by borders drawn on a map. It can be deployed and employed to coordinate a battle or deliver humanitarian aid. Information is truly purple. The U.S. armed services recognize that, when fighting as a joint force, information is a powerful common denominator. **2003 Charles Heyman** (*NPR*) (U.S.) (Mar. 17) **"Talk of the Nation: Military Leadership in Possible War with Iraq"** ▶ I'm quite surprised sometimes when I come to America and I find the interservice rivalry still surprises me in many ways. It doesn't happen here because we are so much smaller as far as armed forces go than the Americans. And nearly all of the senior officer education, senior officer posts are what we call purple. By the time you get to be a brigadier general, you start to be very, very purple and you start to be very, very triservice. **2003 James Dunnigan** *Strategy Page* (July 22) **"The Purple Headquarters Eater"** (Int.) ▶ But since the 1980s, the Department of Defense has been pushing real hard for everyone to think "Purple" (what was good for everyone) than just concentrate on what was best for their particular service. **2005** (*PR Newswire*) (Apr. 7) **"Nationwide Registration for Operation Purple Summer Camps Begins April 15"** (Int.) ▶ Operation Purple is the only summer camp program that focuses on helping kids deal with deployment-related issues and is open to children of personnel from all branches of the U.S. Armed Forces ("purple" is a military term representing inclusion of all branches).

put in blue *v.* in the United Nations, to settle on the draft of a resolution before it is presented for a vote. *Jargon. Politics.*

1996 Colin Keating *Global Policy Forum* (June 5) **"Statement to the General Assembly Working Group on the Security Council"** (Int.) ▶ We think there is an opportunity to utilise modern technology with email and fax to advise all member states of the UN, at a designated point of contact, when texts of resolutions are put in "blue." **1997 Patrick Connole @ NYC** (*Reuters*) (Sept. 11) **"U.S. Envoy to UN Says Iraq Vote Likely Friday"** ▶ We are very close to an agreement on the Iraq resolution. A draft resolution is being put in blue for a probable vote by the Security Council tomorrow. **2002 Philip T. Reeker @ NYC** (*U.S. Dept. of State*) (Oct. 28) **"Briefing for New York Foreign Media"** (Int.) ▶ Question: "Is there any indication that if the discussions within the whole Security Council now won't bear fruit, that the United States might be willing to force a vote to sort of change that text of the resolution to what I believe they call in the United Nations the blue text, printing it on blue paper, and thereby forcing a vote?"...Mr. Reeker: "...We continue to work, as you said, from the US-UK-sponsored resolution, which was put in blue, as your colleague mentioned. And

I still haven't quite figured that out. It is because it's on blue paper or—" Question: "On blue paper (inaudible)." Mr. Reeker: "Blue paper. Anyway, the text was set down and it's an operating text that you've all seen and has been distributed." **2004** *Xinhuanet* **(China) (June 8) "US Makes New Changes to UN Draft on Iraq" (in United Nations) (Int.)** ▶ U.S. Ambassador to the UN John Negroponte told reporters that the new draft, the second in one day, would be put "in blue" Monday night, a UN parlance which means it would be ready for a vote.

Q

qualoid *n.* a newspaper format roughly the size of a traditional tabloid, but with content similar to that of a broadsheet. Also *adj. Jargon. Media.* [*qual*ity + tab*(l)oid*]

1990 *Campaign* (U.K.) (Sept. 28) "Sunday Correspondent; Advertising Must Grab Readers" ▶ The "qualoid" form may just be enough differentiation to help the Corrie escape the continuing broadsheet print warfare. **2002** *Svenska Dagbladet* (Sweden) (Oct. 25) "Tunga nomineringar för SvD," p. 64 ▶ Lena K. Samuelsson nomineras "för att hon lett den journalistiska förnyelsen när SvD utvecklas från missmodig broadsheet till själfull qualoid." **2004** Steve Johnson *Kansas City Star* (Kan., Mo.) (Nov. 12) "For U.S. Newspapers, Future May Be in Tabloid Size" (Int.) ▶ The roughly 18 1/2-by-12 1/2-inch size is also known as the "European midi" (France's *Le Monde* uses it) or, really grimly, as "qualoid," as in quality tabloid.

quinceañera *n.* a coming-out party held for a girl's 15th birthday; a debutante ball or cotillion. *Spanish.* [Spanish *quinceañera*, which also means "a fifteen-year-old girl." The Spanish pronunciation is similar to *keen-say-ah-NYAIR-ah.*]

1978 Lou Cannon @ L.A. *Washington Post* (Mar. 26) "Latin Influence Mounts Throughout Southwest," p. A1 ▶ Well-off Mexican-Americans have adopted the Mexican custom, following a tradition of 16th-century Spain, of presenting their 15-year-old daughters to society at events known as Quinceañera balls. **1984** Benjamin Forgey *Washington Post* (June 14) "Galleries" ▶ The work is a shrine-like assortment of elements from the real world—Cuban and American flags, a striking white gown of the kind a 15-year-old Cuban girl (a "quinceañera") might wear to her coming-out celebration. **1997** Charlene C. Giannetti *The Rollercoaster Years* (Aug. 4), p. 23 ▶ Cuban Americans mark their daughter's turning fifteen with an elaborate party, called a *quince*. The "sweet fifteen bash," which has evolved from the Hispanic *quinceañera*, is a Latino debutante ball, complete with feasting and choreography of mambo and conga dancing. **2005** Thomas E. Franklin *Record* (N.J.) (June 13) "Picture This: 'Quinceañera'" (Int.) ▶ Traditionally, a quinceañera is a young Latina woman's celebration of her 15th birthday—when a girl is symbolically transformed into a woman.

R

racino *n.* a racetrack that offers other forms of gambling in addition to betting on races. *Gambling. Sports. United States.* [*race* track + cas*ino*]

1995 Jamie Wayne *Financial Post* (Toronto, Can.) (July 20) "Greenwood's Glory Reduced to Simulcasts," p. 43 ▶ In Chicago, the owner of Arlington Park talks of turning his track into a "racino," by putting in black jack, crap tables et al. **2004** Dan Ahrens *Investing in Vice* (Feb. 1), p. 54 ▶ At least seventeen states allow either full-scale gambling or what are called "racinos," tracks with slot machine parlors attached. **2004** James Drew *Toledo Blade* (Ohio) (May 30) "Gambling Surrounds Ohio Video Slots Likely to Get Another Vote" (Int.) ▶ West Virginia and New York allow "racinos," horse tracks with video gambling machines, also known as electronic slots.

radcon *n.* a *rad*ical *con*servative. Also **RadCon.** *Politics.*

1997 *Usenet: alt.fan.rush-limbaugh* (Apr. 1) "Re: Clinton Is a Pansy—Bush to Parachute with White Knights" ▶ "Radcon? What does that mean?" "radical conservative. Glad to be of assistance!" **1997** *Usenet: talk.abortion* (July 26) "Re: So Many Idiots (LIBERALS)—So Few Coments" ▶ Presumably, "RadCon" is short for radical conservative. **2004** Steve Weinberg *San Francisco Chronicle* (Calif.) (May 16) "Reich's Optimistic Strategy to Get Democrats Back in Power" (Int.) ▶ Why are so many of these angry workers, who can barely pay their family's bills, voting for radical conservative ("Radcon," in Reich's parlance) Republicans instead of Democrats? Because, Reich answers, the Radcons have "exploited these workers' anger and channeled it toward those familiar targets they want to blame—poor blacks and Latinos, welfare recipients, affirmative action, immigrants, women, Washington bureaucrats, Hillary and Bill and, of course, liberals. Anger is a potent political force. Radcons have been remarkably, and tragically, effective at their scapegoating."

Rafia *n.* a derogatory name for the Provisional Irish Republican Army, a paramilitary and political group seeking the reunification of Ireland. *Ireland. Military. Politics. United Kingdom.* [Republican Army + ma*fia* 'the Italian mob; a criminal organization.']

2004 Suzanne Breen *Belfast News Letter* (Ireland) (Oct. 21) "Ulster—Sicily Without the Sun," p. 15 ▶ Forget romantic notions of the Provos as a liberation army, says McDonald. They're [*sic*] leadership and lieutenants are "the Rafia." **2005** Thomas Harding @ London, England *Sydney Morning Herald* (Australia) (Feb. 22) "Sinn Fein Chiefs 'Sitting at IRA's Top Table'" (Int.) ▶ The Provisional IRA, once regarded as a staunch defender of the Catholic community, is rapidly losing all credibility over allegations of money laundering, theft and murder. It is already being referred to in some Catholic areas as the "Rafia," in reference to the organised crime that has generated millions to bankroll Sinn Fein's political ambitions. **2005** Ben English @ London, England *Herald Sun* (Australia) (Mar. 5) "Brave Siblings Stand Up to IRA" (Int.) ▶ Previously unheard of graffiti of "IRA scum out" emerged on Belfast's streets while a new expression was adopted for the paramilitary force: Rafia—a hybrid of the street word for the Provisionals "Ra" and the Mafia.

rail *n.* a line of powdered drugs intended to be inhaled. *Drugs. Slang.*

1995 *Usenet: alt.bigfoot* (Feb. 7) "Moose in Manhattan" ▶ He discos about, raving throughout his kingdom/and lowers his head to snort a rail. **1997** *Usenet: alt.drugs.hard* (Dec. 6) "Re: Crank and Coke Comparison—Question" ▶ After a biker-rail of meth, i wanna do something. after a biker-rail of blow, i wanna do more blow. **2000** Mark Ames, Matt Taibbi, Edward Limonov *The Exile: Sex, Drugs, and Libel in the New Russia* (Apr. 1), p. 119 ▶ He pulled out a wad of cocaine and poured it onto a mirror. He pulled out two credit cards and started to chop and divide like a Benihana chef, cutting some of the hugest rails I'd ever seen. **2000** Anthony Bourdain *Kitchen Confidential* (May 22), p. 124 ▶ When the restaurant closed, we'd take over the bar, drinking Cristal—which we'd buy at cost—and running fat rails of coke from one end of the bar to the other, then crawling along all fours to snort them. **2002** [aryan_soldat] *EliteFitness.com* (May 14) "My Fuckin Life Is Over!" (Int.) ▶ Fernando has an 8-ball of coke laid out on the bathroom counter, and he is like, "blow a rail, holmes!" I'd never done coke before.

rake *v.* in baseball, to hit well. *Jargon. Sports. United States.* Probably related to *to rake* 'to sweep or traverse with shot' and influenced by *to rake* 'to win at gambling' and *rake* 'money earned from gambling.'

1990 Larry Whiteside *Boston Globe* (Mass.) (May 29) "Go East, Young Man...and Return in a Powerful Way—That Was Cecil Fielder's Route," p. 43 ▶ He rakes pitches like that because he's a low-ball hitter. His power is to right and right-center. They can come inside, but he has the strength like Jim Rice to fight it off. And if they make a mistake.... **1992** Rick Hummel @ Atlanta, Ga. *St. Louis Post-Dispatch* (Mo.) (Aug. 22) "Atlanta—One of the Great Mysteries In," p. 1C ▶ Jose didn't exactly rake the ball but he sent his single over the infield, raising his righthanded average to .404. **1996** Tim Keown *San Francisco Chronicle* (Calif.) (Apr. 6) "For a Big Star, Barry Was Bush League," p. B2 ▶ One guy who can really rake: Scott Brosius. **1996** Jim Street *Seattle Post-Intelligencer* (Wash.) (May 15) "Gooden Enough! Outcast Pitcher Tosses No-Hitter," p. C1 ▶ You have to tip your hat to Doc. To no-hit a team that can flat-out rake the ball is pretty unbelievable. **2002** Howard Bryant *Record* (N.J.) (Feb. 20) "The Yanks 2002 Edition Gets a Workout," p. S3 ▶ "He can really rake that ball to right field," [Joe] Torre said. "He's got a swing that's tough to teach. To cover the ball and yank it to right field is something, and we have a very inviting right field." **2003** Todd Wills *Dallas Morning News* (Tex.) (June 9) "Here's What Scouts Look for When They Grade Prospects and Their 'Tools,'" p. 18 ▶ It's as big a part of Baseball 101 vernacular as "that outfielder has a hose" (a strong throwing arm), "the kid can really rake" (swing that bat) and "he can mash the ball" (hit for power). **2004** Tim Sullivan @ St. Louis, Mo. *San Diego Union-Tribune* (Calif.) (Oct. 28) "Boston's Long Wait Finally Comes to an End" (Int.) ▶ After almost a century in which anguish has accumulated like autumn leaves, New England wakes up this morning toasting a team that, in the current baseball parlance, really "rakes."

rat *n.* a precisely targeted legislative amendment or bill proposed as a political favor. *Connecticut. Politics. United States.* Appears to be specific to Connecticut.

1993 Christopher Keating *Hartford Courant* (Conn.) (June 13) "Special Deals Have Some Legislators on 'Rat' Patrol," p. A1 ▶ State officials who are seeking to find pork-filled amendments say they are currently on "rat patrol." Legislators sometimes disagree whether a bill is a rat or simply represents an effort to help someone who has been genuinely wronged by the system. **1998** *Hartford Courant* (Conn.) (Oct. 20) "While the Cats Were Away...," p. A16 ▶ A rat, in the parlance of Connecticut state legislators, is a bill or an amendment slipped in quietly to favor a friend or a special interest. Two Hartford City Council members recently schemed to sneak through a rat. They had the audacity to think they could get away with it. **2004** Mark Pazniokas *Hartford Courant* (Conn.) (May 12) "Lawmakers OK Borrowing Boost" (Int.) ▶ The Senate passed it only after Democratic leaders agreed to repeal the special favor for Pawelkiewicz—known in legislative parlance as a "rat"—in a separate bill at a future date. **2004** Michele Jacklin *Hartford Courant* (Conn.) (May 26) "Legislative Stalling Becomes a Matter of Degrees" (Int.) ▶ The measure was a "rat," which, in legislative parlance, is a favor-bestowing amendment that supporters sneak through when (wink, wink, nod, nod) no one is looking.

rat line *n.* a covert path or itinerary used for smuggling, escape, or supply. *Crime & Prisons. Jargon. Military.* [This term derives from the tendency of rats to create routes that are out of sight as much as possible, following perimeters and the bases of obstructions.]
1950 Bob Deindorfer @ Vienna, Austria *L.A. Times* (Oct. 15) "Escapes for Sale," p. G9 ▶ I remember a ratline operator helping my nephew escape just after Christmas for two thousand dollars. **1982** William Safire *N.Y. Times* (Dec. 17) "Did Andropov Plot to Intimidate Vatican?" p. P7 ▶ The Bulgarian secret service, which follows KGB orders without question and which had long-established "rat lines" smuggling spies and arms into Italy and Turkey, was the obvious choice. **1983** *Globe and Mail* (Toronto, Can.) (July 5) "U.S. Agents Felt 'No Great Pangs' After Helping Barbie Flee Europe," p. P11 ▶ The former CIC colonel said hundreds of Nazis were brought out of Germany by the same route and "everybody that went through the Rat Line was personally accompanied to the ship by a member of our organization." **2004** Richard Lloyd Parry @ Basra, Iraq *Scotsman* (Scotland) (Oct. 31) "Shells Land Near Black Watch Base" (Int.) ▶ The British troops will be supported by US helicopters and unmanned reconnaissance drones which will scan the desert looking for tracks indicating "rat lines"— military jargon for the routes used by the resistance to transport fighters, arms and money.

rat-racing *n.* a playful form of high-speed flying in which airplanes pursue or attempt to outmaneuver each other, similar to a game of cat-and-mouse. *Military.*
1955 Joseph A. Dear @ Germany *Michigan Evening Sentinel* (Holland, Mich.) (Nov. 15) "Remote Radar Stations Keep Air Force 'Cocked,'" p. 10 ▶ Some of our pilots satisfy their nostalgia by rat racing with Canadian[s]...from another base. **1961** *Mansfield News-Journal* (Ohio) (Apr. 15) "Model Club to Compete," p. 8 ▶ The Mansfield Thunderbirds model plane club expects to send about 20 members to compete in stunt and rat-racing events to be sponsored in Cleveland May 7 by the Cleveland Stunt Men. **1977** John Saar *Washington Post* (June 10) "American 'Rat Racers' Train Hard to Defend South Korea," p. A18 ▶

They call it "rat-racing"—high G-turns that crunch the pilots down in their seats, blasts of afterburner acceleration, simulated missile firings, electronic games of tag staged in the skies five miles up over South Korea. **1991** Jeffrey L. Ethell *Fighter Command* (July 1), p. 12 ▶ A pilot's first taste of "rat racing" in trail, leader trying to shake those following, came with the Texan. **1991** Robert J. Goebel *Mustang Ace: Memoirs of a P-51 Fighter Pilot* (Oct. 1), p. 64 ▶ I've forgotten what we were doing—probably rat-racing, a kind of follow-the-leader in line astern where we chased each other all over the sky. **2000** U.S. Department of Air Force @ Kelly Air Force Base, Texas (*FDCH Regulatory Intelligence Database*) (Aug. 2) "U.S. Pilots, Planes Travel to 'Olympics of the Air' Aboard Air Force C- 5" ▶ She says the experience of "rat-racing around at 150 to 200 knots" in her G-300 is comparable to what she experiences in the SR-71.

rat spill *n.* the accidental importation of rats to a rat-free island (or, rarely, to any rat-free piece of land). *Animals. Environment.*

1991 (*AP*) (Oct. 10) "Federal Biologist Warns of 'Rat Spill'" (in Anchorage, Alaska) (title). **1999** (*AP*) (Jan. 18) "Pribilofs Raise Rodent Defense" (in Anchorage, Alaska) ▶ The agency and local officials have also set up a rat spill-response team to spring into action when there's a shipwreck. **2000** (*U.S. Department of the Interior National Park Service*) (Nov. 17) "Final Environmental Impact Statement for Anacapa Island Restoration Plan...Record of Decision," p. 4 (Int.) ▶ Reacting to a "rat-spill" from a shipwreck or some other introduction requires a rapid response, as does any appearance on Anacapa Island following eradication, or on Prince, Sutil and Santa Barbara Islands. **2004** Sarah Kershaw @ St. Paul, Alaska *N.Y. Times* (Dec. 28) "In Alaskan Islands, Fearing a Spill That Comes on Legs" (Int.) ▶ But worse than an oil spill, in the view of wildlife biologists working furiously to protect millions of exotic animals, the freighter, if it got close enough, could cause an even greater environmental calamity: a rat spill.... Scientists say they now fear rat spills more than oil spills, which can eventually be cleaned up.

rebate shop *n.* a gambling broker that guarantees to return a percentage of every bet to a bettor. *Gambling. Jargon.*

2001 Andrew Beyer *Washington Post* (Feb. 1) "Rebates Knock Betting Off Track," p. D2 ▶ Laurel Vice President Jim Mango traced the bet to the island of St. Kitts, site of a suspected rebate shop. **2004** Chris Young *Toronto Star* (Can.) (Apr. 17) "Complex Betting World," p. E8 ▶ Rebate shops have no such overhead to cover and give most of it back to their customers. Typically, that amounts to between 3 and 12 per cent of the amounts bet, even as high as 18 per cent on some exotic bets. **2004** Joe Drape *N.Y. Times* (Apr. 26) "Horse Racing's Biggest Bettors Are Reaping Richest Rewards" (Int.) ▶ He bets through what are called rebate shops, which are off-shore, on Indian reservations or in states with fewer regulations. Rebate shops offer from 4 percent to 10 percent back on every dollar wagered—win or lose.

receipt *n.* in professional wrestling, a payback, score-settling, or revenge taken for true physical injury or insult. *Entertainment. Jargon. United States.*

1996 *Usenet: rec.sport.pro-wrestling.fantasy* (Apr. 25) "DEWF Thursday Thunder for 4/25/96!!! (Part One)" ▶ This match, as Joey might put it, was a "receipt" for Awesome throwing Vader out of the Extreme Rumble for the DEWF Heavyweight Title. Really. It was gruesome. **2000** John Leland *Newsweek* (Feb. 7) "Our Man Goes to the Mat," p. 54 ▶ If you hurt your opponent for real, he might "get a receipt," or return the favor. "It's like a waltz," yells Ed, counting off a one-two-three rhythm. "Your opponent is really your partner." **2000** Terry Gross *Fresh Air* (NPR) (Apr. 24) "Interview with Bret Hart" ▶ In wrestling, there's a thing called—they're referred to as potatoes, is when you accidentally hurt somebody for real. And, you know, it—one potato's OK, two potatoes is crossing the line, and the third one, you usually give what they call a receipt, which is you give one right back. **2004** Mike Mooneyham *Post and Courier* (Charleston, S.C.) (July 18) "Bret Hart Has Something to Say About Flair's Book" (Int.) ▶ "Personally," Flair says in his book, "I never saw dollar signs on Bret Hart." According to Flair, Hart was too protective of his own image. "(Bret) could have been the president of his own fan club."...That Flair finally issued what in wrestling parlance is known as a "receipt" should have come as no surprise to Hart or his fans.

refi *n.* a refinancing of a mortgage or loan. *Money & Finance.* [Clipping of *refi*nance.]

1986 Robert Guenther *Wall Street Journal* (Apr. 2) "Mortgage-Hunting? Be Ready for Delays and Waiting Lists" ▶ "It's refi-mania," says Felix Beck, chairman of Margaretten & Co., a New Jersey-based mortgage banker. **2003** John Rubino *How to Profit from the Coming Real Estate Bust* (Sept. 20), p. 106 ▶ The 407,000 mortgage brokers/bankers...were busy processing refi applications at the end of 2002. **2005** *Moneyweb* (S. Africa) (June 21) "Rudolf Gouws: Chief Economist, Rand Merchant Bank" (Int.) ▶ If you look elsewhere in the world, house prices rise, consumers then draw more on their bonds, they do "refis" as they call them in the United States.

reflectoporn *n.* a sexual fetish involving the display of nudity in reflective surfaces. *Sexuality.*

2003 Graham Brough *Mirror* (U.K.) (Sept. 9) "Get Your Bids Out for the eBays," p. 18 ► Reflectoporn—the way exhibitionists get their nude bodies seen by millions around the world—swept America first and has now spread to the UK. **2004** *Fleshbot* (May 14) "eBay Item of the Week" (Int.) ► Reflectoporn might have been the big eBay porn craze that wasn't, but we've been seeing a lot of otherwise ordinary auction items modeled by some very extraordinary looking women lately, like this perfectly hideous men's jacket which showed up on eBay Germany last week. **2004** *NewYorkish* (Apr. 8) "The Department of Sad, Sad Hobbies" (Int.) ► This new "craze" is called reflectoporn and here's another explanation: "Sellers take a photo of the object they're auctioning in the nude and their naked body is reflected in its polished surface."

rehat *v.* to outfit military personnel in different uniforms in order to show a change of allegiance or authority. *Military. Politics.*

1995 (*Agence France-Presse*) (Dec. 19) "US Troop Deployment Lags in Bosnia" ► "The French and British had two advantages we did not have. They had substantial numbers of troops on the ground already. They would just rehat their people." He said referring to the switch from UN blue helmets to NATO equipment. **2000** Nancy Soderberg (*Africa News*) (Feb. 7) "Soderberg Remarks to UNSC on Sierra Leone Peacekeeping Force" ► The United States supports the Secretary-General's recommendation to expand the mandate of UNAMSIL to take on the function of the departing ECOMOG forces, and we will vote for the resolution before us today. To ensure there is no gap in security, we support the "rehatting" of two battalions of Nigerian ECOMOG troops remaining in Sierra Leone. **2004** Samantha Power @ Sudan *New Yorker* (Aug. 23) "Dying in Darfur" (Int.) ► One policeman, riding a camel, was wearing the navy-blue trousers of the Sudanese police and the green camouflage top of the Sudanese Army. Others were loitering in the Kas market wearing crisp blue police uniforms, but their turbans, the rifles slung over their shoulders, and their flip-flops gave them away as former janjaweed. In the local parlance, they had been "re-hatted."

relo *n.* a move from one home to another; a person making such a move. [Clipping of *relo*cation.]

1981 Alan S. Oser *N.Y. Times* (Apr. 24) "Sluggish Resale Market for Houses Shown in Employee Relocation Data" ► Such insight was not available when corporations left their employees to handle their own moves, since the figures were too fragmented to collect. To some extent, "relo" services have now become a clearinghouse for resale data. **2002** Emma McLaughlin, Nicola Kraus *The Nanny Diaries* (Mar. 13), p. 244 (March 2003) ▶ The Wall Street kids all get relo money from their companies. You want to beat them out you gotta pay up front. **2005** Peter T. Kilborn *N.Y. Times* (June 1) "The Five-Bedroom, Six-Figure Rootless Life" (Int.) ▶ A rookie "relo," she decides, someone newly relocated to Alpharetta and to its traffic.

renderwall *n.* a bank or cluster of computers devoted to creating animation. *Entertainment. Jargon. Technology.*

1996 *Usenet: comp.unix.solaris* (July 30) "Newsletter Selections" ▶ Remember the movie Toy Story? Well, when Pixar did the rendering on that, they created their own supercomputer to do it. The supercomputer in question was dozens of rack-mounted Sun workstations sans monitors and with their cpus replaced by Ross hyperSPARCs. They called it the RenderWall. **2001** *Onfilm* (New Zealand) (July 30) "Going Postal," p. 15 ▶ We have also added a render wall for our effects and animation. **2001** *Usenet: alt.slack* (Dec. 21) "Re: Oh. My. Bob. LOTR. SPOILER&helllip; But Not Much of a Spoiler" ▶ I was kind of hoping that the CG would be something like "Meet the Feebles" on acid. But there might still be some hope for the Compaq "RenderWall" clusterphuk, if they can hook it up to a ukulele and a kazoo. **2003** Jennifer Hillner *Wired* (Dec.) "The Wall of Fame" (Int.) ▶ Churning out scenes like the destruction of Barad-dûr and the Battle of Pelennor Fields (with thousands of bloodthirsty CG Orcs) took 3,200 processors running at teraflop speeds through 10-gig pipes—that's one epic renderwall.

respeaker *n.* in broadcasting, a person who renarrates, summarizes, or describes a television program for recording in preparation for subtitling. *Media. Television.*

2002 *NHK-TV* (Japan) (Feb.) "First 'Kohaku Utagassen' Closed Captioning Service" (Int.) ▶ A "re-speaker," listening to the performer's speech during the program, utters the content of that speech into the speech recognizer, which automatically produces a caption script. **2003** M.J. Evans *BBC* (U.K.) (July) "Speech Recognition in Assisted and Live Subtitling for Television" (Int.) ▶ Script Capture supplements this with a re-speak system—using recognition trained to the re-speaker's voice—to produce transcripts for programmes for which none exists. ***2004** BBC* (U.K.) (June 6) "Job Specification" (Int.) ▶ A Day in the Life of a Respeaker. **2004** *Yomiuri Shimbun* (Japan)

(Aug. 13) "NHK to Add Closed Captions to Olympics" (Int.) ▶ In live closed-captioned broadcasts, staffers called respeakers translate the original audio content into speech-recognition software that creates the closed captions.

resume on a rope *n.* a backstage pass. *Entertainment. Music. Slang. United States.* [Ref. to the laminated cards on cords worn around the neck that authorize the wearer to have access to restricted areas at concerts.]

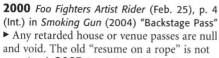

2000 *Foo Fighters Artist Rider* (Feb. 25), p. 4 (Int.) in *Smoking Gun* (2004) "Backstage Pass" ▶ Any retarded house or venue passes are null and void. The old "resume on a rope" is not permitted. **2003** [Kevin] *NadaBlog* (Sept. 14) "Beloit College Show" (Int.) ▶ Ah but Layne, with your "Resume on a Rope" (backstage pass), you could have run of the place.

retcon *v.* to retroactively revise (a plot, storyline, character, event, history, etc.), usually by reinterpreting past events, or by theorizing how the present would be different if past events had not happened or had happened differently. Also *n. Arts. Entertainment. Jargon.* [*ret*roactive + *con*tinuity] Long common in comic books, but now used in historical fiction.

1989 *Usenet: rec.arts.sf-lovers* (Aug. 16) "Re: A New Star Wars Film?" ▶ I'll confirm that: Lucas retconned the opening credits after the release of TESB, once it was clear that the films were doing well enough that the first set would be completed. Had SW bombed, no one would have known the plans for a set of nine. **1989** *Usenet: rec.arts.comics* (Dec. 22) "Re: Infinite Earths" ▶ "Crisis on Infinite Earths" solved a DC crisis all right, but it wasn't the problem of having multiple earths. It was the problem of 50 years of continuity complicating their existing characters.... "Crisis" let DC have good reason to retcon characters to whatever extent needed—heck, it practically demanded it. **2003** David Kipen *San Francisco Chronicle* (Calif.) (Aug. 10) "How Representational Work Was Overshadowed by Abstract Art" (Int.) ▶ In the useful and fast-spreading parlance of comic book fans, Dijkstra has boldly "retconned" most of 20th century American art history. That is, he's given it a new "retroactive continuity," rewritten it so that a discarded early movement suddenly becomes the consummation of everything that came before and a martyr to just about everything after.

reverse cowgirl *n.* a sexual position in which a man lies on his back while his partner faces his feet to straddle him. *Sexuality. Slang.*

1993 *Usenet: alt.sex.movies* (Nov. 23) "Nina Hartley 'DP' and Some More Ramblings on Euro-porn" ▶ Nice, "open" shots are preferred, reverse cowgirl being a favourite, particularly for anals.... It is a tiring position, particularly bad for the thighs; only really light or athletic women, like Candie Evans or Erica Boyer, perform it. **1997** *Usenet: alt.sex.wizards* (June 23) "Position Names?" ▶ *Reverse cowgirl* Gal on top, facing away from guy. **2004** [Disco Dirge] *DVD Talk* (June 26) "Wild on These" (Int.) ▶ Next, the pair performs an act often referred to in the slang jargon as "reverse cowgirl," which seems very funny since there is not a horse in sight.

reward car *n.* an (extravagant, frivolous, or impractical) automobile purchased as a gift to oneself when financial or personal goals have been achieved. *Automotive.*

1995 *Usenet: rec.autos.driving* (Mar. 9) "Re: Questions: Merkur XR4TI" ▶ I have made engine refinement a top priority when I buy my post grad-school reward car. **1996** Mark Savage *Milwaukee Journal Sentinel* (Wisc.) (May 8) "Automakers Play 'Can You Top This?' Convertibles Still Stir Competitive Juices," p. 1 ▶ Our feeling is that Boomers are still in the market for a reward car and there will be a long, stable market for convertibles. **2005** Alex Williams *N.Y. Times* (June 10) "What Women Want: More Horses" (Int.) ▶ There is no single category of female "reward car," as some in the auto industry call such purchases. But analysts see increases in the number of middle-aged women buying all sorts of nonfamily cars.

rexing *n.* organized or competitive rollerskating to dance music; *roller disco*; (*hence*) a leg-scissoring movement in skating sports. *Sports.*

1980 Andrea Kamin *Globe and Mail* (Toronto, Can.) (May 22) "Snapping Feet to the Downbeat at the Rink," p. T1 ▶ He says the term roller disco is hard to define because different regions have different styles of roller disco. In the United States, skaters call it jammin', in the West it is called rexing, and in other parts of Canada it's called boogie. **2000** Audrey Bakewell *Get the Edge* (Jan. 1), p. 81 ▶ The Rexing movement will help to develop agility and increase foot awareness. Rexing is an in-line skating term. It is a combination of In and Out and the Crossover Tuck. With both blades on the ice, push out then glide together, moving into the crossover tuck position. **2005** John Tanasychuk *Sun-Sentinel* (Ft. Lauderdale, Fla.) (July 9) "Jam on a

Roll" (Int.) ▶ Sometimes called "rexing" or "bounce skating," jam skating is to roller skating as snowboarding was once to skiing.

rice bowl *n.* in the military, a jealously protected program, project, department, or budget; a fiefdom. *Military.* [Perhaps related to the Chinese concept of the *rice bowl* as a metaphor for the basic elements required to live, as seen, for example, in the *iron rice bowl*, employment that is guaranteed for life.]

1982 Richard Halloran @ Washington, D.C. *N.Y. Times* (Nov. 23) "How Hornet Was Stripped of Values It Began With" ▶ But some also comes from an institutional, bureaucratic drive to have more airplanes and a bigger share of Navy and Defense Department budgets. "The airsystems people saw that whole program as a gigantic rice bowl they could put their hands into," a critic in the Pentagon said. **1990** Fred Kaplan @ Washington, D.C. *Boston Globe* (Mass.) (July 29) "In House, Bipartisan Drive Is Growing to Slash Defense," p. 2 ▶ Gingrich pledged "to cooperate in any way I can on a bipartisan basis in really rethinking all of this" because the effort is "going to require not only reshaping the rice bowls at the Pentagon but breaking a few of them." **1994** *Defense Daily* (Sept. 15) "Army Seeks Moral High Ground in Briefing to Roles Panel," vol. 184, no. 53 ▶ Attempting to take the moral high ground in a debate that in the past has been characterized by high emotions as each service sought to protect its own "rice bowls," the Army leadership avoided suggesting to the commission ways that the functions the military services perform could be restructured. **1997** Hal Gerhanoff *Journal of Electronic Defense* (Feb. 1) "Empty Rice Bowls," vol. 20, no. 2, p. 10 ▶ The composition of QDR architects is likely to produce another rubber-stamp picture of where spending priorities should remain, thus protecting the iron rice bowls of tactical air supremacy aircraft, carriers and subs, stealth platforms and those other expensive systems better suited to fight the last war than the next one. **2001** Scott C. Truver (*United States Naval Institute: Proceedings*) (Oct. 1) "Where Is the All-Electric Navy?" vol. 127, no. 10, p. 99 ▶ To be sure, there remain hotbeds—maybe "rice bowls" is more apt—of interest in IED and IPS in and out of the Navy.... Several government officials conclude that Secretary Danzig's corporate approach cannot work unless the service overcomes its penchant for rice bowls, and a single agency has the responsibility and authority to make decisions and allocate resources. **2005** Matt Wickenheiser *Portland Press* (Maine) (May 20) "Strategy X Looks at the Big Picture" (Int.) ▶ But funding was sparse, and everyone had their own "rice bowl," he said—a military term describing jurisdictional jealousy.

ridonkulous *adj.* (very) ridiculous. Also **ridonculous, redoncu-lous, redonkulous, redonculus, redonkulus, ridonculus, ridonkulus, redunculous, redunkulous, ridunkulous, riduncu-lous, ridunkulus, redunkulus, redunkulus, ridunkulus.** *Slang.* This word is different from *ridorkulous,* 'extremely dorky.'

1998 *Usenet: alt.fan.backstreet.boys* (Aug. 20) "Another Huge One!!"
▶ Phrases Or Words: ferociously redonculous, and KTBPA. **2000**
Usenet: alt.video.dvd (Dec. 18) "Re: Smoking Pot and Watching DVD
Movies" ▶ I just finished a well-conceived brainstorm that concluded
this thread is ridonkulous only if you continue to read. **2001** *St. Paul
Pioneer Press* (Minn.) (July 20) "How Cold Is It? Oh, Look at That Poor,
Shivering Dog!" p. E3 ▶ The other driver's insurance company is
claiming they have to determine liability...which, to me, is a bit
redonkulous (to steal a word from my brother), seeing as how I was
nowhere near my car. **2004** *Telegraph* (U.K.) (Oct. 16) "Guide to OC
Vocabulary" (Int.) ▶ Ridonkulous—Deserving or inspiring the highest
level of ridicule, as in: "Dude, I cannot believe you live in a
penthouse, man. This place is ridonkulous"—(Seth to Oliver).

rinse *n.* in New Zealand, the drug Gamma-hydroxybutyric acid, also
known as GHB. *Crime & Prisons. Drugs. New Zealand.*

2002 *Usenet: nz.general* (N.Z.) (Oct. 29) "Does Anyone Know What
Drugs Make Up 'Rinse'??" (title). **2003** [Gargoyle] *Twisted* (N.Z.)
(Feb. 4) (Int.) ▶ I've heard that a regular hit of "rinse" (GHB) in
wellington is something like 30ml. **2003** *Dominion Post* (N.Z.)
(Aug. 6) "Coroner Condemns Fatal Fantasy Drug," p. 6 ▶ Some of the
people at Mr. Ferretti's home that night said he had previously sup-
plied them with drugs, including Rinse, a form of Fantasy. **2004**
Dominion Post (N.Z.) (June 8) "New Leads in Nightclub Drug Overdose
Case" (Int.) ▶ Fantasy is a class B drug also known as Rinse, GBH or
GHB, after its chemical name gammahydroxybutyric acid.

roadblock *n.* a program broadcast simultaneously on more than
one television channel. *Entertainment. Jargon. Media.*

1984 Tom Shales *Washington Post* (Oct. 3) "Panning the Reagan Show
TV Privileges Abroad, House Democrats Charge on the Air" ▶ The great
advantage Reagan enjoys is the three-network whammy, what
Matthews calls a "roadblock." When Reagan speaks on all three networks at once, he is making it very difficult for viewers to avoid him,
but the Democrats rarely enjoy this advantage when they finally get
air time to make their responses. **2004** *Electronic Urban Report*
(Apr. 27) "Headlines" (Int.) ▶ The Minnesota Music Man and his
newest label affiliation, Columbia Records, has hooked up with five

Viacom music properties that will conduct what's known in broadcast parlance as a roadblock. MTV, MTV2, BET, VH1 and VH1 Classic will simultaneously broadcast a 30-minute Prince concert special.

road diet *n.* the reduction of a roadway's width or lanes, intended to change traffic patterns. *Architecture. Automotive. Jargon.*

1999 Dan Burden, Peter Lagerwey *Road Diets: Fixing the Big Roads,* p. 3 (Int.) ▶ The Road Diet. "Road dieting" is a new term applied to "skinnying up" patients (streets) into leaner, more productive members of society. **2000** Dan Hulbert *Atlanta Journal and Constitution* (Ga.) (May 19) "Bicycling Advocate Dennis Hoffarth Leads the Campaign to Make Atlanta More Bike-Friendly," p. 1C ▶ DeKalb County says it will convert a section of North Decatur Road from four car lanes to three car and two bicycle lanes, the first "road diet" project of its kind in the metro area. **2001** Rai Demopoulos *London Free Press* (Ontario, Can.) (Apr. 2) "Road Growth Not Always the Answer," p. A13 ▶ When roads were actually closed, or their capacity severely reduced, 20 per cent to 60 per cent of the former traffic disappears entirely. It isn't even siphoned off onto other roads. People just travel less. Some experts scoff, but cases of accidental or deliberate "road diets" prove the point. **2004** Jessica Vanegeren *Post and Courier* (Charleston, S.C.) (Nov. 13) "Why Did the Shopper Cross the Road?" (Int.) ▶ The concept of dropping lanes to improve pedestrian safety, which also tends to benefit street-side businesses, is known as a road diet.

road to Damascus *n.* a religious conversion; a revelation, especially about one's self; in other figurative uses, denoting a change in attitude, perspective, or belief. Also **road to Damascus experience.** From the biblical story of St. Paul, who converted from Judaism to Christianity while traveling on the road to Damascus.

1899 *Chicago Daily Tribune* (June 17) "Delay in Arbitration Plan" (in The Hague), p. 2 ▶ The correspondent of the Daily News at The Hague, who asks whether the Kaiser has found his road to Damascus, says: "A cabinet messenger arrived here this morning from Berlin with fresh instructions to Count Munster. They were of such a nature that several delegates remarked that a new situation had been created thereby and they must write home for fresh instructions." **1910** *State Journal* (Lincoln, Neb.) (Aug. 21), p. 5 ▶ Mr. Roosevelt has always been a progressive, but never an insurgent. Is he now on the road to Damascus? **1979** H.W. Somerville *Globe and Mail* (Toronto, Can.) (Nov. 21) "Parizeau Profile," p. P7 ▶ There is nowhere any mention that on his Road to Damascus, from federalist to separatist, Mr.

Parizeau was defeated as a Progressive Conservative candidate. **1993** Peter Davies *Modern Homosexualities* (Nov. 1) "The Role of Disclosure in Coming Out Among Gay Men," p. 75 ► There are those who regard coming out as a "road to Damascus" experience, a single moment of recognition of one's "true" self, a gestalt shift in which the label of the derided other is applied to one's self. **1995** Dan T. Carter *The Politics of Rage* (Oct. 27), p. 254 ► The Washington summit did not prove a road-to-Damascus experience. Within twenty-four hours, Wallace, back on CBS's *Face the Nation*, once again attacked the media for its use of "unmitigated falsehood" to slander the people of Alabama. **2005** Steven Church *News Journal* (Del.) (Apr. 24) "Big Money, Big Speakers, Big Sound" (Int.) ► I refer to it as a "road to Damascus" experience.... When they hear that sound, they realize they have never heard anything like it before, and it absolutely changes their life.

roasting *n.* group sex involving one woman and more than one man. *Sexuality. United Kingdom.*

2003 *Daily Star* (U.K.) (Oct. 5) "It's Called 'Roasting,'" p. 4 ► Top young footballers driven by lust regularly lure young girls for group sex—and they call their sick post match sex games "roasting."..."It's not unusual for a girl to s**g all of us," said Meikle, who explained that the game gets its name from roasting a chicken. "It gets stuffed." **2005** Alex Peake *Sun* (U.K.) (Apr. 11) "Dyer Fury at Web Sex Slur" (Int.) ► The term "roasting" is slang for group sex between a woman and several men.

robo-call *n.* an automated (telemarketing) phone call. *Technology. Robo*, from *robot*, is a long-standing prefix used to indicate automation or mechanization.

1991 *Usenet: comp.org.eff.talk* (Apr. 13) "Re: Retaliate Against Robot Salesmen (Update)" ► Last time I got robocalled, the discussion went something like: "Would you like blah blah blah insurance information...?" **1994** *Usenet: comp.society.privacy* (July 9) "Re: Question About CallerID" ► If they continue to call (or if it's a robo-call) then (don't know about availability in other states) start hitting *57 (call trace) which logs the number with the phone company as a harassing call. **1995** Laura Brooks *Arizona Daily Star* (Sept. 14) "Voice Mail Is a Boon to Some, But a Hang-Up for Others," p. 1B ► Cochrane's employer recently turned to Robo-call. Last month, Montgomery Ward's credit department switched on an automated...number—and immediately heard the wrath of its customers. **2004** Alexandra Pelosi @ Napoleon, Ohio *Sneaking into the Flying Circus* (Oct. 31), p. 264 (May 3, 2005) ► These women actually believed that a campaign robocall was Arnold himself calling, and from the excitement that her story generated it was clear that people love getting woken up by celebrities. **2005** Justin Fenton *Baltimore Sun* (Md.) (July 27) "Nation in Grip of Record Hot Spell" (Int.) ▶ In the city, an automated message from Mayor Martin O'Malley—a "robo call," his office termed it—alerted seniors to their options regarding relief from the heat.

robotripping *n.* the recreational use of over-the-counter cough syrup for its narcotic effects. Also **roboing.** *Drugs.* This is also known as **dexing** and **tussing,** the latter from the cough syrup brand name "Robitussin."

1991 *Usenet: alt.drugs* (Dec. 22) "Acid and Robitussin" ▶ I have found robotripping to be VERY much like tripping on acid. **1992** *Usenet: alt.drugs* (Feb. 12) "Dextromethorphan Hydrobromide (Delsym)" ▶ I first became interested in the articles about Roboing. I have been doing Robo for about six months. **1992** *Usenet: alt.drugs* (Aug. 26) "Re: Robo" ▶ Drink robo only if you can't get any acid. I've roboed about 20 times in the last six months or so, and I hope I don't ever have to do it again. **1996** *Usenet: alt.drugs.pot* (Aug. 10) "Need Answers on 'Robotrip'" ▶ Anyone who has exact information about Robotripping, could you please e-mail me immediately? I'm curious to its required dosage. **1997** Peggy Fletcher *Salt Lake Tribune* (Utah) (May 4) "U Too Need Jesus, Christian Rockers Say; Concert Rocks for Jesus Christ," p. B1 ▶ He mesmerized the audience with tales of being shot 13 times and attacking opponents while "roboing"—being high on the cough syrup Robitussin. **2005** Sheryl Ubelacker *London Free Press* (Ontario, Can.) (Feb. 28) "Syrup Heads" (Int.) ▶ In fact, the growing use in North America of these drug-store stalwarts has spawned a whole new lexicon, including "robotripping" and popping "Skittles," "Red Devils" and "Triple Cs," the latter the street term for Coricidin Cough and Cold. Those who take them for a high are called "syrup heads."

rocket surgery *n.* a task requiring intelligence or higher education; a difficult undertaking. [A blend of *rocket* science and brain *surgery.*] Often used jocularly in negative constructions similar to "It's not rocket surgery."

1994 *Usenet: alt.prose* (Jan. 29) "Twins" ▶ He usually mutes or ignores the commercials, but one day he finds himself drawn in, watching people do the things he'd always imagined he would do: trapeze artistry, rocket surgery, paleo-indian lifestyles. **1994** Francis X. Clines *N.Y. Times* (Aug. 7) "On Sunday in Boot Camp, Rough Drafts Get Fit to Film," p. 35 ▶ "In a way, movie making is rocket surgery,"

Mr. Gordon says of the Hollywood mélange that beguiles him so. "It's a very quirky art form that intersects with business." **2005** Jim Sullinger @ Topeka, Kan. *Kansas City Star* (Kan., Mo.) (July 3) "Legislative Lingo" (Int.) ▶ One legislator, mixing metaphors in referring to a simple concept, called it "rocket surgery."

rocking chair job *n.* an occupation or employment that requires little work; a sinecure. *Employment.* The *Dictionary of American Regional English* includes the term *rocking-chair money*, 'unemployment compensation or another benefit paid to someone who is not working.' The first 2000 citation probably refers to a job with a great retirement plan.

1919 *N.Y. Times* (Oct. 2) "Urge Pay Increase Before Aldermen," p. 36 ▶ One way to finance a rise in wages, he said, would be to get rid of secretaries to secretaries, rocking chair jobs and jobs that overlapped. **1925** *Washington Post* (Feb. 17) "Batting 'Em Out in the Hot Stove League," p. 21 ▶ It will be no rocking-chair job for whoever does the catching for the St. Louis Browns next season. **1934** *Syracuse Herald* (N.Y.) (Feb. 22) "Draft Dodger Bergdoll Denies Bribery in Escape" (in Philadelphia), p. 2 ▶ I could easily have bribed myself into a rocking chair job in the Army or Navy during the war and would have avoided all the trouble I had. **1951** Edwin Schallert *L.A. Times* (Oct. 7) "In Movie Field, Gene Kelly Proves a Quintuple Threat," p. D10 ▶ I could even welcome just a straight lead for a change, because that's really a rocking-chair job. **1988** Joe Donnelly *Newsday* (Long Island, N.Y.) (Oct. 12) "Meanwhile...A's Wait Pitchers Get in Their Cuts in Workout," p. 138 ▶ Most people seem to think the American League manager has a rocking chair job. That's ridiculous. A manager always has to make a decision on his pitcher. **2000** Rudolph Daniels *Trains Across the Continent* (Dec. 1), 2 ed., p. 219 ▶ *Rocking Chair.* Retire on a pension. *Rocking Chair Job.* Working on a diesel switcher. **2005** Winston Ross *Register-Guard* (Eugene, Ore.) (May 30) "Coastal Towns Seek Formula for Success" (Int.) ▶ A lot of timber workers referred to it as the "rocking chair" industry, because timber workers spent a lot of time on their porches in rocking chairs during the bust time.

roforofo fight *n.* a political battle in which no participant is unsullied; a *mud-slinging contest. Nigeria. Politics.* [This was popularized by, if not originated by, the 1972 song "Roforofo Fight" by Nigerian musician Fela Anikulapo Kuti. The first part of the term is apparently the reduplicated Yoruba word *rofo* 'mud.']

2000 Mideno Bayagbon *Vanguard Daily* (Lagos, Nigeria) (June 21) "13% Derivation War Coming" ▶ The war gongs are already primed, trenches are being dug, and the various troops are moving into positions. Nothing, it seems can stop this fight that promises to be what the late Afro beat musician, Fela Anikulapo Kuti, described as a rofo-rofo fight. **2000** Sufuyan Ojeifo @ Abuja *Vanguard Daily* (Lagos, Nigeria) (Nov. 5) "Na'Abba vs. Obasanjo: The Lingering Blackmail" ▶ Nigeria's Lower Legislative Chamber is involved in what the Yoruba call roforofo fight with the Executive arm of government headed by President Olusegun Obasanjo. Participants in such a fight cannot escape being badly messed up or roundly stained. **2001** [Aiyekooto] *Tempo* (Nigeria) (Feb. 15) "Of Under 50s and Veterans" ▶ I just love reading them—I mean the young ones lambasting the old ones and the old ones almost raining curses on the young ones. That is the politicians and aspiring politicians.... The genesis of this rofo-rofo fight, to my mind, is simply frustration. **2003** Trevor Schoonmaker *Fela: From West Africa to West Broadway* (July 4), p. 192 ▶ In *Roforofo Fight* (1972), Fela Anikulapo-Kuti sings about a very angry friend who, against all the remonstrations of his colleagues, engages in a nasty brawl in a pool of mud with an unspecified assailant. Consequently, the mud (*roforofo*) claims both assailant and defender as the two brawlers come to "look like twins," their separate identities indistinguishable in their grotesque, muddied appearance. **2005** Funke Aboyade *This Day* (Lagos, Nigeria) (June 23) "An Ill Wind..." (Int.) ▶ They are taking no prisoners and what is known in local parlance as a roforofo fight is the only way they know.

rollator *n.* a wheeled walker used by the infirm to increase mobility. *Health.*

1996 Linda S. Mlynarek, Linda C. Mondoux *Nursing Homes* (Sept.) "Pulling Together for Restraint Reduction" (Int.) ▶ To improve this resident's gait, staff worked closely with him, helping him ambulate more regularly. Therapy staff taught him how to use a rollator walker. **1998** Thomas Petzinger Jr. @ Pittsburgh, Pa. *Wall Street Journal* (B1) (Oct. 2) "A New Rolling Walker to Get the Frail Moving Lacks Market Traction" ▶ Unlike a conventional "clomp and stomp" walker, a rollator glides over pavement, carpet, thresholds and grass on large rubber wheels—much like a shopping cart with brakes, but without a big basket. **1998** Jamal Roomi, Abebaw M. Yohannes, Martin J. Connolly *Age and Ageing* (Oxford, Eng.) (Nov.) "The Effect of Walking Aids on Exercise Capacity and Oxygenation in Elderly Patients with Chronic Obstructive Pulmonary Disease," vol. 27, no. 6, p. 703 ▶ We have assessed the effect of Zimmer, rollator and gutter frames on 6-min walking distance and on arterial oxygenation during exercise in elderly patients with COPD. **2004** *Semantic Compositions* (Sept. 28)

"Mechanical Ineptitude" (Int.) ▶ In order to facilitate a day of traipsing around malls, Mom SC therefore decided to surprise MGSC with a device she mistakenly believed to be a wheelchair. In fact, it is something called a "rollator," or a wheeled walker.

rosh katan *n.* an attitude of avoiding responsibility, of extreme self-interest, or of strict adherence to rules to the point of obstruction or absurdity; a person with such an attitude; in British English, a *jobsworth. Hebrew. Israel.* The Hebrew is ראש קטן 'small head.' The term seems to have originated in the Israeli military.

1985 David Bernstein *Times* (London, Eng.) (Aug. 10) "Israel: Exodus from a Land of Lost Promise," p. P9 ▶ This is all part of the phenomenon Israelis call Rosh Katan, literally "small head," an increasing concern with one's own personal life. **1986** Reuven Gal *Portrait of the Israeli Soldier* (Aug. 18), p. 132 ▶ This attitude was known among Israeli troops as "small head" (in Hebrew, "Rosh Katan"), meaning someone who avoids taking responsibility, initiating actions, or diverting from proscribed procedures and instead maintains a "low profile." **1990** Bradley Burston *Jerusalem Post* (Nov. 30) "The Making of the Next CGS," p. 5 ▶ Senior commanders have suggested recently that the demoralization and the Rosh Katan (anti-involvement) doctrine of anti-volunteerism have been potentiated by cuts in training time due to pressures of budget and border/territories patrol priorities. **2004** Tamar Nitzan *Joel on Software* (NYC) (Dec.) (Int.) ▶ As for the expressions (pronounced "rosh katan"—little head, vs. "rosh gadol"—big head). This expression comes from the IDF, and as most military language, doesn't quite translate into normal language. A "rosh katan" (literally "little head," and I actually think it is the original expression which derived most likely from "pinhead," the contrast later came in as a complement) is someone that does exactly what he's told. For instance, someone might be told to clean the barrel of their rifle. A "rosh katan" will strictly clean the barrel, perhaps leaving it useless because the trigger mechanism has sand in it, whereas a "rosh gadol" will clean the entire rifle and lubricate it so it's ready for use and doesn't rust. **2005** Ben Rothschild Neria *The Fool's Page* (Kfar Vradim, Israel) (Jan. 23) "Terms in the Israeli Mind" (Int.) ▶ When someone is "Rosh Katan," it means that he won't do anything unless told to. It means that he won't care for anything unless it hurts him.

rowback *n.* a reversal (of opinion, policy, or stated fact), esp. when intended to be surreptitious.

1963 Frank Johnson *Nevada State Journal* (Reno) (July 3) "Journalistic 'Rowback' Art He Hasn't Mastered," p. 9 ▶ A "rowback" is an important if little-known tool of the journalistic trade. It is the reporter's artgum eraser. If used skillfully enough, the readers will not even realize he has made a correction. **1988** Wilbur G. Landrey *St. Petersburg Times* (Fla.) (June 12) "Kinnock Thinks Again About Nukes," p. 5D ▶ A week ago, Kinnock began a famous rowback.... He still wanted to get rid of the Trident submarine missile systems contracted by Prime Minister Margaret Thatcher, he said in a television interview, "but the fact is that it does not have to be something for nothing. The fact is now that it can be something for something." **2003** Mark Hennessy *Irish Times* (Dublin, Ireland) (Oct. 1) "FF Lobby for Deal on Smoking Ban Grows," p. 7 ▶ The smoking ban, due to come into force in January, yesterday dominated nearly two hours of debate at the weekly Fianna Fail parliamentary party meeting. However, Mr. Martin rejected all calls for a rowback and insisted that the Government had no option but to go ahead with the ban. **2004** William Powers *National Journal* (Apr. 10) "Our Man Dan" ▶ Have you read Okrent on that "squirrelly journalistic dance step known to old-timers as a 'rowback'"? That's when a news outlet tries to cover up an erroneous story with a new story that conveniently neglects to mention the first one.

rubber ear *n.* an attitude or instance of rejection, refusal, or unresponsiveness; *the cold shoulder*. Also *v.*, to reject, refuse, or ignore. *Scotland.* Sometimes constructed similar to *give (someone) the rubber ear* or *get the rubber ear*. Although the first cite is from an American author, the term is far more common among Scots.
1981 William Diehl *Chameleon,* p. 88 ▶ Mooney was getting a rubber ear from listening to all the complaints and excuses, and the phone rang and Mooney snatched it up and snapped, "Forget it!" **1990** *Usenet: eunet.jokes* (Nov. 28) "Translators" ▶ It's helluva difficult tae try an type wi a Scottish accent, so any choobish flames wull just be rubber-eared. **1992** Tom Shields @ Washington, D.C. *Herald* (Glasgow, Scotland) (Feb. 11) "Sutch and Such as Those," p. 12 ▶ Predictably the Democratic Party election organisers are giving Curly a rubber ear. Equally predictably Curly is suing the Democratic Party. **1994** Stephen Mcginty *Herald* (Glasgow, Scotland) (May 21) "Stood Up and Counted," p. 25 ▶ There can be no greater put-down than a stand-up. A dissy, a rubber ear, or cold shoulder, only the names are changed to protect the guilty.... Can you imagine the stench in the streets if every guy or girl rubber-eared on a date, decided to wait until their dates came to their senses? **1998** Denise Mina *Garnethill* (May 1), p. 12 ▶ She was conducting a campaign to have the funding reinstated and was getting the rubber ear everywhere. **2004** Steven Rattray *Scottish Daily Record* (Glasgow, Scotland) (Dec. 8) "Football: Lossie Put the

Shutters Up at Last" ► Steven came up and spoke to me before the game saying he was not feeling too well but I gave him the rubber ear and told him he was playing and to get on with it. **2005** Hugh Reilly *Scotsman* (Glasgow, Scotland) (Apr. 20) "New Scheme with That Sinking Feeling" (Int.) ► It has called for the first module fee of £600 to be paid for by the taxpayer to raise morale among teaching's minions but the Executive has rubber-eared (oops, slipped into Glasgow patois) this request.

Rummy's Dummies *n.* a derogatory name for the U.S. military under the leadership of Secretary of Defense Donald Rumsfeld. *Derogatory. Military. Politics.* "Rummy" is a nickname for Mr. Rumsfeld.

2001 *NY Transfer News Collective* (NYC) (Dec. 21) "Mullah Omar, Entire Taliban Leadership Safe" (Int.) ► It's only the tribal leaders "loyal to the new Afghan government of Karzai" who are getting wiped out at the moment, thanks to the Taliban's superior counterintelligence convincing Rummy's Dummies to bomb them on...the Road to Kabul. Good title for a movie. **2004** *Usenet: soc.sexuality .spanking* (May 9) "Re: Another Paddling Cop" ► Love that "unauthorized photography" charge. It's probably all that will happen to Rummy's Dummies. **2004** Richard Kiefer @ Golden, Colo. *Rocky Mountain News* (Denver, Colo.) (May 26) "Letters" ► Just what did Rummy's dummies think Saddam and his cronies were doing while they were "fighting" a token war against "coalition" forces—knitting prayer shawls? **2005** Tim Appelo *Seattle Weekly* (Wash.) (Mar. 9) "A Rap on War" (Int.) ► The sharpest blow to Rummy's Dummies is a scene, shot long before the recent Rumsfeld press-conference debacle, wherein a gunner in mock-TV-news tones explains how safe he feels.

Rumtopf *n.* a dessert of fruit, rum, and sugar. *Food & Drink. German. United States.* [Ger. 'rum pot.']

1962 *Washington Post, Times Herald* (Aug. 9) "Old-Time Recipe Still Scores Hits," p. C16 ► A fine way to preserve summer fruits is the century-old method called potpourri or rumtopf or fruit crock. It's an assortment of fruits mellowed in liquor and sugar in a stone crock for several months to "ripen." **1972** Lillian Mackesy *Post-Crescent* (Appleton, Wisc.) (Nov. 19) "Holiday Menu," p. C1 ► The Rumtopf (fruit melange...) and Quiche...are easily made, but the lovely meringue and cranberry cream Vacherin...takes a little more loving care. **2004** Marlene Parrish *Plain Dealer* (Cleveland, Ohio) (June 2) "Yum! Rum and Berries Create a Syrupy Treat Come Winter" (Int.) ► If it's late spring, it's time to start a Rumtopf, the German word for rum pot. You store it for fall or winter use.

run the traps *v. phr.* to investigate or pursue all possible options. Also **run the trap line.** *Politics.* This term is especially common in politics. There is an American football term of the same name that refers to a type of offensive play.

1983 William Safire *N.Y. Times Mag.* (Feb. 27) "Right Stuff in the Bully Pulpit," p. 19 ▶ I ran the traps around the lexical trade, even asked my brother, who assured me it wasn't Robert Louis Stevenson. **1984** Allan Cromley *Sunday Oklahoman* (Oklahoma City) (Dec. 2) "Tip's Slips Won't Stop Re-Election" ▶ Jones said he is "running the traps" to determine whether he has the votes to seek a rules change when the Democrats caucus. If successful, he then would have to beat out Panetta, which would be a tough fight. **1991** Rebecca Boren *Seattle Post-Intelligencer* (Wash.) (Nov. 27) "GOP Strategist Reveals He Has AIDS" ▶ I ran the trap line to see how the votes were, and there just weren't enough votes. **1998** Bonny L. Herman *L.A. Times* (May 4) "First a Plan, Then a Solution to Transportation Problems," p. B15 ▶ The Valley Industry and Commerce Assn. (VICA) recently sent a delegation of local business executives to Washington, D.C., to build relationships with—and, we hope, influence—the nation's key legislative decision makers. In so doing, VICA ran the traps, meeting with the administration, Welfare to Work and the Department of Labor, among others. **2000** Duncan Hunter (*Political Transcripts by Federal Document Clearing House*) (Mar. 2) "House Armed Services Committee Holds Hearing on Implementation of Department of Energy Reorganization" ▶ When somebody down in the...operational area wants to affect a change or doesn't want to go along with the policy, they can run the trap line and go up through the back door and try to get somebody in your office to change it. **2001** Jim Barnett *Oregonian* (Portland, Ore.) (Feb. 19) "Wu Tries to Revive Tech Visa Idea," p. D1 ▶ In early 2000, Wu began "running the trap lines" of potential opposition. **2004** Ron Suskind *The Price of Loyalty* (Jan. 13), p. 44 ▶ The need to really "run the traps" on every potential presidential move was more important for this Bush than for his father or Gerald Ford, both of whom had vast experience in the federal government.

rusticle *n.* a stalactite-like underwater accretion formed by cascading rust on sunken iron ships. *Science.* [*rust* + ic*icle*] Nearly all citations found are associated with the RMS *Titanic.*

1999 Ken F. Jarrell, Douglas P. Bayley, Jason D. Correia, Nikhil A. Thomas *BioScience* (July 1) "Recent Excitement About the Archaea," vol. 49, no. 7, p. 530 ▶ Although iron bacteria are of primary importance in extracting the iron that forms the rusticle, the rusticles are composed of a community of perhaps dozens of microbial species.

2003 William J. Broad *Chicago Tribune* (Aug. 10) "Rust and Visitors Join Iceberg as Foes of Doomed Titanic," p. 15 ► Gaping holes have opened up in the *Titanic*'s decks, metal walls have slumped and rivers of rust known as rusticles, which look like brownish icicles hanging from the ship's iron plates, have multiplied so fast that in some places they cover the hull.

S

sack up *v.* to become bold, courageous, or forthright; to **NUT UP**, *man up. Slang.*

1994 *Usenet: alt.romance.chat* (Mar. 11) "Re: Love and Death" ▶ My only response to diablo is to sack up and grow a pair. **1998** *Usenet: alt.sport.lasertag* (Dec. 2) "Re: You Should Not Assume Anything" ▶ I have the balls to jump into the fire instead of letting it fizzle to a spark before stomping on it. When you learn this and sack up maybe, just maybe you'll get some respect for your mediocre smack talent. **2000** *Usenet: misc.fitness.weights* (May 23) "Butch Up Heard in Movie" ▶ I heard the term "butch up" while watching "Die Hard with a Vengeance" last night.... I have transgressed the term to be more encompassing to be used more like "grow some balls," "sack up," "have some integrity," etc. **2004** [Rob] *My "Other" Blog* (Aug. 10) (Int.) ▶ I should probably just sack up and be honest with myself and with her.

sag wagon *n.* at a bicycling event, the vehicle that carries bicyclists who have withdrawn from the event (due to injury, bicycle malfunction, tiredness, etc.). *Sports.*

1967 *Commonwealth Reporter* (Fond du Lac, Wisc.) (June 16) "State Plans New Event on Bikeway," p. 8 ▶ A "sag wagon" will follow the riders to pick up any who have mechanical difficulty or find the ride too strenuous. **1978** James T. Yenckel *Washington Post* (Aug. 27) "Wheeling Away the Days," p. H9 ▶ The van became very important to us during the week.... Because it picked up weary cyclists unable to finish the day's route, it was dubbed the "sag wagon." **1994** *Usenet: dc.biking* (Aug. 24) "PPTC Sep 1994 Ride Schedule" ▶ Non-cycling jobs at Club events (registration, sag wagon, etc.). **2004** Doug Harlow *Morning Sentinel* (Waterville, Maine) (Sept. 16) "Cyclists Visit Waterville En Route to Key West" (Int.) ▶ The cyclists said they carry about 10 pounds of weight with them when they ride. The rest of their equipment and belongings travel with Barrett in the support vehicle or "sag" wagon, as they call it.

sale-manageback *n.* a financial arrangement in which a property is sold, then managed by its former owner for a cut of the profits. Also *attrib. Business. Jargon. Money & Finance.* This is similar to a *sale-leaseback.*

1994 *Lloyd's List* (U.K.) (Apr. 29) "One Ship Line," p. 5 ► Vard, Kloster's parent, is planning a wholesale sell-off of assets to tackle its mountain of debt. What is more saignificant [*sic*] is that Kloster will keep operational management of the ship for a two-year period, which may well be extended if things go well. A sort of "sale and manage back" arrangement into which some industry majors might be tempted for their older tonnage. **1999** *Business Wire* (Nov. 15) "Regent Assisted Living, Inc. Announces 1999 Third Quarter Financials" (in Portland, Ore.) ► During September 1999, Regent sold to its Chairman and Chief Executive Officer its 108-bed Scottsdale, Arizona, community under a sale-manageback arrangement. As a result of the sale, Regent generated approximately $1.2 million of cash available for general working capital requirements.... Regent continues to manage the community pursuant to a long-term agreement. **2005** Martin Flanagan *Scotsman* (Glasgow, Scotland) (Mar. 15) "Finance Directors Calculate Odds on Further Change" (Int.) ► The group has decided that the inelegant neologism "sale and manageback" will create less value for shareholders than the more straightforward "get-shot-of-and-no-mistake."

salvage *v.* to kill or assassinate. *Crime & Prisons. Philippines.* This meaning appears to be specific to the Philippines.

1983 *Globe and Mail* (Toronto, Can.) (Sept. 22) "Church Leads Way as Filipinos Urge Political Reforms," p. P17 ► According to the task force report, 1,082 Filipinos were "extra-legally executed or salvaged (a euphemism for assassinations)" between 1975 and 1983. During the same period, 266 others "disappeared." **2003** *Manila Standard* (Philippines) (Sept. 9) "Use Arnold in a Sentence" ► Ping is quoted as saying it would be "ridiculous for me to execute my own witness." The three-syllable word "execute" shows a marked improvement over that two-syllable Pinoy colloquialism, "salvage." Four-syllable words "assassinate," "exterminate" and "annihilate" cannot be that far behind. **2004** Patricio P. Diaz *Minda News* (Mindanao, Philippines) (July 13) "On Regrettables" (Int.) ► During martial law, "salvage" came into use in the Philippines to mean "to execute or dispose of a person summarily and secretly." Filipino journalists use it that way without regret. I wonder if it will ever be entered into reputable English dictionaries.

sandbox *n.* the Middle East; a country in that region. *Military.* Usually constructed with the definite article: **the sandbox.**

1990 Jim Klobuchar *Star Tribune* (Minneapolis-St. Paul, Minn.) (Sept. 22) "Maps from St. Paul Should Help," p. 1B ► The sergeant isn't excited about war in the desert, but he isn't sure that peace in the desert is a whole lot safer.... He had just three days to do laundry and convalesce before heading back into the sandbox. **1990** David Evans *Chicago Tribune* (Oct. 7) "For GIs, Fun Helps Battle Isolation in 'the Sandbox,'" p. 5 ▶ So what's there to do in what American soldiers here call "the sandbox"?...The Saudi Arabian desert is "the sandbox." ("The only thing missing are swing sets," said one Seabee) and the nomadic local residents are known collectively, and rather affectionately, as "Bedouin Bob." **2003** Amy Schlesing *Arkansas Democrat-Gazette* (June 20) "Arkansas Answers 9/11 Call," p. 1 ▶ More than 150 U.S. troops died in the war with Iraq.... Every soldier, sailor, airman and Marine who has worked and fought in the "sandbox" has a story to tell. **2004** Malcolm Garcia *Oklahoman* (Oklahoma City) (Sept. 20) "War Reopens Old Wounds for Families" (Int.) ▶ Despite the proud family tradition, Edmonds, who suffers from post-traumatic stress disorder, had difficulty accepting Matthew's deployment to the "sand box," as he calls Iraq. **2005** Jonathan Allen *Fort Mill Times* (S.C.) (Mar. 3) "Soldier Writes Home While on Duty in Iraq" (Int.) ▶ More than four months in the Middle East—the "sandbox" as some soldiers call it—hasn't dampened his spirits any.

scanlation *n.* the translation of digitally scanned pages (of *manga*, a style of Japanese comic book, cartoon, and graphic novel); the translated works themselves. *Arts. Entertainment. Technology.* [*scan* + trans*lation*]

2001 [Metamia] *Part Time Pimp Seven* (Nov. 12) (Int.) ▶ ^_^ Lots of pretty fanarts to drool over. I also added some scanlations links. **2004** Jeff Yang *SF Gate* (San Francisco) (June 14) "Manga Nation" (Int.) ▶ Would "Fruits Basket"...have been picked up for U.S. release without its overwhelming popularity on scanlation sites? Possibly— but the built-in fan base scanlators provided has helped turn the series into one of TokyoPop's best-selling titles.

scarlet letter *n.* a license plate that indicates the automobile's owner has been convicted of driving while drunk. *Automotive. Crime & Prisons.* [This is a more specific sense of *scarlet letter* 'a badge or symbol worn to indicate the bearer has committed a crime,' often used figuratively. It originated in Nathaniel Hawthorne's 1850 book *The Scarlet Letter*, in which a scarlet-colored *A* was worn as punishment for adultery.]

1983 Susan Chira @ Albany, N.Y. *N.Y. Times* (May 3) "Further Measures to Curb Drunken Driving Studied in Albany" ▶ The two proposals...call for a study of the possible issuing of "scarlet letter" license plates to people convicted of drunken driving and the possible seizure of cars of people arrested on a charge of drunken driving. **1993** Jim

Massie @ Circleville, Ohio *Columbus Dispatch* (Ohio) (Sept. 2) "Court of Appeal; Fun-Loving Yet Serious Circleville Judge Makes an Impression," p. 1E ▶ The court became the first in Ohio to immobilize the vehicles of repeat OMVI offenders. Adkins also began ordering repeat offenders to put yellow license tags on their automobiles as "scarlet letters," he said. **2005** Amanda Erickson @ Albany, N.Y. *Press & Sun-Bulletin* (Binghamton, N.Y.) (June 17) "DWI Plates Would ID Offenders" (Int.) ▶ Two senators unveiled a measure Thursday that would require drivers convicted of three drunken-driving offenses in a five-year period, or four within 10 years, to purchase license plates with a number code that police could use to identify them as convicted drunken drivers.... In Ohio, the plates are known as "scarlet letters."

schmoopiness *n.* behavior that is excessively cutesy, precious, or adoring. This word—and the noun *schmoopy* 'a term of affection for one who is adored; a person who exhibits schmoopiness' and the adjective *schmoopy* '(excessively) cutesy or adoring'—was popularized by, if not coined for, episode 116 of the television program "Seinfeld," first broadcast Nov. 25, 1995. The words are also frequently spelled with *shmoop-*. Despite the show's setting in New York City and the nebbishness of the character George Constanza, there's no evidence that this word is derived from a real Yiddish word.

1997 *Usenet: alt.tv.x-files* (Dec. 1) "Re: An Assessment of PMP" ▶ I never want to see kissing or any such schmoopiness going on between Mulder and Scully. **1999** Rod Dreher *N.Y. Post* (Sept. 17) "Little Love for 'Game': Costner's Latest Is Way Off Base," p. 43 ▶ "For Love of the Game" is another two-hours-plus Kevin Costner strikeout, a gassy baseball elegy suffocating in Lite-Rock schmoopiness and Costnerian self-regard. **2001** Tom Hill *TV Land to Go* (Dec. 4), p. 209 ▶ This episode is just as rich and thick as the Soup Nazi's mulligatawny, and we didn't even try to include the entire subplot in which George deals with Sheila and her "schmoopiness." **2005** *Johns Hopkins News-Letter* (Baltimore, Md.) (Apr. 15) "Hot at Hopkins" (Int.) ▶ Betsy likes a man who doesn't mind cuddling—or schmoopiness, as she calls it. And after all that schmooping, you'd better not be disrespectful, because disrespect is her pet peeve.

scraper *n.* an automobile, esp. a large passenger vehicle without prestige or current style. *Automotive. California. Slang. United States.* [Despite the obvious suggestion of *scraper*, automobiles called by this term do not seem to be low-riders or *lead sleds*.] This term appears to originate in and be specific to northern California, especially the San Francisco Bay area.

*2003 [ozzie94] @ Oakland, Calif. *CarDomain.com* (Dec. 10) "Ozzie's Oldsmobile: 'The Scraper'" (Int.) ▶ I got rid of the dubbs on my white scraper cause they rubbed too much so i slapped on the 17″ wit vouges from my other scraper. **2004** *Usenet: rec.music.hip-hop* (Jan. 31) "What's Your Area (in Regards to Hip-Hop)?" ▶ Basically just smashed around with my boy and some other folx in his 77 nova scraper (red, white top, red tints, spinners, man it's clean). **2004** [ototpnoy4o8] @ Sacramento, Calif. *Xanga.com* (Mar. 17) (Int.) ▶ I found out AK got locked up...at least that's what DT told me...he got caught ridin in his scraper guess and he didnt have his "L's." **2004** [Afgoutlaw510@yahoo.com] @ Fremont/Union City, Calif. *Craigslist* (Nov. 6) "1988 Chrysler Dynasty !!!!SCRAPER!!!!!!!!!!80k miles only— $1500" (Int.) (title). **2004** Shaheem Reid *MTVNews.com* (Nov. 8) "Hyphy: Crunk, Northern-California Style" (Int.) ▶ Minutes later, a vintage Buick—or, as they call them in the Bay, a Scraper—pulls up and all four doors pop open.

scrumtrelescent *adj.* excellent, fabulous, great. Also **scrumtrilescent.** *Slang.* [This word was popularized by the actor Will Ferrell on the television show "Saturday Night Live" in a skit parodying television presenter James Lipton, host of "Inside the Actor's Studio."]

2001 *Saturday Night Live* (Apr. 7) "Inside the Actor's Studio" (Int.) ▶ That show was delightful. No. No. It was brilliant. No, no, no, no. There is no word to describe its perfection, so I am forced to make one up. And I'm going to do so right now. Scrumtrilescent. **2003** *Usenet: rec.music.phish* (Nov. 13) "Re: Virgin Islands Question?" ▶ My wife and i honeymooned there after getting married on the beach at st. john. This was in mid-to-late May, and the weather was nothing short of scrumtrelescent. **2004** *Usenet: rec.sport.pro-wrestling* (Feb. 25) "Re: Victoria Is Skugly" ▶ She is not skugly, she's Scrumtrelescent! **2004** Charles McGrath *N.Y. Times* (Dec. 31) "Gentlemen, Start Your TV Sets" (Int.) ▶ In Act 2, the crew at West Coast Customs, a Los Angeles shop, filmed sometimes at fast-forward speed, strips the vehicle to bare metal and then renders it "scrumptulescent," as Xzibit would say.

seat of ease *n.* aboard a ship, a board overhanging water for defecation or urination; a toilet.

1869 Richard W. Meade *A Treatise on Naval Architecture and Ship-Building* (Philadelphia, Pa.), 2 ed., p. 467 (Int.) ▶ False Rail.—A rail fayed down upon the upper side of the main or upper rail of the head. It is to strengthen the head-rail, and forms the seat of ease at the after end next to the bow. **1992** Patrick O'Brian *The Truelove*

(May 1), p. 16 (July 1, 1993) ► Taking medicine meant swallowing improbable quantities of calomel, sulphur, Turkey rhubarb (often added to their own surgeon's prescription) and spending the whole of the next day on the seat of ease, gasping, straining, sweating, ruining their lower alimentary tract. **2005** Patricia Smith *Daily News* (Jacksonville, N.C.) (May 23) "QAR Dive Produces Interesting Artifacts" (Int.) ► It's a pissdale; it's essentially a urinal.... Basically it's just a tapered lead tube that leads from the "seat of case" as they called it out into the water.

security theater *n.* highly visible but ineffective antiterrorism or other protection and precaution measures. *Police. Politics.* A *security theater* is also a geopolitical area of military operations (a *theater of operations*) or a local area, such as in a company or home, under protection and surveillance. This term was popularized by, if not coined by, Bruce Schneier, a security expert.

2003 Tyler Hamilton *Toronto Star* (Can.) (Sept. 1) "Security-as-Theatre Intrusive, Ineffective; Smoke and Mirrors Security Fails," p. D4 ► Security expert Bruce Schneier likes to call it "security theatre." "Elected government officials are concerned about re-election and need to be seen by the public as doing something to improve security." **2004** *Spy Blog* (U.K.) (Dec. 8) "Hammersmith Bus Station Metal Detector Trial—More Ineffective 'Security Theatre'?" (Int.) ► Refusal to go through the detector seems to trigger a "you must have something to hide" response, tempered by the usual "ethnic" and "yoof" issues, which leads to a "normal stop and search" by the attendant Police Officers (a rare sight, normally). Yesterday, there were reports of false positives from mobile phones. Is this simply more security theatre? **2004** Seth David Schoen *Vitanuova* (Dec. 16) "In the Superior Court of California, County of San Mateo" (Int.) ► Many aspects of aviation security practice are still stupid and pointless, or, to be more polite and precise, they are security theater.

segotia *n.* good friend, mate, buddy, pal. Also **segocia, segosha.** *Ireland. United Kingdom.* [The historical information in the 2004 cite is plausible but unconfirmed.] The 1966 citation refers to the name of a racehorse.

1966 *Times* (London, Eng.) (Jan. 7) "Grand National Entries," p. 4 ► Me Oul Segocia. **1992** Dick Walsh *Irish Times* (Dec. 5) "Politicians Living in Terror of Real Change," p. 10 ► It's no longer the place where safely returned deputies spend their days, cracking jokes with old segocias before shuffling once more into the back benches for the start of the new Dail. **1999** Kenneth Wright *Herald* (Glasgow, Scotland) (Apr. 21) "Doctor Ross! I Think We're Losing You!" p. 36 ► After tonight's brush with the rules and regs...even his old segocia Carol won't back him up this time. **2002** Jamie O'Neill *At Swim, Two Boys* (Mar. 27) (Int.) ▶ "There was a day, Arthur, and you was pal o' me heart," said he, "me fond segotia." **2004** Diarmaid Ó Muirithe *A Glossary of Irish Slang* (Mar. 4), p. 118 ▶ *Me segotia*, or *me oul' segotia* are phrases as Dublin as they come.... Mr. Paddy O'Neill...was right when he glossed it as a Dublin Fusilier's word. *Me segotia*, Mr. O'Neill claimed, was originally said to children only, which is very important, as it confirms his theory that it was a corruption of some phrase like *mon cher gosse*, my dear child.

set it down *v.* to crash a motorcycle while riding it by dropping from a vertical attitude into a horizontal slide. *Automotive.*

1991 *Usenet: alt.drugs* (May 13) "Driving Under the Influence" ▶ You are not only more likely to set your bike down, but you are more likely to die when you set it down than to just lose some skin. **2004** Greg Lewis *OpinionEditorials.com* (May 12) "Kerry Redux" (Int.) ▶ While he was out riding said $6K bike over the weekend, he, in motorcycle parlance, set it down. Which is to say, he crashed it.

shack *n.* a direct hit on a target by a bomb or missile. *Jargon. Military.* [Perhaps from the actual shacks—'rude cabins or huts'—used in live-fire target practice.]

[**1998** Russell Watson *Newsweek* (Feb. 16) "Battle Stations: Plans Take Shape for an Air War on Iraq, But Success May Be Elusive," p. 38 ▶ Nearly all of them "hit the shack," meaning they came within 20 feet of the targets.] **1999** Ross Roberts (*United States Naval Institute: Proceedings*) (Apr. 1) "Desert Fox: The Third Night," vol. 125, no. 4, p. 36 ▶ I could see the bombs fly to the target on the FLIR...one second.... Direct hit. "Shack!!!" I shouted over the radio. (That's one term we picked up from our Air Force friends.) **2001** Steve Vogel @ Aboard the USS *Carl Vinson Washington Post* (Oct. 29) "Over Afghanistan, Gantlets in the Sky," p. A1 ▶ The operative on the ground radioed confirmation: "That's a shack," slang for a direct hit. **2003** Dave Goldiner *N.Y. Daily News* (Jan. 16) "Doubts Before Bombing." p. 7 ▶ Schmidt: "Shack" [jargon for direct hit].

shearography *n.* a method of detecting surface defects using lasers. *Jargon.* This is most common in the aerospace industries.

1986 Tom Drozda et al. *Tool and Manufacturing Engineers Handbook* (*Vol. 4: Quality Control and Assembly*) (June 1), 4 ed., p. 340 ▶ In shearography, the part being tested is illuminated by an expanding laser beam, and its image is taken with an image-shearing camera.... Two images are taken. One image is made of the part in the unde- formed state, and a second image is made after deformation. The processed film produces a fringe pattern that depicts the gradient of the surface displacements due to the deformation. **1988** William B. Scott *Aviation Week & Space Technology* (Dec. 5) "B-2 Bomber Devel- opment New Design, Production Tools Will Play Key Role in B-2 Cost," vol. 129, no. 23, p. 18 ▶ Skin-to-core bonding problems can be detected by the shearography technique through laser interferometry techniques. **2005** Rosemarie Bernardo *Star Bulletin* (Honolulu, Hawaii) (July 31) "Damien Grad Aids Effort to Fix Shuttle Tank Foam" (Int.) ▶ In the second project, Davis and his team developed a tech- nique called "shearography" to ensure that foam will not come off the tank during launch and ascent. Shearography uses a laser to detect defects.

sheisty *adj.* dishonest, shady, shifty, suspicious. Also **shysty, shi- esty.** *Derogatory. Slang. United States.* [From *shyster*, a dishonest person, esp. a lawyer.]

1993 *Usenet: alt.rap* (July 8) "Re: Pharcyde Show" ▶ The problem is they let EVERYBODY in! I saw kids there where probably no more than 16 years old. Once again, 7-Oasis does some shiesty shit. **1995** *Usenet: rec.arts.comics.misc* (Mar. 29) "why i quit collecting before i got started. hhhrrmmpphh!" ▶ i'll leave the actual collecting to shysty business men who take advantage of everyone they can. [**1999** Mark Whicker *Orange County Register* (Calif.) (Mar. 7) "Holyfield Becomes Champion Talker, Too," p. C1 ▶ "Bean's a shiesty fighter," he said. Shi- esty? "He didn't know what he was doing. So how did I know what he would do?"] **2000** Andrea Comer *Hartford Courant* (Conn.) (Apr. 2) "Outsider's View of Hip-Hop," p. G3 ▶ Their travails, the baby-mama drama, the "sheisty" record execs, the violence that comes closer than most of us will ever experience, are all documented in "Westside." **2003** Derek J. Moore *Press Democrat* (Santa Rosa, Calif.) (Mar. 4) "Lance Salazar Series: Where Are They Now?" p. D8 ▶ Playing in pool halls left him with the impression that most people are "shiesty" and hard to trust. **2004** *Curbed* (NYC) (Aug. 20) "Curbed Readers Report" (Int.) ▶ Regarding yesterday's rant against an unsavory real estate bro- ker, a savory broker emails, "It's too bad that shiesty brokers like the one in the FSBO story ruin the reputation for good, ethical brokers in NYC." **2005** Paul Light *Ultrablog* (Orange County, Calif.) (Jan. 18) "Shiesty?" (Int.) ▶ I've seen several bloggers use the term in different ways. In one case it seemed to mean "crappy," which makes sense if it's from the German "sheisse" (shit), but otter peeps don't use it like that. "She got shiesty on me," one blogger wrote, and in context it seemed to mean "weird" or possibly "suspicious." Definitely not "shitty."

shelf shout *n.* the attention-grabbing aspects of a product's appearance. *Advertising.*

1991 Amanda Burnside *Marketing* (Jan. 31) "Marketing Services Reports on the Creative Packaging Exhibition," p. 25 ▶ The level of interest expressed by the marketing world in the new exhibition is indicative of packaging's growing profile in the marketing mix. As advertising revenues rise and the recession bites, so the need for a point of difference, for competitive edge, for "shelf shout" has never been greater. **2002** Graeme Kennedy *New Zealand Business* (Sept.) "Special Printing, Packaging and Design Report," p. 40 ▶ Graphic design is vital for companies seeking "shelf-shout" for a new product or a striking public face that will reflect the company's quality and integrity through a business card or letterhead.

shi-shi *n.* urine or urination. Also *v.,* **make shi-shi** or **go shi-shi** to urinate. *Hawaii.* Reduplicated *shi,* from the Japanese *shiko* 'urine.' Also imitative of the sound of streaming water.

1992 *Usenet: soc.culture.japan* (Nov. 17) "Re: Hayari Kotoba (Fad Expressions)" ▶ In Hawaii there is a similar thing. When people (esp. old women) have to go to the bathroom they will say "I gotta five-four-four." Say "5-4-4" in Japanese and it's "go shi-shi." **1995** Kathleen Tyau *A Little Too Much Is Enough* (July 1), p. 42 ▶ One day while we were playing in the empty lot next to the sugar-cane fields, I saw Bobby make shi-shi behind a boulder. **2002** Jocko Weyland *The Answer Is Never* (Sept. 1), p. 224 ▶ In the cell next to mine, a husky Samoan girl yelled abuse at the cops, demanding to be taken to the hospital, then informing me she had to go *shi-shi* (piss). **2005** McAvoy Layne *Bonanza* (Incline Village, Nev.) (July 15) "Joe Rides with Lance for a Day in France, or Not," (Int.) ▶ Long about Silver City I realized I had to "make shishi," as they say in the Islands.

shit sheet *n.* a flyer, letter, or other document containing negative or false information about a politician or political organization. *Australia. Politics. Slang.* This term appears to be specific to Australia.

1995 Craig Cooper *Portside Messenger* (Adelaide, Australia) (May 24) "Anger Over Anonymous Pamphlet's 'Libel' of Councillors" ▶ Spence described the pamphlet as a "shit sheet," but said he was not hurt by the comments it made about him. **1999** Janelle Miles @ Gold Coast, Queensland (*AAP Newsfeed*) (Australia) (Feb. 8) ▶ I won't say who they are (but) they were distributing shit sheets amongst our members which said: "The AWU's finished. Join us." **2002** Kate Legge *Australian* (June 22) "Sleepers, Awake!" ▶ There have been two defamation actions, including one over a "shit sheet" of alleged indiscretions by Feeney's rivals. **2004** Steve Lewis *Australian* (Sydney, Australia) (Sept. 20) "Coalition Rolls Out Latham Bogeyman" (Int.) ▶ But this was no ordinary anti-Green rant from the party of free enterprise. In election parlance, Morrison's four-page glossy is known as a "shit sheet."

shmen *n.* a (college or university) freshman. Also plural. *Education.* This term is usually gender-neutral.

1985 William Safire *N.Y. Times Mag.* (Sept. 22) "T'sup on Campus," p. 14 ▶ Let us assume that "wench" is a current sexist way of making a masculine or neuter noun apply to women. We can hypothesize that "shwench" is a feminine form of "shmen." From this breakthrough, we can then ask: What word used frequently by sophomores has "shmen" as its last syllable? **1987** *Orange County Register* (Calif.) (Nov. 26) "Sports People," p. C2 ▶ His best wide receiver was out for the season after injuring a shmen, a sophomore and a converted quarterback to run the deep routes. **2004** Megan Peck *The Dartmouth* (Hanover, Conn.) (Sept. 10) "Storied Dartmouth Traditions Stand Test of Time" (Int.) ▶ The College now officially calls all new students "first-years" in order to be more inclusive and politically correct. However, the unique Dartmouth slang "shmen," which describes all new students, is still part of the common Dartmouth student's lexicon.

shoot a fair one *v. phr.* to have a weaponless physical fight between two people. *Slang. Fair one,* meaning 'a fight,' dates to at least as early as 1958.

[**1994** Gang Starr *Hard to Earn* (Mar. 8) "Suckas Need Bodyguards" ▶ At Madison Square I shot a fair one/so many niggaz knew me that the kid wouldn't dare run.] **1998** Juan Azize (Aug. 20) in *Things Get Hectic* Geoffrey Canada, p. 23 ▶ There was this time, last year, when my boy Duzer was supposed to shoot a fair one with another kid in school, so my little crew got together to keep it a fair fight. **1999** *Usenet: rec.music.hip-hop* (June 22) "Bitch Moves..." ▶ Niggas that NEVER wanna shoot the fair one. Always got an excuse though, "Nah, I dont do that one on one shit no more, I dont got time." Whats so scary about a head-up fight? **2000** *Usenet: rec.music.hip-hop* (Dec. 28) "Re: What Ever Happened to Gangs?" ▶ I always preferred to shoot the fair one 'cause I knew I'd win, but I didn't blame any kid that couldn't fight and said "Fuck that, I'm just gonna shoot your ass," 'cause if I was a dude that couldn't fight I probably would be like that too. **2004** Caroline McGill *A Dollar Outta Fifteen Cent* (Nov. 14), p. 252 ▶ Portia set it off on Michelle, the one who was fucking Wayne, and Simone backed her friends down with the gun so they could shoot a fair one. **2005** Andrew Wolfe *Nashua Telegraph* (N.H.) (Apr. 19) "Man Charged in Murder" (Int.) ▶ The woman said Davis offered to fight Pineda man to man, using a slang term "shoot the fair," after their first scuffle, but Pineda declined.

short eats *n.pl.* small snacks, especially meat or vegetable pastries, eaten in variety in a fashion similar to *dim sum* or *tapas. Food & Drink. Sri Lanka.* While this term is most common in Sri Lanka, it is also used in southern India and other parts of Asia. It dates back at least to the 1960s.

1986 Patricia Stamp, Stephen Katz *Globe and Mail* (Toronto, Can.) (Apr. 23) "It's Lush Eating in Sri Lanka," p. E1 ▶ Order "short eats," a lovely collective noun for various snacks, such as small patties, spring rolls, samosas, fritters, and small desserts of spiced flours, coconut and cashew nuts. **1993** *Usenet: rec.travel* (Sept. 28) "Sri Lanka Travelogue 1993" ▶ Go into a "short-eats" shop, and talk to people there! **1998** *The Hindu* (Sept. 21) "Fragrance and Food" ▶ The small, attractive vegetarian pantry at the entrance serves south Indian short eats like idlis, vadas and different varieties of dosas. **2001** Robert Bradnock *Footprint Sri Lanka Handbook* (Apr. 1), 3 ed., p. 341 ▶ "*Short eats*" a selection of meat and vegetable snacks (in pastry or crumbled and fried) charged as eaten. **2005** Wasantha Ramanayake *Daily News* (Sri Lanka) (Mar. 3) "Intruding Cop Busts Shorteat Vendor's Ears for Saying 'Hello'" (Int.) ▶ The Supreme Court decided to hold a full inquiry into the alleged Police assault on a "shorteats" vendor, who had been found fault for saying "hello" to a Police Sergeant lingering in the vendor's compound in the wee hours.

shoulder peak *n.* a period that precedes or follows regular peaks of heavy use or service, such as in television viewing or electricity consumption. Also **shoulder.** *Jargon. Media. Television.*

1976 *Herald-Times-Reporter* (Manitowoc/Two Rivers, Wisc.) (Feb. 27) "Electricity Rates Must Be Stabilized" ▶ Different rates would be charged electric power users during "super peak hours," "shoulder peak hours," and "off peak hours." **1991** Ian Tinker *Media Week* (20) (June 28) "Vimto Expands into Holiday Market" ▶ Shoulder peak/early peak—returning from the day out and preparing to go out for the evening. This segment also covers the popular soaps. **1999** *Guardian* (U.K.) (July 12) "Was It Worth It?" p. 6 ▶ With better forward-planning and more experimentation, those early successes can perhaps be consolidated with a wider range of programmes into "shoulder peak" as 11 o'clock is now fashionably known. **2004** Oliver Bennet *Independent* (U.K.) (June 28) "Never Judge a Book by Its Clubbers" (Int.) ▶ The show aired at 5pm on a Wednesday, a daytime slot called "shoulder peak" in TV jargon.

shrimp *v.* to suck (toes). *Sexuality.*

1998 *Usenet: alt.showbiz.gossip* (Feb. 1) "Re: Monica's a Psycho?" ▶ No, she did not shrimp my toes.... **2002** *Usenet: alt.discordia* (May 1) "My Date with Eris" ▶ My offer to shrimp her toes was turned down on the grounds that one either knew how to lick webbing or one didn't, and she wasn't going to teach me on the first date. **2004** Richard Ben Cramer *How Israel Lost* (May 4) (Int.) in *MSNBC* (June 16, 2004) "Should Israel Leave the West Bank?" ▶ Even the quieter monied Jews of Wall Street look like homeless next to Bush's pals in the oil bidness—pals who would just as soon see Israel go away so they could more comfortably shrimp the toes of the Arabs.

shut in *n.* in the petroleum industry, a production cap set lower than the available output (of an oil producing site). Also *attrib., v. Jargon.*

1887 *N.Y. Times* (Nov. 2) "A Big Deal in Oil" (in Pittsburg, Pa.), p. 3 ▶ The most important deal ever consummated in the history of the oil business was brought to a head at a late hour last night.... The great shut-down movement was completed in every detail, and the shut-down or shut-in will go into effect to-day. **1899** *L.A. Times* (July 24) "In the Oil Fields," p. 10 ▶ No. 16 flowed 10,000 barrels, which went to waste, before it could be "shut in." **1978** Thomas Kennedy *Globe and Mail* (Toronto, Can.) (Mar. 1) "Oil Supply Held Precarious, Gas Reserves Just Adequate," p. B1 ▶ About 300,000 barrels a day of wellhead capacity, representing about 70 per cent of Western Canada's potential production, is shut in. **2004** Stewart Yerton *Times-Picayune* (Baton Rouge, La.) (Sept. 21) "Dozens of Gulf Oil Platforms Idle" (Int.) ▶ Oil and gas producers moved workers from offshore rigs and platforms located throughout the central and eastern Gulf. This caused a hiatus in production, known as a "shut-in" in industry parlance.

shutter man *n.* in South Korea, a man who makes less money than his wife. *South Korea.* [So-called because the husband's only responsibility is said to be the raising and lowering of the shutters of his wife's shop.]

2004 Antti Leppänen *Hunjangûi karûch'im* (S. Korea) (May 7) "(Social Categories) Paeksu Thoughts" (Int.) ▶ One of the funniest versions of *paeksu* husbands are the so-called shutter men (셔터맨), men who only need to raise and lower the shutter of the shop of their wives. **2005** Shannon Turk @ S. Korea *Hey, I'm in Korea* (Chicago) (Feb. 4) "Korean Is a Language" (Int.) ▶ When a guy is married to a woman who makes more money than him, he is called a "Shutter Man" because all he has to do in the relationship is close the shutter, or rolling metal door, to the shop. This is equivalent to the american slang "Sugar Momma"...ha ha.

silo *other* attributively *silo* and as an adjective **siloed,** kept separate from similar items, especially in the case of funds, a budget line item, a department, etc.; *noun,* something that is kept separate or compartmentalized; *v.,* to keep separate, to **stove pipe.** *Business. Jargon. Money & Finance.*

1989 Keki R. Bhote *National Productivity Review* (Sept. 22) "Motorola's Long March to the Malcolm Baldrige National Quality Award," p. 365 ▶ Integrating related functions to break down artificial department walls and overcome the "vertical silo" syndrome. **1993** John H. Sheridan *Industry Week* (Oct. 4) "A New Breed of M.B.A.," p. 11 ▶ Part of the problem, critics contend, is that B-schools have suffered from a variation of the "functional-silo syndrome" that has hindered many companies' ability to quickly develop integrated responses to change. **1996** Laura Liebeck @ Troy, Mich. *Discount Store News* (Aug. 19) "Kmart Stakes Future on Team Buying," p. 1 ▶ The traditional "silo" approach to buying merchandise at Kmart is being dismantled, replaced by a team-buying concept. **2000** *Managed Medicare & Medicaid* (Feb. 21) "Medicare, Medicaid Rx Cost Survival Tied to Keeping Eye on FDA Pipeline," vol. 6, no. 7 ▶ Come budget time, however, HMO managers and executives may not feel that way as they tend to "silo budget," set a drug budget in isolation of a medical budget, for example. **2000** Barry Holman, Michael Brostek (*Congressional Testimony by Federal Document Clearing House*) (Mar. 9) "Civilian Personnel Readiness" ▶ Structures and work arrangements must be fashioned to avoid "stovepiping" (or "siloing") and draw upon the strengths of the various organizational components. **2003** Eric Chabrow *FSI* (Mar. 4) "State CIOs Losing Faith in Bush Administration Promises" (Int.) ▶ Gerry Washington told conference attendees that federal grants to pay for a health-alert network prevent its use by public-safety authorities, which requires the states to build a duplicate network, wasting taxes. "That's a real problem," Washington said. "We've got to get out of the silo-funding mode." **2003** *Usenet: talk.politics.medicine* (Apr. 28) "Re: Universal Health Care for Iraq But Not for the USA?" ▶ Under a managed care concept the incentives for comprehensive and continuous care override silo budget approaches common in Medicare and Medicaid systems. **2004** *Nottingham Evening Post* (U.K.) (Mar. 4) "Faith, Hope—No Charity Handouts" ▶ But they don't just dole out money and tell communities where to spend it. "That's what you call silo funding—pour money in at the top and let it just come out at the bottom." **2004** Richard S. Whitt *Federal Communications Law Journal* (May 1) "A Horizontal Leap Forward: Formulating a New Communications Public Policy Framework Based on the Network Layers Model," vol. 56, no. 3, p. 587 ▶ The Telecommunications Act of 1996, while largely sticking to the legacy regulatory "silo" regime, took a small step towards the horizontally layered engineering world in several respects. **2004** *LGCnet* (U.K.) (July 29) "Comment—Grip on Purse Strings Starts to Slip" ▶ There is still conflict between the aim of a joined up approach to children's services, and silo funding of schools. **2005** *AME Info FN* (Jan. 23) "Integration and the Customer Data Hub" (Int.) ▶ This information is not—and often simply cannot be—shared across the company, so it is referred to as the "silo" approach. **2005** Madan Sheina *ComputerWire News* (Feb. 11) "CXO Dashboard Breaks Siloed Approach to Risk Management" ▶ Risk management software firm CXO Systems Inc. has launched a new executive dashboard system that it claims will break traditional "siloed" approaches to risk management.

singjay *n.* a reggae performer who disc-jockeys and sings. *Entertainment. Jamaica. Music.* [*sing*er + dee-*jay*]

1984 Richard Harrington *Washington Post* (May 18) "The Startling Eek-a-Mouse," p. 44 ▶ He's a prime practitioner of a reggae style that's come to be known as "sing-jay," combining toasting (Jamaican-style rap) and singing in an elastic scat format that encourages a lot of rhythmically compelling and texturally impressive vocal embellishments. **1998** *Usenet: rec.music.reggae* (Mar. 17) "Re: Peter Metro" ▶ Good early 80's DJ stylee album, a little sing-jay style i would say, check his sweet version on the rougher yet riddim. **2003** Shanel Odum *Vibe Online* (Sept. 2) "Don't Sleep on the Bedroom Brits" (Int.) ▶ I like to speak on music—I'm a sing jay. I'm playing with the freestyle thing right now. **2003** Lady English *New Times Broward-Palm Beach* (Fort Lauderdale, Fla.) (Dec. 11) "Field Marshall" (Int.) ▶ Wayne Marshall is known in Jamaica as a singjay. The term comes from his ability to croon and DJ on a single track. **2004** Dave Stelfox *Independent* (U.K.) (Sept. 21) "Queens of Dancehall" (Int.) ▶ On songs such as "Turn the Other Cheek" and "What a Day" her "sing-jay" style—a blend of bouncy chatting and silken, soulful melody—proves the perfect vehicle for social commentary.

sitzprobe *n.* a first, rough rehearsal of an opera with singers and musicians, but without acting, scenery, or costumes. *Entertainment. German. Music.* [German for 'seated test' or 'sitting trial.']

1966 Reinhard Gerlach *Archiv für Musikwissenschaft* "Richard Strauss: Prinzipien seiner Kompositionstechnik (mit einem Brief von Strauss)," p. 287 ▶ Eine Separatorchesterprobe, eine Sitzprobe, eine Arrangirprobe mit Klavier, 3 Gesammtproben! **1988** *Sydney Morning Herald* (Australia) (May 19) "Half a Mo Won't Do for the Colonel," p. 18 ▶ I looked at the schedule and said, "What's a sitzprobe?" And they said, "Don't you know? Oh dear, you are ignorant." It's a German word which means sitting down and singing with the orchestra. First bandcall, I would have called it. **2005** Jesse Green *N.Y. Times* (Feb. 27) "No Greasepaint, Just the Roar of the Cast" (Int.) ▶ The sitzprobe—the German word originally came into musical theater from the world of opera and literally means "sitting trial"—is actually the rehearsal at which cast and musicians assemble to play through a score for the first time and hear the combined results of their separate endeavors.

skidiot *n.* an unsophisticated or unskilled self-styled black-hat hacker or *cracker* who uses computer- and network-intrusion software made by others; a script kiddie. Also **skiddiot.** *Technology.* [script *kid*die + *idiot*]

2001 *Usenet: rec.games.mame* (Feb. 25) "Re: What's the Name of This Game?" ▶ I unreservedly apologise for even trying to engage this "Skidiot" in even the simplest *reasoning process.* **2003** [method] *Zeropaid* (May 18) "Safest p2p Program" (Int.) ▶ The reason BayTSP can get on KaZaA is because there's a few skiddiot projects already out there for the FastTrack protocol. **2004** [Alistair Tonner Alistair@nerdnet.ca] *Netfilter mail list* (Apr. 18) "TARPIT Question (More Info)" (Int.) ▶ You could TARPIT them there, thus managing to minimize the use of resources on your box, whilst frustrating the scanner/skiddiot/twit on the other end.

skull *v.* in golf, to hit a ball too low and too far, usually the result of striking it above its center. *Sports.*

1950 Charles Curtis *L.A. Times* (Jan. 15) "Smiley Quick, Marty Furgol Fire 69s to Tie with Snead," p. 36 ▶ Howard (Curley) Schmidt...holed out a 6-iron for an eagle 3 at the 18th today. He admitted he had skulled a couple of woods before hitting that one. **1977** Dave Kindred *Washington Post* (Aug. 13) "Pebble Beach Gives Swift Kick to Fragile Dream," p. C1 ▶ Kelly Childs hit his tee shot out of bounds. Later, he hit into a trap and skulled his escape across the green. **2001** Bob

Rotella *Putting Out of Your Mind* (June 5), p. 159 ▶ Many amateurs, I know, worry about skulling or chili-dipping their short shots, particularly from tight lies. **2004** Jeff Potrykus *Milwaukee Journal Sentinel* (Wisc.) (Nov. 11) "Kicking It Up a Notch" (Int.) ▶ In golf parlance, Allen "skulled" both efforts. His right foot hit the ground several inches before the target and he basically hit the top of the ball.

skunk eye *n.* a facial expression of distrust or dislike; STINK EYE. This term seems to have been popularized by American talk show host David Letterman. It is often used with the definite article: **the skunk eye.**

1994 Frazier Moore *Salt Lake Tribune* (Utah) (Nov. 19) "Letterman Heads for Prime Time in First CBS Special," p. C7 ▶ "I came very close," says Dave [Letterman], flashing a skunk-eye in the direction of CBS headquarters. **1996** Usenet: *alt.fan.letterman* (Jan. 14) "Re: Skunk Eye" ▶ "Could someone please be so kind as to explain exactly what a skunk eye is?" "It's kind of an exaggerated, disapproving wink that implies 'I'm skeptical.'" **2000** John Limon *Stand-Up Comedy in Theory, Or, Abjection in America* (Nov. 1), p. 70 ▶ [David Letterman] is also oddly physical: he does facial shtick (the old skunk eye, for example); he plays with his suit; he imposes his body even as far as the camera. **2005** Rodney Rothman *Early Bird* (Apr. 26), p. 193 ▶ The strippers give you the skunk eye because they think you brought the pervert.

sleeve *v.* to decorate an arm with tattoos. *Fashion.* [Directly related to a *sleeve tattoo,* which covers the same arm surface a shirt sleeve might.]

1992 Tom Berg *Orange County Register* (Calif.) (Nov. 26) "Tattoos Are No Longer Just for Bikers and Felons as They Become a Fashion Accessory," p. O15 ▶ Aficionados prefer murals. They'll get "sleeved"—an entire arm's length of tattoos—or go for a chest panel or backpiece. **1995** Usenet: *rec.arts.bodyart* (Mar. 15) "Re: Return of 'Thematic Tattoos'" ▶ I'm also thinking about sleeving in an oriental style. **2002** Usenet: *alt.gothic.fashion* (May 19) "Tattoos for Women Magazine, Help :)" ▶ I am completely sleeved and my back is totally done now. **2004** [misterbeanz (Jay)] *Jay's Journal* (Oct. 31) "A Selfish Weekend Without Bria: Time with the Groove Fam" (Int.) ▶ I used to know a Kiwi tattoo artist back when I was getting sleeved.

slob *n.* a derogatory name for members of the Bloods gang, usually used by members of the Crips. *Crime & Prisons. Derogatory. Slang. United States.*

1993 Usenet: *alt.rap* (Dec. 3) "Heard the 5deuce Mob?" ▶ Theyz the hardest Bay Area shit ta ever come out, bar none. Although I only heard a few songs (East Side Red Rag, Fuck a Slob, Gang Related), theyz the shit.... They're shit iz on the Bloods&Crips tip. **1997** *Usenet: rec.games.video.sega* (Feb. 21) "Re: Street Fighter 3 to be a Saturn EXCLUSIVE!!!" ▶ You're a fucking Slob!!! BK for life motherfucker! This is a crazy CRIPS WORLD!!! **2004** John Stevenson *Herald-Sun* (Durham, N.C.) (June 18) "Terrorized Witnesses Worry DAs" (Int.) ▶ "Slob" is a derogatory street term for Bloods members.

slow elk *n.* stolen cattle butchered for food. *Animals. Food & Drink.*
1931 Paul Jensen *American Speech* (Dec.) "Desert Rats' Word-List from Eastern Idaho," vol. 7, no. 2, p. 120 ▶ A *slow elk* is the cattle *rustler's* (cattle thief's) term for a calf. **1938-39** *LOTJ* "Cow Punchers' Slang and Jargon" (in Utah, Tex., Ore., S.D., Colo., Ariz., Mont.), p. 17 ▶ Slow elk. Beef butchered without owners' consent. **1943** William MacLeod Raine *Chicago Daily Tribune* (Nov. 14) "Courage Stout," p. 22 ▶ Some were homesteaders, decent enough citizens, even if they might at times under the pressure of hunger eat slow elk. That's what they called rustled beef. **1979** A.A. Dornfeld @ Ill. *Chicago Tribune* (May 20) "Tow and Tell with Capt. Pete," p. 41 ▶ Someone else mentioned an unprincipled captain back in the lean '30s who was said to have sent a task force armed with shotguns ashore at rural stretches on dark nights to hunt "slow elk." If successful, the men returned bowed under the weight of beef steaks and roasts. **1989** Edward Hoagland *N.Y. Times* (May 7) "Edward Abbey: Standing Tough in the Desert," p. 7-44 ▶ The potluck stew was from two "slow elk," as he liked to call beef cattle poached from particularly greedy entrepreneurs on the public's wildlands.

slump buster *n.* an unattractive woman sought by a man for sexual relations in order to improve his sports-playing abilities or his involuntarily inactive sex life. *Offensive. Sexuality. Slang. Sports.* [This is a very specific sense of the more general *slump buster* 'something perceived to stop a losing streak, improve sports performance, or to increase sexual activity.' This sense's recent popularity stems from a 1998 interview on Jim Rome's syndicated sports talk show with Mark Grace, former first baseman for the Chicago Cubs, although the term is older than that.]
1994 *Usenet: rec.sport.football.college* (July 11) "A Midsummer's Night's Dream" ▶ I tried to be cordial to her and tell her that I'm sure she was mistaken...was she one that I may have spent some "quality' time with after 2 six-paks during a spring break trip of long ago? Maybe...she was what we used to call a slump-buster? **1998** *Usenet: alt.fan.jim-rome* (July 12) "Re: Get Ready for a Beating" ▶ Are you a slump-buster? Anyone jump on a grenade for the boys, with you lately? **2001** Robert Lipsyte *N.Y. Times* (Oct. 7) "Spoiled Athletes Have

Syndrome All Their Own," p. 15 ▶ Their husbands entertain us with their games and themselves with their "slump-buster" groupies. **2003** Dan Mcgraw *Hamilton Spectator* (Ontario, Can.) (Aug. 7) "All in the Game," p. B1 ▶ Arizona Diamondbacks first baseman Mark Grace commented a few years ago on Jim Rome's sports radio show about the concept of the "slump buster." When a batter is going through a hitting slump, Grace said the player must find an ugly (and preferably fat) woman. Sleep with her, toss her aside and, voilà, the slump is over. It's called "diving on a live grenade," Grace joked. **2005** Maureen Dowd *International Herald Tribune* (Feb. 21) "Back to Beauty and the Beast" (Int.) ▶ "God, I'm 0-for-20. I'm going to get the ugliest girl I can find and have sex with her."...Many of his fellow athletes did seek out "slump busters."..."It could mean the woman was big, or ugly, or a combination of both," Canseco explains.

smearing *n.* a climbing technique in which the soles of the shoes are used flat against the surface being climbed. *Sports.*

1984 David Wilck @ Moose, Wyo. *Christian Science Monitor* (Aug. 29) "Facing Down Fears and Scaling Peaks in the Grand Tetons," p. 19 ▶ Bridwell demonstrates the two types of foot holds: smearing, in which the foot is flat to the rock, and edging, where the boot is used to wedge into the rock. **1984** Jennifer Meadows *Dallas Morning News* (Tex.) (Nov. 2) "Novice Discovers the Pain, Pleasure and Danger of Rock Climbing in Nearby Wichita Mountains," p. 20B ▶ The trick, Sutton explained, to climbing a friction slab, is a motion called "smearing."...With his rump high in the air so that his weight is distributed evenly over the smear spots, the climber spider-walks up the surface. **1990** *Climbing Magazine* (Feb.-Mar.) "DNB: Direct North Buttress, Middle Cathedral Rock, Yosemite Valley" in *Usenet: rec.climbing* (Oct. 2, 1992) Tim Schneider "The DNB" ▶ The most exciting sections entail steep edging and smearing, plus a knack for finding the easiest line. **2005** *News & Star* (Carlisle, Eng.) (Apr. 2) "My Rocky Horror Show" (Int.) ▶ To make progress you have to use a technique called smearing, where you push your foot into the rock and lever yourself up for a handhold.

smile *n.* a line, graphed on a parabolic or bowl-shaped curve, that represents a risk or return relationship in investment markets. *Money & Finance.*

*1999 Gary L. Gastineau, Mark P. Kritzman *Dictionary of Financial Risk Management* (Int.) in IFCI Risk Institute "Glossary" ▶ A reference to the common shape of a graph of at- or out-of-the-money put and call implied volatilities for options with a common expiration date. The name comes from the fact that the furthest out of the money options generally have the highest implied volatilities, causing the ends of the graph to turn up. **2003** Jean-Philippe Bouchaud, Marc Potters *Theory of Financial Risk and Derivative Pricing* (Dec. 11), p. 70 ▶ This has direct consequences for the dynamics of the volatility smile observed on option markets. ***2004** *riskglossary.com* "Volatility Skew" (Int.) ▶ Either the term "volatility smile" or "volatility skew" (or simply skew) may be used to refer to the general phenomena of volatilities varying by strike. Indeed, you may even hear of "volatility smirks" or "volatility sneers," but such names are often as much whimsical as they are descriptive of any particular volatility pattern. **2004** *Australian Financial Review* (May 28) "How to Go Bust in a State of Bliss" (Int.) ▶ Hardly a line of David's trading argot will be intelligible to ordinary mortals, being riddled with references to gamma smiles.

smirting *n.* using smoking as a pretense to flirt. [*sm*oking+ fl*irting*] This word has signs of being factitious: the first appearance of the word so far found is in a press release, and nearly all uses of the word found anywhere in print talk about the word as a phenomenon in itself, whereas a naturally occurring and propagated word would more often be used without explanation.

2003 (*PR Newswire*) (Dec. 3) "Euro RSCG Unveils 15 Global Pop Culture Sightings in a Time of Unease, a Planetwide Outbreak of Pleasure Seeking" (in NYC) ▶ From flash picnics to psychedelic mushrooms, raunchy fashion to "smirting" (smoking and flirting) on sidewalks, we see the quest for personal pleasure moving toward the extremes, where the fun and feeling are most intense, raw, and authentic. **2005** Rachel Tiffen *New Zealand Herald* (July 3) "Smoke Laws Fan Flames of Passion" (Int.) ▶ Indulged in a bit of smirting lately? Yes, that's right, smirting. It's the new phenomenon of smokers ducking outside the pub or workplace and engaging in a bit of good old-fashioned flirting.

smitty *n.* a type of automobile muffler known for its (powerful or resonant) sound. *Automotive. United States.* [Probably from the "Smithy" muffler brand.]

1965 *Daily Northwestern* (Oshkosh, Wisc.) (May 11) (in classifieds) ▶ For Sale. Smitty muffler, $2. **1998** *Usenet: rec.autos.rod-n-custom* (Jan. 8) "Re: Soup Up Ideas for All" ▶ I particularly like the sound of a $15 glasspack! You really don't get to hear them very often anymore. It would be different. But as long as we've got a period theme going, why not some "smitty's"? **1999** *Usenet: rec.outdoors.rv-travel* (Apr. 3) "Re: Banks Exhaust Systems" ▶ My preferred method of quieting an engine is to use a short "turbo" type muffler just behind the engine.

This is followed by a crossover pipe connecting the two banks together and then a "smitty" to bring the remaining tone down. **2004** Mark Davis *Atlanta Journal-Constitution* (Ga.) (June 24) "Hey, Daddy-O, Dig Those Terms" (Int.) ▶ A smitty, he e-mailed, was a "particularly loud, virtually straight-through muffler used by many hot rodders."

smoker's face *n.* a physiognomy deteriorated by habitual tobacco smoking. *Health. Medical. Slang.* [Coined by Dr. Douglas Model.]

1985 Robert Glass (*AP*) (Dec. 20) "Doctor Says Cigarettes Can Cause 'Smoker's Face'" ▶ Cigarette smoking can lead to "smoker's face," a wrinkled, weary, haggard look. **1996** Jane E. Brody *N.Y. Times* (June 19) "Smoker's Face: Another Reason to Quit the Habit," p. C9 ▶ Her face was etched with wrinkles, her features gaunt-looking with prominent underlying bones and her skin shriveled and gray with purplish blotches. Diagnosis: smoker's face. **2004** *Business Times* (Singapore) (May 15) "Eat Your Way to Healthier Skin" (Int.) ▶ The term "smoker's face" was coined in the mid-80s, when studies showed that smokers tend to have similar facial characteristics: Prominent lines and wrinkles from the corners of the eyes ("crow's feet"); sunken cheeks; wrinkle lines perpendicular to the lips; drawn, taut skin that has lost its elasticity; a mottled, slightly reddened, orange and purple complexion or a grey, unnatural pallor.

smoke (someone) up *v. phr.* to share marijuana as a friendly gesture; to enable someone to get high. *Drugs.* Constructed similarly as *to chat (someone) up* 'to flirt (with someone); to make a romantic or sexual play (for someone),' though the latter term is not common in North America.

1993 *Usenet: alt.drugs* (Feb. 14) "Re: Hash" ▶ There was lots of hash around, more or less for free. No one would *sell* us any, but they just loved to smoke us up and send us on our ways with a gram or three in our pockets. **1994** *Usenet: rec.music.gdead* (Jan. 18) "Buckeye/1st Show" ▶ some dude smoked me up and invited me to his van later to party, i dosed real hard. **2004** [phoxylady] *Cannabis.com* (May 8) "Are There Many Girls Who Smoke Pot?" (Int.) ▶ im a girl and i smoke, but the best thing about is that its always with my guy friends and they always smoke me up with whatever (weed, salvia, etc.) for free! **2005** [MC Chris] *Slashdot* (Mar. 22) "MC Chris Answers Your Questions" (Int.) ▶ I smoke too much weed which is bad for my vocal chords. but after every show kids try to smoke me up. Any blue blooded stoner would love this charity.

smurfing *n.* the making of a series of small transactions to escape the regulatory notice a single larger transaction might attract. *Crime & Prisons. Drugs. Money & Finance. United States.*

1985 *Business Week* (NYC) (March 18) "Money Laundering—Who's Involved, How It Works, and Where It's Spreading," p. 74 ► To be more efficient, smurfs target areas where several banks are close to each other and, like most people, they avoid busy banks. "There is very little smurfing in New York City," says Charles Saphos, an Assistant U.S. Attorney in Florida, "because the lines are too long." **1992** Tom Rouillard *Herald* (Rock Hill, S.C.) (Oct. 23) "Nightclub Owner Faces 32 Counts of Dodging IRS" ► Quinn said investigators call "hopping from bank to bank" with cash amounts just under the $10,000 limit "smurfing," after the children's cartoon in which little blue characters hop around. **1994** Michael Grunwald *Boston Globe* (Mass.) (Oct. 13) "Former Representative Fined for Funds Scheme," p. 55 ► By splitting up the transaction—also known as "structuring" or "smurfing"— Marotta evaded regulations requiring banks to file currency transaction reports for withdrawals over $10,000. **1998** Kevin McDermott @ Springfield, Ill. *St. Louis Post-Dispatch* (Mo.) (Jan. 7) "Illinois Finds Record Number of Labs in '97" p. A1 ► Missourians had been caught in Illinois on several occasions "smurfing"—that is, buying anhydrous ammonia, iodine crystals, ether and other ingredients from various sources, far from their labs, to avoid raising suspicion. **2004** Jamie Fetty *Tribune-Star* (Terre Haute, Ind.) (July 29) "Two Men Arraigned in Indy After Allegedly Selling Cold Pills" (Int.) ► Sometimes meth cooks can get around these regulations by what McClintock referred to as "smurfing," stopping from one store to another to pick up one or two packages until they have enough to work with.

snag *n.* in firefighting, a standing dead or burned tree. *Firefighting.* [This is directly related to two older senses: 'a branch stump on a trunk' and 'a dead tree or branch, in the bottom of a body of water, that interferes with navigation or recreation.']

1987 *Seattle Times* (Wash.) (May 17) "Forest-Fire Death Spurs State Review" (in Spokane), p. B5 ► Cash L. Hopkins, 25, an inmate from the Indian Ridge Corrections Center in Snohomish County, was killed Aug. 18 at the Ace Creek fire when a burning snag fell on him. **2000** *Oregonian* (Aug. 18) "Forest Fire Fighters," p. A2 ► Marty Vanausdol cuts down a burned tree—a snag in fire crew parlance—to clear a safe path along a fire line in West Yellowstone, Mont. **2004** Eric Bailey @ Sacramento, Calif. *L.A. Times* (Oct. 5) "Firefighter Crushed to Death as Part of Tree Topples" (Int.) ► A few other team members approached a tree known in forestry parlance as a "snag"—dead or dying timber that poses a threat of falling.

snakebite *v.* to bring (someone) bad luck; to ruin or spoil (a shot, a deal, a game, etc.); *n.* bad luck; unluckiness; a curse. *Sports.* The adjectival forms, **snakebitten** and **snakebit** unlucky or cursed, are common.

1962 Ralph Bernstein @ Philadelphia *Gettysburg Times* (Pa.) (Nov. 9) "Pitt Picked to Lose, Yale to Take Penn" ▶ Temple over Toledo—Hard luck Owls shake the snakebite. **1968** Charles E. Taylor @ Boca Raton, Fla. *Chronicle-Telegram* (Elyria, Ohio) (Jan. 13) "Raiders Respect Green Bay Legend," p. 20 ▶ Even Vince Lombardi—who many say puts the mental snakebite on opponents by being the Green Bay coach—isn't convinced. **1982** Randy Minkoff @ Chicago (*UPI*) (June 22) "Deals Still Possible After Trade Deadline" ▶ He just smiled and recalled that if you snakebite somebody's waiver deal at one time, the time may come when you will want someone and another team will snakebite you. **1984** Edmund Lawler @ Chicago (*AP*) (Sept. 12) ▶ Eckersley's latest bout with snakebite was Tuesday when he limited the Philadelphia Phillies to two runs on five hits. He struck out nine hitters in the eight innings he worked, but it wasn't good enough for his ninth win. **1988** Pohla Smith @ Pittsburgh, Pa. (*UPI*) (Apr. 4) ▶ Philadelphia stranded 11 baserunners, giving them a total of 28 left on base in three games. "Home runs continue to snake bite us," said Manager Lee Eli. **2001** Jeff Barnard *San Diego Union-Tribune* (Calif.) (Jan. 29) "Criminal Past Returns to Haunt Sickly Ex-Con, 70, After 27 Years; California Wants Him to Finish Term," p. A3 ▶ Though his two accomplices have long since been paroled, and a past Oregon governor decided Burns was rehabilitated, California wants Burns to serve out the rest of his life sentence for the 1963 slaying of an officer after a bank robbery. "After 27 years, I couldn't believe California would snake-bite me again," Burns said.

snooker clause *n.* an (undebated) provision or rider covertly attached to legislation, or such legislation itself. Also **snooker bill.** *Politics. United States.* [From *snooker* 'to place in an impossible position; to stymie,' from tactics used in the billiards-like sport of the same name.]

1975 Francis X. Clines *N.Y. Times* (Feb. 18) "Judgeship Battle at Hand for Albany Democrats," p. 21 ▶ This is a "snooker" clause—Albany parlance for a deceitful contrivance—according to Assemblymen Edward H. Lehner of Manhattant and G. Oliver Koppell of the Bronx. **1996** (*PR Newswire*) (Mar. 5) "Support of Veto Override Is a Matter of Principle" (in Tallahassee, Fla.) ▶ Widely known as the "snooker bill," the law was snuck past legislators in the closing hours of the 1994 session. **2004** *N.Y. Times* (Nov. 24) "Snookering the Taxpayers," p. A22 (Int.) ▶ It is called a "snooker clause" in legislative parlance—a last-minute insert into a dense and hurried midnight bill.

snotty *n.* a glass pipe used for smoking marijuana. *Drugs.*

1995 *Usenet: alt.hemp* (Jan. 5) "Re: How Do U Smoke Pot?" ▶ Anyone who smokes pot knows the many advantages to smoking a "Snotty Pipe," nothing beats a cool glass bowl. **1995** *Usenet: alt.drugs.pot* (Mar. 23) "Re: Bong, Pipe, or Joint?" ▶ Glass pipes are the way to go, I think. Especially something with a carb, that changes colour when you smoke, like a Snotty, or something. **2004** *Cigarette Smoking Man from the X-Files* (Oct. 9) "Punk Church" (in Minneapolis-St. Paul, Minn.) (Int.) ▶ Yeah, snotties. They're like a pipe but they have water in it like a bong.

snowflake baby *n.* a child grown and born from a frozen embryo. *Medical.* [The term probably is derived from Snowflakes, an embryo-adoption agency affiliated with Focus on the Family, a conservative Christian organization founded by James Dobson, who is the author of the 2004 citation.]

2003 Suzanne Smalley *Newsweek* (Mar. 24) "A New Baby Debate," p. 53 ▶ Snowflakes, the first embryo-adoption program in the country, began matching donor embryos to infertile women in 1997 with the help of the conservative Christian group Focus on the Family. **2004** James Dobson *CBS-TV* (June 13) "Face the Nation" ▶ They're called snowflake babies, that come from those frozen embryos. **2005** *Democratic Underground* (June 6) "The Top 10 Conservative Idiots" (Int.) ▶ There are currently about 400,000 frozen embryos in storage, and about 9,000 of the 400,000 frozen embryos are available for "adoption" by other people. People who adopt these embryos can get them implanted and attempt to have a so-called "snowflake" baby.

soapedy *n.* a television show that combines elements of a daytime drama and a comedy. *Entertainment. Media. Television.* [*soap* opera + com*edy*]

1999 *(PR Newswire)* (Sept. 7) "Silly Valley Soapedy Continues: 'The Powers That Be' Pondered This Week" (in Palo Alto, Calif.) (title). **2004** Vinay Menon *Toronto Star* (Can.) (May 5) "Why The O.C. Became a Hit" (Int.) ▶ Since premiering in August, the dramedy (or, "soapedy," to use creator Josh Schwartz's neologism) has welcomed millions of weekly viewers to Orange County, Calif., by punching up the ridiculous.

socks and knocks *n.pl.* the oxides of sulfur and nitrogen commonly found in pollution. *Environment. Science.* [A literal pronunciation of the characters that make up the chemical notations SO_x, representing various oxides of sulfur, and NO_x, representing various oxides of nitrogen. A third related term, RO_x, is explained in the 2001 citation.]

1997 Lucille Van Ommering @ Sacramento, Calif. (*Meeting Before the California Air Resources Board*) (May 22), pp. 30-31 (Int.) ▶ That reclaim program is effective for both emissions of knocks and socks. **1997** John D. Dunlap (*Meeting Before the California Air Resources Board*) (Dec. 11), p. 114 (Int.) ▶ Dr. Pitts lecturing some students on the videotape and it is rock, socks and knocks. **2001** Harold H. Schobert *Energy and Society: An Introduction* (Oct. 1), pp. 432-33 ▶ Sulfur is capable of forming more than one oxide..., conveniently lumped together with the symbol SOx. Similarly, nitrogen can produce more than one oxide; they are lumped together as NOx.... Sometimes the generic symbol R is used to represent the metallic elements (such as silicon, aluminum, and iron) present in the various constituents of ash. Then the notation ROx can be taken as a symbol for ash. It's then possible to refer to the potential pollutants as socks, knocks, and rocks. **2002** Mike Bull @ Research Department of the Minnesota House of Representatives *House Research Short Subjects* (St. Paul, Minn.) (Oct.) "Air Quality Regulation in Minnesota," p. 1 (Int.) ▶ The seven criteria pollutants are carbon monoxide (CO); lead; sulphur dioxide (SOx) and nitrogen oxide (NOx) (often called "socks and knocks"). **2004** Doug Abra, Ed Wojczynski *Manitoba Clean Environment Commission Verbatim Transcript* (Can.) (Mar. 2) "Hearing: Wuskwatim Generation and Transmission Project," vol. 2, pp. 506-8 (Int.) ▶ Determining the life cycle socks and knocks is not something that we use at a screening level. **2005** Bill Paul *Motley Fool* (Apr. 21) "Cleaning Up with 'Socks and Knocks'" (Int.) ▶ Readers should understand clearly that if the power industry prevails in its court challenges to the initiative, the huge amount of money expected to be spent primarily on reducing what the industry commonly calls "socks and knocks" might not get spent.

somaticizer *n.* a person whose physical illnesses are caused by neurosis. *Medical.* A *somaticizer* will have genuine physical symptoms of illness whereas a hypochondriac will not.

1988 Alan Wofelt *Death and Grief* (Mar. 1), p. 118 ▶ The somaticizer is the person who converts his or her feelings into physical symptoms. **1995** Nick Cummings *Focused Psychotherapy* (Aug. 1), p. 21 ▶ The

HMO physicians were persuaded to use a less pejorative term, and the designation "somatizer" was substituted to refer to persons who were displacing emotional problems into physical symptoms. **1996** (*U.S. Court of Appeals for 5th Circuit, Western District of Louisiana*) (June 11) "No. 94-40691: Guilbeau v. W.W. Henry Co., et al." (Int.) ▶ The results and Friedberg's analysis indicated that Guilbeau was a somaticizer, meaning that he complained of physical ailments without physical cause.

sonic branding *n.* the association of a piece of music with a product, company, or broadcast program. *Advertising. Music.*

1998 Nick Coleman *Independent* (U.K.) (May 1) "Music: The Tune That Hooked a Generation," p. 14 ▶ "The Wizard" served as the technical model for subsequent efforts at TOTP sonic branding: Tony Gibber's "Get Out of That" in 1991 and, more recently, Vince Clark's "Red Pop Head." Remember how they went? Me neither. [**1999** Martin Croft *Marketing Week* (U.K.) (Feb. 4) "Why Jingles No Longer Jangle," p. 40 ▶ The RAB which obviously has something of a vested interest in the issue is attempting to update the use of sounds in advertising, and has even come up with an alternative name to the slightly downmarket jingle sonic brand triggers.] **2004** Alice Fisher *Telegraph* (U.K.) (Dec. 29) "Tills Are Alive with the Sound of Music" (Int.) ▶ Johnson says writing brand scores is his favourite part of sonic branding. "Writing a sonic logo for a massive company, that's scary."

sonker *n.* a type of berry pie or cobbler. *Food & Drink. North Carolina. United States.* [Perh. fr. Sc./Brit. Eng. *songle, singill, single,* 'a handful of grain or gleanings,' or from Sc. *sonker* 'to simmer, to boil slightly.'] This appears to be specific to the area near Mount Airy, N.C.

1987 James J. Kilpatrick @ Mount Airy, N.C. *Chicago Sun-Times* (Sept. 6) "What Makes Sonker a Sonker After Being Songle or Sonkle?" p. 14 ▶ There is nothing very distinctive about the sonker itself—it may be made with either flour or breadcrumbs—except for this: The filling is whatever's handy at the time. **2004** Richard Creed *Winston-Salem Journal* (N.C.) (May 29) "Berry Good: Granny's Definition Works" (Int.) ▶ I have often wondered why a deep-dish fruit pie is called a cobbler. My online etymological dictionary suggests it is related to a 14th-century word for wooden bowl, cobeler. What is apparently the same dish is called zonker (or sonker) in Surry County.

soup bunch *n.* a bundle of vegetables and herbs used in the preparation of soup. *Food & Drink.* [The English *soup bunch* is probably a calque of the German term *suppenbund.* The word *suppebund* in the 2005 citation is a misspelling. (Thanks to Margaret Marks for the information.)]

1883 *Waukesha Freeman* (Wisc.) (Feb. 1) "Hermann and the Hucksters," p. 12 ▶ "How do you sell these soup bunches?" said he, picking up a peck measure full of herbs. **1909** *Laurel Ledger* (Miss.) (July 8) "Recipes," p. 3 ▶ Vegetable Soup—One-half can tomatoes, cupful of navy beans, one onion, one soup bunch. **1925** Harry Harrison Kroll *A Comparative Study of Upper and Lower Southern Folk Speech* (George Peabody College for Teachers, Tenn.) (Aug.) ▶ *Soup bunch.* Bundle of vegetables. **1992** J.M. Taylor *Hoppin' John's Lowcountry Cooking* (Apr. 1), p. 202 ▶ Some cooks throw a "soup bunch" into the pot while the shank boils. Sold in predominately black neighborhood grocery stores, the bunch is an elaborate *bouquet garni* of mixed vegetables and aromatics for the soup pot. A typical soup bunch includes a carrot, celery, thyme, cabbage, and turnips with their greens. **2003** W.W. Weaver *Country Scrapple* (Sept. 1), p. 99 ▶ Since much of the flavor of rice scrapple is in the boiling stock, you might consider using a traditional Charleston soup bunch. This is a bouquet of herbs and vegetables tied up with string, consisting of parsley, a slice or two of squash, some spring onions or small leeks, a few bay leaves on the stem, and a small parsnip. It is removed when the stock is strained. **2005** Andre Lariviere *Georgia Straight* (Vancouver, B.C., Can.) (Feb. 3) "Chefs Share Passion for the Ugly But Delectable Celery Root" (Int.) ▶ "I still hope it'll become a kitchen staple the way it is in Europe," he says, noting that produce markets in Germany offer a popular bundle of celery root, carrots, and onions as a *suppebund*, or "soup bunch."

sousveillance *n.* the watching of the watchers by the watched; countersurveillance by people not in positions of power or authority. *Technology.* [*sous* French 'under' + surv*eillance.* The word was popularized by, if not coined by, Steve Mann, a professor at the University of Chicago.]

2001 Pauline Tam @ Toronto *Ottawa Citizen* (Can.) (Nov. 19) "Is the Life of a Our Path to Liberation?" p. B6 ▶ You get into a taxi cab, you're under surveillance. There's a camera taking pictures of you. If you were to photograph the cab driver, that would be what I call sousveillance. If you walked into a department store and photographed the clerk, that's a form of sousveillance. **2001** *Usenet: flora.mai-not* (Dec. 24) "FW: 'World Sousveillance Day' Today—Watching the Watchers" ▶ An international coalition that includes artists, scientists, engineers, scholars, and others is declaring December 24, to be

"World Sousveillance Day," or "World Subjectrights Day". **2002** Patrick Di Justo *Wired News* (Nov. 28) "Record the Lens That Records You" (Int.) ► Sousveillance means "to view from below."

spadia *n.* a page wrapped around the spine of a periodical or one of its sections so as to appear as a narrow flap or partial page. Also **spadea**. *Media*. The 1993 citation has it right: a gatefold and a spadia are not the same thing. The word is pronounced *spay-dee-uh*.

1989 *Drug Store News* (Nov. 6) "Harco Drug Targets an Incentive-Driven Private-Label Strategy" (in Northport, Ala.), vol. 11, no. 21, p. 20 ► The ad, called a "spadia," was the equivalent of a full page, folded over the regular circular so that half showed on the front and half on the back. The private-label page pulled off to reveal more private-label items on the reverse side. **1993** Michael R. Fancher *Seattle Times* (Wash.) (Mar. 28) "New 'Gatefold' Ad Not Funny to Readers of Sunday Funnies," p. A2 ► It's a variation on the partial-page ad that wraps around the comics, which is called a spadea (pronounced spay-dee-uh). The gatefold is different. **1996** Mark Fitzgerald *Editor & Publisher* (Mar. 16) "Featherbedding: Fact or Fiction?" p. 12 ► He notes that some of the inserts that gave union mailers their biggest headaches on the new equipment—such as a Montgomery Ward product and the spadia on double Sunday comics sections—have been eliminated since the strike began. **1999** Jeanie Enyart *Presstime* (Oct.) "What Have Been the Most Significant Industry Events and Developments in the Past 20 Years?" p. 33 ► Advertisers now want to reach specific customer groups. Part of the result is the creation of numerous products, including Neighbors editions, Homes magazines, Post-It notes, Comics spadias, TV Book pop-outs and wraps, TV shows and job fairs. **2002** James T. Campbell *Houston Chronicle* (Tex.) (July 29) "What's a Reader Representative, Anyway?" p. A22 ► I've learned more about the Chronilog, comics (that fold that covers half of the Sunday comics is called a "spadia") and the weather page in a little over a month as reader representative than in my entire 14 years at the *Chronicle*. **2004** *Gazette* (Colorado Springs, Colo.) (June 4) "Advertisers Enthusiastic About Color Ads on Sunday Comics" ► About 15 years ago, in response to advertiser requests, comic section printers began using the smaller sheet of newsprint to wrap around the comics section. In the newspaper business this sheet is known as a spadia or gatefold. **2004** Ta-Nehisi Coates *Village Voice* (NYC) (Aug. 17) "Press Clips" (Int.) ► A lucky smattering of folks who picked up the *N.Y. Times* on Monday were treated to a spadia—a strip just wider than a column, overlapping the front page, that announced the day's highlights.... As it happens, the spadia also creates room for what amounts to an ad on page one. If you turned back the flap on Monday's run, you found a full-color pitch from Macy's, right alongside the news from Iraq. The wrap also pushed the hallowed editorial page from its traditional position, instead finishing the front section with a spread of advertising.

spawny *adj.* lucky. *Scotland.*

1992 *Usenet: rec.sport.soccer* (Feb. 7) "Re: Bring Back the Attractiveness in World Cup" ▶ They qualified for the semis by kicking Maradona off the pitch (so when he retaliated he got sent off) and a spawny Rossi hatrick based on defensive errors by Brazil when Italy were getting pissed on. **1994** Irvine Welsh *Trainspotting* (July 11), p. 96 (May 1, 1996) ▶ —Two fuckin aces!—Spawny bastard! You spawny fuckin cunt Renton. **1997** Bill Lecki *Scottish Daily Record* (Jan. 3) "Mbes Aye, Mbes Naw," p. 74 ▶ After his lucky, flukey, jammy, spawny, poxy save against us at Wembley, those initials can only stand for one thing. **1997** Mark Hodkinson *Times* (London, Eng.) (Apr. 21) "Bassett's Petrified Forest Seem Resigned to Their Fate," p. 30 ▶ Many defenders do not a great defence make, as Forest discovered when Bart-Williams sliced a ball against his own post. Deane gleefully poked it into the waiting net as it rebounded along the goal line. Dave Bassett, the Forest general manager, afterwards dubbed the goal "spawny" and the epithet was accurate. **2003** Charlotte Hindle *Lonely Planet Gap Year Book* (Sept. 1), p. 133 ▶ Only spawny gappers find any paid work in the region other than teaching English.

speed table *n.* a flat, raised road surface intended to slow traffic. *Architecture. Automotive.* A speed table is longer and flatter than a speed bump. It sometimes is a part of, or does double-duty as, a raised crosswalk.

1990 *Surveyor* (Feb. 7) "Traffic Management," p. 18 ▶ Bus operators prefer the occasional speed table, not a lengthy series of humps. **2005** Jill R. Goodman @ West Valley, Ariz. *Newzap.com* (Mar. 28) "Speeders Irk Phase I Residents; 'Speed Tables,' Private Security, Radar Signs Are Options" (Int.) ▶ A second traffic mitigation option would be to install a set of elongated speed humps, what transportation officials refer to as "speed tables," which would gradually rise up over six feet until it is three inches high. Then drivers would ride straight along the plateau for about 10 feet and then gradually lower back to street level.

spiedie *n.* a food dish of marinated meat chunks, usually cooked on a skewer and sometimes eaten as a sandwich. Also **spiedi.** *Food & Drink. New York. United States.* [Probably from the Italian *spiedino* 'a skewer' or *spiedo* 'a spit.'] This word in the United States appears to be special to New York State near Binghamton and Syracuse.

1971 *Syracuse Herald-Journal* (N.Y.) (July 9) (in advert.), p. 16 ▶ Spiedi. Marinated Chunks of Meat on a Skewer 55¢. **1981** *Syracuse Herald-Journal* (June 23) (in advert.), p. 6 ▶ State Fair Spiedie Sauce 8 oz. Btl. 89¢. **1983** Fred David *Syracuse Herald-Journal* (N.Y.) (Sept. 2) "State Sets Fall Park Schedule," p. D5 ▶ Spiedie sandwiches—a Southern Tier delight consisting of marinated beef chunks—are $1.50 and difficult to pass up. **2004** Wayne Hansen *Press & Sun-Bulletin* (Binghamton, N.Y.) (Aug. 8) "Local Specialty Puzzling to Some at Fest" (Int.) ▶ What's a Spiedie? It's a tasty treat of marinated meat char-broiled 'n fed on Italian bread.

spin *v.* in horse racing, to renege on an agreement to have a jockey ride a racehorse. *Sports.*

1993 Liz Hafalia *San Francisco Chronicle* (Calif.) (Aug. 27) "The Agent: The Need to Talk a Good Game," p. E2 ▶ To keep the fewest people irate at any one time, Barsotti, who has been an agent for seven years, has rules: "Don't make commitments early, don't spin late." Spin, at the track, means renege on a deal. **1999** Rachel Blount *Star Tribune* (Minneapolis-St. Paul, Minn.) (Aug. 20) "On the Right Track," p. 5C ▶ Agents often make early commitments to more than one horse in a race, figuring that the field will thin out by the time post positions are drawn. But if both horses enter, one of the trainers will be jilted. Jockeys also can back out of a commitment if they get an offer to ride a better horse in another race or at another track. Conversely, trainers sometimes promise a mount to a jockey and then dump him at the last minute for someone else. Those practices, called "spinning," create a daily litany of hard feelings, broken hearts and promises of revenge. **1999** Bob Fortus *New Orleans Times-Picayune* (La.) (Dec. 23) "Jockey Agents Always on Alert 'Spinning' Causes Backstretch Agony," p. D1 ▶ "Spinning" is the racetrack term for maneuvering by which agents change mounts shortly before entries are taken, or trainers change riders. **2004** *Chicago Sun-Times* (Aug. 15) "Dettori Gets Long Shot Home in Beverly D" (Int.) ▶ Prado also earned the ire of Million-winning trainer Michael Matz, who continued to insist that the determined West Coast reinsman had given him a commitment to ride

Kicken Kris in the Million. Instead, Matz insisted, Prado and agent Bob Fries reneged—"spun," in the parlance of the backstretch—six days before the Arlington centerpiece.

spinner *n.* a decorative automobile hubcap or rim that spins independently of the wheel to which it is attached. *Automotive. Jargon.*

1985 Boyd Burchard *Seattle Times* (Wash.) (June 22), p. C1 ▶ Few of the original Mustang spinner hub caps are available, but Lincoln has some used ones priced at $75. **2004** Denny Lee *N.Y. Times* (Apr. 23) "The Dub Generation: Gearheads Go Hip-Hop" (Int.) ▶ It's *Dub*, a niche car magazine with a tiny paid circulation that has nevertheless become the bible of the urban automotive subculture devoted to 20-inch-plus spinners—the outrageously flashy oversize wheels that pop up in nearly every MTV rap video—and the hip-hop attitude they connote.

spit game *v.* to flirt with, hit on, or try to pick up (a woman). *Slang. United States.*

1991 N.W.A. *Niggaz4life* (May 27) "Findum, Fuckum & Flee" ▶ Yo, every bitch I know they wanna get with me/The mothafuckin' notorious D-R-E/Spit game at a bitch while a nigga's around/And you know most hos knows not to clown. **1992** Prince and the New Power Generation "Sexy M.F." ▶ Packing an ass as tight as a grape/I want to spit some game but I said to myself/hmmm.... Just conversate (Yeah!). **1992** *Usenet: rec.music.funky* (July 7) "Go-Go" ▶ The basement was packed w/ a local go-go band and the brothers were working out! The place was packed and everyone was just jumping up and down. Could really spit game and ask a chic to dance...just jump next to her ;-) WILD. **2004** [Ian would say] *MonkeyFilter* (July 9) "Let's Be Friends" (Int.) ▶ I'm entirely comfortable around females; I can't spit game, but I can talk to a stranger in a bar with the same degree of comfort as I have around old friends.

spizerinctum *n.* energy, vigor, or vitality. Also **spizerinktum, spizzerinktum, spizzerinctum, spizarinctum, pizzeringtum, spizzer inktum,** etc. *Health. United States.* [As Merriam-Webster editors pointed out in their May 2005 newsletter, it has been speculated "that the word derives in whole from Latin *specie rectum*, literally, 'the right kind'—but that etymology appears to be a misguided attempt to make something more of good old American slang than is warranted."] The ladies club mentioned in the cites seems to have taken its name from the term, which has existed in one spelling or another since at least as early as 1845.

1891 *Chicago Daily Tribune* (May 18), p. 4 ▶ Jove sits enthroned upon his brow, his head crammed with knowledge; he'll graduate a few weeks hence from Spizzerinctum College. [**1907** *Chicago Daily Tribune* (Jan. 20) "In a Minor Key. The Mayor's Dream," p. B4 ▶ The mayor had a vision,/In his slumbers he was troubled,/Dreamed he saw a huge petition/Signed by more than 80,000/Of the people of they city,/Praying for a referendum./...It was signed by Cephas Wojjers,/ Calthumpian Magruder,/ Garibaldi Mantilini,/...Ananias Spizzerinctum.] **1908** Charles Frederic Goss *Daily News* (Frederick, Md.) (Mar. 18) "On Top," p. 3 ▶ Letting down the bars, he stuck his thumb into the lean ribs of the donkey and when that resentful creature reared and kicked, chuckled with a boundless joy. "You're [*sic*] spizzerinktum hasn't all burned up yet, eh old man?" **1914** *Lincoln Daily Star* (Neb.) (July 9) "Be a Spizzerinktum: It's a Brand New Word, But It Means a Lot—Here Is Its Meaning," p. 7 ▶ "What is a spizzerinktum? I have just been called that and I want to know."..."A spizzerinktum is a person who possesses initiative, vim, vigor, efficiency, intelligent persistency and an overmastering will to succeed," comes the explanation. **1915** *Lincoln Sunday Star* (Neb.) (Feb. 7) "Social Calendar," p. 17 ▶ La Spizzer Inktum will entertain their husbands at dinner Friday evening at 6:30 at the home of Mr. and Mrs. G. I. Smith, 2701 O Street. **1922** *Mexia Evening News* (Tex.) (Oct. 13), p. 2 ▶ Although a live wire, the dengue took much of the spizerinktum out of his being for the time being only, we know. **1936** Jack Wright, Frank Rogers *Morning News* (Florence, S.C.) (May 25) "Kiwanis Club," p. 8 ▶ "On to Washington" will be the next keynote of the program next Thursday with old reliable Kiwanian Frank Key furnishing the "spizzerinktum." **1940** *Chronicle-Telegram* (Elyria, Ohio) (Jan. 20) "How Would You Like to Be the Postman Now?" p. 8 ▶ It may be a letter from Aunt Mehetibelle, a bill for the new car, or an for Spizerinctum's Kill or Cure, but the mail must go through. **1946** *Walla Walla Bulletin* (Wash.) (Mar. 12) "Mrs. J. J. Hamley Dies Sunday in Pendleton," p. 10 ▶ She was a member of the...Spizzerinctum club. **1947** G.C. Graham *Statesville Daily Record* (Feb. 7) "Letters to the Editor," p. P2 ▶ It seems that some of the "dry" leaders of the state are in danger of jeopardizing the cause of sobriety by their weak-knee statements. And, of course, they are being ably assisted by certain headline writer desk men who are most prayerful for the "wet" side. The former gentlemen need a shot of spizerinctum and the latter need the darkness [put] out of their minds. **1956** *Independent* (Pasadena, Calif.) (May 11) "TV Makes Ike 'Look Old'" (in Washington, D.C.) ▶ "I think the country is entitled to know he is young, vigorous, and full of spizerinctum." [Sen. Alexander Wiley (R) Wisc.] said spizerinctum was a word coined by an old banker in his town of Chippewa Falls, Wis., to describe someone full of pep and vitality. **1958** *Independent* (Hawarden, Iowa) (Sept. 25) "Anonymously Yours...," p. 7 ▶ Scientists have concocted a new drug out of rocket fuel, which they claim will give a man renewed energy, like turpentine does a cat.... I'm looking forward to national distribution of this new spizzerinctum builder. **1961** *Evening Sentinel* (Holland, Mich.) (Oct. 13) "Publishers Told Power by Educator" (in Chicago), p. 7 ▶ For the explosive substance in the bomb hydrogen, he substituted knowledge, and for uranium, the fuse, spizzerinctum. This he defined as "energy ambition and the will to succeed." **2004** [Cee Cee] @ Mahtomedi, Minn. *Pioneer Press* (Minneapolis-St. Paul, Minn.) (Oct. 17) "In the Realm of the Coined" (Int.) ▶ Spizerinctum is invisible—an essence or energy of sorts. When beer has lost its foam, soda has lost its fizz or a balloon deflates, it has lost its spizerinctum. I suppose you would say that throughout the wedding preparations and busy weekend, I was overflowing with spizerinctum, but as things are winding down now, I think it has flown the coop for a while.

SPUI *n.* a single point urban interchange, a type of highway exchange. Also **spui.** *Acronym. Architecture. Jargon. United States.*
1995 Karl Cates *Deseret News* (Utah) (Nov. 30) "Life in the Slow Lane," p. A23 ▶ SPUI uses only 2 traffic signals where 4 were previously needed. North and southbound vehicles enter simultaneously. Vehicles also exit to cross street together. **2001** Michael Squires *Las Vegas Review-Journal* (Nev.) (2001) "Planners Say SPUI on Cloverleafs," p. 2B ▶ To increase capacity and avoid such problems, engineers have created a variation on the diamond design known as a single-point urban interchange, or SPUI (pronounced spew-ee).

squadrol *n.* a police vehicle that serves the purposes of both a patrol wagon and squad car. *Automotive. Police.* [*squad* + *patrol*]
1948 *Chicago Daily Tribune* (Feb. 14) "Mail Truck Damages New Police Car; Driver Held," p. A7 ▶ A mail truck driver...was arrested after his truck struck a Deering police station "squadrol," a new combination squad car and patrol wagon, in service a week. The squadrol was damaged. **1952** Pat Englehart *Daily Herald* (Chicago) (June 27) "Reporter 'Taken for a Ride,'" p. 13 ▶ On a recent eight-hour shift, we rode the squadrol with Deputies Joe Lewis and Frank Matz. **1958** *South Bend Tribune* (Ind.) (Mar. 9) "Dick Tracy" (in comic), p. 14 ▶ We'll need an ambulance—and a squadrol. **1972** Tom Hall *Chicago Tribune* (Mar. 12) "Vice in Chicago," p. G43A ▶ As the squadrol was coming to take the prisoners downtown...Sgt. Williams abruptly called for quiet.... The squadrol arrived with its crew of two mildly curious uniformed policemen. **2005** *Chicago Sun-Times* (Apr. 19) "Metro Briefs: Man Shot, Killed by Police," p. 66 ▶ A man who led police on a chase through Chicago's Southwest Side Monday night

died after hitting several parked cars, even striking a police squadrol and pointing a gun at officers.

squick *v.* to disturb, unsettle, make uneasy; to cause disgust or revulsion; to gross (someone) out; to freak (someone) out. Also *noun*, something that causes disgust, revulsion, or uneasiness, or the disgust, revulsion, or uneasiness itself. Also **squick (someone) out**. [There is inconclusive evidence this term may have originated among practitioners of sexual bondage or sadomasochism.]

[**1991** *Usenet: alt.sex.bondage* (Apr. 12) "Squick Was Ten Good Non-Consensual" ▶ There are some things too repulsive to discuss in a public forum—squicking is one of them. I've only been squicked once, and if someone wants me to be a squick-top, they'll have to beg FAR more than for anything else I can think of (though it's not clear that I _could_ bring myself _to_ squick, even consensually).] [**1991** *Usenet: rec.pets* (May 23) "Golden Geysers" ▶ Kit'n Hook, who was my youngest feline till we got Rhiannon, seems to think that expressing his affections to people is best done by squicking them—he comes over for affection, and if I don't put down my book fast enough or pet him intensely enough, he starts licking, and sucking, and licking, and licking, and while, in certain contexts (see alt.sex.bondage for more info) I quite enjoy being tickled, stimulated, and otherwise driven crazy I simply cannot DEAL with being abraded by a cat.] **1991** *Usenet: alt.sex.bondage* (June 17) "Squicking Resux" ▶ More generally, squicking is "that which the bottom cannot endure, whether at that time or in general." Whatever gets a safeword, is squicking. **1991** *Usenet: alt.sex.bondage* (Oct. 25) "Re: Fear of Anger" ▶ What I do in the scene I do because it turns me on, or, because it's something that turns my partner on and doesn't squick me. **1992** *Usenet: alt.peeves* (Aug. 7) "Re: Random Peeve" ▶ I've seen it used as "what tom and ned did with that gopher really squicked me." **1994** Kristin Tillotson *Star Tribune* (Minneapolis-St. Paul, Minn.) (Sept. 11) "No Holes Barred," p. 1E ▶ Don't get squicked (freaked out). **1996** *Usenet: soc.singles* (Jan. 27) "Re: Gorgeous Women: Flesh and Peec-tures" ▶ My squick, I should point out, wasn't a directly personal one (as in, "Oh no, is that evil, nasty man entertaining naughty thoughts about poor, pristine little *me*?").... The squick came more from the idea that this is now a perfectly acceptable way to treat others. **1997** *Usenet: soc.subculture.bondage-bdsm* (Dec. 16) "Re: The New 128 Basic Slave Rules Are Finally Released!" ▶ If I *really* wanted to get over my squick about, oh, Wonder Bread—and found a dom who was interested in such a scene, and agreed to a no-safeword scene in which I'd be force-fed Wonder Bread until I'd eaten twelve loaves, and decided half-way through that this was *really* too much. **2000** *Internet Complete* (Aug.) "Internet Dictionary," p. 931 ▶ Squick (v) To exceed someone's threshold for violent or tasteless imagery. **2001** Jon Carroll *San Francisco Chronicle* (Calif.) (Jan. 23) "Thinking Seriously About Latex," p. FP ▶ I do hate moralizing about people's private lives. I say that because I am about to do that, sort of, and I acknowledge in front the large squick factor. **2002** Andrew Vachss *Only Child* (Oct. 8), p. 171 ▶ There's all that "upskirt" squick, too.... Little perverts walking around with minicams in their briefcases. **2003** Kevin Bentley *Boyfriends from Hell* (Jan. 1), p. 128 ▶ Clearly, doing a diaper scene with a young boy on crack doesn't qualify as "safe," at least not in the minds of normal people. Maybe it even squicks *you*. **2004** Mistress Matisse (July 4) in *The Mammoth Book of Sex Diaries* (Mar. 12, 2005) Maxim Jakubowski, p. 27 ▶ If you squick easily, you should skip this next paragraph. A sound is a medical instrument, a long slender metal rod that's designed to be inserted into the male urethra. **2005** [agregoli] *Ask Metafilter* (June 22) "How Do You Know You Can Mentally Deal with Pregnancy?" (Int.) ▶ I worry that I'll get pregnant and then be so squicked out from having another being moving around in my body that I'll go crazy.

stagette *n.* an unmarried or unbetrothed woman; any woman or girl unaccompanied by a man, especially when socializing as part of a group of women or girls; (*hence*) especially in Canada, a pre-wedding party given for a bride; a bachelorette party. Also **staggette;** *attrib. Canada. United States.* [*stag* 'bachelor' + *-ette*, a diminutive or feminine suffix from Old French.]

1920 *Fayetteville Democrat* (Ark.) (July 14) "Social and Personal," p. 4 ▶ Following an informal "stagette" dance a midnight feast of ices and cakes was served. **1944** *Lethbridge Herald* (Alberta, Can.) (Feb. 28) "'First Niter' Dance on Friday Night," p. 9 ▶ Meet the Stagettes! This is the city's latest service club organization and it is composed of an energetic group of young ladies who announce their "First Niter" Dance Friday night. **1968** *Tri-City Herald* (Pasco, Kennewick, Richland, Wash.) (Nov. 4) "Dolly Hello's It," p. 5 ▶ Mrs. Ed (Mary Lou) Critchlow, right, sat atop the piano alongside chorus girl Mrs. Frank (Millie) Swanberg, at Tri-City Country club which Thursday night will turn itself into a suffragette party at women's division "Staggette." **1983** Salem Alaton *Globe and Mail* (Toronto, Can.) (May 21) "Joining the Brotherhood of Married Man," p. F7 ▶ The old bridal shower is being joined by the stagette. The proceedings are mainly a mimicry of the male event, with an emphasis on drinking and rough talk and a male stripper is becoming mandatory.

staledate *v. intransitive*, to expire; to be unused or unredeemed before a certain date; *transitive*, to set a termination, use-by, or expiration date on something.

1943 *Reno Evening Gazette* (Nev.) (Sept. 9) "Mineral County Grand Jury Files Investigation Report" (in Hawthorne), p. 9 ▶ The general manager should...realize cash wherever possible for all stale-dated and other checks. **1978** Roger C. Gibson *Globe and Mail* (Toronto, Can.) (Apr. 22) "Incorporating a Small Business Could Mean Saving in Tax Dollars," p. B1 ▶ If the loss cannot be fully utilized to reduce income of the corporation in other years (the previous year and the five subsequent years if it is a non-capital loss) the loss will become stale-dated. **1986** Pat Fenner *St. Petersburg Times* (Fla.) (Dec. 18) "Series: Times Action," p. 2 ▶ However, that check has stale-dated, and another check for $15 will be issued to the provider on a priority basis **1995** Steven Alfano *Corporate Cashflow Mag.* (Aug. 1) "The Re-Engineered Treasury: The Pros and Cons of Outsourcing Check Issuance," vol. 16, no. 8, p. 24 ▶ "Stale dating." (Checks are returned unpaid if outstanding beyond a specified number of days.) **1996** Joey Slinger *Toronto Star* (Can.) (July 18) "Eggs-actly! It's Just Big Brotherism," p. A2 ▶ Isn't stale-dating each individual egg an extreme indication of how regulation-happy we're getting? **1999** *Business Wire* (Sept. 22) "Zydacron and Tokyo Broadcasting System Revolutionize Live Broadcasting" (in Manchester, N.H.) ▶ TBS hoped to reduce or eliminate the high cost of remote satellite broadcasts and to avoid the stale dating inherent in studio weather information. **2005** Cory Doctorow *Boing Boing* (Jan. 25) "Why do Newspapers Charge for Yesterday's News?" (Int.) ▶ The NYT often does an extraordinary job of covering the facts, but it doesn't matter a whit to posterity if a link to that job will staledate in a month.

standfirst *n.* in British journalism, introductory or summary information above a newspaper article; a *kicker* (United States); a *précis. Jargon. Media. United Kingdom.* Sometimes wrongly used as a synonym with *lead* (or *lede*), which is part of the article whereas a *standfirst* is not. The content of the May 6, 2003, citation is made of in-house editing notes that ordinarily would not pass through the editorial process onto the news wires.

1990 Jonathan Croall @ Somerset, Eng. *Guardian* (U.K.) (Nov. 6) "Poll Tax Is Further Threatening the Already Much Depleted School Dinner Service" ▶ Standfirst matter: The abolition of school meals is looming for more authorities as they grapple with the effects of the poll tax. Jonathan Croall reports on the struggle to save the service in Somerset. **1996** Mary Edwards *Guardian* (U.K.) (Apr. 16) "Primary: Writing Made Simple," p. 13 ► Each article has a headline printed in large bold letters, followed by a brief description, called a standfirst, and a byline, which is the reporter's name. **2003** Jerry Frank *Lloyd's List* (U.K.) (May 6), p. 2 ► Xxxxxxx—Please write four decks of headline thanks. Please write a standfirst. **2003** Rachel Cooke *Observer* (U.K.) (Sept. 7) "It Will Fit in Your Handbag, But Is Bigger Than Cosmo," p. 9 ► Midway through a communications degree, she landed a job on the Oz teen bible, Dolly, and gave up "spending six weeks learning how to write a standfirst" in favour of doing the job for real.

stashing *n.* in American football, the placing of an uninjured player on the injured reserve list to preserve rights to the player. *Jargon. Sports. United States.*

1976 *N.Y. Times* (Mar. 20) "Csonka, 2 Mates Made Free Agents," p. 21 ► Under the old rules, a club could conceivably maintain valuable trading rights to a player by concealing him or placing him on the injured reserve list. The new rule permits only three injured reservists protection on the list. "This accomplishes the original intent of the 1975 rule to prevent clubs from stashing players on the injured reserve for possible use next year." **1978** *Globe and Mail* (Toronto, Can.) (Mar. 17) "O.J.'s $700,000 No Secret," p. P35 ► They want to get to the Super Bowl in some cases too hard, which is why we have fines for playing games (hiding injuries, etc.) with players and stashing and all. **2004** *EPSN.com* (Oct. 29) "Officials Concerned with IR Increase" (Int.) ► "Stashing" is a term from the past that Tagliabue and his top lieutenants don't want to see become a part of the modern-day NFL lexicon.... For the most part, after all, players on injured reserve are there with legitimate maladies. And for the most part, coaches would rather have those players on the field instead of in treatment.

sticky rice *n.* an East Asian who prefers romantic partners of the same race. Also *attrib. Sexuality.* This term is often derogatory.

1991 *Usenet: soc.motss* (July 10) "Toronto motss.con: A Retrospective" ► He also mentioned a term for an Asian who likes Asians and a White who likes Whites ("sticky rice" and "mashed potato"). [**1995** Richard Lloyd Parry *Independent* (U.K.) (May 30) "Sayonara to Tokyo's Camp Followers," p. 18 ► The young Office Ladies found the city's gay men so cute, they latched on to their club scene. But now the "sticky rice girls" have come unstuck.... A new phenomenon emerged: the okoge. The closest English translation is fag hag, but this doesn't do justice to the expression. Okoge is a culinary term, referring to those irritating grains of rice that stubbornly glue themselves to the bottom of the pot.] ***1996** Au Waipang *Yawning Bread* (Singapore) (Dec.) "Rice and Potatoes" (Int.) ▶ There are some who are "international buffet," most of the rest are "sticky-rice," i.e., East Asians who go for East Asians. They too can be quite specific about their tastes, and even if they think hard about it, they can rarely explain why they find fellow Asians a lot more attractive **1997** *Usenet: bit.listserv.gaynet* (Oct. 4) "Re: Writing Like Idiots Was Re: Living Like Animals" ▶ "Sticky rice" is a gentle joke, and I can tell you with some authority that Asians who date their own race are not considered to be "settling" for something less than a White Man. **2000** Amy Sonnie *Revolutionary Voices* (Oct. 1), p. 48 ▶ Here they have terms like...*sticky rice*.... Gay American culture insists that I am rice and my boyfriend should be a potato. My skin should be smooth, brown, and hairless, and his should resemble that of Wonder bread. If I go against this, I am labeled *sticky rice* and condemned as going against the natural way.

stiffs *n.pl.* in soccer, a reserve or second-string team or its players; a league, figurative or real, of such teams. *Sports. United Kingdom.* [This is directly related to *stiff* 'an ordinary man or sportsman.'] Usually constructed with the definite article: *the stiffs,* similar to baseball's *the minors.*

1993 Phil Daniels *Independent* (U.K.) (Mar. 10) "Steeped in The Stiffs" ▶ They call them The Stiffs. You know, the superstars who can't even make the bench on match days, the would-bes, will-bes, used-to-bes, wannabes and never-will-bes. They are the reserves. **1995** Andrew Longmore *Times* (London, Eng.) (Sept. 14) "Nelson the Author of His Own Misfortunes" ▶ Anything to lighten the prospect of playing in the Stiffs, the reserve team, again. **1996** Glenn Moore *Irish Times* (Apr. 6) "Sellars Moves in a Buyer's Market," p. 16 ▶ With the increase in squads and wages at the big clubs there are plenty of experienced players in the stiffs. **2004** Iain King *Sun* (U.K.) (Mar. 31) "Stephen Won't Have Cald Feat," p. 52 ▶ Once you have played first-team you never want to go back to the reserves. We had reserve teams with the likes of myself, Hugo Viana, Titus Bramble and Shola Ameobi in there. At times we had Pounds 60m worth of talent playing in the stiffs. **2005** Bill Urban *United States National Soccer Players Association* (May 16) "Urban Opinion: Say What?" (Int.) ▶ Having the threat of being forced to play "in the stiffs," "with the B-Team," or "with the scrubs," pick your pejorative, is surely a powerful motivating factor for any modern athlete.

stigmergy *n.* a process via which unorganized actions of individuals serve as stimuli to the actions of other individuals, and, in sum, result in a single outcome; a group of individuals who collectively behave as a sole entity. *Science.*

1959 Pierre-Paul Grassé *Insectes Sociaux* "La reconstruction du nid et les coordinations inter-individuelles chez Belicositermes natalensis et Cubitermes sp. La théorie de la Stigmergie: Essai d," pp. 41-80 ▶ La coordination des tâches, la régulation des constructions ne dépendent pas directement des ouvriers, mais des constructions elles-mêmes. L'ouvrier ne dirige pas son travail, il est guidé par lui. C'est à cette stimulation d'un type particulier que nous donnons le nom de stigmergie (*stigma*: piqûre, *ergon* : travail, oeuvre = oeuvre stimulante). **1967** M. Earl Balis, Irwin H. Krakoff, Peter H. Berman, Joseph Dancis *Science* (May 26) "Urinary Metabolites in Congenital Hyperuricosuria," vol. 156, no. 3778, p. 1123 (Int.) ▶ His hypothesis of "stigmergy" is that building behavior is at first uncoordinated...; when the construction at any one point reaches a certain critical density it attracts other termites topochemically. These focuses of the building material determine where the new pellets of earth used in the building are to be deposited. The constructions built thus act as new determinant stimuli for further construction. **2002** Joe Gregorio *BitWorking* (Dec. 30) "Stigmergy and the World Wide Web" (Int.) ▶ The World Wide Web is human stigmergy. The Web and its ability to let anyone read anything and also to write back to that environment allows stigmeric communication between humans. Some of the most powerful forces on the Web today, Google and weblogs are fundamentally driven by stigmeric communication and their behaviour follows similar natural systems like Ant Trails and Nest Building that are accomplished using stigmergy.

sting jet *n.* a weather formation characterized by high, damaging winds, caused by rapidly descending cool, dry air in contact with warm, moist air. *Jargon.* [As indicated in the citations, Keith Browning, Peter Clark, and Tim Hewson coined the word, based upon the scorpion-tail-like shape of the weather formation when viewed from above.]

2003 Roger Highfield *Daily Telegraph* (U.K.) (June 18) "A Sting in the Tale of the Great Storm," p. 14 ▶ Dubbed the Sting Jet, it is the source of the most damaging winds that scour Britain in winter, uprooting trees, damaging property and taking lives. The name was inspired by an expression first used by Norwegian meteorologists four decades ago.... They talked of the "poisonous tail of the bent-back weather front." Prof. Keith Browning at the University of Reading and Peter Clark and Tim Hewson of the Met Office have found the sting in the tip of this tail and coined the evocative phrase Sting Jet to describe the extraordinary gales that it spawns. **2003** Robert Muir-Wood *Rein-surance* (U.K.) (Sept. 1) "Risk—Weather Models—a Brighter Forecast," p. 53 ► As with many innovations in the understanding of extra-trop-ical cyclone behaviour, the origins of the "sting-jet" start with the insights of Norwegian weather forecasters. Norwegian meteorologist Sigbjorn Gronas has related how he was told by an experienced fore-caster in the 1960s that the most fearsome storms were those that had developed a "bent-back occlusion" in which the warm front, and its associated cloud-head, curl three quarters of an anticlockwise revolu-tion to lie immediately to the south of the cyclone centre—like the first twist of cream on a stirred cup of coffee. Mr. Gronas termed this signature the "scorpion's tail."...it turned out the low-level "sting-jet" was separate and related to intense, small-scale pulses of slantwise convection at the layered interface between the warm moist ascending air—the end of which forms the scorpion's tail—protruding into the "dry intrusion" of air from around the jet stream level that gives the characteristic dry slot at the centre of an intense extra-tropical storm. **2005** Roger Highfield *Telegraph* (U.K.) (Jan. 13) "'Sting Jet' Blamed for Winds" (Int.) ► Research by the Met Office and Prof. Keith Brown-ing, of the University of Reading, discovered the phenomenon and coined the phrase. Sting jets occur in cyclones when there is a dra-matic fall in the barometric pressure.

stink eye *n.* a facial expression of doubt, distrust, or dislike; a dirty look; SKUNK EYE, *the hairy eyeball. Slang.* [There is inconclu-sive evidence that this term originated in Hawaii and spread through beach sports such as surfing and volleyball. In Hawaiian *stink eye* would translate as *maka pilau*, which, according to the *Hawaiian Dictionary* at the Hawaiian Electronic Library, exists as a term meaning 'rotten eyes, one with rotten eyes, a ghost.'] **1962** Dennis R. Dean *English Journal* (May) "Slang Is Language Too!," vol. 51, no. 5, p. 324 ► A dirty look is a *stink eye*. **1987** John Dreyfuss *L.A. Times* (Sept. 27) "'Auntie Louise': Liveliest Living Legend in Hawaii," p. 3 ► You know when you're out of favor if she doesn't give you a peck on the cheek after work.... If she doesn't like you, she gives you the stink eye. **1991** Michael Hiestand *USA Today* (Aug. 22) "ABC's Jackson Not Shy About Expressing Opinion," p. 3C ► Chris Marlowe expects to see some "stink eyes" Saturday. The TV volleyball analyst, working NBC's U.S. championships this weekend, says that piece of beach volleyball lingo—translation: menacing glares—will apply if teams led by Sinjin Smith and Karch Kiraly meet in the Saturday final. "They really hate each other," says Marlowe. **1992** *Usenet: alt.surfing* (Jan. 30) "Re: Only Surfing" ► There had been a family of seven or eight dolphins cruising up and down the local beaches.... I paddled towards them (nothing violent or sudden, just an easy paddle out towards 'em).... The Lead Dude (Bull?) stopped his up and down swimming style, and slowed down a bit, spearing me with stink-eye, and staying on the surface until the rest of the family went by. **1994** David Farber *The 60's: From Memory to History* (Sept. 1), p. 299 ▶ The protestors seemed to give the same "stink eye" to both production and consumption, to the old virtues and the new values. **1995** Bill Adler *Growing Up Asian American* (Jan. 1), p. 82 ▶ Mrs. Vincente studies Joseph with what we called the "stink eye," but he still didn't catch on. She must have considered his behavior insubordinate. **2005** Julian E. Barnes @ Fallujah, Iraq *U.S. News & World Report* (June 18) "Iraq Journal: Filtering Language in Fallujah" (Int.) ▶ The patrol had halted in a particularly unfriendly part of the city where the marines say they get "the stinkeye" a lot.

Stokes basket *n.* a rigid body-sized platform in which a stretcher or litter can be secured for transporting patients, usually in precarious environments. Also **Stokes stretcher, Stokes litter, Stokes.** *Jargon. Medical.*

1909 *Washington Post* (July 16) "His Grit Saves Read," p. 5 ▶ When he was taken out under the trees on the Stokes stretcher he tried to promote a setto between the two young marines at which should have the lighter end to carry. **1941** *Sheboygan Press* (Wisc.) (Sept. 8) "Liner Iroquois Now Hospital Ship," p. 4 ▶ The former liner *Iroquois*...is now being refitted as the Navy's first hospital ship since World War I, bearing the name U.S.S. *Solace.* Injured men are brought aboard the vessel in Stokes basket. **1988** Dennis Smith *Firefighters: Their Lives in Their Own Words* (July 1), p. 156 ▶ They got the Stokes basket down there, a kind of wire basket moulded to the shape of the body, and they floated me on that, then lifted me up and out. **2005** Mindy Blake *KOLD-TV* (Tucson, Ariz.) (May 3) "Man Suffers Severe Tar Burns" (Int.) ▶ They attached what's called a stokes basket to the ladder, and using control ropes above and below, they lowered Gamez to the ground.

stooper *n.* at a racetrack, a person who picks up discarded bet tickets in search of those that represent unclaimed winnings. *Gambling. Sports.*

1940 Damon Runyon *Zanesville Signal* (Ohio) (Apr. 16) "The Brighter Side," p. 14 ▶ This is the stooper. He gets his name from his occupation. He goes around the racing yard between races picking up and examining parimutuel tickets that have been discarded as worthless by the original purchasers. **1985** Hugh A. Mulligan (*AP*) (May 10) "Professional Track Prognosticators Have Uncanny Ability" ▶ "The

Stooper never had a losing day," says Lacombe in ill-concealed envy. "He comes here broke, and the worst he can do is break even. Lots of win tickets go astray. Last year this track turned back $280,000 in uncashed tickets to the state." **2004** John Holl *N.Y. Times* (Aug. 2) "At the Track, Fewer Stoop for the Payoff" (Int.) ► The man, who declined to be interviewed, is part of a horse racing subculture made up of people known as stoopers. Much like people who spend afternoons wandering the beaches with metal detectors searching for treasure in the sand, stoopers spend their day at the track hoping to discover a discarded winning ticket.

stooshie *n.* a fight; a fuss, commotion, or to-do. *Scotland. Scots.* [According to the *Dictionary of the Scots Language*, under the spelling *stashie* this term dates to at least as early as 1824.]

1988 Maev Kennedy *Guardian* (U.K.) (Aug. 15) "Barbara Cartland's 'Pink Monstrosity' Enrages Scots" ► There seems to have been a little bit of a stooshie (a mild altercation, to those South of the Border) on the subject of Barbara Cartland. **1993** Paul Harris, Diana Wildman *Daily Mail* (London, Eng.) (Feb. 4) "Anne's Middle Class Move" ► I don't think people are getting terribly excited about it. Where I come from in Scotland they would say there hasn't been a great stooshy. **1997** Duncan McLean *Bunker Man* (May 1), p. 98 ► Frizzell panicked, lashed out, kicked at the boy's shin. Next thing he kens the boy's on the floor screaming, and the police are interviewing him on an assault charge.... The union had to fight like billy-oh on that one.... It was a right stooshie. In the papers and everything. **2005** Adrian Turpin *Financial Times* (U.K.) (July 1) "On Dangerous Ground" (Int.) ► Another great Scottish word is stooshie, meaning fight. By contesting the received wisdom of the Clearances, Fry has created an almighty stooshie.

stove pipe *v.* to develop, or be developed, in an isolated environment; to solve narrow goals or meet specific needs in a way not readily compatible with other systems. Also *attrib. Business. Jargon. United States.*

[**1987** Brad Bass *Government Computer News* (June 5) "A Review Is Last Hurdle for BASIS," vol. 6, no. 11, p. 1 ► "There are a lot of data processing systems out on Navy bases and stations," he said. "But they're, for lack of a better word, stove-pipe systems that found one specific application and solved that problem very efficiently."] **1993** Sally Atkins *Open Systems Today* (Sept. 20) "In the New Era of Systems Architecture, Apple Is Mr. (Frank Lloyd) Wright," no. 133, p. 88 ► In short, Apple had the sort of confusion present at most older organizations, where databases grew up with stove-piped or isolated islands of proprietary automation. **1994** Linda Taft *Telemarketing* (Feb. 1) "Technology Upgrades That Are Essential for Outstanding Customer Service," vol. 12, no. 8, p. 59 ▶ Each of these systems is supplied by different manufacturers with particular and typically focused disciplines. The various systems get "stove piped" and opportunities resolved within their discipline and sphere of control only. These systems were typically conceived within the vacuum of their own particular discipline and tend not to easily interface with each other. **2004** Keith Cowing *SpaceRef.com* (June 24) "NASA Begins to Transform Itself" (Int.) ▶ The net result was what came to be called "stove piping" where all centers began dueling fiefdoms—all intent on having their own min-NASA complete with efforts which unabashedly duplicated those resident at other centers.

streetism *n.* the living of homeless or unmonitored children on the street, especially when related to drugs, disease, crime, or delinquency. *Ghana. Zimbabwe.* This term appears to be specific to Anglophone Africa.

1996 Catherine Bush @ Addis Ababa, Ethiopia *Globe and Mail* (Toronto, Can.) (Aug. 6) "Circus Mania in Ethiopia," p. C1 ▶ While Circus Ethiopia has sometimes been described as a street-kids circus, Lachance is careful to point out that this is not quite the case. Although the connection to the street is very strong, "you could say that the circus is a preventative measure against streetism," Lachance says. **1997** Agnes Banda @ Lusaka *Times of Zimbabwe* (Aug. 19) "Zambia—70,000 Street Kids—A Day in the Life of One of Them" ▶ It was estimated that there were 35,000 street children in 1991 and that a further 315,000 were at risk of becoming drawn into streetism. **2002** *Accra Mail* (Accra, Ghana) (July 24) "People Should Vote Wisely" ▶ About sixty percent of the youth in the metropolis are unemployed due to lack of skills and the result is "streetism," drug and substance abuse, immorality and armed robbery. **2004** I.K. Gyasi *Ghanaian Chronicle* (Accra, Ghana) (Sept. 13) "Which Way for Education?" (Int.) ▶ Uncontrolled pregnancies outside the marriage circle have led to a flood of births, with the mothers unable to trace the men responsible. The result is what has come to be known in Ghanaian parlance as "streetism."

stripping *n.* a programming technique of broadcasting the same television show, or type of show, in the same time slot on successive nights. *Entertainment. Jargon. Media.*

1989 *Broadcast* (U.K.) (Feb. 10) "Broadcast Looks at the Commercial Stations' Use of Programme Stripping," p. 7 ▶ Roger Laughton, BBC head of co-productions and former head of daytime programming, agreed that stripping produced "more bums on seats but a lower reach." **1991** Georgina Henry *Guardian* (U.K.) "The Shape of Things to Come at ITV," p. 23 ► Stripping [specific programmes in the same slots across the week] is fine in the early evening, though we should stop transmitting Australian soaps then, and develop our own home-grown drama. **2002** Steve Pratt *Newsquest Media Group* (U.K.) (Aug. 31) "In the Picture: I'm an ITV boss...Get Me Out of Here" ► Her scheduling adopted the US method of stripping programmes, show-ing the same type of show at the same time every night so viewers always knew what was on.

stunt up *v.* to enhance or improve with special (eye-catching, flashy) additions. *Slang.*

1991 Georgina Henry *Guardian* (U.K.) "The Shape of Things to Come at ITV," p. 23 ► Stripping will continue, but not much more than we have already. But there will also be "stunting up the schedule": times when we break out of stripping with a one-off movie or event. **1992** Sheena McDonald *Guardian* (U.K.) (Aug. 17) "Scud-FM Goes Critical— BBC Gears Up for Round-the-Clock News Service," p. 25 ► Sceptics recall the reality of Gulf coverage as wastes of half-informed specula-tion by retired military men, punctuated by theatrical press confer-ences stunted up by the US military, complete with video inserts and the wit and wisdom of Stormin' Norman. **1995** Jim Bawden *Toronto Star* (Can.) (July 22) "Mean Streets," p. SW32 ► I found 90 per cent had never pulled a gun in their careers. And of those who did, only 1 per cent ever fired, because you go through a three-stage process of verbal warning, taking the gun out of the holster, clicking it, then, and only then, aiming. On NYPD Blue they blast in every episode. But we're reality—we don't do it to stunt up ratings. **2004** Dick Jones *Dick Jones' Patteran Pages* (May 3) "Business as Usual" (Int.) ► If the pictures were posed—"stunted up," in the parlance—it merely high-lights one relatively mild stage in a consistent pattern of gross behav-iour on the part of a small number of soldiers. The progress from "stunting up" apparent persecution sessions for the amusement of self & others to actually engaging in acts ranging from ritual humiliation through to torturing a victim to death is steady & logical, & for some the movement across the spectrum will be inexorable.

submarine patent *n.* a patent that, when issued, forces compa-nies already using the newly patented technology to pay retroac-tive licensing or rights fees. *Business. Jargon. United States.*

1993 James W. Crowley *Dispatch* (Columbus, Ohio) (Dec. 12) "OSU Could Lose Out in World of Patents," p. 4B ► A man fought with the Patent Office for 15 years while lots of different laser products were being developed. Eventually, makers of laser products were forced to pay him. "We call those 'submarine patents,'" Nickey said. "When he came to the surface, he made a lot of money." **1994** Andrew Pollack @ Tokyo *N.Y. Times* (Jan. 24) "U.S. Agrees to Alter Patents' Period of Coverage," p. D2 ▶ Occasionally, patents take a decade or two to be granted because they are held up in appeals and amendments in the Patent Office. When this happens under the existing system, an inventor can obtain a 17-year monopoly on an invention made long ago and demand payments from companies that have long been using the technology on the assumption that it was not protected by patents. Because these patents remain hidden for a long time and suddenly surface, they have been called "submarine patents." **2004** Robin Bloor *Register* (U.K.) (July 2) "Patents and the Threat to Open Source" (Int.) ▶ Acacia is one of a number of companies that are making a good living by sitting on patents that are actually very general in their application. Individuals can register such patents, with no ability to develop associated product, wait for infringing products to appear, then get a good lawyer and go hunting. Such patents are sometimes referred to as submarine patents.

sub-penny quoting *n.* the practice of offering a decimal of a cent higher than a stock's asking price or another buy order. Also **sub-penny pricing, sub-penny trading.** *Jargon. Money & Finance.*

2000 Judith Burns (*Dow Jones News Service*) (Oct. 26) "NYSE's Grasso Sees Securities Modernization Bill in 2001" ▶ Sub-penny pricing could well occur if some are "tempted to split Mr. Lincoln into further pieces," Grasso warned. He said "that would be tantamount to a neutron bomb" for U.S. markets and could hurt investors if it causes widespread execution problems. **2001** Judith Burns (*Dow Jones News Service*) (May 24) "SEC" ▶ It would be Nasdaq's preference that we don't move to sub-penny quoting. **2004** Sam Ali, Susan Todd (*Newhouse News Service*) (Apr. 26) "SEC Proposals Mean More Than Chump Change to Investors" (Int.) ▶ While the practice of sub-penny quoting is largely invisible, it has led to prevalent cutting, or "stepping ahead" as they call it in the markets.

supermarionation *n.* a form of puppetry using semi-animated doll-like marionettes. *Entertainment. United States.*

1968 *Post* (Frederick, Md.) (Nov. 7) (in advert.), p. D7 ▶ Thunderbirds Are Go.... Supermarionation. Technicolor. **1988** Richard K. Shull *Record* (N.J.) (Mar. 6) "Ask TV Record," p. 4 ▶ I'm trying to remember a children's show called "Fireball XL-5." What can you tell me about it? A. NBC had that show from October 1963 through September 1965 for 39 episodes. The show was done with marionettes and a process called "Supermarionation." **2004** Alan Niester *Globe and Mail* (Toronto, Can.) (July 30) "Thunderbirds Are a No-Go," p. R9 (Int.) ▶ A cheesy puppet show that was filmed in what was laughingly referred to as "supermarionation," the show has mysteriously become something of a cult hit. Despite the fact that the special effects amounted largely to giant puffballs of smoke and cardboard rockets hung from string, the show has managed to remain in syndication these last forty years.

Susmaryosep *n.* an exclamation of surprise, disbelief, or emphasis. *Philippines.* [From Spanish Je*sus, Mary, Joseph.]
1991 *Usenet: soc.culture.filipino* (Apr. 14) "Philippine Environment III: Several Polluting Firms Ordered Closed" ▶ According to officials, SANCANCO had been discharging effluent by 3400 mg/l exceeding the allowable 80 mg/l. Susmaryosep! DENR also said that SANCANCO has been operating without a permit. **1999** Alex L. Lacson *BusinessWorld* (Jan. 27) "Taxing the Underground Economy," p. 4 ▶ In the words of one vendor, who loudly remonstrated that what she earned was not even enough to cover the debts she accumulated as puhunan: "Susmaryosep!" **2004** [Paulemeric] *To Live Without Thinking* (Manila, Philippines) (June 30) "From Acceptable to Exceeds Expectations" (Int.) ▶ There are times when she is very funny because she even translates Filipino terms like "Susmaryosep."

swangaz *n.pl.* spoked automobile tire rims. *Automotive. Hip-Hop.*
1999 *Usenet: rec.music.hip-hop* (July 15) "Re: RapCity: UnderHouston" ▶ H-town is the city of the vehicle fashion show, we got the carfreaks, hoppers, and the boppers 4REAL. You'll some shit you aint seen before i garawn-tee. From candied 'Lacs on swangaz & vogyes to the foreign big- bodies with 4 tv's in the headrests. **2001** *Usenet:rec.music.hip-hop* (Oct. 23) "Re: Balls on a Cadillac Brougham?" ▶ "Bars on a Cadillac Brougham"…"Also known as swangaz…the first spokes the precursors to Daytons." **2005** Kristie Rieken @ Houston *Star-Telegram* (Dallas-Fort Worth, Tex.) (July 2) "Texan Paul Wall Shines in Sea of Rappers" (Int.) ▶ The rapper, whose real last name is Slayton, relies on a dizzying array of local vernacular to describe everything from attractive females (honey dips) to rims (swangaz) and tires (vogues).

swankienda *n.* a mansion or large house. *Architecture. Texas. United States.* [*swank*y + Sp. hac*ienda.* Journalist Maxine Mesinger is often credited with the coinage.] This term appears to be special to the Houston, Texas, area, but has also spread elsewhere.

1968 John Ayres *Port Arthur News* (Tex.) (July 9) "Supper Tagle Talk," p. 4 ▶ High court judges were a dime a dozen at the sumptuous cocktail-buffet tossed by the law partners Marian Rosen (ex of P.A.) and Clyde Woody at the Rosen's swankienda in Houston during the Texas bar convention last week. **1985** Maxine Mesinger *Houston Chronicle* (Tex.) (Mar. 10) "Big City Beat," p. 5 ▶ The Malibu swankienda was still under construction when Tommy lost his battle with cancer more than two years ago, so he never got to enjoy it. **1989** *Late Night with David Letterman* (July 25) "Top 10 Names for the Letterman Estate" in *Usenet: alt.fan.letterman* (July 6, 2002) (mark lee) *"Top Ten 1989 Pt1":* 2. The Swankienda. **1990** *Usenet: rec.arts.tv.soaps* (Nov. 17) "AMC: Just an Observation" ▶ She had it on at her swankienda confronting Adamo, and then bopping about Pine Valley! **2001** Clifford Pugh *Houston Chronicle* (Tex.) (Jan. 20) "'Miss Moonlight' Dies at 75; Columnist Kept Tabs on Celebrities for More Than 4 Decades," p. 3 ▶ In February 1965, the Houston-born columnist landed a rare, exclusive interview with Burt Lancaster (top, left) in Dallas. Later that year, she and celebrity pal Judy Garland (bottom, left) were spied sharing a ride on the way to an undisclosed "swankienda." **2004** Ken Hoffman, Ben Levine *Houston Chronicle* (Nov. 13) "Coined Word Is Reminder of Columnist, Her Colorful Language" (Int.) ▶ I appreciated your "swankienda" reference last week. Maxine Mesinger was my cousin, and it's nice to see that her "phrase" has not been forgotten.

swardspeak *n.* a cant spoken by Filipino gay and transvestite men. *Philippines. Sexuality. Swardspeak* is a mix of Tagalog (Pilipino), Spanish, English, and other languages spoken in the Philippines and dates back to at least as early as the 1970s. *Swardspeak* is pronounced by Filipinos similar to *swards-PEH-ahk.*

1990 Donn V. Hart, Harriet Hart *Crossroads* "Visayan Swardspeak: The Language of a Gay Community in the Philippines," vol. 5, no. 2, p. 27 (title). **1995** Anjie Blardony Ureta *BusinessWorld* (Philippines) (Oct. 12) "Agot's Got It," p. 24 ▶ It would help if Ms. Isidro toned down on the swardspeak. It can get a little disconcerting coming from such a pretty face. **1996** Emily Noelle Ignacio *Contemporary Sociology*

(Jan.) "Social Hierarchies," vol. 25, no. 1, p. 41 ▶ Marginalization is further described in Martin Manalansan's ethnography of *baklas* (loosely translated, male transvestites) in Manhattan. Here, he describes how the appropriation of Spanish, Tagalog, and English into *swardspeak* (the bakla language) illustrates that the bakla are neither on the "inside" nor "outside." **2003** Jana Evans Braziel *Theorizing Diaspora* (Jan. 1), p. 220 ▶ The swardspeak term *ladlad ng kapa* (which literally means "unfurling the cape" and has been unproblematically translated as "coming out") belies how identity is something "worn" and not always "declared." **2005** *Bakla. Bakla. Baket Ka Ginawa?* (May 13) "Gay Speaks on 'Swardspeak'" (Int.) ▶ Isa pa marahil sa naging dahilan ng pagkalat ng swardspeak "nung sixties at seventies eh ang pagpapatungkol nito sa isang luluki na feeling ng "swardspeaker" eh bading din pero hindi aminado: kamiembro ng federasyon, kafatid sa fananampalataya, among others na learn naman nating hanggang ngayon eh No. 1 hobby pa ren ng mga "out" na bading. Ito ang nagpapatunay sa kung gano kahalaga ang "self-identification" o paglantad sa mga vading. **2005** Ayn Veronica L. de Jesus *Manila Times* (Philippines) (Aug. 1) "The 'Jologsification' of Shakespeare" (Int.) ▶ Set in the slums of Barangay Verona, Manila where the jologs culture thrives, the production takes a totally fresh look at the romance of the star-crossed lovers and their warring households, dressed in the latest ukay fashion, uttering sonnets peppered with Filipino "swardspeak."

sweethearting *n.* the granting of special favors or privileges, especially to friends or family; in retail, the giving of unauthorized discounts or the abetting of shoplifting or other theft; the giving of a *sweetheart deal. Business. Crime & Prisons.* [This is a natural outgrowth from existing uses of the attributive and adjectival *sweetheart* 'privileged, exclusive, or preferential' such as in *sweetheart deal* 'a special, exclusive offer or arrangement.'] A more established sense of *sweethearting* is 'courting or wooing.'

1965 Jerry Landauer *Wall Street Journal* (Sept. 23) "Coal 'Sweethearts': UMW Tolerates Pay, Royalties Below Scale in More Small Mines," p. 1 ▶ In the classic "sweetheart" situation, corrupt union leaders accept or extort payoffs from employers in exchange for assuring labor peace or winking at contract violations.... [p. 14] The number of employers paying remarkably low sums into the pension fund yields one indication of how many pensions "sweethearting" may threaten. **1987** Paul Moloney *Toronto Star* (Can.) (Jan. 26) "Chairman Vows to Expose Thefts at Liquor Stores," p. A7 ▶ People come into the store and buy a bottle at a certain price and the cashier rings up a different product at a much lower price. They call that sweethearting in the trade, and that goes on. **2001** *Security* (Feb. 1) "Monitoring System," vol. 38, no. 2, p. 42 ▶ POS/EM Plus helps eliminate employee theft at up to four registers per unit by detecting, documenting and deterring fraud, collusion, sweethearting, coupon misredemption and cash theft. **2001** Mike Hendry *Smart Card Security and Applications* (Apr. 1), 2 ed., p. 255 ▶ *Insiders*, typically employees of the card issuer or scheme operator, have opportunities to copy, analyze, or steal data and hardware, or to give special privileges or benefits to their friends (*sweethearting*). **2002** David D. Perlmutter *Pittsburgh Post-Gazette* (Pa.) (July 10) "The Culture of 'Unethics,'" p. A9 ▶ I'm sure he thinks of himself as an honorable man. And so do they all, big and small:...Bernard Ebbers of WorldCom (suspected of sweethearting himself a $366 million loan). **2005** Jeff Morris *Multichannel Merchant* (June 1) "Minding the Store," vol. 22, no. 6, p. 44 ▶ One of the primary methods used by employees is "sweethearting," theft carried out by collusion between an employee and a customer. It is so named because it most often occurs between a cashier and his family members or friends. With sweethearting, a cashier may fail to charge the customer for some items or may ring up only one item of a multiple purchase.

swellbow *n.* a swollen elbow. *Medical.* [*swell* + el*bow*]

1990 David Rowan *Guardian* (U.K.) (May 19) "Lingua Franca: Monkey Business" ▶ If you fall off your board, you might receive a...swellbow (a swollen elbow). **2002** Scott Sandell *L.A. Times* (F36) (May 9) "The Xs and the Ohs: Athletes' Expertise Was Needed to Turn Action Sports Thrills into an IMAX Ride" ▶ Burnquist has broken 19 bones over the years and endured countless cases of "swellbow," from smacking his elbows. ***2005** *Med Ad News* (June 16) "11th Annual Report on DTC" (Int.) ▶ When they skate, they keep falling on their elbows, and there's a name for it called swellbow. So we give tip cards that explain what swellbow is physiologically and what's happening to their body anatomically, and then how they can treat it.

swivel chair job *n.* a desk job; a sinecure or patronage position; a ROCKING CHAIR JOB. *Employment.* Often derogatory, especially in the military.

1911 *Lincoln Evening News* (Neb.) (Jan. 2) "A Miracle of Re-Birth," p. 8B ▶ Other dilated sarcastically on the difference between a swivel chair job at the city hall and one which kept the holder thereof on his feet all day between counters or in factories under conditions calculated to endow the worker with sore feet, bunions, corns and rheumatism. **1915** *Chicago Daily Tribune* (June 29) "Twelfth St. Condemnation Cases Before Court Today," p. 16 ▶ For such a citizen out of work, the cases offer a swivel chair job at $3 a day. **1920** *Gettysburg Times* (Pa.) (Dec. 15) "Says Youth Did Not Fire Shot," p. 3 ▶ Last year a hero, who had had some swivel-chair job during the war, came up here crowing about his valor. **1927** *Syracuse Herald* (N.Y.) (Feb. 27), p. 8 ▶ Jay F. Gould, Minnesota Game Commissioner, shows his is no swivel chair job. **1943** *N.Y. Times* (June 28) "Senator Assails Big U.S. Payrolls," p. 27 ▶ Senator William Langer...charged yesterday that there are "three-quarters of a million young fellows of draft age now holding down swivel chair jobs instead of being in the armed services where they belong." These young men holding down "cinch jobs"...are "mostly of rather wealthy parentage and of families of rather great influence." **1962** Hal Wood *Western Kansas Press* (Oct. 6) "Tebbetts to New Cleveland Post," p. 5 ▶ Tebbetts subsequently went with the Braves as a vice president in 1959 and remained there in that capacity until September of 1961 when he stepped out of that swivel-chair job to return to the bench as Milwaukee manager.

SWMBO *n.* a woman in authority; a wife. *Acronym.* [She who must be obeyed. The information in the 2004 cite is likely correct as to the popularization and pronunciation of this term, but the earliest use and probable origin is in the H. Rider Haggard novel *She*.] **1986** Geoffrey Kenihan *Advertiser* (Adelaide, Australia) (Oct. 17) "L'Epicurien Advertising Supplement" ▶ But to business. She Who Must Be Obeyed began with Soupe de Poisson Bretonne.... SWMBO and I can rarely agree about anything these days, so we settled for peaceful co-existence and a half bottle each to accompany our main courses. **1990** *Toronto Star* (Apr. 9) "Judi Salem, 52, Managed Law Office," p. A11 ▶ Judi Salem was affectionately known as SWMBO—She Who Must Be Obeyed. **2004** [Grung] *SWIMBO* (Canberra, Australia) (July 1) "Idj's SWMBO" (Int.) ▶ SWMBO. It's pronounced "swimbo." While we might be able to take credit for the initialism and pronunciation, the phrase is actually a phrase Idj first heard and read in the John Mortimer series "Rumpole of the Bailey." In it, Rumpole refers to his wife as "She Who Must Be Obeyed," and, yes, you can hear the capitalization just as Idj wrote it.

T

taco *v.* especially in cycling, to bend or fold (a wheel) in the middle. *Sports.*

1988 Tom Cuthbertson *Anybody's Bike Book* (June 1), p. 122 ▶ If the rim is sprung out of round, so the wheel looks like a potato chip (some people say it's pretzeled, others say tacoed). **1991** *Usenet:*

rec.boats.paddle (Oct. 3) "Inflatable Kayaks" ▶ Flaccid material means you can't brace, and you get tacoed in the smallest of holes. **1995** Charles Walbridge *Whitewater Rescue Manual* (July 1), p. 66 ▶ When a canoe or kayak is caught horizontally against two obstructions...if the current is powerful enough, the boat will be "tacoed," or folded at the center and pushed through the opening. **1997** *Orange County Register* (Mar. 30) "Hot Bike Trails," p. K7 ▶ A little over a year ago, I hit a rock or something, I went flipping over, I scraped up my face and tacoed my front rim. **1997** Scott Steepleton *L.A. Times* (June 13) "Patrol Car Batters Bike; Rider Upset," p. B3 ▶ He ran over the bike and just kept going.... It tacoed my rims, bent my sprocket and it may have bent the frame. **2005** *Ventura County Star* (Calif.) (July 4) "Cycling Through the Lingo" (Int.) ▶ *Taco:* To bend a wheel over on itself into the shape of a taco.

—tacular *suffix* in the forming of nouns, 'an exciting or extravagant event' associated with the root; in the forming of adjectives, an intensifier of the root, 'a lot, great, large, extravagant, excessive.' [From a resegmenting of *spectacular*, in which the syllable *tacular* splinters off of *spec* and becomes a combining form. This true segmenting of the word would ordinarily be *spectacul*, from the Latin *spectacul-um* 'a show, spectacle, something worth observing' and the Latin suffix *-ar* 'of a kind; belonging to.'] Terms created with *—tacular* tend to be jocular one-offs, though some, like *spooktacular* and *craptacular*, appear to have more endurance.

1958 *Lethbridge Herald* (Alberta, Can.) (Oct. 28) (in advert.), p. 14 ▶ We've scared up a spook-tacular selection of grand buys. **1962** *Lima News* (Ohio) (Apr. 10) "'Spring-Tacular' at Bath Friday," p. 5

► The Bath High School band...will present its annual "pops" concert, a "Spring-Tacular." **1970** *Chronic Telegram* (Elyria, Ohio) (Nov. 29) (in advert.), p. 10 ► May's Christmas Sports-Tacular. **1971** *Reno Evening Gazette* (Nev.) (May 18) (in advert.), p. 32 ► Wards Splash-Tacular 30x15' "Leisure Life" Pool with Deluxe Features. **1992** *News Record* (North Hills, Pa.) (Aug. 2) "1992 Pittsburgh Three Rivers Regatta Schedule" ► Digital Music Express Water Ski Tacular. **1994** *Usenet: rec.folk-dancing* (Mar. 18) "NEFFA 1994—New England Folk Festival Schedule" ► Spud-tacular Contras. **1994** *Usenet: alt.music.hardcore* (Mar. 23) "GWARs Tour Dates 94" ► Spew-tacular. **1995** *Usenet: rec.arts.comics.misc* (Aug. 3) "CBG Price Guide: Threat or Menace" ► Sabrina's Halloween Spook-tacular. **1996** *Usenet: rec.sport.paintball* (Apr. 3) "Re: Which Paint Tastes Best?" ► I like the taste of purple premium myself. One time, my friend's brother shot me in the goggles (Scott Intruders) and it squeezed through the little hole in the cheek. Dripped to my mouth. Tast-tacular! **1997** *Usenet: alt.tv.simpsons* (Dec. 22) "'G' Rated Simpsons" ► Although the strangling of Bart is harmless (and VERY old at this point)...the use of the word "craptacular" and the references in Bart's dream raise a flag or two with the rating. **1999** *Usenet: alt.tv.real-world* (June 7) "Re: [RW Ass All-Stars]" ► Miami was Ass-Tacular! **2004** *Varsity Online* (Nov. 26) "Varsity's End-of-Year List-Tacular" (Int.) (title).

takeout *n.* the amount of each bet deducted by a horse-racing track to cover expenses. *Gambling. Jargon.*

1978 James Golla *Globe and Mail* (Toronto, Can.) (Jan. 17) "Backstretch Bookmaking at Racetrack, OPP Charge," p. P35 ► The OJC receives 9.5 cents per dollar wagered through the mutuels and turns back approximately 50 per cent of its takeout to the horsemen in purses. **2004** Joe Drape *N.Y. Times* (Apr. 26) "Horse Racing's Biggest Bettors Are Reaping Richest Rewards" (Int.) ► In the Kentucky Derby on Saturday, for example, Churchill Downs will return to bettors at the track about 82 cents of every dollar wagered in the form of winnings. The remaining 18 cents, known as the takeout, will be used to pay for expenses like racing purses, state taxes and track maintenance.

talent bucket *n.* especially in sports, a team or pool of skilled labor; a person's skill set. *Sports.*

1985 Volney Meece *Oklahoman* (Oklahoma City) (Jan. 26) "Lemons: OCU Should Be a 'Cakewalk' for Loyola" ► Chieftain personnel wasn't too awe-inspiring to start with but OCU was at least competitive until 12 days ago. That's when the bottom started dropping out of the talent bucket. **1997** Jennifer Ezzy *Daily Telegraph* (Sydney, Australia)

(Mar. 12) "Crime Squads in Talent 'Bucket,'" p. 4 ▶ The minutes reveal that some of the 700 detectives will be placed in a "bucket" of talent and handpicked to work in special "strike forces" according to their rank and skill. "The organised crime task force program will operate as a bucket with all staff in it and 'strike forces' will be formed from that bucket." **1999** *Usenet: aus.sport.rugby-league* (Aug. 12) "Re: Dr Who's Who's Who of the NG" ▶ Ted had just about everything the talent bucket could provide, but he wasted most of it. He's my pick for the best natural footballing talent I've ever seen. **2000** Robyn Bryson *Orange County Register* (Calif.) (July 17) "Reventon Super Estrella Rocks the Pond," p. F5 ▶ The stink bomb of the concert was Paulina Rubio. Other than attempting to look sexy with a backdrop of dancers, her talent bucket was empty. **2001** Cathy Fishel *Print* (Sept. 1) "The Midwest," vol. 55, no. 5 ▶ It's common knowledge here that the relatively warmer climes of destinations like San Francisco or Seattle have poked holes in the Midwestern talent bucket for years. **2005** Joe Strauss *St. Louis Post-Dispatch* (Mo.) (June 11) "Cards Insider: Team Shifts Draft Focus, Zero in on Prep Players" (Int.) ▶ When Cardinals vice president of player procurement Jeff Luhnow cites the organization's line of prospects, he refers to the club's "player portfolio." Asked about the team's board for last week's player draft, Luhnow refers to "talent buckets."

talker *n.* a much-discussed topic. *Media. Politics.*

1995 (*AP*) (Oct. 3) "Kansans Watch as Innocent Verdict Comes in for Simpson" ▶ It's a talker. And people are saying it's the trial of the century. **2001** Jason Carroll *CNN* (June 29) "Inside Politics: Vice President Cheney to Undergo Another Heart Procedure" ▶ Ridiculous? Yes. Thought-provoking? No, but it's definitely...a talker in this town. **2002** Bob Longino *Atlanta Journal-Constitution* (Ga.) (Aug. 23) "At the Movies: Neo-Nazi Jew Shocks in 'Believer'" ▶ It's a talker of a film in that it can arrest the eyes. A shocker, as some might say. **2004** Betty Nguyen *CNN* (Dec. 4) "Saturday Morning: Bush, Musharraf Talk Terror War" ▶ It's a talker, and there are new revelations in the steroid scandal looming over major league baseball. **2005** Trip Jennings @ Hartford, Conn. *Republican American* (Waterbury, Conn.) (June 18) "Some Legislators Fish for Votes; Others Are Just Blowing Smoke" (Int.) ▶ A small easy-to-overlook bill suddenly became potentially controversial. In State Capitol parlance, it was a "talker," which can be a kiss of death toward the end of the legislative session, when state lawmakers are trying to ram through hundreds of bills and the threat of a time-consuming debate can hurt a bill's shot at success.

tap-tap *n.* a truck or van used as an independently operated taxi. *Automotive. French-based Creole. Haiti.*

1972 Herbert Gold *N.Y. Times Mag.* (Mar. 12) "Progress in Haiti: Leopards in Sneakers Instead of Tonton Macoutes," p. 34 ► I was cheering them on when a tap-tap, the gaily painted bus, careened into the crowd and knocked a paper mask flying. **1977** Brigitte Weeks *Washington Post* (Apr. 3) "The Haitian Vacation," p. M1 ► Strange little buses called "tap-taps," constructed on flatbed trucks and decorated over every inch with paintings of flowers, animals, Bible stories and proverbs, ply along the Avenue des Salines. **1985** Paul Shell *Daily Oklahoman* (Oklahoma City) (Mar. 13) "Haiti Teaches of Death, Life" ► Once on the road to Aux Cayes we passed a tap-tap (a small pickup truck) wreck and there was a man laying in the road dead. **2004** Mary McCarty @ Leogane, Haiti *Dayton Daily News* (Ohio) (Aug. 4) "Faith Abounds" (Int.) ► She leaves the house at 4 a.m. to catch the "tap-tap," one of the privately-owned vans, buses, and trucks that serve as Haiti's equivalent of public transportation. The always crowded tap-taps—coined for the two-tap system for signaling boarding and exiting—are painted in carnival colors and emblazoned with hopeful messages such as "God is merciful" and "Love is Eternal."

teamgym *n.* a form of group gymnastics that includes trampette, tumbling, and a choreographed floor routine. Also **TeamGym, Team Gym.** *Sports.*

1999 *Nottingham Evening Post* (U.K.) (Mar. 24) "Sportsline" ► The 1999 Teamgym Championships take place at Harvey Hadden Sports Centre this weekend. **2002** Gordon Scott *Edinburgh Evening News* (Scotland) (Apr. 18) "Donor's Cash Is a Boost for Scots," p. 46 ► Team Gym involves teams of gymnasts, aged 16 and over, competing in floor, tumbling and trampette events. ***2004** *Croydon School of Gymnastics* (South Croydon, U.K.) (Feb. 28) "Teamgym" (Int.) ► TeamGym is a relatively new form of gymnastics and has only been in Great Britain since 1998, when the first British TeamGym Championships were held in Aldershot.

teeth arm *n.* a military's fighting troops, such as infantry, cavalry, and armored divisions. *Military. United Kingdom.* Troops not in the *teeth arm* have supporting roles in technical, logistic, and administrative arms.

1981 A.J. Trythall *Journal of Contemporary History* (July) "The Downfall of Leslie Hore-Belisha," vol. 16, no. 3, p. 395 ► Teeth Arm regiments and corps were of course very powerful. For instance, from 1904 to present, all Army Councillors (or Board Members) have been Infantry, Cavalry, Tanks, Gunners or Sappers. **1991** *Independent* (U.K.) (June 10) "Army's System No Longer Suited to Today's Battle-fields" ▶ The six main "teeth" arm units were augmented by soldiers from 10 other regiments. **1992** Gary Gore (Dec. 15) (Int.) in *Morrow Project Journal* (May 24, 1993), vol. 1, no. 1 ▶ Teeth arm units are an Armoured Regiment (8th Canadian Hussars), an Infantry Battalion (1st Battalion Royal Canadian Regiment) and the Canadian Airborne Regiment. **2003** James Gray (*United Kingdom Parliament*) (Oct. 16) "House of Commons Hansard Debates" ▶ The Royal Logistics Corps and the Signals also relied significantly on the T[erritorial] A[rmy]. There were lots of other teeth arm people out there—infantry people and special forces—and all of them were from the TA. **2004** Nowa Omoigui *Omogui.com* (Sept. 20) "Who Is General AO Ogomudia" (Int.) ▶ Signals is a "teeth" arm (in British parlance).... To be a Service Commander in Nigeria requires that one have the right type of commission (regular combatant) and belong to a "teeth arm" (i.e., Infantry, Artillery, Armour, Combat Engineers, Intelligence, or Signals).

telltale *n.* on an automobile's instrument panel, an indicator that relays information about the vehicle to the driver. *Automotive. Jargon.*

1989 Ralph Ong *Electronic Design* (Aug. 4) "Design a Minimum-Space Auto-Instrument Module," p. 53 ▶ The telltales for gas, oil, tempera-ture, and battery voltage—standard, fixed icons that don't change in real time—reside in the PROM memory. **1989** Bill Robinson *Atlanta Journal-Constitution* (Ga.) (Oct. 15) "Studdard's Ambition Burns On: At Age 51, SCCA Driver Wants to Try NASCAR," p. E26 ▶ They've got a "tell-tale" tracking needle on the tachometer. Shows you the highest RPM a driver just reached on the track. **1995** *Usenet: rec.autos .marketplace* (Apr. 7) "Re: Reprogramming Digital Odometers" ▶ The replacement part turns on a little telltale next to the odometer display indicating that the part has been replaced. ***2004** Bob Wallace *Vette* (Aug. 2) "Driving the C6 Shows It Exceeds Expectations" (Int.) ▶ There's less clutter on the faces of the tach and speedo since the idiot lights (Chevrolet refers to them as "telltales") have been moved to a space between the two major gauges.

tent pole *n.* something, such as a commercial undertaking, a story franchise, or a fictional character, that serves as primary support (for a company, television program, etc.), especially a blockbuster movie that compensates for a studio's flops. *Entertainment. Media. United States.*

1986 Gina Mallet *Globe and Mail* (Toronto, Can.) (Mar. 27) "As Stratford's World Turns," p. P58 ▶ As the only major industry in town, it is the tent pole of Stratford's economy. **1987** Aljean Harmetz @ Hollywood (June 4) "Figuring Out the Fates of 'Cop II' and 'Ishtar'" ▶ Mr. Mancuso describes "Beverly Hills Cop II" as a "tent pole" movie. Each year Paramount makes several high-budget films "that because of content, star value or storyline have immediate want-to-see and are strong enough to support your entire schedule," he said. "Ishtar" had none of the strengths of a tent pole. **2003** Hilary Kramer *N.Y. Post* (Aug. 10) "H'Wood Mulls Big-Flick Costs" (Int.) ▶ It's easy to see how big movies—called "tent poles" in industry parlance—can be big risks. "You can't afford too many tent poles in a year." **2004** Jennie Punter *Globe and Mail* (Toronto, Can.) (May 31) "Studios Scurry to Make Movies with International Legs," p. R1 (Int.) ▶ The industry term for a movie (usually but not always a franchise flick) that a major studio expects will be a blockbuster (but often isn't), "tent pole" is a particularly evocative buzzword to toss around these days, especially for those brushing up on ancient texts or history in preparation for a pitch meeting with a major studio. **2004** Jon Gertner *N.Y. Times* (Nov. 14) "Box Office in a Box" (Int.) ▶ A studio like Fox usually works on dozens of DVDs at a time—from minor television shows to $100 million-plus "tent poles" meant to draw everyone in and that entail a marketing blitz mapped out long beforehand. **2005** Patrick D. Healy *N.Y. Times* (Feb. 24) "After Coming Out, a Soap Opera Heroine Moves On" (Int.) ▶ She was most astonished that fans elevated Bianca into one of the serial's "tent poles"—soap parlance for characters who hold enormous sway with viewers.

terminal wean *n.* the intentional reduction of medical life-support, especially mechanical or supplemental respiration, that permits a patient to die. *Medical.*

1992 Robert Zussman *Intensive Care: Medical Ethics and the Medical Profession* (July 15), p. 109 ▶ In twelve cases they performed a procedure called, in only mildly obscurantist language, a "terminal wean." (Although neither doctors nor nurses literally "pull the plug," the process is dramatic enough. After a doctor or, more often, a nurse turns down the respirator setting, death usually follows quickly, most often in an hour or two.) **1995** Dean Gianakos *Chest* (Nov. 1) "Terminal Weaning (from Ventilator Therapy)," vol. 108, no. 5, p. 1405 ▶ Physicians often withdraw patients from mechanical ventilators when therapy has been judged futile or the patient requests discontinuation. Withdrawal occurs in two ways: physicians either extubate patients immediately or wean them over a period of hours (terminal weaning). **1997** John M. Luce *Western Journal of Medicine* (Dec. 1) "Withholding and Withdrawal of Life Support from Critically Ill Patients," vol. 167, no. 6, p. 411 ▶ Of physicians who withdrew ventilators, 33% preferred the gradual withdrawal of supplemental oxygen and positive end-expiratory pressure treatment before removing the ventilator, a process called terminal weaning. **2004** Nell Boyce *U.S. News & World Report* (Jan. 12) "Science Calls at the Deathbed," vol. 136, no. 1, p. 50 ▶ They cover studies on both brain-dead people and "terminal wean" patients, who still have brain function but will die soon after being taken off life support. **2005** Marc Lallanilla *ABC News* (U.S.) (Mar. 21) "Most End-of-Life Cases Avoid Courtrooms" (Int.) ▶ Ending the care of a patient—also known as "terminal wean"—is a decision made daily in most hospitals.

terp *n.* an interpreter.

1992 *Usenet: bit.listserv.deaf-l* (Nov. 25) "Re: Question for All of You..." ▶ One of the most pleasant and rewarding contacts we (husband and I) had with deaf signers was at a lunch where one of the other hearing people who signed (actually a terp, but off duty) was willing to both sign and voice interpret back and forth for us. **2002** David Zucchino @ Sardak, Afghanistan *L.A Times* (Oct. 13) "The Untold War," p. A1 ▶ With the help of a helmeted "terp"—an Afghan interpreter—the lieutenant explained that he had come to search for Al Qaeda and Taliban gunmen and weapons. **2004** Linda Robinson *U.S. News & World Report* (May 10) "The War in the Shadows," vol. 136, no. 16, p. 38 ▶ The "terp," as the grunts call their Afghan interpreter, sums up the atmosphere. **2004** Sabrina Tavernise @ Baghdad, Iraq *Times Argus* (Barre, Vt.) (Sept. 19) "Hit Men Target Iraqis Working for Americans" (Int.) ▶ Interpreters are referred to as "terps" and are replaced in a seemingly endless flow of manpower as soon as they are killed.

therapism *n.* a culture or an ideal of mental therapy, empathy, or sharing of feelings, especially as a cure. *Health.* This term was popularized, although probably not coined by, novelist Fay Weldon.

1986 Janice G. Raymond *A Passion for Friends*, pp. 155-56 in *Women Without Men* (May 1, 1993) Donald J. Greiner, p. 112 ▶ Therapism is an overvaluation of feeling. In a real sense, it is a tyranny of feelings where women have come to believe that what really counts in their life is their "psychology."...We might say that therapism promotes a psychological hypochondria with women as the major seekers of emotional health. **1995** Susan C. Jarratt (May 18) "In Excess: Radical

Extensions of Neopragmatism" in *Rhetoric, Sophistry, Pragmatism* Steven Mailloux, p. 216 ► Some are put off by the New Age rhetoric of crystals, spiritualism, and therapism. **1997** Fay Weldon *Guardian* (U.K.) (Jan. 11) "Mind at the End of Its Tether" ► Once we saw ourselves as serving God, then science, then the state: now we turn inwards and serve ourselves, worship our individuality. This is what I mean by Therapism. It is a religion which began a hundred years ago in the consulting rooms of psychotherapists, and which now, in its wider social and political context, sweeps all before it. **1998** Fay Weldon *Harper's Magazine* (May 1) "Where Women Are Women and So Are Men," vol. 296, no. 1776, p. 65 ► The first step that women took in their emancipation was to adopt traditional male roles: to insist on their right to wear trousers, not to placate, not to smile, not to be decorative. The first step men have taken in their self-defense is to adopt the language of Therapism: a profoundly female notion this—that all things can be cured by talk. **2005** Andrew Ferguson *Bloomberg.com* (June 21) "Can U.S. Companies End Emotional Correctness?" (Int.) ► "Therapism," they write, is a doctrine that "valorizes openness, emotional self-absorption and the sharing of feelings."

386 generation *n.* the age group of South Koreans who were born in the 1960s, attended university in the 1980s, and are now serving in positions of power. *South Korea.*

1999 *Korea Herald* (Seoul, S. Korea) (Jan. 6) "1999—The Sideways Year" ► The "386 generation" of people born in the 1960s and the "shinsedae" of people born in the 1970s will demand changes in traditional top-down decision making in Korean organizations. **1999** *Korea Times* (Seoul, S. Korea) (June 11) "Student Activists in 1980s Gear Up for New Social Movement" ► Many of them were imprisoned while staging anti-government and unification activities in the 1980s. They belong to the so-called "386 Generation." **2004** Kim So-young *Korea Herald* (Seoul, S. Korea) (Aug. 19) "Minister Preaches Market Economy to Lawmakers" (Int.) ► The 386 generation refers to those who were in their thirties when the term was coined, attended college in the 1980s and were born in the 1960s. **2004** Kim Gi-hyeon @ Moscow *Dong-A Ilbo Daily* (Seoul, S. Korea) (Aug. 24) "The Long-Lost Civilian Revolution" ► The so-called "386-generation" members who had once led the movement for democracy are now in several government positions.

thrillionaire *n.* a rich person who pursues expensive and dangerous pastimes. *Money & Finance.* [*thrill* + *millionaire*]

[**1997** David Gordois *News of the World* (Apr. 6) "Carole Is Butlin Thrillionaire!" p. 60 (title).] **1998** Michael Corcoran *Austin American-Statesman* (Tex.) (Sept. 19) "Austinites Peek into the Remains of

Titanic Wreck," p. E1 ► Thrillionaire Richard Garriott and a handful of others defied a court order and toured the wreckage of the *Titanic* last week. The 37-year-old Origin Systems co-founder paid a reported $65,000 for the trip. **2005** John Schwartz *N.Y. Times* (June 14) "Thrillionaires: The New Space Capitalists" (Int.) ► The SpaceShipOne flight made him the best-known member of a growing club of high-tech thrillionaires, including the Amazon founder Jeff Bezos, who find themselves with money enough to fulfill their childhood fascination with space.

throw down *n.* evidence, especially a weapon, planted by police on a suspect or at a crime scene. *Crime & Prisons. Police. Slang.* A more common meaning of *throw down* is "a fight."

1985 *Baton Rouge Morning Advocate* (La.) (Mar. 20) "Settlement Approved," p. 5B ► A Louisiana woman who sued the city because a "throw-down" gun was planted near her son after he was fatally shot by police. **1993** *Usenet: talk.politics.misc* (Mar. 5) "Re: What the Media Isn't Saying About Events in Waco" ► This has been a major embarrassment for the BATF. They would need to prove what they claim just to save face. Just like a cop carrying a "throw-down." **1996** *New Orleans Times-Picayune* (La.) (Apr. 21) "Accused Cop Has Record of Larceny," p. B1 ► It's a Saturday night special, judge.... It's not a mystery that a gun with no serial numbers is used by criminals. It's used as a throw-down. **1997** Sydney P. Freedberg *Miami Herald* (Oct. 3) "Third Cop Arrested in Miami Gun Case," p. B1 ► Police in Miami arrest narcotics Detective Jorge Castello, third officer connected with "throw-down" case, on charges of lying about shooting of homeless man Daniel Hoban who allegedly pointed gun at officers. **2000** David Klinger (*NPR*) (Feb. 15) "Talk of the Nation: Analysis: Growing Problem of Police Misconduct and Its Impact on Effective Policing" ► Nobody had a throw-down gun.... if you don't know the difference between a backup gun and a throw-down, you have no business talking on this show, sir. **2002** Stefano Esposito *News Tribune* (Tacoma, Wash.) (July 5) "Controversy Dogs Ruston Police Chief" ► He also said Reinhold showed some city employees a handgun he called a "throw-down piece," a weapon he would plant at the scene if an officer shot an unarmed suspect. **2004** Lise Olsen *Houston Chronicle* (Tex.) (Nov. 13) "Lawyers Claim Officer Planted Gun on Victim," p. 1 ► Kallinen contends the deputy may have planted an untraceable "throw-down gun" and emptied Romero's pockets of other items, including his cell phone. **2005** William C. Lhotka *St. Louis Post-Dispatch* (Mo.) (Mar. 4) "Ex-Officer Is Sentenced in Shooting" (Int.) ► Prosecutor John Quarenghi hinted throughout the trial that Zeigler had the dope in the black bag to use as a "throw down"—street language for planting evidence on a suspect.

throw red meat *v.* to appease, satisfy, rally, or excite one's (political) supporters. *Politics. United States.* Usually transitive: *throw read meat* to the lions, the wolves, the sharks, etc.

1958 *Salisbury Times* (Md.) (Oct. 17) "All They Need Is Red Meat," p. 6 ▶ Will it finally penetrate even the thick heads of rabble-rousers who have been throwing red meat to lions and hyenas that rabble-rousers, themselves, can be turned into red meat? **1973** Nick Thimmesch *Sheboygan Press* (Wisc.) (Jan. 4) "Spiro Agnew Goes Low Key," p. 38 ▶ His immediate strategy is to cut down the number of speaking engagements, particularly those fund-raising affairs where he is obligated to throw red meat out for Republicans hungry to feast on those no-good Democrats and other bad guys. **1986** Jack W. Germond, Jules Witcover *Seattle Times* (Wash.) (Apr. 28) "Linking Libya, Nicaragua—Bad History, Bad Politics," p. A8 ▶ Throwing red meat the other night to members of the Heritage Foundation, the conservative think tank, Reagan said: "I hope every member of Congress will reflect on the fact that the Sandinistas have been training, supporting and directing as well as sheltering terrorists." **2004** Stephen Koff *Plain Dealer* (Cleveland, Ohio) (July 11) "Senate Debates Gay Marriage Ban This Week" (Int.) ▶ The gay-marriage issue could create a minor sideshow to Kerry's formal nomination and keep the conservative Republican base energized during a time when the national political spotlight will be on Kerry, not Bush. Congressional aides have referred to it as throwing "red meat" to the base.

thulp *v.* to overcome in a contest, sport, or fight; to beat, drub, or subdue; to finish off or exhaust. *India.* [Often said to be a blend of *"thu*mp to a p*ulp."*] Usually transitive: *to thulp someone or something.*

1991 *Usenet: soc.culture.indian* (Apr. 20) "Politics & Religion" ▶ Most have expressed fervent hopes that the BJP would get badly thulped in the forthcoming elections. **1992** *Usenet: soc.culture.indian* (Aug. 22) "Kaduk's Revenge" ▶ He would capture this or the other miscreants and punish them by "thulping" them and breaking their bones. **1999** *New Zealand in India* (India) (Oct.-Nov.) "Kiwi Nets, Lost in the City and Small Town Fame" (Int.) ▶ I made my bad throat worse by thulping mint and coffee ice cream. **2001** [phunti] *Tulleeho.com* (New Delhi, India) (Oct. 23) "Off Beat Places to Get Smashed In" (Int.) ▶ Talking of kashmir, one of the best places to get thulped is a houseboat on dal lake.... you let the houseboat owner know what you wanted to eat in the next meal and they made it. being a veg had some downsides but still they rose magnificently to the task. liquor is freely available in the valley. **2002** Vinay Kamat *Times of India* (June 1) "The Serial Killer Waits to Draw First Blood" ▶ In Italy, unknown Cameroon thulped Maradona's boys 12 years ago in the World Cup opener. ***2004** *Saras 97–IIT Madras* (Apr. 4) "IIT M Slang" (in IIT Madras, India) (Int.) ▶ *Thulp*—Comes from "THUmp into puLP." To beat the shit out of something. **2004** [lakesidey] *Coffee Time* (India) (Oct. 11) "Strenuous Sunday" (Int.) ▶ I went for a quiz (and was thulped in embarrassing fashion after making the finals with inordinate ease). ***2004** *Ganga Hostel IIT Madras* (Dec. 20) "Lingo...and All That 'Fart'" (in Madras, India) (Int.) ▶ *Thulp:* extremely widely connotative word—from physically beat to mentally exhaust with everything in between. **2005** *Usenet: comp.dsp* (May 5) "Really OT: Ann Coulter Heckler Responds!" ▶ Basically this was a story of University of Texas student Ajay Raaj heckling Ann Coulter during a Q/A session and getting thulped by cops.

thumper *n.* a grenade launcher; (*hence*) a gun known more for its power or noise than for its precision; any gun. *United States.*
[**1986** Joe Doggett *Houston Chronicle* (Tex.) (Nov. 20) "Is the .270 Caliber the 'Top Gun' of Texas?" p. 10 ▶ The .243 has excellent accuracy, minimal recoil, and surprising clout (with a 100-grain factory bullet), making it a good choice for a light-framed youngster or lady, or any shooter skittish of "kick." But it's not the buck-thumper that the bigger guns are.] **1989** Barbara Reynolds *USA Today* (Jan. 27) "Fear Is Knowing an AK-47 Owner," p. 11A ▶ I've had to join the arms race and get a "thumper," a 40 mm over-the-shoulder grenade launcher. **1992** Peter Hernon *St. Louis Post-Dispatch* (Mo.) (June 2) "Gang Slang Police Compile New Glossary of Street Talk," p. 1A ▶ That banger's thumper is a double-deuce, and he packs a gauge. Translation: That gang member's pistol is a .22, and he carries a shotgun. **1994** *Usenet: rec.guns* (Apr. 7) "Re: Charter Arms Bulldog 44spl." ▶ To make things even more out of balance, the Ruger has a .449" bore. It is a real shooter tho when .455" bullets are used and I use it for my "thumper" loads. **1995** *Usenet: rec.games.mecha* (Oct. 18) "New Cappellan Mech!" ▶ Originally the designers wanted to mount a "long tom" or a "thumper" as the mech's "main gun" but these proved far too "large" so they settled for the Schlong 2,000 Large Pulse Laser. **1996** *Usenet: rec.guns* (June 16) "Re: HARD KICKING 45-70's & 444 Marlins" ▶ The key to shooting any powerful gun, and especially a thumper, is to roll with it, not fight it. **2004** [Mugzi AKA Mugzilla] *Raptalk.net* (June 30) "Re: i guess i'll be tha first..." (Int.) ▶ what is 30/30? what do that mean? well it's a protector a pumkin buster a

thumper a wig splitter meaning a Heater. **2004** Matt O'Connor, David Heinzmann *Chicago Tribune* (Aug. 7) "Patterson Virulently Answers Charges" (Int.) ▶ Aaron Patterson brokered a heroin deal and talked of his need to acquire "thumpers," street slang for guns, federal prosecutors alleged Friday.

thunder run *n.* a high-speed military convoy using offensive tactics and heavy weaponry to reach a destination; generally, a route or trip involving extreme effort or danger. *Military.* [The etymological information in the 2001 citation is unverified. There is a theatrical device also called a *thunder run*, a trough down which cannonballs are rolled in order to simulate the sound of thunder.] This term dates from at least as early as the Vietnam War.

1971 *Lima News* (Lima, Ohio) (Nov. 27) "Bugle Notes: Limalanders in Service," p. 10 ▶ He participated in Operation Thunder Run in which the company set the tonnage mile and maintenance record in running two truck convoys from its home base at Frankfurt, Germany, to Alconbury and Warrington in England. **1986** Michael Precker (Aug. 4) "Bush, Entourage Visit Sinai Peacekeepers," p. 1A ▶ Another pastime is provided by the base's 14 bars, including at least one operated by each national contingent. "When you hit them all in one night, they call it the Thunder Run," said Sutton, a truck driver who delivers supplies to remote outposts in the desert. **1991** Rich Roberts *L.A. Times* (June 19) "The Other Side of the Kern 'March Miracle' Means Plenty of Water, But Plenty of Water Means Danger," p. 6 ▶ The Kern is designated a national "Wild and Scenic River."...That is followed by the Upper Kern, a series of several defined runs. The last takeout is at Riverside Park in town. The sections vary from Class III to IV, with one Class V portion—Thunder Run. **2001** Kregg P. Jorgenson *Very Crazy, G.I.!* (Jan. 30), p. 205 ▶ They were called Thunder Runs, high-speed gauntlet races by the mechanized infantry units of the army's 1st Infantry Division along Highway 13, northwest of Saigon. The tactic was used to throw off the Viet Cong and North Vietnamese Army units, which had frequently staged ambushes along the remote highway and the secondary roads that fed into it. The name Thunder Run came from the Big Red One's fire support bases—named Thunder One, Thunder Two, and Thunder Three— that dotted the route from Quan Loi south to Lai Khe. **2003** Ralph Kinney Bennett *Tech Central Station* (May 13) "Tanks for the Memory" (Int.) ▶ One of the enduring images of the recent war in Iraq is a column of M-1A1 Abrams tanks barreling down the streets of Baghdad on a "thunder run," deep into the city. **2004** Simon Dunstan *Vietnam Tracks* (Mar. 1), rev. ed., p. 84 ▶ At night the outposts scattered along the route, consisting of a few vehicles and an infantry squad, were vulnerable to attack, so continuous patrols known as "thunder runs" were maintained. A run involved AFV's moving in column with tanks in the van and other vehicles at close intervals, moving at high speed and undertaking "reconnaissance by fire" along the roadsides to trigger potential ambushes.... As in all operations in Vietnam, it was essential to avoid establishing a pattern while "thunder running." **2004** John Kifner *N.Y. Times* (May 11) "The Marines Enter Falluja, with Peace Their Aim" (Int.) ► The plan for the convoy had gone through a number of permutations. At first it was seen by planners as a show of strength, with preparations worthy of a major invasion, including tank support and air cover—a "thunder run," as they called it, into the city. **2004** Tommy Franks *American Soldier* (July 1), p. 517 ► "Looks to me like a 'Thunder Run,'" I said, recalling reconnaissance-in-force operations of that name I'd seen near the Y Bridge in Vietnam in 1968.... A "Thunder Run" was a unit of armor and mechanized infantry moving at high speed through a built-up area like a city. The purpose was to either catch the enemy off guard *or* overwhelm him with force. **2005** Sean D. Naylor *DefenseNews.com* (U.S.) (Mar. 21) "Making the Best Tank Better" (Int.) ► Tucker cited an Abrams with the 3rd Infantry Division (Mechanized) that took part in the first "thunder run" into Baghdad as an example.

tick-tacker *n.* at a horse track, a person (often a tout) who communicates information to others by hand signals. *Slang. Sports.*
[**1926** Bert E. Collyer *Washington Post* (Aug. 6) "Collyer Gives Sprinter Chance," p. 14 ► The lads who fondle the ticktack clocks—when most of us are warming feathers—slip me this as the "best sprinter at Coney Island."] **1988** Steve Crawley *Sun Herald* (Sydney, Australia) (May 1) "How Two Fingers Strode the Turf," p. 110 ► They were the days of meat pies and trams, of the Flat and the Leger. Tick-tackers. "You could sit on the sidelines and watch forever," said Bert. **1995** Max Presnell *Sydney Morning Herald* (Australia) (June 23) "Just Like a Day at Manchester, and Look What Happened To It," p. 60 ► Perhaps the tick-tackers—sharp little blokes with white gloves who conveyed betting information with their hands from vantage points—and a few other key ingredients were missing, but the feel was similar.... Ticktackers were tolerated on British tracks long after being barred in Australia because the racing over there needed the custom. **2004** Max Presnell *Sydney Morning Herald* (Australia) (June 24) "Randwick's Last Tout: Nine Tips But None the Winner" (Int.) ► Tick-tackers lasted longer. Usually wearing white gloves for better visibility, tick-tackers conveyed prices from one enclosure to another by hand signals.

tie-down *n.* one of a series of questions that encourage a customer to agree to a purchase. *Business.*

1985 *Washington Post* (Oct. 15) "The Pitch" ▶ The Tie-Down. The "don't you agree?" or "isn't that so?" attached to a statement: "You can change your life, don't you agree?" It softens the presumptuousness of a statement, and builds agreement. **1990** Dennis McCann *The Art and Science of Resort Sales* (July 1), p. 33 ▶ When making your presentation you can keep guests involved with the use of "tie downs." Finish statements with, isn't it? doesn't it? wouldn't you? The tie down requires an answer from your guests. **2005** Mike Adams *Self SEO* (July 2) "An Internet Marketing Secret: Using Tie Downs to Increase Sales" (Int.) ▶ One very old direct sales principle is to get people to say yes to multiple little questions. This gets them agreeing with you and also gets them used to saying yes. Psychologically, they will then be more likely to say yes when you ask for the sale. One sales technique for achieving that is the tie-down.

tiger kidnapping *n.* the abduction or holding of a hostage to persuade another person to aid in a crime. *Crime & Prisons.*

1995 Grania Langdon-Down *Financial Times* (U.K.) (Apr. 8) "On the Trail of the Fraudsters," p. II ▶ In western Europe the threat is more from "tiger" kidnaps, in which, for example, the wife of a bank manager is held hostage to force him to open the safe. **1999** Tony Thompson *Observer* (U.K.) (Nov. 14) "Gangs Bring Wave of Kidnaps to Britain," p. 12 ▶ More than 80 per cent of "tiger" kidnappings involve ethnic minorities. There has been a particular problem with Chinese nationals who have entered the country illegally. They are often snatched by gangs linked to the Triads and then their families in China are pressured into paying a ransom. **2002** Mo Hayder *The Treatment* (Feb. 19), p. 5 ▶ "It isn't a custody kidnap. He's their child—no exes involved." "A tiger then?" "Not a tiger either." Tiger kidnaps meant ransom demands and the Peaches were not in an extortionist's financial league. **2002** Ruth O'Callaghan *Sunday Times* (London, Eng.) (Dec. 22) "Tiger Kidnapping—the New Threat—Small Business" ▶ Gardai call such incidents, where a hostage is taken and forced to help thieves, tiger kidnapping. **2005** Jonathan McCambridge *Belfast Telegraph* (N. Ireland) (Jan. 12) "Anatomy of a Bank Robbery" (Int.) ▶ Police intelligence reports and underworld crime gangs share the same use of terminology—a tiger kidnapping is what they both call a crime where a hostage is held to force the victim to take part in a robbery.... The origins of the tiger kidnapping spread back well over two decades. The term was first used in London for a particular type of crime against illegal immigrants, usually from the Middle East. When these immigrants reached London they were kidnapped by armed gangs who told their families back home that their relatives would be killed unless large ransoms were paid.

time famine *n.* across a society, a lack of free or leisure time. *Business. Jargon.*

1986 Jolie Solomon *Wall Street Journal* (Apr. 21) "Working at Relaxation: In Spite of Unprecedented Affluence, Americans Labor to Find the Time for Leisure Pursuits" ▶ "Time famine," as some sociologists call it, is an extraordinary paradox. Despite shorter workdays, the proliferation of labor-saving devices and unmatched financial resources, true leisure remains elusive. **2004** Carol Kleiman *Houston Chronicle* (Tex.) (July 2) "Flexibility Is Cure for 'Time Famine'" (Int.) ▶ In the institute's study, a new phrase is referred to what seems to reflect the condition of many working people: It's "time famine." The research shows that "67 percent of employed parents say they don't have enough time with their husbands or wives—up from 50 percent in 1992—and 55 percent say they don't have enough time for themselves."

tiny heart syndrome *n.* cowardice; reluctance to fight or to fully commit (to an undertaking or challenge). *Military.*

2000 Usenet: *alt.sport.weightlifting* (July 14) "Re: OT—Endurance Training" ▶ The only people who don't are mostly people who aren't trying. They called it THS, or tiny heart syndrome when I was in basic. **2004** [Whitey] *MilitaryForums.co.uk* (Mar. 28) "Bush Takes Heat for WMD Jokes" (Int.) ▶ They found the WMD. Saddam had them in his arse. No I thought the joke could have been made funnier. In bad taste? Well if you are a queer with teeny tiny heart syndrome. Our military bitched for 12 years for a war, they got one, a good one too, so I don't think it was a bad joke. **2005** John F. Burns @ Baghdad, Iraq *N.Y. Times* (Mar. 21) "There Are Signs the Tide May Be Turning on Iraq's Street of Fear" (Int.) ▶ The complaints among American officers about "tiny heart syndrome"—a caustic reference to some Iraqi units' unwillingness to expose themselves to combat—have diminished.

tip drill *n.* an unattractive person, male or female, esp. one who is used for sex or money. *Derogatory. Hip-Hop. Sexuality. United States.* [There are two supposed etymologies circulating. Neither can be verified. One says *tip drill* refers to a practice routine by the same name in basketball or football, in which the ball is quickly passed, bounced, or rebounded from player to player. The other says it refers to the power tool of the same name, which has a twisted head but a smooth shaft or body. The latter may be influenced by *tool*, a derogatory name for someone who is dense, easily taken advantage of, or otherwise operating at a sub-par capacity.]

2003 Nelly *Da Derrty Versions: The Reinvention* (Nov. 25) "E. I. [Tip-drill Remix]" (Int.) ▶ I said it must be ya ass cause it ain't ya face/I need a tip drill, I need a tip drill.... It must be ya money, cause it ain't ya face/You a tip drill, nigga you a tip drill. **2004** [Dr. Jo Koster's WRIT 102 Class] @ Winthrop Univ. *Winthrop Slang Dictionary Spring 2004* (Rock Hill, S.C.) (Int.) ▶ *tip drill* A girl or boy that is unattractive from the neck up but is good enough to have sexual intercourse with. Used by African Americans and appropriated by some whites. **2004** [GullyNotRude] *FromTheHeart* (May 11) "This Not Beef This Turkey" (Int.) ▶ My dumb ass friend told ugly boy I like him I think I'm like hell the fuck naw, so I wrote ugly a letter telling his dumb ass why I'm looking at him and hes not cute to me. He took it to the heart, hey who could blame him, I called him a TIP DRILL. **2004** Nick Kiewik *The Productivity Vortex* (Lexington, Va.) (May 15) "Hate the Player, Not the Game" (Int.) ▶ How can he really respect those guys when he knows they're all hung like frightened hamsters? Obviously Condol is not "hung" in any fashion, but yo that tip drill can eat a.... **2004** Ytasha Womack *Chicago Tribune* (May 26) "The Beat Goes On" (Int.) ▶ "If you take offense, it's like you're saying you are a tip drill," a street term for a woman in whom men only have a sexual interest.

tip-on *n.* a promotional item, such as a magnet or game piece, affixed to the cover of a publication. *Advertising. Jargon.*

1993 Susan Hovey *Folio* (Mar. 1) "Special Promotions Boost Local Newsstand Sales," p. 15 ▶ One tactic is the tip-on, a small paper square affixed to the cover that highlights an article of interest to readers in that area. **1998** Mary Cowlett *PR Week* (June 19) "A Clean Start for Pore Perfect," p. 8 ▶ Attenborough also distributed postcards with tip-on samples in cinemas and used the Clothes Show Live in December and the Cosmopolitan Show in April to demonstrate the product to the public. **2001** Lee Hammel *Worcester Telegram & Gazette* (U.K.) (Apr. 6) "Phone Book Advertisers Reach Out in New Ways," p. A1 ▶ Bell Atlantic, which merged with GTE to form Verizon last summer, began offering what Verizon Information Services calls a "magnetic tip-on" on the front cover of the phone book about a year and a half ago, according to spokeswoman Heidi Jaquish. **2004** Richard Prior *Financial News & Daily Record* (Jacksonville, Fla.)

(Aug. 11) "Attorneys Favor High-Visibility Advertising" (Int.) ▶ One firm has taken the whole back page; another is featured on the spine. A refrigerator magnet—or "tip-on," in BellSouth parlance—is adhered to the front.

TMPMITW *n.* the president of the United States of America. *Acronym. Politics. Slang. United States.* [the most powerful man in the world]

2002 Ben Domenech *The Ben File* (Oct. 10) "The Real West Wing" (Int.) ▶ Outside of the occasional state visit, there's really only bustle when POTUS or VPOTUS (TMPMITW) walk through. It's good when you don't hear anything—that means nothing's wrong. **2004** *Spectre AWOL* (Apr. 7) "Yousa Tinkin Yousa People Gonna DIE?" (Int.) ▶ As an added bonus, Jar Jar McClellan has a way of distilling the complex philosophies and intellectual reasonings of TMPMITW (The Most Powerful Man in the World) into digestible bites while still conveying the nuance and thoughtfulness underneath. **2004** Joseph Curl *Wonkette* (Washington, D.C.) (May 5) "WH Pool Report: The President Never Did Get His Morning Papers Edition" (Int.) ▶ As your pool stood around in the parking lot of the Somerset Inn on W. Big Beaver Road, waiting for TMPMITW, Scott McClellan got an early-morning briefing about the news from yeoman Josh Deckard, who pointed out important passages as he handed the press secretary a ream of paper.

toe-popper *n.* a small antipersonnel land mine that tends to wound the feet and legs. *Military.*

1967 *L.A. Times* (Dec. 14) "Booby Traps Taking Toll in Vietnam" (in Washington, D.C.), p. F4 ▶ "Toe-popper wounds"—in which toes are explosively amputated—are a typical result of ingenious booby traps used by the Viet Cong in Vietnam. **2002** David H. Hackworth *Steel My Soldiers' Hearts* (May 7), p. 17 ▶ The VC use anything and everything to build their devil's devices. There were toe poppers—normally a single bullet no bigger than a pencil, set on top of a nail; step on it, and the bullet is pushed down into the nail and fired through your foot. **2003** *Capital* (Annapolis, Md.) (Mar. 23) "Afghan Air Base Heavily Mined, Hazardous" (in Bagram, Afghanistan), p. A2 ▶ Nearly a quarter-century of fighting has left Bagram littered with mines and unexploded ordnance, from the tiny, flesh-shredding toe-popper land mines to rusting 500-pound Soviet bombs sticking out of the fields just beyond the runway. **2005** *Potomac News* (Woodbridge, Va.) (May 16) "Lane Ranger" (Int.) ▶ The practice mines were not fully charged and most were defused, Hall said. "The army referred to them as 'toe poppers.'"

toe-touch *n.* a trip taken by a reporter merely to acquire the proper dateline on a story, even though all reporting is done somewhere else or by someone else. *Jargon. Media.*

2003 Jack Shafer *Slate* (May 23) "Rick Bragg's 'Dateline Toe-Touch'" (Int.) ▶ Visiting a scene just long enough to claim a dateline for an article based on somebody else's uncredited reporting—let's call it a "dateline toe-touch"—may not be as egregious as writing stories date-lined Palestine, W.Va., without leaving your Brooklyn apartment, as Jayson Blair did. **2003** N.Y. Times Co. *Siegal Committee Report* (July 30), p. 28 (Int.) ▶ When a correspondent travels, it should be to report for the newspaper. If deadline constraints mean that the reporter will make no significant contribution to someone else's work, we should skip the trip—the "toe touch" that serves only to justify a dateline artificially beneath the byline. **2004** Greg Mitchell, Joe Strupp @ NYC *Editor & Publisher* (Mar. 9) "'E&P' Puts Readers' Questions to Jayson Blair" (Int.) ▶ You talk a lot about the practice back then of the "toe-touch"—someone reporting a story from their home desk and then traveling only briefly to the city where the story is set just to "get the dateline." You say editors "often" ordered that to be done.

tomato can *n.* an inferior boxer. *Slang. Sports. United States.*

1955 Jack Gregson *N.Y. Herald Tribune* (Nov. 6) "A Glossary of Fight Terms for TV Fans," p. 23 (Int.) in *ADS-L* (Dec. 10, 2001) Barry Popik "War on Poverty (1955); The Way It Is; Fight Terms" ▶ "Tomato Can"—an inferior fighter. This reference is generally made by one manager describing another manager's fighter. [**1983** *Globe and Mail* (Toronto, Can.) (Feb. 11) "Boxer Cannot Find His Size," p. P19 ▶ I've learned my lesson the hard way. I don't want to end up looking like a tomato can when my career is over.] **1987** Jack Fiske *San Francisco Chronicle* (Calif.) (Aug. 5) "Now Everyone Wants to Take a Shot at Foreman," p. 61 ▶ Carlos DeLeon's one-round KO of a tomato can, who quit after a hook to the body, on the Tyson-Tony Tucker card, was not conclusive enough to showcase him as a future opponent for Tyson. **2004** Dave Hackenberg *Toledo Blade* (Ohio) (May 4) "Nonde-script Heavies Make Tyson Interesting" (Int.) ▶ McBride is, to be gra-cious, a journeyman. In boxing parlance he is a tomato can. He hasn't fought anyone, to speak of, yet has kissed plenty of canvas.

tom-walkers *n.pl.* stilts.

1921 Paul Stevenson *Atlanta Constitution* (Ga.) (Aug. 6) "'Tom Walker' Fad Hits Oakland City; Kids Stepping High," p. 4 ▶ What are "Tom walkers," you say? Why, bless your heart, don't go talking about "stilts" out there in Oakland City. They are "Tom walkers" to every-body and every kid. **1925** Harry Harrison Kroll *A Comparative Study of Upper and Lower Southern Folk Speech* (George Peabody College for Teachers, Tenn.) (Aug.), p. 77 ▶ *Tom-walkers.* Stilts. "We been walking on Tom-walkers to-day." **1961** Jim Baker *Coshocton Tribune* (Ohio) (Apr. 29) "The American Journal," p. 6 ▶ "Tin Can Tom Walkers." Time was when tin cans were as useful after being emptied as they were before. Yesterday's children used cans for many playthings— things like "tom walkers." A good "tromp" collapsed the can firmly around the heel, where it clung tightly until kicked off against a curb-stone. **1974** *Daily Times-News* (Burlington, N.C.) (Apr. 19), p. B15 ▶ Kenneth klops around on stilts, or some people still call them Tom-walkers.

toolie *n.* in Australia, an older man who preys on or interferes with teenagers celebrating the end of final year secondary school exams. *Australia. Derogatory. Education. Slang.* [Perhaps related to *tool* 'a stupid person' by comparison with *schoolie* 'a student cel-ebrating the end of final year exams.' Alternately, it could be influ-enced by *tool v.,* 'to drive (an automobile); to cruise (around),' par-ticularly given the predatory undertones of *toolie.*]

2002 Tracey Gibbons *Sunday Mail* (Queensland, Australia) (Nov. 24) "Teenagers Blame 'Toolies,'" p. 4 ▶ Schoolies say the violence on the Gold Coast in the past week has been caused by "toolies"—the name they use for the older gatecrashers ruining their party. **2003** (*AAP*) (Australia) (May 11) "State Government to Crack Down on Schoolies" (in Brisbane) ▶ "The big problem is the sleazy predators who try to take advantage of our kids—'toolies,' as the schoolies call them. I don't need to spell out that teenage girls are particularly vulnerable to these creeps." **2004** *CBC* (Canada) (Nov. 27) "Australia's 'Schoolies' Warned About Drinking" (in Sydney, Australia) (Int.) ▶ About half of those arrested have been people referred to as "toolies," older men who take advantage of the Schoolies Week celebrations.

tools of ignorance *n.* a baseball catcher's mask, shin guards, and chest padding. *Sports. United States.*

1936 *Arcadia Tribune* (Calif.) (May 2) "Breadmen to Face Locals," p. 1 ▶ Leroy Zimmerman, star local high school graduate, will perform on the mound for the Corpe squad with Max Purcell donning the tools of ignorance to handle his slants. **1937** Bob Ray *L.A. Times* (Mar. 27) "The Sports X-Ray," p. A11 (Int.) in *ADS-L* (June 3, 2004) Barry Popik "Sometimes you eat the bear..." (1904); 'Tools of Ignorance'" ▶ Ball players call a catcher's paraphernalia "the tools of ignorance." **2003** Vince Staten *Why Is the Foul Pole Fair?* (Apr. 1), p. 266 ▶ Bresnahan's shin guards were the final pieces of the "tools of ignorance," that great descriptive phrase for the catcher's equipment. There are conflicting stories about who came up with that wonderful moniker: Some sources credit Herold "Muddy" Ruel, a Senators catcher who caught for Walter Johnson and later became a lawyer. The more likely—and earlier—story, from the "Diamond Jargon" column in the August 1939 issue of *Baseball Magazine* accepts Yankee catcher Bill Dickey as the true author. Dickey supposedly coined the term while donning his gear and brooding over why anyone would want to be a catcher in July heat. I like the Dickey story because it was published sixteen years before the Ruel claim.

top-hatting *n.* in roulette and casino gambling, the surreptitious placing of a bet after the outcome has been decided; PAST-POSTING. *Gambling.*

1990 Oliver Gillie *Independent* (U.K.) (July 9) "Self-Delusion Keeps the Chips Going Down," p. 4 ▶ The most common form of cheating is top-hatting. One of a team creates a diversion during the pay-off in roulette while another member of the team slips a late bet on the winning number. [**1992** Mark Honigsbaum *Guardian* (U.K.) (Jan. 4) "Lingua Franca Poker-Faced Diplomats" ▶ The sages at Binion's say the fastest way to make a buck is by top-hatting, or marking the back of the cards with your fingernails.] **2000** Tefo Mothibeli *Business Day* (S. Africa) (Apr. 27) "Stopping Illegal Gambling May Net Gauteng Millions" ▶ The long-term goal of the unit is to be involved in the handling of crimes peculiar to the gambling industry as a whole. Examples of these would be late betting, top hatting, theft of credit cards from slot machines and theft of jackpot cups. **2005** Justin Davenport *Scotsman* (Glasgow, Scotland) (Aug. 9) "Gang Guilty of Swindling Casinos with 'Top Hatting' Deception" (Int.) ▶ The film, which played a part in all three men pleading guilty, showed "top hatting"—dropping chips onto a gaming table a split second after the roulette ball has dropped—in slow motion. The deception relies on the dealer, casino inspector, security staff and other players all being distracted at the vital point when the ball drops.

totopo *n.* a baked corn tortilla. *Food & Drink. Mexico. Spanish. United States.*

1986 *Toronto Star* (Can.) (Oct. 4) "Let Hot Bean Soup Kick Off Fiesta" (recipe) ▶ 8 totopo (corn chips) crumbled. ***2004** [Ricardo J. Salvador] *Culture and Society of México FAQ* "What Is the Recipe for the Tortilla?" (Int.) ▶ A totopo is a tortilla that is made with salt in the dough and is then baked dry, rather than pliable. This toasted tortilla was made specifically for travellers, as it keeps without spoiling.

*2004 [Marcela Coronado Malagón] *Unidad de Estudios Sobre Empresas, Migración y Empleo en el Campo* (*UESEMEC*) (Universitaria, México) "La Guerra del Totopo" (Int.) ▶ El totopo es una especie de tortilla tostada de maíz de diversos tamaños, elaborado con masa de maíz preferentemente de la variedad zapalote, maíz criollo de la región.

totty shot *n.* a picture or brief broadcast of a (nude, semi-nude, or attractive) woman, used to appeal to male readers or viewers. *Entertainment. Media. United Kingdom.* [*totty* 'girl or woman, esp. one who is loose, or a prostitute.']

1998 Stephen Plaice *Guardian* (U.K.) (Oct. 24) "Through the Spyhole," p. 4 ▶ Soft-porn totty-shots happily co-exist on cell walls with baby-snaps and postcards. **2003** Andrew McGuinness *Campaign* (U.K.) (Apr. 25) "Dad—An Expert's View," p. 10 ▶ I was particularly impressed that they even managed to get the lads' mags stalwart of a naked "totty shot" in, even if it was rather worthily dressed up in an advice column from a midwife. **2004** Mark Campanarios *Football365.com* (U.K.) (June 11) "Euro 2004: Reasons It's Going to Be Ace" (Int.) ▶ The Totty Shots. Lest I be accused of sexism here, that is the unofficial slang term for the shot of a woman in the crowd used to spice up TV coverage.

trace *v.* to swear or to curse (at someone or something). *English-based Creole. Jamaica.*

2001 Barbara Blake Hannah *Jamaica Observer* (Kingston, Jamaica) (Aug. 22) "Memories of a Summer Music Festival" (Int.) ▶ As that genre of Jamaican music has increased in popularity, the style has become one of tenement-yard-style tracing, and those Jamaicans who are accustomed to a daily life in which such "tracing matches" are commonplace, applaud the winners who act out their hate battles on the dance hall stage. **2001** *Jamaica Gleaner* (Kingston, Jamaica) (Aug. 23) "Montel Talk!" (Int.) ▶ Tracing war. A who upset CeCile?...Massa all under the hair dryer she a cuss and carry on. **2002** [Mad Bull] *The Mad Bull's Blog* (Sept. 5) "A Happy Ending!" (Int.) ▶ She got a warning that she'd be evicted if she didn't pay her rent within a certain time. She had paid her rent, however, and checks with her bank indicated that the cheque had been encashed fairly promptly too. She therefore wrote her landlord a letter "tracing him off" as we say here...(cussing him out). **2002** Peach @ Brooklyn, N.Y. *Brown Angel Dancehall Heaven* (Oct. 2) (Int.) ▶ I know I went overboard and went against my own rules for dissing that little "punk" but I had to get those jokes off my chest. See how the "punk" just knew it was me who banned his narrow minded butt and it wasn't even me. I informed Capone to never take a post off if a person is tracing me. **2004** Lloyd B. Smith *Jamaica Observer* (Kingston, Jamaica) (May 18) "What's in a Word?" (Int.) ▶ Then again, Jamaicans love to "trace" (verbally attack someone) and there is no other way to win this war of words than to resort to the use of bad words.

trapo *n.* a traditional politician believed to be corrupt. *Derogatory. Philippines. Politics. Tagalog.* [< Tgl. 'dirty rag, old rag' < Span. 'cleaning cloth.']

1990 *Economist* (U.K.) (June 16) "Philippines; At Arm's Length" (in Manila), p. 37 ▶ In theory, at least, Mrs. Aquino has declared her political debts either paid or cancelled: Kabisig can now provide a platform for cleaner forms of political ambition than those of the trapos. **1991** Henry F. Carey *Christian Science Monitor* (Boston, Mass.) (Aug. 19) "Aquino's Challenge: Electoral Reform," p. 18 ▶ In the 1987 legislative elections, the National Movement for Free Elections (NAMFREL)—which exposed President Ferdinand Marcos's attempts to rig the 1986 elections—did not contest the election of many traditional politicians, derogatorily called trapos (Tagalog for "dirty rag"). **2004** Dean Jorge Bocobo *Philippine Commentary* (Philippines) (May 31) "Hear No Evil, See No Evil, Speak No Evil" (Int.) ▶ The very term "trapo" must have been invented because of Jose de Venecia. A trapo through and through even before trapo entered the lexicon, he was already a trapo in Ferdinand Marcos's Batasang Pambansa, the martial law era "parliament."

Trashcanistan *n.* Afghanistan; any poor Middle Eastern country or central Asian republic. *Politics. Slang.*

1994 *Usenet: alt.folklore.urban* (Apr. 6) "Re: Laser Tattoo=NPR Hoax? Gotta Be..." ▶ The story from 1992 was unprecedented strife in an obscure republic in Central Asia, "Trashcanistan." **2000** Michael Sivy *Money Magazine* (Jan. 1) "Forecast 2000 Profits Are Strong. Inflation Is Tame. Are We in a New Era? Sure. But You Still Need a Smart Strategy to Cash In," pp. 63+ ▶ Be sure to have exposure to international economies. You don't have to buy shares in the Trashcanistan Fund to be a global investor. **2003** Scott Baldauf *The Nation* (NYC) (Apr. 28) "Letter from Afghanistan," p. 24 ▶ Outside the wire surrounding their bases, soldiers jokingly trade names for their temporary home: Trashcanistan, Asscrackistan. **2003** Robert Kirby *Salt Lake Tribune* (Utah) (Dec. 1) "Make It a Bloodless Christmas," p. C1 ▶ Mail early. If it has to be in Trashcanistan by Christmas, even overnight express won't get there in time if you mail it Christmas Eve. **2004** *Australian* (Apr. 28) "See You Later, Succour" (Int.) ▶ Stephen Kotkin, director of Russian Studies at Princeton University, has coined the term Trashcanistan to describe the tin-pot kleptocracies and autocracies that emerged out of the debris of the Soviet Union.

trout pout *n.* prominent lips resulting from cosmetic surgery. *Medical.*

2002 Sharon Marshall *News of the World* (U.K.) (Dec. 15) "From Beauty to Old Trout" ► [Leslie Ash,] the new star of BBC1's Mersey-beat police drama admits fins haven't been the same since surgery to plump up her lips left her with what she describes as "my trout pout." **2003** *The Age* (Australia) (Feb. 6) "'Trout Pout' Surgery Warning" (Int.) ► Actress Leslie Ash has warned women to beware the perils of cosmetic surgery after her lip enhancement procedure went disastrously wrong. The *Merseybeat* star said she had been through hell since implants left her with an over-sized "trout pout." **2003** Leigh Purves, Nadia Brooks, Amy Watts *Daily Star* (U.K.) (May 18) "Lovely Liz Bares All," p. 16 ► Trout-pout Liz is desperate to rival screen siren Sharon Stone, who whipped fans into a frenzy with her infamous no-knickers scene in smash hit thriller "Basic Instinct." **2004** Jeremy Clarkson *Times* (London, Eng.) (May 2) "You're All on Probation, This Is the British Nation," p. 15 ► I'm a celebrity and I want to get out, have your face altered, get a trout pout, be famous for doing nothing at all. [**2004** *Derby Evening Telegraph* (U.K.) (Sept. 3) "New v50 Is a More Sporting Estate," p. 56 ► "It's good to see Volvo has moved away from the boxy models of the past," he said. He described the grille as a "trout pout."]

trufan *n.* a dedicated and loyal follower (of an entertainer, cult, credo, hobby, pastime, genre, etc.). *Entertainment. Slang. Technology.*

1978 Patricia Byrd *American Speech* (Spring) "Star Trek Lives: Trekker Slang," vol. 53, no. 1, p. 55 (Int.) ► 1976 Fisher *Strekfan's* Glossary 6 "*Trufan:* The total fan, one who embraces every aspect of fandom. This has another meaning in SFandom but the single definition has been prevalent in STrekdom so far." **1983** *Usenet: net.sf-lovers* (Jan. 7) "Re: Cursing Ministers" ► I repeat my contention that absence of critical sense is one of the marks of the fringefan, and introduce the corollary (observable from the earliest days of anything recognizable as fandom) that argumentativeness is one of the common denominators of the [trufan] (I hate that term but it carries a useful sense). **1989** *Usenet: rec.music.misc* (May 14) "Re: Toyah" ► "Are there any fans of Toyah out there?"…"A Scottish friend of mine claims to have felt her breasts in concert (is that a tru-fan or a lecher? no need to answer)." **2003** Cory Doctorow *Boing Boing* (Sept. 18) "New Haunted Mansion Book Probably *Won't* Suck" (Int.) ▶ Jeff Baham has interviewed the author, who appears to be a real Mansion trufan who set out to write a comprehensive historical document about the bestest ride the Imagineers ever built.

tsori *n.* a problem, trouble, worry. Also **tsouri**. *Yiddish.*

1948 in *The Naked and the Dead* (May 1, 1998) Norman Mailer, p. 54 ▶ We're supposed to be the chosen people…. Chosen! Chosen for *tsoris*! **1989** Judy Blume *Wifey* (July 15), p. 28 ▶ You don't know how lucky you are to have girls instead of boys. With boys you wind up with tsouris. **2005** Michael Lee *Washington Post* (June 19) "Brown May Remain in Detroit" (Int.) ▶ "This has been phenomenal for me. I mean, I don't have too many left, and I've had tsoris my whole life. I'm doing exactly what I want to do," Brown said, using a Yiddish word for problems. **2005** Whitney McKnight @ Marlton, N.J. *Christian Science Monitor* (July 25) "Swearing Got Me Hired—and Fired" (Int.) ▶ Very satisfying if you are venting about how much *agita* and *tsuriss* (pain and trouble) your *schlumperdick pischk* (big fat mouth) causes you.

tumshie *n.* a stupid or foolish person. *Derogatory. Scotland. Slang. United Kingdom.* [Originally jocular or colloquial Scots for 'turnip.' Common insult *tumshie-head* and other comparisons of a head to a turnip probably preceded the stand-alone *tumshie*.]

[**1947** *Dictionary of the Scots Language* (Int.) ▶ A jocular or colloq. name for a turnip.] **1993** Mary Lockhart *Herald* (Glasgow, Scotland) (Mar. 23) "Eggs and the Oaf," p. 16 ▶ We are given a blustering blundering tumshie, jingling keys and flapping his arms against his sides like a penguin on ecstasy. **1996** Charles Duncan *Scottish Daily Record* (Scotland) (May 22) "The Voice of Scotland," p. 14 ▶ While doing my weekly shopping in our local supermarket, I was choosing a turnip and was appalled at the price of one—70-90p depending on size and they were tiny!…You'd be a right "tumshie" to pay that much for a neep! **1996** M. C. Beaton (June 1) "Death of a Macho Man," 1997 reissue ed., p. 3 ▶ Now we all hae tae listen tae that big tumshie, blethering on and on and on. **1996** *Usenet: rec.arts.drwho* (Dec. 2) "Re: Kill Files" ▶ Whit ur ye bluhtherung aboot ya tumshie. **1999** *Usenet: rec.audio.opinion* (Dec. 26) "Re: The Great LP vs CD Debate/War" ▶ Och, ye muckle tumshie, hae ye nae sense avah? **1999** *Usenet: soc.culture.scottish* (Dec. 29) "Re: Bye for Now, You Losers"

▸ Well good riddance you auld tumshie. **2000** *Usenet: uk.rec.climbing* (July 19) "Re: Wh&s Run Amok" ▸ No an insult would be if I called you a "richt sasenach Tumshie, wi a heid the' size o' ben macduhi." Then you would have every right to be offended. **2004** Simon Pia *Scotsman* (Scotland) (Nov. 3) "Yes, Folks, Tumshie Is the New Numpty" (Int.) ▸ Forget about these two tumshies, Bush and Kerry.... Indeed, the Diary even prefers the term "tumshie" to "numpty."...We are assured, a great afternoon for anyone feeling depressed—if Bush wins—at a tumshie as leader of the free world.

tuner car *n.* a stock or factory-default automobile with, or suitable for, aftermarket modifications (to enhance speed, power, or style). *Automotive.* A *tuner* is someone who makes special modifications to a car.

1993 *Usenet: rec.autos* (July 21) "Monster Miata" ▸ I saw a little blurb on a tuner car called the Monster Miata. It's a Miata with a Ford 302 dropped-in and, optionally, some "looks" packages. **1995** John M. Clor *AutoWeek* (Mar. 13) "Ex Post Factory: Tuners Can Give You a Lift Over Stock, But You Need to Do Some Homework," p. 15 ▸ If you're dropping $100K on a tuner car, a warranty may not worry you too much. **1996** *Usenet: rec.autos.driving* (Oct. 28) "Re: Modern American Muscle Cars VS Ferraris" ▸ At least in ten to twenty years I can still get money back out of the Porsche where the "tuner car" will have lost nearly all of its value. **1999** Matt Nauman *Knight Ridder Tribune Business News* (Mar. 26) "Accessories Help Owners Personalize Their Camrys" ▸ Although the Camry certainly isn't as popular as a tuner car as the Honda Civic, Acura Integra or Mitsubishi Eclipse with young, male drivers, magazine editor Nosek expects that it will become a popular platform for modification. [**1999** *Usenet: rec.autos.market place* (Oct. 20) "17″ Icw Racing Tuner Rims" ▸ Sweet ooking skinny 9 spoke, tuner style, you can change the color of the center cap, the center caps are chrome right now.] **2003** Thos. L. Bryant *Road & Track: Ford Mustang Portfolio 1994-2002* (Jan. 1), p. 2 ▸ Steve Saleen stresses that his cars are not tuner cars.... S351s are sold only as entire cars, not a bunch of pieces. And though they are certainly modified Ford Mustangs, they are production cars, not one-offs with specially ported and polished heads and other tweaks that might help the car eke out a few extra mph. **2005** Steve Spalding *Detroit Free Press* (Mich.) (Jan. 13) "Cobo's Basement Is a Tuner Wonderland" (Int.) ▸ Loosely and somewhat inaccurately, this is called the tuner car section, so designated because of the displays of sport or tuner versions of Subaru, Scion and Honda compact cars.

turkey *n.* a pet project funded via pork barrel politics. *Florida. Politics. United States.* This appears to be specific to Florida.

[**1982** Denise Gamino *Daily Oklahoman* (Okla.) (Nov. 23) "Skiatook Project Labeled One of 12 Turkeys of the Year" ▶ The country's major environmental groups Monday declared open season on a $112 million Oklahoma water project they say is one of 12 "Turkeys of the Year" that should be bagged by Congress.] **1998** *Florida Times-Union* (May 1) "Pork and Turkey," p. A12 ▶ The Legislature marred an otherwise good session by producing a record number of "turkeys," which are a Florida term for projects that have been inserted by legislative prerogative. In many cases, they involve spending state dollars for projects local governments should fund.... Another type of turkey is one that was not recommended by a state agency through the normal process. **2004** Linda Kleindienst, Mark Hollis *Sun-Sentinel* (Fla.) (May 1) "Late-Night Flurry of Bills Breaks Florida House Logjam" (Int.) ▶ While generally pleased with the budget, Bush acknowledged that it does contain several special projects known in legislative parlance as "turkeys."

turkey bacon *n.* a private security guard or officer; a *rent-a-cop*. Also plural. *Police. Slang.*

2001 [Dwarf Invasion (braindamage)] *Dance Party* (Winterpark, Fla.) (Oct. 20) "The Mall with Alicia and Julia" (Int.) ▶ The turkey bacon security guard yelled at us. **2002** Max Dobberstein *Irate Weirdos* (Sept. 19) "Turkey Bacon" (Int.) ▶ My fellow weirdos, you must join me in my quest to expand our language just slightly. From now on, I ask that you now refer to all rent-a-cops as turkey bacon. For those who don't know, turkey bacon is processed, smoked turkey meat cut into strips that resemble, but only barely function as, bacon. **2002** [Eleanor] *Black Skulls, Pink Ruffles—Goth vs Martha Stewart* (Oct. 30) "Introducing...Gothmommy" (Int.) ▶ A nice security guard stops them, and I stopped calling security guards "Turkey bacon rent-a-cops." **2003** [Wesoby] *Michael Buffington* (Portland, Ore.) (Mar. 5) "Stupidity Is Not Patriotism" (Int.) ▶ i agree, this man was treated screwed. turkey bacon (rent-a-cops) suck ass. they're all a bunch of wannabes who couldn't cut it as real cops. as for the police, come on, i'm sure they could've handled that a lot better. damn piggies. [**2003** "Early Show" CBS-TV (Dec. 4) "Slang Dictionary to the Rescue" (in Calif.) (Int.) ▶ Another word a girl offered was: "turkey bacon." She explained, "Undercover police. 'Put that away! I think those guys are turkey bacon.'"] **2004** [firegeek] *Nu Fud Friday* (Feb. 10) "I Laugh in the Face of Security!!!! *Still Laughing*" (Int.) ▶ That young security guard!! Trying to be all bad...especially when he knows he's just turkey bacon!!

twidget *n.* a soldier or other military individual whose job primarily involves using or maintaining electronics. *Military. United States.*

1995 P.T. Deutermann *Edge of Honor* (May 1), p. 110 ▶ A twidget was anybody who wasn't an engineer, and therefore, according to the snipes, not a real man. **1996** Alex Lee *Force Recon Command: 3D Force Recon Company in Vietnam, 1969-70* (Nov. 1), p. 152 ▶ As the Marines laughingly said, once they had become fans of the use of sensors, "If you want it done right, keep the 'twidgets' out of the field!" **2002** Douglas Morgan *Tiger Cruise* (Mar. 1), p. 63 ▶ At this evening's muster, ET2 Fred Larousse, one of *Cushing's* twidgets— electronic technicians—and the senior man on the BAF, was holding forth on the subject of security alerts. **2004** Peter Hall *Express-Times* (N.J.) (June 20) "Cullen 'Kind of an Oddball' in Navy" (Int.) ▶ Cullen was a "twidget"—someone who made fine adjustments to computers rather than turning a wrench to fix the ship's heavy equipment.

two-spirited *adj.* homosexual, transgendered, or transsexual. *Gay. Native American. Sexuality. United States.* [Claimed to be derived from Native American usage.]

1991 *Usenet: rec.arts.comics.strips* (Apr. 1) "Re: FBOFW" ▶ The aboriginal people considered us "Mystics." They call us "two spirited"— meaning that we're blessed with both female and male spirits!! **1996** Ellen Lewin *Women Writing Culture* (Jan.) "Writing Lesbian Ethnography," p. 329 ▶ Issues of similarity and difference are played out in a different way in Sabine Lang's account of the difficulties she faced trying to carry out research among Native American "two-spirited" women. **2004** Sheila Mullowney *Newport Daily News* (R.I.) (May 17) "'Queer' Label Still Raises Questions" (Int.) ▶ It can be used to describe both gender identity and sexual orientation and increasingly is being used in a new, wide-ranging alphabet soup...transgender, transsexual, two-spirited (a Native American reference), queer and questioning.

U

unass *v.* to dismount or disembark (a vehicle); to get off of (something); to unseat (someone); to leave (somewhere). *Military. Slang.* This term dates back to at least the 1960s and the Vietnam War. It is especially associated with the military, from where it has spread to politics and aeronautics.

1989 Richard West *Independent* (U.K.) (Nov. 29) "Misfortunes of War: 'About Face'—David H. Hackworth & Julie Sherman" ▶ Airmobile assaults were both exciting and frightening. Each one was a gut-churning event not dissimilar to the moment before you unassed a plane with a parachute on your back. **1990** *Usenet: rec.autos.driving* (Nov. 15) "Re: Getting Rear Ended" ▶ "I'll take 'un-assing the A.O.' to mean 'helping up the arresting officer.'"..."Get a clue. The phrase is Army slang for 'leaving the area of operations.'" **1992** *Usenet: sci .military* (Dec. 30) "Re: Sheridan" ▶ The crew felt they would be more useful elsewhere and dismounted the tank in record time. (We called it "Unassed the vehicle.") **1993** *Usenet: sci.space* (Aug. 14) "Re: Engine Failures and Safety" ▶ There have been numerous cases of the plane making an acceptable touchdown while significant passenger casualties are taken before they can un-ass the aircraft. **1993** *Usenet: alt.war* (Oct. 13) "Re: Barefooted Warriors in Somalia" ▶ Un-ass the place and leave them to fight over the food and die! **1997** *Usenet: soc.culture.african.american* (Dec. 20) "Re: The National Debt to Slavery" ▶ But all these kinte-cloth pillbox hat mumia fans aren't going to get two feet trying to convince anyone to un-ass several BILLION dollars, with the weak shit I've seen bandied about here. **1999** *Usenet: alt.war.vietnam* (Dec. 16) "Re: Vietnam F.A.Q." ▶ Move it. Move it. Move it! Unass my chow line. **2004** *Usenet: rec.outdoors.rv-travel* (Sept. 23) "Re: OT—Should We Remain in the UN" ▶ Trying to unass the 3rd world leader of it because we don't like him sure would be "sending a message" to the rest of the world "community," wouldn't it? **2004** *Argghhh!* (Nov. 14) "Monteith Provides This Dope About the Ferret" (Int.) ▶ The Saracen swapped the engine from the rear to front for reasons of easy debussing (dismounting, "un-assing" in US military parlance) by the PBI (Poor Bloody Infantry) carried in the back area.

unblind *v.* to reveal the identity of a subject involved in a blind study, in which the subject is ordinarily anonymous. *Science.*

1982 *Science* (Jan. 29) "Harvard Delays in Reporting Fraud," vol. 215, no. 4532, p. 480 (Int.) ▶ Late in September 1981, the Harvard team sent its portion of the AMPIM data to the NIGH in preparation for a group meeting in Bethesda at which the participants would, for the first time, discuss unblinded results. **1988** *Medical World News* (Feb. 8), vol. 29, no. 3, p. 76 ▶ I know you're on the research end of things, not economic policy, but if at two years you unblind the study and the drug is having a positive effect, at some point those patients will have to start paying for it themselves, and at current prices it would be prohibitively expensive for many. **2004** *Izzle Pfaff* (Apr. 22) "Dreamlike Occurrences That Were Not Actually Dreams" (Int.) ▶ When a patient is on a double-blind study, there are certain times when the doctor needs to "unblind" them, which is just revealing whatever crap the patient was getting: drug or placebo, etc.

unk-unk *n.* especially in engineering, something, such as a problem, that has not been and could not have been imagined or anticipated; an *unk*nown *unk*nown. *Science.* The *Barnhart Dictionary of New English Since 1963* (Barnhart/Harper & Row, New York, 1973) gives this term as a plural and defines it as "a series of unknowns, especially of inexplicable calamities." The term is now common as a singular and has spread from the aerospace engineering business to be used in military, government, and corporate environments. The two letter *K*s are not silent as they would be in *unknown*, but are audible and hard, as in the end of *drunk*.

1969 Harold B. Jyers *Fortune* (Aug.) "For Lockheed Everything's Coming Up Unk-Unks," p. 77 in *Urban Establishment* (Mar. 1, 1982) Frederic Cople Jaher, p. 703 (title). **1970** *Time* (Mar. 9) "Aerospace: End of the Gravy Years," p. 63 (Int.) ▶ Aerospace-men have come down with a severe case of what they call the "unk-unks"—the "unknown unknowns." **1980** *N.Y. Times* (Dec. 17) "The Vague General Haig," p. A34 ▶ There is an old Navy term for the truly imponderable: UNK-UNK for unknown-unknown. Of the ten men Mr. Reagan has nominated so far, Mr. Donovan stands out as the "UNK-UNK" of the team. This is not to say that he cannot do a good job—only that he lacks evident qualifications. **1985** *U.S. News & World Report* (Dec. 9) "'Unk-Unks' and 'Golden Arches': The New Lingo of Star Wars," p. 49 ▶ Many phrases, in fact, were culled from books and movies that depict imaginary space battles and often describe "unk-unks"—the "unknown unknowns" that no one can predict but seem likely to occur. **1994** Robert J. Thomas *What Machines Can't Do* (Mar. 1),

p. 149 ▶ What caused most apprehension, however, was what aircraft designers refer to as the "unk-unks," the unknown-unknowns, the problems you cannot anticipate because you don't even know they exist. **2002** Alexander Kossiakoff *Systems Engineering* (Nov. 15), p. 82 ▶ Many unknowns are evident at the beginning, and may be called "known unknowns." These are identified early as potential problem areas and are therefore singled out for examination and resolution.... However, many other problem areas are only identified later when they are discovered during system development. These unanticipated problems are often identified as "unknown unknowns" are "unk-unks" to distinguish them from the group of "known unknowns" that were recognized at the outset and dealt with.

Utah claw *n.* a female hairstyle typified by bangs projecting outward from the forehead. *Fashion. Slang. United States.*

1994 *Usenet: alt.usage.english* (Mar. 7) "Re: 'Bad Hair Day'" ▶ "It was often used in reference to something I came to refer to as the "stiffened frontal bang facade," a hair tiara set in place with blow drier, hair spray and teasing comb. The heights these can sometimes reach is quite ridiculous."..."I grew up in an area of West Virginia where such hairstyles are quite popular. We always used to refer to the tall, teased bangs as 'joke-catchers' (kept the joke from going over one's head). A friend from Idaho whom I met in college informed me that her circle of high school friends had dubbed the style of bangs the 'Utah Claw.'" **1999** *Usenet: alt.radio.talk.dr-laura* (Nov. 16) ▶ "Very proud to say she has never had a spiral perm nor big, crunchy bangs."..."Around here we call it the Utah Claw." **2000** *Usenet: alt.tv.sopranos* (Mar. 17) "Re: Application to Live in New Jersey" ▶ Do you have the equivalent of what we know here as the Utah Claw—long straight hair styled down with the bangs flipped up defying gravity and lacquered with hair spray to withstand hurricane winds? **2001** Anne Marie Cruz @ NYC *ESPN The Magazine* (July 27) "Splits and Giggles" (Int.) ▶ "We have great theme parties. The last one was the white trash party. I had my hair like this," she says, as she forces her bangs into a four-inch clump off her forehead. "The Utah claw!" exclaims Nicole in recognition. You could practically smell the hairspray. **2003** Jesse McKinley *N.Y. Times* (Mar. 2) "A Night Out with Tiffani Thiessen," p. 9-4 (Int.) ▶ "She had the Utah claw," Mr. Simington explained, describing bangs that shot up toward the heavens. **2003** [Dandle] *CTcentral.com* (Conn.) (Oct. 10) "Town Talk: Should Humans Be Playing with Tigers?" (Int.) ▶ Actually, it was a "Utah

Claw" that led to Roy Horn's injury. According to the owner of the Mirage, the tiger became distracted by a woman with big hair in the front row. (I can sympathize; I also can't help but stare at a white-trash woman with a hairdo that she hasn't changed in 20 years.) **2004** [Jessica] *Very Mom* (Murray, Utah) (Aug. 4) "The Fartkeeper" (Int.) ▶ I never did perfect the "Utah Claw" it always fell over by 2nd period—but oh, I tried. Me and Aqua Net, we tried!

utzy *adj.* uncomfortable, bothered, uneasy. *United States. Yiddish.* [Probably from the Yiddish *utz* 'to tease, bother, nag,' related to the German *uzen* 'to tease, to kid,' and perhaps reinforced by *antsy*.]

1989 Nina J. Easton *L.A. Times* (Jan. 30) "'Rain Man' Sends a Global Message" ▶ Shelley Long, wearing more fabric on her shoulders than on her legs: "I get a little utzy." (Translation: She misses the constant work of a TV series.) **2003** *Usenet: alt.pagan* (Aug. 10) "Re: The Pagan Way" ▶ Getting all utzy due to non-perfected English seems a little passive-aggressive to me. **2003** *Usenet: rec.arts.sf.fandom* (Aug. 12) "Re: Going to Torcon" ▶ Plus these are the same people who had to go to a strange hospital when the grandmother who was with them at a convention slipped and broke her wrist, so they're understandably "utzy" about travel in general. **2004** Susan Dominus *N.Y. Times* (Aug. 29) "What Women Want to Watch" (Int.) ▶ Mr. Graff, now 53, thought he had retired back in 1999 when he sold Spice to Playboy TV for a neat $100 million, moved to a small town near the Berkshires and took over an old country store. "I sliced bologna, sold mice traps, penny candy," he says. "It was my Norman Rockwell moment." And then? "I got utzy," he says. "I got bored."

vacation diplomacy *n.* the use of a non-state trip by a politician or diplomat to show friendliness with the nation being visited. *China. Politics.*

1993 *Kyodo News International* (June 6) "China Warns U.S. of Taiwan Leader's Visit" (in Beijing) ▶ The Chinese spokesman accused Taiwan authorities of using "transit diplomacy" and "vacation diplomacy" as a way to create "two Chinas" or "one China, one Taiwan," Xinhua said. **1994** *Xinhua News Agency* (China) (Sept. 17) "Commentary Exposes Taiwan's 'Sports Diplomacy'" (in Beijing) ▶ Xinhua news agency today carries a commentary titled, "What are the Taiwan authorities up to while going in for 'sports diplomacy'?" which reads as follows: Over the past few years, the Taiwan authorities have pursued their so-called "substantial diplomacy" and "pragmatic diplomacy" as well as "vacation diplomacy," "transit diplomacy," "ceremony diplomacy" and "money diplomacy." **2004** Wang Jianmin *China Daily* (Beijing, China) (July 23) "Taiwan Trip Tightens Tension" (Int.) ▶ In 1990, Hao Po-tsun, then "president of Executive Yuan," visited Singapore on vacation, which set the precedent for what later came to be called "vacation diplomacy."

Vanna White veto *n.* a form of line-item veto that permits an elected official to strike single letters in legislation. *Politics. Wisconsin.* [Vanna White is hostess for the TV game show "Wheel of Fortune," where she is responsible for revealing letters on a large board at the direction of contestants.] This term is specific to Wisconsin, where this type of veto—also called a *pick-a-letter veto* and similar to the *digit veto*, which allowed the striking of single numerals—is no longer permitted by state law.

1990 Craig Gilbert *Milwaukee Journal* (Wisc.) (Mar. 25) "Vote to Decide on Use of Partial Veto," p. 1 ▶ The power is the governor's partial veto, which includes the unusual ability to take a bill and change its meaning by vetoing the individual letters of words. The result can be the creation of whole new words and a whole new law. Democrats have dubbed the practice the "Vanna White veto." **2005** David Callender *Capital Times* (Madison, Wisc.) (Aug. 6) "Doyle Detects New Love: The Veto" (Int.) ▶ The governor also used to be able to strike individual letters to create new words—the so-called "Vanna White veto," named after the letter-turner on "Wheel of Fortune"—but those powers were reined in under a 1990 constitutional amendment.

veisalgia *n.* a hangover. *Health. Medical.* [Norwegian *kveis* 'uneasiness following debauchery' + Greek *algia* 'pain.' This word was coined by the authors of the first cite. There may be a double-entendre in the word *kveis*, as it is also a word for a parasitic worm found in fish.]

2000 Jeffrey G. Wiese; Michael G. Shlipak; Warren S. Browner *Annals of Internal Medicine* (June 6) "The Alcohol Hangover," vol. 132, no. 11, pp. 897-902 (Int.) ► Perhaps the most alarming feature of veisalgia is its high prevalence. **2004** Rita Rubin *USA Today* (June 28) "Hangover Helper: An Extract of Prickly Pear Cactus" (Int.) ► In a 2000 journal article, Wiese and co-authors coined a term for such hangovers: veisalgia, from the Norwegian word *kveis*, meaning "uneasiness following debauchery," and *algia*, Greek for "pain."

vernac *adj.* provincial; culturally backwards, unfashionable, or unrefined. Also *n. India.* [From *vernacular* 'typical of a place or of a people, especially everyday language,' which is sometimes colloquially abbreviated as *vernac.*] The derogatory uses of this term are closely tied to the ongoing debate over the role and use of English in India.

1997 Vikram Chandra *Love and Longing in Bombay* (Mar. 1), p. 120 ► They had argued and talked and laughed about what to call their parts, she hated *lund* and *chut*, how vernac and crude and vulgar she said. **1997** *Economic Times* (India) (Dec. 7) "What Are Ken and Barbie Watching Tonight?" ► "There is the image, that to be successful, you have to speak English, wear a certain kind of clothes, frequent certain kind of places. Says 14-year-old Rachna: "I can't think of mixing with the vernac types. What do we talk about. And how?" **1998** Kishore Singh *Business Standard* (India) (Oct. 24) "Sponsorship for the Theatre of the Absurd" ► "They wanted a famous name from Mumbai to put on the marquee. I even organised that," she said. "I got them a star performer, but they didn't like him, said he was too vernac." "Meaning what?" "Meaning he did serious theatre and gave interviews in Hindi and Marathi. They dumped him, and got me someone else instead." **2000** Monojit Lahiri *Statesman* (India) (Aug. 11) "Khan + Kaushik = Magic" ► I remember with anger and frustration, the long hours I spent pleading with some sponsors to consider my productions, to no avail. Any other language apart from English, is considered infra dig and vernac! English, no matter how dumb the production is, remains cool! **2001** Saisuresh Sivaswamy *Rediff* (India) (Feb. 13) "Tears for Fears" (Int.) ▶ It is often said if you want to sample true creative talent in India—or in any other multi-linguistic country—you have to go vernacular. "Vernac" may be pejorative to us English-speaking elite, but just as true writing flourishes in the local milieu, so does cartooning. **2003** *Usenet: rec.sport.cricket* (Jan. 26) "Re: India vs. Pak WC 03" ▶ You mean to say "The Indian team morale IS down"...you PAKI vernac!!! **2003** Leela Prasad *South Asian Folklore* (Mar. 1) "Character Stereotypes," p. 109 ▶ Through their circulation among a fluent English-speaking, often convent-educated community, these joking questions highlight the processes of insider/outsider demarcation common to stereotyping in general. They characterize, for instance, the Tamilian or the Gujarati as having pronounced regional accents when speaking English (creating thus the figure of "the vernac"). ***2004** Donna Rubinoff @ University of Colorado-Boulder *Education and "Human Capital"* (June 23) (Int.) ▶ English Medium Schools in India: alienation from families and common people? Non English mediums school kids called "vernacs" or HMT's (Hindi Medium Type = Hindustan Machine Tools). ***2004** Philip Lutgendorf @ University of Iowa *Who Wants to Be a Goddess?* (July 13) (Int.) ▶ By the 1970s mythological movies were seen as downmarket and vernac, suitable only for films made in other ethnic Indian languages. (Vernac is short for vernacular. It is a common Indian English word for a person of an ethnic Indian background without much education, English or sophistication who speaks only a local "vernacular" language. The equivalent of a country bumpkin or backwoods bozo.)

Verwaltungsvereinfachungsmassnahmen *n.* an anti-bureaucratese, anti-bafflegab campaign. *Austria. Business. German. Germany. Jargon. Politics.* Ger. *Verwaltungs* 'administration' + *vereinfachungs* 'reduction' + *massnahmen* 'measures'.

2000 *CDU/CSU Fraktion* (Germany) (Oct. 12) "Verbesserung des "Meister-BAfoeG" dringend erforderlich" (in Berlin) ▶ Verwaltungsvereinfachungsmassnahmen sollen ebenfalls zu einem Zulauf an Antragstellern und damit potentiellen Existenzgruendern fuehren. Es bleibt abzuwarten, ob die bisher untaetige Bundesregierung aufgrund dieses Vorstosses der Opposition aus ihrer Lethargie erwacht. **2004** Don Hill @ Prague, Czech Republic *Radio Free Europe/Radio Liberty* (June 9) "Writing Campaigns Encouraging Bureaucrats to Come in from the Fog" (Int.) ▶ They've assigned the effort to rid their writing of fogginess a

name. It is Verwaltungsvereinfachungsmassnahmen—that is, "simplified administrative procedures."

vineyard seating *n.* terraced rows of seats very close to a performance stage or platform. *Architecture. Entertainment.*

1996 *Building* (U.K.) (Aug. 6) "Sound System: Bridgewater Concert
Hall Open to Public," p. 8 ► The 2,400-seat auditorium, home of the
Halle Orchestra, is designed to combine the acoustic advantages of
the standard "shoebox" and terraced "vineyard" seating arrangements. **2002** Pierre Ruhe @ Philadelphia, Pa. *Atlanta Journal-
Constitution* (Ga.) (Jan. 13) "A Sound Space: Philadelphia's New
Kimmel Center Holds Lessons for Atlanta," p. 1L ► There's also talk
that the ASO will ask for a "vineyard seating" hall, where the audience can sit behind and to the sides of the stage on shallow terraces—
a cozier arrangement for the audience, but a trickier job for the
acoustician. **2004** Charles Ward *Houston Chronicle* (Tex.) (June 13)
"Symphony Reaches Out to Audience" (Int.) ► Designers of new
venues, such as Los Angeles' Walt Disney Concert Hall, surround the
stage with terraces of seats that get listeners as close to the players as
possible. The buzzword is "vineyard" seating.

vinyl village *n.* a neighborhood or town of plain or cheaply made
buildings. *Architecture.*

1992 Richard N. Gambrill @ Columbia *Baltimore Sun* (Md.) (Mar. 29)
"Don't Cut Education," p. 13 ► It doesn't take a sharp eye to also see
great blue heron, Canada geese, mallards and barred owls. Red fox are
also not uncommon. These creatures inhabit the heart of our vinyl
village and appear to be doing quite well in spite of us! **1996** D.R.
Burgoyne *Virginian-Pilot* (Norfolk, Va.) (Dec. 6) "Chesapeake Clipper:
Letters to the Editor—Chesapeake," p. 2 ► "Vinyl villages" (a term I
borrowed from a friend) line Cedar Road, where builders are more
concerned with making money than making homes aesthetically
appealing or by saving the trees that will take another generation to
grow back. **2001** Kenneth B. Hall, Gerald A. Porterfield *Community by
Design* (Mar. 12), p. 78 ► There are so many barriers to producing
good design solutions that the path of least resistance has led us to
vinyl villages of franchised architecture surrounded by seas of asphalt.
2005 Stuart A. Hirsch *Indianapolis Star* (Ind.) (Mar. 17) "Development
Plan Criticized" (Int.) ► Other opponents called it a "vinyl village," a
pejorative term opponents of building projects often use, implying
that homes with vinyl siding are built with substandard materials and
would eventually blight the landscape.

visibility whip *n.* a worker responsible for precisely orchestrat-
ing the presentation of placards, chants, and other demonstrations

of support among delegates at a political convention, especially during speeches. *Politics. United States.*

1988 *Omaha World-Herald* (Neb.) (July 19) "'Dukakis Can Talk State Issues' Kerrey Backs National Ticket" ▶ Beatty Brasch of Omaha said her assignment at the Democratic National Convention is "visibility whip," or cheerleader, of the Nebraska delegation. "It is extremely important that we demonstrate at the right time and that we are spontaneous," she told the delegation. **1996** Brad Cain (*AP*) (Aug. 29) "Week's Worth of Politicking Just the Ticket for Delegate Couple" ▶ Eymann is the state delegation's "visibility whip." It's her job to coordinate which slogans the delegates chant, or the signs that they hold up at the right moment. On Wednesday night, it was her job to make sure delegates held up large cardboard pictures of salmon, fir trees and wheat when it came time for the Oregon delegation to cast its votes to nominate President Clinton. **2004** *National Journal* (July 27) "Convention Dispatches: Definitely Thinkin' About Tomorrow..." (Int.) ▶ Take, for example, the "America's Future" signs brought out for President Clinton's speech Monday night. Hotline sources report that DNCC "visibility whips" were under strict orders not to pass them out even one second before New York Sen. Hillary Clinton finished her introduction.

visquene *n.* a kind of airproof and waterproof plastic sheeting.

1989 Don Hamilton *Oregonian* (Portland, Ore.) (Nov. 27) "Add Ice, the Skaters and Swirl," p. 1 ▶ Here are the layers of the rink itself:— The vapor barrier. This is placed directly on the stage. It's actually a sheet of a material called visquene and is designed to protect the wooden stage from the cold and wet. **1991** Bob Lancaster *Arkansas Democrat-Gazette* (Little Rock) (July 17) "Forget What Clinton Says, He's Running Until He's Not Running" ▶ This vision of the Clinton presidency is still under construction in his mind, with, scaffolding and tarps and visquene still scattered about. **2004** Stan Maddux *South Bend Tribune* (Ind.) (Dec. 14) "Experts to Look at Severed Leg" (Int.) ▶ A crew installing new water and electrical lines at Swan Lake Memorial Gardens uncovered the leg wrapped in heavy plastic or a material commonly referred to as visquene.

vog *n.* volcanic smog. *Environment.*

1987 John Edward Young *Christian Science Monitor* (Boston, Mass.) (Jan. 9) "Peering into Kilauea's Caldron," p. B4 ▶ Clouds of acrid volcanic smoke begin to mix with Hilo's humid fog. It's a mixture referred to as "vog" around these parts. **1988** Charles Petit *San Francisco Chronicle* (Calif.) (Jan. 13) "Hawaiians Determined to Save Bit of Paradise," p. 1/Z1 ▶ With the exception of places on the Big Island where "vog," or volcanic smog, occasionally smarts the eyes, air pollution is almost nonexistent, thanks to trade winds and thousands of miles of surrounding ocean. **2005** Corvallis, Ore. *ScienceDaily* (Mar. 16) "Long-Spewing Hawaiian Volcano May Be Health Risk" (Int.) ▶ The island of Hawaii does have a monitoring system and a Vog index, the researchers point out, but it is measured only along the Kona Coast, not in Kau. This "volcano-smog" index—Vog is a locally coined term—also is based on aerosol visibility, not SO2.

vogue *n.* a tire. *Automotive. Hip-Hop.* [From the automobile tire brand *Vogue*, usually sold as whitewalls and often used on Cadillacs and other town cars.] Usually plural: *vogues.*

*1994 (Apr. 1) in *Usenet: alt.rap* Malcolm D. Moore "Re: Unnaground Bay Shit" ▶ Iz all about the playahz in the 9quad—playin them hoes and rollin on Vogues. **1996** Outkast *ATLiens* (song) (Aug. 27) "Elevators (Me & You)" ▶ Rollin' down the strip on Vogues/comin' up slammin' Cadillac doors. **1999** *Usenet: rec.music.hip-hop* (July 15) "Re: RapCity: UnderHouston" ▶ H-town is the city of the vehicle fashion show, we got the carfreaks, hoppers, and the boppers 4REAL. You'll some shit you aint seen before i garawn-tee. From candied 'Lacs on swangaz & vogyes to the foreign big- bodies with 4 tv's in the headrests. **2001** *Usenet: rec.music.hip-hop* (Oct. 24) "Re: Balls on a Cadillac Brougham?" ▶ I mean, those stock hubs are practically rims, and most years look saucy as fuck. And they're hard to take off, even without the locks! That and some vogues and you're set. **2005** Kristie Rieken @ Houston *Star-Telegram* (Dallas-Fort Worth) (July 2) "Texan Paul Wall Shines in Sea of Rappers" (Int.) ▶ The rapper, whose real last name is Slayton, relies on a dizzying array of local vernacular to describe everything from attractive females (honey dips) to rims (swangaz) and tires (vogues).

voodoo poll *n.* an opinion-tallying system whose results are easily manipulated or are otherwise untrustworthy. *Politics.*

1990 David Zizzo *Sunday Oklahoman* (Oklahoma City) (July 29) "2 Republican Candidates for Governor Battle Over Poll," p. 16 ▶ Cole previously had called a Hargis poll showing Hargis leading in Tulsa "a shell game." Hunter said this week's poll for Price was a "voodoo poll." **1995** *Economist* (U.K.) (June 17) "Special—Democracy and Technology—Electioneering" ▶ The telephone has made opinion polling vastly easier and faster. It has encouraged not only the carefully structured poll, which confronts a large random sample with a well-designed question, but what Robert Worcester, head of MORI, Britain's largest polling firm, calls the "voodoo poll," whereby newspaper readers or television viewers are encouraged to telephone with their opinions on some burning issue of the day. Charging a premium rate for the call makes money, too. **1995** Robert M. Worcester *Independent* (U.K.) (July 23) "Condon and the Voodoo Poll," p. 22 ▶ To test the system, I rang nine times in the two minutes given to register a "yes" vote (although I would not normally participate in such a "voodoo" poll). **2005** [Anthony Wells] *UK Polling Report* (Feb. 24) "Voodoo Polling Corner" (Int.) ▶ "Voodoo polls" is a term coined by Sir Bob Worcester to refer to phone-in, click-on or "press-the-red-button" polls, the sort of thing you see on Sky News, the AOL home-page or in the tabloid press. These polls have no statistical validity whatsoever, they do not attempt to be representative of the population, they are entirely self-selecting and they are spectacularly easy to fix by getting partisan supporters to repeatedly ring them. No one should mistake them for a worthwhile indication of public opinion.

vuzvuz *n.* a derogatory name for an Ashkenazic Jew. Also *adj.;* **vusvus.** *Derogatory. Hebrew. Religion.* This term is usually used within the religion, especially by Sephardic Jews. The etymological information in the 1998 and 2005 citations is unverified.

1984 *Usenet: net.religion.jewish* (July 17) "Re: Test for Jewishness" ▶ Yet another mindless leftist VusVus cosmopolitan stupidity. Humans have slaughtered each other for universalistic reasons (as in revolutionary France, Russia or China) as least as often as they have slaughtered each for narrow tribal reasons. Groveling cosmopolitan VusVusim were stunned when the Nazis came for them. **1998** A.J. Gilboa *Mendele: Yiddish Literature and Language* (July 22) "Frenk" (Int.) ▶ Speaking of pejoratives, have you heard the term "vuzvuz" applied to Ashkenazim? Apparently derived from the frequent use of "vus? vus?" in Yiddish. I am not sure that there is any real insult attached to this, though. I often say to people who ask about my origins: Ani? Ani vuzvuz. For that matter, some of my Sephardic friends and colleagues often refer to themselves as frenkim. Perhaps the insult has worn off and all that is left is the wry humour? **2000** [María] *The Jewish Palestinian Encounter* (Nov. 20) (Int.) ▶ And now, since when Iraq is the Mediterranean, no disrespect intended? since when Ovadia is a Med? Again the Ashkenaziut showing its ear! "Anything not vuzvuz is the Med, ya'ani Sefardim, Españolim, the lot." **2005** [Danya] *Jerusalem Syndrome* (Jan. 29) "Today's Hebrew Lesson" (Int.) ▶ I have a new favorite word. It's slang, but not (as it was explained to me, though it'd be useful to know if someone else out there disagrees) derogatory, for an Ashkenazi person. The word is "vuzvuz," ie "That vuzvuz over there by the bus stop...." Why that word, you might ask? Because the Askenazim always asking, "Vus is dis? Vus is dat?" I'm not kidding. That's really the reason.

W

wab *n.* a Mexican. Also *v.*, **wab** or **wab out** to dress or behave like a stereotypical Mexican. *Derogatory.* [Usually said to be a shortening of *wetback*, perhaps from the abbreviation *w.b.*] This term appears to be most common in California.

1998 William Finnegan *Cold New World* (May 12), p. 216 (June 7, 1999) ▶ "I just hope Victoria doesn't look like a little wab." Wab—short for wetback—was, I had already discovered, the single most popular local youth insult. "Whenever my mom has Victoria for more than a couple of hours, she's totally wabbed out—ribbons everywhere, little sandals, frilly socks." **2001** Gustavo Arellano *OC Weekly* (Calif.) (Feb. 2) "The Mexican-American War, Every Sunday in Anaheim" ▶ You half-baked beaners should learn English, damn it! You fat, piss-drunk, chicharron-eating wabs! None of you belong here! I see a lot of wasted space in my country [gesturing at his own muscular chest] occupied by you wabs jabbing his finger at the audience! All of you Mexicans can kiss my great white ass! **2001** Theresa Walker *Orange County Register* (Calif.) (May 15) "The Sounds of 'Silence' Series: Teens," p. 1 ▶ I hate being called "wab," it's a slur for Mexicans, like wetback. **2005** Gustavo Arellano *OC Weekly* (Calif.) (July 22) "iAsk a Mexican!" (Int.) ▶ "Wab" is a slur that assimilated Mexicans use to describe and deride recently arrived Mexicans.... The etymology of wab is unknown—could either be a mongrelization of "wetback" or "wop."

wad *v.* to crash (a motorcycle). *Automotive. Slang.* [Perhaps from the crumpled vehicle that can result from such a wreck.]

1998 Usenet: *rec.motorcycles.dirt* (Sept. 7) "XR400 Used for Furniture Repair" ▶ All of the sudden, I dropped into "the zone" and found myself riding a perfect 15MPH constant-speed balanced wheelie. After about 100-150 ft. on the back wheel, I got nervous and set it down. (I panicked—figured something was bound to happen that would cause me to wad if I didn't get back on two wheels!) **1999** [TrackDude] *Motorcycle Online's Reader Feedback BBS* (Feb. 26) "February 1999 600cc Shootout BBS, Archive One" (Int.) ▶ I know the R1 gets your wheaties but she's a handful for inexperienced riders. Be careful and try not to wad that expensive little toy. **2001** Mark Pittman *Utah Sport Bike Association* (Nov.) "Dave Palazzolo" (Int.) ▶ All it is going to take is one senator's son to wad his R1 (or something) at 160 mph and kill himself or the congressman's daughter goes for a ride with a squid on a GSX-R1000 who target fixates into a rock wall and bam! **2002** [joe c] @ Baltimore, Md. *Caferacer.net Forum* (Nov. 3) "How Much Do You Like That 550/4" (Int.) ► ehhh...just buy that bike for 7500, that way we can have another really expensive honda to wad next year.

wags *n.* the *wives* and *girlfriends* of an all-male sports team. *Acronym. Sports. United Kingdom.*

2004 Niamh Bugler *IC Wales* (June 24) "Telly Gets a Sporting Makeover" (Int.) ► She's got plenty of time to become as polished, pretty and vacant as the WAGs (wives and girlfriends) of the rest of the England squad—why make her clone up any faster than she needs to? **2004** Lousie France *Guardian* (U.K.) (Oct. 3) "Success Isn't All It's Cracked Up to Be" (Int.) ► Pictures of the wives and girlfriends (or Wags as the FA's acronym calls them) of the Euro 2004 England team, or of the wives and girlfriends of the 1999 US Ryder Cup team, for instance, show a classic feminine look where every woman is tanned, polished, thin.... She is not allowed to complain or to step out of line. If she does—such as Posh Spice's decision not to move to Madrid—she's criticised or ostracized (witness the glee when Mrs. Beckham missed the boat on booking into the same hotel as the other Wags in Portugal because it was full).

waps *n.pl.* a woman's breasts. *Sexuality. Slang. United Kingdom.*

1998 Usenet: *alt.music.black-sabbath* (Apr. 16) "Re: Rock n Roll Doctor and No Bone Movies" ► Close with the flaps meaning titties, they are waps. **2000** Usenet: *alt.sports.soccer.manchester.united.scum-haters* (June 25) "At the End of the Day 227" ► We never get to see much during a streak, do we? There's always some copper there with his fucking helmet, sticking it over the fanny, and some doddering old get dressed in Union Jack clothes to put his coat over her waps. **2004** Annabel Crabb @ London, England *Sydney Morning Herald* (Australia) (July 3) "Gag Denied in 'Sexism in City' Case" (Int.) ► A preliminary hearing into her sexual discrimination case against the international finance giant heard that senior colleague Nathaniel Norgren indeed congratulated her on her waps—British slang for breasts—at an office Christmas lunch last year.

watermelon *n.* a communist masquerading as an environmental activist. *Derogatory. Politics. Slang. United States.*

1983 Oakland Ross *Globe and Mail* (Toronto, Can.) (June 4) "El Salvador: Election Just a Sideshow to Real Fight," p. P9 ► Major Robert D'Aubuisson, leader of the ultra right Nationalist Republican Alliance

(ARENA), likes to compare the Christian Democrats to a watermelon. "Green (the Christian Democrats' official color) on the outside," he says, "and red on the inside." **1991** Harry Vaughn *San Francisco Chronicle* (Calif.) (Mar. 25) "Letters to the Editor: 'Hate Campaign,'" p. A20 ▶ The keynote speaker, William H. Holms, presented a talk entitled, "Wimps, Weirdos and Watermelons," in which he stated environmentalists were just a bunch of unemployed welfare-leeching Communists. He suggested that the timber industry should join forces with the farming and mining (oil) industries and mount a "hate campaign" against the environmental community, which he portrayed as "green on the outside and red on the inside." **2004** [Dean Esmay] *Dean's World* (Apr. 25) "Fun with Political Hate Speech" (Int.) ▶ We have one for the greens—"watermelons" (green on the outside, red on the inside, i.e. closet commies).

wear one *v. phr.* in baseball, to be hit by a pitch. *Sports.*

2001 Todd Jones *Sporting News* (St. Louis, Mo.) (Sept. 3) "The Closer," p. 18 ▶ From Day One, you are taught how to send a message to the other team. You work on the beanball.... It's totally barbaric, and it's hard to explain, but it is crucial for your hitters to know that you will protect them if the other team starts hitting your guys. No one likes to talk about it, but it is something that has to be done. After you do it, the first guy to tell you thanks is the hitter on your team who had to wear one. **2003** Teddy Greenstein *Chicago Tribune* (May 16) "Colon Earns Teammates' Respect; Shuts Down O's, Answers Plunking," p. 1 ▶ Baltimore reliever Jorge Julio plunked Magglio Ordonez in the back. Now it was Colon's turn.... "When the best player on your team keeps getting hit, whether it's accidental or not, someone's going to have to wear one."...Colon's decision to retaliate could help unify a team that's already on the rise. **2005** [capeleague] *Royal Rooters of Redsoxnation.net* (Feb. 19) "Wells Takes His Shots at CFY" (Int.) ▶ Regardless if Unit hits someone or not, I say Schilling makes Sheffield "wear one" on his first at bat. **2005** Troy E. Renck @ L.A. *Denver Post* (Colo.) (May 2) "Rockies Take Hit in More Than L Column" (Int.) ▶ They expected someone to "wear one"—baseball parlance for getting plunked—after their pitchers hit seven Dodgers batters in their previous series, but took exemption to the 24-year-old's timing.

wedgie *n.* jocularly, a standard bicycle. *Sports.* [So-called because a rider astride a standard bicycle is likely to have a *wedgie*, where underpants ride up into the crack of the buttocks.]

1993 *Usenet: rec.bicycles.soc* (July 19) "Re: Recumbents (was: Is Touring Dying?)" ▶ Great bikes (for "wedgie riders") if you enjoy riding a bike where the leather encased saddle is wedged between the cheeks of your butt giving you that wonderful pain in your backside. **1996** Stephanie Dunnewind *Columbian* (Vancouver, Wash.) (Oct. 15) "Sit Back & Enjoy the Ride" ▶ The way recumbent riders make it sound, traditional bikes are just one step up from the torture rack. One common name is "wedgie bike." **2005** Sharon Tummins *Daily News* (Galveston County, Tex.) (July 17) "The View from a Different Angle" (Int.) ▶ Last year I converted from a road bike (fondly called a "wedgie") to a recumbent (proudly called a "bent").

weeded *adj.* busy, swamped, **in the weeds.** *Food & Drink.* This term appears to be specific to the restaurant business.

1995 *Usenet: alt.games.marathon* (Feb. 17) "Re: Top Ten Signs You've Been Playing Marathon Too Long" ▶ I'm a waiter at TGI Friday's. "Weeded" is jargon for being so busy you can't even think of what you came into the kitchen to get. As in "in the weeds" like you're "swimming" (another useful bit of nomenclature for the same thing) in a lake, and being tangled in seaweed. **1997** *Usenet: alt.food.waffle-house* (May 14) "Closest W.H. to D.C." ▶ The poor old waitress was getting weeded with only 3 tables including me; she was at the end of a double shift I think. **2000** Anthony Bourdain *Kitchen Confidential* (May 22), p. 223 ▶ *Weeded* means "in the weeds." **2002** [Jina] @ Houston, Texas *B4-U-Eat* (July 24) "Cheddar's" (Int.) ▶ I have been to this restaurant several times. Service is not always great, but they are so incredibly busy that I am pretty forgiving. However, my most recent visit was incredibly frustrating. The waiter was severely "weeded." He spent a lot of time in the kitchen and was rarely to be seen on the floor.

wet *n.* a recreational drug made of marijuana, PCP, and formaldehyde. *Crime & Prisons. Drugs. Slang. United States.*

1995 James F. McCarty *Cleveland Plain Dealer* (Ohio) (Apr. 30) "The Self-Destruction of David Allen," p. 8 ▶ Allen was "running with a crowd doing a lot of drugs": marijuana, crack, PCP and a potent concoction called "Wet," which is marijuana laced with formaldehyde. **2002** Lewis Goldfrank, et al. *Goldfrank's Toxicologic Emergencies* (Apr. 26), p. 1036 ▶ PCP was infrequently incorporated into marijuana cigarettes.... These are being sold on the street under varying names such as "Illy" in Connecticut, "Hydro" in New York City, "Dip" in New Jersey, "Wet" in Philadelphia, and "Fry" in Texas. The cigarettes are treated with "embalming fluid," allegedly to enhance the drug's euphoric effects. Embalming fluid, which contains formalin (formaldehyde in methanol), is used as a medium to ease a uniform distribution of PCP in these cigarettes. **2004** David Hunt *Daily*

Courier (Connellsville, Pa.) (May 7) "Fayette County: Edwards Claims Police Coerced Confession" (Int.) ► According to court documents, Edwards and Larry Sr. were locked in a dispute over a drug called "wet," the slang term for a mixture of PCP and formaldehyde. It is used to lace marijuana or other smoking materials to enhance the high they produce.

whale *n.* a serious, heavily funded bettor; a *high roller. Gambling. Slang.*

1990 Robert Johnson *Wall Street Journal* (June 28), p. A1 ► In the parlance of the casino industry, a huge bettor like Mr. Kashiwagi is a "whale," which surely makes Mr. Trump his Ahab. **2004** Joe Drape *N.Y. Times* (Apr. 26) "Horse Racing's Biggest Bettors Are Reaping Richest Rewards" (Int.) ► In horse-playing parlance, Maury Wolff is a whale, one of the thousand or so professional bettors who collectively wager as much as $1.5 billion a year on thoroughbred races in the United States. He will not attend the Kentucky Derby at Churchill Downs on Saturday. In fact, he and the other whales rarely set foot in a racetrack. **2005** Adam Levy, Jeannine DeFoe *Bloomberg.com* (Mar. 2) "Harrah's, MGM Mirage Duel for Supremacy on the Las Vegas Strip" (Int.) ► Lanni courts the casino's best clients—"whales," in industry parlance—taking semiannual trips to Hong Kong, Taipei, Shanghai and Singapore, where he hosts as many as three dinners in one night. **2005** Suzette Parmley @ Atlantic City, N.J. *Philadelphia Inquirer* (Pa.) (Mar. 11) "Upping the Ante in Atlantic City" (Int.) ► Anthony Patrone, president of marketing at Resorts, said the range of available funds for players at the blackjack tournament last weekend was from $25,000 to $300,000. "Mini-whales," as he calls them. Whales is casino slang for gamblers who can lose millions.

whickerbill *n.* **1.** (the foreskin of) a penis; **2.** an unsophisticated person or rustic; **3.** a thin, raised edge on an airfoil or fan blade that adds downward force. Also **wicker bill, whickerbill, wickerbill.** Similar synonyms for the first two senses are *peckerhead* and *peckerwood*, both in a literal definition '(a part of) a penis' and in a more derogatory one, 'an unsophisticated person; a redneck.' Another synonym for the second sense is *scissorbill*.

1925 Harry Harrison Kroll *A Comparative Study of Upper and Lower Southern Folk Speech* (George Peabody College for Teachers, Tenn.) (Aug.), p. 82 ► *Whicker bill*. A rustic, servant, poor white trash. Miss. **1939** J.C. Short @ Galena, Mo. *Down in the Holler* (Oct.) in *Pissing in* *the Snow and Other Ozark Folktales* (Jan. 1, 1987) Vance Randolph, p. 91 ▶ "Does whickerbills count?" says he. The boys argued awhile, but there ain't no denying that a whickerbill is part of a man's prick.... Jack pulled out the God-awfullest tool you ever seen, only on a jackass.... Randolph notes that "whickerbill" is the Ozark word for prepuce. **1948** Bill Pucker *Independent* (Murphysboro, Ill.) (Jan. 28), p. 7 ▶ News from Our Whickerbill Correspondent. Goat Gap, Illinois, Speshul to Interdependent. It if twernt for Nudge Squat sayin what Nudge said to the Thumpit twins, Nudge would soon be at his spring plowin. [**1960** Cliff Farrell *Evening Sentinel* (Holland, Mich.) (Aug. 19) "The Lean Rider," p. 14 ▶ "If a little thing like that'll cold-chill you, then you jest naturally won't tolerate what I'm going to do to this whicker-bill next."...He moved to the steer and pressed down the hot curved end of the iron, forming an insignia. The steer bawled mournfully.] **1971** Albert Murray *South to a Very Old Place,* p. 172 in *Making Mark Twain Work in the Classroom* (May 1, 1999) J. S. Leonard, p. 172 ▶ As for the part about being a nigger, the most obvious thing about that was that you were not a whicker-bill different like them old peckerwoods were. **1984** David B. Kalinich *Surviving in Corrections* (Sept. 1), p. 173 ▶ *Wicker Bill or Hillbilly*—Person from the South. **1998** Usenet: *rec.org.mensa* (Mar. 11) "Re: Circumcision" ▶ The biggest advantage of being uncircumcised is that with practice, you can jerk on your wickerbill and cause it to emit a quacking sound. You can be the life of the party. **1998** Usenet: *ca.politics* (Dec. 16) "Re: Nazi's Were/Tim Starr Can't Clean the Poop Off His Shoes or Out of His Mind" ▶ Since you've read Dr Sooos, does this mean you dribble in your cornflakes, and fondle your whickerbill at dusk on full moon evenings, or what? **2002** Ralph Wiley *ESPN.com* (May 22) "A One-Man Rainbow Coalition" (Int.) ▶ Asian-Americans feel a sense of pride, accomplishment, even of authorship of Tiger Woods at work. Everyone does. Bony whicker-bill ranchers out in West Texas eating chicken-fried steak do, too. **2002** William S. Webster @ South Georgia College *Webster's Home Page* (Douglas, Ga.) (Nov. 12) "Dirty Joke" (Int.) ▶ He and my father's nickname for penis was "wickerbill," which made sex seem ridiculous, like it was a misshapen bird beak in your pants that you sometimes dangled into the dark holes of outhouses, something funnier even than a big nose or butt and a lot less reliable. [**2002** Usenet: *alt.politics.democrats* (Dec. 30) "Re: Why I Want Hillary for President?" ▶ A Wickerbill is a bird that pecks his own shit!] **2003** Bobby Unser *Winners Are Driven* (Feb. 14), p. 15 ▶ Dan hand-cut and shaped a couple of pieces of sheet metal that looked like angle-irons—just 90 degree bent pieces of aluminum. He had us mount them on the back edges of the rear wing of the car.... His simple "wicker-bill" invention—also known as the Gurney Flap—

had given us another four miles per hour. **2003** [6 shot] *SDH Water-fowl Forums* (Aug. 28) "Duckin" (Int.) ▶ I think it is up to the guide to show good judgement and decide based on talking if this is a duck hunter or some wickerbill. **2003** Shawn Brouse *Daily Item* (Sunbury, Pa.) (Sept. 26) "World of Outlaws Invade Mid-State Next Week" (Int.) ▶ The only thing that could temper this review is the reintroduction of the allowance of wickerbills on the top wings for the locals in the Open. A wickerbill produces a downforce or dragging effect on the car, planting it to the speedway surface. **2004** [Le D'Nah] *Petlovers forum* (May 21) "Hello Everyone!" (Int.) ▶ Let the "good ol' boys" pull each others' wickerbill, the internet is a big place and there is room for all kinds. **2004** Sterling Johnson *Watch Your F*cking Language* (Nov. 3), p. 83 ▶ In Arkansas, whickerbill is a common term for the foreskin.

whip *n.* an automobile. *Black English. Hip-Hop. Slang. United States.*

1997 *Usenet: rec.music.hip-hop* (Nov. 19) "Re: You Know You Ghetto When..." ▶ When you start your whip with a screwdriver. **2000** *Usenet: rec.music.hip-hop* (Dec. 29) "Re: OTP: Subway Trains v. Your Whip" ▶ Trains and walking when it comes to the daily grind. Whips when it's free time. I can understand the appeal of pushing your own whip 'round town though. I brought a car back in March and I've gone overboard putting money into it. **2004** Denny Lee *N.Y. Times* (Apr. 23) "The Dub Generation: Gearheads Go Hip-Hop" (Int.) ▶ "It has some of the hottest whips on the planet," she added, using the current East Coast slang for car.

white knowledge *n.* information acquired without conscious effort. [This term originated in science fiction writing and is associated with author Terry Pratchett, who probably coined it.]

1995 *Usenet: alt.fan.pratchett* (Feb. 12) "Re: IT Annotations (Spoiler)" ▶ I think it's just a joke; the storming of the winter palace in the Russian Revolution is far more ingrained into people's "white knowledge." **1997** Neil Gaiman *Neverwhere* (July 1), p. 9 ▶ He continued, slowly, by a process of osmosis and white knowledge (which is like white noise, only more useful) to comprehend the city, a process that accelerated when he realized that the actual City of London itself was no bigger than a square mile. **1999** *Usenet: rec.arts.sf.written.robert-jordan* (Mar. 13) "Re: More on Verin" ▶ _Why_ must you use the Socratic method to introduce the Old Testament? I mean, granted, most of your students will have absorbed the basics in a white knowledge sort of manner—I did, and I've never read it. **2000** [Cassady Toles] (*Unknown Armies RPG Mailing List*) (Sept. 25) "Pacific NW Clio

Sites" (Int.) ▶ My friend Alexai describes the existence of a certain white knowledge that everyone has, but doesn't know where they got it. **2004** Priti Trivedi @ Toms River, N.J. *Fractured Blog* (Oct. 15) "See How Busy We Are?" (Int.) ▶ The production team is slowly picking up the lingo, so that last night when Chad asked for a "Half apple" I actually knew 1. what he was talking about 2. where it was and 3. where he needed to put it. That's amazing! Okay, so maybe apple boxes was a bad example, but the amount of "white knowledge" we're all picking up on this movie is what keeps us going when the going gets tough. Or cold.

white space *n.* an underserved business market or undeveloped product category. *Business. Jargon.*

1989 *Computing* (U.K.) (July 27) "Resellers Feel Pinch as DEC Tightens Belt," p. 11 ▶ "Hamilton and ADL have provided extra competition, while Snergy has gone for niche markets," he said. DEC's green and white space policy meant that Rapid had to move into a different market area. "We were strong in green space," Dunne explained, "so we had to cut a market in white space which has taken us a long time." **1993** Christopher Lorenz *Financial Times* (U.K.) (Oct. 15) "Management—Avoiding the IBM Trap," p. 18 ▶ A group of 150 people were handpicked for what he and Alberthal call "their ability to think outside the box."...They were broken into five "waves" of 30, focusing on different issues...a search for "white space" (uncontested new competitive areas). **2004** Diane Stafford *Kansas City Star* (Kan., Mo.) (Nov. 23) "Increased Pay Gets Devoured by Inflation" (Int.) ▶ White space—a high-growth or unserved market or outside-the-box business opportunity. **2004** Mary Lou Roberts *iSeries Network* (U.S.) (Dec. 7) "Will Pennsylvania Casinos Gamble on the iSeries?" (Int.) ▶ Just about everyone in the iSeries community agrees that the key to survival of the platform is growth in new business opportunities—the "white space" as the hardware vendors refer to it. Let's hope that the iSeries ISVs and resellers will fill that white space with slot machines.

whoadie *n.* a casual, familiar form of address for a friend. Also **wodie, wody.** *Black English. Hip-Hop. Louisiana. United States.* [< *wardie* 'resident of a political ward.'] This term appears to originate in the hip-hop scene of New Orleans, La.

1997 *Usenet: neworleans.general* (Nov. 23) "Re: N.O.L.A. Slang...peep it out" ▶ wodie. **1997** *Usenet: rec.music.hip-hop* (Nov. 23) "Re: SOUTH SLANG...peep it out" ▶ "wodie"—just like dog or bruh.... Whazzatnin wodie. [**1998** *Usenet: rec.music.hip-hop* (Jan. 8) "Re: Regional Slang" ▶ wody (long O).] **2000** *Usenet: alt.sport.qzar* (Feb. 26) "Re: 2's

Results in Pleasanton..." ▶ My block hot baby my block burn. My block on fire whoadie what about yerz? **2000** *UBB Developer's Network* (Dec.) "Spotlight" (Int.) ▶ A "wodie" is basically a New Orleans slang for "associate" or "homie," and it's pronounced WHOA-DEE. **2001** Bryant Gumbel, Alonzo Westbrook "CBS News: The Early Show" (Feb. 19) "Staying in Step with Slang" ▶ GUMBEL: What about a whoadie. WESTBROOK: A term of familiar address from male to male or female to female. **2004** *Yahoo! Finance* (June 22) "Cash Money Records Dominates the Radio Airwaves" (in New York) (Int.) ▶ Cash Money introduced a number of words like "bling bling" and "Whoadie" into the hip hop lexicon.

winker *n.* the anus; the posterior or buttocks. A similar term is *brown eye.*

1995 *Usenet: alt.tasteless* (Mar. 27) "Processed Cheeze" ▶ When I finally got the *really hard part* past my winker (marvelous emanations from my prostate noted in the process) the second half was much softer. **2001** Emma Tom *Australian* (Feb. 3) "Gettin' It Down Pat, Italian Style," p. 13 ▶ Whackin' a young lady on the winker-stinker should only be illegal if she isn't a looker. **2003** Roshan McArthur @ L.A. *Sunday Mirror* (U.K.) (June 1) "Down-There Hair Care," p. 23 ▶ She says, "Cindee, will you wax my butt?" I flipped her over on her hands and knees and slapped her winker with wax and—yank, yank—she was clean as a whistle. **2005** Tristan Taormino *Village Voice* (NYC) (July 11) "Britesmile for Bungholes" (Int.) ▶ We've been bleaching lots of Texan winkers.... Anal bleaching is based on the idea that there is one perfect shade of ass.

witches' knickers *n.pl.* plastic bags that have caught in trees or bushes. *Environment. Slang. United Kingdom.*

2000 Katharine Blake *Irish Times* (Dec. 23) "Degradable Witches' Knickers," p. 66 ▶ Two-thirds of this is plastic carrier bags, which end up in landfill or blowing about in trees and hedges (now known colloquially as "witches knickers"). **2004** [T. Feran] *Plain Dealer* (Cleveland, Ohio) (May 2) "Writer Branches Out to Snagging Bags" (Int.) ▶ A woman told them that in Ireland bags in trees are called witches' knickers. **2004** Margie Wylie *Times-Picayune* (New Orleans,

La.) (Oct. 21) "Blight of Bags Bringing Bans," p. 1 ▶ Alaskans call them "tundra ghosts" and "landfill snowbirds." In China, they're "white pollution." South Africans have sarcastically dubbed them their "national flower." Snagged in treetops in Ireland, they become "witches' knickers."

wizzo *n.* among military aircraft personnel, a weapons systems operator. *Acronym. Jargon. Military. Technology. United States.* [Pronunciation of the first letters of *w*eapons *s*ystems *o*perator or *o*fficer.]

1986 Russel Watson, John Barry, John Walcott *Newsweek* (Apr. 28) "Reagan's Raiders," p. 26 ▶ A skilled "Wizzo"—weapons-systems operator—can achieve good accuracy with only one aiming device, but the planners established the "double lock" rule to make sure the right targets were hit. **1991** *Tulsa Tribune* (Okla.) (Jan. 18) "Combat Beginner Says Strike Awesome," p. 17A ▶ His "wizzo" weapons system officer, Maj. Billy Wilhite, 36, of Monroe, La., said, "Nobody has ever shot at us before." **2004** Michael Shinabery *Alamogordo News* (N.Mex.) (Dec. 16) "American F-4s Future Is Mothballed" (Int.) ▶ Lt. Col. Mark Buccigrossi's back-seat wizzo—vernacular for the acronym WSO, or weapons system officer/navigator—in the F-4 Phantom.

woobie *n.* a security blanket; a *blankie*; a favorite toy or object. Also **wooby**. *Colloquial. United States.*

1989 *Usenet: rec.arts.movies* (Dec. 2) "Batman (Spoiler)" ▶ The scene where he was trying to tell Vicky Vale that he was really Batman reminded me of Mr. Mom where Keaton is trying to explain to his son that he'll get him another "wooby." **1999** Rita Kempley *Washington Post* (Oct. 1) "'Grouchland': Everything's A-Okay," p. C5 ▶ The resident villain, Huxley (Mandy Patinkin, suitably silly in a scenery-chewing turn), steals Elmo's "wooby"—his word for the blanket—thus forcing the littlest Muppet on a perilous quest to retrieve it. **1999** *Times-Picayune* (New Orleans, La.) (Dec. 5) "Myers' Family Comes Together to Help Heal Grief" (in Cincinnati, Ohio) ▶ In the same way that each member of the family chose something that represented them and placed it in Chip's casket, Adam and Holly and their children chose Connor's pacifier and Janie's "woobie." **2004** Gwen Schmidt *Library Squirrel* (Can.) (Nov. 20) "The Woobie" (Int.) ▶ I don't actually even know how to spell the word "woobie." All I know is that the Engineer always used it to mean "a shirt that is really warm and comfortable, but that is in such bad shape that you could never wear it outside your house."

woo-woo *adj.* concerned with emotions, mysticism, or spiritualism; other than rational or scientific; mysterious; *new agey.* Also *n.,* a person who has mystical or new age beliefs.

1986 Carol M. Ostrom *Seattle Times* (Wash.) (June 20) "In the Spirit—New Age Adherents Follow a Personal Path," p. E1 ▶ Of course, not everyone who thinks that science doesn't tell all would think it's reasonable to believe, as Gibson does, that one can program crystals with thought energy. But Gibson says there is ample evidence—both scientific and subjective—that crystals can help in healing and transformation. "You can say it's woo-woo," she says with a laugh. "But it works. I go with what works." **1990** *Usenet: ran.ragforum* (May 28) "Thoughts on the Bombing" ▶ My thoughts on this past weekend... (emotional but not too woo woo). There is no logic to the outrage, the helplessness, the constant frustration, and the relentless struggle that we as activists feel on an ongoing basis and for this particular event in our lives. **1992** Howie Movshovitz *Denver Post* (Colo.) (May 29) "Muddled 'Poison Ivy' Implies More Than It Delivers," p. 6F ▶ The movie jumbles Cooper's occasional poor insights with something like a bad book on adolescent psychology, a worse self-help book and a thoroughly unoriginal horror story. You can see the movie reaching for importance and a kind of woo-woo seriousness. **1995** Sean Mitchell *L.A. Times* (Dec. 31) "Following Her Instincts," p. 10 ▶ I didn't give a good audition either. I've always felt that [the late] Jean Rosenthal, who was the real Ginger, helped me get the part. That sounds kind of woo-woo, but we're in L.A., so what the hell. **1996** *Usenet: bit.listserv.dorothyl* (Mar. 22) "Theater/Blanche/Starving/Mr. Moto" ▶ Some of the spirituality stuff was a bit "woo woo la la" for my tastes, but not so much so that it was a problem. **1999** Lee Caroll, Jan Tober *Indigo Children* (May 1), p. 131 ▶ She considers my metaphysical matters rather woo-woo. **2001** Julia McCord *Omaha World-Herald* (Neb.) (July 22) "Charity Event Rubs Donors the Right Way," p. 5B ▶ When a friend suggested 10 years ago that Deb Oetken get a massage, she scoffed. "Yeah, right!" she thought to herself. "What kind of woo-woo stuff is that?" **2002** Eric Mortenson *Oregonian* (Portland) (Mar. 22) "Gresham's 2002-03 Budget Draft Balances with Whacks and Freezes," p. C2 ▶ Not to get too woo-woo about symbolism, but the boiler broke down at Gresham City Hall on Thursday, providing an appropriately chilly atmosphere as interim City Manager Rob Fussell prepared his budget message. **2003** *Usenet: rec.arts .mystery* (Apr. 9) "Re: Connolly, _White Road_" ▶ To be a proper woo-woo, you must follow these rules:...Never look for the simplest, most obvious cause of something.... Always favor the conspiracy angle over the boring angle.... Don't accept mainstream science.... Memorize all the sci-babble terms used in the Star Trek series.... Always claim that the other guy is "closed-minded." **2004** David Ramsdale *Red Hot Tantra* (Mar. 1), p. 118 ► Leave it to his kooky sister to think that sitting around with a bunch of woo-woos was going to get him a date. **2005** [Mimi Smartypants] *Mimi Smartypants* (Chicago) (Apr. 6) (Int.) ► I am curious how they handle this particular song, since surely our slightly woo-woo preschool, which decorated paper Easter eggs for "spring" while seemingly making an effort not to actually mention Easter, does not sing the "Teddy Bear, Teddy Bear, say your prayers" line that I learned back in the jump rope days.

worm poll *n.* a continuous survey taken of a live audience to measure reactions to a political speech or debate. *Media. Politics.*

[**1996** *San Antonio Express-News* (Tex.) (June 5) "A Worm Poll: Sorry, Dennis Rodman: Many Respondents to an Online Poll Say They Want You in a Bulls Uniform Next Season, But Not at a $10 Million Price Tag" (title).] **1996** Ruth Laugesen *Dominion* (New Zealand) (Oct. 8) "Clark Wins 'Worm' Poll," p. 1 ► Labour leader Helen Clark was last night judged a two-time winner by undecided voters operating an electronic "worm" in the final TVNZ leaders' debate, with Alliance leader Jim Anderton close on her heels. **2002** Alister Browne *Evening Standard* (New Zealand) (July 23) "Worm Poll Cannot Be Trusted," p. 3 ► The poll of 696 people showed 27 percent remained undecided. Similarly with the "worm" TV studio audience, there was no way of figuring who people were going to vote for or whether their emotional reactions would turn into a solid preference. **2004** (*AAP Bulletins*) (Australia) (Sept. 12) "The Worm Turns for Latham in Debate" (in Canberra) ► Opposition Leader Mark Latham was the runaway winner in tonight's live televised debate with Prime Minister John Howard, the "worm" poll of audience members showed. **2005** David Rowan *Times* (London, Eng.) (Apr. 9) "A Guide to...Election-speak" (Int.) ► The swingometer, meanwhile, has been surpassed by on-screen *worm polls*, tracking audience reaction to speeches in real time. **2005** *Guardian* (U.K.) (Apr. 11) "Breaking the Code," p. 8 ► Those who like nothing better than an evening watching "The West Wing" know the format. Voters turn a dial to say if they are pleased, indifferent or hostile as they listen to a speech. A "worm poll" describes the lines which slither across the screen to record their instant reaction.

yampee *n.* the crust of mucous that forms in the corner of the eye. *Trinidad & Tobago.*

1992 *Usenet: soc.culture.caribbean* (Feb. 20) "Trini Words for the WEEK" ▶ *YAMPEE*—Mucus, found in the corner of the eyes after a sleep. **2003** Kevin Baldeosingh *Kevin Baldeosingh—Caribbean Writer, Author, Journalist, Trinidad and Tobago* (Nov. 7) "Freudian Slips" (Int.)

▶ You en see all dem Creole eye have yampee in em! **2004** [Hook] *UrlUnknown* (Apr. 18) "Ever Been Talking to a Hot Guy and..." (Int.) ▶ U trying to tell me that some sweaty, pimple-faced jackass with snat running down dey nose, yampee in dey eyes and headflakes all over dey clothes will have a chance with u?! **2004** [imusic] *CaribbeanCricket.com* (Sept. 25) "England and Vaughn—Chokers!!!!!" (Int.) ▶ Belittlin de opposition doh take away de yampee in we own eye. **2005** Roger James *TnTisland.com* (Trinidad & Tobago) (Jan. 5) "Trini Xmas Special #5: Parang! Parang!" (Int.) ▶ So wash dem glasses and bring out de rum. Before yuh blink and wipe de yampee out yuh eye, Dem boys go be in front we gate singing "Cy, Cy,Cy."

Yankee dime *n.* a (perfunctory) kiss. *Slang. United States.* This term appears to originate in the South.

1900 *Landmark* (Statesville, N.C.) (Aug. 28) "A Great Day at Troutman's," p. 3 ▶ When the boys and girls husked corn together and the boys hustled like the very mischief to get the first red ear—wonder why?—and then attended the girls home from these husking bees and night singings, bidding them good-night in the moonlight at the front gate and going home with a bran[d]-new Yankee dime, feeling prouder and more independent than any of the present generation. **1928** *Indiana Weekly Messenger* (Pa.) (June 7) "Colloquial," p. 6 ▶ "Yankee dime" is a slang term used in some sections of the United States, particularly in the South, to denote a kiss, just as "Dutch quarter" is used to mean a hug. In some sections "Quaker nickel" is employed in the same sense as "Yankee Dime." **2004** Merle Kessler *DBMT* (San Francisco) (Sept. 29) "Yankee Dime" (Int.) ▶ Yankee

Dime—This is Texas slang, apparently (I read it in the Lone Star Iconoclast!) for an insincere kiss. President Bush sure knows how to spend those.

yard sale *n.* especially in skiing or other snow-based sports, a fall or spill; a *wipeout. Slang. Sports.* [Perhaps from the appearance of "sporting goods spread out all over the yard."]

1988 Bob MacDonald *Boston Globe* (Mass.) (Jan. 31) "A Turn for the Better After a Year Off the Slopes, a Skier Bravely Undergoes Six Days of Basic Training," p. 18 ▶ responded to her praise with a "face plant" and "yard sale"—falling flat while my skis and poles went in four directions. It might have hurt if we both hadn't been laughing so hard. **1991** *Usenet: rec.skiing* (Jan. 3) "Re: Ski Goggles" ▶ On the other hand, goggles can be a pain, tend to fog up at the wrong moments and are just another piece of hardware to recover after a "yard sale" type fall. **1997** *Usenet: alt.magick* (Oct. 21) "Re: T'ai-Chi Skiing: The Dance of the Cosmos" ▶ The "yard sale" resulted completely from the fact that I was going too fast, given the fact that I was coming down from an easy slope where all the folks around me were going waaaay slower, and doing occasional panic stops. **2004** Tamara Miller @ Vail Mountain *Vail Daily* (Colo.) (Nov. 27) "Skiers and Boarders Unite in Battle Against the Fall" (Int.) ▶ A good fall always makes for a good story. But boarders and skiers agreed that wearing a helmet is essential for making your average yard sale nothing more than a goofy tale to tell your friends. **2005** *Ventura County Star* (Calif.) (July 4) "Cycling Through the Lingo" (Int.) ▶ *Yard sale:* A horrendous crash that leaves all of your belongings scattered as if on display for sale. Also a skiing term.

yips *n.* nervousness that interferes with precision playing, especially in golf; a case of nerves; the jitters. *Sports.* [Golfer Sam Snead has been credited with coining this word, but while he certainly used it, no evidence has been found to support the claim.] Usu. with the definite article: **the yips.**

1937 Bill Braucher @ New York *Hammond Times* (Ind.) (July 3) "Tales in Tidbits," p. 9 ▶ Carl Hubbell says he got the "yips" so bad during his recent slump that he was walking into closed doors. **1940** Hutt Martin *Nevada State Journal* (Reno) (Aug. 11) "It's Well Worth While to Practice on Getting Out of Golfing Trouble," p. 14 ▶ The grass between the ball and the blade will cause a bit of run so allow for it and practice this shot at least twenty times the next time you go out, not that you will perfect it that quickly but having practiced it—it won't give you those mental yips the next time you're in that spot. **1984** Jim Lassiter *Daily Oklahoman* (Oklahoma City) (June 15) "Moody a Winner on Seniors Tour Moody Finds New Life on Seniors Tour" ▶ He had what they call the "yips.."...If you're a golfer and you have the "yips," you don't have to be told what they are. You also don't have to be told you're in trouble. **2004** Barry Horn *Dallas Morning News* (Tex.) (July 3) "Rangers' Bierbrodt Tries to Put Shooting Behind Him" (Int.) ▶ After winning his first game against the Mariners on June 23, pitching six encouraging innings, Bierbrodt's control looked lost again. In 1 2/3 innings Monday, he walked five batters. Once more, some misses could be measured in feet. In baseball, such misfiring is referred to as "yips." They cost one-time Pittsburgh star Steve Blass his career. Most recently, St. Louis pitcher Rick Ankiel was afflicted with the yips in 2000.

Yuma *n.* In Cuba, a nickname for the United States; an American. *Cuba. Spanish.* [The etymological information in the 1996 cite and last 2004 cite is unverified. Another claim that it comes from a corrupted pronunciation by Cubans of the English words "united states" is less likely.] In Spanish, the word is used with the definite article: *La Yuma.*

1991 Don Rosen *Orange County Register* (Calif.) (May 19) "After Treacherous Voyage, Refugees Seek Fresh Start in Irvine," p. H9 ▶ For years they dreamed of coming to "la yuma," as the United States is known in Cuba. **1996** *Usenet: soc.culture.cuba* (Jan. 21) "Re: What Does Gusano Mean?" ▶ Tu si te las sabes todas, desde el Rosita de Hornedo hasta lo de la Yuma. Efectivamente, no se si te recuerdas, se trataba de una pelicula de Glenn Ford, "The 3:10 to Yuma" Asi creo que se llamaba. Esta pelicula cuando la echaron formo tremendo revuelo, pues en los cines en esos dias lo que estaban "echando" era pura bazofia del campo socialista. Se formaron tremendas colas y la gente comenzo a popularizar y asociar Yuma con USA. **2004** Anita Snow @ Cojimar, Cuba *Miami Herald* (Fla.) (Aug. 11) "Repeat of '94 'Rafter' Crisis Less" (Int.) ▶ The upheaval of 1994 began when thousands of Cubans crowded Havana's sea wall to cheer on the latest of many ferry hijackings by passengers bent on reaching "La Yuma"— slang for the United States. ***2004** Tom Miller *Traveler's Tales* (Aug. 12) "Cuba: Introduction" (Int.) ▶ In Cuban street slang, yuma means a foreigner, more specifically, someone from a non-Spanish speaking European or North American country, and most particularly, from the United States. When someone asks my brother-in-law where his sister went, he might say, "Se fue pa' la yuma." She went to the United States. Or an American tourist strolling down Havana's Prado might hear, "¡Oye, yuma! ¡Ven acá!" Hey 'merican, com'ere! Yuma is a word unknown in Mexico or any other Spanish-speaking country that I know of.... The Cuban street-slang yuma derives directly from the film 3:10 to Yuma.

yumptious *adj.* delicious. *Food & Drink.* [*yum*my + scr*umptious*]
1957 Nancy and Temple Fielding *Syracuse Herald-American* (N.Y.) (Aug. 4) "Next Time You're in Belgium Try This Pint-Size Restaurant" ▶ The other chose, as usual, the "Sabayon Fielding"—a yumptious creation which the inventor was kind enough to name in our honor several years ago. **1980** William Safire *N.Y. Times Mag.* (Sept. 21) "On Language: Living in Synonymy," p. 16 ▶ This scholarly, no-frills econiche for neologisms makes yumptious reading from here to Bosnywash. **1990** *Usenet: soc.singles* (Apr. 11) "Re: A Stupid Poll for the Ages" ▶ Fresh ground, mornings, with Oatmeal, brown sugar, nuts, yumptious. **1991** Tom Shales *Dallas Morning News* (Tex.) (Dec. 8) "TV Is a Weighty Problem When You're on a Diet," p. 4C ▶ One of the newest cereals is made in the shape of yumptious, scrumptious cinnamon minibuns. **2005** *St. Paul Pioneer Press* (Minn.) (Feb. 15) "Anyone Got the Dope on Humbums?" (Int.) ▶ You could slaver them with butter or powdered sugar or jam.... Humbums were yumptious.

Z

zeitgeber *n.* a naturally occurring cue, such as light or temperature, that regulates biological rhythms; something that influences or regulates the timing or rhythm of something else. *Biology. German. Germany. Jargon. Science.* [*zeit* 'time' + *geber* 'giver.' Coined by scientist Jürgen Aschoff, ca. 1954.]

1958 Colin Pittendrigh, Victor Bruce, Peter Kaus (*Proceedings of the Natl. Acad. of Sciences*) (*U.S.*) (Sept. 15) "On the Significance of Transients in Daily Rhythms," vol. 44, no. 9, p. 966 (Int.) ▶ Light and temperature are the only periodic or quasi-periodic environmental variables to which endogenous oscillation can be coupled: in nature they entrain the endogenous oscillation, thereby controlling period and establishing appropriate phase. They are, to use Aschoff's phrase, the principal *Zeitgeber*. **1962** Miklos D. F. Udvardy *American Midland Naturalist* (Apr.) "Biology and Comparative Physiology of Birds," vol. 67, no. 2, pp. 507-8 (Int.) ▶ No reference is made to diurnal activity, Orstreue, Zeitgeber, and other terms of the last thirty years. **2003** Franz Halberg *Journal of Circadian Rhythms* (Sept. 24) "Transdisciplinary Unifying Implications of Circadian Findings in the 1950s" (Int.) ▶ All three of us redefined our terms, they a *zeitgeber* and I a synchronizer (as primary or secondary), respectively, as an external agent, usually a cycle that does not "give" time and merely synchronizes existing body time with its own. **2004** Alison Stein Wellner *Inc.com* (NYC) (June) "The Time Trap," p. 42 (Int.) ▶ These "external pacers" are known among academics as *zeitgebers*—German for "time givers" and they exert tremendous influence on your company. Zeitgebers can include anything from the fiscal year to the production schedule of a supplier to the school calendar in your community, and every company possesses a unique set of them.

zhing-zhong *n.* merchandise made in Asia; cheaply made, inexpensive, or substandard goods. *Business. Slang. Zimbabwe.*

*2004 [The Woodpecker] *Standard* (Zimbabwe) (July 22) "Christmas Comes Early for People of Tsholotsho" (Int.) ▶ Shavings can only advise that, judging from what we hear, the "Zhing Zhong" condoms may not be that protective to Zimbabweans, many of whom are of bigger built than your average Chinese man. **2004** *Financial Gazette* (Harare, Zimbabwe) (July 29) "Save Us from 'Zhing-Zhongs,' Say

Leather Industry Players" (Int.) ▶ A deluge of cheap counterfeits, nick-named "zhing-zhongs," imported mainly from Asia, has threatened the viability of the country's leather industry. **2004** Vincent Kahiya *Zimbabwe Independent* (Harare) (July 30) "Locals Exposed" (Int.) ▶ Zhing-zhong is the street lingo for products from Asia—mainly China—which have hit the country.

ziatype *n.* a photo-printing process that uses palladium and platinum and does not require developer fluid. *Arts.* [The process was created by photographer Richard Sullivan of Santa Fe, New Mexico. Technical details of ziatype can be found at his web site, bostick-sullivan.com/ziatype.htm, where it is explained that "the Ziatype was named for the ancient New Mexico Anasazi pueblo people's symbol for the sun. The Zia is the familiar circular image with 4 sets of 4 rays seen on the flag of New Mexico."]

1997 *Usenet: Paul Romaniuk* (Oct. 2) "Paper Negatives" ▶ I'm getting interested in trying some alternative processes like kallitype and ziatype. For this, I'll need to convert 35 mm negs and positives to 8X10, 11X14 etc. paper negatives for the contact printing. **1998** Richard Farber *Historic Photographic Processes* (Oct. 1), p. 112 ▶ Richard Sullivan announced a palladium and gold POP (and developing-out) process in 1996 called the *Ziatype*. Lithium chloropalladite is used for cool tones and the addition of sodium tungstate to give warm brown to sepia tones. **1998** Sil Horwitz *PSA Journal* (Nov. 1) "Tools for Photographers" ▶ Continuing with "alternative" photography, Richard Sullivan and Carl Weese are the authors of a new definitive work, The New Platinum Print.... This covers the complete field of chemical and procedural controls of color and contrast for expressive photographic printing in platinum, palladium, and gold, introducing the new Ziatype process, while explaining in detail the traditional methods. **2005** Robert McFarlane *Sydney Morning Herald* (Australia) (May 17) "From the Mean Streets to Silent Meadows" (Int.) ▶ Kersey uses several processes for printing his pictures, from traditional silver gelatin prints to a mysterious, little-known technique called a ziatype.

Select Bibliography

Allsopp, Richard. *Dictionary of Caribbean English Usage*. New York: Oxford University Press, 1996.

Barnhart, Clarence L., Steinmetz, Sol, and Barnhart, Robert K., eds. *The Barnhart Dictionary of New English Since 1963*. Bronxville, N.Y.: Barnhart/Harper & Row, 1973.

Barnhart, Clarence L., Steinmetz, Sol, and Barnhart, Robert K., eds. *Second Barnhart Dictionary of New English*. Bronxville, N.Y.: Barnhart/Harper & Row, 1980.

Bluestein, Gene. *Anglish/Yinglish*. 2nd ed. Lincoln, Neb.: University of Nebraska Press, 1998.

Bolton, Kingsley. *Chinese Englishes*. Cambridge: Cambridge University Press, 2003.

Cassidy, Frederick G., ed. *Dictionary of American Regional English, vol. I*. Cambridge, Mass.: Belknap Press of Harvard University Press, 1985.

Cassidy, Frederick G., and Hall, Joan Houston, eds. *Dictionary of American Regional English, vol. II*. Cambridge, Mass.: Belknap Press of Harvard University Press, 1991.

————. *Dictionary of American Regional English, vol. III*. Cambridge, Mass.: Belknap Press of Harvard University Press, 1996.

Cassidy, Frederick, and Le Page, Robert. *Dictionary of Jamaican English*. 2nd ed. Kingston, Jamaica: University of West Indies Press, 2002.

Cruz, Bill, and Teck, Bill, eds. *Official Spanglish Dictionary*. New York: Fireside, 1998.

De Bhaldraithe, Tomás, ed. *English-Irish Dictionary*. Dublin: An Gum, Baile Atha Cliath, 1959.

Dictionary of Scots Language. Edinburgh, Scotland: Scottish Language Dictionaries Limited, 2004. Available at dsl.ac.uk/dsl.

Foley, Joseph. *New Englishes: The Case of Singapore*. Singapore: Singapore University Press, 1988.

Görlach, Manfred. *Dictionary of European Anglicisms*. New York: Oxford University Press, 2001.

Görlach, Manfred. *English in Europe*. New York: Oxford University Press, 2004.

Green, Jonathon. *Cassell's Dictionary of Slang.* London: Cassell, 1998.

Gupta, Anthea Fraser. *The Step-Tongue: Children's English in Singapore.* U.K.: Multilingual Matters Limited, 1994.

Hall, Joan Houston, ed. *Dictionary of American Regional English, vol. IV.* Cambridge, Mass.: Belknap Press of Harvard University Press, 2002.

Harkavy's Manual Dictionary. New York: Hebrew Publishing Co., 1894.

HarperCollins German Dictionary. 2nd ed. New York: HarperCollins, 1991.

Jarman, Beatriz Galimberti, and Russell, Roy, eds. *Oxford Spanish Dictionary.* Oxford: Oxford University Press, 2003.

Library of Congress, Manuscript Division, Washington D.C. Papers of the Works Progress Administration, *Lexicon of Trade Jargon,* boxes A798-A804.

Lighter, J. E., ed. *Historical Dictionary of American Slang, vols. I & II.* New York: Random House, 1994 & 1997.

Macquarie Dictionary. 3rd ed. New South Wales, Australia: Macquarie University, Macquarie Library, 1997.

Manessy, Gabriel. *Le français en Afrique noire.* Paris: Harmattan, 1994.

Mathews, Mitford M., ed. *A Dictionary of Americanisms on Historical Principles.* Chicago: University of Chicago Press, 1951.

McArthur, Tom. *Oxford Guide to World English.* New York: Oxford University Press, 2002.

Mencken, H. L. *The American Language.* New York: Alfred A. Knopf, 1948.

Merriam-Webster's Collegiate Dictionary. 11th ed. New York: Merriam-Webster, 2003.

Metcalf, Allan. *Predicting New Words.* Boston: Houghton Mifflin, 2002.

Montgomery, Michael, and Hall, Joseph S., eds. *Dictionary of Smoky Mountain English.* Knoxville, TN: University of Tennessee Press, 2004.

Moore, Bruce, ed. *Australian Oxford Dictionary.* 2nd ed. Melbourne: Oxford University Press, 2004.

New Revised Velásquez Spanish and English Dictionary. Clinton, N.J.: New Win Publishing, 1985.

Ooi, Vincent B.Y., ed. *Evolving Identities: The English Language in Singapore and Malaysia.* Singapore: Times Academic Press, 2001.

Orsman, H.W., ed. *Dictionary of New Zealand English.* Auckland: Oxford University Press, 1997.

Oxford Duden German Dictionary. 2nd ed. New York: Oxford University Press, 2001.

Oxford English Dictionary Online. Available at oed.com; Oxford University Press, 2003-2005. Includes draft entries that are posted quarterly.

Partridge, Eric, and Beale, Paul, eds. *A Dictionary of Slang and Unconventional English.* 8th ed. New York: Macmillan, 1984.

Rosten, Leo. *Hooray for Yiddish!* New York: Simon & Schuster, 1982.

Sáez, Julia Sanmartín. *Diccionario de Argot.* Madrid: Espasa, 2003.

Safire, William. *Safire's New Political Dictionary.* New York: Random House, 1993.

Stavans, Ilan. *Spanglish: The Making of a New American Language.* New York: Rayo of HarperCollins, 2003.

Tongue, R. K. *The English of Singapore and Malaysia.* 2nd ed. Singapore: Eastern Universities Press, 1979.

Weinreich, Uriel. *Modern English-Yiddish, Yiddish English Dictionary.* New York: YIVO, 1968.

Weiser, Chaim M. *Frumspeak.* New York: Rowman and Littlefield, 2004.

WordNet, Cognitive Science Laboratory, Princeton University. Available at http://wordnet.princeton.edu.

Full-Text Digital Resources

African-American Poetry, http://collections.chadwyck.com
American National Corpus, http://americannationalcorpus.org
Black Drama, Alexander Street Press, alexanderstreet2.com/bldrlive
Documenting the American South (University of North Carolina),
    http://docsouth.unc.edu
Early English Books Online (Chadwyck-Healey), http://eebo.chad
    wyck.com
Eighteenth-Century Collections Online (Gale), gale.com/Eighteenth
    Century
JSTOR, jstor.org
LexisNexis, lexisnexis.com
Literature Online, http://lion.chadwyck.com
Making of America (Cornell University), http://moa.umdl.umich
    .edu
Making of America (University of Michigan), http://moa.umdl
    .umich.edu
netLibrary, netlibrary.com
NewspaperARCHIVE, newspaperarchive.com
Paper of Record, paperofrecord.com
ProQuest, proquest.com
Women Writers Online, wwp.brown.edu/texts/wwoentry.html

For Further Information

One place where some of today's English-language professionals, amateurs, and gadabouts hash out the serious and frivolous questions of modern language is on the e-mail list of the American Dialect Society (ADS).

ADS, founded in 1889 at Harvard University, has always had on its member roster a comfortable mixture of professionals and amateurs. Although such language greats as Sir William Craigie (the third editor of the *Oxford English Dictionary* and chief editor of the *Dictionary of American English*) sat on the ADS advisory board and although the society included writers such as H. L. Mencken (among other works, author of *The American Language*, last edition published 1948, and editor of the journal *The American Mercury*), in the 1930s and 1940s the pages of the ADS journal *American Speech* were heavy with the names of now-forgotten contributors and commentators who by their own admission were dilettantes.

The pages of the journal are now held to much stricter academic standards; the e-mail list (ADS-L), however, is its egalitarian counterweight. Even more than the society, ADS-L subscribers represent all facets and professions of English usage and study: lexicographers, etymologists, editors, reporters, professors, students, linguists, grammarians, and interested nonscholarly observers and word-lovers. Now going on its fifteenth year, membership to the e-mail list continues to be freely open and includes participants from around the world.

The content of the list—whose daily messages can measure in the hundreds—has an excellent signal to noise ratio, meaning that idle chatter, spam, or flame wars are kept to a minimum. Many of the messages contain antedatings—recently found citations that prove a lexical item existed before the dates currently given in dictionaries. (Most often, these dates are compared against the *Oxford English Dictionary*, which is simultaneously the most-lauded and most-corrected dictionary in English.) Other messages discuss catchphrases, odd usages, pet peeves and bugaboos, comments on the language of public figures, memories of favorite family words, and, every couple of years, a fresh outbreak of the *coke* vs. *soda* vs. *pop* debate. And, of course, it's not just lexicons and vocabularies that get attention: changes in the sound and structure of American language are a constant topic.

That kind of collaborative atmosphere, where the professional and the amateur can mingle, brings together all sorts of personalities. Any new member to the list will note in particular the word-hunters, the men and women who hunt down new language and post their results to the e-mail list. They share many traits: a bit of obsessiveness, a drive for truth and accuracy, an eagerness to defy conventional wisdom and overturn popular beliefs, and a good level of computer aptitude. They also do not limit themselves to fun and quirky new words but recognize the value of researching humdrum everyday words, too. Their collegiality means they collaborate by sharing their findings freely, but their competitive spirit compels them to search just a bit harder for the antedatings, or look a bit deeper for new words and changing language, so they can have "eureka" moments.

You can join the society or subscribe to its e-mail list at americandialect.org.